Authoritative, Accessible ...
... and Affordable

An entirely NEW, concise business law text from the author team that sets the standard for readability and reliability

Carefully crafted from the ground up to provide a less encyclopedic alternative to most other texts on the market, Jeffrey F. Beatty and Susan S. Samuelson's *Introduction to Business Law, 2e* covers the full range of essential business law topics in a series of fast-paced and brief chapters. Comprehensive breadth of topical coverage is presented in a cost-effective, manageable format.

Filled with fascinating stories and engaging cases, Beatty and Samuelson's text continually reveals the many applications of business law. Their renowned and respected writing style captivates students and makes even the most difficult concepts easy to understand. *Introduction to Business Law, 2e* was developed with business students in mind as opposed to law students. The result is a text that appeals directly to your students' interests—and in turn one that drives their retention and learning of business law.

Preview

Turn the page for a preview of

THOMSON
WEST

Introduction to Business Law

Making Business Law Relevant and Engaging

Averaging 10 pages long, the text's chapters are very concise and dynamic. Students will find the text easy to read and understand, and will be able to quickly and easily digest the manageable content of each chapter. And each chapter's story-telling introductions will intrigue them from the first page. Beatty and Samuelson introduce each chapter's topic using either a fictional or a real story that students can easily relate to. Each story illustrates the issues to be discussed and provides important context. Students are captivated by the stories, read them and remember them, and come to class more eager to question, discuss and learn.

The Beatty and Samuelson hallmark writing style conveys legal material in a superb conversational narrative that engages students like no other text. The authors use interesting stories, illustrations, scenarios, and a direct-to-student voice—all peppered with good dose of humor. A common student response is "I had no idea business law could be so interesting."

Engaging

Beatty and Samuelson include a wealth of interesting cases that
bring the law to life. All cases are summarized in the
authors' own language, making it easy for
students to quickly understand
the key legal issues and
the outcomes
of the cases.

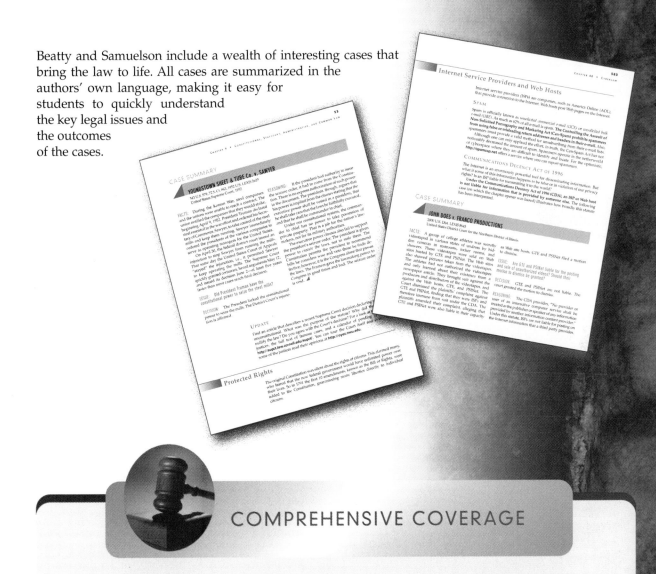

COMPREHENSIVE COVERAGE

Beatty and Samuelson's comprehensive range of coverage provides complete treatment of all
critical business law topics, including the following:

- ■ Two tort chapters
- ■ Nine contracts chapters
- ■ Four negotiable instrument chapters
- ■ Two agency chapters
- ■ Four business organization chapters
- ■ Three property chapters
- ■ Separate employment law and employment discrimination chapters
- ■ Separate estate planning and insurance chapters

Meaningful Features Help Students Meet Essential Pedagogical Goals

You Be the Judge

Students learn to think independently and build their critical thinking skills with You Be the Judge. These sections provide the facts of a case and conflicting appellate arguments. The court's decision appears only in the Instructor's Manual, giving students the opportunity to review both sides and reach their own decision.

Cyberlaw

Cyberlaw discussions examine the legal considerations of today's electronic world. Beatty and Samuelson pull examples from courts and statute books that are full of fascinating cyberlaw issues, such as the right of employers to read workers' e-mail, determining when an electronic signature is valid, and more.

At Risk

Because the best lawsuit is the one that never happens, the authors give future businesspeople insight into how they can stay out of court. At Risk sections provide detailed methods to avoid a particular problem; other times they challenge students to formulate their own approach to dispute prevention.

Ethics

The authors help teach students to ask ethical questions about cases, legal issues, and commercial practices. Discussions of ethics are highlighted throughout the text, rather than relegated to a single chapter.

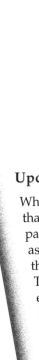

Updates

When it's possible to see that a law may change in a particular area, the authors ask students to research the latest developments. These Update indicators ensure that students are kept current as courts continue to decide cases, and legislatures continue to pass statutes.

INTEGRATED FEATURES

All features are treated as an essential part of the text and are integrated into the chapter flow, reducing the likelihood that they will be skipped over as the student is reading.

Practice Makes Perfect

Robust end-of-chapter activities act as a built-in Study Guide to encourage students to practice and succeed in their course. The authors challenge student understanding with problems that include true/false, multiple-choice, and short-answer questions, including an Ethics question and Role Reversal. Role Reversal questions ask students to formulate their own test questions, helping to reinforce what they already understand. Also included is an Internet Research Problem.

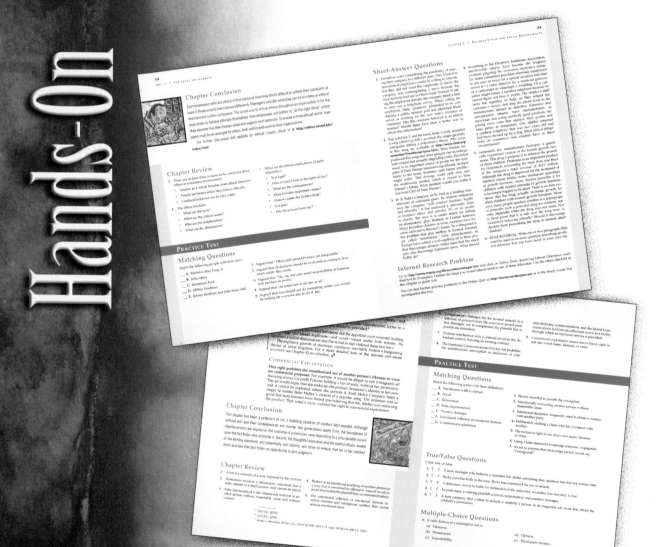

Put the Power of the Web to Work in Your Course

Book Companion Website
http://beatty.westbuslaw.com

When you adopt *Introduction to Business Law*, you and your students will have access to a rich array of teaching and learning resources that you won't find anywhere else. This outstanding site features chapter-specific tutorial quizzes and web links, an online glossary, and more!

West Legal Studies in Business Resource Center
http://www.westbuslaw.com

This website offers a unique and robust online resource for instructors and students, including customer service and product information, links to all text-supporting websites, and other cutting-edge resources such as NewsEdge and Court Case Updates.

LegalTrac™

An excellent resource for research and writing assignments, LegalTrac draws on a wide variety of the most highly regarded legal publications, LegalTrac provides indexing for approximately 875 titles including major law reviews, legal newspapers, bar association journals, and international legal journals, as well as law-related articles from over 1,000 additional business and general interest titles. LegalTrac is available as an optional package with a new text.

Business & Company Resource Center
http://www.bcrc.swlearning.com

Now you can give your students access to a dynamic database of information and resources. The Business & Company Resource Center supplies online access (available as an optional package with a new text) to a wide variety of global business information, including competitive intelligence, career and investment opportunities, business rankings, company histories, and much more.

WebTutor™ ToolBox

WebTUTOR ToolBox

Preloaded with content and available via a free access code when packaged with this text, WebTutor™ ToolBox pairs all the content of this text's rich Book Companion Website with sophisticated course management functionality. Contact your Thomson South-Western representative for information on packaging WebTutor ToolBox with this text.

West's Digital Video Library
http://digitalvideolibrary.westbuslaw.com

Featuring 60+ segments on the most important topics in Business Law, West's Digital Video Library helps students make the connection between their textbook and the business world. Four types of clips are represented: 1) Legal Conflicts in Business feature modern business scenarios; 2) Ask the Instructor clips offer concept review; 3) Drama of the Law present classic legal situations; and 4) LawFlix features segments from widely-recognized, modern-day movies. Access to West's Digital Video Library is free when bundled with a new text.

Online Enhancements

Course Preparation, Student Assessment

Instructor's Manual

0-324-31144-3

This essential manual includes special features to enhance class discussion and student progress.

- Dialogues, a series of questions-and-answers on pivotal cases and topics
- Action learning ideas that include interviews, quick research projects, drafting exercises, classroom activities, commercial analyses, and other suggested assignments that get students out of their chairs and into the diverse settings of business law
- Lively skits from various chapters that students can perform in class, with no rehearsal, to put legal doctrine in a real-life context
- A chapter theme and a quote of the day
- Updates of text material, as well as new cases and examples
- Answers to You Be the Judge cases from the text and to the Practice Test questions found at the end of each chapter

Instructor's Resource CD-ROM

0-324-31149-4

Includes all of the key supplements that accompany this text: Instructor's Manual, test bank in Word and ExamView®, and Microsoft® PowerPoint® slides.

ExamView® Computerized Testing

Create, deliver, and customize tests and study guides (both print and online) in minutes with this easy-to-use assessment and tutorial system. You can build tests of up to 250 questions using up to 12 question types.

Test Bank

0-324-31145-1

by Carol Cromer. Includes hundreds of essay, short-answer, and multiple-choice problems.

Westlaw® Access

http://www.westlaw.com

Westlaw®, West Group's vast online source of value-added legal and business information, contains over 15,000 databases of information spanning a variety of jurisdictions, practice areas, and disciplines. Qualified instructors may receive ten complimentary hours of Westlaw for their course (certain restrictions apply; contact your Thomson representative for details).

Lecture/Presentation

Microsoft® PowerPoint® Presentation Slides

These slides let you incorporate concepts from the book right into your lectures. Available at http://beatty.westbuslaw.com.

West Legal Studies in Business Video Library (VHS)

Videos on many business law issues are available (with some restrictions) to qualified adopters of this text. For more detailed information about the videos, please visit: http://www.westbuslaw.com/video.

Student Learning Support

Black's Law Dictionary: Handbook of Basic Law Terms

0-324-03737-6

This paperback dictionary is a helpful reference guide to business law terminology and can be packaged for a small additional cost with any new West Legal Studies in Business text.

Student Guide to the Sarbanes-Oxley Act

0-324-32365-4

This brief overview for undergraduate business students explains the Sarbanes-Oxley Act, what is required of whom, and how it might affect students in their business life. Available as an optional package with the text.

The Wall Street Journal

0-324-17970-7

Help your students connect coursework to the real world! For a nominal additional cost, new copies of the text can be packaged with a card entitling students to a 15-week subscription to both the print and online versions of *The Wall Street Journal*.

Solutions Designed for the Way You Teach Today's Students...

The Resource Integration Guide

From the day you choose to adopt a Thomson West text through the final exams, we are committed to providing the best materials available to support your teaching and your students' learning. In addition to multimedia, video, and print supplements, this text is supported by a free *Resource Integration Guide*—saving you time by showing how to use this book's extensive ancillary package to enhance your course.

YOUR **RESOURCE INTEGRATION GUIDE**

BEGINS HERE

Resource Integration Guide

The Legal Environment

CLASS PREPARATION/ LECTURE TOOLS	TESTING TOOLS/ COURSE MANAGEMENT	STUDENT MASTERY/ HOMEWORK & TUTORIALS	BEYOND THE BOOK
Instructor's Manual • Suggested Additional Assignments such as a poll on student attitudes about law and lawyers in Ch. 1 or researching examples of libel in Ch. 5 • Chapter Themes and Quotes of the Day • Action Learning activities, such as interviews, skits, negotiations • Questions for Class • Answers to You Be the Judge and Practice Tests	**Test Bank** • Includes true/false, multiple choice, and fact pattern essay questions for each of the eight chapters in the unit	**Integrated Study Guide** • At the end of each textbook chapter, several types of questions support students' different learning styles: matching, true/false, multiple choice, and short answer. • Answers appear in the Instructor's Manual.	**West Legal Studies in Business Resource Center** http://www.westbuslaw.com • This Web site offers a unique, rich and robust online resource for instructors and students. The site provides customer service and product information, links to all text-supporting Web sites, and other cutting-edge resources such as *NewsEdge* and **Court Case Updates**.
Instructor's Resource CD-ROM • Contains the Instructor's Manual, Test Bank, PowerPoint® slides	**ExamView®** • Computerized version of the Test Bank. • Instructors can add or edit questions, instructions, and answers, and select questions by previewing them on the screen, selecting them randomly, or selecting them by number. Instructors can also create and administer quizzes online, whether over the Internet, a local area network (LAN), or a wide area network (WAN).	**Book Companion Website** http://beatty.westbuslaw.com • Interactive quizzes, web links, glossary, court case updates	**West's Digital Video Library** http://digitalvideolibrary.westbuslaw.com • Featuring 60+ segments on the most important topics in Business Law, West's Digital Video Library helps students make the connection between their textbook and the business world. New to this edition are LawFlix, twelve scenes from Hollywood movies with instructor materials for each film clip. Included are goals for the clips, questions for students (with answers for the instructor), background on the film and the scene, and fascinating trivia about the film, its actors and its history.
Book Companion Website http://beatty.westbuslaw.com • Interactive quizzes, web links, glossary, court case updates, downloadable PowerPoint® slides	**WebTutor™ ToolBox** • Preloaded with content, WebTutor™ ToolBox pairs all the content of the book's Companion Web site with all the sophisticated course management functionality of Blackboard® or WebCT™.		**The Business and Company Resource Center (BCRC)** http://bcrc.swlearning.com • A premier online business research tool that allows you to seamlessly search thousands of periodicals, journals, references, financial information, industry reports, company histories and much more.
			LegalTrac™ • An excellent resource for research and writing assignments, *LegalTrac™* provides indexing for approximately 875 titles including major law reviews, legal newspapers, bar association journals and international legal journals, and also contains law-related articles from over 1,000 additional business and general interest titles.

CLASS PREPARATION/ LECTURE TOOLS	TESTING TOOLS/ COURSE MANAGEMENT	STUDENT MASTERY/ HOMEWORK & TUTORIALS	BEYOND THE BOOK
Instructor's Manual • Suggested Additional Assignments such as a skit based on the opening scenario in Ch. 10 or analyzing an actual lease in Ch. 14 • Chapter Themes and Quotes of the Day • Action Learning activities, such as interviews, skits, negotiations • Questions for Class • Answers to You Be the Judge and Practice Tests	**Test Bank** • Includes true/false, multiple choice, and fact pattern essay questions for each of the nine chapters in the unit	**Integrated Study Guide** • At the end of each textbook chapter, several types of questions support students' different learning styles: matching, true/false, multiple choice, and short answer. • Answers appear in the Instructor's Manual.	**West Legal Studies in Business Resource Center** http://www.westbuslaw.com • This Web site offers a unique, rich and robust online resource for instructors and students. The site provides customer service and product information, links to all text-supporting Web sites, and other cutting-edge resources such as *NewsEdge* and **Court Case Updates**.
Instructor's Resource CD-ROM • Contains the Instructor's Manual, Test Bank, PowerPoint® slides	**ExamView®** • Computerized version of the Test Bank. • Instructors can add or edit questions, instructions, and answers, and select questions by previewing them on the screen, selecting them randomly, or selecting them by number. Instructors can also create and administer quizzes online, whether over the Internet, a local area network (LAN), or a wide area network (WAN).	**Book Companion Website** http://beatty.westbuslaw.com • Interactive quizzes, web links, glossary, court case updates	**West's Digital Video Library** http://digitalvideolibrary.westbuslaw.com • Featuring 60+ segments on the most important topics in Business Law, West's Digital Video Library helps students make the connection between their textbook and the business world. New to this edition are LawFlix, twelve scenes from Hollywood movies with instructor materials for each film clip. Included are goals for the clips, questions for students (with answers for the instructor), background on the film and the scene, and fascinating trivia about the film, its actors and its history.
Book Companion Website http://beatty.westbuslaw.com • Interactive quizzes, web links, glossary, court case updates, downloadable PowerPoint® slides	**WebTutor™ ToolBox** • Preloaded with content, WebTutor™ ToolBox pairs all the content of the book's Companion Web Site with all the sophisticated course management functionality of Blackboard® or WebCT™.		**The Business and Company Resource Center (BCRC)** http://bcrc.swlearning.com • A premier online business research tool that allows you to seamlessly search thousands of periodicals, journals, references, financial information, industry reports, company histories and much more.
			LegalTrac™ • An excellent resource for research and writing assignments, *LegalTrac™* provides indexing for approximately 875 titles including major law reviews, legal newspapers, bar association journals and international legal journals, and also contains law-related articles from over 1,000 additional business and general interest titles.

Commercial Transactions

CLASS PREPARATION/ LECTURE TOOLS	TESTING TOOLS/ COURSE MANAGEMENT	STUDENT MASTERY/ HOMEWORK & TUTORIALS	BEYOND THE BOOK
Instructor's Manual • Suggested Additional Assignments such as rewriting a warranty in plain English in Ch. 20 or researching laws on exempt property in bankruptcy in Ch. 27 • Chapter Themes and Quotes of the Day • Action Learning activities, such as interviews, skits, negotiations • Questions for Class • Answers to You Be the Judge and Practice Tests	**Test Bank** • Includes true/false, multiple choice, and fact pattern essay questions for each of the ten chapters in the unit	**Integrated Study Guide** • At the end of each textbook chapter, several types of questions support students' different learning styles: matching, true/false, multiple choice, and short answer. • Answers appear in the Instructor's Manual.	**West Legal Studies in Business Resource Center** http://www.westbuslaw.com • This Web site offers a unique, rich and robust online resource for instructors and students. The site provides customer service and product information, links to all text-supporting Web sites, and other cutting-edge resources such as *NewsEdge* and **Court Case Updates**.
Instructor's Resource CD-ROM • Contains the Instructor's Manual, Test Bank, PowerPoint® slides	**ExamView®** • Computerized version of the Test Bank. • Instructors can add or edit questions, instructions, and answers, and select questions by previewing them on the screen, selecting them randomly, or selecting them by number. Instructors can also create and administer quizzes online, whether over the Internet, a local area network (LAN), or a wide area network (WAN).	**Book Companion Website** http://beatty.westbuslaw.com • Interactive quizzes, web links, glossary, court case updates	**West's Digital Video Library** http://digitalvideolibrary.westbuslaw.com • Featuring 60+ segments on the most important topics in Business Law, West's Digital Video Library helps students make the connection between their textbook and the business world. New to this edition are LawFlix, twelve scenes from Hollywood movies with instructor materials for each film clip. Included are goals for the clips, questions for students (with answers for the instructor), background on the film and the scene, and fascinating trivia about the film, its actors and its history.
Book Companion Website http://beatty.westbuslaw.com • Interactive quizzes, web links, glossary, court case updates, downloadable PowerPoint® slides	**WebTutor™ ToolBox** • Preloaded with content, WebTutor™ ToolBox pairs all the content of the book's Companion Web site with all the sophisticated course management functionality of Blackboard® or WebCT™.		**The Business and Company Resource Center (BCRC)** http://bcrc.swlearning.com • A premier online business research tool that allows you to seamlessly search thousands of periodicals, journals, references, financial information, industry reports, company histories and much more.
			LegalTrac™ • An excellent resource for research and writing assignments, *LegalTrac™* provides indexing for approximately 875 titles including major law reviews, legal newspapers, bar association journals and international legal journals, and also contains law-related articles from over 1,000 additional business and general interest titles.

Agency and Employment Law

CLASS PREPARATION/ LECTURE TOOLS	TESTING TOOLS/ COURSE MANAGEMENT	STUDENT MASTERY/ HOMEWORK & TUTORIALS	BEYOND THE BOOK
Instructor's Manual • Suggested Additional Assignments such as writing out an example of apparent authority in Ch. 29 or debating a unionization proposal in Ch. 32 • Chapter Themes and Quotes of the Day • Action Learning activities, such as interviews, skits, negotiations • Questions for Class • Answers to You Be the Judge and Practice Tests	**Test Bank** • Includes true/false, multiple choice, and fact pattern essay questions for each of the five chapters in the unit	**Integrated Study Guide** • At the end of each textbook chapter, several types of questions support students' different learning styles: matching, true/false, multiple choice, and short answer. • Answers appear in the Instructor's Manual.	**West Legal Studies in Business Resource Center** http://www.westbuslaw.com • This Web site offers a unique, rich and robust online resource for instructors and students. The site provides customer service and product information, links to all text-supporting Web sites, and other cutting-edge resources such as *NewsEdge* and **Court Case Updates**.
Instructor's Resource CD-ROM • Contains the Instructor's Manual, Test Bank, PowerPoint® slides	**ExamView®** • Computerized version of the Test Bank. • Instructors can add or edit questions, instructions, and answers, and select questions by previewing them on the screen, selecting them randomly, or selecting them by number. Instructors can also create and administer quizzes online, whether over the Internet, a local area network (LAN), or a wide area network (WAN).	**Book Companion Website** http://beatty.westbuslaw.com • Interactive quizzes, web links, glossary, court case updates	**West's Digital Video Library** http://digitalvideolibrary.westbuslaw.com • Featuring 60+ segments on the most important topics in Business Law, West's Digital Video Library helps students make the connection between their textbook and the business world. New to this edition are LawFlix, twelve scenes from Hollywood movies with instructor materials for each film clip. Included are goals for the clips, questions for students (with answers for the instructor), background on the film and the scene, and fascinating trivia about the film, its actors and its history.
Book Companion Website http://beatty.westbuslaw.com • Interactive quizzes, web links, glossary, court case updates, downloadable PowerPoint® slides	**WebTutor™ ToolBox** • Preloaded with content, WebTutor™ ToolBox pairs all the content of the book's Companion Web site with all the sophisticated course management functionality of Blackboard® or WebCT™.		**The Business and Company Resource Center (BCRC)** http://bcrc.swlearning.com • A premier online business research tool that allows you to seamlessly search thousands of periodicals, journals, references, financial information, industry reports, company histories and much more.
			LegalTrac™ • An excellent resource for research and writing assignments, *LegalTrac™* provides indexing for approximately 875 titles including major law reviews, legal newspapers, bar association journals and international legal journals, and also contains law-related articles from over 1,000 additional business and general interest titles.

Business Organizations and Government Regulation

CLASS PREPARATION/ LECTURE TOOLS	TESTING TOOLS/ COURSE MANAGEMENT	STUDENT MASTERY/ HOMEWORK & TUTORIALS	BEYOND THE BOOK
Instructor's Manual • Suggested Additional Assignments such as researching initial filing fees in local states in Ch. 33 or finding annual reports on the SEC Web site in Ch. 36 • Chapter Themes and Quotes of the Day • Action Learning activities, such as interviews, skits, negotiations • Questions for Class • Answers to You Be the Judge and Practice Tests	**Test Bank** • Includes true/false, multiple choice, and fact pattern essay questions for each of the seven chapters in the unit	**Integrated Study Guide** • At the end of each textbook chapter, several types of questions support students' different learning styles: matching, true/false, multiple choice, and short answer. • Answers appear in the Instructor's Manual.	**West Legal Studies in Business Resource Center** http://www.westbuslaw.com • This Web site offers a unique, rich and robust online resource for instructors and students. The site provides customer service and product information, links to all text-supporting Web sites, and other cutting-edge resources such as *NewsEdge* and **Court Case Updates**.
Instructor's Resource CD-ROM • Contains the Instructor's Manual, Test Bank, PowerPoint® slides	**ExamView®** • Computerized version of the Test Bank. • Instructors can add or edit questions, instructions, and answers, and select questions by previewing them on the screen, selecting them randomly, or selecting them by number. Instructors can also create and administer quizzes online, whether over the Internet, a local area network (LAN), or a wide area network (WAN).	**Book Companion Website** http://beatty.westbuslaw.com • Interactive quizzes, web links, glossary, court case updates	**West's Digital Video Library** http://digitalvideolibrary.westbuslaw.com • Featuring 60+ segments on the most important topics in Business Law, West's Digital Video Library helps students make the connection between their textbook and the business world. New to this edition are LawFlix, twelve scenes from Hollywood movies with instructor materials for each film clip. Included are goals for the clips, questions for students (with answers for the instructor), background on the film and the scene, and fascinating trivia about the film, its actors and its history.
Book Companion Website http://beatty.westbuslaw.com • Interactive quizzes, web links, glossary, court case updates, downloadable PowerPoint® slides	**WebTutor™ ToolBox** • Preloaded with content, WebTutor™ ToolBox pairs all the content of the book's Companion Web site with all the sophisticated course management functionality of Blackboard® or WebCT™.		**The Business and Company Resource Center (BCRC)** http://bcrc.swlearning.com • A premier online business research tool that allows you to seamlessly search thousands of periodicals, journals, references, financial information, industry reports, company histories and much more.
			LegalTrac™ • An excellent resource for research and writing assignments, *LegalTrac™* provides indexing for approximately 875 titles including major law reviews, legal newspapers, bar association journals and international legal journals, and also contains law-related articles from over 1,000 additional business and general interest titles.
			Student Guide to the Sarbanes-Oxley Act This brief overview for undergraduate business students explains the Sarbanes-Oxley Act, what is required of whom, and how it might affect students in their business life.

CLASS PREPARATION/ LECTURE TOOLS	TESTING TOOLS/ COURSE MANAGEMENT	STUDENT MASTERY/ HOMEWORK & TUTORIALS	BEYOND THE BOOK
Instructor's Manual • Suggested Additional Assignments such as finding cookies on a hard drive in Ch. 40 or drafting a deed in Ch. 42 • Chapter Themes and Quotes of the Day • Action Learning activities, such as interviews, skits, negotiations • Questions for Class • Answers to You Be the Judge and Practice Tests	**Test Bank** • Includes true/false, multiple choice, and fact pattern essay questions for each of the seven chapters in the unit	**Integrated Study Guide** • At the end of each textbook chapter, several types of questions support students' different learning styles: matching, true/false, multiple choice, and short answer. • Answers appear in the Instructor's Manual.	**West Legal Studies in Business Resource Center** http://www.westbuslaw.com • This Web site offers a unique, rich and robust online resource for instructors and students. The site provides customer service and product information, links to all text-supporting Web sites, and other cutting-edge resources such as *NewsEdge* and **Court Case Updates**.
Instructor's Resource CD-ROM • Contains the Instructor's Manual, Test Bank, PowerPoint® slides	**ExamView®** • Computerized version of the Test Bank. • Instructors can add or edit questions, instructions, and answers, and select questions by previewing them on the screen, selecting them randomly, or selecting them by number. Instructors can also create and administer quizzes online, whether over the Internet, a local area network (LAN), or a wide area network (WAN).	**Book Companion Website** http://beatty.westbuslaw.com • Interactive quizzes, web links, glossary, court case updates	**West's Digital Video Library** http://digitalvideolibrary.westbuslaw.com • Featuring 60+ segments on the most important topics in Business Law, West's Digital Video Library helps students make the connection between their textbook and the business world. New to this edition are LawFlix, twelve scenes from Hollywood movies with instructor materials for each film clip. Included are goals for the clips, questions for students (with answers for the instructor), background on the film and the scene, and fascinating trivia about the film, its actors and its history.
Book Companion Website http://beatty.westbuslaw.com • Interactive quizzes, web links, glossary, court case updates, downloadable PowerPoint® slides	**WebTutor™ ToolBox** • Preloaded with content, WebTutor™ ToolBox pairs all the content of the book's Companion Web site with all the sophisticated course management functionality of Blackboard® or WebCT™.		**The Business and Company Resource Center (BCRC)** http://bcrc.swlearning.com • A premier online business research tool that allows you to seamlessly search thousands of periodicals, journals, references, financial information, industry reports, company histories and much more.
			LegalTrac™ • An excellent resource for research and writing assignments, *LegalTrac™* provides indexing for approximately 875 titles including major law reviews, legal newspapers, bar association journals and international legal journals, and also contains law-related articles from over 1,000 additional business and general interest titles.

UPDATED BANKRUPTCY COVERAGE

INTRODUCTION
to
BUSINESS LAW

Second Edition

Jeffrey F. Beatty
Boston University

Susan S. Samuelson
Boston University

THOMSON

WEST

Australia · Brazil · Canada · Mexico · Singapore · Spain · United Kingdom · United States

Introduction to Business Law, Second Edition
Jeffrey F. Beatty and Susan S. Samuelson

VP/Editorial Director: Jack W. Calhoun

Publisher: Rob Dewey

Acquisitions Editor: Steven Silverstein, Esq.

Developmental Editor: Bob Sandman

Executive Marketing Manager: Lisa L. Lysne

Production Project Manager: Brian Courter

Manager of Technology, Editorial: Vicky True

Technology Project Editor: Pam Wallace

Web Coordinator: Scott Cook

Manufacturing Coordinator: Charlene Taylor

Production House: Interactive Composition Corporation

Printer: Globus
Minster, OH

Art Director: Michelle Kunkler

Internal Designer: Lou Ann Thesing

Cover Designer: Kathy Heming

Cover Image: © Steve Dunwell/
The Image Bank

For permission to use material from this
text or product, submit a request online at
http://www.thomsonrights.com.

Library of Congress Control Number:
2005937141

For more information about our
products, contact us at:

Thomson Learning Academic Resource
Center
1-800-423-0563

Thomson Higher Education
5191 Natorp Boulevard
Mason, Ohio 45040
USA

Contents: Overview

Contents

Preface

Our goal in writing this book was to capture the passion and excitement, the sheer enjoyment, of the law. Business law is notoriously complex, and as authors we are obsessed with accuracy. Yet this intriguing subject also abounds with human conflict and hard-earned wisdom, forces that can make a law book sparkle. We are grateful to the faculty who tell us that this introductory business law text is like no other-a book that is precise and authoritative *yet a pleasure to read*. Here are some of the book's key features:

Strong Narrative

The law is full of great stories, and we use them. Your students and ours should come to class excited. In Chapter 3, on dispute resolution (page 30), we explain litigation by tracking a double indemnity lawsuit. An executive is dead. Did he drown accidentally, obligating the insurance company to pay? Or did the businessman commit suicide, voiding the policy? The student follows the action from the discovery of the body, through each step of the lawsuit, to the final appeal. The chapter offers a detailed discussion of dispute resolution, but it does so by exploiting the human drama that underlies litigation.

Students read stories and remember them. Strong narratives provide a rich context for the remarkable quantity of legal material presented. When students care about the material they are reading, they persevere. We have been delighted to find that they also arrive in class eager to question, discuss, and learn.

Authoritative

We insist, as you do, on a law book that is indisputably accurate. A professor must teach with assurance, confident that every paragraph is the result of exhaustive research and meticulous presentation. Dozens of tough-minded people spent thousands of hours reviewing this book, and we are delighted with the stamp of approval we have received from trial and appellate judges, working attorneys, scholars, and teachers.

We reject the cloudy definitions and fuzzy explanations that can invade judicial opinions and legal scholarship. To highlight the most important rules, we use bold print, and then follow with vivacious examples written in clear, forceful English. (See, for example, the description of assault, on page 97.)

Comprehensive

Staying comprehensive means staying current. Look, for example, at the important field of corporate governance. We present a clear path through the thicket of new issues, such as board composition, executive compensation, and shareholder proposals. We want tomorrow's business leaders to anticipate the challenges that await them and then use their knowledge to avert problems.

This book also provides a strong narrative flow. Like you, we are here to teach. We do not use boxes because, in our experience, they disrupt the flow of the text. Students inform us that a box indicates peripheral material, that is, material they routinely skip; we prefer to give them an uncluttered whole. Each chapter also contains several Internet addresses, offering students a quick link to additional knowledge. These addresses, however, are woven into the body of the text, to reinforce the point that new technology and research methods are an integral part of a lively discipline. We believe that a well-written chapter is seamless and cohesive.

A Book for Students

We have written this book as if we were speaking directly to our students. We provide black letter law, but we also explain concepts in terms that hook students. Over the years, we have learned how much more successfully we can teach when our students are intrigued. No matter what kind of a show we put on in class, they are only learning when they want to learn.

Every chapter begins with a story, either fictional or real, to illustrate the issues in the chapter and provide context. Chapter 40 on Cyberlaw begins with the true story of a college student who discovers nude pictures of himself online. These photos had been taken in the locker room without his knowledge. What privacy rights do any of us have? Does the Internet jeopardize them? Students want to know-right away.

Most of today's undergraduates were not yet born when Jimmy Carter was president. They come to college with varying levels of preparation; many now arrive from other countries. We have found that to teach business law most effectively we must provide its context. Chapter 38 on Accountants explains how a changing culture within Arthur Andersen led to the firm's downfall during the Enron scandal.

At the same time, we enjoy offering "nuts and bolts" information that grabs students. In Chapter 39, on Consumer Law, we bring home the issue of credit history by providing phone numbers and Web sites that students can use to check their own credit reports (page 566).

Students respond enthusiastically to this approach. One professor asked a student to compare our book with the one that the class was then using. This was the student's reaction: "I really enjoy reading the [Beatty & Samuelson] textbook and I have decided that I will give you this memo ASAP, but I am keeping the book until Wednesday so that I may continue reading. Thanks! :-)"

Humor

Throughout the text we use humor-judiciously-to lighten and enlighten. Not surprisingly, students have applauded-but is wit appropriate? How dare we employ levity in this venerable discipline! We offer humor because we take law seriously. We revere the law for its ancient traditions, its dazzling intricacy, its relentless though imperfect attempt to give order and decency to our world. Because we are confident of our respect for the law, we are not afraid to employ some levity. Leaden prose masquerading as legal scholarship does no honor to the field.

Humor also helps retention. We have found that students remember a contract problem described in a fanciful setting, and from that setting recall the underlying principle. By contrast, one widget is hard to distinguish from another.

Features

We chose the features for our book with great care. As mentioned above, all features are considered an essential part of the text, and are woven into its body. Also, each feature responds to an essential pedagogical goal. Here are some of those goals and the matching feature.

YOU BE THE JUDGE

GOAL: Get them thinking independently. When reading case opinions, students tend to accept the court's "answer." Judges, of course, try to reach decisions that appear indisputable, when in reality they may be controversial-or wrong. From time to time we want students to think through the problem and reach their own answer. Most chapters contain a You Be the Judge feature, providing the facts of the case and conflicting appellate arguments. The court's decision, however, appears only in the Instructor's Manual.

Since students do not know the result, discussions tend to be more free-flowing. For instance, many commentators feel that *Smith v. Van Gorkom*, the landmark case on the business judgment rule, was wrongly decided. However, when students read the court's opinion, they rarely consider the opposing side. Now, with the case presented as You Be the Judge in Chapter 35 (page 508), the students disagree with the court at least half the time. They are thinking.

CYBERLAW

GOAL: Master the present and anticipate the future. The computer has changed all of our lives forever, and the courts and statute books are full of fascinating cyberlaw issues. Do employers have the right to read workers' e-mail? When does an electronic signature satisfy the statute of frauds? Cyberlaw is fully discussed in Chapter 40 on Cyberlaw and Chapter 41 on Intellectual Property. Finally, throughout the text we discuss still more cyberlaw issues as they relate to the particular topic; icons highlight those sections.

AT RISK

GOAL: Help managers stay out of court. As every lawyer knows, the best lawsuit is the one that never happens. Some of our students are already in the workforce, and the rest soon will be, so we offer ideas on avoiding legal disputes. Sometimes we provide detailed methods to avoid the particular problem; other times we challenge the students to formulate their own approach to dispute prevention. For example, this feature in Chapter 5 on Intentional Torts (page 72) helps future managers think about plans to deal with suspected shoplifters.

ETHICS

GOAL: Make ethics real. We ask ethical questions about cases, legal issues, and commercial practices. Is it fair for one party to void a contract by arguing, months after the fact, that there was no consideration? Do managers have ethical obligations to older workers for whom employment opportunities may be limited? What is wrong with bribery? We do not have definitive answers but believe that asking the questions and encouraging discussion reminds students that ethics is an essential element of justice, and of a satisfying life.

UPDATE

GOAL: To keep students current. As we go to press, this book is accurate and up-to-date. Inevitably, however, during the book's three-year life span some changes will occur. Courts will decide cases, legislatures will pass statutes. In some cases, we ask students to research the latest developments. For example, in Chapter 20 on Product Liability, we discuss the Consumer Product Safety Commission. We ask students to search for CPSC news online or visit the agency's Web site.

CASES

GOAL: Bring case law alive. Each case begins with a summary of the facts followed by a statement of both the issue and the decision. Next comes a summary of the court's opinion. We have written this ourselves, to make the judges' reasoning accessible to all readers, while retaining the court's focus and the decision's impact. We cite cases using a modified bluebook form. In the principal cases in each chapter, we provide the state or federal citation, the regional citation, and the LEXIS or Westlaw citation. We also give students a brief description of the court. Because many of our cases are so recent, some will have only a regional reporter and a LEXIS or Westlaw citation.

PRACTICE TESTS

GOAL: Encourage students to practice! To support students' different learning styles, we provide several types of questions at the end of each chapter: matching, multiple choice, True/False, and short answer. In addition, the following questions are included in each chapter:

- Internet Research Problem. This question sends students to an Internet address where they can explore issues from the chapter.

- Ethics. This question highlights the ethical issues of a dispute and calls upon the student to formulate a specific, reasoned response.

- CPA Questions. For topics covered by the CPA exam, administered by the American Institute of Certified Public Accountants, the practice tests include questions from previous CPA exams.

- Role Reversal. Students are asked to formulate their own test questions. Crafting questions is a good way to reinforce what they already understand, and recognize areas that they need to review.

Answers to the odd-numbered questions are available on the Beatty *Introduction to Business Law* Web site at **http://beatty.westbuslaw.com/**. Here is why. Students often ask us how to study for exams. Reviewing the problems in the end-of-chapter practice tests is helpful, but without the answers students have no way of being sure they are on the right track. The answers to the even-numbered questions appear only in the Instructor's Manual so that faculty can assign them for written or oral presentation.

Teaching Materials

For more information about any of these ancillaries, contact your Thomson Learning/West Legal Studies in Business Sales Representative for more details, or visit the Beatty *Introduction to Business Law* Web site at **http://beatty. westbuslaw. com/**.

Instructor's Manual

(ISBN: 0-324-31144-3) We have included special features to enhance class discussion and student progress:

- Dialogues. These are a series of questions-and-answers on pivotal cases and topics. The questions provide enough material to teach a full session. In a pinch, you could walk into class with nothing but the manual and use the Dialogues to conduct an exciting class.

- Action learning ideas. Interviews, quick research projects, drafting exercises, classroom activities, commercial analyses, and other suggested assignments that get students out of their chairs and into the diverse settings of business law.

- Skits. Various chapters have lively skits that students can perform in class, with no rehearsal, to put legal doctrine in a real-life context.

- A chapter theme and a quote of the day.

- Updates of text material.

- New cases and examples.

- Answers to You Be the Judge cases from the text and to the Practice Test questions found at the end of each chapter.

Test Bank

(ISBN: 0-324-31145-1) The test bank offers hundreds of essay, short answer and multiple choice problems, and may be obtained in hard copy or electronic format.

ExamView Testing Software-Computerized Testing Software

This testing software contains all of the questions in the printed test bank. This easy-to-use test creation software program is compatible with Microsoft Windows. Instructors can add or edit questions, instructions, and answers; and select questions by previewing them on the screen, selecting them randomly, or selecting them by number. Instructors can also create and administer quizzes online, whether over the Internet, a local area network (LAN), or a wide area network (WAN). The ExamView testing software is available on the Instructor's Resource CD.

Instructor's Resource CD (IRCD)

(ISBN: 0-324-31149-4) The IRCD contains the ExamView testing software files, the test bank in Microsoft Word files, the Instructor's Manual in Microsoft Word files, and the Microsoft PowerPoint Lecture Review Slides.

Microsoft PowerPoint Lecture Review Slides

PowerPoint slides are available for use by instructors for enhancing their lectures. Download these slides at **http://beatty.westbuslaw.com/**. The PowerPoint slides are also available on the IRCD.

West's Digital Video Library

Featuring 60+ segments on the most important topics in business law, West's Digital Video Library helps students make the connection between their textbook and the business world. Access to West's Digital Video Library is free when bundled with a new text, and students with used book can purchase access to the video clips online. New to this edition are LawFlix, twelve scenes from Hollywood movies with instructor materials for each film clip. The clips were chosen by the author and the IM materials were written by the author and include elements such as goals for the clips, questions for students (with answers for the instructor), background on the film and the scene, and fascinating trivia about the film, its actors and its history. For more information about West's Digital Video Library, visit **http://digitalvideolibrary.westbuslaw.com**.

West Legal Studies in Business Resource Center

This Web site offers a unique, rich and robust online resource for instructors and students. Visiting **http://www.westbuslaw.com** provides customer service and product information, links to all text-supporting Web sites, and other cutting-edge resources such as *NewsEdge* and Court Case Updates.

LegalTrac

An excellent resource for research and writing assignments, *LegalTrac*(tm) provides indexing for approximately 875 titles including major law reviews, legal newspapers, bar association journals, and, international legal journals, and also contains law-related articles from over 1,000 additional business and general interest titles. *LegalTrac*(tm) is available as an optional package with a new text.

The Business & Company Resource Center

The Business & Company Resource Center (BCRC) is a premier online business research tool that allows you to seamlessly search thousands of periodicals, journals, references, financial information, industry reports, company histories and much more. Visit **http://bcrc.swlearning.com** to learn more about this powerful tool. *BCRC* is available as an optional package with a new text.

A Handbook of Basic Law Terms, Black's Law Dictionary Series

This paperback dictionary, prepared by the editor of the popular *Black's Law Dictionary*, can be packaged for a small additional cost with any new *West Legal Studies in Business* text.

Student Guide to the Sarbanes Oxley Act

This brief overview for undergraduate business students explains the Sarbanes Oxley Act, what is required of whom, and how it might affect students in their business life. It is available as an optional package with the text.

Westlaw®

Westlaw®, West Group's vast online source of value-added legal and business information, contains over 15,000 databases of information spanning a variety of jurisdictions, practice areas and disciplines. Qualified instructors who adopt *West Legal Studies in Business* textbooks may receive ten complimentary hours of Westlaw for their course (certain restrictions apply).

West Legal Studies in Business VHS Video Library

VHS videotapes on many business law issues are available (with some restrictions) to qualified adopters of *West Legal Studies in Business* texts. For more detailed information about the videos, please visit **http://video.westbuslaw.com**.

Interaction with the Authors

This is our standard: Every professor who adopts this book must have a superior experience. We are available to help in any way we can. Adopters of this text often call us or e-mail us to ask questions, obtain a syllabus, offer suggestions, share pedagogical concerns, or inquire about ancillaries. One of the pleasures of working on this project has been our discovery that the text provides a link to so many colleagues around the country. We value those connections, are eager to respond, and would be happy to hear from you.

To the Student

Each Practice Test contains one Role Reversal feature, in which we challenge you to create your own exam question. Your professor may ask you to submit the questions in writing or electronically, or to prepare an overhead slide. The goal is to think creatively and accurately. The question should be challenging enough that the average student will need to stop and think, but clear enough that there is only one answer. Questions can be formatted as essay, short answer or multiple choice.

For a multiple choice question, the first step is to isolate the single issue that you want to test. For example, in the unit on contract law, you do not want to ask a question that concerns five different aspects of forming an agreement. A good question will focus exclusively on one issue, for example, whether a job offer has to be in writing (some do, others do not). Create a realistic fact pattern that raises the issue. Provide one answer that is clearly correct. Add additional answers that might seem plausible but are definitely incorrect.

Some exam questions are very direct, and test whether a student knows a definition. Other questions require deeper analysis. Here are two multiple choice questions. The first is direct.

Question: Which contract is governed by the Uniform Commercial Code?

a. An agreement for an actor to appear in a movie for a $600,000 fee.

b. An agreement for an actor to appear in a movie for a fee of $600,000 plus 2% of box office.

c. An agreement for the sale of a house.

d. An agreement for the sale of 22,000 picture frames.

e. An agreement for the rental of an apartment.

As you will learn later on, the correct answer is (d), because the Code applies to the sale of goods, not to employment contracts or real estate deals.

The next question is more difficult, requiring the student to spot the issue of law involved (product liability), remember how damages are awarded in such cases (generally, without regard to fault), and make a simple calculation.

Question: Lightweight Corp. manufactures strings of Christmas tree lights and sells 3.5 million sets per year. Every year, between 10 and 20 of the company's strings have a manufacturing defect that causes a consumer injury. Maxine receives a severe shock from a Lightweight string of lights. She sues. The evidence at trial is that: 1) Lightweight's safety record is the best in the industry; 2) all competing companies have a higher rate of injuries; 3) the lights that injured Maxine arrived at her house in the factory box, untouched by anyone outside of Lightweight; 4) Maxine operated the lights properly. Maxine's medical bills amount to $200,000; her lost income is $100,000; and her pain and suffering amounts to $600,000. What is the probable outcome at trial?

a. Maxine will win $200,000.

b. Maxine will win $100,000.

c. Maxine will win $900,000.

d. Maxine will win nothing.

e. Lightweight might win damages for a frivolous lawsuit.

As you will learn, the correct answer is (c). Lightweight is responsible under product liability law regardless of its careful work and excellent record. Maxine is entitled to all of her damages. Notice that the same question could be used in essay format, simply by deleting the multiple choice answers.

Acknowledgments

We are grateful to the following reviewers who gave such helpful comments on the manuscript of this book:

Alan Questell
Richmond Community College

Thomas L. Severance
MiraCosta College

Cornelia Farrell Scuderi
Kaplan University

Jeffrey F. Beatty
Phone: (617) 353-6397
E-mail: jfbeatty@bu.edu

Boston, Massachusetts
OCTOBER, 2005

Susan S. Samuelson
Phone: (617) 353-2033
E-mail: ssamuels@bu.edu

THE LEGAL ENVIRONMENT

UNIT 1

Introduction to Law

Law is powerful. Law is essential. And law is fascinating. We hope this book will persuade you of all three ideas.

Three Important Ideas About Law

POWER

The law displays its muscle every day, to people from all walks of life. A driver is seriously injured in an automobile accident, and the jury concludes the car had a design defect. The jurors award her $29 million. A senior vice-president congratulates himself on a cagey stock purchase but is horrified to receive, not profits, but a prison sentence. A homeless person, ordered by local police to stop panhandling, ambles into court and walks out with an order permitting him to beg on the city's streets. The strong reach of the law touches us all. To understand something that powerful is itself power.

Suppose, some years after graduation, you are a midlevel manager at Sublime Corp., which manufactures and distributes video games and related hardware and software. You are delighted with this important position in an excellent company—and especially glad you bring legal knowledge to the job. Sarah, an expert at computer-generated imagery, complains that Rob, her boss, is constantly touching her and making lewd comments. That is sexual harassment, and your knowledge of *employment law* helps you respond promptly and carefully. You have dinner with Jake, who has his own software company. Jake wants to manufacture an exciting new video game in cooperation with Sublime, but you are careful not to create a binding deal. (*Contract law.*) Jake mentions that a similar game is already on the market. Do you have the right to market one like it? That answer you already know. (*Intellectual property law.*)

The next day a letter from the Environmental Protection Agency asks how your company disposes of toxic chemicals used to manufacture computer drives. You can discuss it efficiently with in-house counsel, because you have a working knowledge of administrative law. LuYu, your personnel manager, reports that a silicon chip worker often seems drowsy; she suspects drug use. Does she have the right to test him? (*Constitutional law* and *employment law.*) On the other hand, if she fails to test him, could Sublime Corp. be liable for any harm the worker does? (*Tort law* and *agency law.*)

In a mere week, you might use your legal training a dozen times, helping Sublime to steer clear of countless dangers. During the coming year you encounter many other legal issues, and you and your corporation benefit from your skills.

It is not only as a corporate manager that you will confront the law. As a voter, investor, juror, entrepreneur, and community member, you will influence and be affected by the law. Whenever you take a stance about a legal issue, whether in the corporate office, the voting booth, or as part of local community groups, you help to create the social fabric of our nation. Your views are vital. This book will offer you knowledge and ideas from which to form and continually reassess your legal opinions and values.

IMPORTANCE

We depend upon laws for safe communities, functioning economies, and personal liberties. An easy way to gauge the importance of law is to glance through any newspaper, and read about nations that lack a strong system of justice. Notice that these countries cannot insure physical safety and personal liberties. They also fail to offer economic opportunity for most citizens. We may not always like the way our legal system works, but we depend on it for a functioning society.

FASCINATION

Law is intriguing. When the jury awarded $29 million against an auto manufacturer for a defective car design, it certainly demonstrated the law's power. But was the jury's decision right? Should a company have to pay that much for one car accident? Maybe the jury was reacting emotionally. Or perhaps the anger caused by terrible trauma should be part of a court case. These are not abstract speculations for philosophers. Verdicts such as this may cause each of us to pay more for our next automobile. Then again, we may be driving safer cars.

Sources of Contemporary Law

It would be nice if we could look up "the law" in one book, memorize it, and then apply it. But the law is not that simple. Principles and rules of law actually come from many different sources. Why is this so?

We inherited a complex structure of laws from England. Additionally, ours is a nation born in revolution and created, in large part, to protect the rights of its people from the government. The Founding Fathers created a national government but insisted the individual states maintain control in many areas. As a result, each state has its own government with exclusive power over many important areas of our lives. What the Founding Fathers created was **federalism: a double-layered system of government, with the national government and state governments each exercising important but limited powers.** To top it off, the Founders guaranteed many rights to the people alone, ordering national and state governments to keep clear. They achieved all of this in one remarkable document, the United States Constitution.

CONSTITUTIONS

United States Constitution

The United States Constitution, adopted in 1789 by the original 13 colonies, is the supreme law of the land.[1] Any law that conflicts with it is void. This Federal Constitution, as it is also known, does three basic things. First, it establishes the national government of the United States, with its three branches. The Constitution creates the Congress, with a Senate and a House of Representatives, and prescribes what laws Congress may pass. The same document establishes the office of the president and the duties that go with it. And it creates the third branch of government, the federal courts, describing what cases they may hear.

Second, the Constitution ensures the states retain all power not given to the national government. This simple idea has meant that state governments play an important role in all of our lives. Major issues of family law, criminal law, property law, and many other areas are regulated predominantly by the various states.

Third, the Constitution guarantees many basic rights to the American people. Most of these rights are found in the amendments to the Constitution. The First

---

[1] The complete text of the Constitution appears in Appendix A.

Amendment guarantees the rights of free speech, free press, and the free exercise of religion. The Fourth, Fifth, and Sixth Amendments protect the rights of any person accused of a crime. Other amendments ensure that the government treats all people equally and that it pays for any property it takes from a citizen. Merely by creating a limited government of three branches and guaranteeing basic liberties to all citizens, the Constitution became one of the most important documents ever written.

State Constitutions

In addition to the Federal Constitution, each state has a constitution that establishes its own government. All states have an executive (the governor), a legislature, and a court system. Thus there are two entire systems of government affecting each of us: a federal government, with power over the entire country, and a state government, exercising those powers that the United States Constitution did not grant to the federal government. This is federalism at work.

STATUTES

The second important source of law is statutory law. The Constitution gave to the United States Congress the power to pass laws on many subjects. **Laws passed by Congress are called statutes.** For example, the Constitution allows Congress to pass statutes about the military: to appropriate money, reorganize divisions, and close bases. You can find any federal statute, on any subject, at the Web site of the United States House of Representatives, which is **http://www.house.gov/**.

    State legislatures also pass statutes. Each state constitution allows the legislature to pass laws on a wide variety of subjects. All state legislatures, for example, may pass statutes about family law issues such as divorce and child custody.

COMMON LAW AND EQUITY

The common law originated in England, as lawyers began to record decisions and urge judges to follow earlier cases. As judges started to do that, the earlier cases, called precedent, took on steadily greater importance. Eventually, judges were obligated to follow precedent. **The principle that precedent is binding on later cases is *stare decisis,* which means "let the decision stand."** *Stare decisis* makes the law predictable, and this in turn enables businesses and private citizens to plan intelligently. We will see this principle at work later in this chapter.

    Sometimes a judge refused to hear a case, ruling that no such claims were legal. The injured party might then take his case to the Chancellor, in London, whose status in the king's council gave him unique, flexible powers. This Court of Chancery had no jury. The court's duty was to accomplish what "good conscience" required, that is, an equitable result. This more creative use of a court's power became known as equity.

    Principles of equity traveled to the colonies along with the common-law rules. All states permit courts to use equitable powers. An example of a contemporary equitable power is an **injunction,** a court order that someone stop doing something. Suppose a music company is about to issue a new compact disk by a well-known singer, but a composer claims that the recording artist has stolen his song. The composer, claiming copyright violation, could seek an injunction to prevent the company from issuing the compact disk. Every state has a trial court that can issue injunctions and carry out other equitable relief. There is no jury in an equity case.

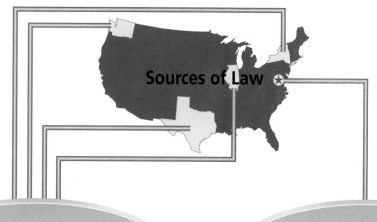

Sources of Law

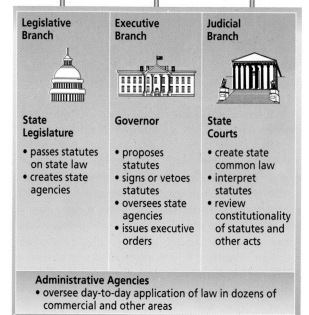

50 State Governments

State Constitution
- establishes the state government
- guarantees the rights of state residents

Legislative Branch

State Legislature
- passes statutes on state law
- creates state agencies

Executive Branch

Governor
- proposes statutes
- signs or vetoes statutes
- oversees state agencies
- issues executive orders

Judicial Branch

State Courts
- create state common law
- interpret statutes
- review constitutionality of statutes and other acts

Administrative Agencies
- oversee day-to-day application of law in dozens of commercial and other areas

One Federal Government

United States Constitution
- establishes limited federal government
- protects states' power
- guarantees liberty of citizens

Legislative Branch

Congress
- passes statutes
- ratifies treaties
- creates administrative agencies

Executive Branch

President
- proposes statutes
- signs or vetoes statutes
- oversees administrative agencies
- issues executive orders

Judicial Branch

Federal Courts
- interpret statutes
- create (limited) federal common law
- review the constitutionality of statutes and other legal acts

Administrative Agencies
- oversee day-to-day application of law in dozens of commercial and other areas

Federal Form of Government. Principles and rules of law come from many sources. The government in Washington creates and enforces law throughout the nation. But 50 state governments exercise great power in local affairs. And citizens enjoy constitutional protection from both state and federal government. The Founding Fathers wanted this balance of power and rights, but the overlapping authority creates legal complexity.

ADMINISTRATIVE LAW

In a society as large and diverse as ours, the executive and legislative branches of government cannot oversee all aspects of commerce. Congress passes statutes about air safety, but U.S. senators do not stand around air traffic towers, serving coffee to keep everyone awake. The executive branch establishes rules concerning how foreign nationals enter the United States, but presidents are reluctant to sit on the dock of the bay, watching the ships come in. **Administrative agencies** do this day-to-day work.

Most administrative agencies are created by Congress or by a state legislature. Familiar examples at the federal level are the Federal Communications Commission (FCC), which regulates most telecommunications; the Federal Trade Commission (FTC), which oversees interstate trade; and the Immigration and Naturalization Service (INS), which controls our nation's borders. At the state level, regulators set insurance rates for all companies in the state, control property development and land use, and regulate many other issues.

Criminal and Civil Law

It is a crime to embezzle money from a bank, to steal a car, to sell cocaine. **Criminal law concerns behavior so threatening that society outlaws it altogether.** Most criminal laws are statutes, passed by Congress or a state legislature. The government itself prosecutes the wrongdoer, regardless of what the bank president or car owner wants. A district attorney, paid by the government, brings the case to court. The injured party, for example the owner of the stolen car, is not in charge of the case, although she may appear as a witness. The government will seek to punish the defendant with a prison sentence, a fine, or both. If there is a fine, the money goes to the state, not to the injured party.

Civil law is different, and most of this book is about civil law. **The civil law regulates the rights and duties between parties.** Tracy agrees in writing to lease you a 30,000-square-foot store in her shopping mall. She now has a legal duty to make the space available. But then another tenant offers her more money, and she refuses to let you move in. Tracy has violated her duty, but she has not committed a crime. The government will not prosecute the case. It is up to you to file a civil lawsuit. Your case will be based on the common law of contract. You will also seek equitable relief, namely an injunction ordering Tracy not to lease to anyone else. You should win the suit, and you will get your injunction and some money damages. But Tracy will not go to jail.

Some conduct involves both civil and criminal law. Suppose Tracy is so upset over losing the court case that she becomes drunk and causes a serious car accident. She has committed the crime of driving while intoxicated, and the state will prosecute. Tracy may be fined or imprisoned. She has also committed negligence, and the injured party will file a lawsuit against her, seeking money.

LAW AND MORALITY

Law is different from morality, yet the two are obviously linked. There are many instances when the law duplicates what all of us would regard as a moral position. It is negligence to drive too fast in a school district, and few would dispute the moral value of that law. And similarly with contract law: If the owner of land agrees in writing to sell property to a buyer at a stated price, the seller must go through with the deal, and the legal outcome matches our moral expectations.

On the other hand, we have had laws that we now clearly regard as immoral. Seventy-five years ago, a factory owner could legally fire a worker for any reason at all—including, for example, her religion. Today, we would say it is immoral to fire a worker because of her faith—and the law prohibits it.

Finally, there are legal issues where the morality is not so clear. Suppose you serve alcohol to a guest who becomes intoxicated and then causes an automobile accident, seriously injuring a pedestrian. Should you, the social host, be liable? This is an issue of tort liability, which we examine in Chapter 5. As with many topics in this book, the problem has no easy answer. As you learn the law, you will have an opportunity to reexamine your own moral beliefs. One of the goals of Chapter 2, on ethics, is to offer you some new tools for that task.

Working with the Book's Features

In this section we introduce a few of the book's features, and discuss how you can use them effectively. We will start with cases.

ANALYZING A CASE

A law case is the decision a court has made in a civil lawsuit or criminal prosecution. Cases are the heart of the law and an important part of this book. Reading them effectively takes practice. The following decision in a civil suit is a good place to start.

This case begins with violence outside a nightclub. Lindie Osborne, an innocent young woman out for a night on the town, is viciously struck by a drunken karate expert. Obviously the thug who attacked her is responsible for the harm done. But is the nightclub also liable? That is no theoretical question, because the hooligan is likely to have little or no money.

CASE SUMMARY

OSBORNE v. STAGES MUSIC HALL, INC.

312 Ill. App. 3d 141; 726 N.E.2d 728; 2000 Ill. App. LEXIS157; 244 Ill. Dec. 753
Illinois Court of Appeals, 2000

FACTS: Stages Music Hall owned the Metro Club in Chicago. Karl Trujillo and his friend Daniel Hosneola became intoxicated while at the Metro and got into a violent fight with eight of the club's bouncers. Trujillo, trained in the martial arts, knocked down two of the employees, but the bouncers finally ejected the young men, who remained outside the door, clamoring for readmission.

Meanwhile, Lindie Osborne and her friend Michelle Becht were leaving the Metro. As Becht exited, one of the young men slapped her in the face. Osborne hurried outside, but as she approached her friend, Trujillo spun on his heel and kicked her in the face. Osborne fell to the ground. The two men left the scene but were later arrested.

Osborne suffered two facial fractures that required permanent plates and pins to be inserted in her jaw, which was wired shut for six weeks. She sued Stages, but the trial court gave a directed verdict for Stages, meaning that it dismissed the case. The court declared that Stages had no duty to protect Osborne because the incident took place on a public sidewalk, and because Trujillo's assault was not foreseeable. Osborne appealed.

ISSUE: Did Stages have a duty to protect Osborne from Trujillo's attack?

DECISION: Yes, Stages did have a duty to protect Osborne. Reversed and remanded to the trial court.

REASONING: An injured plaintiff can only recover if the defendant had a duty to her. In deciding whether to impose this burden, courts examine the foreseeability of the injury and the consequences to the defendant.

Metro's bouncers knew that Trujillo and Hosneola were intoxicated, combative, and angry.

After they ejected the two men, they made no effort to supervise the area outside the club, even though earlier in the evening they had erected barriers to control foot traffic. In other words, they exported the club's problem to the sidewalk, and then allowed two female patrons to walk directly into the danger. The club was obligated to guard against such a foreseeable assault. Stages did have a duty to Osborne.

The burden on Stages is not excessive. It might have been enough for the club simply to warn the two women of the peril. A jury should decide exactly what steps a bar must take in these circumstances. The case is remanded for a new trial. ◢

Analysis

Let's take it from the top. The case is called *Osborne v. Stages Music Hall, Inc.* Lindie Osborne is the plaintiff, the person who is suing. Stages Music Hall, Inc., which owns the Metro Club, is being sued, and is called the defendant. In this example, the plaintiff's name happens to appear first, but that is not always true. When a defendant loses a trial and files an appeal, *some* courts reverse the names of the parties.

The next line gives the legal citation, which indicates where to find the case in a law library. We explain in the footnote how to locate a book if you plan to do research.[2]

The *Facts* section provides a background to the lawsuit, written by the authors of this text. The court's own explanation of the facts is often many pages long, and may involve complex matters irrelevant to the subject covered in this book, so we relate only what is necessary.

The *Issue* section is very important. It tells you what the court had to decide—and why you are reading the case.

The *Decision.* This is the court's answer to the issue posed. A court's decision is often referred to as its *holding.* The court rules that Stages did have a duty to Osborne. The court *reverses* the trial court's decision, meaning it declares the lower court's ruling wrong and void. The judges also *remand* the case to the trial court, that is, send it back down to the lower court, for a new trial. If this court had agreed with the trial court's decision, the judges would have *affirmed* the lower court's ruling, meaning to uphold it.

---

[2] If you want to do legal research, you need to know where to find particular legal decisions. A case citation guides you to the correct volume(s). The full citation of our case is: *Osborne v. Stages Music Hall, Inc.*, 312 Ill. App. 3d 141, 726 N.E.2d 728, 2000 Ill. App. Lexis 157. The string of numbers identifies three different books in which you can find the full text of this decision. The first citation is to "Ill.App.3d," which means the official court reporter of the state of Illinois, third set. Illinois, like most states, reports its law cases in a series of numbered volumes. After the volumes reach the number 999, most reporters start over with a second set of volumes and then a third. This case appears in volume 312 of the third set of Illinois reporters. If you go to a law library and find that book, you can then turn to page 141 and—*voilà!*—you have the case. The decision is also reported in another set of volumes, called the regional reporters. This series of law reports is grouped by geographic region. Illinois is included in the northeast region, so our case appears in volume 726 of the second set of the northeast reporter, at page 728. Finally, most cases are now available online. The third citation is to the electronic law library operated by LEXIS. Once you are connected to the LEXIS service, typing "2000 Ill. App. Lexis 157" in the appropriate box will bring the Metro Club and its rowdy patrons right into your computer.

The *Reasoning.* This section explains why the court reached its decision. The actual written decision may be three paragraphs or 75 pages. Some judges offer us lucid prose, while others seem intent on torturing the reader. Judges frequently digress and often discuss matters that are irrelevant to the issue on which this text is focusing. For those reasons, we have taken the court's explanation and cast it in our own words. If you are curious about the full opinion, you can always look it up.

Let us examine the reasoning. The court begins with a general point of law, applicable to many cases. The judges point out that a defendant is liable only if he has a duty to the plaintiff. Whether there is such a duty depends on the foreseeability of the injury and the potential burden placed on the defendant. The judges are emphasizing that courts do not reach decisions arbitrarily. They attempt to make thoughtful choices, consistent with earlier rulings, that make good sense for the general public.

The court then describes the key facts that it will use to decide whether Stages had a duty to Osborne. The judges note that the club's bouncers knew the two disorderly men were drunk and dangerous. Yet after evicting the men from the club, the bouncers neither supervised the sidewalk, nor warned departing patrons of the obvious danger. The bouncers rid themselves of an unpleasant problem and left it for everyone else to cope with the resulting risk. The court concludes that an injury was easy to foresee, and that as a result Stages did have a duty to Osborne. Finally, the judges explain that imposing a duty on the club is not a particularly heavy burden, because the club might have fulfilled this duty simply by warning its patrons of the danger.

Why does the court not specify what Metro should have done? The judges are leaving that decision to the jury, which will have several questions to answer: What would a reasonable club have done to prevent the harm? Did the Metro club do enough? (Almost certainly not, since they did nothing.) How severe were Osborne's injuries? How much money does the Metro owe her? The jury will consider all of these questions, if the parties go through with the second trial. In all likelihood, though, now that an appeals court has ruled that Metro *did* have a duty, the defendant will be eager to settle out of court. The most important issue of the case is decided: Metro does not escape liability merely because the attack occurred outside.

UPDATE

In this feature, we ask students to find a current article on an issue discussed in the text. The goal is for you to apply the principles of this course to current events—this material is very real! You may use periodicals from the library or articles from any electronic database. The article should be dated within the past two months.

Find an article on nightclub liability. What did the club allegedly do or fail to do? Is this a civil or criminal case? What outcome do you anticipate? How could the owner have avoided the problem?

"YOU BE THE JUDGE"

Many cases involve difficult decisions for juries and judges. Often both parties have legitimate, opposing arguments. Most chapters in this book will have a feature called "You Be the Judge," in which we present the facts of a case but not the court's holding. We offer you two opposing arguments based on the kinds of claims the lawyers made in court. We leave it up to you to debate and decide which position is stronger or to add your own arguments to those given. The following case is another negligence lawsuit, with issues similar to those in the Osborne case. A suicide caused a distraught family to sue a rock singer and music producer. Once again the defendants asked the judge to dismiss the case. They pointed out, correctly, that a negligence case requires a plaintiff to prove that the defendant could have foreseen the type of harm that occurred. Could Ozzy Osbourne have foreseen this sad outcome to one of his songs? You be the judge.

YOU BE THE JUDGE

McCOLLUM v. CBS, INC.

202 Cal. App. 3d 989, 249 Cal. Rptr. 187, 1988 Cal. App. LEXIS 909
California Court of Appeal, 1988

FACTS: John McCollum, 19 years old, was an alcoholic with serious emotional problems. He listened over and over to music recorded by Ozzy Osbourne on CBS records, particularly two albums called *Blizzard of Oz* and *Diary of a Madman.* He usually listened to the music on the family stereo in the living room because the sound was most intense there. One Friday evening, though, he went to his bedroom and lay on his bed, listening to more Osbourne music. He placed a loaded .22 caliber handgun to his right temple and pulled the trigger.

McCollum's parents sued Osbourne and CBS records, claiming that they negligently aided and encouraged John to commit suicide. The parents' argument was that Osbourne's songs were designed to appeal to unstable youths, and that the message of some of his music explicitly urged death. One of the songs John had listened to before his death was "Suicide Solution," which included these lyrics:

Wine is fine but whiskey's quicker
Suicide is slow with liquor
Take a bottle drown your sorrows
Then it floods away tomorrows
Now you live inside a bottle
The reaper's travelling at full throttle
It's catching you but you don't see
The reaper is you and the reaper is me
Breaking law, knocking doors
But there's no one at home
Made your bed, rest your head
But you lie there and moan
Where to hide, Suicide is the only way out
Don't you know what it's really about.[3]

The trial court dismissed the lawsuit, ruling that the plaintiff had not made out a valid negligence claim. The court ruled the First Amendment's free speech provision protected the rights of Osbourne and CBS to publish any music they wanted. In addition, the court found that the defendants could not have foreseen that anyone would respond to the lyrics by taking his own life. With no foreseeability, the court ruled, the plaintiffs' case must fail. The parents appealed.

YOU BE THE JUDGE: **Was McCollum's suicide foreseeable?**

ARGUMENT FOR THE PARENTS: Your honors, for years Ozzy Osbourne has been well known as the "madman" of rock and roll. The words and music of his songs revolve around bizarre, antisocial beliefs, emphasizing death and satanic worship. Many of his songs suggest that life is hopeless and suicide is not only acceptable but desirable. Now one of his devoted fans has acted on Osbourne's advice and killed himself. The defendants share responsibility for this tragic death.

Osbourne and CBS knew that many of Osbourne's fans struggled with self-identity, alienation, and substance abuse. Both defendants aggressively targeted this market and reaped enormous profits. They realized that the confused youths who adored Osbourne were precisely those most vulnerable to vicious advice. Yet in spite of their knowledge, both defendants churned out songs such as "Suicide Solution," urging troubled, chemically addicted young people to kill themselves. Not

---

[3] Words and music by John Osbourne, Robert Daisley, and Randy Rhoads. TRO © Copyright 1981 Essex Music International, Inc., New York, New York and Kord Music Publishers, London, England. Used by permission.

only was it foreseeable that one of Osbourne's fans would sooner or later take his life, it was inevitable. The only way to ensure this doesn't occur again is to permit a jury to hear the parents' case and, if it is persuaded by the evidence, to award the grieving parents damages.

ARGUMENT FOR OSBOURNE AND CBS: Your honors, we all agree that this death was tragic and unnecessary. But the plaintiffs delude themselves if they think Mr. Osbourne and CBS bear any responsibility. The fact is that John McCollum was deeply troubled and alcoholic. He was responsible for his life— and for his own death. Next to the young man himself, of course, those who bear the greatest responsibility for his sad life and gruesome end are his parents, the plaintiffs in this case. Mr. Osbourne

and CBS sympathize with the parents' bereavement, but not with their attempt to foist responsibility onto others.

If the plaintiffs' farfetched foreseeability argument were the law—which it is not—every singer, writer, and film and television producer would be at risk of several thousand lawsuits every year. Under their theory, a producer who made a bank robbery movie would be liable for every robbery that took place afterward, as would every author or singer who ever mentioned the subject. The First Amendment was written to ensure that we do have access to arts and entertainment, and to prohibit efforts at silencing artists with outlandish lawsuits. This death was never foreseeable, and no jury should ever hear the case. ▗

Chapter Conclusion

We depend upon the law to give us a stable nation and economy, a fair society, a safe place to live and work. But while law is a vital tool for crafting the society we want, there are no easy answers about how to create it. In a democracy, we all participate in the crafting. Legal rules control us, yet we create them. A working knowledge of the law can help build a successful career—and a solid democracy.

Chapter Review

1. Our federal system of government means that law comes from a national government in Washington, D.C. and from 50 state governments.

2. The primary sources of contemporary law are:

   • United States Constitution and state constitutions.

   • Statutes, which are drafted by legislatures.

   • Common law, which is the body of cases decided by judges, as they follow earlier cases, known as precedent; and

   • Administrative law, the rules and decisions made by federal and state administrative agencies.

3. Criminal law concerns behavior so threatening to society that it is outlawed altogether. Civil law deals with duties and disputes between parties, not outlawed behavior.

PRACTICE TEST

Matching Questions

Match the following terms with their definitions:

___ **A.** Statute

___ **B.** Administrative Agencies

___ **C.** Common law

___ **D.** *Stare decisis*

___ **E.** United States Constitution

1. Law created by judges.

2. Let the decision stand.

3. A law passed by Congress or a state legislature.

4. The supreme law of the land.

5. The Internal Revenue Service; the Federal Communications Commission; the Federal Trade Commission.

True/False Questions

Circle true or false:

1. T F The idea that current cases must be decided based on earlier cases is called legal positivism.

2. T F Civil lawsuits are brought to court by the injured party, but criminal cases must be prosecuted by the government.

3. T F Congress established the federal government by passing a series of statutes.

4. T F The federal government has three branches: executive, legislative, and administrative.

5. T F Law is different from morality, but the two are closely linked.

Multiple-Choice Questions

6. More American law comes from one country than from any other. Which country?

(a) France.

(b) England.

(c) Germany

(d) Spain

(e) Canada

7. Under the United States Constitution, power that is not expressly given to the federal government is retained by

(a) The courts

(b) The Congress

(c) The Founding Fathers

(d) The states and the people

(e) International treaty

8. The 25 nations of the European Union sometimes struggle to create a unified policy that works for all of the countries, while still permitting each member nation to maintain adequate power over its own affairs. With what legal principle are they struggling?

(a) Jurisprudence

(b) Precedent

(c) Strict construction.

(d) Federalism

(e) Morality

9. Judges use precedent to create what kind of law?

(a) Common law

(b) Statutes

(c) National law

(d) Local law

(e) Empirical law

10. Rebecca leaves a store at night and enters the store's parking lot. Before she can reach her car, she is robbed at gunpoint. Rebecca sues the store. When a court decides whether the store had a *duty* to prevent this harm, what issue will the judges focus on?

    (a) Federalism

    (b) Equity

    (c) Legal realism

    (d) Morality

    (e) Foreseeability

Short-Answer Questions

11. Union organizers at a hospital wanted to distribute leaflets to potential union members, but hospital rules prohibited leafletting in areas of patient care, hallways, cafeterias, and any areas open to the public. The National Labor Relations Board (NLRB) ruled that these restrictions violated the law and ordered the hospital to permit the activities in the cafeteria and coffee shop. The NLRB cannot create common law or statutory law. What kind of law was it creating?

12. Bill and Diane are hiking in the woods. Diane walks down a hill to fetch fresh water. Bill meets a stranger, who introduces herself as Katrina. Bill sells a kilo of cocaine to Katrina, who then flashes a badge and mentions how much she enjoys her job at the Drug Enforcement Administration. Diane, heading back to camp with the water, meets Freddy, a motorist whose car has overheated. Freddy is late for a meeting where he expects to make a $30 million profit; he's desperate for water for his car. He promises to pay Diane $500 tomorrow if she will give him the pail of water, which she does. The next day, Bill is in jail and Freddy refuses to pay for Diane's water. Explain the criminal law/civil law distinction and what it means to Bill and Diane. Who will do what to whom, with what results?

13. The stock market crash of 1929 and the Great Depression that followed were caused in part because so many investors blindly put their money into stocks they knew nothing about. During the 1920s it was often impossible for an investor to find out what a corporation was planning to do with its money, who was running the corporation, and many other vital things. Congress responded by passing the Securities Act of 1933, which required a corporation to divulge more information about itself before it could seek money for a new stock issue. What kind of law did Congress create? Explain the relationship between voters, Congress, and the law.

14. Ethics: The greatest of all Chinese lawgivers, Confucius, did not esteem written laws. He believed that good rulers were the best guarantee of justice. Does our legal system rely primarily on the rule of law or the rule of people? Which do you instinctively trust more? Confucius himself was an extraordinarly wise man. How does that fact influence your analysis?

15. Role Reversal: Each Practice Test contains one Role Reversal feature, in which we challenge you to create your own exam question. The goal is to think creatively and accurately. Crafting questions is a good way to reinforce what you understand and recognize the areas you need to review. Your professor may ask you to submit the questions in writing or electronically or to prepare an overhead slide.

    The question should be challenging enough that the average student will need to stop and think, but clear enough that there is only one answer. Useful questions can be formatted as essay, short answer, or multiple choice. Notice that some exam questions are very direct, while others require deeper analysis. Here are two examples. The first focuses on a definition.

    Question: An injunction is:

    (a) A decision by an appeals court affirming the trial court.

    (b) A decision by an appeals court reversing a trial court.

    (c) A decision by an appeals court sending a decision back down to a lower court.

    (d) A theory of law requiring that current cases be decided based on earlier decisions.

    (e) A judge's order that someone stop doing something.

    As you know, the correct answer is "e."

    The next question demands that the student spot the issue of law involved (foreseeability) and correctly apply it to the facts provided.

    Question: Marvin asks Sheila, a qualified auto mechanic, to fix his engine, which constantly stalls (stops) while driving. When Marvin returns, Sheila informs him that the engine is now "Perfect—runs like a top." Marvin drives home along Lonesome

Highway. Suddenly the car stalls. Sheila has not fixed it. Marvin pulls over and begins the long walk to the nearest telephone. A blimp flies overhead, advertising "Top" brand tires. Tragically, the blimp suddenly plummets to earth and explodes 20 feet from Marvin, seriously injuring him. Marvin sues Sheila. Sheila's best defense is that:

(a) The falling blimp is so bizarre that Sheila could never have foreseen it.

(b) Sheila made reasonable efforts to fix the engine.

(c) Marvin should have checked the engine himself.

(d) Marvin should have carried a cell phone with him in case of emergencies.

(e) Sheila is a qualified mechanic and her work is presumptively sufficient.

The correct answer is "a." Notice that the same facts could be used as an essay question, simply by deleting the multiple-choice answers. Now it is your turn for Role Reversal: draft a multiple-choice question focusing on federalism.

Internet Research Problem

Take a look at **http://www.courttv.com**. Find two current cases that interest you: one civil, one criminal. Explain the different roles played by each type of law, and summarize the issues in the respective cases.

You can find further practice problems in the Online Quiz at **http://beatty.westbuslaw.com** or in the Study Guide that accompanies this text.

Business Ethics and Social Responsibility

Arthur Haupt is a 79-year-old retired waiter who lives with his black cat, Max, in a tidy, 650-square-foot apartment in Chicago's Rienzi Plaza apartment building. He works 20 hours a week, shelving books at Loyola University's law library, earning $6.95 an hour. He also gets Social Security and two modest pensions. His total income last year was $18,713. His monthly rent in this federally subsidized apartment is $352. Market rent for an equivalent apartment would be as high as $1,644.

Last fall, Haupt's landlord notified him that he might be evicted. Nationally, landlords have taken about 125,000 units out of the federal subsidy program. At the same time, demand for subsidized housing is rising, in part because big cities such as Chicago are tearing down their old public housing projects and telling residents to find subsidized apartments instead. Where will Arthur Haupt go?

The landlord, Sheldon Baskin, is not a bad guy. Twenty years ago, he and his partners signed a contract with the federal government, promising to build and maintain an apartment building for low-income Chicagoans. In exchange, the government guaranteed a steady stream of rent. But now the contract on Rienzi Plaza is set to expire. Baskin could make a

larger profit on the building, either by selling it, converting it to condominiums, or renting to unsubsidized tenants who could pay more. What does Baskin owe to his investors?

The Rienzi tenants and community groups have begun looking for a white knight—someone who could buy the building and preserve its low-income housing. Two for-profit organizations that specialize in investing in "affordable" housing expressed interest in buying Rienzi, but neither has made an offer.

Meanwhile, Mr. Baskin asked government officials how much more rent they would pay if he extended his contract for five years. Officials said they would have to hire an outside consultant to do a market study, a task that would take months—long past the deadline by which federal regulations require Mr. Baskin to announce his decision.[1] ◼

Business is an enormously powerful tool that corporate managers can use to accomplish many goals. They may wish to earn a good living, even to become wealthy, but they can also use their business skills to cure the ill, feed the hungry, entertain the bored, and in many other ways affect their community, their country, and their world.

This book is primarily about the impact of law on business. But law is only one set of rules that governs business; ethics is another. **Ethics is the study of how people ought to act.** Law and ethics are often in harmony. Most reasonable people agree that murder should be prohibited. But law and ethics are not always compatible. In some cases, it might be *ethical* to commit an *illegal* act; in others, it might be *unethical* to be *legal*. A 75-year-old man confined to a wheelchair robbed a bank in San Diego of $70 so that he could buy heart medicine. That was illegal—was it unethical?

Or what about Martin Luther King, Jr., who was arrested in Birmingham, Alabama in 1963 for leading illegal sit-ins and marches to protest laws that discriminated against African Americans. When eight local clergymen criticized his activities, King offered this defense:

> [W]hen you suddenly find your tongue twisted as you seek to explain to your six-year-old daughter why she can't go to the public amusement park that has just been advertised on television, and see tears welling up when she is told that Funtown is closed to colored children . . . [W]hen you take a cross-country drive and find it necessary to sleep night after night in the uncomfortable corners of your automobile because no motel will accept you . . . How can [we] advocate breaking some laws and obeying others? . . . I agree with St. Augustine that "an unjust law is not law at all."[2]

The other chapters of this book focus on legal issues, but this chapter concentrates on ethics. In all of the examples in this chapter, the activities are *legal*, but are they *ethical?*

---

[1] Based on the article: Jonathan Eig, "Landlord's Dilemma: Help Poor Tenants or Seek More Profits." *The Wall Street Journal,* July 17, 2001, p. 1.

[2] Martin Luther King, Jr., "Letter from Birmingham Jail." *The Christian Century,* June 12, 1963.

Why Bother with Ethics?

Business schools teach students how to maximize the profitability of an enterprise, large or small. Some people argue that, in the *long run,* ethical behavior does indeed maximize profitability. But they must mean the *very* long run, because to date there is little evidence that ethical behavior necessarily pays financially, either in the short or the long run.

For instance, when a fire destroyed the Malden Mills factory in Lawrence, Massachusetts, its 70-year-old owner, Aaron Feuerstein, could have shut down the business, collected the insurance money, and sailed off into retirement. But a layoff of the factory's 3,000 employees would have been a major economic blow to the region. So instead Feuerstein kept the workers on the payroll making the company's patented Polartec fabric, while he rebuilt the factory. However, five years after the fire, Malden Mills filed bankruptcy papers. The company was not able to pay off the loans it had incurred to keep the business going.

In contrast, unethical behavior is no bar to financial success. The first antitrust laws in America were designed, at least in part, to restrain John D. Rockefeller's unethical activities. Yet, four generations later, his name is still synonymous with wealth and his numerous heirs can live comfortably on their inheritance from him.

If ethical behavior does not necessarily pay and unethical behavior sometimes does, why bother with ethics?

SOCIETY AS A WHOLE BENEFITS FROM ETHICAL BEHAVIOR

John Akers, the former chairman of IBM, argues that, without ethical behavior, a society cannot be economically competitive. He puts it this way:

> *Ethics and competitiveness are inseparable. No society anywhere will compete very long or successfully with people stabbing each other in the back; with people trying to steal from each other; with everything requiring notarized confirmation because you can't trust the other fellow; with every little squabble ending in litigation; and with government writing reams of regulatory legislation, tying business hand and foot to keep it honest. There is no escaping this fact: the greater the measure of mutual trust and confidence in the ethics of a society, the greater its economic strength.[3]*

PEOPLE FEEL BETTER WHEN THEY BEHAVE ETHICALLY

Every businessperson has many opportunities to be dishonest. Consider how one person felt when he *resisted* temptation:

> *Occasionally a customer forgot to send a bill for materials shipped to us for processing . . . It would have been so easy to rationalize remaining silent. After all, didn't they deserve to lose because of their inefficiency? However, upon instructing our staff to inform the parties of their errors, I found them eager to do so. Our honesty was beneficial in subtle ways. The "inefficient" customer remained loyal*

---

[3] David Grier, "Confronting Ethical Dilemmas," unpublished manuscript of remarks at the Royal Bank of Canada, Sept. 19, 1989.

for years . . . [O]ur highly moral policy had a marvelously beneficial effect on our employees. Through the years, many an employee visited my office to let me know that they liked working for a "straight" company.[4]

Profitability is generally not what motivates managers to care about ethics. Managers want to feel good about themselves and the decisions they have made; they want to sleep at night. Their decisions—to lay off employees, install safety devices in cars, burn a cleaner fuel—affect peoples' lives.

The Web site **http://www.yourtruehero.org** offers examples of ordinary people who have inspired others with their ethical behavior.

UNETHICAL BEHAVIOR CAN BE VERY COSTLY

Unethical behavior is a risky business strategy—it may lead to disaster. An engaged couple made a reservation, and put down a $1,500 deposit, to hold their wedding reception at a New Hampshire restaurant. Tragically, the bride died of asthma four months before the wedding. Invoking the terms of the contract, the restaurant owner refused to return the couple's deposit. In a letter to the groom, he admitted, "Morally, I would of course agree that the deposit should be returned." When newspapers reported this story, customers deserted the restaurant and it was forced into bankruptcy—over a $1,500 disagreement.[5] Unethical behavior does not always damage a business, but it certainly has the potential of destroying a company overnight. So why take the risk?

Even if unethical behavior does not devastate a business, it can cause other, subtler damage. In one survey, a majority of those questioned said that they had witnessed unethical behavior in their workplace and that this behavior had reduced productivity, job stability, and profits. Unethical behavior in an organization creates a cynical, resentful, and unproductive workforce.

So why bother with ethics? Because society benefits when managers behave ethically. Because ethical managers have happier, more satisfying lives. And because unethical behavior can destroy a business faster than a snake can bite.

What Is Ethical Behavior?

It is one thing to decide, in theory, that being ethical is good; in practice, it can be much more difficult to make the right decisions. Supreme Court Justice Potter Stewart once said that he could not define pornography, but he knew it when he saw it. Many people feel the same way about ethics—that somehow, instinctively, they know what is right and wrong. In real life, however, ethical dilemmas are often not black and white, but many shades of gray. The purpose of this section is to analyze the following ethics checklist as an aid to managers in making tough decisions:

- What are the facts?

- What are the critical issues?

---

[4] Hugh Aaron, "Doing the Right Thing in Business." *The Wall Street Journal,* June 21, 1993, p. A10.

[5] John Milne, "N.H. Restaurant Goes Bankrupt in Wake of Wedding Refund Flap." *The Boston Globe,* Sept. 9, 1994, p. 25.

- Who are the stakeholders?
- What are the alternatives?
- What are the ethical implications of each alternative?
  - Is it legal?
  - How would it look in the light of day?
  - What are the consequences?
  - Does it violate important values?
  - Does it violate the Golden Rule?
  - Is it just?
  - Has the process been fair?

ANALYZING THE ETHICS CHECKLIST

What Are the Facts?

Although this question seems obvious, people often forget in the heat of battle to listen to (and, more importantly, to hear) all the different viewpoints. It is crucial to discover the facts, firsthand, from the people involved.

What Are the Critical Issues?

In analyzing ethical dilemmas, expand your thinking to include all the important issues. Avoid a narrow focus that encompasses only one or two aspects. In the case of the New Hampshire restaurant that refused to refund a deposit, the owner focused on the narrow legal issue. His interpretation of the contract was correct. But if the owner had expanded his thinking to include consideration for his customers, he might have reached a different decision.

Who Are the Stakeholders?

Stakeholders are all the people potentially affected by the decision. That list might include subordinates, bosses, shareholders, suppliers, customers, members of the community in which the business operates, society as a whole, or even more remote stakeholders, such as future generations.

What Are the Alternatives?

The next step is to list the reasonable alternatives. A creative manager may find a clever solution that is a winner for everyone. What alternatives might be available to Sheldon Baskin, the landlord who faced a dilemma in the opening scenario?

What Are the Ethical Implications of Each Alternative?

Is the Alternative Legal?   Illegal may not always be synonymous with unethical, but, as a general rule, you need to think long and hard about the ethics of any illegal activities.

How Would the Alternative Look in the Light of Day?   If your activities were reported on the evening news, how would you feel? Proud? Embarrassed? Horrified? Undoubtedly, sexual harassment would be virtually eliminated if people thought that their parents, spouse, or partner would shortly see a video replay of the offending behavior.

What Are the Consequences of This Alternative?   Ask yourself: Am I hurting anyone by this decision? Which alternative will cause the greatest good (or the least harm) to the most people? For example, you would like to fire an incompetent employee. That decision will clearly have adverse consequences for him. But the other employees in your division will benefit, and so will the shareholders of your company. You should look with a particularly critical eye if an alternative benefits you while harming others.

This approach to decision making was first developed by two 19th-century English philosophers, Jeremy Bentham and John Stuart Mill. Bentham and Mill argued that all decisions should be evaluated according to how much happiness they create. This philosophy is called **utilitarianism.**

Does the Alternative Violate Important Values?   In addition to consequences, consider fundamental values. It is possible to commit an act that does not harm anyone else, but is still the wrong thing to do. Suppose, for instance, that you are away from home and have the opportunity to engage in a temporary sexual liaison. You are absolutely certain that your spouse will never find out and your partner for the night will have no regrets or guilt. There would be no negative consequences, but you believe that infidelity is wrong, regardless of the consequences, so you resist temptation.

Some people question whether, as a diverse, heterogeneous society (not to mention world), we have common values. But throughout history, and across many different cultures, common values do appear, such as: consideration, courage, integrity, and self-control. Although reasonable people may disagree about a precise list of important values, most would agree that values matter. Try compiling your own list of values and then check it periodically to see if you are living up to it in your business and personal life.

Does the Alternative Violate the Golden Rule?   We all know the Golden Rule: Do unto others as you would have them do unto you. If one of the alternatives you are considering would be particularly unpleasant when done to you, reconsider.

Immanuel Kant, an 18th-century German philosopher, took the Golden Rule one step further with a concept he called the **categorical imperative.** According to Kant, you should not do something unless you would be willing for everyone else to do it, too (and not just to you). Imagine that you could cheat on an exam without getting caught. You might gain some short-term benefit—a higher grade. But what would happen if everyone cheated? The professor would have to make the exams harder or curve everyone's grade down. If your school developed a reputation for cheating, you might not be able to find a job after graduation. Cheating works only if most people are honest. To take advantage of everyone else's honesty is contemptible.

Is the Alternative Just?   Are you respecting individual rights such as liberty (privacy, free speech, and religious freedom), welfare (employment, housing, food, education), and equality? Would it be just to fire an employee because her political views differ from your own?

Has the Process Been Fair?   Unequal outcomes are acceptable, provided they are the result of a fair process. At the end of a poker game, some players have won and others lost, but no one can complain that the result was unfair, unless players cheated. In a business context, a fair process means applying the same set of rules to everyone. If three of your subordinates are vying for the same promotion, it would be unfair to let one state her case to you but not the others.

Applying the Ethics Checklist: Making Decisions

An organization has responsibilities to customers, employees, shareholders, and society generally, both here and overseas. The purpose of this section is to apply the ethics checklist to actual business dilemmas. The checklist does not lead to one particular solution; rather it is a method to use in thinking through ethics problems. The goal is for you to reach a decision that satisfies you.

ORGANIZATION'S RESPONSIBILITY TO SOCIETY

Facts.   In the United States, teenagers routinely list alcohol commercials among their favorite advertisements. Adolescents who frequently see ads for alcohol are more likely to believe that drinkers are attractive, athletic, and successful. They are also more likely to drink, drink excessively, and drink in hazardous situations, such as when driving a car.

Then Secretary of Health and Human Services, Louis W. Sullivan publicly denounced the test marketing of Uptown, a high-tar cigarette targeted at African Americans. He called it "contemptible that the tobacco industry has sought to increase their market" among minorities because this population was "already bearing more than its fair share of smoking-related illness and mortality." Comedian Jay Leno joked that R. J. Reynolds named the cigarette Uptown "because the word 'genocide' was already taken."[6]

A promotion for Request Jeans shows a man pinning a naked woman against a shower wall. In Canada, an advertisement features childlike model Kate Moss lying naked on a couch. Above the couch is a picture of the product being promoted—Calvin Klein's Obsession for Men.

Critical Issues.   Is it ethical to entice teenagers into drinking or African Americans into smoking? What about glorifying rape to sell jeans?

Stakeholders.   Ad designers are primarily responsible to their firms and the firms' clients. After all, designers are paid to sell product, not to make the world a better place. But do the designers have any responsibility to the people who see the advertisements? Or to society as a whole?

Alternatives.   Firms have at least four alternatives in dealing with issues of ethics in advertising. They can:

• Ignore ethics and simply strive to create promotions that sell the most product

• Try, in a general way, to minimize racism, sexism, and other exploitation

---

[6] Richard W. Pollay, Jung S. Lee, and David Carter-Whitney, "Separate, But Not Equal: Racial Segmentation in Cigarette Advertising," *Journal of Advertising,* Mar. 1992, vol. 21, no. 1, p. 45.

- Include, as part of the development process, a systematic, focused review of the underlying messages contained in their advertisements; or

- Refuse to create any ads that are potentially demeaning, insensitive, or dangerous, recognizing that such a stand may lead to a loss of clients.

Ethical Implications.   All of these alternatives are perfectly legal. And, far from the ad executives being embarrassed if the ads see the light of day, the whole purpose of ads is to be seen. As for the consequences, the ads may help clients sell their products. But a manager might question whether these ads violate fundamental values. Are they showing consideration for others? Do they encourage self-control? As for the Golden Rule, how would an advertising executive feel about an ad in which he was being sexually assaulted? Are these ads just? Do they violate principles of equality? Is the process by which they have been created fair? Have those who may be adversely affected by them had an opportunity to be heard?

Organization's Responsibility to Its Customers

In this chapter's opening scenario, landlord Sheldon Baskin faced a dilemma: His contract with the federal government was set to expire, so he would soon have the right to evict the poor and elderly tenants in Rienzi Plaza. What would you do if you were Baskin? What obligation does he have to the tenants? To his investors? Is it fair to them if he decides to subsidize the rents of low-income tenants? What about the community? Does it benefit from having elderly members? How will Baskin feel about himself if he puts these elderly tenants out on the street? Or if *The Wall Street Journal* runs a front-page article about his eviction plans? On the other hand, could he argue that it is the government's responsibility to house the poor and elderly? Is there any compromise solution?

Organization's Responsibility to Its Employees

Which deal would you rather have?

- *Plan A:* Your company has a 401(k) pension plan. Federal law permits you to contribute a certain amount tax free each year. You can then invest that money in a choice of mutual funds. In addition, for every dollar you put in, your employer will contribute a dollar of company stock. However, you cannot sell this company stock until you are 50 years old. The good news is that, if the stock market—and your company—prosper, your retirement years will indeed be golden. The downside is that if the stock market or your company declines, you could be like one of the tenants in Rienzi Plaza, unable to pay your rent.

- *Plan B:* The amount of your pension is guaranteed by the company, regardless of how the market performs. This guarantee is backed up by a federal agency. In addition, as part of your annual bonus, you are given company stock that you can sell at any time. Moreover, when you invest in your special 401(k) plan, the company guarantees a minimum annual return of 12%.

Enron Corp. offered Plan A to its rank-and-file employees; Plan B was reserved for top executives. At one point, 60% of the assets in the Plan A 401(k) was invested in Enron stock. As this stock plummeted in value from $80 a share to under $1, many employees were unable to sell out because they had not yet turned 50. Even worse, as the stock price sank, the company imposed a month-long "blackout" prohibiting all employees from selling any stock in the 401(k) while a new plan administrator took over. Less than a month after the blackout ended, the company filed for bankruptcy. As a result, the 401(k) plans lost $1.3 billion of their $2.1 billion worth.

Is it ethical for top executives to set up two such different pension/savings plans for company employees? Supporters of 401(k) plans argue that offering top executives a better pension is no more unfair than paying them higher wages. Moreover, the 401(k) plans are better than nothing, which is what companies would offer if these plans were not available. One could even argue that these plans are good for employees: The matching employer contributions entice many workers into saving money that they might otherwise just spend. And the plans are good for employers: A company can meet its obligations with transfers of company stock, which are much cheaper to make than the cash payments required by traditional plans. Moreover, companies like having their stock in the friendly hands of employees. The younger employees whom companies want to attract rarely object to a 401(k) pension plan because they do not appreciate the significant disadvantages—and companies have not been eager to educate them.

Should companies do more than meet the minimum requirements of the pension laws? How much more? Would a generous pension plan for all employees benefit the company by attracting valuable workers or harm the company by decreasing its profits?

ORGANIZATION'S RESPONSIBILITY TO ITS SHAREHOLDERS

Ford Motor Company was founded by William C. Ford, Jr.'s great-grandfather, Henry. The younger Ford is an avid environmentalist and also head of the company that bears his name. He shares the concern of many environmentalists that automobile exhaust contributes to global warming. Ford Motor recently announced that it would increase the fuel economy of its sport utility vehicles (SUVs) by 25% (about 5 miles per gallon). This decision comes shortly after Congress, partly in response to lobbying by automobile manufacturers, refused to increase national fuel economy standards.

About a fifth of the vehicles Ford sells each year are SUVs. Because these heavy cars are gas inefficient, Ford has barely been able to meet existing federal standards. To achieve the higher fuel economy it has announced, the company will make more auto parts out of lighter aluminum and will redesign the SUV engines. The cost of implementing these changes could be substantial, but the company has decided not to pass the costs on to consumers. The plan is controversial within the company itself, because some insiders believe that consumers would prefer more powerful cars to more gas-efficient ones.

Milton Friedman, a Nobel laureate in economics, famously observed, "The one and only social responsibility of business is to increase its profits."[7] He argued that an executive should act for the benefit of the owners of the company. His primary responsibility is to them. If an individual wishes to support other responsibilities, such as a charity, a church, a city, or a country, let him do so with his own time and money, not that of the shareholders.

---

[7] Milton Friedman, "The Social Responsibility of Business Is to Increase Its Profits," *The New York Times Magazine*, Sept. 13, 1970, p. 32.

If you were a shareholder of Ford Motor Company, would you support the fuel efficiency initiative? Perhaps you would prefer to earn higher returns on your stock so that you could give money to other projects you consider more compelling (finding an AIDS vaccine, for example). Should William Ford, who inherited his company stock, have the right to spend company funds to support his pet projects? If the air needs to be cleaner or the schools richer, why shouldn't private donors or public institutions be responsible, not one company's shareholders?

Do executives have an obligation to be socially responsible? Ford officials argue that their fuel economy initiative may be profitable—it might increase sales enough to make up for the lower profit per car. Moreover, an environmentally friendly image may help sales of all its cars, not just SUVs. By voluntarily increasing its own fuel standards, Ford may head off tighter federal regulation.

UPDATE

Find a current news article about fuel economy standards. Have other automobile manufacturers (here and abroad) followed Ford's lead? Did Ford sales increase enough to offset the cost of making these design changes? Did Ford's stock price rise or fall after the company announced its intention to increase fuel economy?

ORGANIZATION'S RESPONSIBILITY OVERSEAS

An American company's ethical obligations do not end at the border. What ethical duties does an American manager owe to stakeholders in countries where the culture and economic circumstances are very different?

Here is a typical story from Guatemala:

"My father left home a long time ago. My mother supported me and my five brothers and sisters by selling tortillas and corn. Our house was a tin shack on the side of the road. We were crowded with all of us in one room, especially when it rained and the roof and sides leaked. One day the police came and cleared us all out. The owners of the land said we couldn't come back unless we paid rent. How could we afford that? I was 12 and my mother said it was time for me to work. But most people won't hire children. "Lots of other kids shine shoes or beg, but I heard that the maquila [clothing factory] was willing to hire children if we would work as hard as older people.

"I can keep up with the grown-ups. We work from 6:00 in the morning to 6:30 at night, with half an hour break at noon. We have no other breaks the whole rest of the day. If I don't work fast enough, they hit me, not too hard, and threaten to fire me. Sometimes, if there is too much work to do, they'll lock the doors and not let us out until everything is finished.

"I earn $30 a week and without that money, we would not have enough to eat. My mother hopes all of my brothers and sisters can get jobs in the factory, too. Of course, I'd rather be in school where I could wear a uniform and have friends. Then I could get a job as a clerk at the medical clinic. I would find people's files and tell them how long before the doctor could see them."

This description paints a distasteful picture indeed: Children being beaten as they work 12-hour days. Should American companies (and consumers) buy goods that are produced in sweatshop factories? Jeffrey Sachs, a leading economist and adviser to developing nations, says, "My concern is not that there are too many sweatshops but that there are too few."[8] Why would he support sweatshops and child labor?

Historically, poor children have worked. Indeed, for many people and for many centuries, the point of having children was to create a supply of free labor to help support the family. In England in 1860, almost 40% of 14-year-old boys worked, and that was not just a few hours at Burger Box, but more likely 60 hours a week. That percentage is higher than in Africa or India today. For a child in a desperately poor family, the choice is not work or school, it is work, starvation, or prostitution. (For a history of sweatshops in America, work your way over to **http://americanhistory.si.edu/sweatshops/**.)

Industrialization has always been the first stepping-stone out of dire poverty— it was in England, it is now in the Third World. Eventually, higher productivity leads to higher wages. During the past 50 years, Taiwan and South Korea welcomed sweatshops. During the same period, India resisted what it perceived to be foreign exploitation. Although all three countries started at the same economic level, Taiwan and South Korea today have much lower levels of infant mortality and much higher levels of education than India.[9]

When governments or customers try to force Third World factories to pay higher wages, the factory owners typically either relocate to lower-wage countries or mechanize, thereby reducing the need for workers. In either case, the local economy suffers.

The difference, however, between the 21st and the 19th centuries is that now there are wealthy countries able to help their poorer neighbors. In the 19th century, England was among the richest countries, so it was on its own to solve its economic problems. Is America ethically obligated to assist people around the world who live in abject poverty? Already, owing to pressure from activists, many companies have introduced better conditions in their factories. Workers are less likely to be beaten. They can go to the bathroom without asking permission. They might even receive rudimentary medical care. Manufacturing processes use fewer dangerous chemicals. Factories are cleaner, with better lighting and more ventilation. But hours are still long and wages low.

Many of these sweatshops produce clothing. As a consumer, how much would you be willing to pay in higher clothing prices to eliminate sweatshops and child labor? As a taxpayer, how much are you willing to pay in taxes to subsidize Third World incomes so that sweatshops and child labor are no longer necessary?

---

[8] Allen R. Meyerson, "In Principle, A Case for More 'Sweatshops,'" *The New York Times*, June 22, 1997, p. E5.

[9] The data in this and the preceding paragraph are from Nicholas D. Kristof and Sheryl WuDunn, "Two Cheers for Sweatshops," *The New York Times Magazine*, Sept. 24, 2000, p. 70.

Chapter Conclusion

Even employees who are ethical in their personal lives may find it difficult to uphold their standards at work if those around them behave differently. Managers wonder what they can do to create an ethical environment in their companies. The surest way to infuse ethics throughout an organization is for top executives to behave ethically themselves. Few employees will bother to "do the right thing" unless they observe that their bosses value and support such behavior. To ensure a more ethical world, managers must be an example for others, both within and outside their organizations.

For further discussion and updates on ethical issues, check in at **http://ethics.acusd.edu/ index.html**.

Chapter Review

1. There are at least three reasons to be concerned about ethics in a business environment:

   • Society as a whole benefits from ethical behavior.

   • People feel better when they behave ethically.

   • Unethical behavior can be very costly.

2. The ethics checklist:

   • What are the facts?

   • What are the critical issues?

   • Who are the stakeholders?

   • What are the alternatives?

• What are the ethical implications of each alternative?

   • Is it legal?

   • How would it look in the light of day?

   • What are the consequences?

   • Does it violate important values?

   • Does it violate the Golden Rule?

   • Is it just?

   • Has the process been fair?

PRACTICE TEST

Matching Questions

Match the following people with their views:

___ **A.** Martin Luther King, Jr.

___ **B.** John Akers

___ **C.** Immanuel Kant

___ **D.** Milton Friedman

___ **E.** Jeremy Bentham and John Stuart Mill

1. Argued that "Ethics and competitiveness are inseparable."

2. Argued that all decisions should be evaluated according to how much utility they create.

3. Argued that "The one and only social responsibility of business is to increase its profits."

4. Argued that "An unjust law is not law at all."

5. Argued that you should not do something unless you would be willing for everyone else to do it, too.

Short-Answer Questions

1. Executives were considering the possibility of moving their company to a different state. They wanted to determine if employees would be willing to relocate, but they did not want the employees to know the company was contemplating a move because the final decision had not yet been made. Instead of asking the employees directly, the company hired a firm to carry out a telephone survey. When calling the employees, these "pollsters" pretended to be conducting a public opinion poll and identified themselves as working for the new state's chamber of commerce. Has this company behaved in an ethical manner? Would there have been a better way to obtain this information?

2. Rap artist Ice-T and his band, Body Count, recorded a song called *Cop Killer,* in which the singer gleefully anticipates slitting a policeman's throat. (The lyrics to this song are available at **http://www.cleat.org/remember/TimeWarner/lyrics.html**.) Time Warner, Inc. produced this song and other gangsta rap recordings with violent and sexually degrading lyrics. Recorded music is an important source of profits for the company. If Time Warner renounces rap albums, its reputation in the music business—and future profits—might suffer. This damage could spill over into the multimedia market, which is crucial to Time Warner's future. What decision would you make if you were CEO of Time Warner?

3. H. B. Fuller Company of St. Paul is a leading manufacturer of industrial glues. Its mission statement says the company "will conduct business legally and ethically." It has endowed a university chair in business ethics and donates 5% of its profits to charity. But now it is under attack for selling its shoemakers' glue, Resistol, in Central America. Many homeless children in these countries have become addicted to Resistol's fumes. So widespread is the problem that glue sniffers in Central America are called "resistoleros." Glue manufacturers in Europe have added a foul-smelling oil to their glue that discourages abusers. Fuller fears that the smell may also discourage legitimate users. What should Fuller do?

4. According to the Electronic Industries Association, questionable returns have become the toughest problem plaguing the consumer electronics industry. Some consumers purchase electronic equipment to use once or twice for a special occasion and then return it—a radar detector for a weekend getaway or a camcorder to videotape a wedding. Or a customer might return a cordless telephone because he cannot figure out how it works. The retailer's staff lacks the expertise to help, so they refund the customer's money and ship the phone back to the manufacturer labeled as defective. Excessive and unwarranted returns force manufacturers to repackage and reship perfectly good products, imposing extra costs that squeeze their profits and raise prices to consumers. One retailer returned a cordless telephone that was two years old and had been chewed up by a dog. What ethical obligations do consumers and retailers have in these circumstances?

5. Genentech, Inc. manufactures Protropin, a genetically engineered version of the human growth hormone. This drug's purpose is to enhance the growth of short children. Protropin is an important product for Genentech, accounting for more than one third of the company's total revenue of $217 million. Although the drug is approved for the treatment of children whose bodies make inadequate quantities of growth hormone, many doctors prescribe it for children with normal amounts of growth hormone who simply happen to be short. There is no firm evidence that the drug actually increases growth for short children with normal growth hormone. Moreover, many people question whether it is appropriate to prescribe such a powerful drug for cosmetic reasons, especially when the drug may not work. Nor is there proof that it is safe over the long term. Is Genentech behaving ethically? Should it discourage doctors from prescribing the drug to normal, short children?

6. ROLE REVERSAL: Write one or two paragraphs that could be used as an essay question describing an ethical dilemma that you have faced in your own life.

Internet Research Problem

Go to **http://www.mapnp.org/library/ethics/ethxgde.htm** and click on Ethics Tools: Resolving Ethical Dilemmas (with Real-to-Life Examples). Outline the steps you would take to resolve one of these dilemmas. Use the ethics checklist in this chapter to guide you.

You can find further practice problems in the Online Quiz at **http://beatty.westbuslaw.com** or in the Study Guide that accompanies this text.

Courts, Litigation, and Alternative Dispute Resolution

Tony Caruso had not returned for dinner, and his wife, Karen, was nervous. She put on some sandals and hurried across the dunes, a half mile to the ocean shore. She soon came upon Tony's dog, Blue, tied to an old picket fence. Tony's shoes and clothing were piled neatly nearby. Karen and friends searched frantically throughout the evening. A little past midnight, Tony's body washed ashore, his lungs filled with water. A local doctor concluded he had accidentally drowned.

Karen and her friends were not the only ones distraught. Tony had been partners with Beth Smiles in an environmental consulting business, Enviro-Vision. They were good friends, and Beth was emotionally devastated. When she was able to focus on business issues, Beth filed an insurance claim with the Coastal Insurance Group. Beth hated to think about Tony's death in financial terms, but she was relieved that the struggling business would receive $2 million on the life insurance policy.

Several months after filing the claim, Beth received this reply from Coastal: "Under the policy issued to Enviro-Vision, we are liable in the amount of $1 million in the event of Mr. Caruso's death. If his death is accidental, we are liable to pay double indemnity of $2 million. But pursuant to section H(5) death by suicide is not covered. After a thorough investigation, we have concluded that Anthony Caruso's death was an act of suicide. Your claim is denied in its entirety." Beth was furious. She was convinced Tony was incapable of suicide. And her company could not afford the $2 million loss. She decided to consult her lawyer, Chris Pruitt.

Three Fundamental Areas of Law

This case is a fictionalized version of several real cases based on double indemnity insurance policies. In this chapter we follow Beth's dispute with Coastal from initial interview through appeal, using it to examine three fundamental areas of law: the structure of our court systems, litigation, and alternative dispute resolution.

When Beth Smiles meets with her lawyer, Chris Pruitt brings a second attorney from his firm, Janet Booker, who is an experienced **litigator,** that is, a lawyer who handles court cases. If they file a lawsuit, Janet will be in charge, so Chris wants her there for the first meeting. Janet probes about Tony's home life, the status of the business, his personal finances, everything. Beth becomes upset that Janet doesn't seem sympathetic, but Chris explains that Janet is doing her job: She needs all the information, good and bad.

LITIGATION VERSUS ALTERNATIVE DISPUTE RESOLUTION

Janet starts thinking about the two methods of dispute resolution: litigation and alternative dispute resolution. **Litigation** refers to lawsuits, the process of filing claims in court, trying the case, and living with the court's ruling. **Alternative dispute resolution** is any other formal or informal process used to settle disputes without resorting to a trial. It is increasingly popular with corporations and individuals alike because it is generally cheaper and faster than litigation.

Alternative Dispute Resolution

Janet Booker knows that even after expert legal help, vast expense, and years of work, litigation may leave clients unsatisfied. If she can use alternative dispute resolution (ADR) to create a mutually satisfactory solution in a few months, for a fraction of the cost, she is glad to do it. In most cases the parties **negotiate,** whether personally or through lawyers. Fortunately, the great majority of disputes are resolved this way. Negotiation often begins as soon as a dispute arises and may last a few days or several years.

MEDIATION

Mediation is the fastest-growing method of dispute resolution in the United States. Here, a neutral person, called a mediator, attempts to coax the two disputing parties toward a voluntary settlement.

A mediator does not render a decision in the dispute, but uses a variety of skills to prod the parties toward agreement. Mediators must earn the trust of both parties, listen closely, diffuse anger and fear, explore common ground, cajole the parties into different perspectives, and build the will to settle. Good mediators do not need a law degree, but they must have a sense of humor and low blood pressure.

ARBITRATION

In this form of ADR, the parties agree to bring in a neutral third party, but with a major difference: The arbitrator has the power to impose an award. The arbitrator allows each side equal time to present its case and, after deliberation, issues a binding decision, generally without giving reasons. Unlike mediation, arbitration ensures that there will be a final result, although the parties lose control of the outcome. Arbitration is generally faster and cheaper than litigation.

Parties in arbitration give up many rights that litigants retain, including discovery. *Discovery*, as we see below, allows the two sides in a lawsuit to obtain, before trial, documentary and other evidence from the opponent. Arbitration permits both sides to keep secret many files that would have to be divulged in a court case, potentially depriving the opposing side of valuable evidence. A party may have a stronger case than it realizes, and the absence of discovery may permanently deny it that knowledge.

Janet Booker proposes to Coastal Insurance that they use ADR to expedite a decision in their dispute. Coastal rejects the offer. Coastal's lawyer, Rich Stewart, insists that suicide is apparent.

It is a long way to go before trial, but Janet has to prepare her case. The first thing she thinks about is where to file the lawsuit.

Court Systems

The United States has more than 50 systems of courts. One nationwide system of *federal* courts serves the entire country. In addition, each *state* has its court system. The state and federal courts are in different buildings, have different judges, and hear different kinds of cases. Each has special powers and certain limitations.

STATE COURTS

The typical state court system forms a pyramid, as Exhibit 3.1 shows. You may use the Internet to learn the exact names and powers of the courts in your state. Go to **http://www.state.[name of state].gov**, and click on "agencies," "courts," or a similar link.

Trial Courts

Almost all cases start in trial courts, the ones endlessly portrayed on television and in film. There is one judge and there will often (but not always) be a jury. This is the only court to hear testimony from witnesses and receive evidence. **Trial courts determine the facts of a particular dispute and apply to those facts the law given by earlier appellate court decisions.**

In the Enviro-Vision dispute, the trial court will decide all important facts that are in dispute. Did Tony Caruso die? Did he drown? Assuming he drowned, was his death accidental or suicide? Once the jury has decided the facts, it will apply the law to those facts. If Tony Caruso died accidentally, contract law provides that Beth Smiles is entitled to double indemnity benefits. If the jury decides he killed himself, Beth gets nothing.

Jurisdiction refers to a court's power to hear a case. A plaintiff may start a lawsuit only in a court that has jurisdiction over that kind of case. Some state trial courts have very limited jurisdiction, while others have the power to hear almost any case. In Exhibit 3.1, notice that some courts have power only to hear cases of small claims, domestic relations, and so forth.

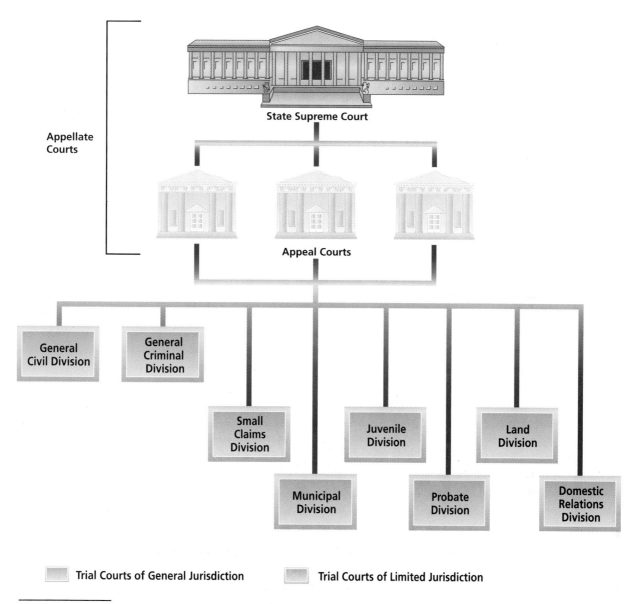

Exhibit 3.1

Appellate Courts

Appellate courts are entirely different from trial courts. Three or more judges hear the case. There are no juries, ever. These courts do not hear witnesses or take new evidence. They hear appeals of cases already tried below. **Appeal courts generally accept the facts given to them by trial courts and review the trial record to see if the court made errors of law.**

An appeal court reviews the trial record to make sure that the lower court correctly applied the law to the facts. If the trial court made an **error of law,** the appeal court may require a new trial. Suppose the jury concludes that Tony Caruso committed suicide, but votes to award Enviro-Vision $1 million because it feels sorry for Beth Smiles. That is an error of law: If Tony committed suicide, Beth is entitled to nothing. An appellate court will reverse the decision, declaring Coastal the victor.

The party that loses at the trial court generally is entitled to be heard at the intermediate court of appeals. The party filing the appeal is the **appellant.** The party opposing the appeal (because it won at trial) is the **appellee.** A party that loses at the court of appeals may *ask* the state supreme court to hear an appeal, but the state's highest court may choose not to accept the case.

FEDERAL COURTS

As discussed in Chapter 1, federal courts are established by the United States Constitution, which limits what kinds of cases can be brought in any federal court. For our purposes, two kinds of civil lawsuits are permitted in federal court: federal question cases and diversity cases.

Federal Question Cases

A claim based on the United States Constitution, a federal statute, or a federal treaty is called a federal question case.[1] Federal courts have jurisdiction over these cases. If the Environmental Protection Agency orders Logging Company not to cut in a particular forest, and Logging Company claims that the agency has wrongly deprived it of its property, that suit is based on a federal statute (a law passed by Congress) and is thus a federal question. Enviro-Vision's potential suit merely concerns an insurance contract. The federal district court has no federal question jurisdiction over the case.

Diversity Cases

Even if no federal law is at issue, federal courts have jurisdiction when (1) the plaintiff and defendant are citizens of different states and (2) the amount in dispute exceeds $75,000. The theory behind diversity jurisdiction is that courts of one state might be biased against citizens of another state. To ensure fairness, the parties have the option of federal court.

Enviro-Vision is located in Oregon and Coastal Insurance is incorporated in Georgia.[2] They are citizens of different states and the amount in dispute far exceeds $75,000. Janet could file this case in United States District Court based on diversity jurisdiction.

Trial Courts

United States District Courts are the primary trial courts in the federal system. The nation is divided into about 94 districts, and each has a district court. States with smaller populations have one district, while those with larger populations have several districts. There are also specialized trial courts such as Bankruptcy Court,

---

[1] 28 U.S.C. §1331 governs federal question jurisdiction and 28 U.S.C. §1332 covers diversity jurisdiction.

[2] For diversity purposes, a corporation is a citizen of the state in which it is incorporated and the state in which it has its principal place of business.

Tax Court, and others which are, you will be happy to know, beyond the scope of this book.

Appellate Courts

United States Courts of Appeals.   These are the intermediate courts of appeals. As the map below shows, they are divided into "circuits," most of which are geographical areas. For example, an appeal from the Northern District of Illinois would go to the Court of Appeals for the Seventh Circuit. You will find an interactive map of the District and Circuit Courts at **http://www.uscourts.gov/links.html**.

United States Supreme Court.   This is the highest court in the country. There are nine justices on the Court. One justice is the chief justice and the other eight are associate justices. When they decide a case, each justice casts an equal vote. For a face-to-face meeting with Supreme Court justices, past and present, introduce yourself to **http://oyez.nwu.edu.**

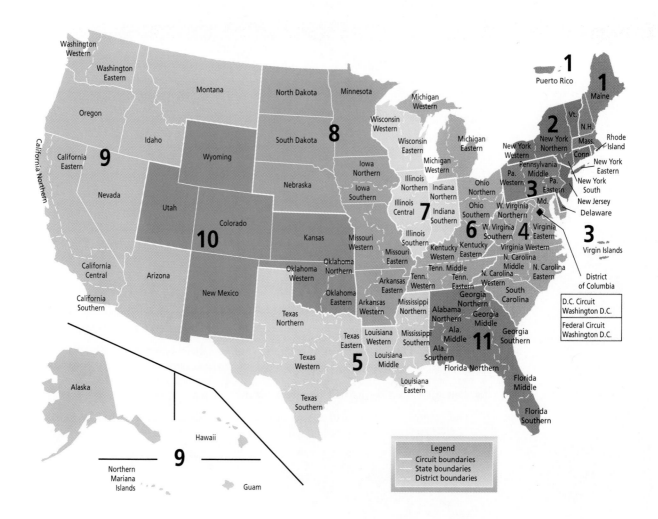

Litigation

Janet Booker decides to file the Enviro-Vision suit in the Oregon trial court. She thinks that a state court judge may take the issue more seriously than a federal district court judge.

PLEADINGS

The documents that begin a lawsuit are called the **pleadings.** The most important are the complaint and the answer.

Complaint

The plaintiff files in court a **complaint,** which is a short, plain statement of the facts she is alleging and the legal claims she is making. The purpose of the complaint is to inform the defendant of the general nature of the claims and the need to come into court and protect his interests.

Janet Booker files the complaint, as shown below. Since Enviro-Vision is a partnership, she files the suit on behalf of Beth, personally.

STATE OF OREGON

CIRCUIT COURT

Multnomah County   Civil Action No._____

Elizabeth Smiles,

Plaintiff

JURY TRIAL DEMANDED

v.

Coastal Insurance Company, Inc.,

Defendant

COMPLAINT

Plaintiff Elizabeth Smiles states that:

1. She is a citizen of Multnomah County, Oregon.

2. Defendant Coastal Insurance Company, Inc., is incorporated under the laws of Georgia and has as its usual place of business 148 Thrift Street, Savannah, Georgia.

3. On or about July 5, 2006, plaintiff Smiles ("Smiles"), Defendant Coastal Insurance Co, Inc. ("Coastal") and Anthony Caruso entered into an insurance contract ("the contract"), a copy of which is annexed hereto as Exhibit "A." This contract was signed by all parties or their authorized agents, in Multnomah County, Oregon.

4. The contract obligates Coastal to pay to Smiles the sum of two million dollars ($2 million) if Anthony Caruso should die accidentally.

5. On or about September 18, 2006, Anthony Caruso accidentally drowned and died while swimming.

6. Coastal has refused to pay any sum pursuant to the contract.

7. Coastal has knowingly, willingly and unreasonably refused to honor its obligations under the contract.

WHEREFORE, plaintiff Elizabeth Smiles demands judgment against defendant Coastal for all monies due under the contract; demands triple damages for Coastal's knowing, willing, and unreasonable refusal to honor its obligations; and demands all costs and attorney's fees, with interest.

ELIZABETH SMILES,

By her attorney,

[Signed]

Janet Booker

Pruitt, Booker & Bother

983 Joy Avenue

Portland, OR

October 18, 2006

Answer

Coastal has 20 days in which to file an answer. Coastal's **answer is a brief reply to each of the allegations in the complaint.** The answer tells the court and the plaintiff exactly what issues are in dispute. Since Coastal admits that the parties entered into the contract that Beth claims they did, there is no need for her to prove that in court. The court can focus its attention on the issue that Coastal disputes: whether Tony Caruso died accidentally.

If the defendant fails to answer in time, the plaintiff will ask for a **default judgment,** meaning a decision that the plaintiff wins without a trial.

Class Actions

Suppose Janet uncovers evidence that Coastal denies 80% of all life insurance claims, calling them suicide. She could ask the court to permit a **class action.** If the court granted her request, she would represent the entire group of plaintiffs, including those who are unaware of the lawsuit or even unaware they were harmed. Class actions can give the plaintiffs much greater leverage, since the defendant's potential liability is vastly increased. Because Janet has no such evidence, she decides not to pursue a class action.

Discovery

Discovery is the critical, pre-trial opportunity for both parties to learn the strengths and weaknesses of the opponent's case.

The theory behind civil litigation is that the best outcome is a negotiated settlement and that parties will move toward agreement if they understand the opponent's case. That is likeliest to occur if both sides have an opportunity to examine the evidence their opponent will bring to trial. Further, if a case does go all the way to trial, efficient and fair litigation cannot take place in a courtroom filled, like a piñata, with surprises. In television dramas, witnesses say astonishing things that amaze the courtroom. In real trials, the lawyers know in advance the answers to practically all questions asked because discovery has allowed them to see the opponent's documents and question its witnesses. The following are the most important forms of discovery.

Interrogatories.   These are written questions that the opposing party must answer, in writing, under oath.

Depositions.   These provide a chance for one party's lawyer to question the other party, or a potential witness, under oath. The person being questioned is the **deponent.** Lawyers for both parties are present.

Production of Documents and Things.   Each side may ask the other side to produce relevant documents for inspection and copying; to produce physical objects, such as part of a car alleged to be defective; and for permission to enter on land to make an inspection, for example, at the scene of an accident.

Physical and Mental Examination.   A party may ask the court to order an examination of the other party, if his physical or mental condition is relevant, for example, in a case of medical malpractice.

Janet Booker begins her discovery with interrogatories. Her goal is to learn Coastal's basic position and factual evidence and then follow up with more detailed questioning during depositions. Her interrogatories ask for every fact Coastal relied on in denying the claim. She asks for the names of all witnesses, the identity of all documents, and the descriptions of all things or objects that they considered. She requests the names of all corporate officers who played any role in the decision and of any expert witnesses Coastal plans to call.

Coastal has 30 days to answer Janet's interrogatories. Before it responds, Coastal mails to Janet a notice of deposition, stating its intention to depose Beth Smiles. Beth and Janet will go to the office of Coastal's lawyer, and Beth will answer questions under oath. But at the same time Coastal sends this notice, it sends 25 other notices of deposition. It will depose Karen Caruso as soon as Beth's deposition is over. Coastal also plans to depose all seven employees of Enviro-Vision; three neighbors who lived near Tony and Karen's beach house; two policemen who participated in the search; the doctor and two nurses involved in the case; Tony's physician; Jerry Johnson, Tony's tennis partner; Craig Bergson, a college roommate; a couple who had dinner with Tony and Karen a week before his death; and several other people.

Rich, the Coastal lawyer, proceeds to take Beth's deposition. It takes two full days. He asks about Enviro-Vision's past and present. He learns that Tony appeared to have won their biggest contract ever from Rapid City, Oregon, but that he then lost it when he had a fight with Rapid City's mayor. He inquires into Tony's mood, learns that he was depressed, and probes in every direction he can to find evidence of suicidal motivation. Janet and Rich argue frequently over questions and whether Beth should have to answer them. At times Janet is persuaded and permits Beth to answer; at other times she instructs Beth not to answer. For example, toward the end of the second day, Rich asks Beth whether she and Tony had been sexually involved. Janet instructs Beth not to answer. This fight necessitates a trip into court. As both lawyers know, **the parties are entitled to discover anything that could reasonably lead to valid evidence.** Rich wants his questions answered, and files a motion to compel discovery. The judge will have to decide whether Rich's questions are reasonable.

A **motion** is a formal request to the court. Before, during, and after trial, both parties will file many motions. A **motion to compel discovery** is a request to the court for an order requiring the other side to answer discovery. The judge rules that Beth must discuss Tony's romantic life only if Coastal has evidence that he was involved with someone outside his marriage. Because the company lacks any such evidence, the judge denies Coastal's motion.

At the same time, the judge hears Beth's **motion for a protective order.** Beth claims that Rich has scheduled too many depositions; the time and expense are a huge burden to a small company. The judge limits Rich to 10 depositions. Rich cancels several depositions, including that of Craig Bergson, Tony's old roommate. As we will see, Craig knows crucial facts about this case, and Rich's decision not to depose him will have major consequences.

Judges rule on many discovery motions, often with dramatic effect, as the following case demonstrates.

CASE SUMMARY

KLUPT v. KRONGARD

126 Md. App. 179; 728 A.2d 727; 1999 Md. App. LEXIS 86
Court of Special Appeals of Maryland, 1999

FACTS: Carle Klupt invented a disposable cardboard videocassette. He formed a corporation, Sharbar, Inc., to develop and market the product. Alvin Krongard and a few associates paid $115,000 to Klupt for a chance to participate in the manufacture and sale of the cassette. Three years later, Krongard and his associates sued Klupt and Sharbar, claiming that the defendants had fraudulently persuaded them to enter into the deal, in other words, had lied in order to get their investment. Klupt, in turn, sued the plaintiffs, asserting that the Krongard group had actually attempted to seize control of the business in violation of their agreement.

The plaintiffs served requests on Klupt for all documents (in writing or any other medium) relating to oral or written communications between the parties. The plaintiffs also scheduled a deposition of Klupt, but the defendant repeatedly objected to dates. Klupt also changed lawyers from time to time, causing further delay. When the trial court ordered him to appear on a specific date, Klupt claimed he had another deposition scheduled for the same date, but that later turned out to be false.

When he finally appeared for deposition, Klupt produced only four pages of notes from phone conversations with the plaintiffs. He then managed to delay the deposition six more months. When it resumed, Klupt was forced to concede that in fact he had tape-recorded all of his phone calls for many years and had possessed hundreds of recorded calls between the parties. However, in the gap between depositions, he had destroyed the tapes.

Arguing that this was gross abuse of the discovery process, the plaintiffs moved to dismiss Klupt's claims. The trial court granted the motion, and Klupt appealed.

ISSUE: Did the trial court abuse its discretion by dismissing Klupt's claims?

DECISION: Affirmed. The trial court did not abuse its discretion by dismissing Klupt's claims.

REASONING: Appellate courts prefer not to second-guess trial judges on discovery rulings, and will reverse only when the lower court has abused its discretion. However, dismissing a claim is a grave penalty, appropriate only in cases of extraordinary misconduct.

During discovery, Klupt prepared false, back-dated memoranda. He also deliberately concealed many tapes from the court and even from his own lawyer. The tapes were clearly subject to discovery, because they were reasonably calculated to enable the other party to find admissible evidence. Klupt admitted that he had smashed the tapes with a hammer, at a time when the lawsuit was already several months old. The trial judge did not abuse his discretion in dismissing Klupt's claims. ◢

Summary Judgment

When discovery is completed, both sides may consider seeking summary judgment. **Summary judgment is a ruling by the court that no trial is necessary because there are no essential facts in dispute.** The purpose of a trial is to determine the facts of the case, that is, to decide who did what to whom, why, when, and with what consequences. If there are no relevant facts in dispute, then there is no need for a trial.

Suppose Joe sues EZBuck Films, claiming that the company's new movie, *Lover Boy*, violates the copyright of a screenplay that he wrote, called *Love Man*. Discovery establishes that the two stories are suspiciously similar. But EZBuck's lawyer also learns that Joe sold the copyright for *Love Man* to HotShot Pix. EZBuck may or may not have violated a copyright, but there is no need for a trial because Joe cannot win even if there is a copyright violation. He does not own the copyright. When EZBuck moves for summary judgment, the court will grant the motion, terminating the case before trial.

In the following case, the defendant won summary judgment, meaning that the case never went to trial. And yet, this was only the beginning of trouble for that defendant, William Jefferson Clinton.

CASE SUMMARY

◤ JONES v. CLINTON

990 F. Supp. 657, 1998 U.S. Dist. LEXIS 3902
United States District Court for the Eastern District of Arkansas, 1998

FACTS: In 1991, Bill Clinton was governor of Arkansas. Paula Jones worked for a state agency, the Arkansas Industrial Development Commission (AIDC). When Clinton became president, Jones sued him, claiming that he had sexually harassed her. She alleged that, in May 1991, the governor arranged for her to meet him in a hotel room in Little Rock, Arkansas. When they were alone, he put his hand on her leg and slid it toward her pelvis. She escaped from his grasp, exclaimed, "What are you doing?" and said she was "not that kind of girl." She was upset and confused, and sat on a sofa near the door. She claimed that Clinton approached her, "lowered his trousers and underwear, exposed his penis and told her to kiss it." Jones was horrified, jumped up, and said she had to leave. Clinton responded by saying, "Well, I don't want to make you do anything you don't want to do," and pulled his pants up. He added that if she got in trouble for leaving work, Jones should "have Dave call me immediately and I'll take care of it." He also said, "You are smart. Let's keep this between ourselves." Jones remained at AIDC until February 1993, when she moved to California because of her husband's job transfer.

President Clinton denied all of the allegations. He also filed for summary judgment, claiming that Jones had not alleged facts that justified a trial. Jones opposed the motion for summary judgment.

ISSUE: Was Clinton entitled to summary judgment or was Jones entitled to a trial?

DECISION: Jones failed to make out a claim of sexual harassment. Summary judgment is granted for the president.

REASONING: To establish this type of sexual harassment case, a plaintiff must show that her refusal to submit to unwelcome sexual advances resulted in specific harm to her job.

Jones received every merit increase and cost-of-living allowance for which she was eligible. Her only job transfer involved a minor change in working conditions, with no reduction in pay or benefits. Jones claims that she was obligated to sit in a less private area, often with no work to do, and was the only female employee not to receive flowers on Secretary's Day. However, even if these allegations are true, all are trivial and none is sufficient to create a sexual harassment suit. Jones has demonstrated no specific harm to her job. ◢

In other words, the court acknowledged that there were factual disputes, but concluded that even if Jones proved each of her allegations, she would still lose the case, because her allegations fell short of a legitimate case of sexual harassment. Jones appealed the case. Later the same year, as the appeal was pending and the House of Representatives was considering whether to impeach President Clinton, the parties settled the dispute. Clinton, without acknowledging any of the allegations, agreed to pay Jones $850,000 to drop the suit.

Janet and Rich each consider moving for summary judgment, but both correctly decide that they would lose. There is one major fact in dispute: Did Tony Caruso commit suicide? Only a jury may decide that issue. As long as there is some evidence supporting each side of a key factual dispute, the court may not grant summary judgment.

Well over 90% of all lawsuits are settled before trial. But the parties in the Enviro-Vision dispute seem unable to compromise, and are headed for trial.

Trial

ADVERSARY SYSTEM

Our system of justice assumes that the best way to bring out the truth is for the two contesting sides to present the strongest case possible to a neutral factfinder. Each side presents its witnesses and then the opponent has a chance to cross-examine. The **adversary system** presumes that by putting a witness on the stand and letting both lawyers "go at" her, the truth will emerge.

The judge runs the trial. Each lawyer sits at a large table near the front. Beth, looking tense and unhappy, sits with Janet. Rich Stewart sits with a Coastal executive. In the back of the courtroom are benches for the public. Today there are only a few spectators. One is Tony's old roommate, Craig Bergson, who has a special interest in the trial.

RIGHT TO JURY TRIAL

Not all cases are tried to a jury. As a general rule, both plaintiff and defendant have a right to demand a jury trial when the lawsuit is one for money damages. For example, in a typical contract lawsuit, such as Beth's insurance claim, both plaintiff and defendant have a jury trial right whether they are in state or federal court. Even in such a case, though, the parties may waive the jury right, meaning they agree to try the case to a judge.

If the plaintiff is seeking an equitable remedy, such as an injunction (an order not to do something), there is no jury right for either party. Equitable rights come from the old Court of Chancery in England, where there was never a jury. Even today, only a judge may give an equitable remedy.

Although jury selection for some cases takes many days, in the Enviro-Vision case the first day of the hearing ends with the jury selected. In the hallway outside the court, Rich offers Janet $200,000 to settle. Janet reports the offer to Beth and they agree to reject it. Craig Bergson drives home, emotionally confused. Only three weeks before his death, Tony had accidentally met his old roommate and they had had several drinks. Craig believes that what Tony told him answers the riddle of this case.

OPENING STATEMENTS

The next day, each attorney makes an opening statement to the jury, summarizing the proof he or she expects to offer, with the plaintiff going first. Janet focuses on Tony's successful life, his business and strong marriage, and the tragedy of his accidental death.[3]

Rich works hard to establish a friendly rapport with the jury. He expresses regret about the death. Nonetheless, suicide is a clear exclusion from the policy. If insurance companies are forced to pay claims they did not bargain for, everyone's insurance rates will go up.

BURDEN OF PROOF

In civil cases, the plaintiff has the **burden of proof.** That means that the plaintiff must convince the jury that its version of the case is correct; the defendant is not obligated to disprove the allegations.

The plaintiff's burden in a civil lawsuit is to prove its case by a **preponderance of the evidence.** The plaintiff must convince the jury that his or her version of the facts is at least *slightly* more likely than the defendant's version. Some courts describe this as a "51–49" persuasion, that is, that plaintiff's proof must "just tip" credibility in its favor. By contrast, in a criminal case, the prosecution must demonstrate **beyond a reasonable doubt that the defendant is guilty.** The burden of proof in a criminal case is much tougher because the likely consequences are, too. See Exhibit 3.2.

PLAINTIFF'S CASE

Since the plaintiff has the burden of proof, Janet puts in her case first. She wants to prove two things. First, that Tony died. That is easy, since the death certificate clearly demonstrates it and since Coastal does not seriously contest it. Second, in order to win double indemnity damages, she must show that the death was

---

[3] Janet Booker has dropped her claim for triple damages against Coastal. To have any hope of such a verdict, she would have to show that Coastal had no legitimate reason at all for denying the claim. Discovery has convinced her that Coastal will demonstrate some rational reasons for what it did.

Exhibit 3.2
Burden of Proof. In a civil lawsuit, a plaintiff wins with a mere preponderance of the evidence. But the prosecution must persuade a jury beyond a reasonable doubt in order to win a criminal conviction.

accidental. She will do this with the testimony of the witnesses she calls, one after the other. Her first witness is Beth. When a lawyer asks questions of her own witness, it is **direct examination.** Janet brings out all the evidence she wants the jury to hear: that the business was basically sound, though temporarily troubled, that Tony was a hard worker, why the company took out life insurance policies, and so forth.

Then Rich has a chance to **cross-examine** Beth, which means to ask questions of an opposing witness. He will try to create doubt in the jury's mind. He asks Beth only questions for which he is certain of the answers, based on discovery. Rich gets Beth to admit that the firm was not doing well the year of Tony's death; that Tony had lost the best client the firm ever had; that Beth had reduced salaries; and that Tony had been depressed about business.

Janet uses her other witnesses, Tony's friends, family, and coworkers, to fortify the impression that his death was accidental.

DEFENDANT'S CASE

Rich now puts in his case, exactly as Janet did, except that he happens to have fewer witnesses. He calls the examining doctor, who admits that Tony could have committed suicide by swimming out too far. On cross-examination, Janet gets the doctor to acknowledge that he has no idea whether Tony intentionally drowned. Rich also questions several neighbors as to how depressed Tony had seemed and how unusual it was that Blue was tied up. Some of the witnesses Rich deposed, such as the tennis partner Jerry Johnson, have nothing that will help Coastal's case, so he does not call them.

Craig Bergson, sitting in the back of the courtroom, thinks how different the trial would have been had he been called as a witness. When he and Tony had the fateful drink, Tony had been distraught: Business was terrible, he was involved in an extramarital affair that he could not end, and he saw no way out of his problems. He had no one to talk to and had been hugely relieved to speak with Craig. Several times Tony had said, "I just can't go on like this. I don't want to, anymore." Craig thought Tony seemed suicidal and urged him to see a therapist Craig knew. Tony had said that it was good advice, but Craig is unsure whether Tony sought any help.

This evidence would have affected the case. Had Rich Stewart known of the conversation, he would have deposed Craig and the therapist. Coastal's case would have been far stronger, perhaps overwhelming. But Craig's evidence will never be heard. Facts are critical. Rich's decision to depose other witnesses and omit Craig may influence the verdict more than any rule of law.

CLOSING ARGUMENT

Both lawyers sum up their case to the jury, explaining how they hope the jury will interpret what they have heard. Judge Rowland instructs the jury as to its duty. He tells them that they are to evaluate the case based only on the evidence they heard at trial, relying on their own experience and common sense.

He explains the law and the burden of proof, telling the jury that it is Beth's obligation to prove that Tony died. If Beth has proven that Tony died, she is entitled to $1 million; if she has proven that his death was accidental, she is entitled to $2 million. However, if Coastal has proven suicide, Beth receives nothing. Finally, he states that if they are unable to decide between accidental death and suicide, there is a legal presumption that it was accidental. Rich asks Judge Rowland to rephrase the "legal presumption" part, but the judge declines.

VERDICT

The jury deliberates informally, with all jurors entitled to voice their opinion. Some deliberations take two hours; some take two weeks. Many states require a unanimous verdict; others require only, for example, a 10–2 vote in civil cases.

This case presents a close call. No one saw Tony die. Yet even though they cannot know with certainty, the jury's decision will probably be the final word on whether he took his own life. After a day and a half of deliberating, the jury notifies the judge that it has reached a verdict. Rich Stewart quickly makes a new offer: $350,000. Beth hesitates but turns it down.

The judge summons the lawyers to court, and Beth goes as well. The judge asks the foreman if the jury has reached a decision. He states that it has: The jury finds that Tony Caruso drowned accidentally, and awards Beth Smiles $2 million.

Appeals

Two days later, Rich files an appeal to the court of appeal. The same day, he phones Janet and increases his settlement offer to $425,000. Beth is tempted but wants Janet's advice. Janet says the risks of an appeal are that the court will order a new trial, and they would start all over. But to accept this offer is to forfeit over $1.5 million. Beth is unsure what to do. The firm desperately needs cash now. Janet suggests they wait until oral argument, another eight months.

Rich files a brief arguing that there were two basic errors at the trial: first, that the jury's verdict is clearly contrary to the evidence; and second, that the judge gave the wrong instructions to the jury. Janet files a reply brief, opposing Rich on both issues. In her brief, Janet cites many cases that she claims are **precedent:** earlier decisions by the state supreme court on similar or identical issues.

APPEAL COURT OPTIONS

The court of appeal can **affirm** the trial court, allowing the decision to stand. The court may **modify** the decision, for example, by affirming that the plaintiff wins but decreasing the size of the award. (That is unlikely here; Beth is entitled to $2 million or nothing.) The court might **reverse and remand,** meaning it nullifies the lower court's decision and returns the case to the trial court for a new trial. Or it could simply **reverse,** turning the loser (Coastal) into the winner, with no new trial.

Janet and Beth talk. Beth is very anxious and wants to settle. She does not want to wait four or five months, only to learn that they must start all over. With Beth's approval, Janet phones Rich and offers to settle for $1.2 million. Rich snorts, "Yeah, right." Then he snaps, "750,000. Take it or leave it. Final offer." After a short conversation with her client, Janet calls back and accepts the offer.

Litigation

1. Pleadings	2. Discovery	3. Pretrial Motions
Complaint	Interrogatories	Class action
Answer	Depositions	Summary judgment
	Production of documents and things	
	Physical and mental examinations	
4. Trial	5. Jury's Role	6. Appeals
Voir dire	Judge's instructions	Affirm
Opening statements	Deliberation	Modify
Plaintiff's case	Verdict	Reverse
Defendant's case		Remand
Closing argument		

Chapter Conclusion

No one will ever know for sure whether Tony took his own life. Craig Bergson's evidence might have tipped the scales in favor of Coastal. But even that is uncertain, since the jury could have found him unpersuasive. After two years, the case ends with a settlement and uncertainty—both typical lawsuit results. The vaguely unsatisfying feeling about it all is only too common and indicates why litigation is best avoided—by reasonable negotiation.

Chapter Review

1. Alternative dispute resolution (ADR) is any formal or informal process to settle disputes without a trial. Mediation and arbitration are the two most common forms.

2. There are many systems of courts, one federal and one in each state. A federal court will hear a case only if it involves a federal question or diversity jurisdiction.

3. Trial courts determine facts and apply the law to the facts; appeal courts generally accept the facts found by the trial court and review the trial record for errors of law.

4. A complaint and an answer are the two most important pleadings, that is, documents that start a lawsuit.

5. Discovery is the critical pretrial opportunity for both parties to learn the strengths and weaknesses of the opponent's case. Important forms of discovery include interrogatories, depositions, production of documents and objects, physical and mental examinations, and requests for admission.

6. A motion is a formal request to the court.

7. Summary judgment is a ruling by the court that no trial is necessary because there are no essential facts in dispute.

8. Generally, both plaintiff and defendant may demand a jury in any lawsuit for money damages.

9. The plaintiff's burden of proof in a civil lawsuit is preponderance of the evidence, meaning that its version of the facts must be at least slightly more persuasive than the defendant's. In a criminal prosecution, the government must offer proof beyond a reasonable doubt in order to win a conviction.

10. The verdict is the jury's decision in a case.

11. An appeal court has many options. The court may affirm, upholding the lower court's decision; modify, changing the verdict but leaving the same party victorious; reverse, transforming the loser into the winner; and/or remand, sending the case back to the lower court.

PRACTICE TEST

Matching Questions

Match the following terms with their definitions:

___ **A.** Arbitration

___ **B.** Diversity jurisdiction

___ **C.** Mediation

___ **D.** Interrogatories

___ **E.** Deposition

1. A pretrial procedure involving written questions to be signed under oath.

2. A form of ADR in which the parties themselves craft the settlement.

3. A pretrial procedure involving oral questions answered under oath.

4. The power of a federal court to hear certain cases between citizens of different states.

5. A form of ADR which leads to a binding decision.

True/False Questions

Circle true or false:

1. T   F   One advantage of arbitration is that it provides the parties with greater opportunities for discovery than litigation does.

2. T   F   In the United States there are many separate courts, but only one court *system,* organized as a pyramid.

3. T   F   If we are listening to witnesses testify, we must be in a trial court.

4. T   F   About one half of all lawsuits settle before trial.

5. T   F   In a lawsuit for money damages, both the plaintiff and the defendant are generally entitled to a jury.

Multiple-Choice Questions

6. A federal court has the power to hear

   (a) Any case.

   (b) Any case between citizens of different states.

   (c) Any criminal case.

   (d) Appeals of any cases from lower courts.

   (e) Any lawsuit based on a federal statute.

7. Before trial begins, a defendant in a civil lawsuit believes that even if the plaintiff proves everything he has alleged, the law requires the defendant to win. The defendant should

   (a) Request arbitration.

   (b) Request a mandatory verdict.

   (c) Move for recusal.

   (d) Move for summary judgment.

   (e) Demand mediation.

8. In a civil lawsuit

   (a) The defendant is presumed innocent until proven guilty.

   (b) The defendant is presumed guilty until proven innocent.

   (c) The plaintiff must prove her case by a preponderance of the evidence.

   (d) The plaintiff must prove her case beyond a reasonable doubt.

   (e) The defendant must establish his defenses to the satisfaction of the court.

9. Mack sues Jasmine, claiming that she caused an automobile accident. At trial, Jasmine's lawyer is asking her questions about the accident. This is

   (a) An interrogatory

   (b) A deposition

   (c) Direct examination

   (d) Cross-examination

   (e) Opening statement

10. Jurisdiction refers to

   (a) The jury's decision.

   (b) The judge's instructions to the jury.

   (c) Pretrial questions posed by one attorney to the opposing party.

   (d) The power of a court to hear a particular case.

   (e) A decision by an appellate court to send the case back to the trial court.

Short-Answer Questions

11. State which court(s) have jurisdiction as to each of these lawsuits:

    (a) Pat wants to sue his next-door neighbor Dorothy, claiming that Dorothy promised to sell him the house next door.

    (b) Paula, who lives in New York City, wants to sue Dizzy Movie Theatres, whose principal place of business is Dallas. She claims that while she was in Texas on holiday, she was injured by their negligent maintenance of a stairway. She claims damages of $30,000.

    (c) Phil lives in Tennessee. He wants to sue Dick, who lives in Ohio. Phil claims that Dick agreed to sell him 3,000 acres of farmland in Ohio, worth over $2 million.

    (d) Pete, incarcerated in a federal prison in Kansas, wants to sue the United States government. He claims that his treatment by prison authorities violates three federal statutes.

12. Students are now suing schools for sexual harassment. The cases raise important issues about the limits of discovery. In a case in Petaluma, California, a girl claimed that she was harassed for years and that the school knew about it and failed to act. According to press reports, she alleges that a boy stood up in class and asked, "I have a question. I want to know if [Jane Doe] has sex with hot dogs." In discovery, the school district sought the parents' therapy records, the girl's diary, and a psychological evaluation of the girl. Should they get those things?

13. ETHICS: Trial practice is dramatically different in Britain. The lawyers for the two sides, called solicitors, do not go into court. Courtroom work is done by different lawyers, called barristers. The barristers are not permitted to interview any witnesses before trial. They know the substance of what each witness intends to say, but do not rehearse questions and answers, as in the United States. Which approach do you consider more effective? More ethical? What is the purpose of a trial? Of pretrial preparation?

14. You plan to open a store in Chicago, specializing in beautiful rugs imported from Turkey. You will work with a native Turk who will purchase and ship the rugs to your store. You are wise enough to insist on a contract establishing the rights and obligations of both parties and would prefer an ADR clause. But you want to be sensitive to different cultures and do not want a clause that will magnify a problem or alienate the parties. Is there some way you can accomplish all of this?

15. Claus Scherer worked for Rockwell International and was paid over $300,000 per year. Rockwell fired Scherer for alleged sexual harassment of several workers, including his secretary, Terry Pendy. Scherer sued in United States District Court, alleging that Rockwell's real motive in firing him was his high salary.

Rockwell moved for summary judgment, offering deposition transcripts of various employees. Pendy's deposition detailed instances of harassment, including comments about her body, instances of unwelcome touching, and discussions of extramarital affairs. Another deposition, from a Rockwell employee who investigated the allegations, included complaints by other employees as to Scherer's harassment. In his own deposition, which he offered to oppose summary judgment, Scherer testified that he could not recall the incidents alleged by Pendy and others. He denied generally that he had sexually harassed anyone. The district court granted summary judgment for Rockwell. Was its ruling correct?

16. ROLE REVERSAL: Write a multiple-choice question that illustrates the unique significance of summary judgment. First, be sure you understand when and why a party is entitled to summary judgment.

Internet Research Problem

You may be called for jury duty before long. Read the summary of the juror's responsibilities at **http://www.placer.ca.gov/courts/jury.htm**. Some people try hard to get out of jury duty. Why is that a problem in a democratic society?

You can find further practice problems in the Online Quiz at **http://beatty.westbuslaw.com** or in the Study Guide that accompanies this text.

Constitutional, Statutory, Administrative, and Common Law

Gregory Johnson was angry. On a public street in Dallas, the young man lit an American flag on fire, protesting the nearby political convention. Law officers arrested and convicted him of violating Texas law, but Johnson appealed his case all the way to the United States Supreme Court, claiming that the First Amendment protected this form of demonstration. Did it? Should it? Which has a higher social value, Johnson's urge to protest, or the government's decision to protect the flag? How do we decide the issue? Where do we find the law that will answer this question? In this chapter, we look at four vital sources of law: the United States Constitution, statutes, administrative agencies, and the common law.

Let us consider a very different—yet related—question. What if a state legislature passes a law prohibiting new construction along a lakefront? This measure will protect the environment, and keep beaches open for all of us. In the process, though, it will render some very expensive waterfront property worthless, because the owners will not be able to build. Whose interest is more important, that of the public or that of the property owners?

Does your state have the power to prohibit flag burning? If so, does that mean it could outlaw a campaign poster on your front lawn? Prohibit political protest entirely? Ban waterfront development? How much power have we granted to the government? What rights do the people retain? Those important questions lead to our first law source.

CONSTITUTIONAL LAW

Government Power

The Constitution of the United States is the greatest legal document ever written. No other written constitution has lasted so long, governed so many, or withstood such challenge.

In 1783, 13 American colonies gained surprising independence from Great Britain. Four years later, the colonies sent delegates to craft a new constitution, but the men (no women among them) faced conflicts on a basic issue. How much power should the federal government be given? The Framers, as they have come to be called because they made or "framed" the original document, had to compromise. **The Constitution is a series of compromises about power.**

SEPARATION OF POWERS

One method of limiting power was to create a national government divided into three branches, each independent and equal. Each branch would act as a check on the power of the other two, avoiding the despotic rule that had come from London. Article I of the Constitution created a Congress, which was to have legislative power. Article II created the office of president, defining the scope of executive power. Article III established judicial power by creating the Supreme Court and permitting additional federal courts.

Consider how the three separate powers balance one another: Congress was given the power to pass statutes, a major grant of power. But the president was permitted to veto legislation, a nearly equal grant. Congress, in turn, had the right to override the veto, ensuring that the president would not become a dictator. The president was allowed to appoint federal judges and members of his cabinet, but only with a consenting vote from the Senate.

FEDERALISM

The national government was indeed to have considerable power, but it would still be *limited* power. Article I, section 8, enumerates those issues on which Congress may pass statutes. If an issue is not on the list, Congress has no power to legislate. Thus Congress may create and regulate a post office because postal service is on the list. But Congress may not pass statutes regulating child custody in a divorce: That issue is not on the list. Only the states may legislate child custody issues.

Power Granted

CONGRESSIONAL POWER

Article I of the Constitution creates the Congress with its two houses. Representation in the House of Representatives is proportionate with a state's population, but each state elects two senators. Congress may perform any of the functions enumerated in Article I, section 8, such as imposing taxes, spending money, creating copyrights, supporting the military, declaring war, and so forth. None of these rights is more important than the authority to raise and spend money (the "power of the purse"), because every branch of government is dependent upon Congress for its money.

One of the most important items on this list of congressional powers concerns trade.

Interstate Commerce

"The Congress shall have power to regulate commerce with foreign nations, and among the several states." This is the **Commerce Clause: Congress is authorized to regulate trade between states.** For example, if Congress passed a law imposing a new tax on all trucks engaged in interstate transportation, the law is valid. Congress can regulate television broadcasts because many of them cross state lines.

States have less power in this area. **A state statute that discriminates against interstate commerce is unconstitutional and void.** Suppose that Ohio, in order to protect its dairy industry, imposes a special tax on milk produced outside the state. That law discriminates against interstate trade, and violates the Commerce Clause.

EXECUTIVE POWER

Article II of the Constitution defines the executive power. Once again the Constitution gives powers in general terms. **The basic job of the president is to enforce the nation's laws.** Three of his key powers concern appointment, legislation, and foreign policy.

Appointment

As we see later in this chapter, administrative agencies play a powerful role in business regulation. The president nominates the heads of most of them. These choices dramatically influence what issues the agencies choose to pursue and how aggressively they do it. For example, a president who believes that it is vital to protect our natural resources may appoint a forceful environmentalist to run the Environmental Protection Agency, whereas a president who dislikes federal regulations will choose a more passive agency head.

Legislation

The president and his advisers propose bills to Congress and lobby hard for their passage. The executive also has the veto power.

Foreign Policy

The president conducts the nation's foreign affairs, coordinating international efforts, negotiating treaties, and so forth. The president is also the commander in chief of the armed forces, meaning that he heads the military.

JUDICIAL POWER

Article III of the Constitution creates the Supreme Court and permits Congress to establish lower courts within the federal court system. Federal courts have two key functions: adjudication and judicial review.

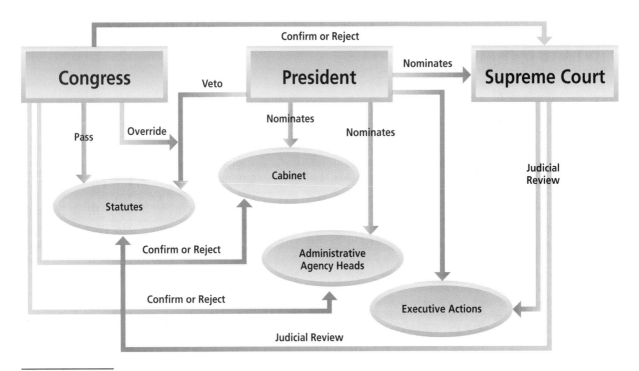

Exhibit 4.1

The Constitution established a federal government of checks and balances. Congress may pass statutes; the president may veto them; and Congress may override the veto. The president nominates cabinet officers, administrative heads, and Supreme Court justices, but the Senate must confirm his nominees. Finally, the Supreme Court (and lower federal courts) exercise judicial review over statutes and executive actions. Unlike the other checks and balances, judicial review is not provided for in the Constitution, but is a creation of the Court itself in *Marbury v. Madison*.

Adjudicating Cases

The federal court system hears criminal and civil cases. All prosecutions of federal crimes begin in United States District Court. That same court has limited jurisdiction to hear civil lawsuits, a subject discussed in Chapter 3, on dispute resolution.

Judicial Review

Judicial review refers to the power of federal courts to declare a statute or governmental action unconstitutional and void. The courts can examine acts from any branch of federal or state government. If Ohio did pass a tax on milk produced in other states, a federal court would declare the law void, as a violation of the Commerce Clause. Exhibit 4.1 illustrates the balance among Congress, the president, and the Court.

Is judicial review good for the nation? Those who oppose it argue that federal court judges are all appointed, not elected, and that we should not permit judges to nullify a statute passed by elected officials because that diminishes the people's role in their government. Those who favor judicial review insist that there must be one cohesive interpretation of the Constitution and the judicial branch is the logical one to provide it. This dispute about power simmers continuously beneath the surface and occasionally comes to the boil.

CASE SUMMARY

YOUNGSTOWN SHEET & TUBE Co. v. SAWYER

343 U.S. 579, 72 S. Ct. 863, 1952 U.S. LEXIS 2625
United States Supreme Court, 1952

FACTS: During the Korean War, steel companies and the unions were unable to reach a contract. The union notified the companies that they would strike, beginning April 9, 1952. President Truman declared steel essential to the war effort and ordered his Secretary of Commerce, Sawyer, to take control of the steel mills and keep them running. Sawyer immediately ordered the presidents of the various companies to serve as operating managers for the United States.

On April 30, the federal district court issued an injunction to stop Sawyer from running the mills. That same day the United States Court of Appeals "stayed" the injunction, i.e., it permitted Sawyer to keep operating the mills. The Supreme Court quickly granted certiorari, heard arguments May 12, and issued its decision June 2—at least five years faster than most cases reach final decision.

ISSUE: **Did President Truman have the constitutional power to seize the steel mills?**

DECISION: The President lacked the constitutional power to seize the mills. The District Court's injunction is affirmed.

REASONING: If the president had authority to issue the seizure order, it had to come from the Constitution. There is no express authorization of such power in the document. The president, though, argues that his power is implied from the clauses stating that the executive power shall be vested in a president, that he shall take care that the laws be faithfully executed, and that he shall be commander in chief.

Under our constitutional system, the commander in chief has no power to take possession of private property. That is a job for the nation's lawmakers, not for its military authorities.

The executive power clauses also fail to support the president's seizure order. The president is given power to *execute* the laws, not to *make* them. The Constitution permits the president to recommend bills he considers wise and veto those he finds defective; however, it is the Congress alone that passes the laws. The Framers gave the lawmaking power to Congress in good times and bad. The seizure order is void. ◢

UPDATE

Find an article that describes a recent Supreme Court decision declaring a statute unconstitutional. What was the purpose of the statute? Why did the justices nullify the law? Do you agree with the Court's decision? For a look at the current justices, the full text of famous cases, and a calendar of pending cases, see **http://supct.law.cornell.edu/supct/**. You can tour the Court itself and even hear some of the justices read their opinions at **http://oyez.nwu.edu**.

Protected Rights

The original Constitution was silent about the rights of citizens. This alarmed many, who feared that the new federal government would have unlimited power over their lives. So in 1791 the first 10 amendments, known as the Bill of Rights, were added to the Constitution, guaranteeing many liberties directly to individual citizens.

The amendments to the Constitution protect the people of this nation from the power of state and federal government. The **First Amendment** guarantees rights of free speech, free press, and religion; the **Fourth Amendment** protects against illegal searches; the **Fifth Amendment** ensures due process; the **Sixth Amendment** demands fair treatment for defendants in criminal prosecutions; and the **Fourteenth Amendment** guarantees equal protection of the law. We consider the First, Fifth, and Fourteenth Amendments in this chapter and the Fourth, Fifth, and Sixth Amendments in Chapter 7, on crime.

The "people" who are protected include citizens and, for most purposes, corporations. Corporations are considered persons and receive most of the same protections. The great majority of these rights also extend to citizens of other countries who are in the United States.

Constitutional rights generally protect only against governmental acts. The Constitution generally does not protect us from the conduct of private parties, such as corporations or other citizens. Constitutional protections apply to federal, state, and local governments.

FIRST AMENDMENT: FREE SPEECH

The First Amendment states that "Congress shall make no law . . . abridging the freedom of speech . . ." In general, we expect our government to let people speak and hear whatever they choose. The Framers believed democracy would only work if the members of the electorate were free to talk, argue, listen, and exchange viewpoints in any way they wanted. If a city government prohibited an antiabortion group from demonstrating, its action would violate the First Amendment. Government officers may not impose their political beliefs on the citizens. The government may regulate the *time, place,* and *manner* of speech, for example by prohibiting a midnight rally, or insisting that demonstrators remain within a specified area. But outright prohibitions are unconstitutional.

"Speech" includes symbolic conduct. Does that mean flag burning is permissible? You be the judge.

CASE SUMMARY

TEXAS v. JOHNSON

491 U.S. 397, 109 S. Ct. 2533, 1989 U.S. LEXIS 3115
United States Supreme Court, 1989

FACTS: Outside the Republican National Convention in Dallas, Gregory Johnson participated in a protest against policies of the Reagan administration. Participants gave speeches and handed out leaflets. Johnson burned an American flag. He was arrested and convicted under a Texas statute that prohibited desecrating the flag, but the Texas Court of Criminal Appeals reversed on the grounds that the conviction violated the First Amendment. Texas appealed to the United States Supreme Court. The Court concluded that flag burning *was* in fact symbolic speech, and that it *could* therefore receive First Amendment protection. The question was, *should* it be protected? ◢

YOU BE THE JUDGE

Does the First Amendment protect flag burning?

ARGUMENT FOR TEXAS: For more than 200 years, the American flag has occupied a unique position as the symbol of our nation, a special place that justifies a governmental prohibition against flag burning. In the Revolutionary War, the flag served to unite the struggling colonies. More recently, in the First and Second World Wars, thousands of our countrymen and women died defending the flag. Nearly 6,000 Americans died just on the small island of Iwo Jima, in order to raise a flag there.

No other American symbol has been so universally admired and honored. Surely it is the height of hypocrisy to burn this glorious emblem of freedom and then demand in a courtroom that the liberty which the flag symbolizes guarantees the right to destroy the banner itself.

ARGUMENT FOR JOHNSON: The government may not prohibit the expression of an idea simply because society finds it offensive. Could the government prohibit the burning of state flags? Copies of the Constitution? How are we to decide which symbols deserve special treatment? Judges are not entitled to force their own political perspectives on the populace.

The way to preserve the flag's special role is not to punish those who feel differently about these matters. It is to persuade them that they are wrong. We do not consecrate the flag by punishing its desecration, for in doing so we dilute the freedom that this cherished emblem represents. ▰

Fifth Amendment: Due Process and The Takings Clause

Ralph is a first-semester senior at State University, where he majors in finance. With a 3.6 grade point average and outstanding recommendations, he has an excellent chance of admission to an elite business school—until his life suddenly turns upside down. Professor Watson, who teaches Ralph in marketing, notifies the school's dean that the young man plagiarized material that he included in his recent paper. Dean Holmes reads Watson's report and sends Ralph a brief letter: "I find that you have committed plagiarism in violation of school rules. Your grade in Dr. Watson's marketing course is an 'F.' You are hereby suspended from the University for one full academic year."

Ralph is shocked. He is convinced he did nothing wrong, and wants to tell his side of the story, but Dean Holmes refuses to speak with him. What can he do? The first step is to read the Fifth Amendment.

Two related provisions of the Fifth Amendment, called the Due Process Clause and the Takings Clause, prohibit the government from arbitrarily depriving us of our most valuable assets. Together, they state: "No person shall be . . . deprived of life, liberty, or property without due process of law; nor shall private property be taken for public use, without just compensation." We will discuss the civil law aspects of these clauses, but due process also applies to criminal law. The reference to "life" refers to capital punishment. The criminal law issues of this subject are discussed in Chapter Seven, on crime.

PROCEDURAL DUE PROCESS

The government deprives citizens or corporations of their property in a variety of ways. The Internal Revenue Service may fine a corporation for late payment of taxes. The Customs Service may seize goods at the border. As to liberty, the government may take it by confining someone in a mental institution or by taking a child out of the home because of parental neglect. **The purpose of procedural due process is to ensure that before the government takes liberty or property, the affected person has a fair chance to oppose the action.**

The Due Process Clause protects Ralph because State University is part of the government. Ralph is entitled to due process. Does this mean that he gets a full court trial on the plagiarism charge? No. **The type of hearing the government must offer depends upon the importance of the property or liberty interest.** The more important the interest, the more formal the procedures must be. Regardless of how formal the hearing, one requirement is constant: The fact finder must be neutral.

In a criminal prosecution, the liberty interest is very great. A defendant can lose his freedom or even his life. The government must provide the defendant with a lawyer if he cannot afford one, adequate time to prepare, an unbiased jury, an opportunity to present his case and cross-examine all witnesses, and many other procedural rights.

A student faced with academic sanctions receives less due process, but still has rights. State University has failed to provide Ralph with due process. The school has accused the young man of a serious infraction. The school must promptly provide details of the charge, give Ralph all physical evidence, and allow him time to plan his response. The university must then offer Ralph a hearing, before a neutral person or group, who will listen to Ralph (as well as Dr. Watson) and examine any evidence the student offers. Ralph is not, however, entitled to a lawyer or a jury.

THE TAKINGS CLAUSE

Kabrina owns a 10-acre parcel of undeveloped land on Lake Halcyon. She plans to build a 20-bedroom inn of about 35,000 square feet—until the state environmental agency abruptly halts the work. The agency informs Kabrina that, to protect the lake from further harm, it will allow no shoreline development except single-family houses of 2,000 square feet or less. Kabrina is furious. Does the state have the power to wreck Kabrina's plans? To learn the answer, we look to another section of the Fifth Amendment.

The Takings Clause prohibits a state from taking private property for public use without just compensation. A town wishing to build a new football field *does* have the right to boot you out of your house. But the town must compensate you. The government takes your land through the power of eminent domain. Officials must notify you of their intentions and give you an opportunity to oppose the project and to challenge the amount the town offers to pay. When the hearings are done, though, the town may write you a check and grind your house into goalposts, whether you like it or not.

If the state actually wanted to take Kabrina's land and turn it into a park, the Takings Clause would force it to pay the fair market value. However, the state is not trying to seize the land—it merely wants to prevent large development.

"My land is worthless," Kabrina replies. "You might just as well kick me off my own property!" **A regulation that denies *all beneficial use* of property is a taking, and requires compensation.** Has the government denied Kabrina all beneficial use? No, it has not. Kabrina retains the right to build a private house. The environmental agency has decreased the value of the land, but owes her nothing. Had the state forbidden *any construction* on her land, it would have been obligated to pay Kabrina.

Fourteenth Amendment: Equal Protection Clause

Shannon Faulkner wanted to attend The Citadel, a state-supported military college in South Carolina. She was a fine student who met every admission requirement that The Citadel set except one: She was not a male. The Citadel argued that its long and distinguished history demanded that it remain all male. Faulkner responded that she was a citizen of the state and ought to receive the benefits that others got, including the right to a military education. Could the school exclude her on the basis of gender?

The Fourteenth Amendment provides that "No State shall . . . deny to any person within its jurisdiction the equal protection of the laws." This is the **Equal Protection Clause,** and it means that, generally speaking, all levels of government must treat people equally. Unfair classifications among people or corporations will not be permitted. **Regulations based on gender, race, or fundamental rights are generally void.** Shannon Faulkner won her case and was admitted to The Citadel. The Court found no justification for discriminating against women. Any regulation based on race or ethnicity is *certain* to be void. Similarly, all citizens enjoy the *fundamental right* to travel between states. If Kentucky limited government jobs to those who had lived in the state for two years, it would be discriminating against a fundamental right, and the restriction would be struck down.

ETHICS | Today over 800 high school girls wrestle competitively. Some join female clubs but others have no such opportunity and compete with boys—or seek to. Some schools allow girls to join the boys' wrestling team, but others refuse, citing moral reasons, concern for the girls' safety, and the possibility of sexual harassment. If a particular school has no female team, should girls be permitted to wrestle boys? Do they have an equal protection right to do so? ◼

STATUTORY LAW

Most new law is statutory law. Statutes affect each of us every day, in our business, professional, and personal lives. When the system works correctly, this is the one part of the law over which we the people have control. We elect the local legislators who pass state statutes; we vote for the senators and representatives who create federal statutes. If we understand the system, we can affect the largest source of contemporary law. If we live in ignorance of its strengths and pitfalls, we delude ourselves that we participate in a democracy.

As we saw in Chapter 1, there are many systems of government operating in the United States: a national government and 50 state governments. Each level of government has a legislative body. In Washington, D.C., Congress is our national legislature. Congress passes the statutes that govern the nation. In addition, each state has a legislature, which passes statutes for that state only. In this section we look at how Congress does its work creating statutes. State legislatures operate similarly, but the work of Congress is better documented and obviously of national importance.

COMMITTEE WORK

Congress is organized into two houses, the House of Representatives and the Senate. Either house may originate a proposed statute, which is called a **bill.** After a bill has been proposed, it is sent to an appropriate committee.[1]

If you visit either house of Congress, you will probably find half a dozen legislators on the floor, with one person talking and no one listening. This is because most of the work is done in committees. Both houses are organized into dozens of committees, each with special functions. The House currently has about 27 committees (further divided into about 150 subcommittees) and the Senate has approximately 20 committees (with about 86 subcommittees). For example, the armed services committee of each house oversees the huge defense budget and the workings of the armed forces. Labor committees handle legislation concerning organized labor and working conditions. Banking committees develop expertise on financial institutions. Judiciary committees review nominees to the federal courts. There are dozens of other committees, some very powerful, because they control vast amounts of money, and some relatively weak.

When a bill is proposed in either house, it is referred to the committee that specializes in that subject. Why are bills proposed in the first place? For any of several reasons:

- *New Issue, New Worry.* During the early years of this millennium, voters were increasingly irate about abuses in campaign financing, and, after years of hearings, Congress finally passed legislation designed to reduce excessive political donations.

- *Unpopular Judicial Ruling.* If Congress disagrees with a judicial interpretation of a statute, the legislators may pass a new statute to modify or "undo" the court decision. For example, if the Supreme Court misinterprets a statute about musical copyrights, Congress may pass a new law correcting the Court's error.

- *Criminal Law.* When legislators perceive that social changes have led to new criminal acts, they may respond with new statutes. The rise of Internet fraud has led to many new statutes outlawing such things as computer trespass and espionage, fraud in the use of cell phones, identity theft, and so on.

Congressional committees hold hearings to investigate the need for new legislation and consider the alternatives. Suppose a congressman believes that a growing number of American corporations locate their headquarters offshore to escape taxes. She requests committee hearings on the subject, hoping to discover the extent of the problem, its causes, and possible remedies. After hearings, if the committee votes in favor of the bill, it goes to the full body, meaning either the House of Representatives or the Senate. If the full body approves the bill, it goes to the other house.

---

[1] See the chart of state and federal governments in Chapter 1. A vast amount of information about Congress is available on the Internet. The House of Representatives has a Web page at **http://www.house.gov/**. The Senate's site appears at **http://www.senate.gov**. Each page provides links to current law, pending legislation, votes, committees, and more.

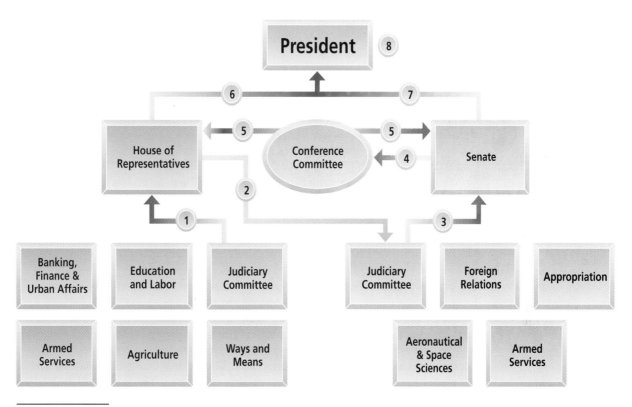

The two houses of Congress are organized into dozens of committees, a few of which are shown here. The path of the 1964 Civil Rights Act (somewhat simplified) was as follows: (1) The House Judiciary Committee approved the bill and sent it to the full House; (2) the full House passed the bill and sent it to the Senate, where it was assigned to the Senate Judiciary Committee; (3) the Senate Judiciary Committee passed an amended version of the bill and sent it to the full Senate; (4) the full Senate passed the bill with additional amendments. Since the Senate version was now different from the bill the House passed, the bill went to a Conference Committee. The Conference Committee (5) reached a compromise and sent the new version of the bill back to both houses. Each house passed the compromise bill (6 and 7) and sent it to the president, who signed it into law (8).

The bill must be voted on and approved by both branches of Congress. Assuming both houses pass it, the bill goes to the president. If the president signs the bill, it becomes law. If the president opposes the bill, he will veto it, in which case it is not law. When the president vetoes a bill, Congress has one last chance to make it law: an override. Should both houses re-pass the bill, each by a two thirds margin, it becomes law over the president's veto.

COMMON LAW

Jason observes a toddler wander onto the railroad tracks and hears a train approaching. He has plenty of time to pull the child from the tracks with no risk to himself, but chooses to do nothing. The youngster is killed. The child's family sues Jason for his callous behavior, and a court determines that Jason owes—nothing. How can that be?

Jason and the toddler present a classic legal puzzle: What, if anything, must a bystander do when he sees someone in danger? We will examine this issue to see how the common law works.

The common law is judge-made law. It is the sum total of all the cases decided by appellate courts. The common law of Pennsylvania consists of all cases decided by appellate courts in that state. The Illinois common law of bystander liability is all of the cases on that subject decided by Illinois appellate courts. Two hundred years ago, almost all of the law was common law. Today, most new law is statutory. But common law still predominates in tort, contract, and agency law, and it is very important in property, employment, and some other areas.

We focus on appellate courts because they are the only ones to make rulings of law, as discussed in Chapter 3. In a bystander case, it is the job of the state's highest court to say what legal obligations, if any, a bystander has. The trial court, on the other hand, must decide facts: Was this defendant able to see what was happening? Was the plaintiff really in trouble? Could the defendant have assisted without peril to himself?

STARE DECISIS

Nothing perks up a course like Latin. *Stare decisis* **means "let the decision stand."** It is the essence of the common law. The phrase indicates that once a court has decided a particular issue, it will generally apply the same rule in future cases. Suppose the highest court of Arizona must decide whether a contract for a new car, signed by a 16-year-old, can be enforced against him. The court will look to see if there is precedent, that is, whether the high court of Arizona has already decided a similar case. The Arizona court looks and finds several earlier cases, all holding that such contracts may not be enforced against a minor. The court will apply that precedent and refuse to enforce the contract in this case. Courts do not always follow precedent but they generally do: *Stare decisis.*

Two words explain why the common law is never as easy as we might like: *predictability* and *flexibility*. The law is trying to accommodate both goals. The need for predictability is apparent: People must know what the law is. If contract law changed daily, an entrepreneur who leased factory space and then started buying machinery would be uncertain if the factory would actually be available when she was ready to move in. Will the landlord slip out of the lease? Will the machinery be ready on time? The need for predictability created the doctrine of *stare decisis*.

Yet there must also be flexibility in the law, some means to respond to new problems and changing social mores. In this new millennium, we cannot be encumbered by ironclad rules established before electricity was discovered. These two ideas may be obvious but they also conflict: The more flexibility we permit, the less predictability we enjoy. We will watch the conflict play out in the bystander cases.

BYSTANDER CASES

This country inherited from England a simple rule about a bystander's obligations: You have no duty to assist someone in peril unless you created the danger. In *Union Pacific Railway Co. v. Cappier,*[2] through no fault of the railroad, a train struck a man, severing an arm and a leg. Railroad employees saw the incident

---

[2] 66 Kan. 649, 72 P. 281 (1903).

happen but did nothing to assist him. By the time help arrived, the victim had died. In this 1903 case the court held that the railroad had no duty to help the injured man. The court declared that it was legally irrelevant whether the railroad's conduct was inhumane.

As harsh as this judgment might seem, it was an accurate statement of the law at that time in both England and the United States: Bystanders need do nothing. With a rule this old and well established, no court was willing to scuttle it. What courts did do was seek openings for small changes.

Eighteen years after the Kansas case of Cappier, the court in nearby Iowa found the basis for one exception. Ed Carey was a farm laborer, working for Frank Davis. While in the fields, Carey fainted from sunstroke and remained unconscious. Davis simply hauled him to a nearby wagon and left him in the sun for an additional four hours, causing serious permanent injury. The judges said that was not good enough. Creating a modest exception in the bystander rule, the court ruled that when an employee suffers a serious injury *on the job*, the employer must take reasonable measures to help him. Leaving a stricken worker in the hot sun was not reasonable, and Davis was liable.[3]

And this is how the common law changes: bit by tiny bit. In the 1970s, changes came more quickly.

CASE SUMMARY

TARASOFF v. REGENTS OF THE UNIVERSITY OF CALIFORNIA

17 Cal. 3d 425, 551 P.2d 334, 131 Cal. Rptr. 14
Supreme Court of California, 1976

FACTS: On October 27, 1969, Prosenjit Poddar killed Tatiana Tarasoff. Tatiana's parents claimed that two months earlier Poddar had confided his intention to kill Tatiana to Dr. Lawrence Moore, a psychologist employed by the University of California at Berkeley. They sued the university, claiming that Dr. Moore should have warned Tatiana and/or should have arranged for Poddar's confinement.

ISSUE: Did Dr. Moore have a duty to Tatiana Tarasoff?

DECISION: Yes, Dr. Moore had a duty to Tatiana Tarasoff.

REASONING: Under the common law, one person generally owes no duty to control the conduct of another or to warn anyone who is in danger. However, courts make an exception when the defendant has a special relationship to a dangerous person or potential victim. A therapist is someone who has just such a special relationship with a patient.

No one can be expected to do a perfect job. A therapist must only exercise the reasonable degree of skill, knowledge, and care ordinarily possessed by others in the field. In this case, however, there is no dispute about whether Dr. Moore could have foreseen violence. He actually predicted Poddar would kill Tatiana. Once a therapist determines that a patient poses a serious danger of violence, he must make reasonable efforts to protect the victim. The Tarasoffs have stated a legitimate claim against Dr. Moore. ◢

---

[3] *Carey v. Davis*, 190 Iowa 720, 180 N.W. 889 (1921).

The Tarasoff exception applies in the limited circumstance of a special relation-ship, such as therapist–patient. Does the decision mean an end to the bystander rule? By no means. Ernesto Parra was a customer at the Jiminez Restaurant when food became lodged in his throat. The employees did not use the Heimlich ma-neuver or any other method to try to save him. Parra choked to death. Was the restaurant liable? No, said the Illinois Appeals Court. The restaurant had no oblig-ation to do anything.[4] The bystander rule, that hardy oak, is alive and well.

Administrative Law

Before beginning this section, please return your seat to its upright position. Stow the tray firmly in the seat back in front of you. Turn off any radios, CD players, or other electronic equipment. Sound familiar? Administrative agencies affect each of us every day in hundreds of ways. They have become the fourth branch of gov-ernment. Supporters believe that they provide unique expertise in complex areas; detractors regard them as unelected government run amok.

Many administrative agencies are familiar. The Federal Aviation Administra-tion, which requires all airlines to ensure that your seats are upright before takeoff and landing, is an administrative agency. The Internal Revenue Service haunts us every April 15. The Environmental Protection Agency regulates the water quality of the river in your town. The Federal Trade Commission oversees the commer-cials that shout at you from your television set.

Other agencies are less familiar. You may never have heard of the Bureau of Land Management, but if you go into the oil and gas industry, you will learn that this powerful agency has more control over your land than you do. If you develop real estate in Palos Hills, Illinois, you will tremble every time the Appearance Commission of the City of Palos Hills speaks, since you cannot construct a new building without its approval. If your software corporation wants to hire an Argentine expert on databases, you will get to know the complex workings of the Immigration and Naturalization Service: No one lawfully enters this country without its nod of approval.

Administrative agencies use three kinds of power to do the work assigned to them: they make rules, investigate, and adjudicate.

Rule Making

One of the most important functions of an administrative agency is to make rules. In doing this, the agency attempts, prospectively, to establish fair and uniform be-havior for all businesses in the affected area. **To create a new rule is to promulgate it.** Agencies promulgate two types of rules: legislative and interpretive.

Legislative Rules

These are the most important agency rules, and they are much like statutes. Here, an agency is changing the law by requiring businesses or private citizens to act in

---

[4] 230 Ill. App. 3d 819, 595 N.E.2d 1186, 1992 Ill. App. LEXIS 935 (1992).

a certain way. For example, the Federal Communications Commission (FCC) promulgated a rule requiring all cable television systems with more than 3,500 subscribers to develop the capacity to carry at least 20 channels and to make some of those channels available to local community stations. This legislative rule has a heavy financial impact on many cable systems. As far as a cable company is concerned, it is more important than most statutes passed by Congress. Legislative rules have the full effect of a statute.

Interpretive Rules

These rules do not change the law. They are the agency's interpretation of what the law already requires. But they can still affect all of us.

In 1977, Congress passed the Clean Air Act in an attempt to reduce pollution from factories. The act required the Environmental Protection Agency (EPA) to impose emission standards on "stationary sources" of pollution. But what did "stationary source" mean? It was the EPA's job to define that term. Obscure work, to be sure, yet the results could be seen and even smelled, because the EPA's definition would determine the quality of air entering our lungs every time we breathe. Environmentalists wanted the term defined to include every smokestack in a factory so that the EPA could regulate each one. The EPA, however, developed the "bubble concept," ruling that "stationary source" meant an entire factory, but not the individual smokestacks. As a result, polluters could shift emission among smokestacks in a single factory to avoid EPA regulation. Environmentalists howled that this gutted the purpose of the statute, but to no avail. The agency had spoken, merely by interpreting a statute.

Investigation

Agencies do an infinite variety of work, but they all need broad factual knowledge of the field they govern. Some companies cooperate with an agency, furnishing information and even voluntarily accepting agency recommendations. For example, the United States Product Safety Commission investigates hundreds of consumer products every year and frequently urges companies to recall goods that the agency considers defective. Many firms comply. (For an up-to-the-minute report on dangerous products and company compliance, proceed carefully to **http://www.cpsc.gov/index.html**.)

Other companies, however, jealously guard information, often because corporate officers believe that disclosure would lead to adverse rules. To force disclosure, agencies use subpoenas and searches. **A subpoena is an order to appear at a particular time and place to provide evidence.** A subpoena *duces tecum* requires the person to appear and bring specified documents. Businesses and other organizations intensely dislike subpoenas and resent government agents plowing through records and questioning employees. Nonetheless, a subpoena is generally lawful if it is *relevant* to a valid investigation, does not create an *unreasonable burden* on the company, and does not seek *privileged material*, such as a document in which an executive admits committing a crime.

ADJUDICATION

To **adjudicate** a case is to hold a hearing about an issue and then decide it. Agencies adjudicate countless cases. The FCC adjudicates which applicant for a new television license is best qualified. The Occupational Safety and Health Administration (OSHA) holds adversarial hearings to determine whether a manufacturing plant is dangerous.

Most adjudications begin with a hearing before an **administrative law judge** (ALJ). There is no jury. An ALJ is an employee of the agency but is expected to be impartial in her rulings. All parties are represented by counsel. The rules of evidence are informal, and an ALJ may receive any testimony or documents that will help resolve the dispute.

After all evidence is taken, the ALJ makes a decision. The losing party has a right to appeal to an appellate board within the agency. The appellate board has the power to make a *de novo* decision, meaning it may ignore the ALJ's decision. A party unhappy with that decision may appeal to federal court.

Chapter Conclusion

The legal battle over power never stops. When may a state outlaw waterfront development? Prohibit symbolic speech? Other issues are just as thorny, such as when a bystander is liable to assist someone in peril, or whether a government agency may subpoena corporate documents. Some of the questions will be answered by that extraordinary document, the Constitution, while others require statutory, common law or administrative responses. There are no easy answers to any of the questions, because there has never been a democracy so large, so diverse, or so powerful.

Chapter Review

1. The Constitution is a series of compromises about power.

2. Article I of the Constitution creates the Congress and grants all legislative power to it. Article II establishes the office of president and defines executive powers. Article III creates the Supreme Court and permits lower federal courts; the article also outlines the powers of the federal judiciary.

3. Under the Commerce Clause, Congress may regulate interstate trade. A state law that interferes with interstate commerce is void.

4. The president's key powers include making agency appointments, proposing legislation, conducting foreign policy, and acting as commander in chief of the armed forces.

5. The federal courts adjudicate cases and also exercise judicial review, which is the right to declare a statute or governmental action unconstitutional and void.

6. The First Amendment protects most freedom of speech, although the government may regulate the time, place, and manner of speech.

7. Procedural due process is required whenever the government attempts to take liberty or property.

8. The Takings Clause prohibits a state from taking private property for public use without just compensation.

9. The Equal Protection Clause generally requires the government to treat people equally.

10. Bills originate in congressional committees and go from there to the full House of Representatives or Senate. If both houses pass the bill, the legislation normally must go to a conference committee to resolve differences between the two versions. If the president signs the bill, it becomes a statute; if he vetoes it, Congress can pass it over his veto with a two thirds majority in each house.

11. *Stare decisis* means "let the decision stand," and indicates that once a court has decided a particular issue, it will generally apply the same rule in future cases.

12. The common law evolves in awkward fits and starts, because courts attempt to achieve two contradictory purposes: predictability and flexibility.

13. The common-law bystander rule holds that, generally, no one has a duty to assist someone in peril unless the bystander himself created the danger. Courts have carved some exceptions during the last 100 years, but the basic rule still stands.

14. Congress creates federal administrative agencies to supervise many industries. Agencies promulgate rules and investigate and adjudicate cases.

PRACTICE TEST

Matching Questions

Match the following terms with their definitions:

___**A.** Statute
___**B.** Equal Protection Clause
___**C.** Judicial review
___**D.** Takings Clause
___**E.** Stare decisis
___**F.** Promulgate

1. The power of federal courts to examine the constitutionality of statutes and acts of government.
2. Part of the Constitution that requires compensation in eminent domain cases.
3. The rule that requires courts to rule based on precedent.
4. The act of an administrative agency creating a new rule.
5. A law passed by a legislative body.
6. Generally prohibits regulations based on gender, race, of fundamental rights.

True/False Questions

Circle true or false:

1. T F The government may not prohibit a political rally, but it may restrict when and where the demonstrators meet.

2. T F The Due Process Clause requires that any citizen is entitled to a jury trial before any right or property interest is taken.

3. T F The government has the right to take a homeowner's property for a public purpose.

4. T F A subpoena is an order punishing a defendant who has violated a court ruling.

5. T F A bystander who sees someone in peril must come to that person's assistance, but only if he can do so without endangering himself or others.

6. T F Administrative agencies play an advisory role in the life of many industries but do not have the legal authority to enforce their opinions.

Multiple-Choice Questions

7. Colorado passes a hotel tax of 8% for Colorado residents and 15% for out-of-state visitors. The new law

(a) Is valid, based on the Supremacy Clause.

(b) Is void, based on the Supremacy Clause.

(c) Is valid, based on the Commerce Clause.

(d) Is void, based on the Commerce Clause.

(e) Is void, based on the Takings Clause.

8. Suppose a state legislature approves an education plan for the next year budgets $35 million for boys' athletics and $25 million for girls' athletics. Legislators explain the difference by saying, "In our experience, boys simply care more about sports than girls do." The new plan is

(a) Valid.

(b) Void.

(c) Permissible, based on the legislator's statutory research.

(d) Permissible, though unwise.

(e) Subject to the Takings Clause.

9. Congress has passed a new bill but the president does not like the law. What could happen next?

(a) The president must sign the bill whether he likes it or not.

(b) The president may veto the bill, in which case it is dead.

(c) The president may veto the bill, but Congress may attempt to override the veto.

(d) The president may ask the citizens to vote directly on the proposed law.

(e) The president may discharge the Congress and order new elections.

10. Which of these is an example of judicial review?

(a) A trial court finds a criminal defendant guilty.

(b) An appeals court reverses a lower court's ruling.

(c) An appeals court affirms a lower court's ruling.

(d) A federal court declares a statute unconstitutional.

(e) A Congressional committee interviews a potential Supreme Court justice.

11. Martine, a psychiatrist, is convinced that Lance, her patient, intends to kill his own father.

(a) Martine may not contact the father, because she is obligated to protect patient–therapist confidentiality.

(b) Martine *may* contact the father, but she is *not obligated* to take any steps at all.

(c) Martine must warn the father.

(d) Martine may seek judicial review of the case.

(e) Martine may warn Lance not to do anything but she herself may not become involved.

12. What is an example of a subpoena?

(a) A court order to a company to stop polluting the air.

(b) A court order requiring a deponent to answer questions.

(c) A federal agency demands various internal documents from a corporation.

(d) The president orders troops called up in the national defense.

(e) The president orders Congress to pass a bill on an expedited schedule.

Short-Answer Questions

13. In the early 1970s, President Nixon became embroiled in the Watergate dispute. He was accused of covering up a criminal break-in at the national headquarters of the Democratic Party. Nixon denied any wrongdoing. A United States District Court judge ordered the president to produce tapes of conversations held in his office. Nixon knew that complying with the order would produce damaging evidence, probably destroying his presidency. He refused, claiming executive privilege. The case went to the Supreme Court. Nixon strongly implied that even if the Supreme Court ordered him to produce the tapes, he would refuse. What major constitutional issue did this raise?

14. Gilleo opposed American participation in the war in the Persian Gulf. She displayed a large sign on her front lawn that read, "Say No to War in the Persian Gulf, Call Congress Now." The city of Ladue prohibited signs on front lawns, and Gilleo sued. The city claimed that it was regulating "time, place, and manner." Explain that statement, and decide who should win.

15. Hiller Systems, Inc. was performing a safety inspection on board the M/V *Cape Diamond*, an oceangoing

vessel, when an accident occurred involving the fire extinguishing equipment. Two men were killed. The Occupational Safety and Health Administration (OSHA), a federal agency, attempted to investigate, but Hiller refused to permit any of its employees to speak to OSHA investigators. What could OSHA do to pursue the investigation? What limits were there on what OSHA could do?

16. Federal antitrust statutes are complex, but the basic goal is straightforward: to prevent a major industry from being so dominated by a small group of corporations that they destroy competition and injure consumers. Does Major League Baseball violate the antitrust laws? Many observers say that it does. A small group of owners not only dominate the industry, but actually own it, controlling the entry of new owners into the game. This issue went to the United States Supreme Court in 1922. Justice Holmes ruled,

perhaps surprisingly, that baseball is exempt from the antitrust laws, holding that baseball is not "trade or commerce." Suppose that a congressman dislikes this ruling and dislikes the current condition of baseball. What could he do?

17. ETHICS: Suppose you were on a state supreme court and faced with a restaurant choking case. Should you require restaurant employees to know and employ the Heimlich maneuver to assist a choking victim? If they do a bad job, they could cause additional injury. Should you permit them to do nothing at all? Is there a compromise position? What social policies are most important?

18. ROLE REVERSAL: Write an exam question that involves any two of these important Fifth Amendment protections: procedural due process, the Takings Clause, and the Equal Protection Clause.

Internet Research Problem

Research some pending legislation in Congress. Go to **http://www.senate.gov**, and click on bills. Choose some key words that interest you, and see what your government is doing. Read the summary of the bill, if one is provided, or go to the text of the bill, and scan the introduction. What do the sponsors of this bill hope to accomplish? Do you agree or disagree with their goals?

You can find further practice problems in the Online Quiz at **http://beatty.westbuslaw.com** or in the Study Guide that accompanies this text.

Intentional Torts and Business Torts

In a small Louisiana town, Don Mashburn ran a restaurant called Maison de Mashburn. *The New Orleans States-Item* newspaper reviewed his eatery, and here is what the article said:

"'Tain't Creole, 'tain't Cajun, 'tain't French, 'tain't country American, 'tain't good. I don't know how much real talent in cooking is hidden under the mélange of hideous sauces which make this food and the menu a travesty of pretentious amateurism but I find it all quite depressing. Put a yellow flour sauce on top of the duck, flame it for drama and serve it with some horrible multi-flavored rice in hollowed-out fruit and what have you got? A well-cooked duck with an ugly sauce that tastes too sweet and thick and makes you want to scrape off the glop to eat the plain duck. [The stuffed eggplant was prepared by emptying] a shaker full (more or less) of paprika on top of it. [One sauce created] trout à la green plague [while another should have been called] yellow death on duck."

Mashburn sued, claiming that the newspaper had committed libel, damaging his reputation and hurting his business.[1] Trout à la green plague will be the first course on our menu of tort law. Mashburn learned, as you will, why filing such a lawsuit is easier than winning it. ◾

This odd word "tort" is borrowed from the French, meaning "wrong." And that is what it means in law: A tort is a wrong. More precisely, **a tort is a violation of a duty imposed by the civil law.** When a person breaks one of those duties and injures another, it is a tort. The injury could be to a person or her property. Libel is one example of a tort where, for example, a newspaper columnist falsely accuses someone of being an alcoholic. A surgeon who removes the wrong kidney from a patient commits a different kind of tort, called negligence. A business executive who deliberately steals a client away from a competitor, interfering with a valid contract, commits a tort called interference with a contract. A con artist who tricks money out of you with a phony offer to sell you a boat commits fraud, yet another tort.

Because tort law is so broad, it takes a while to understand its boundaries. To start with, we must distinguish torts from criminal law.

It is a crime to steal a car, to embezzle money from a bank, to sell cocaine. As discussed in Chapter 1, society considers such behavior so threatening that the government itself will prosecute the wrongdoer, whether or not the car owner or bank president wants the case to go forward. A district attorney, who is paid by the government, will bring the case to court, seeking to send the defendant to prison and/or to fine him. If there is a fine, the money goes to the state, not to the victim.

In a tort case, it is up to the injured party, the plaintiff, to seek compensation. She must hire her own lawyer, who will file a lawsuit. Her lawyer must convince the court that the defendant breached some legal duty and ought to pay money damages to the plaintiff. The plaintiff has no power to send the defendant to jail. Bear in mind that a defendant's action might be both a crime *and* a tort. The con artist who tricks money out of you with a fake offer to sell you a boat has committed the tort of fraud. You may file a civil suit against him and will collect money damages if you can prove your case. The con artist has also committed the crime of fraud. The state will prosecute, seeking to imprison and fine him.

Tort law is divided into categories. In this chapter we consider **intentional torts,** that is, harm caused by a deliberate action. The newspaper columnist who wrongly accuses someone of being a drunk has committed the intentional tort of libel. The con artist who tricks money from you has committed the intentional tort of fraud. In the next chapter we examine **negligence and strict liability,** which are injuries caused by neglect and oversight rather than by deliberate conduct.

---

[1] *Mashburn v. Collins*, 355 So.2d 879 (La. 1977).

Intentional Torts

DEFAMATION

The First Amendment guarantees the right to free speech, a vital freedom that enables us to protect other rights. But that freedom is not absolute. Courts have long recognized that we cannot permit irresponsible speech to harm another's reputation. Free speech should not include the right to falsely accuse your neighbor of selling drugs. That sounds sensible enough, yet once we say that free speech and personal reputation both deserve protection, we have guaranteed perpetual conflict.

The law of defamation concerns false statements that harm someone's reputation. Defamatory statements can be written or spoken. Written defamation is **libel.** Suppose a newspaper accuses a local retail store of programming its cash registers to overcharge customers, when the store has never done so. That is libel. Oral defamation is **slander.** If Professor Wilson, in class, refers to Sally Student as a drug dealer, and Sally has never sold anything stronger than Arm & Hammer, he has slandered her. (Defamatory comments made on television and radio are considered libel, because the vast audiences mean that the damage is similar to that done by newspapers.)

There are four elements to a defamation case. **An element is a fact that a plaintiff must prove to win a lawsuit.** The plaintiff in any kind of lawsuit must prove all of the elements to prevail. The elements in a defamation case are:

- *Defamatory statement.* This is a statement likely to harm another person's reputation. When Professor Wisdom accuses Sally of dealing drugs, that will clearly harm her reputation.

- *Falseness.* The statement must be false to be defamatory. If Sally Student actually sold marijuana to a classmate, then Professor Wisdom has a defense to slander.

- *Communicated.* The statement must be communicated to at least one person other than the plaintiff. If Wisdom speaks only to Sally and accuses her of dealing drugs, there is no slander. But there is if he shouts the accusation in a crowded hall.

- *Injury.* In slander cases, the plaintiff generally must show some injury. Sally's injury would be lower reputation in the school, embarrassment, and humiliation. But in libel cases, the law is willing to assume injury. Since libel is written, and more permanent, courts award damages even without proof of injury.

Opinion

Remember that the plaintiff must demonstrate a "false" statement. Opinions, though, cannot be proven true or false. For that reason, **opinion is generally a valid defense in a defamation suit.**

Mr. Mashburn, who opened the chapter suing over his restaurant review, lost his case. The court held that a reasonable reader would have understood the statements to be opinion only. "A shaker full of paprika" and "yellow death on duck" were not to be taken literally but were merely the author's expression of his personal dislike. What about a crude description of a college official, appearing in the school's newspaper? You be the judge.

YOU BE THE JUDGE

YEAGLE v. COLLEGIATE TIMES

255 Va. 293, 497 S.E.2d 136, 1998 Va. LEXIS 32
Virginia Supreme Court, 1998

FACTS: Sharon Yeagle was assistant to the vice-president of student affairs at the Virginia Polytechnic Institute and State University. The state had an academic honors program called the Governor's Fellows Program, and one of Yeagle's duties was to help students apply. The school newspaper, the *Collegiate Times*, published an article describing the university's success at placing students in the Fellows Program. The article included a block quotation in larger print, attributed to Yeagle. Underneath Yeagle's name was the phrase "Director of Butt Licking."

Yeagle sued the *Collegiate Times*, alleging that the vulgar phrase defamed her. The trial court dismissed the case, ruling that no reasonable person would take the words literally, and that the phrase conveyed no factual information. Yeagle appealed to the Virginia Supreme Court.

YOU BE THE JUDGE: Was the phrase defamatory, or was it deliberate exaggeration that no reasonable person would take literally?

ARGUMENT FOR YEAGLE: The disgusting phrase that the *Collegiate Times* used to describe Ms. Yeagle is defamatory for several reasons. The conduct described by the words happens to be a crime in Virginia, a violation of the state sodomy statute. Thus the paper is accusing her of criminal offenses

that she has never committed. That is defamation, and in itself entitles Ms. Yeagle to damages.

If, however, defendants argue that the phrase must be interpreted figuratively, then the newspaper has accused Ms. Yeagle of currying favor, or directing others to do so, in a uniquely degrading fashion. The *Collegiate Times* is informing its readers that she performs her job in a sleazy, unprofessional manner evidently because she cannot succeed by merit. The paper is suggesting that she is devoid of integrity and capable of achieving goals only by devious, deviant methods.

ARGUMENT FOR COLLEGIATE TIMES: Statements are only defamatory if a reasonable reader would understand them as asserting facts that can be proven true or false. There is no such statement in this case, and no defamation. No reasonable reader, after finishing an article about the Fellows Program, would believe that Ms. Yeagle was actually the director as described, or even that there is such a job.

The paper chose to inject humor into its coverage of a mundane issue, for the entertainment of its readers. The great majority of the paper's readers appreciate lively language that is at times irreverent. For anyone who is quick to take offense, the proper recourse is not to file suit, but to put down the paper. ▮

Public Personalities

The rules of the game change for those who play in the open. Public officials and public figures receive less protection from defamation. An example of a public official is a police chief. A public figure is a movie star, for example, or a multimillionaire playboy constantly in the news. In the landmark case *New York Times Co. v. Sullivan*, the Supreme Court ruled that the free exchange of information is vital in a democracy and is protected by the First Amendment to the Constitution. If the information wounds public people, that may just be tough luck.

The rule from the *New York Times v. Sullivan* case is that a public official or public figure can win a defamation case only by proving actual malice by the defendant. **Actual malice means that the defendant knew the statement was false or acted with reckless disregard of the truth.** If the plaintiff merely shows that the defendant newspaper printed incorrect statements, even very damaging ones, that will not suffice to win the suit. In the *New York Times v. Sullivan* case, the police chief of Birmingham, Alabama claimed that the *Times* falsely accused him of racial violence in his job. He lost because he could not prove that the *Times* had acted with actual malice. If he had shown that the *Times* knew the accusation was false, he would have won.

FALSE IMPRISONMENT

False imprisonment is the intentional restraint of another person without reasonable cause and without consent. False imprisonment cases most commonly arise in retail stores, which sometimes detain employees or customers for suspected theft. Most states now have statutes governing the detention of suspected shoplifters. **Generally, a store may detain a customer or worker for alleged shoplifting provided there is a reasonable basis for the suspicion and the detention is done reasonably.** To detain a customer in the manager's office for 20 minutes and question him about where he got an item is lawful. To chain that customer to a display counter for three hours and humiliate him in front of other customers is unreasonable, and false imprisonment.

AT **RISK**

Assume that you are a junior vice-president of a chain of 15 retail clothing stores, all located in your state. The president has asked you to outline a sensible plan, to be given to all employees, for dealing with suspected shoplifters. Here are some ideas to consider:

• There are competing social values. Shoplifting is very costly to our society, causing businesses to lose anywhere from $5 billion to $25 billion annually. On the other hand, no one wants to shop in a "police state" environment.

• What is a "reasonable" suspicion of shoplifting? What if a clerk sees a customer hurry out, wearing a sweater identical to those on display? Must the clerk have seen the customer pick up the sweater? Put it on?

• What is "reasonable" detention? Can you tackle someone running through the parking lot? Can you shoot him?

Some people in our society are biased against others, based on race or gender, while others are entirely free of such prejudices. How do you take that into account? ▪▪

BATTERY AND ASSAULT

These two torts are related, but not identical. **Battery is an intentional touching of another person in a way that is unwanted or offensive.** There need be no intention to hurt the plaintiff. If the defendant intended to do the physical act, and a reasonable plaintiff would be offended by it, battery has occurred.

Suppose an irate parent throws a chair at a referee during his daughter's basketball game, breaking the man's jaw. It is irrelevant that the father did not intend to injure the referee. But a parent who cheerfully slaps the winning coach on the back has not committed battery, because a reasonable coach would not be offended.

Assault occurs when a defendant does some act that makes a plaintiff fear an imminent battery. It is assault even though the battery never occurs. Suppose Ms. Wilson shouts "Think fast!" at her husband and hurls a toaster at him. He turns and sees it flying at him. His fear of being struck is enough to win a case of assault, even if the toaster misses. If the toaster happens to strike him, Ms. Wilson has also committed battery.

FRAUD

Fraud is injuring another person by deliberate deception. It is fraud to sell real estate knowing that there is a large toxic waste deposit underground, of which the buyer is ignorant. Fraud is a tort, but it typically occurs during the negotiation or performance of a contract, and it is discussed in detail in Unit 2, on contracts.

INTENTIONAL INFLICTION OF EMOTIONAL DISTRESS

A credit officer was struggling in vain to locate Sheehan, who owed money on his car. The officer finally phoned Sheehan's mother, falsely identified herself as a hospital employee, and said she needed to find Sheehan because his children had been in a serious auto accident. The horrified mother provided Sheehan's whereabouts, which enabled the company to seize his car. But Sheehan himself spent seven hours frantically trying to locate his supposedly injured children, who in fact were fine. He was not injured physically, but he sued for his emotional distress—and won. **The intentional infliction of emotional distress results from extreme and outrageous conduct that causes serious emotional harm.** The credit company was liable for the intentional infliction of emotional distress.[2] The following case arose in a setting that guarantees controversy—an abortion clinic.

CASE SUMMARY

JANE DOE AND NANCY ROE v. LYNN MILLS

212 Mich. App. 73, 536 N.W.2d 824, 1995 Mich. App. LEXIS 313
Michigan Court of Appeals, 1995

FACTS: Late one night, an antiabortion protestor named Robert Thomas climbed into a Dumpster located behind the Women's Advisory Center, an abortion clinic. He found documents indicating that the plaintiffs were soon to have abortions at the clinic. Thomas gave the information to Lynn Mills. The next day, Mills and Sister Lois Mitoraj created signs, using the women's names, indicating that they were about to undergo abortions, and urging them not to "kill their babies."

Doe and Roe (not their real names) sued, claiming intentional infliction of emotional distress (as well as breach of privacy, discussed later in this chapter). The trial court dismissed the lawsuit, ruling that the defendants' conduct was not extreme and outrageous. The plaintiffs appealed.

ISSUE: Have the plaintiffs made a valid claim of intentional infliction of emotional distress?

DECISION: The plaintiffs have made a valid claim of intentional infliction of emotional distress.

REASONING: A defendant is liable for the intentional infliction of emotional distress only when his conduct is outrageous in character, extreme in degree, and utterly intolerable in a civilized community. A good test is whether the average member of the community would respond to the defendant's conduct by exclaiming, "Outrageous!"

These defendants have a constitutional right to protest against abortions, but they have no such right to publicize private matters. Their behavior here might well cause the average person to say, "Outrageous!" The plaintiffs are entitled to a trial, so that a jury can decide whether the defendants have inflicted emotional distress. ◢

---

[2] *Ford Motor Credit Co. v. Sheehan,* 373 So. 2d 956, 1979 Fla. App. LEXIS 15416 (Fla. Dist. Ct. App. 1979).

Damages

COMPENSATORY DAMAGES

Mitchel Bien, a deaf mute, enters the George Grubbs Nissan dealership, where folks sell cars aggressively. Very aggressively. Maturelli, a salesman, and Bien communicate by writing messages back and forth. Maturelli takes Bien's own car keys, and the two then test drive a 300ZX. Bien says he does not want the car, but Maturelli escorts him back inside and fills out a sales sheet. Bien repeatedly asks for his keys, but Maturelli only laughs, pressuring him to buy the new car. Minutes pass. Hours pass. Bien becomes frantic, writing a dozen notes, begging to leave, threatening to call the police. Maturelli mocks Bien and his physical disabilities. Finally, after four hours, the customer escapes.

Bien sues for the intentional infliction of emotional distress. Two former salesmen from Grubbs testify that they have witnessed customers cry, yell, and curse as a result of the aggressive tactics. Doctors state that the incident has traumatized Bien, dramatically reducing his confidence and self-esteem and preventing his return to work even three years later.

The jury awards Bien damages. But how does a jury calculate the money? For that matter, why should a jury even try? Money can never erase pain or undo a permanent injury. The answer is simple: Money, however inexact and ineffective, is the only thing a court has to give. A successful plaintiff generally receives **compensatory damages, meaning an amount of money that the court believes will restore him to the position he was in before the defendant's conduct caused an injury.** Here is how damages are figured.

First, a plaintiff receives money for medical expenses that he has proven by producing bills from doctors, hospitals, physical therapists, and psychotherapists. If a doctor testifies that he needs future treatment, Bien will offer evidence of how much that will cost. The **single recovery principle** requires a court to settle the matter once and for all, by awarding a lump sum for past and future expenses.

Second, the defendants are liable for lost wages, past and future. The court takes the number of days or months that Bien has missed (and will miss) work and multiplies that times his salary.

Third, a plaintiff is paid for pain and suffering. Bien testifies about how traumatic the four hours were and how the experience has affected his life. He may state that he now fears shopping, suffers nightmares, and seldom socializes. To bolster the case, a plaintiff uses expert testimony, such as the psychiatrists who testified for Bien. In this case, the jury awarded Bien $573,815, calculated as in the following table.[3]

---

[3] The compensatory damages are described in *George Grubbs Enterprises v. Bien,* 881 S.W.2d 843, 1994 Tex. App. LEXIS 1870 (Tex. Ct. App. 1994). In addition to the compensatory damages described, the jury awarded $5 million in punitive damages. The Texas Supreme Court reversed the award of punitive damages, but not the compensatory. Id., 900 S.W.2d 337, 1995 Tex. LEXIS 91 (Tex. 1995). The high court did not dispute the appropriateness of punitive damages, but reversed because the trial court failed to instruct the jury properly as to how it should determine the assets actually under the defendants' control, an issue essential to punitive damages but not compensatory damages.

Past medical	$ 70.00
Future medical	6,000.00
Past rehabilitation	3,205.00
Past lost earning capacity	112,910.00
Future lost earning capacity	34,650.00
Past physical symptoms and discomfort	50,000.00
Future physical symptoms and discomfort	50,000.00
Past emotional injury and mental anguish	101,980.00
Future emotional injury and mental anguish	200,000.00
Past loss of society and reduced ability to socially interact with family, former fiancee, and friends, and hearing (i.e., nondeaf) people in general	10,000.00
Future loss of society and reduced ability to socially interact with family, former fiancee, and friends, and hearing people	5,000.00
TOTAL	$573,815.00

PUNITIVE DAMAGES

The Ford Bronco II that Pamela Ammerman was riding in rolled over. Pamela suffered a crushed pelvis, skull fractures, and brain damage that left her with manic depression and suicidal tendencies. She sued Ford. The jury concluded that the car rolled over because it was defectively designed, and that the company knew of the dangers but recklessly hurried the car into production, against the advice of its own engineers, in order to maximize profits. They awarded Pamela $4 million in compensatory damages plus a larger sum in punitive damages.

Punitive damages are not designed to compensate the plaintiff for harm, because compensatory damages will have done that. **Punitive damages are intended to punish the defendant for conduct that is extreme and outrageous.** Courts award these damages in relatively few cases. When an award of punitive damages is made, it is generally in a case of intentional tort, although as the Ammerman case illustrates, they also occur in negligence suits. The idea behind punitive damages is that certain behavior is so unacceptable that society must make an example of it. A large award of money should deter the defendant from repeating the mistake and others from ever making it.

The jury awarded Pamela Ammerman $13.8 million in punitive damages (beyond the compensatory damages). Ford appealed—and lost. The court concluded that the jury reasonably concluded that the company had acted with callous indifference to the lives of its customers.

Although a jury has wide discretion in awarding punitive damages, the U.S. Supreme Court has ruled that a verdict must be reasonable. In awarding punitive damages, a court must consider three "guideposts":

- The reprehensibility of the defendant's conduct.

- The ratio between the harm suffered and the award. Generally, the punitive award should not be more than nine times the compensatory award.

- The difference between the punitive award and any civil penalties used in similar cases.

Business Torts

TORTIOUS INTERFERENCE WITH A CONTRACT

Competition is the essence of business. Successful corporations compete aggressively, and the law permits and expects them to. But there are times when healthy competition becomes illegal interference. This is called **tortious interference with a contract.** To win such a case, a plaintiff must establish four elements:

- There was a contract between the plaintiff and a third party.

- The defendant knew of the contract.

- The defendant improperly induced the third party to breach the contract or made performance of the contract impossible; and

- There was injury to the plaintiff.

Because businesses routinely compete for customers, employees, and market share, it is not always easy to identify tortious interference. There is nothing wrong with two companies bidding against each other to buy a parcel of land, and nothing wrong with one corporation doing everything possible to convince the seller to ignore all competitors. But once a company has signed a contract to buy the land, it is improper to induce the seller to break the deal. The most commonly disputed issues in these cases concern elements one and three: Was there a contract between the plaintiff and another party? Did the defendant improperly induce a party to breach it? Defendants will try to show that the plaintiff had no contract.

INTRUSION

Intrusion into someone's private life is a tort if a reasonable person would find it offensive. Peeping through someone's windows or wiretapping his telephone are obvious examples of intrusion. In a famous case involving a "paparazzo" photographer and Jacqueline Kennedy Onassis, the court found that the photographer had invaded her privacy by making a career out of photographing her. He had bribed doormen to gain access to hotels and restaurants she visited, had jumped out of bushes to photograph her young children, and had driven powerboats dangerously close to her. The court ordered him to stop.[4] Nine years later the paparazzo was found in contempt of court for again taking photographs too close to Ms. Onassis. He agreed to stop once and for all—in exchange for a suspended contempt sentence.

CYBERLAW

Robert Konop, a pilot for Hawaiian Airlines, was distressed with the demands his company was making on employees, and also with his union's response. On a private Web site, he criticized both parties and urged fellow pilots to switch to a different union. Konop gave his colleagues passwords to the site, while denying access to management and union officials. Hawaiian Airlines Vice-President James Davis surreptitiously visited the site by using the name and password of two pilots, with their consent. Davis entered the site at least 20 times in this fashion. Konop sued, claiming

---

[4] *Galella v. Onassis*, 487 F. 2d 986, 1973 U.S.App.LEXIS 7901 (2d Cir. 1973).

a violation of two important statutes:

- The Electronic Communications Privacy Act, which prohibits the unauthorized interception or disclosure of wire and electronic communications;[5] and

- The Stored Communications Act, which prohibits unauthorized access to a facility through which an electronic service is provided.[6]

The district court dismissed the claims, but the appellate court reversed, holding that Konop had raised legitimate—and novel—issues under both statutes. He deserved a trial to demonstrate that Davis had in fact violated these two laws.[7]

The explosive growth of electronic commerce inevitably fosters a burgeoning docket of novel litigation. For a more detailed look at the statutes and issues involved, see Chapter 42 on cyberlaw. ◾

COMMERCIAL EXPLOITATION

This right prohibits the unauthorized use of another person's likeness or voice for commercial purposes. For example, it would be illegal to run a magazine ad showing actress Gwyneth Paltrow holding a can of soda, without her permission. The ad would imply that she endorses the product. Someone's identity is her own, and it cannot be exploited unless she permits it. Ford Motor Company hired a singer to imitate Bette Midler's version of a popular song. The imitation was so good that most listeners were fooled into believing that Ms. Midler was endorsing the product. That, ruled a court, violated her right to commercial exploitation.

Chapter Conclusion

This chapter has been a potpourri of sin, a bubbling cauldron of conduct best avoided. Although tortious acts and their consequences are diverse, two generalities apply. First, the boundaries of intentional torts are imprecise, the outcome of a particular case depending to a considerable extent upon the fact finder who analyzes it. Second, the thoughtful executive and the careful citizen, aware of the shifting standards and potentially vast liability, will strive to ensure that his or her conduct never provides that fact finder an opportunity to give judgment.

Chapter Review

1. A tort is a violation of a duty imposed by the civil law.

2. Defamation involves a defamatory statement that is false, uttered to a third person, and causes an injury.

3. False imprisonment is the intentional restraint of another person without reasonable cause and without consent.

4. Battery is an intentional touching of another person in a way that is unwanted or offensive. Assault involves an act that makes the plaintiff fear an imminent battery.

5. The intentional infliction of emotional distress involves extreme and outrageous conduct that causes serious emotional harm.

---

[5] 18 U.S.C. §2511.

[6] 18 U.S.C. §2701.

[7] *Konop v. Hawaiian Airlines, Inc.*, 236 F.3d 1035, 2001 U.S. App. LEXIS 191 (9th Cir. 2001).

6. Compensatory damages are the normal remedy in a tort case. In unusual cases, the court may award punitive damages, not to compensate the plaintiff but to punish the defendant.

7. Tortious interference with a contract involves the defendant unfairly harming an existing contract.

8. The Electronic Communications Privacy Act prohibits the unauthorized interception or disclosure of wire and electronic communications, and the Stored Communications Act bars unauthorized access to a facility through which an electronic service is provided.

9. Commercial exploitation means the exclusive right to use one's own name, likeness, or voice.

PRACTICE TEST

Matching Questions

Match the following terms with their definitions:

___ **A.** Interference with a contract

___ **B.** Fraud

___ **C.** Defamation

___ **D.** False imprisonment

___ **E.** Punitive damages

___ **F.** Intentional infliction of emotional distress

___ **G.** Commercial exploitation

1. Money awarded to punish the wrongdoer.

2. Intentionally restraining another person without reasonable cause.

3. Intentional deception, frequently used to obtain a contract with another party.

4. Deliberately stealing a client who has a contract with another.

5. Violation of the exclusive right to use one's own name, likeness, or voice.

6. Using a false statement to damage someone's reputation.

7. An act so extreme that an average person would say, "Outrageous!"

True/False Questions

Circle true or false:

1. T F A store manager who believes a customer has stolen something may question him but not restrain him.

2. T F Becky punches Kelly in the nose. Becky has committed the tort of assault.

3. T F A defendant cannot be liable for defamation if the statement, no matter how harmful, is true.

4. T F In most cases, a winning plaintiff receives compensatory and punitive damages.

5. T F A beer company that wishes to include a celebrity's picture in its magazine ads must first obtain the celebrity's permission.

Multiple-Choice Questions

6. A valid defense in a defamation suit is

(a) Falseness.

(b) Honest error.

(c) Improbability.

(d) Opinion.

(e) Third-party reliance.

7. Joe Student, irate that on an exam he received a B- rather than a B, stands up in class and throws his laptop at the professor. The professor sees it coming and ducks just in time; the laptop smashes against the chalkboard. Joe has committed

(a) Assault.

(b) Battery.

(c) Negligence.

(d) Slander.

(e) No tort, because the laptop missed the professor.

8. Marsha, a supervisor, furiously berates Ted in front of 14 other employees, calling him "a loser, an incompetent, a failure as an employee and as a person." She hands around copies of Ted's work and for twenty minutes mocks his efforts. If Ted sues Marsha, his best claim will be

(a) Assault.

(b) Battery.

(c) Intentional infliction of emotional distress.

(d) Negligence.

(e) Interference with a contract.

9. Rodney is a star player on the Los Angeles Lakers basketball team. He has two years remaining on his four-year contract. The Wildcats, a new team in the league, try to lure Rodney away from the Lakers by offering him more money, and Rodney agrees to leave Los Angeles. The Lakers sue. The Lakers will

(a) Win a case of defamation.

(b) Win a case of commercial exploitation.

(c) Win a case of intentional interference with a contract.

(d) win a case of negligence.

(e) Lose.

10. While Mark is driving, he drinks from a bottle of whiskey, becoming intoxicated. Because he is drunk, he swerves into the wrong lane, causing an accident and seriously injuring Janet. Which statement is true?

(a) Janet could sue Mark, who might be found guilty in her suit.

(b) Janet and the state could start separate criminal cases against Mark.

(c) Janet could sue Mark, and the state could prosecute Mark for drunk driving.

(d) The state could sue Mark but only with Janet's consent.

(e) The state could prosecute Mark and sue him at the same time, for drunk driving.

Short-Answer Questions

11. Benzaquin had a radio talk show in Boston. On the program, he complained about an incident earlier in the day, in which state trooper Fleming had stopped his car, apparently for lack of a proper license plate and safety sticker. Even though Benzaquin explained that the license plate had been stolen and the sticker had fallen onto the dashboard, Fleming refused to let him drive the car away, and Benzaquin and his daughter and two young grandsons had to find other transportation. On the show, Benzaquin angrily recounted the incident, then made the following statements about Fleming and troopers generally: "arrogants wearing trooper's uniforms like tights"; "little monkey, you wind him up and he does his thing"; "we're not paying them to be dictators and Nazis"; "this man is an absolute barbarian, a lunkhead, a meathead." Fleming sued Benzaquin for defamation. Comment.

12. Caldwell was shopping in a K-Mart store, carrying a large purse. A security guard observed her look at various small items such as stain, hinges, and antenna wire. On occasion she bent down out of sight of the guard. The guard thought he saw Caldwell put something in her purse. Caldwell removed her glasses from her purse and returned them a few times. After she left, the guard approached her in the parking lot and said that he believed she had store merchandise in her pocketbook, but was unable to say what he thought was put there. Caldwell opened the purse, and the guard testified that he saw no K-Mart merchandise in it. The guard then told Caldwell to return to the store with him. They walked around the store for approximately 15 minutes, while the guard said six or seven times that he saw her put something in her purse. Caldwell left the store after another store employee indicated she

could go. Caldwell sued. What kind of suit did she file, and what should the outcome be?

13. Tata Consultancy of Bombay, India is an international computer consulting firm. It spends considerable time and effort recruiting the best personnel from India's leading technical schools. Tata employees sign an initial three-year employment commitment, often work overseas, and agree to work for a specified additional time when they return to India. Desai worked for Tata, but then quit and formed a competing company, which he called Syntel. His new company contacted Tata employees by phone, offering more money to come work for Syntel, bonuses, and assistance in obtaining permanent resident visas in the United States. At least 16 former Tata employees left their work without completing their contractual obligations and went to work for Syntel. Tata sued. What did it claim, and what should be the result?

14. Johnny Carson was for many years the star of a well-known television show, The Tonight Show. For about 20 years, he was introduced nightly on the show with the phrase, "Here's Johnny!" A large segment of the television-watching public associated the phrase with Carson. A Michigan corporation was in the business of renting and selling portable toilets. The company chose the name "Here's Johnny Portable Toilets," and coupled the company name with the marketing phrase, "The World's Foremost Commodian." Carson

sued. What claim is he making? Who should win, and why?

15. ETHICS: Fifteen-year-old Terri Stubblefield was riding in the backseat of a Ford Mustang II when the car was hit from behind. The Mustang was engulfed in a ball of fire, and Terri was severely burned. She died. Terri's family sued Ford, alleging that the car was badly designed—and that Ford knew it. At trial, Terri's family introduced evidence that Ford knew the fuel tank was dangerous and that it could have taken measures to make the tank safe. There was evidence that Ford consciously decided not to remedy the fuel tanks in order to save money. The jury awarded $8 million in punitive damages to the family. Ford appealed. Should the punitive damages be affirmed? What are the obligations of a corporation when it knows that one of its products may be dangerous? Should we require a manufacturer to improve the safety of its cars if doing so will make them too expensive for many drivers? What would you do if you were a midlevel executive and saw evidence that your company was endangering the lives of consumers to save money? What would you do if you were on a jury and saw such evidence?

16. ROLE REVERSAL: Write a multiple-choice question about defamation in which one and only one element is missing from the plaintiff's case. Choose a set of answers that forces the student to isolate the missing element.

Internet Research Problem

Using the Internet, find a recent case in which a court awarded punitive damages for the intentional tort of assault, battery, intentional infliction of emotional distress, or false imprisonment. What facts led to the punitive damages award? Make your own award of punitive damages, and then compare your judgment with the court's.

You can find further practice problems in the Online Quiz at **http://beatty.westbuslaw.com** or in the Study Guide that accompanies this text.

Negligence and Strict Liability

Party time! A fraternity at the University of Arizona welcomed new members, and the alcohol flowed freely. Several hundred people danced and shrieked and drank, and no one checked for proof of age. A common occurrence—but one that ended tragically. A minor student drove away, intoxicated, and slammed into another car. The other driver was gravely injured. The drunken student was obviously liable, but his insurance did not cover the huge medical bills. The injured man also sued the fraternity. Should the organization be legally responsible? The issue is one of negligence law. In this contentious area, courts continually face one question: When someone is injured, how far should responsibility extend?

CHAPTER
6

Negligence

We might call negligence the "unintentional" tort because it concerns harm that arises by accident. A person, or perhaps an organization, does some act, not expecting to hurt anyone, yet someone is harmed. Should a court impose liability? The fraternity members who gave the party never wanted—or thought—that an innocent man would suffer terrible damage. But he did. Is it in society's interest to hold the fraternity responsible?

Before we can answer this question, we need some guidance. Things go wrong all the time, and people are hurt in large ways and small. Society needs a method of analyzing negligence cases consistently and fairly. One of America's greatest judges, Benjamin Cardozo, offered his thoughts more than 75 years ago. His decision still dominates negligence thinking today, so we will let him introduce us to Helen Palsgraf.

CASE SUMMARY

PALSGRAF v. LONG ISLAND RAILROAD CO.

248 N.Y. 339, 162 N.E. 99, 1928 N.Y. LEXIS 1269
New York Court of Appeals, 1928

FACTS: Helen Palsgraf was waiting on a railroad platform. As a train began to leave the station, a man carrying a package ran to catch it. He jumped aboard but looked unsteady, so a guard on the car reached out to help him as another guard, on the platform, pushed from behind. The man dropped the package, which struck the tracks and exploded—since it was packed with fireworks. The shock knocked over some heavy scales at the far end of the platform, and one of them struck Palsgraf. She sued the railroad. The jury found that the guards had acted negligently, and held the railroad liable. The company appealed.

ISSUE: Assuming the guards did a bad job assisting the passenger, was the railroad liable for the injuries to Ms. Palsgraf?

DECISION: No, the railroad was not liable because it had no duty to Palsgraf. Reversed.

REASONING: To win a negligence suit, an injured plaintiff must show that the defendant had a duty *specifically to her,* not to anyone else. There is no such thing as responsibility to society in general.

The guard's conduct was not a wrong to Palsgraf, even though it might have been a wrong to the man holding the package. The guard could not realize that the package might injure a passenger at the far end of the platform. If the guard had grabbed the package and deliberately hurled it to the ground, he would never have expected to hurt a distant passenger. Here, where his act was *un*intentional, he obviously cannot be liable. ◢

To win a negligence case, the plaintiff must prove *all five* of these elements:

- *Duty of due care.* The defendant had a duty of due care *to this plaintiff.* This is Judge Cardozo's point in the Palsgraf case.

- *Breach.* The defendant breached her duty.

- *Factual cause.* The defendant's conduct actually caused the injury.

- *Foreseeable harm.* It was foreseeable that conduct like the defendant's might cause this type of harm.

- *Injury.* The plaintiff has actually been hurt.

DUTY OF DUE CARE

The first issue may be the most difficult in all of tort law: Did the defendant have a duty of due care to the injured person? Judges draw an imaginary line around the defendant and say that she owes a duty to the people within this circle, but not to those outside it. The test is generally "foreseeability." **If a defendant can foresee injury to a particular person, she has a duty to him.** If she cannot foresee the harm, there is usually no duty.

Some cases are easy. Suppose Glorious University operates a cafeteria. Does the school have a duty of due care to its diners? Absolutely. Management can foresee that a grimy kitchen will cause serious illness, so the university has a duty to each of its patrons. On the other hand, assume the school bookstore sells a road map of Greece to a student. During spring break, the student drives recklessly along a narrow country lane in Greece, injuring a farmer. The university could never have foreseen harm to a Greek farmer merely from selling a map, so it had no duty to the man.

Let us apply these principles to the fraternity case.

CASE SUMMARY

HERNANDEZ v. ARIZONA BOARD OF REGENTS

177 Ariz. 244, 866 P.2d 1330, 1994 Ariz. LEXIS 6
Arizona Supreme Court, 1994

FACTS: At the University of Arizona, the Epsilon Epsilon chapter of Delta Tau Delta fraternity gave a welcoming party for new members. The fraternity's officers knew that the majority of its members were under the legal drinking age, but permitted everyone to consume alcohol. John Rayner, who was under 21 years of age, left the party. He drove negligently and caused a collision with an auto driven by Ruben Hernandez. At the time of the accident, Rayner's blood alcohol level was 0.15, exceeding the legal limit. The crash left Hernandez blind, severely brain damaged, and quadriplegic.

Hernandez sued Rayner, who settled the case, based on the amount of his insurance coverage. The victim also sued the fraternity, its officers and national organization, all fraternity members who contributed money to buy alcohol, the university, and

others. The trial court granted summary judgment for all defendants and the court of appeals affirmed. Hernandez appealed to the Arizona Supreme Court.

ISSUE: Did the fraternity and the other defendants have a duty of due care to Hernandez?

DECISION: Yes, the defendants did have a duty of due care to Hernandez. Reversed and remanded.

REASONING: Historically, Arizona and most states have considered that *consuming* alcohol led to liability, but not *furnishing* it. However, the common law also has had a long-standing rule that a defendant could be liable for supplying some object to a person who is likely to endanger others. Giving a car to an intoxicated youth is an example of such behavior.

The youth might easily use the object (the car) to injure other people.

There is no difference between giving a car to an intoxicated youth and giving alcohol to a young person with a car. Both acts involve minors who, because of their age and inexperience, are likely to endanger third parties. Furthermore, furnishing alcohol to a minor violates several state statutes. The defendants did have a duty of due care to Hernandez and to the public in general. ◢

ETHICS

In most states, anyone serving alcohol to a minor is liable for injuries that result to a third party. One of the intriguing aspects of the common law is that every answer prompts another question. Should a homeowner who serves alcohol to an *adult* friend be liable for resulting harm? New Jersey has answered this question "Yes." In that state, if an adult pours drinks for a friend, aware that he is becoming drunk, and the friend injures a third party, the host is fully liable. However, the great majority of states to consider this issue have reached the opposite conclusion, holding that a social host is not liable for harm caused by an adult drinker. Why do most states distinguish between adult and underage guests, holding a social host liable only for serving minors? Using the ethics checklist, ask yourself: What are the consequences of serving alcohol to an adult guest? Which values are in conflict? Which of those values are most important to you? ▪

UPDATE

Online, find a recent case of social host liability. How did the accident occur? What was the outcome? In your view, was the outcome fair? ▪

Landowner's Duty

The common law applies special rules to a landowner for injuries occurring on her property. In most states, the owner's duty depends on why the injured person came onto the property.

- *Lowest Liability: Trespasser.* A **trespasser** is anyone on the property without consent. A landowner is only liable to a trespasser for intentionally injuring him or for some other gross misconduct. The landowner has no liability to a trespasser for mere negligence. Jake is not liable if a vagrant wanders onto his land and is burned by defective electrical wires.

- *Higher Liability: Licensee.* A **licensee** is anyone on the land for her own purposes but with the owner's permission. A social guest is a typical licensee. A licensee is entitled to a warning of hidden dangers that the owner knows about. If Juliet invites Romeo for a late supper on the balcony and fails to mention that the wooden railing is rotted, she is liable when her hero plunges to the courtyard.

- *Highest Liability: Invitee.* An **invitee** is someone on the property as of right because it is a public place or a business open to the public. The owner has a duty of reasonable care to an invitee. Perry is an invitee when he goes to the town beach. If riptides have existed for years and the town fails to post a warning, it is liable if Perry drowns. Perry is also an invitee when he shops at Daphne's Boutique. Daphne is liable if she ignores spilled coffee that causes Perry to slip.

CRIME AND TORT: LANDOWNER'S LIABILITY

Law shows us trends in social issues. Regrettably, a major concern of tort law today is how to respond to injury caused by criminals. If a criminal assaults and robs a pedestrian in a shopping mall, that act is a crime and may be prosecuted by the state. But prosecution leaves the victim uncompensated. The assault is also an intentional tort (discussed in Chapter 5), and the victim could file a civil lawsuit against the criminal. But most violent criminals have no assets. Given this economic frustration and the flexibility of the common law, it is inevitable that victims of violence look elsewhere for compensation. Because crimes now occur in offices, shopping malls, and parking lots, plaintiffs increasingly seek compensation from the owners of these facilities.

CASE SUMMARY

ANN M. v. PACIFIC PLAZA SHOPPING CENTER

6 Cal. 4th 666, 863 P.2d 207, 1993 Cal. LEXIS 6127
Supreme Court of California, 1994

FACTS: Ann M. worked at the Original 60 Minute Photo Company in the Pacific Plaza Shopping Center, a strip mall in San Diego. About 25 commercial tenants occupied the center. She was the only employee on duty one day when a man walked in "just like a customer," pulled a knife, went behind the counter, and raped her. He robbed the store, fled, and was never caught.

Ann M. sued Pacific Plaza, claiming that it negligently failed to provide security patrols in the common areas of the shopping center. Under the terms of the lease, Pacific Plaza had exclusive control of these areas, and the right to police them if it chose.

ISSUE: Did Pacific Plaza have a duty to Ann M. to provide security patrols?

DECISION: No, Pacific Plaza did not have a duty to Ann M. to provide security patrols.

REASONING: Deciding the scope of a landlord's duty involves a balancing act. The law must weigh any potential harm to tenants against the burden imposed on the landlord. Hiring security guards is very expensive. Violent criminal acts must be clearly foreseeable before the courts impose such an expensive obligation.

Before Ann M. was raped, tenants and employees of the shopping center had been concerned about their safety. Some evidence indicated that criminals had robbed banks, snatched purses, and pulled down women's pants in the shopping center. However, Pacific Plaza's own records revealed no criminal activity at all. As a result, violent criminal assaults were not foreseeable, and the landlord had no duty to provide security guards. ◢

AT RISK | The court found Pacific Plaza not liable, because it could not have foreseen the harm. If this brutal crime occurred again at the same mall, would it be foreseeable? What advice would you give to Pacific Plaza? Now consider some other retail store or office with which you are familiar. What steps could the employer take to diminish the likelihood of workplace violence? ◼

BREACH OF DUTY

The second element of a plaintiff's negligence case is **breach of duty**. Courts apply the *reasonable person* standard: **A defendant breaches his duty of due care by failing to behave the way a reasonable person would under similar circumstances.** Reasonable "person" means someone of the defendant's occupation. A taxi driver must drive as a reasonable taxi driver would. An architect who designs a skyscraper's safety features must bring to the task far greater knowledge than the average person possesses.

Two medical cases illustrate the reasonable person standard. A doctor prescribes a powerful drug without asking his 21-year-old patient about other medicines she is currently taking. The patient suffers a serious drug reaction from the combined medications. The physician is liable for the harm. A reasonable doctor always checks current medicines before prescribing new ones.

On the other hand, assume that an 84-year-old patient dies on the operating table in an emergency room. While the surgeon was repairing heart damage, the man had a fatal stroke. If the physician followed normal medical procedures, and acted with reasonable speed, he is not liable. A doctor must do a reasonable professional job, but cannot guarantee a happy outcome.

FACTUAL CAUSE AND FORESEEABLE HARM

A plaintiff must also show that the defendant's breach of duty *caused* the plaintiff's harm. Courts look at two issues to settle causation: Was the defendant's behavior the *factual cause* of the harm? Was *this type of harm foreseeable?*[1]

Factual Cause

Nothing mysterious here. **If the defendant's breach physically led to the ultimate harm, it is the factual cause.** Suppose that Dom's Brake Shop tells Customer his brakes are now working fine, even though Dom knows that is false. Customer drives out of the shop, cannot stop at a red light, and hits Bicyclist crossing at the intersection. Dom is liable to Bicyclist. Dom's unreasonable behavior was the *factual cause* of the harm. Think of it as a row of dominoes. The first domino (Dom's behavior) knocked over the next one (failing brakes), which toppled the last one (the cyclist's injury).

Suppose, alternatively, that just as Customer is exiting the repair shop, Bicyclist hits a pothole and tumbles off her cycle, avoiding Customer's auto. Bicyclist's injuries stem from her fall, not from the auto. Customer's brakes still fail, and Dom has breached his duty to Customer, but Dom is not liable to Bicyclist. She would have been hurt anyway. No factual causation.

Foreseeable Type of Harm

For the defendant to be liable, the *type of harm* must have been reasonably foreseeable. In the case above, Dom could easily foresee that bad brakes would cause an automobile accident. He need not have foreseen exactly what happened. He did not know there would be a cyclist nearby. What he could foresee was this general type of harm involving defective brakes. Because the accident that occurred was of the type he could foresee, he is liable.

By contrast, assume the collision of car and bicycle produces a loud crash. Two blocks away, a pet pig, asleep on the window ledge of a 12th-story apartment, is startled by the noise, awakens with a start, and plunges to the sidewalk, killing a

---

[1] Courts often refer to these two elements, grouped together, as *proximate cause* or *legal cause*. However, as many judges have acknowledged, those terms have created legal confusion, so we use *factual cause* and *foreseeable type of harm*, the issues on which most decisions ultimately focus.

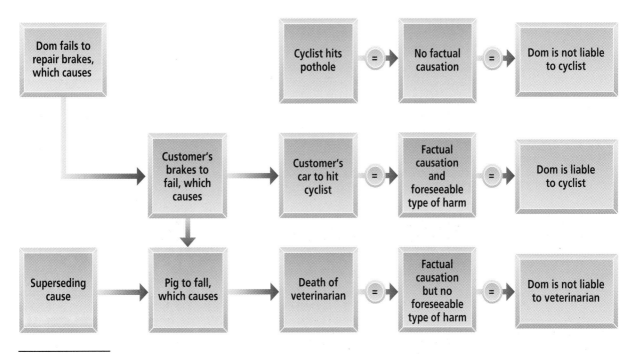

Exhibit 6.1

veterinarian who was making a house call. If the vet's family sues Dom, should it win? Dom's negligence was the factual cause: It led to the collision, which startled the pig, which flattened the vet. Most courts would rule, though, that Dom is not liable. The *type of harm* is too bizarre. Dom could not reasonably foresee such an extraordinary chain of events, and it would be unfair to make him pay for it. See Exhibit 6.1.

Res Ipsa Loquitur

Normally, a plaintiff must prove factual cause and foreseeable type of harm in order to establish negligence. But in a few cases, a court may be willing to infer that the defendant caused the harm, under the doctrine of *res ipsa loquitur* ("the thing speaks for itself"). Suppose a pedestrian is walking along a sidewalk when an air conditioning unit falls on his head from a third-story window. The defendant, who owns the third-story apartment, denies any wrongdoing, and it may be difficult or impossible for the plaintiff to prove why the air conditioner fell. In such cases, many courts will apply *res ipsa loquitur* and declare that the facts imply that the defendant's negligence caused the accident. If a court uses this doctrine, then the defendant must come forward with evidence establishing that it did not cause the harm.

Because *res ipsa loquitur* dramatically shifts the burden of proof from plaintiff to defendant, it applies only when (1) the defendant had exclusive control of the thing that caused the harm; (2) the harm normally would not have occurred without negligence; and (3) the plaintiff had no role in causing the harm. In the air conditioner example, most states would apply the doctrine and force the defendant to prove she did nothing wrong.

INJURY

Finally, a plaintiff must prove that he has been injured. In some cases, injury is obvious. For example, Ruben Hernandez suffered grievous harm when struck by a drunk driver. But in other cases, injury is unclear. **The plaintiff must persuade the court that he has suffered a harm that is genuine, not one that is merely speculative.**

UPDATE

A federal judge awarded $4 million to a California man who suffered severe brain damage after merchandise fell on him at a Wal-Mart store. Todd Caranto, a former Air Force medical corpsman, was Christmas shopping when more than a dozen heavy boxes of toys tumbled off high shelves and knocked him to the floor. The accident resulted in permanent brain damage and left the 26-year-old father of two unable to take care of himself. Caranto will require total care, 24 hours a day, for the rest of his life. He can walk but is unable to speak or communicate with anyone around him.

Find a current personal injury case that resulted in a jury verdict. How large was the award? What factors do you think most affected the jury's decision. How could the harm have been avoided? Are there lessons that a business can take from the case? ◼

The following lawsuit concerns a woman's fear of developing AIDS, a worry that can be overwhelming. The court must still decide, however, whether the cause of the unhappiness is genuine injury or mere speculation.

CASE SUMMARY

REYNOLDS v. HIGHLAND MANOR, INC.

24 Kan. App. 2d 859, 954 P.2d 11, 1998 Kan. App. LEXIS 20
Kansas Court of Appeals, 1998

FACTS: Angelina Reynolds and her family checked into a Holiday Inn, but since the air conditioner did not work they requested a room change. As they were repacking their luggage, Reynolds felt for items left under the bed, and picked up what she thought was a candy wrapper. Reynolds felt a "gush" as she retrieved the item, which unfortunately turned out to be a wet condom. She screamed and quickly washed her hands. There was a second condom under the bed. Reynolds and her husband rushed to an emergency room, taking the condoms with them. Hospital staff said that they were unable to test the contents of the condoms. A doctor examined Reynolds's hand, which had a burn on the middle finger and bloody cuticles, but told her that there was nothing he could do if she had been exposed to infectious diseases.

The condom was never tested. Reynolds sued the motel, claiming among other things that she feared she would die of AIDS. The trial court dismissed the case, ruling that there was no showing of injury. Reynolds appealed.

ISSUE: Has Reynolds demonstrated injury?

DECISION: No, Reynolds has not demonstrated injury. Affirmed.

REASONING: A plaintiff may win a suit based on fear of a future disease or condition, but only if her anxiety is reasonable. She must show a substantial probability that her present injury will develop into a future ailment. If the medical evidence indicates that will not happen, the plaintiff loses.

Reynolds tested HIV-negative four times, including one result obtained more than a year after the incident at the motel. The condom never tested positive. It is more than 99% probable that Reynolds will never become HIV-positive. As a result, her fear of contracting AIDS is legally unreasonable, and she may not recover damages. ◀

DAMAGES

The plaintiff's damages in a negligence case are generally **compensatory damages,** meaning an amount of money that the court believes will restore him to the position he was in before the defendant's conduct caused an injury. In unusual cases, a court may award **punitive damages,** that is, money intended not to compensate the plaintiff but to punish the defendant. We discussed both forms of damages in Chapter 5.

Defenses

ASSUMPTION OF THE RISK

Quick, duck! Close call—that baseball nearly knocked your ear off. If it had, the home team would owe you . . . nothing. Here at the ballpark, there is always a slight chance of injury, and you are expected to realize it. Wherever there is an obvious hazard, a special rule applies. **Assumption of the risk: A person who voluntarily enters a situation that has an obvious danger cannot complain if she is injured.** If you are not willing to tolerate the risk of being hurt by a batted ball, stay home and watch the game on television. And while you are here—pay attention, will you?

Suppose that Good Guys, a restaurant, holds an ice-fishing contest on a frozen lake, to raise money for accident victims. Margie grabs a can full of worms and strolls to the middle of the lake to try her luck, but slips on the ice and suffers a concussion. When she returns to consciousness, Margie should not bother filing suit—she assumed the risk.

CONTRIBUTORY AND COMPARATIVE NEGLIGENCE

Sixteen-year-old Michelle Wightman was out driving at night, with her friend Karrie Wieber in the passenger seat. They came to a railroad crossing, where the mechanical arm had descended and warning bells were sounding, in fact, had been sounding for a long time. A Conrail train, SEEL-7, had suffered mechanical problems and was stopped 200 feet from the crossing, where it had stalled for roughly an hour. Michelle and Karrie saw several cars ahead of them go around the barrier and cross the tracks. Michelle had to decide whether she would do the same.

Long before Michelle made her decision, the train's engineer had seen the heavy Saturday night traffic crossing the tracks, and realized the danger. A second train had passed the crossing at 70 miles per hour, without incident. SEEL-7's conductor and brakeman also understood the peril, but rather than posting a flagman, who could have stopped traffic when a train approached, they walked to the far end of their train to repair the mechanical problem. A police officer had come upon the scene, told his dispatcher to notify Conrail of the danger, and left.

Michelle decided to cross the tracks. She slowly followed the cars ahead of her. TV-9, a freight train traveling at 60 miles per hour, struck the car broadside, killing both girls instantly.

Michelle's mother sued Conrail for negligence. The company claimed that it was Michelle's foolish risk that led to her death. Who wins when both parties are partly responsible? It depends on whether the state uses a legal theory called contributory negligence. **Under contributory negligence, if the plaintiff is even**

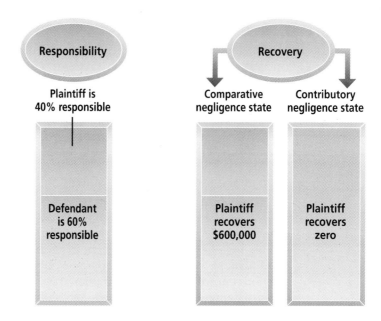

Exhibit 6.2
Defendant's negligence injures plaintiff, who suffers $1 million in damages.

slightly **negligent she recovers nothing.** If Michelle's death occurred in a contributory negligence state, and the jury considered her even minimally responsible, her estate would receive no money.

Critics attacked this rule as unreasonable. A plaintiff who was 1% negligent could not recover from a defendant who was 99% responsible. So most states threw out the contributory negligence rule, replacing it with comparative negligence. **In a comparative negligence state, a plaintiff may generally recover even if she is partially responsible.** The jury will be asked to assess the relative negligence of the two parties.

Michelle died in Ohio, which is a comparative negligence state. The jury concluded that reasonable compensatory damages were $1 million. It also concluded that Conrail was 60% responsible for the tragedy and Michelle 40%. See Exhibit 6.2. The girl's mother received $600,000 in compensatory damages.[2]

Strict Liability

Some activities are so naturally dangerous that the law places an especially high burden on anyone who engages in them. A corporation that produces toxic waste can foresee dire consequences from its business that a stationery store cannot. This higher burden is **strict liability.** There are two main areas of business that incur strict liability: ultrahazardous activity and defective products. We discuss **defective products** in Chapter 20, on product liability.

---

[2] *Wightman v. Consolidated Rail Corporation,* 86 Ohio St. 3d 431, 715 N.E.2d 546 (Ohio, 1999).

ULTRAHAZARDOUS ACTIVITY

Ultrahazardous activities include using harmful chemicals, operating explosives, keeping wild animals, bringing dangerous substances onto property, and a few similar activities where the danger to the general public is especially great. **A defendant engaging in an ultrahazardous activity is virtually always liable for any harm that results.** Plaintiffs do not have to prove duty or breach or foreseeable harm. Recall the deliberately bizarre case we posed earlier of the pig falling from a window ledge and killing a veterinarian. Dom, the mechanic whose negligence caused the car crash, could not be liable for the veterinarian's death because the plunging pig was not foreseeable. But if the pig had been jolted off the window ledge by Sam's Blasting Company doing perfectly lawful blasting for a new building down the street, Sam would be liable. Even if Sam had taken extraordinary care, he would lose. The "reasonable person" rule is irrelevant in a strict liability case.

YOU BE THE JUDGE

NEW JERSEY DEPARTMENT OF ENVIRONMENTAL PROTECTION v. ALDEN LEEDS, INC.

153 N.J. 272; 708 A.2d 1161; 1998 N.J. LEXIS 212; 46 ERC(BNA) 1447
Supreme Court of New Jersey, 1998

FACTS: The Alden Leeds company packages, stores, and ships swimming pool chemicals. The firm does most of its work at its facility in Kearns, New Jersey. At any given time, about 21 different hazardous chemicals are present.

The day before Easter, a fire of unknown origin broke out in "Building One" of the company's site, releasing chlorine gas and other potentially dangerous by-products into the air. There were no guards or other personnel on duty. The fire caused $9 million in damage to company property. Because of the danger, the Department of Environmental Protection (DEP) closed the New Jersey Turnpike along with half a dozen other major highways, halted all commuter rail and train service in the area, and urged residents to stay indoors with windows closed. An unspecified number of residents went to local hospitals with respiratory problems.

Based on New Jersey's air pollution laws, the DEP fined Alden Leeds for releasing the toxic chemicals. The appellate court reversed, declaring that there was no evidence the company had caused the fire or the harm. The case reached the state's high court.

YOU BE THE JUDGE: Is the company responsible for the harm?

ARGUMENT FOR ALDEN LEEDS: Alden Leeds did nothing wrong. Why should the company pay a fine? The firm was licensed to use these chemicals, and did so in a safe manner. There is no evidence the company caused the fire. Sometimes accidents just happen. Do not penalize a responsible business simply to make somebody pay. The state should go after careless firms that knowingly injure the public. Leave good companies alone so they can get on with business and provide jobs.

ARGUMENT FOR THE DEPARTMENT OF ENVIRONMENTAL PROTECTION: This accident made innocent people sick and caused massive difficulties for tens of thousands. It makes no difference why the accident happened. That is the whole point of strict liability. When a company chooses to participate in an ultrahazardous activity, it accepts full liability for anything that goes wrong, regardless of the cause. If you want the profits, you accept the responsibility. Alden Leeds must pay.

Chapter Conclusion

Negligence issues necessarily remain in flux, based on changing social values and concerns. There is no final word on what is an ultrahazardous activity, or how much security a shop owner must provide, or whether a social host can be liable for the destruction caused by a guest. What is clear is that a working knowledge of these issues and pitfalls can help everyone—business executive and ordinary citizen alike.

Chapter Review

1. The five elements of negligence are duty of due care, breach, factual causation, foreseeable type of harm, and injury.

2. If the defendant could foresee that misconduct would injure a particular person, he probably has a duty to her.

3. In most states, a landowner's duty of due care is lowest to trespassers; higher to a licensee (anyone on the land for her own purposes but with the owner's permission); and highest of all to an invitee (someone on the property as of right).

4. A defendant breaches his duty of due care by failing to behave the way a reasonable person would under similar circumstances.

5. If an event physically led to the ultimate harm, it is the factual cause.

6. For the defendant to be liable, the type of harm must have been reasonably foreseeable.

7. The plaintiff must persuade the court that he has suffered a harm that is genuine, not speculative.

8. In a contributory negligence state, a plaintiff who is even slightly responsible for his own injury recovers nothing; in a comparative negligence state, the jury may apportion liability between plaintiff and defendant.

9. A defendant is strictly liable for harm caused by an ultrahazardous activity or a defective product. Ultrahazardous activities include using harmful chemicals, blasting, and keeping wild animals. Strict liability means that if the defendant's conduct led to the harm, the defendant is liable, even if she exercises extraordinary care.

PRACTICE TEST

Matching Questions

Match the following terms with their definitions:

___ **A.** Breach.

___ **B.** Strict liability.

___ **C.** Compensatory damages.

___ **D.** Invitee.

___ **E.** Negligence.

1. Money awarded to an injured plaintiff.

2. Someone who has a legal right to enter upon land.

3. A defendant's failure to perform a legal duty.

4. A tort caused accidentally.

5. Legal responsibility that comes from performing ultrahazardous acts.

True/False Questions

Circle true or false:

1. T   F   There are five elements in a negligence case, and a plaintiff wins who proves at least three of them.

2. T   F   Max, a 19-year-old sophomore, gets drunk at a fraternity party and then causes a serious car accident. Max can be found liable and so can the fraternity.

3. T   F   Some states are comparative negligence states but the majority are contributory negligence states.

4. T   F   A landowner might be liable if a dinner guest fell on a broken porch step, but not liable if a trespasser fell on the same place.

5. T   F   A defendant can be liable for negligence even if he never intended to cause harm.

6. T   F   When Ms. Palsgraf sued the railroad, the court found that the railroad should have foreseen what might go wrong.

Multiple-Choice Questions

7. In which case is a plaintiff most likely to sue based on strict liability?

   (a) Defamation.

   (b) Injury caused on the job.

   (c) Injury caused by a tiger that escapes from a zoo.

   (d) Injury caused by defendant's careless driving.

   (e) Injury caused partially by plaintiff and partially by defendant.

8. Martha signs up for a dinner cruise on a large commercial yacht. While the customers are eating dinner, the yacht bangs into another boat. Martha is thrown to the deck, breaking her wrist. She sues. At trial, which of these issues is likely to be the most important?

   (a) Whether the yacht company had permission to take Martha on the cruise.

   (b) Whether the yacht company improperly restrained Martha.

   (c) Whether Martha feared an imminent injury.

   (d) Whether the yacht's captain did a reasonable job of driving the yacht.

   (e) Whether Martha has filed similar suits in the past.

9. Dolly, an architect, lives in Pennsylvania, which is a comparative negligence state. While she is inspecting a construction site for a large building she designed, she is injured when a worker drops a hammer from two stories up. Dolly was not wearing a safety helmet at the time. Dolly sues the construction company. The jury concludes that Dolly has suffered $100,000 in damages. The jury also believes that Dolly was 30% liable for the accident, and the construction company was 70% liable. Outcome?

   (a) Dolly wins nothing.

   (b) Dolly wins $30,000.

   (c) Dolly wins $50,000.

   (d) Dolly wins $70,000.

   (e) Dolly wins $100,000.

10. A taxi driver, hurrying to pick up a customer at the airport, races through a 20 mph hospital zone at 45 mph, and strikes May, who is crossing the street in a pedestrian crosswalk. May sues the driver and the taxi company. What kind of suit is this?

   (a) Contract.

   (b) Remedy.

   (c) Negligence.

   (d) Assault.

   (e) Battery.

Short-Answer Questions

11. At approximately 7:50 p.m., bells at the train station rang and red lights flashed, signaling an express train's approach. David Harris walked onto the tracks, ignoring a yellow line painted on the platform instructing people to stand back. Two men shouted to Harris, warning him to get off the tracks. The train's engineer saw him too late to stop the train, which was traveling at approximately 99 mph. The train struck and killed Harris as it passed through the station. Harris's widow sued the railroad, arguing that the railroad's negligence caused her husband's death. Evaluate the widow's argument.

12. A new truck, manufactured by General Motors Corp., stalled in rush hour traffic on a busy interstate highway because of a defective alternator, which caused a complete failure of the truck's electrical system. The driver stood nearby and waved traffic around his stalled truck. A panel truck approached the GMC truck. Immediately behind the panel truck, Davis was driving a Volkswagen fastback. Because of the panel truck, Davis was unable to see the stalled GMC truck. The panel truck swerved out of the way of the GMC truck, and Davis drove straight into it. The accident killed him. Davis's widow sued GMC. GMC moved for summary judgment, alleging (1) no duty to Davis; (2) no factual causation; and (3) no foreseeable harm. Comment on the three defenses that GMC has raised.

13. A prison inmate bit a hospital employee. The employee sued the state for negligence and lack of supervision, claiming a fear of AIDS. The plaintiff had tested negative for the AIDS virus three times, and there was no proof that the inmate had the virus. Comment on the probable outcome.

14. Van Houten owned a cat and allowed it to roam freely outside. In the three years he had owned it, it had never bitten anyone. The cat entered Pritchard's garage. Pritchard attempted to move it outside his garage, and the cat bit him. As a direct result of the bite, Pritchard underwent four surgeries, was fitted with a plastic finger joint, and spent more than $39,000 in medical bills. He sued Van Houten, claiming both strict liability and ordinary negligence. Please evaluate his claims.

15. ETHICS: Koby, age 16, works after school at Fast-Food, from 4 p.m. until 11 p.m. On Friday night, the restaurant manager sees that Koby is exhausted, but insists that he remain until 4:30 a.m., cleaning up, then demands that he work Saturday morning from 8 a.m. until 4 p.m. On Saturday afternoon, as Koby drives home, he falls asleep at the wheel and causes a fatal car accident. Should FastFood be liable? What important values are involved in this issue? How does the Golden Rule apply?

16. ROLE REVERSAL: Create a short-answer question that focuses on either factual cause, foreseeable type of harm, or *res ipsa loquitur.*

Internet Research Problem

Everyone knows that drunk driving is bad, but many people still do it. Proceed to **http://www.madd.org/**. Find something that you did not know about drunk driving. What role should the law play in this problem, and what role should parents, students, and schools play?

You can find further practice problems in the Online Quiz at **http://beatty.westbuslaw.com** or in the Study Guide that accompanies this text.

Criminal Law
and Procedure

Crime can take us by surprise. Stacey tucks her nine-year-old daughter, Beth, into bed. Promising her husband, Mark, that she will be home by 11 p.m., she jumps into her car and heads back to Be Patient, Inc. She puts a compact disk in the player of her $85,000 sedan and tries to relax. Be Patient is a health care organization that owns five geriatric hospitals. Most of its patients use Medicare, and Stacey supervises all billing to their largest client, the federal government.

She parks in a well-lighted spot on the street and walks to her building, failing to notice two men, collars turned up, watching from a parked truck. Once in her office, she goes straight to her computer and works on billing issues. Tonight's work goes more quickly than she expected, thanks to new software she helped develop. At 10:30 p.m., she emerges from the building with a quick step and a light heart, walks to her car—and finds it missing.

A major crime has occurred during the 90 minutes Stacey was at her desk, but she will never report it to the police. It is a crime that costs Americans countless dollars each year, yet Stacey will not even mention it to friends or family. Stacey is the criminal.

When we think of crime, we imagine the drug dealers and bank robbers endlessly portrayed on television. We do not picture corporate executives sitting at polished desks. "Street crimes" are indeed serious threats to our security and happiness. But when measured only in dollars, street crime takes second place to white-collar crime, which costs society tens of billions of dollars annually.

The hypothetical about Stacey is based on many real cases and is used to illustrate that crime does not always dress the way we expect. Her car was never stolen; it was simply towed. Two parking bureau employees, watching from their truck, saw Stacey park illegally and did their job. It is Stacey who committed a crime—Medicare fraud. Stacey has learned the simple but useful lesson that company profits rise when she charges the government for work that Be Patient has never done. For months she billed the government for imaginary patients. Then she hired a computer hacker to worm into the Medicare computer system and plant a "Trojan horse," a program that seemed useful to Medicare employees but actually contained a series of codes opening the computer to Stacey. Stacey simply entered the Medicare system and altered the calculations for payments owed to Be Patient. Every month, the government paid Be Patient about $10 million for imaginary work. Stacey's scheme was quick and profitable—and a distressingly common crime.

Crime, Society, and Law

CIVIL LAW/CRIMINAL LAW

Conduct is criminal when society outlaws it. When a state legislature or Congress concludes that certain behavior threatens the population generally, it passes a statute forbidding that behavior, in other words, declaring it criminal. Medicare fraud, which Stacey committed, is a crime because Congress has outlawed it.

Prosecution

Suppose the police arrest Roger and accuse him of breaking into a video store and stealing 25 video cameras, videos, and other equipment. The owner of the video store is the one harmed, but it is the government that prosecutes crimes. The local prosecutor will decide whether or not to charge Roger and bring him to trial.

Jury Right

The facts of the case will be decided by a judge or jury. A criminal defendant has a right to a trial by jury for any charge that could result in a sentence of six months or longer. The defendant may demand a jury trial or may waive that right, in which case the judge will be the fact finder.

Punishment

In a civil lawsuit, the plaintiff seeks a verdict that the defendant is liable for harm caused to her. But in a criminal case, the government asks the court to find the defendant guilty of the crime. If the judge or jury finds the defendant guilty, the court will punish him with a fine and/or a prison sentence. The fine is paid to the government, not to the injured person (although the court will sometimes order restitution, meaning that the defendant must reimburse the victim for harm suffered). It is generally the judge who imposes the sentence. If the jury is not persuaded of the defendant's guilt, it will acquit him, that is, find him not guilty.

Felony/Misdemeanor

A felony is a serious crime, for which a defendant can be sentenced to one year or more in prison. Murder, robbery, rape, drug dealing, wire fraud, and embezzlement are felonies. A misdemeanor is a less serious crime, often punishable by a year or less in a county jail. Driving without a license and simple possession of one marijuana cigarette are considered misdemeanors in most states.

THE PROSECUTION'S CASE

In all criminal cases, the prosecution faces several basic issues.

Conduct Outlawed

Virtually all crimes are created by statute. The prosecution must demonstrate to the court that the defendant's alleged conduct is indeed outlawed by a statute. Returning to Roger, the alleged video thief, the state charges that he stole video cameras from a store, a crime clearly defined by statute as burglary.

Burden of Proof

In a civil case, the plaintiff must prove her case by a preponderance of the evidence. But in a criminal case, the government must prove its case beyond a reasonable doubt. This is because the potential harm to a criminal defendant is far greater. The stigma of a criminal conviction will stay with him, making it more difficult to obtain work and housing.

Actus Reus

Actus reus means the "guilty act." The prosecution must prove that the defendant voluntarily committed a prohibited act. Suppose Mary Jo files an insurance claim for a stolen car, knowing that her car was not stolen. That is insurance fraud. Filing the claim is the *actus reus:* Mary Jo voluntarily filled out the insurance claim and mailed it. At a bar, Mary Jo describes the claim to her friend, Chi Ling, who laughs and replies, "That's great. It'll serve the company right." Has Chi Ling committed a crime? No. She may be cynical, but Chi Ling has committed no *actus reus.*

Mens Rea

The prosecution must also show *mens rea,* a "guilty state of mind," on the defendant's part. This is harder to prove than *actus reus*—it requires convincing evidence about something that is essentially psychological. Precisely what "state of mind" the prosecution must prove varies, depending on the crime. Most crimes require a showing of **general intent,** meaning that the defendant intended to do the prohibited physical action (the *actus reus*). Suppose Miller, a customer in a bar, picks up a bottle and smashes it over the head of Bud. In a trial for criminal assault, the *mens rea* would simply be the intention to hit Bud. The prosecution need not show that Miller intended serious harm, only that he intended the blow.

Some crimes require **specific intent.** The prosecution must prove that the defendant willfully intended to do something beyond the physical act. For example, burglary requires proof that the defendant entered a building at night and intended to commit a felony inside, such as stealing property.

DEFENSES

A criminal defendant will frequently dispute the facts that link her to the crime. For example, she might claim mistaken identity (that she merely resembles the real criminal) or offer an alibi (that she can prove she was elsewhere when the crime was committed). In addition, a defendant may offer legal defenses. One of the most controversial is the insanity defense.

Insanity

In most states, a defendant who can prove that he was insane at the time of the criminal act will be declared not guilty. This reflects the moral basis of our criminal law. Insane people, though capable of great harm, historically have not been considered responsible for their acts. A defendant found to be insane will generally be committed to a mental institution. If and when that hospital determines that he is no longer a danger to society, he will, in theory, be released.

States use different rules to gauge sanity. The most common test is the M'Naghten Rule. The defendant must show (1) that he suffered a serious, identifiable mental disease and that because of it (2) he did not understand the nature of his act or did not know that it was wrong. Suppose Jerry, a homeless man, stabs Phil. At trial, a psychiatrist testifies that Jerry suffers from chronic schizophrenia, that he does not know where he is or what he is doing, and that when he stabbed Phil he believed he was sponging down his pet giraffe. If the jury believes the psychiatrist, it may find Jerry not guilty by reason of insanity.

What if the alleged mental defect is a result of the defendant's own behavior? You be the judge.

YOU BE THE JUDGE

BIEBER v. PEOPLE

856 P.2d 811, 1993 Colo. LEXIS 630 Supreme Court of Colorado, 1993

FACTS: Donald Bieber walked up to a truck in which William Ellis was sitting and shot Ellis, whom he did not know, in the back of his head. He threw Ellis's body from the truck and drove away. Shortly before and after the killing, Bieber encountered various people in different places. He sang "God Bless America" and the "Marine Hymn" to them and told them he was a prisoner of war and was being followed by communists. He told people he had killed a Communist on "War Memorial Highway." The police arrested him.

Bieber had a long history of drug abuse. Several years before the homicide, Bieber voluntarily sought treatment for mental impairment, entering a hospital and saying he thought he was going to hurt someone. He was later released into a long-term drug program.

Bieber was charged with first-degree murder. He pleaded not guilty by reason of insanity. An expert witness testified that he was insane, suffering from "amphetamine delusional disorder" (ADD), a recognized psychiatric illness resulting from long-term use of amphetamines and characterized by delusions. At trial, Bieber's attorney argued that he was not intoxicated at the time of the crime but that he was insane due to ADD. The trial court refused to instruct that Bieber could be legally insane due to ADD, and the jury found Bieber guilty of first-degree murder. He appealed.

YOU BE THE JUDGE: May a jury find that a defendant with ADD is legally insane?

ARGUMENT FOR BIEBER: It is morally and legally proper to distinguish between people who commit a crime out of viciousness and those who suffer serious mental illness. Mr. Bieber suffered from a serious psychotic illness recognized by the American Psychiatric Association. There was overwhelming evidence that he was out of control and did not know what he was doing at the time of the homicide. The fact that ADD is brought about by years of amphetamine use should make no difference in an insanity case. This man's reason was destroyed by a serious illness. He should not be treated the same as a cold-blooded killer.

ARGUMENT FOR THE STATE: Your honors, there is no qualitative difference between a person who drinks or takes drugs knowing that he or she will be momentarily "mentally defective" as an immediate result and one who drinks or takes drugs knowing that he or she may be "mentally defective" as an eventual, long-term result. In both cases, the person is aware of the possible consequences of his or her actions.

As a matter of public policy, we must not excuse a defendant's actions, which endanger others, based upon a mental disturbance or illness that he or she actively and voluntarily contracted. If anything, the moral blameworthiness would seem to be even greater with respect to the long-term effects of many, repeated instances of voluntary intoxication occurring over an extended period of time. We ask that you affirm. ▮

Crimes That Harm Business

LARCENY

It is holiday season at the mall, the period of greatest profits—and the most crime. At the Foot Forum, a teenager limps in wearing ragged sneakers and sneaks out wearing Super Rags, valued at $195. Down the aisle at a home furnishing store, a man is so taken by a $375 power saw that he takes it.

Larceny is the trespassory taking of personal property with the intent to steal it. "Trespassory taking" means that someone else originally had the property. The Super Rags are personal property (not real estate), they were in the possession of the Foot Forum, and the teenager deliberately left without paying, intending never to return the goods. That is larceny. By contrast, suppose Fast Eddie leaves Bloomingdale's in New York, descends to the subway system, and jumps over a turnstile without paying. Larceny? No. He has "taken" a service—the train ride—but not personal property.

FRAUD

Robert Dorsey owned Bob's Chrysler in Highland, Illinois. He ordered cars from the manufacturer, the First National Bank of Highland paid Chrysler, and Dorsey—supposedly—repaid the loans as he sold autos. Dorsey, though, began to suffer financial problems, and the bank suspected he was selling cars without repaying his loans. A state investigator notified Dorsey that he planned to review all dealership records. One week later a fire engulfed the dealership. An arson investigator discovered that an electric iron, connected to a timer, had been placed on a pile of financial papers doused with accelerant.

The saddest part of this true story is that it is only too common. Some experts suggest that 1% of corporate revenues are wasted on fraud alone. Dorsey was convicted and imprisoned for committing two crimes that cost business billions of dollars annually—fraud and arson.[1]

Fraud refers to various crimes, all of which have a common element: the deception of another person for the purpose of obtaining money or property from him. Robert Dorsey's precise violation was bank fraud, a federal crime. It is **bank fraud** to use deceit to obtain money, assets, securities, or other property under the control of any financial institution.

Wire fraud and **mail fraud** are additional federal crimes, involving the use of interstate mail, telegram, telephone, radio, or television to obtain property by deceit. For example, if Marsha makes an interstate phone call to sell land that she does not own, that is wire fraud.

Finally, Stacey, the hospital executive described in the chapter's introduction, committed a fourth type of fraud. **Medicare fraud** includes using false statements, bribes, or kickbacks to obtain Medicare payments from the federal or state government.

Arson

Robert Dorsey, the Chrysler dealer, committed a second serious crime. Arson is the malicious use of fire or explosives to damage or destroy any real estate or personal property. It is both a federal and a state crime. Dorsey used arson to conceal his bank fraud. Most arsonists hope to collect on insurance policies. Every year thousands of buildings burn, particularly in economically depressed neighborhoods, as owners try to make a quick kill or extricate themselves from financial difficulties. We involuntarily subsidize their immorality by paying higher insurance premiums.

EMBEZZLEMENT

This crime also involves illegally obtaining property, but with one big difference: The culprit begins with legal possession. **Embezzlement is the fraudulent conversion of property already in the defendant's possession.** A bank teller is expected to handle thousands of bills every day. But when she decides to tidy her cash drawer by putting all the wrinkled hundred-dollar bills in her pocket, she has embezzled.

COMPUTER CRIME

CYBERLAW

A 29-year-old computer whiz stole a car—using his keyboard. The man infiltrated a telephone company network and rigged a radio station's call-in promotion, winning himself a splendid new Porsche. He also damaged court-ordered wiretaps of alleged gangsters and may even have jammed the phones on an Unsolved Mysteries television episode in which he was the featured fugitive! The ascent of the Internet

---

[1] *United States v. Dorsey*, 27 F.3d 285 (7th Cir. 1994).

inevitably brings with it new forms of crime. Various federal statutes criminalize this behavior.

- The **Computer Fraud and Abuse Act** prohibits using a computer to commit theft, espionage, trespass, fraud, and damage to another computer. An angry employee who hacks into his company's central computer system and damages the billing system has violated this law.

- The **Access Device Fraud Act** outlaws the fraudulent use of cards, codes, account numbers, and other devices to obtain money, goods, or services. For example, it is a violation of this act to reprogram a cellular telephone so that calls are charged to an improper account.

- The **Identity Theft and Assumption Deterrence Act** bars the use of false identification to commit fraud or other crime. A waiter who uses stolen credit card numbers to buy airline tickets has violated this act. The Federal Trade Commission receives about 100,000 complaints of identity theft every year, so you should guard identifying data carefully.

- The **Wire and Electronic Communications Interception Act** makes it a crime to intercept most wire, oral, and electronic communications. (This law does not prohibit recording your own conversations.) We warned you not to tape your roommate's conversations! ▪

Crimes Committed by Business

A corporation can be found guilty of a crime based on the conduct of any of its agents, who include anyone undertaking work on behalf of the corporation. An agent can be a corporate officer, an accountant hired to audit a statement, a sales clerk, or almost any other person performing a job at the company's request.

If an agent commits a criminal act within the scope of his employment and with the intent to benefit the corporation, the company is liable. This means that the agent himself must first be guilty. The normal requirements of *actus reus* and *mens rea* apply. If the agent is guilty, the corporation is, too. The most common punishment for a corporation is a fine. This makes sense in that the purpose of a business is to earn a profit, and a fine, if large enough, hurts.

CASE SUMMARY

WISCONSIN v. KNUTSON, INC.

196 Wis. 2d 86, 537 N.W.2d 420, 1995 Wis. App. LEXIS 1223
Wisconsin Court of Appeals, 1995

FACTS: Richard Knutson, Inc. (RKI) was constructing a sanitary sewer line for the city of Oconomowoc. An RKI crew attempted to place a section of corrugated metal pipe in a trench in order to remove groundwater. The backhoe operator misjudged the distance from the backhoe's boom to the overhead power lines and failed to realize that he had placed the the boom in contact with the wires. A crew member attempted to attach a chain to the backhoe's bucket and was instantly electrocuted.

The state charged RKI with negligent vehicular homicide under a statute that says: "Whoever causes the death of another human being by the negligent operation or handling of a vehicle is guilty of a Class E felony." The jury convicted, and RKI appealed, claiming that a corporation could not be held guilty under the statute.

ISSUE: May a corporation be guilty of vehicular homicide under the statute?

DECISION: Yes, a corporation can be found guilty of vehicular homicide. Affirmed.

REASONING: Corporations are a dominant part of life in the United States, and criminal responsibility is one of the primary ways we regulate our affairs. It would be unfair to assign guilt to a group of people within a company while ignoring the corporate culture that may have prompted the illegal conduct. Because crime can be profitable, firms may pressure workers to break the law. Corporations must be held responsible for the harm they cause. Furthermore, because many corporations are so large, identifying guilty employees within a company may be impossible.

Here, if RKI had enforced OSHA's written safety regulations, or if the company had complied with the procedures outlined in its contract, the victim would never have died. RKI's failure to take elementary precautions for its employees was a substantial cause of this electrocution. ◢

COMPLIANCE PROGRAMS

The Federal Sentencing Guidelines are the detailed rules that judges must follow when sentencing defendants convicted of crimes in federal court. The guidelines instruct judges to determine whether, at the time of the crime, the corporation had in place a serious compliance program, that is, a plan to prevent and detect criminal conduct at all levels of the company. A company that can point to a detailed, functioning compliance program may benefit from a dramatic reduction in the fine or other punishment meted out. Indeed, a tough compliance program may even convince federal investigators to curtail an investigation and to limit any prosecution to those directly involved, rather than attempting to get a conviction against high-ranking officers or the company itself.

WORKPLACE CRIMES

The workplace can be dangerous. Working on an assembly line exposes factory employees to fast-moving machinery. For a roofer, the first slip may be the last. The invisible radiation in a nuclear power plant can be deadlier than a bullet. The most important statute regulating the workplace is the federal Occupational Safety and Health Act of 1970 (OSHA), which sets safety standards for many industries. May a state government go beyond standards set by OSHA and use the criminal law to punish dangerous conditions? The courts of Illinois answered that question with a potent "yes," permitting a *murder prosecution* against corporate executives who had caused the death of a worker by forcing him to work with life-threatening chemicals, including bubbling vats of sodium cyanide.

RICO

The Racketeer Influenced and Corrupt Organizations Act (RICO) is one of the most powerful and controversial statutes ever written. Congress passed the law primarily to prevent gangsters from taking money they earned illegally and investing it in legitimate businesses. But RICO has expanded far beyond the original intentions of Congress and is now used more often against ordinary businesses than against organized criminals.

The government may prosecute both individuals and organizations for violating RICO. For example, the government may prosecute a mobster, claiming that he has run a heroin ring for years. It may also prosecute an accounting firm, claiming that it lied about corporate assets in a stock sale to make the shares appear more valuable than they really were. If the government proves its case, the defendant can be hit with large fines and a prison sentence of up to 20 years.

What is a violation of this law? RICO prohibits using two or more racketeering acts to accomplish any of these goals: (1) investing in or acquiring legitimate businesses with criminal money; (2) maintaining or acquiring businesses through criminal activity; or (3) operating businesses through criminal activity.

What does that mean in English? It is a two-step process to prove that a person or an organization has violated RICO.

- The prosecutor must show that the defendant committed two or more racketeering acts, which are any of a long list of specified crimes: embezzlement, arson, mail fraud, wire fraud, and so forth. If a stockbroker told two customers that Bronx Gold Mines was a promising stock, when she knew that it was worthless, that would be two racketeering acts.

- The prosecutor must show that the defendant used these racketeering acts to accomplish one of the three purposes listed above. If the stockbroker gave fraudulent advice and used the commissions to buy advertising for her firm, that would violate RICO.

ENVIRONMENTAL CRIMES

Federal and state statutes prohibit many forms of air and water pollution. Some of the laws create criminal liability. For example, the Clean Water Act (CWA), a federal statute, is designed to protect the waters that we use for recreation and commerce, including lakes, rivers and oceans. The CWA prohibits discharging raw sewage without a permit, an issue in the following case.

CASE SUMMARY

UNITED STATES v. WEITZENHOFF

35 F.3d 1275 (9th Cir. 1994)
Ninth Circuit Court of Appeals

FACTS: Michael Weitzenhoff and Thomas Mariani managed the East Honolulu Community Services Sewage Treatment Plant, located near Sandy Beach, a popular playground on the island of Oahu. The plant treats four million gallons of residential wastewater each day by removing solids and other harmful pollutants from the sewage, so that the resulting effluent can be safely discharged into the ocean. During treatment, sludge accumulates in the bottom of the tanks. The sludge is supposed to be re-treated, or else shipped to a separate facility.

When the sludge levels became unmanageable, Weitzenhoff and Mariani ordered workers to discharge the untreated matter directly into the ocean. Lifeguards promptly complained about foul odors coming from the ocean water; swimmers became sick. During an FBI investigation, Weitzenhoff and Mariani admitted authorizing the discharge. They were convicted of "knowingly violating" the discharge provisions, and sentenced to several years in prison. On appeal, they argued that they could not be found guilty because they were unaware that their conduct was illegal.

ISSUE: Can the defendants be guilty of "knowingly violating" a CWA provision they knew nothing about?

DECISION: Yes, the defendants can be guilty of violating the CWA whether or not they knew of its criminal provisions. Affirmed.

REASONING: The term *knowingly* requires only that the defendants knew they were discharging the pollutants, not that they were aware of the legal consequences. Weitzenhoff and Mariani personally authorized the discharge. Congress included the term *knowingly* in the CWA so that those who realized they were polluting the water would receive harsher penalties than those who accidentally caused pollution. ◢

Weitzenhoff and Mariani knew what they were doing. Other cases have found corporate officers guilty of *unintended* water pollution, that is, for their mere negligence in allowing harmful substances to enter the water.[2] Anyone involved in an industry that could potentially cause pollution must beware of the criminal law.

The Criminal Process

How does the government investigate and prosecute criminal cases? The steps vary from case to case, but the summary in Exhibit 7.1 highlights the important steps.

Informant

Yasmin is a secretary to Stacey, the Be Patient executive who opened this chapter. She speaks to Moe, an FBI agent. She reports that Stacey routinely charges the government for patients who do not exist. Moe prepares an affidavit for Yasmin to sign, detailing everything she told him. An affidavit is simply a written statement signed under oath.

WARRANT

Moe takes Yasmin's affidavit to a United States magistrate, an employee of the federal courts who is similar to a judge. Moe asks the magistrate to issue search warrants for Be Patient's patient records. A search warrant is written permission from a neutral official, such as the magistrate, to conduct a search. A warrant must specify with reasonable certainty the place to be searched and the items to be seized.

Probable Cause

The magistrate will issue a warrant only if there is probable cause. Probable cause means that, based on all of the information presented, it is likely that evidence of crime will be found in the place mentioned. The magistrate will look at Yasmin's affidavit to determine (1) whether the informant (Yasmin) is reliable and (2) whether she has a sound basis for the information. The magistrate issues the warrant.

---

[2] *United States v. Hanousek*, 176 F.3d 1116 (9th Cir. 1999).

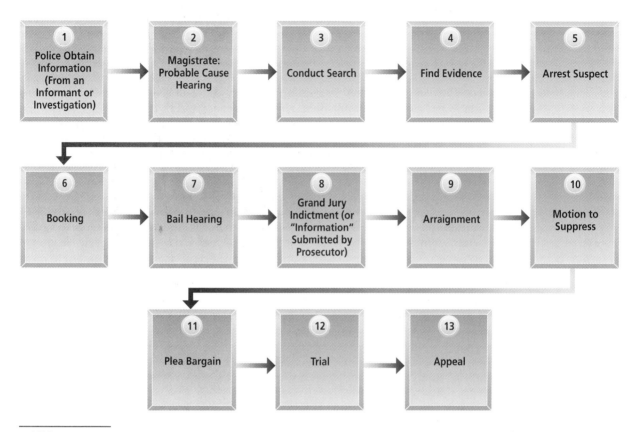

Exhibit 7.1

SEARCH AND SEIZURE

Armed with the warrants, Moe and other agents arrive at Be Patient hospitals, show the warrants, and take away the appropriate records. The search may not exceed what is described in the warrant. The agents cart the records back to headquarters and enter the data into a computer. The computer compares the records of actual patients with the bills submitted to the government and indicates that 10% of all bills are for fictional patients. Moe summarizes the new data on additional affidavits and presents the affidavits to the magistrate, who issues arrest warrants.

Fourth Amendment

The Fourth Amendment prohibits the government from making illegal searches and seizures. This amendment protects individuals, corporations, partnerships, and other organizations. In general, the police must obtain a warrant before conducting a search. If the police search without one, they have probably violated the Fourth Amendment.

Exclusionary Rule

Under the exclusionary rule, evidence obtained illegally may not be used at trial against the victim of the search. Suppose when Yasmin called the FBI, Moe simply drove straight to one of Be Patient's hospitals and grabbed patient records. Moe lacked a warrant, the search was illegal, and the evidence would be excluded from trial.

ARREST

Moe arrives at Be Patient and informs Stacey that she is under arrest. He informs her of her right to remain silent. He drives Stacey to FBI headquarters, where she is booked; that is, her name, photograph, and fingerprints are entered in a log. She is entitled to a prompt bail hearing. A judge or magistrate will set an amount of bail that she must pay in order to go free pending the trial. The purpose of bail is to ensure that Stacey will appear for all future court hearings.

Self-Incrimination

The Fifth Amendment bars the government from forcing any person to testify against himself. In other words, the police may not use mental or physical coercion to force a confession out of someone. Society does not want a government that engages in torture. Such abuse might occasionally catch a criminal, but it would grievously injure innocent people and make all citizens fearful of the government that is supposed to represent them. Before the police obtain a confession, the defendant must be told that he has the right to remain silent; that anything he says can be used against him at trial; that he has the right to a lawyer; and that if he cannot afford a lawyer, the court will appoint one for him.

INDICTMENT

Moe turns all of his evidence over to Larry, the local prosecutor for the United States. Larry presents the evidence to a grand jury. It is the grand jury's job to determine whether there is probable cause that this defendant committed the crime with which she is charged. The grand jury votes to indict Stacey. An indictment is the government's formal charge that the defendant has committed a crime and must stand trial. The grand jury is persuaded that there is probable cause that Stacey billed for 1,550 nonexistent patients, charging the government for $290 million worth of services that were never performed. The grand jury indicts her for (1) Medicare fraud, (2) mail fraud, (3) computer crimes, and (4) RICO violations. It also indicts Be Patient, Inc., and other employees.

ARRAIGNMENT

Stacey is ordered back to court. A clerk reads her the formal charges of the indictment. The judge asks whether Stacey has a lawyer, and of course she does. If she did not, the judge would urge her to get one quickly. If a defendant cannot afford a lawyer, the court will appoint one to represent her free of charge. The judge now asks the lawyer how Stacey pleads to the charges. Her lawyer answers that she pleads not guilty to all charges.

Plea Bargaining

Sometime before trial, the two attorneys will meet to consider a plea bargain. A plea bargain is an agreement between prosecution and defense that the defendant will plead guilty to a reduced charge, and the prosecution will recommend to the judge a relatively lenient sentence. Based on the RICO violations alone, Stacey faces a possible 20-year prison sentence, along with a large fine and a devastating forfeiture order. The government makes this offer: Stacey will plead guilty to 100 counts of mail fraud; Be Patient will repay all $290 million and an additional $150 million in fines; the government will drop the RICO and computer crime charges and recommend to the judge that Stacey be fined only $1 million and sentenced to three years in prison. In the federal court system, about 75% of all prosecutions end in a plea bargain. In state court systems the number is often higher.

Stacey agrees to the government's offer. The judge accepts the plea, and Stacey is fined and sentenced accordingly. A judge need not accept the bargain, but usually does.

TRIAL AND APPEAL

When there is no plea bargain, the case must go to trial. The mechanics of a criminal trial are similar to those for a civil trial, described in Chapter 3, on dispute resolution. It is the prosecution's job to convince the jury beyond a reasonable doubt that the defendant committed every element of the crime charged.

THE PATRIOT ACT OF 2001

In response to the devastating attacks of September 11, 2001, Congress passed a sweeping antiterrorist law known as the Patriot Act. The statute was designed to give law enforcement officials greater power to investigate and prevent potential terrorist assaults. The bill raced through Congress nearly unopposed. Proponents hailed it as a vital weapon for use against continuing lethal threats. Opponents argued that the law was passed in haste and threatened the liberties of the very people it purported to shield. They urged that the statute gave law officers too much power, permitting them to conduct searches, intercept private Internet communications, and examine financial and academic records—all with little or no judicial oversight. Supporters of the law responded that its most controversial sections were scheduled to expire in four years. In the meantime, they said, constitutional protections governed the law as they did all others.

As this book goes to press, it is difficult to assess the full impact of the Patriot Act. In an early legal test, a federal judge permitted the government to use secret evidence in its effort to freeze the assets of Global Relief Foundation, a religious organization suspected of terrorist activity. The group, which claimed to be purely humanitarian, asserted that it could hardly defend itself against unseen evidence. Finding "acute national security concerns," the judge allowed the government to introduce the evidence in private, without the foundation ever seeing it.

Chapter Conclusion

Business crime appears in unexpected places, with surprising suspects. A corporate executive aware of its protean nature is in the best position to prevent it. Classic fraud and embezzlement schemes are often foiled with commonsense preventive measures. Federal sentencing guidelines make it eminently worthwhile for corporations to establish aggressive compliance programs. Sophisticated computer and money laundering crimes can be thwarted only with determination and the cooperation of citizens and police agencies. We can defeat business crime if we have the knowledge and the will.

UPDATE

Find a recent case involving the Patriot Act. What were the precise issues? How did the court rule and why? ◾

Chapter Review

1. The rationales for punishment include restraint, deterrence and retribution.

2. In all prosecutions, the government must establish that the defendant's conduct was outlawed, that the defendant committed the actus reus, and that he had the necessary mens rea.

3. In addition to factual defenses, such as mistaken identity or alibi, a defendant may offer various legal defenses, such as insanity, entrapment.

4. Larceny is the trespassory taking of personal property with the intent to steal.

5. Fraud refers to a variety of crimes, all of which involve the deception of another person for the purpose of obtaining money or property.

6. Arson is the malicious use of fire or explosives to damage or destroy real estate or personal property.

7. Embezzlement is the fraudulent conversion of property already in the defendant's possession.

8. Computer crime statutes prohibit computer trespass and fraud; wrongful use of cards, codes, and identification; and most intercepting or taping of conversations.

9. If a company's agent commits a criminal act within the scope of her employment and with the intent to benefit the corporation, the company is liable.

10. RICO prohibits using two or more racketeering acts to invest in legitimate business or carry on certain other criminal acts. RICO permits civil lawsuits as well as criminal prosecutions.

PRACTICE TEST

Matching Questions

Match the following terms with their definitions:

___ **A.** Larceny

___ **B.** RICO

___ **C.** Felony

___ **D.** *Mens rea*

___ **E.** M'Naughten Rule

___ **F.** Embezzlement

1. A statute designed to prevent the use of criminal proceeds in legitimate businesses.

2. Fraudulently keeping property already in defendant's possession.

3. A test used to gauge a defendant's sanity.

4. The most serious type of crime, usually punishable by a year or more in prison.

5. The trespassory taking of personal property.

6. A guilty state of mind.

True/False Questions

Circle true or false:

1. T   F   Both the government and the victim are entitled to prosecute a crime.

2. T   F   A misdemeanor is a less serious crime, punishable by less than a year in jail.

3. T   F   In all criminal cases, the prosecution must prove *actus reus*.

4. T   F   Corporate officers can be convicted of crimes; corporations themselves cannot be.

5. T   F   An affidavit is the government's formal charge of criminal wrongdoing.

Multiple-Choice Questions

6. The insanity defense

    (a) is available in less than 5 states nationwide.

    (b) means that if the jury finds that a defendant was insane at the time of the crime, the defendant goes free.

    (c) means that if the jury finds that a defendant was insane at the time of the crime, the defendant is locked in prison for the same time period as if he had been found guilty.

    (d) means that if the jury finds that a defendant was insane at the time of the crime, the defendant will be locked in a mental hospital until he is no longer a danger to society.

    (e) used to be the law in all states, but has now been outlawed by court rulings.

7. Probable cause means

    (a) substantial evidence that the person signing the affidavit has legitimate reasons for requesting the warrant.

    (b) substantial similarity between the items sought and the items found.

    (c) substantial likelihood that a crime has taken place or is about to take place.

    (d) trustworthy evidence that the victim of the search is known to have criminal tendencies.

    (e) that based on all of the information presented it is likely that evidence of crime will be found in the place mentioned.

8. Police believe that Jay is dealing drugs from his apartment. They search his apartment without a warrant and find 3 kilos of cocaine. The cocaine

    (a) Will be excluded from Jay's trial.

    (b) Is valid evidence provided the police reasonably believed Jay was a drug dealer.

    (c) Is valid evidence provided the police had spoken to neighbors before searching.

    (d) Was improperly obtained but may be used in Jay's trial.

    (e) May not be used in Jay's trial but may be used during his sentencing.

9. A prosecutor concerned that he may lack sufficient evidence to obtain a conviction may agree to

    (a) An affidavit.

    (b) A warrant.

    (c) An appeal.

    (d) An indictment.

    (e) A plea bargain.

10. Professor asks Janice, his teaching assistant, to please drive the professor's car to the repair shop. Janice gets in and drives, not to the garage, but 1,400 miles further west, to Las Vegas. Janice has committed

    (a) Fraud

    (b) Embezzlement

    (c) Larceny

    (d) RICO violation

    (e) Access Device Fraud

Short-Answer Questions

11. Arnie owns a two-family house in a poor section of the city. A fire breaks out, destroying the building and causing $150,000 damage to an adjacent store. The state charges Arnie with arson. Simultaneously, Vickie, the store owner, sues Arnie for the damage to her property. Both cases are tried to juries, and the two juries hear identical evidence of Arnie's actions. But the criminal jury acquits Arnie, while the civil jury awards Vickie $150,000. How did that happen?

12. ETHICS: Nineteen-year-old David Lee Nagel viciously murdered his grandparents, stabbing them repeatedly and slitting their throats, all because they denied him use of the family car. He was tried for murder and found not guilty by reason of insanity. He has lived ever since in mental hospitals. In 1994 he applied for release. The two psychiatrists who examined him stated that he was no longer mentally ill and was a danger neither to society nor to himself. Yet the Georgia Supreme Court refused to release him, seemingly because of the brutality of the killings. Comment on the court's ruling. What is the rationale for treating an insane defendant differently from others? Do you find the theory persuasive? If you do, what result must logically follow when psychiatrists testify that the defendant is no longer a danger? Should the brutality of the crime be a factor in deciding whether to prolong the detention? If you do not accept the rationale for treating such defendants differently, explain why not.

13. Federal law requires that all banks file reports with the IRS anytime a customer engages in a cash transaction in an amount over $10,000. It is a crime for a bank to "structure" a cash transaction, that is, to break up a single transaction of more than $10,000 into two or more smaller transactions (and thus avoid the filing requirement). In *Ratzlaf v. United States*, 510 U.S. 135, 114 S. Ct. 655 (1994), the Supreme Court held that in order to find a defendant guilty of structuring, the government must prove that he specifically intended to break the law, that is, that he knew that what he was doing was a crime and meant to commit it. Congress promptly passed a law "undoing" Ratzlaf. A bank official can now be convicted on evidence that he structured a payment, even with no evidence that he knew it was a crime. The penalties are harsh. (1) Why is structuring so serious? (2) Why did Congress change the law about the defendant's intent?

14. Northwest Telco Corp. (Telco) provides long-distance telephone service. Customers dial a general access number, then enter a six-digit access code and then the phone number they want to call. A computer places the call and charges the account. On January 10, 1990, Cal Edwards, a Telco engineer, noticed that Telco's general access number was being dialed exactly every 40 seconds. After each dialing, a different six-digit number was entered, followed by a particular long-distance number. This continued from 10 p.m. to 6 a.m. Why was Edwards concerned?

15. Kathy Hathcoat was a teller at a Pendleton, Indiana bank. In 1990 she began taking home money that belonged in her cash drawer. Her branch manager, Mary Jane Cooper, caught her. But rather than reporting Hathcoat, Cooper joined in. The two helped cover for each other by verifying that their cash drawers were in balance. They took nearly $200,000 before bank officials found them out. What criminal charge did the government bring against Hathcoat?

16. ROLE REVERSAL: Write a short-answer question that focuses on the elements of a RICO violation.

Internet Research Problem

A Web site devoted to Internet crime is **http://www.digitalcentury.com/encyclo/update/crime.html**. Find a current crime that might victimize you. What steps should you take to avoid harm?

You can find further practice problems in the Online Quiz at **http://beatty.westbuslaw.com** or in the Study Guide that accompanies this text.

International Law

The day after Anfernee graduates from business school, he opens a shop specializing in sports caps and funky hats. Sales are brisk, but Anfernee is making little profit because his American-made caps are expensive. Then an Asian company offers to sell him identical merchandise for 45% less than the American suppliers charge. Anfernee is elated, but quickly begins to wonder. Why is the new price so low? Are the foreign workers paid a living wage? Could the Asian company be using child labor? The sales representative requests a $50,000 cash "commission" to smooth the export process in his country. That sounds suspicious. The questions multiply without end. Will the contract be written in English or a foreign language? Must Anfernee pay in dollars or some other currency? The foreign company wants a letter of credit. What does that mean?

Anfernee should put this lesson under his cap: The world is now one vast economy, and negotiations quickly cross borders. Transnational business grows with breathtaking speed. The United States now exports more than $700 billion worth of goods each year, and an additional $300 billion worth of services. Leading exports include industrial machinery, computers, aircraft and other transportation equipment, electronic equipment, and chemicals.

Here are the leading trading partners of the United States:

Rank	Country	Total Trade (exports plus imports), 2003, in billions of U.S. dollars.
1	Canada	$394
2	Mexico	236
3	China	181
4	Japan	170
5	Germany	97
6	United Kingdom	77
7	Korea	61
8	Taiwan	49
9	France	46
10	Italy	36

Source: United States Census Bureau, **http://www.census.gov**

Who are the people who do all this trading? Anfernee's modest sports cap concern is at one end of the spectrum. At the other are multinational enterprises (MNEs), that is, companies doing business in several countries simultaneously.

MNEs and Power

An MNE can take various forms. It may be an Italian corporation with a wholly owned American subsidiary that manufactures electrical components in Alabama and sells them in Brazil. Or it could be a Japanese company that licenses a software company in India to manufacture computer programs for sale throughout Europe. One thing is constant: the power of these huge enterprises. Each of the top 10 MNEs earns annual revenue greater than the gross domestic product of two thirds of the world's nations. More than 200 MNEs have annual sales exceeding $1 billion and more cash available at any one time than the majority of countries do. Money means power. This corporate might can be used to create jobs, train workers, and build lifesaving medical equipment. Such power can also be used to corrupt government officials, rip up the environment, and exploit already impoverished workers. International law is vital.

Trade Regulation

Nations regulate international trade in many ways. In this section we look at export and import controls that affect trade out of and into the United States. **Exporting** is shipping goods or services out of a country. The United States, with its huge farms, is the world's largest exporter of agricultural products. **Importing** is shipping goods and services into a country. The United States suffers trade deficits every year because the value of its imports exceeds that of its exports, as the following table demonstrates.

U.S. International Trade in Goods and Services, in millions of dollars
(Details may not equal totals due to seasonal adjustment and rounding.)

Year	Balance			Exports			Imports		
	Total	Goods	Services	Total	Goods	Services	Total	Goods	Services
2001	−362,692	−427,188	64,496	1,006,653	718,712	287,941	1,369,345	1,145,900	223,445
2002	−421,735	−482,895	61,160	975,940	681,833	294,107	1,397,675	1,164,728	232,947
2003	−496,508	−547,552	51,044	1,020,503	713,122	307,381	1,517,011	1,260,674	256,337

Source: United States Census Bureau, **http://www.census.gov**

EXPORT CONTROLS

You and a friend open an electronics business, intending to purchase goods in this country for sale abroad. A representative of Interlex stops in to see you. Interlex is an Asian electronics company, and the firm wants you to obtain for it a certain kind of infrared dome. The representative explains that this electronic miracle helps helicopters identify nearby aircraft. You find a Pennsylvania company that manufactures the domes, and you realize that you can buy and sell them to Interlex for a handsome profit. Any reason not to? As a matter of fact, there is.

All nations limit what may be exported. In the United States, several statutes do this, including the **Arms Export Control Act** (AECA). This statute permits the president to create a list of controlled goods, all related to military weaponry. No one may export any listed item without a license.

The AECA prohibits exports of the infrared domes. The equipment is used in the guidance system of one of the most sophisticated weapons in the American defense arsenal. Foreign governments have attempted to obtain the equipment through official channels, but the American government has placed the domes on the list of restricted military items. When a U.S. citizen did send such goods to a foreign country, he was convicted and imprisoned.

IMPORT CONTROLS

Tariffs

Tariffs are the most widespread method of limiting what may be imported into a nation. **A tariff is a duty (a tax) imposed on goods when they enter a country.** Nations use tariffs primarily to protect their domestic industries. Because the company importing the goods must pay this duty, the importer's costs increase, making the merchandise more expensive for consumers. This renders domestic products more attractive. High tariffs unquestionably help local industry, but they proportionately harm local buyers. Consumers benefit from zero tariffs, because the unfettered competition drives down prices.

Tariffs change frequently and vary widely from one country to another. Even within one nation, tariffs may be low on some products and high on others. Average tariffs for American goods entering Turkey have dropped from 11% to 6% in the last decade. However, duties on fruit imported into Turkey are often over 100% and are more than 200% on meats. At the other extreme, two thirds of all U.S. products entering Mexico are duty free. Almost all trade between Canada and the United States is done with zero tariffs, which is partly why the two nations do more bilateral commerce than any others in the world.

Classification. The U.S. Customs Service imposes tariffs at the point of entry into the United States. A customs official inspects the merchandise as it arrives and **classifies** it, in other words, decides precisely what the goods are. This decision is critical because the tariff will vary depending on the classification, as Nissan's experience demonstrates.

CASE SUMMARY

MARUBENI AMERICA CORP. v. UNITED STATES

35 F.3d 530, 1994 U.S. App. LEXIS 24288
United States Court of Appeals for the Federal Circuit, 1994

FACTS: One of Japan's major auto manufacturers, Nissan, found itself in the late 1980s behind the competition in the market for four-wheel-drive sport utility vehicles. In order to catch up quickly, Nissan used its "Hardbody" truck line as the basis for designing and building its "Pathfinder" sport utility vehicle. The Pathfinder incorporated the Hardbody's frame side rails, front cab, and front suspension.

When the 1989 models arrived in the United States, the Customs Service had to classify them. The service uses a tariff schedule to do this, which is a long list of goods, carefully described, with each type of good assigned a particular duty. The tariff schedule gave the Customs Service two possible classifications:

Section 8704.31.00: Motor vehicle for the transport of goods.

Section 8703.23.00: Motor cars and other motor vehicles principally designed for the transport of persons, including stations wagons and racing cars.

The "transport of persons" tariff was 2.5%, but the "transport of goods" duty was exactly 10 times higher. The Customs Service concluded that the Pathfinder was similar to a pickup truck, declared it a "transport of goods" vehicle, and imposed the 25% duty, ruining Nissan's hope for profits. The company appealed. Customs appeals go first to the Court of International Trade (CIT) in Washington. The CIT trial included test drives of the Pathfinder

and comparison vehicles (including the Hardbody), as well as videotapes of competing vehicles and expert testimony about engineering, design, and marketing. (Indeed, the court's work was so thorough that the next time your car needs servicing you might ask the CIT to take a look at it.) The CIT reversed the Customs Service, declaring the Pathfinder a passenger car. The service appealed to the federal court of appeals.

ISSUE: Is the Pathfinder a vehicle for passengers or for the transport of goods?

DECISION: The Pathfinder is a passenger vehicle.

REASONING: Although the Pathfinder is derived from Nissan's Hardbody truck line, the vehicle is intended primarily to carry passengers. The company relied on its truck design only because it was desperate to catch up in a market it had entered late. Nissan made major changes to the original design. The company added a rear passenger seat, meaning that the gas tank and spare tire had to be relocated. This, in turn, reduced cargo space. Nissan also added a new rear suspension, with new crossbeams, to provide a smooth ride for passengers. The new design included a carpeted cargo area and a separate window in the tailgate to accommodate small packages. By contrast, the Hardbody truck bed is designed for loading with a forklift. The CIT correctly concluded that Nissan's new vehicle is meant for passengers. ◢

Valuation.   After classifying the imported goods, customs officials impose the appropriate duty *ad valorem,* meaning "according to the value of the goods." In other words, the Customs Service must determine the value of the merchandise before it can tax a percentage of that value. This step can be equally contentious, since goods will have different prices at each stage of manufacturing and delivery. The question is supposed to be settled by the transaction value of the goods, meaning the price actually paid for the merchandise when sold for export to the United States (plus shipping and other minor costs). But there is often room for debate, so importers use customs agents to help negotiate the most favorable valuation.

Dumping

Dumping means selling merchandise at one price in the domestic market and at a cheaper, unfair price in an international market. Suppose a Singapore company, CelMaker, makes cellular telephones for $20 per unit and sells them in the United States for $12 each, vastly undercutting domestic American competitors. CelMaker may be willing to suffer short-term losses in order to drive out competitors for the American market. Once it has gained control of that market, it will raise its prices, more than compensating for its initial losses. And CelMaker may get help from its home government. Suppose the Singapore government prohibits foreign cellular phones from entering Singapore. CelMaker may sell its phones for $75 at home, earning such high profits that it can afford the temporary losses in America.

In the United States, the Commerce Department investigates suspected dumping. If the Department concludes that the foreign company is selling items at **less than fair value,** and that this harms an American industry, it will impose a **dumping duty** sufficiently high to put the foreign goods back on fair footing with domestic products.

Quotas

A **quota** is a limit on the quantity of a particular good that may enter a nation. For example, the United States, like most importing nations, has agreements with many developing nations, placing a quota on imported textiles. In some cases, textile imports from a particular country may grow by only a small percentage each year. Without such a limit, textile imports from the developing world would increase explosively because costs are so much lower there. As part of the GATT treaty (discussed below), the wealthier nations pledged to increase textile imports from the developing countries.

Money and politics are a volatile mix, as demonstrated by all recorded history from 3000 B.C. to the present. As long as nations have existed, they have engaged in disputes about quotas and tariffs. And that is why more than 100 countries negotiated and signed the GATT treaty.

General Agreement on Tariffs and Trade (GATT)

What is GATT? The greatest boon to American commerce in a century. The worst assault on the American economy in 200 years. It depends on whom you ask. Let's start where everyone agrees.

GATT is the General Agreement on Tariffs and Trade. This massive international treaty has been negotiated on and off since the 1940s to eliminate trade barriers and bolster commerce. GATT has already had considerable effect. In 1947, the worldwide average tariff on industrial goods was about 40%. Now it is about 4%

(although agricultural duties still average over 40%). The world's economies have exploded over that half century. Proponents of GATT applaud the agreement. Opponents scoff that both lower duties and higher trade would have arrived without GATT.

In 1994, the United States and 125 other countries signed the treaty. A **signatory** is a nation that signs a treaty. However, a signatory is not bound by the agreement until it is **ratified,** that is, until the nation's legislature votes to honor it. In the United States, Congress voted to ratify GATT. If the latest round of cuts is fully implemented, average duties in all signatories should drop to about 3.7%. Further, nearly half of all trade in industrial goods will be duty free, at least in developed countries. That must be good—or is it?

Trade

Leading supporters of GATT suggest that its lower tariffs vastly increase world trade. The United States should be one of the biggest beneficiaries because for decades this country has imposed lower duties than most other nations. American companies will for once compete on equal footing.

But opponents claim that the United States will be facing nations with unlimited pools of exploited labor. These countries will dominate labor-intensive merchandise such as textiles, eliminating millions of American jobs.

World Trade Organization and the Environment

GATT created the **World Trade Organization (WTO)** to resolve trade disputes. The WTO is empowered to hear arguments from any signatory nation about tariff violations or nontariff barriers. This international "court" may order compliance from any nation violating GATT and may penalize countries by imposing trade sanctions.

Here is how the WTO decides a trade dispute. Suppose that the United States believes that Brazil is unfairly restricting trade. The United States asks the WTO's Dispute Settlement Body (DSB) to form a panel, which consists of three nations uninvolved in the dispute. After the panel hears testimony and arguments from both countries, it releases its report. The DSB generally approves the report, unless either nation appeals. If there is an appeal, the WTO Appellate Body hears the dispute and generally makes the final decision, subject to approval by the entire WTO. No single nation has the power to block final decisions. If a country refuses to comply with the WTO's ruling, affected nations may retaliate by imposing punitive tariffs.

ETHICS

Child labor is an even more wrenching issue. The practice exists to some degree in all countries and is common throughout the developing world. The International Labor Organization, an affiliate of the United Nations, estimates that 120 million children between the ages of 5 and 14 work full time, and 130 million more labor part time. As the world generally becomes more prosperous, this ugly problem has actually increased. Children in developing countries typically work in agriculture and domestic work, but many toil in mines and others in factories, making rugs, glass, clothing, and other goods.

The rug industry highlights this tragedy. Tens of millions of children, some as young as four, toil in rug workrooms, seven days a week, 12 hours a day. Many, shackled to the looms they operate, are essentially slaves, working for pennies a day or, in some cases, for no money at all. As we confront such brutal conditions, we must bear in mind that child labor is truly universal. The United Farm Workers union estimates that 800,000 underage children help their migrant parents harvest U.S. crops—work that few Americans are willing to do. ◾

WTO Summary

The WTO continues to grow, adding China (and a quarter of the world's population) early in this millennium. The WTO has resolved many trade disputes that otherwise might have caused bitter tariff wars. The United States has been the most active user of the dispute settlement process, bringing almost one quarter of all cases to the WTO. The United States has prevailed in the majority of its cases, though not all. For example, as a result of WTO consultations, Japan changed its law to grant full copyright protection to sound recordings, a case worth about $500 million annually to the American recording industry.

In a case that did not settle, India was ordered to eliminate import bans on 2,700 types of goods, including consumer products, textiles, agricultural products, petrochemicals, and other commodities. On the other hand, Japan prevailed in another case brought by the United States, when a WTO panel determined, contrary to assertions made on behalf of Eastman Kodak, that Japan did not discriminate against imported film.

UPDATE | Find a current trade dispute that the United States has brought to the WTO. What are the issues and respective positions? ◾

REGIONAL AGREEMENTS

Many regional agreements also regulate international trade. We will briefly describe the two that most closely affect the United States.

The European Union

The **European Union (EU)** used to be known as the Common Market. The original six members—Belgium, France, Luxembourg, the Netherlands, West Germany, and Italy—have been joined by 19 additional countries. See the map on page 118.

The EU is one of the world's most powerful associations, with a prosperous population of over 460 million. Its sophisticated legal system sets Union-wide standards for tariffs, dumping, subsidies, antitrust, transportation, and many other issues. The first goals of the EU were to eliminate trade barriers between member nations; establish common tariffs with respect to external countries; permit the free movement of citizens across its borders; and coordinate its agricultural and fishing policies for the collective good. The EU has largely achieved these goals. Most but not all of the EU countries have adopted a common currency, the euro. During the next decade, the Union will focus on further economic integration and effective coordination of foreign policy.

NAFTA

In 1993, the United States, Canada, and Mexico signed the **North American Free Trade Agreement (NAFTA).** The principal goal was to eliminate almost all trade barriers, tariff and nontariff, among the three nations. Like GATT, this trilateral

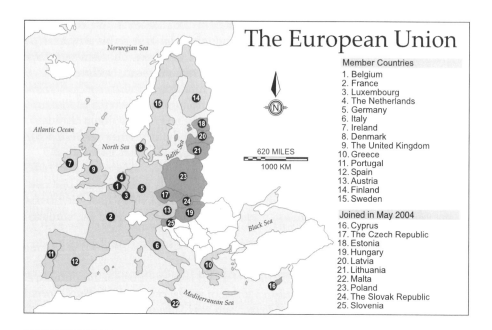

EU Members.

(three-nation) compact has been controversial, and there will probably never be agreement on NAFTA's value because the treaty has enriched some while impoverishing others. Unquestionably, trade among the three nations has increased enormously. Mexico now sells more to the United States than do Germany and the United Kingdom combined.

Opponents of the treaty argue that NAFTA costs the United States jobs and lowers the living standards of American workers by forcing them to compete with low-paid labor. For example, Swingline Staplers closed a factory in Queens, New York after 75 years of operation and moved to Mexico. Instead of paying its American workers $11.58 per hour, Swingline pays Mexican workers 50 cents an hour to do the same job. Proponents contend that although some jobs are lost, many others are gained, especially in fields with a future, such as high technology. They claim that as new jobs invigorate the Mexican economy, consumers there will be able to afford American goods for the first time, providing an enormous new market.

International Sales Agreements

Cowboy boots are hot in France. Big Heel, Inc., your small company in Tucson, Arizona, makes superb boots with exquisite detailing, and you realize that France could be a bonanza.

Le Pied D'Or, a new, fast-growing French chain of shoe stores, is interested in buying 10,000 pairs of your boots, at about $300 per pair. You must focus on two principal issues: the sales contract and letters of credit. You are wise enough to know that you must have a written contract—$3 million is a lot of money for Big Heel.

This is a contract for the sale of goods. Goods are things that can be moved, such as boots, airplanes, pencils, and computers. A sale of goods is governed by different law than the sale of real estate (e.g., a house) or services (e.g., accounting).

What Law Governs the Sale of Goods?

Potentially, three conflicting laws could govern your boot contract: Arizona law, French law, and an international treaty. Each is different, and it is therefore essential to negotiate which law will control.

Because this contract is for the sale of goods, your local law is the **Arizona Uniform Commercial Code (UCC).** The UCC is discussed throughout Units 2 and 3, on contracts and commercial transactions. It is a statute that has taken the common law principles of contract and modified them to meet the needs of contemporary business. Article 2 of the UCC governs the sale of goods. American business lawyers are familiar with the UCC and will generally prefer that it govern. French law is based on **Roman law** and the **Napoleonic Code** and is obviously different. French lawyers and business executives are naturally partial to it. How to compromise? Perhaps by using a neutral law.

The **United Nations Convention on Contracts for the International Sale of Goods (CISG)** is the result of 50 years of work by various international groups, all seeking to create a uniform, international law on this important subject. Finally, in 1980, a United Nations conference adopted the CISG, though it became the law in individual nations only if and when they adopted it. The United States and most of its principal trading partners have adopted this important treaty.

The **CISG applies automatically to any contract for the sale of goods between two parties, from different countries, each of which is a signatory.** France and the United States have both signed. Thus the CISG automatically applies to the Big Heel–Pied D'Or deal unless the parties specifically opt out. If the parties want to be governed by other law, they must state very clearly that they exclude the CISG and elect, for example, the UCC.

Should the parties allow the CISG to govern? They need to understand how the CISG differs from other law. Big Heel's lawyer will point out that there are key differences between the CISG and the UCC, such as whether a contract must be in writing to be enforceable (yes, under the UCC, for contracts worth $500 or more); whether one bargaining party may revoke its offer before the other accepts (often not, under the CISG); whether a successful plaintiff can force the other side to actually complete the contract (CISG) or must take only money damages (UCC); and so forth. ◾

Choice of Forum

The parties must decide not only what law governs, but where disagreements will be resolved. The French and American legal systems are dramatically different. In a French civil lawsuit, generally neither side is entitled to depose the other or to obtain interrogatories or even documents, in sharp contrast to the American system where such discovery methods dominate litigation. American lawyers, accustomed to discovery to prepare a case and advance settlement talks, are unnerved by the French system. Similarly, French lawyers are dismayed at the idea of spending two years taking depositions, exchanging paper, and arguing motions, all at great expense. At trial, the contrasts grow. In a French civil trial, there is generally no right to a jury. The rules of evidence are more flexible (and unpredictable), neither side employs its own expert witnesses, and the parties themselves never appear as witnesses.

Final Choices

The parties must select a language for the contract and a currency for payment. Language counts, because legal terms seldom translate literally. Currency is vital, because the exchange rate may alter between the signing and payment.

The parties agree that the contract price will be paid in U.S. dollars. Pied D'Or is unfamiliar with the UCC and absolutely refuses to make a deal unless either French law or the CISG governs. Your lawyer recommends accepting the CISG, provided that the contract is written in English and that any disputes will be resolved in Arizona courts. Pied D'Or reluctantly agrees. You have a deal!

Letter of Credit

Because Pied D'Or is new and fast growing, you are not sure it will be able to foot the bill. Your lawyer recommends that payment be made by letter of credit. Here is how the letter will work.

Big Heel demands that the contract include a provision requiring payment by **confirmed irrevocable letter of credit.** Le Pied D'Or agrees. The French company now contacts its bank, La Banque Bouffon, and instructs Bouffon to issue a letter of credit to Big Heel. The letter of credit is a promise by the bank itself to pay Big Heel, if Big Heel presents certain documents. Banque Bouffon, of course, expects to be repaid by Pied D'Or. The bank is in a good position to assess Pied D'Or's creditworthiness, since it is local and can do any investigating it wants before issuing the credit. It may also insist that Pied D'Or give Bouffon a mortgage on property, or that Pied D'Or deposit money in a separate Bouffon account.

But at Big Heel, you are still not entirely satisfied about getting paid because you don't know anything about Bouffon. That is why you have required a *confirmed* letter of credit. Bouffon will forward its letter of credit to Big Heel's own bank, the Bandito Trust Company of Tucson. Bandito examines the letter and then confirms the letter. This is *Bandito's own guarantee* that it will pay Big Heel. Bandito will do this only if it knows, through international banking contacts, that Bouffon is a sound bank. The risk has now been spread to two banks, and at Big Heel you are confident of payment.

Why do banks do this? For a fee. When will Bandito pay Big Heel? As soon as Big Heel presents documents indicating that the boots have been placed on board a ship bound for France.

The following case shows why sellers often demand a letter of credit.

CASE SUMMARY

CENTRIFUGAL CASTING MACHINE CO., INC. v. AMERICAN BANK & TRUST CO.

966 F.2d 1348, 1992 U.S. App. LEXIS 13089
United States Court of Appeals for the Tenth Circuit, 1992

FACTS: Centrifugal Casting Machine Co. (CCM) entered into a contract with the State Machinery Trading Co. (SMTC), an agency of the Iraqi government. CCM agreed to manufacture cast iron pipe plant equipment for a total price of $27 million. The contract specified payment of the full amount by confirmed irrevocable letter of credit. The Central Bank of Iraq then issued the letter, on behalf of SMTC (the "account party") to be paid to CCM (the "beneficiary"). The Banca Nazionale del Lavorov (BNL) confirmed the letter.

Following Iraq's invasion of Kuwait on August 2, 1990, President George H. W. Bush issued two executive orders blocking the transfer of property in the

United States in which Iraq held any interest. In other words, no one could use, buy, or sell any Iraqi property or cash. When CCM attempted to draw upon the letter of credit, the United States government intervened. The government claimed that like all Iraqi money in the United States, this money was frozen by the executive order. The United States District Court rejected the government's claim, and the government appealed.

ISSUE: Is CCM entitled to be paid pursuant to the letter of credit?

DECISION: CCM is entitled to payment. Affirmed.

REASONING: The United States claims that it is freezing Iraqi assets to punish international aggres-

sion. That is a legitimate foreign policy argument. However, no court has the power to rewrite basic principles of international trade.

A letter of credit has unique value for two reasons. First, the bank that issues the letter is substituting its credit for that of the buyer. Because the bank is promising to pay with its own funds, the seller is confident of receiving its money.

Second, the bank's obligation to pay on the letter of credit is entirely separate from the underlying bargain between buyer and seller. The bank must pay, even if the seller has breached the contract or the buyer has gone bankrupt. The money in this case came from the bank that issued the letter; the government may not seize it. Any other ruling would undermine all letters of credit. ◢

Foreign Corrupt Practices Act

Foreign investment is another major source of international commerce. Assume that Fonlink is an American communications corporation that wants to invest in the growing overseas market. As a Fonlink executive, you travel to a small, new republic that was formerly part of the Soviet Union. You meet a trade official who tells you that Fonlink is the perfect company to install a new, nationwide telephone/digital system for his young country. You are delighted with his enthusiasm. Over lunch, the official tells you that he can obtain an exclusive contract for Fonlink to do the work, but you will have to pay him a commission of $750,000. Such a deal would be worth millions of dollars for Fonlink, and a commission of $750,000 is economically sensible. Should you pay it?

The **Foreign Corrupt Practices Act (FCPA) makes it illegal for an American businessperson to give "anything of value" to any foreign official in order to influence an official decision.** The classic example of an FCPA violation is bribing a foreign official to obtain a government contract. You must find out exactly why the minister needs so much money, what he plans to do with it, and how he will obtain the contract.

You ask these questions, and the trade official responds, "I am a close personal friend of the minister of the interior. In my country, you must know people to make things happen. The minister respects my judgment, and some of my fee will find its way to him. Do not trouble yourself with details."

Bad advice. A prison sentence is not a detail. The FCPA permits fines of $100,000 for individuals and $1 million for corporations, as well as prison sentences of up to five years. If you pay money that "finds its way to the minister," you have violated the act.

It is sad but true that in many countries bribery is routine and widely accepted. When Congress investigated foreign bribes to see how common they were, more than 300 U.S. companies admitted paying hundreds of millions of dollars in bribes to foreign officials. Legislators concluded that such massive payments distorted competition among American companies for foreign contracts, interfered with the free market system, and undermined confidence everywhere in our way of doing business. The statutory response was simple: Foreign bribery is illegal, plain and simple. The FCPA has two principal requirements:

- *Bribes.* The statute makes it illegal for U.S. companies and citizens to bribe foreign officials to influence a governmental decision. The statute prohibits giving anything of value and also bars using third parties as a conduit for such payments.

- *Record Keeping.* All publicly traded companies—whether they engage in international trade or not—must keep detailed records that prevent hiding or disguising bribes. These records must be available for U.S. government officials to inspect.

Transparency International, an international nonprofit agency based in Germany, publishes a "Corruption Perception Index," gauging how much dishonesty businesspeople and scholars encounter in different nations. In 2003, the agency listed 133 nations on its index. The 10 highest-ranking countries (perceived least corrupt) were Finland, Iceland, Denmark, New Zealand, Singapore, Sweden, the Netherlands, Australia, Norway, and Switzerland. The agency listed the United States as the 18th least corrupt nation. The 10 countries ranking lowest (perceived most corrupt) were Angola, Azerbaijan, Cameroon, Georgia, Tajikstan, Myanmar, Paraguay, Haiti, Nigeria, and Bangladesh. The full index is available from Transparency International at **http://www.transparency.org**.

Chapter Conclusion

Overseas investment, like sales abroad, offers potentially great rewards but significant pitfalls. A working knowledge of international law is essential to any entrepreneur or executive seriously considering foreign commerce. As the WTO lowers barriers, international trade will increase, and your awareness of these principles will grow still more valuable.

Chapter Review

1. The AECA restricts exports from the United States that would harm national security or foreign policy.

2. A tariff is a duty (tax) imposed on goods when they enter a country. The U.S. Customs Service classifies goods when they enter the United States and imposes appropriate tariffs.

3. Most countries, including the United States, impose duties for goods that have been dumped (sold at an unfairly low price in the international market).

4. The General Agreement on Tariffs and Trade (GATT) is lowering the average duties worldwide. Propo-

nents see it as a boon to trade; opponents see it as a threat to workers and the environment.

5. GATT created the World Trade Organization (WTO), which resolves disputes between signatories to the treaty.

6. A sales agreement between an American company and a foreign company may be governed by the UCC, by the law of the foreign country, or by the United Nations Convention On Contracts For The International Sale Of Goods (CISG). The CISG differs from the UCC in several important respects.

7. A confirmed, irrevocable letter of credit is an important means of facilitating international sales contracts, because the seller is assured of payment by a local bank as long as it delivers the specified goods.

8. The Foreign Corrupt Practices Act (FCPA) makes it illegal for an American business person to bribe foreign officials.

PRACTICE TEST

Matching Questions

Match the following terms with their definitions:

___ **A.** Signatory

___ **B.** NAFTA

___ **C.** Tariff

___ **D.** CISG

___ **E.** Dumping

1. A trade agreement between Mexico, the United States and Canada.

2. Selling goods at a cheaper, unfair price internationally.

3. An international convention that governs the sale of goods.

4. A nation that signs a treaty.

5. A duty imposed on imports.

True/False Questions

Circle true or false:

1. T F A problem for many international merchants is that tariffs have been rising for the last decade.

2. T F The United States imports more goods and services (combined) than it exports.

3. T F "Valuation" is the process by which the Customs Services decides the nature of goods being imported into the United States.

4. T F The United States helped negotiate GATT but ironically has refused to sign the agreement.

5. T F Decisions of the WTO are non-binding recommendations.

Multiple-Choice Questions

6. With which country does the United States trade more than any other?

(a) Mexico

(b) Germany

(c) China

(d) United Kingdom

(e) Canada

7. The Commerce Department alleges that Interlex, a foreign company, is selling palm pilots in the United States for less than the cost of production. The department is charging Interlex with

(a) A NAFTA violation.

(b) Dumping.

(c) An FCPA infraction.

(d) An AECA violation.

(e) A CISG violation.

8. "Choice of Forum" refers to

(a) The exporting venue.

(b) The importing venue.

(c) The country where legal disputes will be settled.

(d) The method of payment in an international contract.

(e) An inter-banking agreement designed to insure payment for goods.

9. The WTO rules that the nation of Lugubria must lower tariffs on software from the United States from 45% to 8%, but Lugubria refuses to comply. What can the U.S. do?

   (a) Nothing, because the WTO's ruling is only a recommendation.

   (b) Appeal to the United Nations.

   (c) Appeal to the World Court.

   (d) Impose retaliatory tariffs.

   (e) File suit in Federal court in the U.S.

10. Your Chicago company negotiates an agreement with a British company for the sale goods. The contract does not specify the law that governs the agreement. If there is a dispute, what law *will* govern?

   (a) The UCC.

   (b) The CISG.

   (c) British law.

   (d) Illinois law.

   (e) EU law.

Short-Answer Questions

11. Jean-François, a French wine exporter, sues Bob Joe, a Texas importer, claiming that Bob Joe owes him $2 million for wine. Jean-François takes the witness stand to describe how the contract was created. Where is the trial taking place?

12. Blondek and Tull were two employees of an American company called Eagle Bus. They hoped that the Saskatchewan provincial government would award Eagle a contract for buses. To bolster their chances, they went to Saskatchewan and paid $50,000 to two government employees. Back in the United States, they were arrested and charged with a crime. Suppose they argue that even if they did something illegal, it occurred in Canada, and that Canada is the only nation that can prosecute them. Comment on the defense.

13. Sports Graphics, Inc., imports consumer goods, including "Chill" brand coolers, which come from Taiwan. Chill coolers have an outer shell of vinyl, with handles and pockets, and an inner layer of insulation. In a recent federal lawsuit, the issue was whether Chill coolers were technically "luggage" or "articles used for preparing, serving or storing food or beverages." Who were the parties to this dispute likely to be, and why did they care about such a technical description of these coolers?

14. ETHICS: Hector works in Zoey's importing firm. Zoey overhears Hector on the phone say, "OK, 30,000 ski parkas at $80 per parka. You've got yourself a deal. Thanks a lot." When Hector hangs up, Zoey is furious, yelling, "I told you not to make a deal on those Italian ski parkas without my permission! I think I can get a better price elsewhere." "Relax, Zoey," replies Hector. "I wanted to lock them in, to be sure we had some in case your deal fell through. It's just an oral contract, so we can always back out if we need to." Is that ethical? How far can a company go to protect its interests? Does it matter that another business might make serious financial plans based on the discussion? Apart from the ethics, is Hector's idea smart?

15. Continental Illinois National Bank issued an irrevocable letter of credit on behalf of Bill's Coal Company For $805,000, with the Allied Fidelity Insurance Co. as beneficiary. Bill's Coal Co. then went bankrupt. Allied then presented to Continental documents that were complete and conformed to the letter of credit. Continental refused to pay. Since Bill's Coal was bankrupt, there was no way Continental would collect once it had paid on the letter. Allied filed suit. Who should win?

16. ROLE REVERSAL: Draft an essay or short-answer question that focuses on how a confirmed, irrevocable letter of credit works.

Internet Research Problem

At **http://www.sweatshops.org**, read about the worldwide problem of sweatshops. Is this a serious problem? If so, what role should the law play in its resolution? What can one student do about it?

You can find further practice problems in the Online Quiz at **http://beatty.westbuslaw.com** or in the Study Guide that accompanies this text.

CONTRACTS

UNIT 2

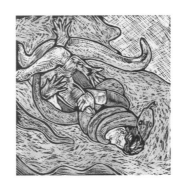

Introduction to Contracts

In Marina del Rey, California, Cassandra sits on the sunny deck of her waterside condominium, sipping a mocha latte while watching spinnakers fill with the warm Pacific wind. She has just received an offer of $1.7 million to buy her condominium. Cassandra has decided to counteroffer for $1.9 million. She is in high spirits because she assumes that at the very worst she has $1.7 million guaranteed, and that represents a huge profit to her. Cassandra plans to buy a cheaper house in North Carolina and invest her profits so that she can retire early. She opens the newspaper, notices a headline "Hard Body Threatens Suit," and turns the page, thinking that a corporate lawsuit in Ohio is of no concern to her. She is mistaken and may learn some hard lessons about contract law.

A year earlier, Jerusalem Steel had signed a contract with Hard Body, a manufacturer of truck and bus bodies. Jerusalem was to deliver 20,000 tons of steel to Hard Body's plant in Joy, Ohio. Hard Body relied on the contract, hiring 300 additional workers even before the steel was delivered, so that the plant would be geared up and ready to produce buses when the metal arrived. To help deal with the new workers, Hard Body offered a midlevel personnel job to Nicole. Hard Body told Nicole, "Don't worry, we expect your job to last forever." Nicole, in turn, relied on that statement to quit her old job in Minneapolis, move to Joy, and sign an agreement with Jasper to purchase his house for $450,000. Based on that sales contract, Jasper phoned his offer to Cassandra's real estate agent for $1.7 million. See Exhibit 9.1.

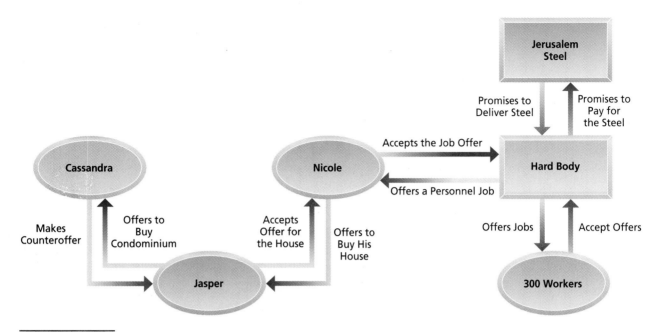

Exhibit 9.1
Contracts are intended to make business matters more predictable. Frequently, a series of contracts becomes mutually dependent.

But in the year since Jerusalem signed its contract, the price of the specified steel has gone up 60%. Jerusalem now refuses to deliver the steel unless the price is renegotiated. Hard Body has insisted on the original contract price. Hard Body cannot afford to buy steel at the current price, which would make its deal to produce buses unprofitable. If Hard Body receives no steel, does it have a valid lawsuit against Jerusalem? May the company force Jerusalem to deliver the steel? If it cannot get steel, may Hard Body lay off the newly hired workers? May it fire Nicole, or does she have a job for life? If Nicole loses her paycheck, will the law force her to buy a house she no longer wants? Jasper will never get such a good price from anyone else, because with no work at Hard Body property prices in Joy will plummet. May Jasper refuse to buy Cassandra's condo, or is he committed for $1.7 million?

Contracts

Throughout this unit on contracts, we will consider issues like those raised in the Cassandra–Hard Body story. Parties enter into contracts attempting to control their future. **Contracts exist to make business matters more predictable.**

JUDICIAL ACTIVISM VERSUS JUDICIAL RESTRAINT

We will see that courts generally, but not always, do what we expect. In most contract cases, judges do their best simply to enforce whatever terms the parties have agreed to. This is judicial restraint—a court taking a passive role and requiring the parties to fulfill whatever obligations they agreed to, whether the deal was wise or foolish. For example, if a real estate developer contracts with a builder to erect 10 expensive homes, but the housing market collapses before construction begins, a judge will order the developer to pay for the houses, even though the expense will cause him devastating losses. **Judicial restraint makes the law less flexible but more predictable.**

On the other hand, courts sometimes practice judicial activism. In contract law, this means that a court will ignore certain provisions of a contract, or an entire agreement, if the judge believes that enforcing the deal would be unjust. Since judicial activism is always phrased in terms of "doing justice," it has an initial appeal. For example, when one party deceives the other with a misleading contract, it may be appropriate for a court to rewrite the agreement. But when a court practices judicial activism, it may diminish our ability to control our own future—which is the whole point of creating a contract. **Judicial activism makes the law more flexible but less predictable.**

ISSUES (AND ANSWERS)

The chain of contracts connecting Jerusalem Steel and Cassandra illustrates various contract problems. We consider each problem in detail in this unit, but here we briefly identify the issues and summarize the answers. A contract has four elements:

- **Agreement.** One party must make a valid offer, and the other party must accept it.

- **Consideration.** There has to be bargaining that leads to an exchange between the parties.

- **Legality.** The contract must be for a lawful purpose.

- **Capacity.** The parties must be adults of sound mind.

The chapters that follow cover each of the elements in sequence. Contract cases often raise several other important issues, which we examine in later chapters:

- **Consent.** Neither party may trick or force the other into the agreement.

- **Written contracts.** Some contracts must be in writing to be enforceable.

- **Third party interests.** Some contracts affect people other than the parties themselves.

- **Performance and discharge.** If a party fully accomplishes what the contract requires, his duties are discharged.

- **Remedies.** A court will award money or other relief to a party injured by a breach of contract.

When we apply these principles to the problem at this chapter's beginning, we see that Jerusalem Steel is almost certainly bound by its agreement. A rise in price is generally no excuse to walk away from a contract. Hard Body has made the bargain precisely to protect itself in case of a price rise. These are issues of offer and acceptance, consideration, and discharge, discussed in later chapters. Can Hard Body force Jerusalem to deliver the steel? Probably not, as we learn in Chapter 17, on remedies. Hard Body is entitled to money damages if it is forced to buy steel at higher prices. If Hard Body is unable to obtain steel in the rising market, may it lay off its workers? Very likely, as Chapter 10, on agreement, indicates. Can it fire Nicole? The statement about expecting her job to last forever almost certainly creates no lifetime employment. What about the fact that she quit her job in reliance on this one? That raises an issue called promissory estoppel, which we discuss later in this chapter.

Must Nicole go through with her purchase of Jasper's house? Probably, as Chapter 14, on written contracts, demonstrates. Do Jasper and Cassandra have a contract? No, because the agreement must be in writing to be enforceable. Even if there is no settled price, is Cassandra safe in assuming she has $1.7 million guaranteed? Not at all, as the chapter on agreement explains. If Cassandra had read this unit, she would be faxing a written contract to Jasper rather than waiting for her latte to cool.

CONTRACTS DEFINED

Contract law is a study in promises. Is Nicole entitled to a lifetime job at Hard Body? Is Jasper obligated to buy Cassandra's condominium? Contract law determines which promises to enforce. **A contract is a promise that the law will enforce.**

As we look more closely at the elements of contract law, we will encounter some intricate issues. This is partly because we live in a complex society, which conducts its business in an infinite variety of ways. It is also due to the constant tug between predictability and fairness, described above. Remember, though, that we are usually interested in answering three basic questions of common sense, all relating to promises:

- Is it certain that the defendant promised to do something?

- If she did promise, is it fair to make her honor her word?

- If she did not promise, are there unusual reasons to hold her liable anyway?

Types of Contracts

BILATERAL AND UNILATERAL CONTRACTS

In a bilateral contract, both parties make a promise. Suppose a producer says to Gloria, "I'll pay you $2 million to star in my new romantic comedy, *A Promise for a Promise,* which we are shooting three months from now in Santa Fe." Gloria says, "It's a deal." That is a bilateral contract: one promise in exchange for another promise. The producer is now bound to pay Gloria $2 million, and Gloria is obligated to show up on time and act in the movie. The vast majority of contracts are bilateral contracts.

In a unilateral contract, one party makes a promise that the other party can accept only by doing something. These contracts are less common. Suppose the movie producer says to Leo, "I'll give you a hundred bucks if you mow my lawn this weekend." Leo is not promising to do it. If he mows the lawn, he has accepted the offer and is entitled to his hundred dollars. If he spends the weekend at the beach, neither he nor the producer owes anything.

EXPRESS AND IMPLIED CONTRACTS

In an express contract, the two parties explicitly state all important terms of their agreement. Most contracts are express contracts. The contract between the producer and Gloria is an express contract, because the parties explicitly state what Gloria will do and how much she will be paid. Some express contracts are oral, as that one was, and some are written. Obviously, it is good business sense always to make express contracts, and wise to put them in writing. We emphasize, however, that *many oral contracts are fully enforceable.*

In an implied contract, the words and conduct of the parties indicate that they intended an agreement. Suppose every Friday, for two months, the producer asks Leo to mow his lawn, and loyal Leo does so each weekend. Then for three more weekends, Leo simply shows up without the producer asking, and the producer continues to pay for the work done. But on the 12th weekend, when Leo rings the doorbell to collect, the producer suddenly says, "I never asked you to mow it. Scram." The producer is correct that there was no express contract, because the parties had not spoken for several weeks. But a court will probably rule that the conduct of the parties has implied a contract. Not only did Leo mow the lawn every weekend, but the producer even paid on three weekends when they had not spoken. It was reasonable for Leo to assume that he had a weekly deal to mow and be paid. Naturally, there is no implied contract thereafter.

Today, the hottest disputes about implied contracts continue to arise in the employment setting. Many corporate employees have **at-will contracts** with their companies. This means that the employees are free to quit at any time and the company has the right to fire them at any time, for virtually any reason. But often a company provides its workers with personnel manuals that guarantee certain rights. The manual may assure all workers that they will have a hearing and a chance to present evidence on their behalf before being fired. Is that a binding promise? You decide.

YOU BE THE JUDGE

FEDERAL EXPRESS CORP. v. DUTSCHMANN

846 S.W.2d 282, 1993 Tex. LEXIS 9
Supreme Court of Texas, 1993

FACTS: When Marcie Dutschmann began working as a courier at Federal Express, she received an *Employment Handbook and Personnel Manual* stating that her employment was at will and "would continue as long as it was mutually satisfactory to both parties." The manual specified that it created no contractual rights. But it also described a "Guaranteed Fair Treatment Policy" (GFTP). According to the GFTP, any employee who was terminated would have a hearing at a board of review, at which he could appear and present evidence.

Federal Express fired Dutschmann in October 1987, claiming that she had falsified delivery records. She responded that her termination was in retaliation for her complaints of sexual harassment. She attempted to appeal her termination through the GFTP, but Federal Express did not allow her the kind of hearing that the handbook described. Dutschmann sued. At trial, Federal Express argued that Dutschmann was an employee at will and that the company was free to fire her at any time without a hearing. Dutschmann contended that the employee handbook and manual created an implied contract giving her the right to present witnesses and evidence. The jury found that the handbooks did create an implied contract and that Federal Express had not given her a fair hearing. The court of appeals affirmed. Federal Express appealed to the Texas Supreme Court.

YOU BE THE JUDGE: Did the employee handbook and manual create an implied contract guaranteeing a fair hearing?

ARGUMENT FOR FEDERAL EXPRESS: Your honors, when Federal Express created its employee manuals, it was well aware that some state courts have ruled that these handbooks may create an implied contract. And that is why Federal Express wrote employee manuals including the following statements: "The employee's employment is at will and will continue as long as it is mutually satisfactory to both parties. This manual does not create any contractual rights. Its use is intended only as a reference." That manual states that it is intended "solely as a guide for management and employees and is not a contract of employment and that no such contract may be implied from its provisions." We think that language is about as clear as it is possible to be, but we didn't stop there. At the inception of Ms. Dutschmann's employment, she signed an agreement stating that she understood the employee manuals did not constitute a contract.

Freedom to contract means freedom, among other things, to create at-will employment. Ms. Dutschmann signed an agreement saying she understood her position. It is time for her to keep her word.

ARGUMENT FOR Ms. DUTSCHMANN: Your honors, the manuals do state that the employment is at will. But those manuals then go on to say that all employees are guaranteed certain rights, including the rights to a fair, thorough termination hearing. The company refused to hear her evidence and refused to see her documents, because they knew she could prove sexual harassment. So they just fired her, pretending that there was no booklet and no guarantee of a hearing.

Federal Express is trying to have it both ways. The company creates these handsome, glossy booklets, filled with assurances of fair dealing. The booklets describe reasonable, sensible ways of treating employees and guarantee those rights to all employees. But then Federal Express comes into court and argues that a guarantee is not a guarantee, and a hearing is not a hearing.

Federal Express knew that guaranteeing fair treatment was a proven way to attract and retain good employees. Would Ms. Dutschmann have gone to work for Federal Express if she had been told she might be sexually harassed and then fired without a fair hearing? Of course not. Federal Express created an implied contract and the company should honor its promise. ▰

UPDATE   Besides Dutschmann and the company, who are their other stakeholders? What alternatives were available to Federal Express? What are the most important values involved in this dispute? If there are conflicting values, which are most important? ▰

EXECUTORY AND EXECUTED CONTRACTS

A contract is executory when one or more parties has not fulfilled its obligations. Recall Gloria, who agrees to act in the producer's film beginning in three months. The moment Gloria and the producer strike their bargain, they have an executory bilateral express contract. A contract is executed when all parties have fulfilled their obligations. When Gloria finishes acting in the movie and the producer pays her final fee, their contract will be fully executed.

Remedies Created by Judicial Activism

Now we turn away from true contracts and consider two remedies created by judicial activism: promissory estoppel and quasi-contract. We emphasize that these remedies are exceptions. Most of the agreements that courts enforce are the express contracts that we have already studied. Nonetheless, the next two remedies have grown in importance over the last 100 years. In each case, a sympathetic plaintiff can demonstrate an injury. The harm has occurred in a setting where a contract might well have been made. But the crux of the matter is this: There is no contract. The plaintiff cannot claim that the defendant breached the agreement, because none ever existed. The plaintiff must hope for more "creative" relief.

The two remedies can be confusingly similar. The best way to distinguish them is this:

- In promissory estoppel cases, the defendant made a promise that the plaintiff relied on.

- In quasi-contract cases, the defendant did not make any promise, but did receive a benefit from the plaintiff.

PROMISSORY ESTOPPEL

A fierce fire swept through Dana and Derek Andreason's house in Utah, seriously damaging it. The good news was that agents for Aetna Casualty promptly visited the Andreasons and helped them through the crisis. The agents reassured the couple that all of the damage was covered by their insurance, instructed them on which things to throw out and replace, and helped them choose materials for repairing other items. The bad news was that the agents were wrong: The Andreasons' policy had expired six weeks before the fire. When Derek Andreason presented a bill for $41,957 worth of meticulously itemized work that he had done under the agents' supervision, Aetna refused to pay.

The Andreasons sued—but not for breach of contract. There was no contract; that was exactly the problem. So they sued Aetna under the legal theory of **promissory estoppel: Even when there is no contract, a plaintiff may use promissory estoppel to enforce the defendant's promise if he can show that:**

- The defendant made a promise knowing that the plaintiff would likely rely on it.

- The plaintiff did rely on the promise; and

- The only way to avoid injustice is to enforce the promise.

Aetna made a promise to the Andreasons, namely, its assurance that all the damage was covered by insurance. The company knew that the Andreasons would rely on that promise, which they did by ripping up a floor that might have been salvaged, throwing out some furniture, and buying materials to repair the house.

Is enforcing the promise the only way to avoid injustice? Yes, ruled the Utah Court of Appeals. The Andreasons' conduct was reasonable and based entirely on what the Aetna agents told them. Under promissory estoppel, the Andreasons received virtually the same amount they would have obtained had the insurance contract been valid.[1]

Promissory estoppel is an important development of 20th-century law. This is judicial activism, helping people by crafting new remedies. But, as is true whenever the rules are "bent," it means that the outcome of a particular case is less predictable.

QUASI-CONTRACT

Don Easterwood leased over 5,000 acres of farmland in Jackson County, Texas from PIC Realty for one year. The next year he obtained a second one-year lease. Each year, Easterwood farmed the land, harvested the crops, and prepared the land for the following year's planting. Toward the end of the second lease, he and PIC began discussing the terms of another lease. While they negotiated, Easterwood prepared the land for the following year, cutting, plowing, and disking the soil. But the negotiations for a new lease failed, and Easterwood moved off the land. He sued PIC Realty for the value of his work preparing the soil.

Easterwood had neither an express nor an implied contract for the value of his work. How could he make any legal claim? By relying on the legal theory of a quasi-contract: **Even when there is no contract, a court may use quasi-contract to compensate a plaintiff who can show that:**

- The plaintiff gave some benefit to the defendant

- The plaintiff reasonably expected to be paid for the benefit and the defendant knew this; and

- The defendant would be unjustly enriched if he did not pay.

If a court finds all these elements present, it will generally award the value of the goods or services that the plaintiff has conferred. The damages awarded are called *quantum meruit,* meaning that the plaintiff gets "as much as he deserved." The court is awarding money that it believes the plaintiff morally ought to have, even though there was no valid contract entitling her to it. This again is judicial activism, with the courts inventing a "quasi" contract where no true contract exists.

Don Easterwood testified that in Jackson County, it was quite common for a tenant farmer to prepare the soil for the following year but then be unable to farm the land. In those cases, he claimed, the landowner compensated the farmer for the work done. Other witnesses agreed that this was the local custom. The court ruled that all elements of quasi-contract had been satisfied. Easterwood gave a benefit to PIC because the land was ready for planting. Jackson County custom caused Easterwood to assume he would be paid, and PIC Realty knew it. Finally, said the court, it would be unjust to let PIC benefit without paying anything. The court ordered PIC to pay the fair market value of Easterwood's labors.

---

[1] *Andreason v. Aetna Casualty & Surety Co.,* 848 P.2d 171 (Utah App. 1993).

Four Theories of Recovery

Theory	Did the Defendant Make a Promise?	Is There a Contract?	Description
Express Contract	Yes	Yes	The parties intend to contract and agree on explicit terms.
Implied Contract	Not explicitly	Yes	The parties do not formally agree, but their words and conduct indicate an intention to create a contract.
Promissory Estoppel	Yes	No	There is no contract, but the defendant makes a promise that she can foresee will induce reliance; the plaintiff relies on it; and it would be unjust not to enforce the promise.
Quasi-Contract	No	No	There is no intention to contract, but the plaintiff gives some benefit to the defendant, who knows that the plaintiff expects compensation; it would be unjust not to award the plaintiff damages.

Sources of Contract Law

COMMON LAW

Express and implied contracts, promissory estoppel, and quasi-contract were all crafted, over centuries, by appellate courts deciding one contract lawsuit at a time. In this country, the basic principles are similar from one state to another, but there have been significant differences concerning most important contract doctrines.

In part because of these differences, the 20th century saw the rise of two major new sources of contract law: the Uniform Commercial Code and the Restatement of Contracts.

UNIFORM COMMERCIAL CODE

Business methods changed quickly during the first half of the 20th century. Executives used new forms of communication, such as telephone and wire, to make deals. Corporations conducted business across state borders and around the world. Executives, lawyers, and judges wanted a body of law for commercial transactions that reflected modern business methods and provided uniformity throughout the United States. That desire gave birth to the Uniform Commercial Code (UCC), created in 1952. The drafters intended the UCC to facilitate the easy formation and enforcement of contracts in a fast-paced world. The Code governs many aspects of commerce, including the sale of goods, negotiable instruments, and secured transactions. Every state has adopted at least part of the UCC to govern commercial transactions within that state. For our purposes in studying contracts, the most important part of the Code is Article 2. The entire UCC is available online at **http://www.law.cornell.edu/ucc/ucc.table.html**.

UCC Article 2 governs the sale of goods. "Goods" means anything movable, except for money and securities. Goods include pencils, commercial aircraft, books, and Christmas trees. Goods do not include land or a house, because neither is movable, nor do they include a stock certificate. A contract for the sale of 10,000 sneakers is governed by the UCC; a contract for the sale of a condominium in

Marina del Rey is governed by the California common law and its statute of frauds. Thus, when analyzing any contract problem as a student or business executive, you must note whether the agreement concerns the sale of goods. Most of the time the answer is clear, and you will immediately know whether the UCC or the common law governs. In some cases, as in a mixed contract for goods and services, it is not so obvious. **In a mixed contract, Article 2 governs only if the primary purpose was the sale of goods.** In the following case, the court had to decide the primary purpose.

CASE SUMMARY

PASS v. SHELBY AVIATION, INC.

2000 Tenn. App. LEXIS 247
Tennessee Court of Appeals, 2000

FACTS: Max Pass was flying a single-engine Piper airplane that he owned when he encountered turbulence, lost control of the aircraft, and crashed, killing his wife and himself. Pass's parents filed suit against Shelby Aviation, which had serviced the Piper four months before the tragedy. Among other things, Shelby had replaced both rear wing attach-point brackets. The parents asserted that the brackets were defective because they lacked the necessary bolts.

The primary claim in their suit was breach of warranty under the UCC. A warranty is an assurance that a product will work properly, and Article 2 of the Code establishes several warranties for goods. In other words, the Passes claimed that Shelby's use of faulty parts cost two lives. The company moved to dismiss, claiming that the UCC did not apply, because the contract had been one for services. If the common law governed the contract, there were no warranties and the parents had no valid claim. The trial court denied the motion and Shelby appealed.

ISSUE: Did the UCC or the common law govern this contract?

DECISION: The common law governed. Reversed and remanded.

REASONING: This contract, like many others, involved a mix of goods and services. To decide whether the UCC or the common law governs, we determine whether the predominant purpose of the agreement was for services or for the sale of goods.

Shelby's invoice states that "the following repair work" will be done, using necessary material. A box is checked indicating an "annual 100 hour periodic inspection." The document also includes a list of services performed and parts used. Only about 37% of the charges were for parts. Overall, the invoice emphasizes the inspection and repair of the airplane.

Shelby's business appears to be primarily service. All the parts sold to Pass were ordered specifically for his airplane except for one, which the customer himself supplied. If Shelby were in the business of selling parts, it would not have accepted one from Pass. The predominant purpose of this contract was services, and Shelby is entitled to judgment on the UCC warranty claims. ◢

The common law governs contracts for services, employment, real estate and certain other things, and so each chapter in this unit will analyze the relevant common law principles. But the sale of goods is obviously a major element in business nationwide, and therefore each chapter will also discuss appropriate aspects of the Code.

RESTATEMENT (SECOND) OF CONTRACTS

In 1932 the American Law Institute (ALI), a group of lawyers, scholars, and judges, drafted the Restatement of Contracts, attempting to codify what its members regarded as the best rulings of contract law. Where courts had disagreed, for example, about when to enforce promissory estoppel, the drafters of the Restatement chose what they considered the wisest decisions. The Restatement was a treatise and never became the law anywhere. But because of the eminence of those who wrote it, the Restatement influenced many courts as they decided contract cases.

In 1979, the ALI issued a new version, the Restatement (Second) of Contracts. Like its predecessor, the Restatement (Second) is not the law anywhere, and in this respect it differs from the common law and the UCC. But the Restatement (Second) influences lawyers as they draft contracts and judges as they decide cases; we, too, will seek its counsel throughout the chapters on contracts.

Chapter Conclusion

Contracts govern countless areas of our lives. Understanding contract principles is especially important, because courts no longer rubber-stamp any agreement that two parties have made. If we know the issues that courts scrutinize, the agreement we draft is likelier to be enforced. We thus achieve greater control over our affairs—the very purpose of a contract.

Chapter Review

A contract is a promise that the law will enforce. Contracts are intended to make business matters more predictable. Analyzing a contract generally involves inquiring into some or all of these issues:

1. What is the subject of the agreement?
   - If the contract is for the sale of goods, UCC Article 2 governs.
   - If the contract is for services, employment, or real estate, the common law governs.

2. Did the parties intend to contract?
   - If the parties formally agreed and stated explicit terms, there is probably an express contract.
   - If the parties did not formally agree but their conduct, words, or past dealings indicate that they intended a binding agreement, there may be an implied contract.

3. If there is an agreement, is there any reason to doubt its enforceability?

4. If there is no contract, are there other reasons to give the plaintiff damages?
   - A claim of promissory estoppel requires that the defendant made a promise knowing that the plaintiff would likely rely, and the plaintiff did so. It would be wrong to deny recovery.
   - A claim of quasi-contract requires that the defendant received a benefit, knowing that the plaintiff would expect compensation, and it would be unjust not to grant it.

PRACTICE TEST

Matching Questions

Match the following terms with their definitions:

___ **A.** Quasi-contract

___ **B.** Implied contract

___ **C.** Express contract

___ **D.** Promissory estoppel

___ **E.** Bilateral contract

1. An agreement with all terms stated explicitly

2. A judicial remedy based on a defendant's promise on which the plaintiff reasonably relied.

3. An agreement based on one promise in exchange for another.

4. A judicial remedy based on a benefit given by the plaintiff to the defendant.

5. An agreement based on the words and actions of the parties.

True/False Questions

Circle true or false:

1. T F An express contract is an example of judicial activism.

2. T F To be enforceable, all contracts must be in writing.

3. T F Maria agrees to photograph Caitlin's children, and Caitlin agrees to pay $800 for the pictures. This is a bilateral contract.

4. T F Abdul hires Sean to work in his store, and agrees to pay him $9 per hour. This agreement is governed by the UCC.

5. T F A principal purpose of contracts is to make business matters more predictable.

Multiple-Choice Questions

6. Which contract is governed by the Uniform Commercial Code?

(a) An agreement for an actor to appear in a movie for a $600,000 fee.

(b) An agreement for an actor to appear in a movie for a fee of $600,000 plus 2% of box office.

(c) An agreement for the sale of a house.

(d) An agreement for the sale of 22,000 picture frames.

(e) An agreement for the rental of an apartment.

7. Mark, a newspaper editor, walks into the newsroom and announces to a group of five reporters: "I'll pay a $2,000 bonus to the first reporter who finds definitive evidence that Senator Blue smoked marijuana at the celebrity party last Friday." Anna, the first reporter to produce the evidence, claims her bonus based on

(a) Unilateral contract.

(b) Promissory estoppel.

(c) Quasi-contract.

(d) Implied contract.

(e) Express contract.

8. What are the elements of a contract?

(a) Express, implied, quasi-contract, promissory estoppel.

(b) Agreement, consideration, legality, capacity.

(c) Common law, UCC, Restatement.

(d) Bilateral, unilateral, express, implied.

(e) The reasonable expectations of similarly placed parties.

9. Raul has finished the computer he promised to perform for Tanya, and she has paid him in full. This is

(a) An express contract.

(b) An implied contract.

(c) An executed contract.

(d) A bilateral contract.

(e) No contract.

10. Business affairs can be made less certain because of

(a) Restatement of Contracts.

(b) UCC.

(c) Judicial activism.

(d) Judicial restraint.

(e) Executory contracts.

Short-Answer Questions

11. Pennsylvania contracted with Envirotest Systems, Inc., an Arizona company, to build 86 automobile emissions inspection stations in 25 counties, and operate them for seven years. This contract is worth hundreds of millions of dollars to Envirotest. But suddenly, Pennsylvania legislators opposed the entire system, claiming that it would lead to long delays and high expenses for motorists. These lawmakers urged that Pennsylvania simply stop construction of the new system. Was Pennsylvania allowed to get out of the contract because its legislators concluded that the whole system is unwise?

12. Central Maine Power Company made a promotional offer in which it promised to pay a substantial sum to any homeowner or builder who constructed new housing heated with electricity. Motel Services, Inc., which was building a small housing project for the city of Waterville, Maine, decided to install electrical heat in the units in order to qualify for the offer. It built the units and requested payment for the full amount of the promotional offer. Is Central Maine obligated to pay? Why or why not?

13. Interactive Data Corp. hired Daniel Foley as an assistant product manager at a starting salary of $18,500. Over the next six years Interactive steadily promoted Foley until he became Los Angeles branch manager at a salary of $56,116. Interactive's officers repeatedly told Foley that he would have his job as long as his performance was adequate. In addition, Interactive distributed an employee handbook that specified "termination guidelines," including a mandatory seven-step, pretermination procedure. Two years later Foley learned that his recently hired supervisor, Robert Kuhne, was under investigation by the FBI for embezzlement at his previous job. Foley reported this to Interactive officers. Shortly thereafter, Interactive fired Foley. He sued, claiming that Interactive could only fire him for good cause, after the seven-step procedure. What kind of a claim is he making? Should he succeed?

14. The Hoffmans owned and operated a successful small bakery and grocery store. They spoke with Lukowitz, an agent of Red Owl Stores, who told them that for $18,000 Red Owl would build a store and fully stock it for them. The Hoffmans sold their bakery and grocery store and purchased a lot on which Red Owl was to build the store. Lukowitz then told Hoffman that the price had gone up to $26,000. The Hoffmans borrowed the extra money from relatives, but then Lukowitz informed them that the cost would be $34,000. Negotiations broke off and the Hoffmans sued. The court determined that there was no contract because too many details had not been worked out— the size of the store, its design, and the cost of constructing it. Can the Hoffmans recover any money?

15. ETHICS: John Stevens owned a dilapidated apartment that he rented to James and Cora Chesney for a low rent. The Chesneys began to remodel and rehabilitate the unit. Over a four-year period, they installed two new bathrooms, carpeted the floors, installed new septic and heating systems, and rewired, replumbed, and painted. Stevens periodically stopped by and saw the work in progress. The Chesneys transformed the unit into a respectable apartment. Three years after their work was done, Stevens served the Chesneys with an eviction notice. The Chesneys counterclaimed, seeking the value of the work they had done. Are they entitled to it? Comment on the law and the ethics.

16. ROLE REVERSAL: Write a multiple-choice question that requires use of the predominant factor test to determine whether a contract is one for goods or services.

Internet Research Problem

Visit **http://www.law.cornell.edu/states/listing.html**. Select a state. Then click on judicial opinions. Search for a case concerning "quasi-contract." What are the details of the quasi-contract dispute? Who won and why?

You can find further practice problems in the Online Quiz at **http://beatty.westbuslaw.com** or in the Study Guide that accompanies this text.

Agreement

Interior. A glitzy café, New York. Evening. Bob, a famous director, and Katrina, a glamorous actress, sit at a table, near a wall of glass looking onto a New York sidewalk that is filled with life and motion. Bob sips a margarita while carefully eying Katrina. Katrina stares at her wine glass.

Bob (smiling confidently): *Body Work* is going to be huge—for the right actress. I know a film that's gonna gross a hundred million when I'm holding one. I'm holding one.

Katrina (perking up at the mention of money): It is quirky. It's fun. And she's very strong, very real.

Bob: She's you. That's why we're sitting here. We start shooting in seven months.

Katrina (edging away from the table): I have a few questions. That nude scene.

Bob: The one on the toboggan run?

Katrina: That one was OK. But the one in the poultry factory—very explicit. I don't work nude.

Bob: It's not really nude. Think of all those feathers fluttering around.

Katrina: It's nude.

Bob: We'll work it out. This is a romantic comedy, not tawdry exploitation. Katrina, we're talking $2.5 million. A little accommodation, please. $600,000 up front, and the rest deferred, the usual percentages.

Katrina: Bob, my fee is $3 million. As you know. That hasn't changed.

Katrina picks up her drink, doesn't sip it, places it on the coaster, using both hands to center it perfectly. He waits, as she stares silently at her glass.

BOB: We're shooting in Santa Fe, the weather will be perfect. You have a suite at the Excelsior plus a trailer on location.

KATRINA: I should talk with my agent. I'd need something in writing about the nude scene, the fee, percentages—all the business stuff. I never sign without talking to her.

Bob shrugs and sits back.

BOB: A *lot* of people love that role. (That jolts her.) I have to put this together fast. We can get you the details you want in writing.

Katrina looks at Bob. He nods reassuringly. Bob sticks out his hand, smiling. Katrina hesitates, lets go of her drink, and *shakes hands,* looking unsure. Bob signals for the check. ◾

Do Bob and Katrina have a deal? They seem to think so. But is her fee $2.5 million or $3 million? What if Katrina demands that all nude scenes be taken out, and Bob refuses? Must she still act in the film? What if Bob auditions another actress the next day, likes her, and signs her? Does he owe Katrina her fee?

Bob and Katrina have acted out a classic problem in agreement, one of the basic issues in contract law. Their lack of clarity means that disputes are likely and lawsuits possible. Similar bargaining goes on every day around the country and around the world. Some of the negotiating is done in person; more is done by phone, fax, and e-mail. This chapter highlights the most common sources of misunderstanding and litigation so that you can avoid making deals you never intended—or "deals" that you cannot enforce.

There almost certainly is no contract between Bob and Katrina. Bob's offer was unclear. Even if it was valid, Katrina counteroffered. When they shook hands, it is impossible to know what terms each had in mind.

Meeting of the Minds

As courts dissect a negotiation that has gone awry, they examine the intent of the parties. **The parties can form a contract only if they had a meeting of the minds.** This requires that they (1) understood each other and (2) intended to reach an agreement.

Keep in mind that judges must make objective assessments of the respective intent of each party. A court will not try to get inside Katrina's head and decide what she was thinking as she shook hands. It will look at the handshake objectively, deciding how a reasonable person would interpret the words and conduct. Katrina may honestly have meant to conclude a deal for $3 million with no nude scenes, while Bob might in good faith have believed he was committing himself to $2.5 million and absolute control of the script. Neither belief will control the outcome. A reasonable person observing their discussion would not have known what terms they agreed to, and hence there is no agreement.

Offer

Bargaining begins with an offer. **An offer is an act or statement that proposes definite terms and permits the other party to create a contract by accepting those terms.**

The person who makes an offer is the **offeror.** The person to whom he makes that offer is the **offeree.** The terms are annoying but inescapable because, like handcuffs, all courts use them. In most contract negotiations, two parties bargain back and forth, maybe for minutes, perhaps for months. Each may make several offers, revoke some proposals, suggest counteroffers, and so forth. For our purposes, the offeror remains the one who made the first offer, and the offeree is the one who received it.

Two questions determine whether a statement is an offer:

- Did the offeror intend to make a bargain?

- Are the terms of the offer definite?

PROBLEMS WITH INTENT

Zachary says to Sharon, "Come work in my English language center as a teacher. I'll pay you $500 per week for a 35-hour week, for nine months starting Monday." This is a valid offer. Zachary intends to make a bargain and his offer is definite. If Sharon accepts, the parties have a contract that either one can enforce. By contrast, we will consider several categories of statements that are generally not valid offers.

Invitations to Bargain

An invitation to bargain is not an offer. Suppose Martha telephones Joe and leaves a message on his answering machine, asking if Joe would consider selling his vacation condo on Lake Michigan. Joe faxes a signed letter to Martha saying, "There is no way I could sell the condo for less than $150,000." Martha promptly sends Joe a cashier's check for that amount. Does she own the condo? No. Joe's fax was not an offer. It is merely an invitation to bargain. Joe is indicating that he would be happy to receive an offer from Martha. He is not promising to sell the condo for $150,000 or for any amount.

Letters of Intent

In complex business negotiations, the parties may spend months bargaining over dozens of interrelated issues. It may be tempting during the negotiations to draft a **letter of intent,** summarizing the progress made thus far. But is such a letter binding? As the following case illustrates, an ambiguous letter of intent is often an invitation to court.

CASE SUMMARY

QUAKE CONSTRUCTION v. AMERICAN AIRLINES

141 Ill. 2d 281, 565 N.E.2d 990 1990 Ill. LEXIS 151
Supreme Court of Illinois, 1990

FACTS: Jones Brothers Construction was the general contractor on a job to expand American Airlines' facilities at O'Hare International Airport. Jones Brothers invited Quake Construction to bid on the employee facilities and automotive maintenance shop ("the project"). Quake bid, and Jones Brothers sent a letter of intent that stated, among other things:

"We have elected to award the contract for the subject project to your firm as we discussed on April 15, 1985. A contract agreement outlining the detailed terms and conditions is being prepared and will be available for your signature shortly. Your scope of work includes the complete installation of expanded lunchroom, restroom and locker facilities for

American Airlines employees as well as an expansion of American Airlines' existing Automotive Maintenance Shop. The entire project shall be complete by August 15, 1985.

"This notice of award authorizes the work set forth in the [attached] documents at a lump sum price of $1,060,568.00. Jones Brothers Construction Corporation reserves the right to cancel this letter of intent if the parties cannot agree on a fully executed subcontract agreement."

The parties never signed the fully written contract, and ultimately Jones Brothers hired another company. Quake sued, seeking to recover the money it spent in preparation and its loss of anticipated profit.

ISSUE: Was Jones Brothers' letter of intent a valid offer?

DECISION: The letter is ambiguous, and the case is remanded for the trial court to determine what the parties intended.

REASONING: Whether a letter of intent creates a binding contract depends on what the parties meant when they wrote it. If the parties intended the letter to create an enforceable agreement, then it does. However, if the letter says that the parties will *not* be bound until a more formal document is signed, then the letter is unenforceable. In deciding what the parties intended, a court should consider the normal practice in the industry, the amount of detail in the letter, and whether the letter states that a more formal contract is essential.

This letter of intent is ambiguous. The document states that Jones was awarding the project to Quake, and that work could begin within just a few days. Even the cancellation clause suggests a binding agreement, since otherwise there would be nothing to cancel. On the other hand, the letter refers several times to the signing of a more formal contract, and this indicates that the parties did not consider this document binding. It is impossible to tell what the parties meant. In the trial court, the parties must use other evidence to demonstrate their intentions. ◢

So after several years of litigation, Jones Brothers and Quake had to go back to court to prove their intent. At times, ambiguity in a letter of intent is deliberate, because one party is hoping to obtain the other side's commitment while leaving itself an escape hatch. As the interminable Quake litigation demonstrates, that is a dangerous game.

Advertisements

Mary Mesaros received a notice from the United States Bureau of the Mint, announcing a new $5 gold coin to commemorate the Statue of Liberty. The notice contained an order form stating:

"VERY IMPORTANT—PLEASE READ: YES, Please accept my order for the U.S. Liberty Coins I have indicated. I understand that all sales are final and not subject to refund. Verification of my order will be made by the Department of the Treasury, U.S. Mint. If my order is received by December 31, 1985, I will be entitled to purchase the coins at the Pre-Issue Discount price shown."

Mesaros ordered almost $2,000 worth of the coins. But the Mint was inundated with so many requests for the coin that the supply was soon exhausted. Mesaros and thousands of others never got their coins. This was particularly disappointing because the market value of the coins doubled shortly after their issue. Mesaros sued on behalf of the entire class of disappointed purchasers. Like most who sue based on an advertisement, she lost.

An advertisement is generally not an offer. An advertisement is merely a request for offers. The consumer makes the offer, whether by mail, as above, or by arriving at a merchant's store ready to buy. The seller is free to reject the offer.

Note that while the common law regards advertisements as mere solicitations, consumers do have protection from those shopkeepers intent upon deceit. Almost every state has some form of **consumer protection statute.** These statutes outlaw false advertising. For example, an automobile dealer who advertises a remarkably low price but then has only one automobile at that price has probably violated a consumer protection statute because the ad was published in bad faith, to trick consumers into coming to the dealership. The United States Mint did not violate any consumer protection statute because it acted in good faith and simply ran out of coins.

PROBLEMS WITH DEFINITENESS

It is not enough that the offeror intends to enter into an agreement. **The terms of the offer must be definite.** If they are vague, then even if the offeree "accepts" the deal, a court does not have enough information to enforce it and there is no contract.

You want a friend to work in your store for the holiday season. This is a definite offer: "I offer you a job as a sales clerk in the store from November 1 through December 29, 40 hours per week at $10 per hour." But suppose, by contrast, you say: "I offer you a job as a sales clerk in the store from November 1 through December 29, 40 hours per week. We will work out a fair wage once we see how busy things get." Your friend replies, "That's fine with me." This offer is indefinite and there is no contract. What is a fair wage? $6 per hour? $15 per hour? How will the determination be made? There is no binding agreement.

The following case presents a problem with definiteness. You be the judge.

YOU BE THE JUDGE

LEMMING v. MORGAN

228 Ga. App. 763, 492 S.E.2d 742, 1997 Ga. App. LEXIS 1264
Georgia Court of Appeals, 1997

FACTS: Larry Lemming and Jackson Morgan were good friends who became business associates— and then ex-friends. According to Lemming, he and Morgan orally agreed to form a partnership. Lemming would use his business connections and influence to locate real estate that was ripe for development. He would help Morgan obtain financing and then assist in developing and reselling the property. Morgan would temporarily hold the property in his name alone because Lemming was going through a divorce and also had tax problems. The two men agreed that, "if and when Lemming's divorce and tax problems subsided," Morgan would transfer to Lemming one half of all property and one half of all profits.

Lemming claims that over a five-year period, he located five properties, which he helped Morgan develop and resell. Then Morgan refused to give Lemming his one half stake. Lemming leaped into court. Morgan denied that the parties had ever formed a partnership. The trial court granted summary judgment for Morgan, ruling that even if the parties had made the agreement Lemming described, it was too indefinite to enforce. Lemming appealed.

YOU BE THE JUDGE: Assuming the parties reached the agreement Lemming described, was it sufficiently definite to create a contract?

ARGUMENT FOR LEMMING: Both parties understood exactly what the deal was. Mr. Lemming was temporarily unable to hold property in his name. But he was willing to help run the business, and Morgan eagerly exploited his friend's expertise. For five years Mr. Lemming did everything he could to make the business a success, and that is what has caused the problem: The business succeeded. Now the trial court says that Morgan can keep 100% of the profits. In other words, even if both parties *intended* to split the money, and Mr. Lemming *did his share* to create the profit, he earns nothing because of some technical contract rule. Surely, the law is not designed to encourage such deceit.

ARGUMENT FOR MORGAN: The rule requiring definite terms is more than a technicality. To be enforceable, a promise must be sufficiently definite that a court can determine who was supposed to do what. Even if Mr. Morgan made the agreement Lemming describes, it is so vague that no court could possibly enforce it. Exactly when was Mr. Morgan supposed to transfer the property to Lemming? How was the division to be made? Would one person receive certain properties? Which ones? If there were profits, how were they to be calculated, and when paid? Mr. Morgan was the only one who borrowed money, bought the land, paid all interest and taxes, and assumed full liability. Why should Lemming be entitled to half, when Mr. Morgan bore all the risk?

ETHICS: Why did Lemming want all property listed in Morgan's name? Analyze the agreement by using the ethics checklist from Chapter 2. Was the agreement legal? How would it look in the light of day? Generally, vague terms creep into negotiations unobserved, because the parties want to conclude the deal and get to work. What happens when ambiguity is deliberate? ▟

UCC AND OPEN TERMS

Throughout this unit, we witness how the Uniform Commercial Code makes the law of sales more flexible. There are several areas of contract law where imperfect negotiations may still create a binding agreement under the Code, even though the same negotiations under the common law would have yielded no contract. "Open terms" is one such area.

Yuma County Corp. produced natural gas. Yuma wanted a long-term contract to sell its gas so that it could be certain of recouping the expenses of exploration and drilling. Northwest Central Pipeline, which operated an interstate pipeline, also wanted a deal for 10 or more years so it could make its own distribution contracts, knowing it would have a steady supply of natural gas in a competitive market. But neither Yuma nor Northwest wanted to make a long-term price commitment, because over a period of years the price of natural gas could double—or crash. Each party wanted a binding agreement without a definitive price. If their negotiations had been governed by the common law, they would have run smack into the requirement of definiteness—no price, no contract. But because this was a sale of goods, it was governed by the UCC.

UCC §2-204(3): Even though one or more terms are left open, a contract for sale does not fail for indefiniteness if the parties have intended to make a contract and there is a reasonably certain basis for giving an appropriate remedy.

Yuma County and Northwest drafted a contract with alternative methods of determining the price. In the event that the price of natural gas was regulated by the Federal Energy Regulatory Commission (FERC), the price would be the highest allowed by the FERC. If the FERC deregulated the price (as it ultimately did), the contract price would be the average of the two highest prices paid by different gas producers in a specified geographic area. Under the UCC, this was an enforceable agreement.

If the contract lacks a method for determining missing terms, the Code itself contains gap-filler provisions, which are rules for supplying missing terms. Some of the most important gap-filler provisions of the Code are these:

- If the parties do not settle on a price, the Code establishes a **reasonable price.** This will usually be the market value or a price established by a neutral expert or agency (UCC §2-305).

- Delivery, time, and payment. The place of delivery is the seller's business. The time for shipping goods is usually a reasonable time, based on the normal trade practice. And payment is normally due when and where the buyer receives the goods (UCC §§2-308 through 2-310).

- Warranties. The Code includes a **warranty of merchantability,** which means that the goods must be of at least average, passable quality in the trade. Ten thousand pairs of sneakers must be such that a typical shoe store would accept them (UCC §§2-312 through 2-317).

TERMINATION OF OFFERS

As we have seen, the great power that an offeree has is to form a contract by accepting an offer. But this power is lost when the offer is revoked or rejected.

Termination by Revocation

In general, the offeror may revoke the offer any time before it has been accepted. **Revocation is effective when the offeree receives it.** Douglas County, Oregon sought bids on a construction job involving large quantities of rock. The Taggart Company discovered a local source of supply with cheap rock and put in a bid. Shortly thereafter, Taggart discovered that the local rock was no longer for sale. Taggart hand-delivered a written revocation of its bid. Later, the county opened all bids and accepted Taggart's low offer—but lost the case. By delivering its revocation, Taggart terminated the county's power to accept.

Termination by Rejection

If an offeree rejects an offer, the rejection terminates the offer. Suppose a major accounting firm telephones you and offers a job, starting at $80,000. You respond, "Nah. I'm gonna work on my surfing for a year or two." The next day you come to your senses and write the firm, accepting its offer. No contract. Your rejection terminated the offer and ended your power to accept.

Counteroffer. Frederick faxes Kim, offering to sell a 50% interest in the Fab Hotel in New York for only $335 million. Kim faxes back, offering to pay $285 million. Moments later, Kim's business partner convinces her that Frederick's offer was a bargain, and she faxes an acceptance of his $335 million offer. Does Kim have a binding deal? No. **A counteroffer is a rejection.** When Kim offered $285 million, she rejected Frederick's offer. Her original fax created a new offer, for $285 million, which Frederick never accepted. The parties have no contract at any price.

Acceptance

As we have seen, when there is a valid offer outstanding, the offeree can create a contract by accepting. **The offeree must say or do something to accept.** Silence, though golden, is not acceptance. Marge telephones Vick and leaves a message on his answering machine: "I'll pay $75 for your law textbook from last semester. I'm desperate to get a copy, so I will assume you agree unless I hear from you by 6 o'clock tonight." Marge hears nothing by the deadline and assumes she has a deal. She is mistaken. Vick neither said nor did anything to indicate that he accepted.

MIRROR IMAGE RULE

If only he had known! A splendid university, an excellent position as department chair—gone. And all because of the mirror image rule.

Ohio State University wrote to Philip Foster offering him an appointment as a professor and chair of the art history department. His position was to begin July 1, and he had until June 2 to accept the job. On June 2, Foster telephoned the Dean and left a message accepting the position, effective July 15. Later, Foster thought better of it and wrote the university, accepting the school's starting date of July 1. Too late! Professor Foster never did occupy that chair at Ohio State. The court held that since his acceptance varied the starting date, it was a counteroffer. And a counteroffer, as we know, is a rejection.

Was it sensible to deny the professor a job over a mere 14-day difference? Sensible or not, that is the law. **The common-law mirror image rule requires that acceptance be on precisely the same terms as the offer.** If the acceptance contains terms that add or contradict the offer, even in minor ways, courts generally consider it a counteroffer. The rule worked reasonably well 100 years ago, when parties would write an original contract and exchange it, penciling in any changes. But now that businesses use standardized forms to purchase most goods and services, the rule creates enormous difficulties. Sellers use forms they have prepared, with all conditions stated to their advantage, and buyers employ their own forms, with terms they prefer. The forms are exchanged in the mail or electronically, with neither side clearly agreeing to the other party's terms.

The problem is known as the "battle of forms." Once again, the UCC has entered the fray, attempting to provide flexibility and common sense for those contracts involving the sale of goods.

UCC AND THE BATTLE OF FORMS

UCC §2-207 dramatically modifies the mirror image rule for the sale of goods. Under this provision, an acceptance that adds additional or different terms will often create a contract. The full rule is beyond the scope of this chapter, but it is important to understand its basic features because most goods are bought and sold with standardized forms. One thing we see is that the Code gives different treatment to merchants than consumers. **A merchant is anyone who routinely deals in the goods involved,** such as a wholesaler or retailer.

Additional or Different Terms

One basic principle of the common law of contracts remains unchanged: The key to creation of a contract is a valid offer that the offeree intends to accept. If there is no intent to accept, there is no contract. The big change brought about by UCC §2-207 is this: **For the sale of goods, the mirror image rule does not apply. The acceptance may include new terms.**

Additional terms are those that bring up new issues not contained in the original offer. Additional terms in the acceptance are considered proposals to add to the contract. Assuming that both parties are merchants, the additional terms will generally become part of the contract unless the other side rejects them.

Example A. Wholesaler writes to Manufacturer, offering to buy "10,000 wheelbarrows at $50 per unit. Payable on delivery, 30 days from today's date." Manufacturer writes back, "We accept your offer of 10,000 wheelbarrows at $50 per unit, payable on delivery. Interest at normal trade rates for unpaid balances." Manufacturer clearly intends to form a contract. The company has added a new term about interest rates, but there is still a valid agreement. If Wholesaler is late in paying, it owes interest at the current rate.

Example B. Same offer and acceptance. This time, though, when Wholesaler receives the form mentioning interest rates, it rejects the added term. Wholesaler sends an e-mail, saying, "We do not accept that interest rate." There is no contract.

Different terms are those that contradict terms in the offer. For example, if the seller's form clearly states that no warranty is included, and the buyer's form insists that the seller warrants all goods for three years, the acceptance contains *different* terms. An acceptance may contain different terms and still create a contract. **The majority of states hold that different (contradictory) terms cancel each other out.** Neither term is included in the contract. Instead, the neutral terms from the Code itself are "read into" the contract. These are the gap-filler terms discussed above. Suppose the forms have contradictory clauses about where the goods will be delivered. The different terms cancel each other out, and the gap-filler clause from the UCC is substituted. The place of delivery is the seller's business.

CYBERLAW

Clickwraps and Shrinkwraps. You want to purchase Attila brand software and download it to your computer. You type in your credit card number and other information, agreeing to pay $99. Attila also requires that you "read and agree to" all of the company's terms. You click "I agree," without having read one word of the terms. Three frustrating weeks later, tired of trying to operate defective Attilaware, you demand a refund and threaten to sue. The company breezily replies that you are barred from suing, because the terms you agreed to included an arbitration clause. To resolve any disputes, you must travel to Attila's hometown, halfway across the nation, use an arbitrator that the company chooses, pay one half the arbitrator's fee, and also pay Attila's legal bills if you should lose. The agreement makes it financially impossible for you to get your money back. Is that contract enforceable?

You have entered into a "clickwrap" agreement. Similar agreements, called "shrinkwraps," are packaged inside many electronic products. A shrinkwrap notice might require that before inserting a purchased CD into your computer, you must read and agree to all terms in the brochure. Clickwraps and shrinkwraps often include arbitration clauses. They frequently limit the seller's liability if anything goes wrong, saying that the manufacturer's maximum responsibility is to refund the purchase price (even if the software destroys your hard drive).

Most of the courts that have analyzed these issues have ruled that clickwrap and shrinkwrap agreements are indeed binding, even against consumers. Some of the judges have relied on §2-207 to reach that conclusion, while others have used different UCC provisions. The courts have emphasized that sellers are entitled to offer a product on any terms they wish, and that shrinkwrap and clickwrap are the most efficient methods of including complicated terms in a small space. At least one court has refused to enforce such contracts against a consumer, stating that the buyer never understood or agreed to the shrinkwrapped terms. However, the trend is toward enforcement of these agreements. Think before you click! ◗

COMMUNICATION OF ACCEPTANCE

The offeree must communicate his acceptance for it to be effective. Generally acceptance may be made in person or by mail, telephone, e-mail, or fax. If Masako e-mails Eric an offer to sell 20,000 pairs of jeans for $20 each, he may mail, fax, or e-mail his acceptance. However, if Masako's offer demands one method of acceptance (such as in writing, by mail) then the acceptance must comply.

Acceptance is generally effective upon dispatch, meaning the moment it is out of the offeree's control. Eric prints a copy of the offer that Masako e-mailed. He writes "I accept" on the document, signs it, and mails it back to Masako. The moment he places the envelope in the mailbox, he has accepted. Suppose he mails his acceptance at 2:05 p.m. and then, at 2:15 p.m., Masako telephones to revoke her offer. Result? A binding contract, created the moment the envelope fell into the mailbox.

Chapter Conclusion

The law of offer and acceptance can be complex. Yet for all its fault, the law is not the principal source of dispute between parties unhappy with negotiations. Most litigation concerning offer and acceptance comes from lack of clarity on the part of the people negotiating. Letters of intent are often an effort to "have it both ways," that is, to ensure the other side's commitment without accepting a corresponding obligation. Similarly, the "battle of the forms" is caused by corporate officers seeking to make a deal and hurry things forward without settling details. These, and the many other examples discussed, are all understandable given the speed and fluidity of the real world of business. But the executive who insists on clarity is likelier in the long run to spend more time doing business and less time in court.

Chapter Review

1. The parties can form a contract only if they have a meeting of the minds, which requires that they understand each other and intend to reach an agreement.

2. An offer is an act or statement that proposes definite terms and permits the other party to create a contract by accepting those terms.

3. Invitations to bargain and advertisements are generally not offers. A letter of intent may or may not be an offer, depending upon the exact language and whether it indicates that the parties have reached an agreement.

4. The terms of the offer must be definite, although under the UCC the parties may create a contract that has open terms.

5. An offer may be terminated by revocation or rejection.

6. The offeree must say or do something to accept. Silence is not acceptance.

7. The common-law mirror image rule requires acceptance on precisely the same terms as the offer. Under the UCC, an offeree may often create a contract even when the acceptance includes terms that are additional to or different from those in the offer.

8. Clickwrap and shrinkwrap agreements are generally enforceable.

9. If the offer does not specify a type of acceptance, the offeree may accept in any reasonable method.

PRACTICE TEST

Matching Questions

Match the following terms with their definitions:

___ **A.** Mirror image rule.

___ **B.** Letter of intent.

___ **C.** Gap-filler.

___ **D.** Counteroffer.

___ **E.** Clickwrap.

1. A communication between negotiating parties that summarizes their progress and may imply a binding agreement.

2. An agreement made online by a consumer who may not understand its terms.

3. One method of rejecting an offer.

4. A common law principle requiring the acceptance to be on exactly the terms of the offer.

5. Terms supplied by the UCC for use in sale-of-goods contracts.

True/False Questions

Circle true or false:

1. T F Shrinkwraps are typically enforceable even if the buyer does not bother to read them.

2. T F An acceptance must be made in the same manner as the offer, that is, in writing, by phone, etc.

3. T F If an offer demands a reply within a stated period, the absence of a reply indicates acceptance.

4. T F An offer may generally be revoked at any time before it is accepted.

5. T F Without a meeting of the minds there cannot be a contract.

Multiple-Choice Questions

6. Alejandro sees an ad in the newspaper, with a beautiful sweater pictured: "Versace sweaters, normally $600, today only: $300." He phones the store and says that he wants two sweaters, a black one and a gray one. When he arrives at the store, the sweaters are sold out. He sues. Alejandro will

(a) Win, because the store never revoked its offer.

(b) Win, because he accepted within a reasonable time.

(c) Win, because there was a meeting of the minds.

(d) Lose, because he needed to accept in person.

(e) Lose, because the store never made an offer.

7. On Monday night, Louise is talking on her cell phone with Bill. "I'm desperate for a manager in my store," says Louise. "I'll pay you $45,000 per year, if you can start tomorrow morning. What do you say?"

"It's a deal," says Bill. "I can start tomorrow at 8 a.m. I'll take $45,000 and I also want 10% of any profits you make above last year's." Just then Bill loses his cell phone signal. The next morning he shows up at the store, but Louise refuses to hire him. Bill sues. Bill will

(a) Win, because there was a valid offer and acceptance.

(b) Win, based on promissory estoppel.

(c) Lose, because he rejected the offer.

(d) Lose, because the agreement was not put in writing.

(e) Lose, because Louise revoked the offer.

8. Tanya is having lunch with three friends. "I am going to sell my Ferrari," she says. "I expect to get between $125,000 and $150,000." An hour later, Mike emails Tanya: "I agree to buy your Ferrari for $150,000." He promptly arrives at Tanya's house with a cashier's check for the full amount, but she refuses to sell. Mike sues. Mike will

(a) Win.

(b) Lose, because Tanya never made a definite offer.

(c) Lose, because he should have accepted in person.

(d) Lose, because Tanya revoked her offer.

(e) Lose, because Tanya owns the car.

9. Reggie is hiring an accountant for his firm. During any negotiations that take place

(a) The UCC governs.

(b) The Restatement of Contracts governs.

(c) The mirror image rule applies.

(d) A letter of intent is mandatory.

(e) Either party may accept while making a counteroffer.

10. A wholesaler sells a retailer 25 parrots. Both sides use preprinted forms. The wholesaler's form says, "No warranty of any kind." The retailer's form says, "All birds fully warranted." Result?

(a) There is no contract.

(b) There is a contract with no warranty.

(c) There is a contract with full warranty.

(d) There is a contract and the birds must be of average quality in the trade.

(e) There is a contract and the parties must re-negotiate the warranty issue.

Short-Answer Questions

11. Arnold owned a Pontiac dealership and wanted to expand by obtaining a Buick outlet. He spoke with Patricia Roberts and other Buick executives on several occasions. He now claims that those discussions resulted in an oral contract that requires Buick to grant him a franchise, but the company disagrees. His strongest evidence of a contract is the fact that Roberts gave him forms on which to order Buicks. Roberts answered that it was her standard practice to give such forms to prospective dealers, so that if the franchise were approved, car orders could be processed quickly. Is there a contract?

12. The Tufte family leased a 260-acre farm from the Travelers Insurance Co. Toward the end of the lease, Travelers mailed the Tuftes an option to renew the lease. The option arrived at the Tuftes' house on March 30, and gave them until April 14 to accept. On April 13, the Tuftes signed and mailed their acceptance, which Travelers received on April 19. Travelers claimed there was no lease and attempted to evict the Tuftes from the farm. May they stay?

13. Northrop is a huge defense firm, and Litronic manufactures electronic components such as printed wire boards. Northrop requested Litronic to submit an offer on certain printed boards. Litronic sent its offer form, stating a price and including its preprinted warranty clause, which limited its liability to 90 days. Northrop orally accepted the offer, then sent its own purchase order form, which contained a warranty clause holding the seller liable with no time limit. Six months after the goods were delivered, Northrop discovered they were defective. Northrop sued, but Litronic claimed it had no liability. Was there a contract? If not, why not? If there was a contract, what were its warranty terms?

14. The Dukes leased land from Lillian Whatley. Toward the end of their lease, they sent Ms. Whatley a new

contract, renewing the lease for three years and giving themselves the option to buy the land at any time during the lease for $50,000. Ms. Whatley crossed out the clause giving them an option to buy. She added a sentence at the bottom, saying, "Should I, Lillian Whatley, decide to sell at end [sic] of three years, I will give the Dukes the first chance to buy." Then she signed the lease, which the Dukes accepted in the changed form. They continued to pay the rent until Ms. Whatley sold the land to another couple for $35,000. The Dukes sued. Are the Dukes entitled to the land at $50,000? At $35,000?

15. Academy Chicago Publishers (Academy) approached the widow of author John Cheever about printing some of his unpublished stories. She signed a contract, which stated:

"The Author will deliver to the Publisher on a mutually agreeable date one copy of the manuscript of the Work as finally arranged by the editor and satisfactory to the Publisher in form and content . . . .

"Within a reasonable time and a mutually agreeable date after delivery of the final revised manuscript, the Publisher will publish the Work at its own expense, in such style and manner and at such price as it deems best, and will keep the Work in print as long as it deems it expedient."

Within a year, Academy had located and delivered to Mrs. Cheever more than 60 unpublished stories. But she refused to go ahead with the project. Academy sued for the right to publish the book. The trial court ruled that the agreement was valid; the appeals court affirmed; and the case went to the Illinois Supreme Court. Was Academy's offer valid, and was the contract enforceable?

16. ROLE REVERSAL: Write a multiple-choice question focusing on UCC 2-207.

Internet Research Problem

Search the Internet for an auction with a ring selling for over $500. Is the site reliable? Who is actually selling the item? If you were to pay for the ring, would you receive it? If you were unhappy with your purchase, what remedies would you have? How can you ascertain the Web site's reliability?

You can find further practice problems in the Online Quiz at **http://beatty.westbuslaw.com** or in the Study Guide that accompanies this text.

Consideration

We have all made promises that we soon regretted. Mercifully, the law does not hold us accountable for everything we say. Yet some promises must be enforced. Which ones? The doctrine of consideration exists for one purpose: to distinguish promises that are binding from those that are not. Which of these four promises should a court enforce?

PROMISE ONE. In a delirious burst of affection, Professor Parsley says to a class of 50 students, "You've been a great class all semester. Next week I'm going to mail each of you a check for $1,000." But that night, the professor reconsiders and decides that her class is actually a patch full of cabbage heads whose idea of work is getting out of bed before noon. The following day, in class, Parsley announces that she has changed her mind. Mike, a student, sues for his $1,000. Should a court enforce the professor's promise?

PROMISE TWO. After class, Parsley promises a student, Daisy, a part-time job as a researcher for the rest of the semester. "You can start on Monday," she says, "and we'll work out pay and all the details then." "You mean I can give up my job at Burger Bucket?" asks an elated Daisy. "Sure thing," chirps the prof. But on Monday, Parsley informs Daisy that she has lost the funding for her research and can offer no job. Daisy is unable to get back her position at Burger Bucket and sues Parsley.

PROMISE THREE. Professor Parsley announces in class that she will be selling her skis at the end of the semester for $450. After class, Arabella says she would like to buy the skis but can only afford to pay $250. Parsley frowns and mutters, "They're worth a lot more than that." But Arabella looks so heartbroken that Parsley adds, "OK, what the heck. You can have them May 15." On that date Arabella shows up with the cash, but Parsley explains that another student offered her the full $450 for the skis and she sold them. Arabella purchases a nearly identical pair for $475 and sues Parsley.

PROMISE FOUR. The professor makes no promise at all. In fact, she announces in class that she will be unable to attend the next session because her favorite racehorse, Preexisting Duty, is running in the third race at the local track and she wants to be there. The students are crushed at the idea of missing a class. Sam wails, "Don't do this to us, Professor! I'll pay you 20 bucks if you'll be here to teach us." Other students chime in, and in a groundswell of tears and emotion, the students promise a total of $1,000 if Parsley will do her job. She agrees. When she arrives to teach the next class, 50 suddenly sullen students refuse to pay, and she sues. ∎

Society could enforce *all* promises in the interests of simple morality. Or should it enforce only those where the two sides engaged in some bargaining? Does it matter whether someone relied on a promise? Should the outcome be different if someone is promising to do what she is already obligated to do? These are important policy questions, affecting promises for a hundred dollars and deals for a billion; their answers lie in the law of consideration.

A Bargain and an Exchange

Consideration is a required element of any contract. **Consideration means that there must be bargaining that leads to an exchange between the parties.** "Bargaining" indicates that each side is obligating itself in some way to induce the other side to agree. Generally, a court will enforce one party's promise only if the other party did something or promised something in exchange. Without an exchange of mutual obligations, there is usually no deal.

How would the four Parsley examples in the introduction work out? In the first case, Mike loses. There is no consideration because the students neither bargained for Parsley's promise nor gave anything in exchange for it. In the second case, there is also no contract because none of the terms were definite. What were Daisy's hours, her salary, her duties? Daisy cannot sue on a contract, but she does have a claim of promissory estoppel, the one major exception to the rule of consideration. Because Daisy relied on Parsley's promise, a court may give her some compensation. In case three, Arabella should win. A bargain and an exchange occurred. The professor promised to sell the skis at a given price, then broke her promise. Arabella will probably recover $225, the difference between the contract price and what she was forced to pay for substitute skis. Finally, in the fourth case, the professor loses. Clearly, bargaining and an exchange took place, but the professor only promised to do something that she was already obligated to do. The law does not respect such a promise.

When trying to enforce a defendant's promise, the plaintiff must show that she did something or promised something in exchange for that promise. What sort of action or promise is good enough? It need not be much. **Consideration can be anything that someone might want to bargain for.** As we explore this idea, we need to use two more legal terms: promisor, meaning the person who makes the promise, and promisee, the person to whom the promise is made. In consideration cases, a court is typically trying to determine whether the promisee should be able to enforce the promise, and the decision will depend upon whether the promisee gave consideration.

The thing bargained for can be another promise or action. Usually, the thing bargained for is another promise. Suppose an employer says to a valued computer technician, "I will give you 1% of the company's stock, effective in 60 days, if you promise to be on-call 24/7." The technician agrees. Two months later, the employer is obligated to hand over the stock, regardless of whether he has taken advantage of his worker's availability. The pair had a typical bilateral contract. See Exhibit 11.1.

The thing bargained for can be an action, rather than a promise. Suppose Professor Parsley says to Wade, "If you plow my driveway by tonight, I'll pay you $150." Her offer seeks an action, not a promise. If Wade plows the driveway, his work is consideration and the parties have a binding contract.

The thing bargained for can be a benefit to the promisor or a detriment to the promisee. Suppose Professor Parsley says to the class, "You're all in terrible shape. I offer $25 to anyone who enters next week's marathon and finishes the race." "No way," shouts Joanne. "But I'll do it for $100." Parsley agrees and Joanne completes the entire race. Her running was of no particular benefit to Parsley, but it was clearly a detriment to Joanne, so Parsley owes her $100.

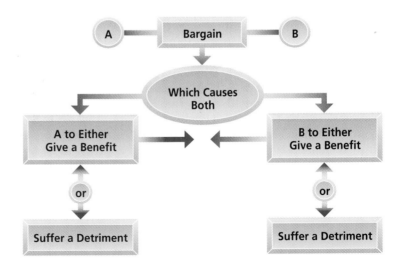

Exhibit 11.1
There is consideration to support a contract when A and B bargain, and their bargaining causes both A and B either to give a benefit to the other or to suffer a detriment.

The thing bargained for can be a promise to do something, but it can also be a promise to refrain from doing something. Leroy, who runs a beauty parlor, offers Chloe $75,000 not to open a beauty parlor within 30 miles. Chloe's promise not to compete is consideration.

The most famous of all consideration lawsuits began in 1869, when a well-meaning uncle made a promise to his nephew. Ever since *Hamer v. Sidway* appeared, generations of American law students have dutifully inhaled the facts and sworn by its wisdom; now you, too, may drink it in.

CASE SUMMARY

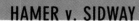 **HAMER v. SIDWAY**

124 N.Y. 538, 27 N.E. 256, 1891 N.Y. LEXIS 1396
New York Court of Appeals, 1891

FACTS: This is a story with two Stories. William Story wanted his nephew to grow up healthy and prosperous. In 1869, he promised the 15-year-old boy (also William Story) $5,000 if the lad would refrain from drinking liquor, using tobacco, swearing, and playing cards or billiards for money until his 21st birthday. (In that wild era—can you believe it?—the nephew had a legal right to do all those things.) The nephew agreed and, what is more, he kept his word. When he reached his 21st birthday, the nephew notified his uncle that he had honored the agreement. The uncle congratulated the young man and promised to give him the money, but said he would wait a few more years before handing over the cash, until the nephew was mature enough to handle such a large sum. The uncle died in 1887 without having paid, and his estate refused to honor the promise. Because the nephew had transferred his rights in the money, it was a man named Hamer who eventually sought to collect from the uncle's estate. The estate argued that since the nephew had given no consideration for the uncle's promise, there was no enforceable contract. The trial court found for the plaintiff, and the uncle's estate appealed.

ISSUE: Did the nephew give consideration for the uncle's promise?

DECISION: Yes, the nephew's conduct was valid consideration and the contract must be enforced.

REASONING: The uncle's estate argues that the conduct, far from harming the boy, actually aided him. Because it is wise to avoid tobacco, alcohol, and gambling, the nephew's decision to give up those vices could never be consideration. But the estate's argument is unpersuasive. What matters is simply this: Did one party do something or refrain from doing something at the request of the other party? If so, that conduct or forbearance is consideration.

Before making the agreement, the nephew had lawfully used alcohol and tobacco. When his uncle promised him $5,000, the nephew gave up the activities, restricting his freedom for several years. The contract must be enforced, whether or not anyone benefited. ◢

ADEQUACY OF CONSIDERATION

John Tuppela was a gold prospector in Alaska, but mental problems overwhelmed him and a court ordered him institutionalized in Oregon. Four years later, Tuppela emerged (with a court-appointed guardian supervising his assets) and learned two things: The guardian had sold the mine for pennies, and shortly thereafter, gold had been discovered on his property, which was now valued at over half a million dollars. Tuppela turned to his lifelong friend, Embola, saying, "If you will give me $50 so I can go to Alaska and get my property back, I will pay you $10,000 when I win the property." Embola advanced the $50.

Tuppela won back his mine, and asked the guardian to pay the full $10,000 to Embola, but the guardian refused, saying the $50 advance was too small to support such a huge payment. Embola sued.

Courts seldom inquire into the adequacy of consideration. The question of adequacy is for the parties as they bargain, not for the courts. Embola won, and the guardian paid him the full $10,000.

Mutuality of Obligations

Generally, both sides must be committed to the agreement to make it enforceable. Though courts will not inquire into the adequacy of consideration, they will insist that it be genuine. In some cases a party appears to make a commitment but actually does not. The result: no contract. Here we examine the major issues concerning mutuality.

ILLUSORY PROMISE

Annabel calls Jim and says, "I'll sell you my bicycle for 325 bucks. Interested?" Jim says, "I'll look at it tonight in the bike rack. If I like what I see, I'll pay you three and a quarter in the morning." At sunrise, Jim shows up with the $325 but Annabel refuses to sell. Can Jim enforce their deal? No. He said he would buy the bicycle if he liked it, keeping for himself the power to get out of the agreement for any reason at all. He is not committing himself to do anything, and the law considers his promise illusory, that is, not really a promise at all. **An illusory promise is not consideration.** Because he has given no consideration, there is no contract and neither party can enforce the deal. Is the promise in the following case illusory?

YOU BE THE JUDGE

CULBERTSON v. BRODSKY

788 S.W.2d 156, 1990 Tex. App. LEXIS 1008
Texas Court of Appeals, 1990

FACTS: Sam Culbertson had some Texas real estate to sell. He and Frederick Brodsky signed an option contract. Brodsky was to deliver a check for $5,000, representing "earnest money," to a bank. The bank would hold the check in escrow for 60 days. During that period, the bank would not cash it. Brodsky could inspect the property and perform engineering studies to determine whether the real estate could be used for his purposes. If he decided that the land was of no use to him, he could terminate the agreement and demand return of his earnest money. Ultimately, Brodsky decided that he did want to buy the land, but Culbertson refused to sell, claiming that Brodsky gave no consideration to support their contract. The trial court gave judgment for Brodsky, ordering Culbertson to convey the land. Culbertson appealed.

YOU BE THE JUDGE: **Did Brodsky give valid consideration that makes Culbertson's promise enforceable?**

ARGUMENT FOR CULBERTSON: Your honors, Mr. Brodsky made a very sly promise, since it was in fact no promise at all. Brodsky insisted on keeping the right to terminate this phony agreement at any time, for any reason. Mr. Culbertson was expected to leave the property off the market for 60 valuable days while Brodsky took his own sweet time to inspect the land. Please note that he didn't even lose the use of the $5,000. The bank was not permitted to cash the check until Brodsky made up his mind. Brodsky had no obligation at all, and thus never formed a contract.

ARGUMENT FOR BRODSKY: Your honors, it is rather disingenuous of Mr. Culbertson to pose as an injured party here. He is, in fact, a sophisticated property owner. He voluntarily entered into a contract with Mr. Brodsky for one reason: It was in his own interest. He concluded that the best way to "land" Mr. Brodsky was first to "hook" him with an option contract. He wanted Mr. Brodsky to show serious interest, and demanded earnest money. He got it. He insisted that Mr. Brodsky's check be held in escrow. He got it. Culbertson hoped that Mr. Brodsky would perform the necessary tests and conclude he wanted to buy it. And that is precisely what happened. This is a binding deal. ▌

SALES LAW: REQUIREMENTS AND OUTPUT CONTRACTS

You decide to open a "novelty T-shirt" business. You will buy plain white T-shirts from a wholesaler and then arrange for them to be printed with funny pictures and quotes. Your single biggest expense will be the wholesale cost of the T-shirts. How many will you need? You have no idea whether sales will soar or slide. Your solution may be a requirements contract.

In a requirements contract, the buyer agrees to purchase 100% of her goods from one seller. The seller agrees to sell the buyer whatever quantity she reasonably needs. The quantity is not stated in the contract, though it may be estimated, based on previous years or best calculations.

The common law regarded requirements contracts as void because the buyer could purchase a vast quantity or none at all. She was making no commitment, and hence, giving no consideration. Common-law courts refused to enforce requirements contracts, as well as their counterpart, output contracts. **In an output contract, the seller guarantees to sell 100% of its output to one buyer, and the buyer agrees to accept the entire quantity.** For example, a timber company might agree to sell all of its wood products to a lumber wholesaler. The common law frowned because now it was the seller who was making no real commitment.

The problem with the common-law rule was that many merchants valued these contracts. From the buyer's viewpoint, a requirements contract provides flexibility. The buyer can adjust purchases based on consumer demands. For a seller, the requirements agreement will ensure him at least this one outlet and will prevent competitors from selling to this buyer. Output contracts have similar value.

The UCC responded in a forthright fashion: **Section §2-306 expressly allows output and requirements contracts in the sale of goods.** However, the Code places one limitation on how much the buyer may demand (or the seller may offer):

> *"A term which measures the quantity by the output of the seller or the requirements of the buyer means such actual output or requirements as may occur in good faith . . ."*

The "good faith" phrase is critical. A buyer must make its requirement demands in good faith, based on the expectations the parties had when they signed the deal. A seller has the same obligation in an output contract.

PAST CONSIDERATION

Past consideration is generally no consideration. If one party makes a promise based on what the other party has already done, there is no exchange, and there will usually be no enforceable contract. It all goes back to our basic definition of consideration, which requires bargaining and an exchange of obligations.

CASE SUMMARY

DEMENTAS v. ESTATE OF TALLAS

95 Utah Adv. Rep. 28, 764 P.2d 628, 1988 Utah App. LEXIS 174
Utah Court of Appeals, 1988

FACTS: Jack Tallas came to the United States from Greece in 1914. He lived in Salt Lake City for nearly 70 years, achieving great success in insurance and real estate. When he died, he left a large estate. During the last 14 years of his life, Tallas was a close friend of Peter Dementas, who helped him with numerous personal and business chores. Two months before his death, Tallas met with Dementas and dictated a memorandum to him, in Greek, stating:

> *"PETER K. DEMENTAS, is my best friend I have in this country and since he came to the United States he treats me like a father and I think of him as my own son. He takes me in his car grocery shopping. He drives me to the doctor and also takes me every week to Bingham to pick up my mail, collect the rents and manage my properties. For all the services Peter has given me all these years, I owe to him the amount of $50,000 (Fifty Thousand Dollars.) I will shortly change my will to include him as my heir."*

Tallas signed the memorandum, but he did not in fact alter his will to include Dementas. The estate refused to pay, and Dementas sued. The trial was entertaining, thanks to Judge Dee, whose remarks included: "It's hearsay, I agree, but its damn good hearsay, and I want to hear it." Urging a lawyer to hurry up, the judge snapped, "Go on to your next

question. This witness—who is supposed to be one witness for 15 minutes—is now into the second day, and we've still got the same witness . . . At the rate we're going, I will have long retired and been happily fishing in Wyoming." Finally hearing something worthwhile from the witness, he interrupted, "Wait a minute. Wait. Wait. Wait. Now, the fact finder has finally got a fact. He said, 'I did it a lot of times.' I've identified a fact in a day and a half. Let's go to the next witness and see if we can find another one in this case."

Unfortunately for Dementas, when the testimony ground to a halt, Judge Dee ruled that there was no consideration to support Tallas's promise. Dementas appealed.

ISSUE: Was there consideration to make Tallas's promise enforceable?

DECISION: There was no consideration to support the promise. Affirmed.

REASONING: Consideration refers to a legal detriment that has been bargained for and exchanged for a promise. Any detriment, no matter how economically inadequate, will support a promise. The trial judge correctly stated: "If Tallas thought it was worth 50,000 bucks to get one ride to Bingham, that's Tallas's decision. The only thing you can't do is take it with you."

On the other hand, services performed *before* the promise is made, with no intention of inducing that promise, are not consideration. This is so because no bargaining has taken place. No one has said if you will do this for me, I will do that for you. Dementas gave no consideration for Tallas's statement, so the promise may not be enforced. ◢

PROMISSORY ESTOPPEL

You enjoy your job in human resources at a major company in Minnesota, although the pay is disappointing. Then an old college friend, Ralph, phones and invites you to come to his glitzy new company in Miami. "Come on down. The weather is better and you'll make much more than you're making now." You ask Ralph if he's serious and he replies, "Darn right I am. See you in two weeks." A fortnight later you quit your job and hustle to Miami, only to learn that Ralph has hired someone else.

Do you have an enforceable contract? No. You and Ralph never exchanged promises. You gave no consideration. Ralph never asked you for a promise and you have done nothing to benefit him. Furthermore, there are no definite terms, or indeed any agreement at all. Your only hope is *promissory estoppel.* This doctrine is a result of judicial activism and requires a plaintiff to prove that:

- The offeror made a promise knowing the offeree was likely to rely.

- The offeree did in fact rely; and

- The only way to avoid injustice is to enforce the promise.

A court *may* award you some damages because Ralph made a promise knowing you were likely to rely, and that you did in fact rely, with serious consequences to your career. Remember, though, that promissory estoppel is very much the exception to the rule. Courts use it only to avoid serious injustice, and it is never a remedy you can count on.

PREEXISTING DUTY

You are building your dream house, a shingle and glass mansion nestled on a hillside overlooking 300 acres of postcard-perfect wilderness. The builder has agreed to finish the project by September 1, and you have already sold your current house, scheduled the moving company, and committed yourself at a new job. But in July, the builder announces he cannot finish the job. You're furious. He replies that transporting material has proven more expensive than he anticipated, and also that his carpenters and electricians have raised their rates. He can complete the work only if you agree to pay an extra $90,000, on top of the $850,000 you have already promised. You cannot afford the extra money and bitterly resent paying. But you desperately need the house finished, so you agree. On September 1 you move in, and the builder arrives to collect the final $90,000. Must you pay?

No. The builder gave no consideration to support your promise to pay the extra $90,000. It is true that the builder promised to finish by September 1, and true that a promise to do something is normally valid consideration. But the builder was already obligated to finish on September 1. He has not taken on any increased burden. **A promise to do something the promisor is already obligated to do is not valid consideration.**

Of course, exceptions are the spice of law, and the preexisting obligation rule provides us with a rack full. Courts have created these exceptions because a rigid application of the rule may interfere with legitimate business goals.

Exception: Additional Work

When a promisor agrees to do something above and beyond what he is obligated to do, his promise is valid consideration. Thus, if the builder asked for $90,000 extra but agreed that he would landscape the two acres surrounding the house, his promise is consideration. If you agree to pay the extra $90,000, you have created a binding contract.

Exception: Unforeseen Circumstances

Hugo has a deal to repair major highways. Hugo hires Hal's Hauling to cart soil and debris. Hal's trucks begin work, but after crossing the work site several times they sink to their axles in sinister, sucking slime. Hal demands an additional 35% payment from Hugo to complete the job, pointing out that the surface was dry and cracked and that neither Hal nor Hugo was aware of the subsurface water. Hal howls that he must use different trucks with different tires and work more slowly to permit the soil to dry. Hugo hems and haws and finally agrees. But when the hauling is finished, Hugo refuses to pay the extra money. Is Hugo liable?

Yes. **When *unforeseeable changes* cause one party to make a promise regarding an unfinished project, that promise is often valid consideration.** Even though Hal is only promising to finish what he was already obligated to do, many courts will declare his promise to be valid consideration, because neither party knew of the subsoil mud. Hal was facing a situation quite different from what the parties anticipated. Hal has given consideration and Hugo is bound by *his* promise to pay extra money. Because this is an exception to the rule, some courts will refuse to apply it. Others will use this exception only when unforeseeable *physical* circumstances change the very nature of the work to be done, and dramatically increase one party's expenses. Recall from the earlier example that a contractor who merely discovers that some of his costs are higher than he expected is *not* entitled to extra payment for doing the work he promised to perform. Any party seeking additional money for work already due faces a tough battle.

 Unexpected problems such as subsoil water often arise in construction cases. A well-drafted contract will reduce the chances of a dispute. The parties should state in their agreement what conditions they expect to find, how they anticipate the work to proceed, and how they will compensate a party that encounters unexpected problems. For example, in the hauling contract, Hugo and Hal should have agreed on the following:

- A description of the surface and subsurface conditions that they anticipated.

- The type of equipment necessary to haul it and the approximate time needed to transport a given quantity, such as "two hours per hundred cubic yards."

- A provision for periodic review of the conditions actually encountered; and

- A summary of how they will adjust the price—if at all—in the event the hauler encounters unexpected hardship. ◾

Exception: Modification

If both parties agree that a modification is necessary, the surest way to accomplish that is to rescind the original contract and draft a new one. **To rescind means to cancel.** Thus, if neither party has completed its obligations, the agreement to rescind will terminate each party's rights and obligations under the old contract. This should be done in writing. Then the parties sign the new agreement. Most courts will enforce a rescission and modification unless it appears that one party unfairly coerced the other into the changes.

Once again the UCC has changed the common law, making it easier for merchants to modify agreements for the sale of goods. UCC §2-209 provides:

- An agreement modifying a contract for the sale of goods needs no consideration to be binding.

- A signed agreement which excludes modification or rescission except by a signed writing cannot be otherwise modified or rescinded.

Here is how these two provisions work together. Mike's Magic Mania agrees to deliver 500 rabbits and 500 top hats to State University, for the school's Sleight of Hand 101 course. The goods, including 100 cages and 1,000 pounds of rabbit food, are to arrive no later than September 1, in time for the new semester, with payment on delivery. By September 20 no rabbits have appeared, in or out of hats. The university buys similar products from another supply house at a 25% steeper price, and sues MMM for the difference. Mike claims that in early September the dean had orally agreed to permit delivery in October. The dean is on sabbatical in Tahiti and cannot be reached for comment. Is the alleged modification valid?

Under the common law, the modification would have been void, because MMM gave no consideration for the extended delivery date. However, this is a sale of goods, and under UCC §2-209, an oral modification may be valid even without consideration. Unfortunately for Mike, though, the original agreement included a clause forbidding oral modification. Any changes had to be in writing, signed by both parties. Mike never obtained such a document. Even if the dean did make the oral agreement, the university wins.

Settlement of Debts

You claim that your friend Felicity owes you $90,000, but she refuses to pay. Finally, when you are desperate, Felicity offers you a cashier's check for $60,000—provided you accept it as full settlement. To get your hands on some money, you agree and cash the check. The next day you sue Felicity for $30,000. Who wins? First, an ethical question.

ETHICS | Even if you think you have a chance of winning, is it right to accept the money as full settlement and then sue for the balance? From the Chapter 2 ethics checklist: Which values are in conflict? Which of these values are most important? Under what circumstances would you feel ethically correct in suing for the balance? When would you consider it wrong? ▪■

As to the legal outcome, it will depend principally upon one major issue: Was Felicity's debt liquidated or unliquidated?

LIQUIDATED DEBT

A **liquidated debt** is one in which there is no dispute about the amount owed. A loan is a typical example. If a bank lends you $10,000, and the note obligates you to repay that amount on June 1 of the following year, you clearly owe that sum. The debt is liquidated.

In cases of liquidated debt, if the creditor agrees to take less than the full amount as full payment, her agreement is not binding. The debtor has given no consideration to support the creditor's promise to accept a reduced payment, and therefore the creditor is not bound by her word. The reasoning is simply that the debtor is already obligated to pay the full amount, so no bargaining could reasonably cause the creditor to accept less. If Felicity's debt to you is liquidated, your agreement to accept $60,000 is not binding, and you will successfully sue for the balance.

UNLIQUIDATED DEBT: ACCORD AND SATISFACTION

A debt is **unliquidated** for either of two reasons: (1) the parties dispute whether any money is owed, or (2) the parties agree that some money is owed but dispute how much. When a debt is unliquidated, for either reason, the parties may enter into a binding agreement to settle for less than what the creditor demands.

Such a compromise will be enforced if:

- The debt is unliquidated and;

- The parties agree that the creditor will accept as full payment a sum less than she has claimed; and;

- The debtor pays the amount agreed upon.

This agreement is called an **accord and satisfaction.** The accord is the agreement to settle for less than the creditor claims. The satisfaction is the actual payment of that compromised sum. An accord and satisfaction is valid consideration to support the creditor's agreement to drop all claims. Each party is giving up something: the creditor gives up her full claim, and the debtor gives up his assertion that he owed little or nothing.

Chapter Conclusion

This old doctrine of consideration is simple to state but subtle to apply. The parties must bargain and enter into an exchange of promises or actions. If they do not, there is no consideration and the courts are unlikely to enforce any promise made. A variety of exceptions modify the law, but a party wishing to render its future more predictable—the purpose of a contract—will rely on a solid bargain and exchange.

Chapter Review

1. A promise is normally binding only if it is supported by consideration, which requires a bargaining and exchange between the parties.

2. The "thing" bargained for can be another promise or an action—virtually anything that a party might seek.

It can create a benefit to the promisor or a detriment to the promisee.

3. The courts will seldom inquire into the adequacy of consideration.

4. An illusory promise is not consideration.

5. Past consideration is generally no consideration.

6. Under the doctrine of promissory estoppel, reliance may permit a party to enforce a promise even when there is no consideration; but this is an exception and courts are reluctant to grant it.

7. Under the doctrine of preexisting duty, a promise to do something that the promisor is already legally obligated to perform is generally not consideration.

8. A liquidated debt is one in which there is no dispute about the amount owed.

9. For a liquidated debt, a creditor's promise to accept less than the full amount is not binding.

10. For an unliquidated debt, if the parties agree that the creditor will accept less than the full amount claimed and the debtor performs, there is an accord and satisfaction and the creditor may not claim any balance.

PRACTICE TEST

Matching Questions

Match the following terms with their definitions:

___ **A.** Liquidated debt

___ **B.** Consideration

___ **C.** Accord and satisfaction

___ **D.** Illusory promise

___ **E.** Preexisting duty

1. A promise made by one party which in reality obligates him to do nothing.

2. Something the promisor is already obligated to do.

3. A debt in which the amount is undisputed.

4. Payment of an agreed upon sum that is less than what the creditor originally claimed.

5. Bargaining that leads to an exchange between the parties.

True/False Questions

Circle true or false:

1. T   F   As long as one party gives consideration, there is a binding contract.

2. T   F   Valid consideration requires that each party suffer a detriment and give a benefit to the other.

3. T   F   An illusory promise is no consideration.

4. T   F   Promising to do something that one is already obligated to do is generally not consideration.

5. T   F   A creditor who agrees to take less than the full amount of a liquidated debt is not bound by her agreement.

Multiple-Choice Questions

6. Terrance admits that he owes Natasha money, but the two disagree over the size of his debt. This is

(a) An accord and satisfaction.

(b) A preexisting duty.

(c) A liquidated debt.

(d) An unliquidated debt.

(e) An unforeseen circumstance.

7. Rollo is building a swimming pool for Tatiana for $65,000. When the job is half finished, he tells her that he needs an extra $15,000 (a total of $80,000) to finish the pool. She agrees to pay, but when the pool is finished, Tatiana refuses to pay more than $65,000.

(a) Tatiana is obligated to pay the full $80,000.

(b) Tatiana is only obligated to pay $65,000.

(c) Tatiana is obligated to pay $80,000 if Rollo performed additional work.

(d) Tatiana is obligated to pay only if she had a preexisting duty to do so.

(e) Tatiana is not obligated to pay anything, because Rollo has committed fraud.

8. At Lorenza's 90th birthday party, she gives a speech to the 25 guests, praising her maid, Anna. "Anna has worked faithfully for me for 55 years. In appreciation, next week I am going to give Anna $100,000." Anna is ecstatic, but next week, Lorenza changes her mind. Is Anna entitled to the money?

   (a) Yes, provided the witnesses agree she made the promise.

   (b) Yes, provided Lorenza *intended* to make the gift.

   (c) Yes, because there is adequate consideration: Anna's work and Lorenza's promise.

   (d) Yes, provided Lorenza actually has the money.

   (e) No.

9. At 10 p.m., Professor suddenly realizes that he has forgotten to write the final exam, to be given at 8 a.m. He calls a former student and says, "I'm desperate. Help me out tonight. We'll work from 11 until 7 a.m. I'll pay you $100." Student, realizing professor is desperate, demands $1,000. "That's absurd," Professor responds—but ends up paying it because he has no choice. When the exam is written, Professor pays student $100. Student sues. Student

   (a) Wins $900.

   (b) Wins $900 provided the agreement was in writing.

   (c) Wins nothing because Student gave insufficient consideration.

   (d) Wins nothing because Professor gave insufficient consideration.

   (e) Wins nothing because he knowingly took advantage of the dire circumstances.

10. Two merchants have a two-year contract for the sale of 500,000 gallons of gasoline. One now wishes to modify the agreement. The original contract says nothing about modification. This contract

   (a) May not be modified.

   (b) May only be modified in writing.

   (c) May only be modified if the side requesting the change gives new consideration.

   (d) May be modified without new consideration.

   (e) May only be modified by accord and satisfaction.

Short-Answer Questions

11. An aunt saw her eight-year-old nephew enter the room, remarked what a nice boy he was, and said, "I would like to take care of him now." She promptly wrote a note, promising to pay the boy $3,000 upon her death. Her estate refused to pay. Is it obligated to do so?

12. Elio Pino took out a health insurance policy with the Union Bankers Insurance Company Eighteen months later he became ill, suffered medical expenses, and filed a claim for benefits. Union Bankers wrote Pino this letter:

    "Dear Mr. Pino:
    While servicing your claim, we learned that the medical facts on the application for this policy were not complete. If we had known the complete health history, we couldn't have issued this insurance. We must place you and ourselves back where we were when you applied for the policy and consider that the insurance was never in effect. (We are refunding the premiums you've paid us.)"

    Pino deposited the refund check, which was much less than his claim, and then sued for the full claim. Bankers Insurance argued that Pino had entered into an accord and satisfaction. The trial court gave summary judgment for the insurer, and Pino appealed. Did Pino enter into an accord and satisfaction by cashing the insurance company check?

13. Tindall operated a general contracting business in Montana. He and Konitz entered into negotiations for Konitz to buy the business. The parties realized that Konitz could succeed with the business only if Tindall gave support and assistance for a year or so after the purchase, especially by helping with the process of bidding for jobs and obtaining bonds to guarantee performance. Konitz bought the business and Tindall helped with the bidding and bonding. Two years later, Tindall presented Konitz with a contract for his services up to that point. Konitz did not want to sign but Tindall insisted. Konitz signed the agreement, which said: "Whereas Tindall sold his contracting business to Konitz and thereafter assisted Konitz in bidding and bonding without which Konitz would have been unable to operate, NOW THEREFORE Konitz agrees to pay Tindall $138,629." Konitz later refused to pay. Comment.

14. Eagle ran convenience stores. He entered into an agreement with Commercial Movie in which Commercial would provide Eagle with videotape cassettes for rental. Eagle would pay Commercial 50% of the rental revenues. If Eagle stopped using Commercial's service, Eagle could not use a competitor's services for 18 months. The agreement also provided: "Commercial shall not be liable for compensation or damages of any kind, whether on account of the loss by Eagle of profits, sales or expenditures, or on account of any other event or cause whatsoever." Eagle complied with the agreement for two years but then began using a competitor's service, and Commercial sued. Eagle claimed that the agreement was unenforceable for lack of consideration. Did Eagle's argument fly?

15. ETHICS: Melnick built a house for Gintzler, but the foundation was defective. Gintzler agreed to accept the foundation if Melnick guaranteed to make future repairs caused by the defects. Melnick agreed but later refused to make any repairs. Melnick argued that his promise to make future repairs was unsupported by consideration. Who will win the suit? Is either party acting unethically? Which one, and why?

16. ROLE REVERSAL: Write a short-answer question that focuses on one of these consideration issues: illusory promise, preexisting duty, or accord and satisfaction.

Internet Research Problem

Go to **http://www.law.cornell.edu/ucc/ucc.table.html** and click on Article 2. Find your way to §2-209, concerning contract modification. Write a clear, one- or two-paragraph explanation of subsections (1) and (2). Explain what these subsections mean (in English) and how they work together.

You can find further practice problems in the Online Quiz at **http://beatty.westbuslaw.com** or in the Study Guide that accompanies this text.

Legality

Soheil Sadri, a California resident, did some serious gambling at Caesar's Tahoe casino in Nevada. And lost. To keep gambling, he wrote checks to Caesar's and then signed two memoranda pledging to repay money advanced. After two days, with his losses totaling more than $22,000, he went home. Back in California, Sadri stopped payment on the checks and refused to pay any of the money he owed Caesar's. The casino sued. In defense, Sadri claimed that California law considered his agreements illegal and unenforceable. He was unquestionably correct about one thing: **A contract that is illegal is void and unenforceable.** ▪

In this chapter we examine a variety of contracts that may be void. Illegal agreements fall into two groups: those that violate a statute, and those that violate public policy.

Contracts That Violate a Statute

WAGERS

Gambling is big business. Almost all states now permit some form of wagering, from casinos to racetracks to lotteries, but some people disapprove. With citizens and states divided over the ethics of gambling, it is inevitable that we have conflicts such as the dispute between Sadri and Caesar's. The basic rule, however, is clear: **A gambling contract is illegal unless it is specifically authorized by state statute.**

In California, as in many states, gambling on credit is not allowed. In other words, it is illegal to lend money to help someone wager. A contract based on a gambling debt is unenforceable. But in Nevada, gambling on credit is legal, and debt memoranda such as Sadri's are enforceable contracts. Caesar's sued Sadri in California (where he lived). The result? Here is what the court said:

> *"There is a special reason for treating gambling on credit differently from gambling itself. Gambling debts are characteristic of pathological gambling, a mental disorder which is recognized by the American Psychiatric Association and whose prevalence is estimated at 2 to 3 percent of the adult population. Characteristic problems include extensive indebtedness and consequent default on debts and other financial responsibilities . . . and financially motivated illegal activities to pay for gambling. In our view, this is why enforcement of gambling debts has always been against public policy in California and should remain so, regardless of shifting public attitudes about gambling itself. If Californians want to play, so be it. But the law should not invite them to play themselves into debt."*[1]

Caesar's lost and Sadri kept his money. The dispute is a useful starting place from which to examine contract legality because it illustrates two important themes. First, morality is a significant part of contract legality. In refusing to enforce an obligation that Sadri undeniably had made, the California court relied on the human and social consequences of gambling and on the ethics of judicial enforcement of gambling debts. Second, "void" really means just that: A court will not intercede to assist either party to an illegal agreement, even if its refusal leaves one party obviously shortchanged.

INSURANCE

Another market in which "wagering" unexpectedly pops up is that of insurance. You may certainly insure your own life for any sum you choose. But may you insure someone else's life? **Anyone taking out a policy on the life of another must have an insurable interest in that person,** meaning some legitimate reason for

---

[1] *Metropolitan Creditors Service of Sacramento v. Sadri,* 15 Cal.App. 4th 1821, 19 Ca. Rptr. 2d 646 (Cal.Ct.App.1993).

fearing his death. A common reason for insuring someone else is that the other person owes you money. You want to be sure you are paid if something happens to her.

Juanita, a college student, has never met Joe Loony, a movie star, but she knows two things: He is a distinguished actor, and he is prone to reckless behavior. Juanita takes out a $300,000 life insurance policy on Joe's life, with herself as the beneficiary (the person who gets the money if the insured dies). Six months later, Joe is killed in a car accident. Dutiful Juanita is briefly sad, then sprints to the insurance office, where she collects . . . nothing. She had no insurable interest in Joe, and the law considers her policy nothing but an unenforceable gambling contract.

LICENSING STATUTES

You sue your next-door neighbor in small claims court, charging that he keeps a kangaroo in his backyard and that the beast has disrupted your family barbecues by leaping over the fence, demanding salad, and even punching your cousin in the ear. Your friend Foster, a graduate student from Melbourne, offers to help you prepare the case, and you agree to pay him 10% of anything you recover. Foster proves surprisingly adept at organizing documents and arguments. You win $1,200 and Foster demands $120. Must you pay? The answer is determined by the law of licensing.

States require licenses for anyone who practices a profession, such as law or medicine, works as a contractor or plumber, and for many other kinds of work. These licenses are required in order to protect the public. **When a licensing requirement is designed to protect the public, any contract made by an unlicensed worker is unenforceable.** Foster cannot enforce his contract for $120.

States use other licenses simply to raise money. For example, most states require a license to open certain kinds of retail stores. This requirement does not protect the public, because the state will not investigate the store owner the way it will examine a prospective lawyer or electrician. The state is simply raising revenue. **When a licensing requirement is designed merely to raise revenue, a contract made by an unlicensed person is generally enforceable.**

Many cases, such as the following one, involve contractors seeking to recover money for work they did without a license.

CASE SUMMARY

CEVERN, INC. v. FERBISH

666 A.2d 17, 1995 D.C. App. LEXIS 183
District of Columbia Court of Appeals, 1995

FACTS: Cevern, Inc. was a small contractor. The company was bonded and insured, as local law required, but it did not have a license to do home improvement work. Cevern applied for such a license, and this is what then happened:

- August 24: The District of Columbia regulatory agency certified that Cevern met all of the

requirements for a license (but it did not yet grant the license).

- August 27: Cevern's agents met with Robert Ferbish and Viola Stanton, and the parties signed a contract for Cevern to do extensive work on the Ferbish-Stanton home (to re-Ferbish it).

- August 31: The owners made an advance payment of $7,000 for the work. Cevern immediately began work on the project, digging a ditch and perhaps erecting a wall.

- September 5: Cevern paid its licensing fee and received the home improvement license.

Ferbish and Stanton later paid an additional $7,000 for Cevern's work but claimed that it was defective. When the owners refused to make a final payment of $10,295, the company sued. Ferbish counterclaimed for the $14,000 already paid, alleging that he and Stanton had spent an additional $43,000 to repair poor-quality work.

The trial court gave summary judgment for Ferbish and Stanton, ruling that Cevern's contract was void and unenforceable because the company had been unlicensed when the parties made the agreement. The judge ordered restitution (repayment) of the $14,000 the owners had paid. Cevern appealed.

ISSUE: Was the contract void because Cevern was unlicensed when the parties reached agreement?

ARGUMENT FOR CEVERN: We concede that unlicensed contractors generally may not enforce contracts. That rule makes sense, to discourage unqualified companies from doing work that might endanger the public. This is no such case. The District's regulatory agency had already declared that Cevern met all licensing requirements. Cevern had only to pay the fee and collect its license. The company promptly did this and had the license in hand when it performed the bulk of the work.

It is the homeowners who seek to pull a fast one: They wish to take advantage of a technical licensing rule to obtain first-rate work for free. Unfair! Even if the court refuses to enforce the contract, we urge alternatively that it permit Cevern to collect quasi-contract damages. The owners have benefited and know that Cevern expected payment.

ARGUMENT FOR THE OWNERS: An unlicensed contractor may never enforce contracts. This old rule is designed to protect the public from shoddy work, and it should be enforced for two reasons. First, a contractor may easily comply. All the company needs to do is demonstrate its competence, fill out certain forms, and pay a fee. Second, to permit this builder to recover for unlicensed work would encourage other unqualified contractors to try the same ruse: begin the work with glib assurances of a pending license, then hope for the best. The court should deny quasi-contract damages for the same reason: A void contract deserves no reward. ◢

USURY

Henry Paper and Anthony Pugliese were real estate developers. They bought a $1.7 million property in West Palm Beach, Florida, intending to erect an office building. They needed $1 million to start construction but were able to raise only $800,000. Walter Gross, another developer, agreed to lend them the final $200,000 for 18 months at 15% interest. Gross knew the partners were desperate for the money, so at the loan closing, he demanded 15% equity (ownership) in the partnership, in addition to the interest. Paper and Pugliese had no choice but to sign the agreement. The two partners never repaid the loan, and when Gross sued, the court ruled they need never pay a cent. It pays to understand usury.

Usury laws prohibit charging excess interest on loans. A lender who charges a usurious rate of interest may forfeit the illegal interest, or all interest, or, in some states, the entire loan. Florida permits interest rates of up to 18% on loans such as Gross's. A lender who charges more than 18% loses the right to collect any interest. A lender who exceeds 25% interest forfeits the entire debt. Where was the usury? Just here: When Gross insisted on a 15% share of the partnership, he was simply extracting additional interest and disguising it as partnership equity. The Paper-Pugliese partnership had equity assets of $600,000. A 15% equity, plus interest payments of 15% over 18 months, was the equivalent of a per annum interest rate of

45%. Gross probably thought he had made a deal that was too good to be true. And in the state of Florida, it was. He lost the entire debt.

ETHICS | Is it fair for Paper and Pugliese to sign a deal and then walk away from it? Analyze the issue by using these items from the checklist in the ethics chapter: Who are the *stakeholders?* Has the process been *fair?* ∎

Contracts That Violate Public Policy

In the preceding section, we saw that courts refuse to enforce contracts that violate a statute. In this section we examine cases in which no statute applies but where a *public policy* prohibits certain contracts. In other words, we focus primarily on the common law.

RESTRAINT OF TRADE

Free trade is the basis of the American economy, and any bargain not to compete is suspect. The two most common settings for legitimate noncompetition agreements are the sale of a business and an employment relationship.

Sale of a Business

Kory has operated a real estate office, Hearth Attack, in a small city for 35 years, building an excellent reputation and many ties with the community. She offers to sell you the business and its goodwill for $300,000. But you need assurance that Kory will not take your money and promptly open a competing office across the street. With her reputation and connections, she would ruin your chances of success. You insist on a noncompete clause in the sale contract. In this clause, Kory promises that for one year she will not open a new real estate office or go to work for a competing company within a 10-mile radius of Hearth Attack. Suppose, six months after selling you the business, Kory goes to work for a competing realtor, two blocks away. You seek an injunction to prevent her from working. Who wins?

When a noncompete agreement relates to the sale of a business, it is enforceable if reasonable in time, geographic area, and scope of activity. In other words, a court will not enforce a noncompete agreement that lasts an unreasonably long time, covers an unfairly large area, or prohibits the seller of the business from doing a type of work that she never had done before. Measured by this test, Kory is almost certainly bound by her agreement.

If, on the other hand, the noncompetition agreement had prevented Kory from working anywhere within 200 miles of Hearth Attack, and she started working 50 miles away, a court would refuse to enforce the contract. The geographic restriction is unreasonable, since Kory never previously did business 50 miles distant.

Employment

When you sign an employment contract, the document may well contain a noncompete clause. Employers have legitimate worries that employees might go to a competitor and take with them trade secrets or other proprietary information. Some employers, though, attempt to place harsh restrictions on their employees, perhaps demanding a blanket agreement that the employee will never go to work for a competitor. Once again, courts look at the reasonableness of restrictions placed on an employee's future work. Because the agreement now involves the very livelihood of the worker, a court scrutinizes the agreement more closely.

A noncompete clause in an employment contract is generally enforceable only if it is essential to the employer, fair to the employee, and harmless to the general public. Judges invariably enforce these agreements to protect trade secrets and confidential information. They may protect customer lists that have been expensive to produce. Courts rarely restrain an employee simply because he wants to work for a competitor, and they disfavor agreements that last too long or apply in a very wide area. The following chart summarizes the factors that courts look at in all types of noncompetition agreements.

The Legality of Noncompetition Clauses ("Noncompetes")

Type of Noncompetition Agreement	When Enforceable	
Not ancillary to a sale of business or employment	Never	
Ancillary to a sale of business	If reasonable in time, geography, and scope of activity	
Ancillary to employment	Contract is *more* likely to be enforced when it involves: • Trade secrets or confidential information: these are almost always protected • Customer lists developed over extended period of time and carefully protected • Limited time and geographical scope • Vital to protect the employer's business	Contract is *less* likely to be enforced when it involves: • Employee who already had the skills when he arrived, or merely developed general skills on the job • Customer lists that can be derived from public sources • Excessive time or geographical scope • Unduly harsh on the employee or contrary to public interest

Suppose that Gina, an engineer, goes to work for Fission Chips, a silicon chip manufacturer that specializes in defense work. She signs a noncompete agreement promising never to work for a competitor. Over a period of three years, Gina learns some of Fission's proprietary methods of etching information onto the chips. She acquires a great deal of new expertise about chips generally. And she periodically deals with Fission Chips's customers, all of whom are well-known software and hardware manufacturers. Gina accepts an offer from WriteSmall, a competitor. Fission Chips races into court, seeking an injunction that would prevent Gina from (1) working for WriteSmall; (2) working for any other competitor; (3) revealing any of Fission's trade secrets; (4) using any of the general expertise she acquired at Fission Chips; and (5) contacting any of Fission's customers.

This injunction threatens Gina's career, and no court will grant such a broad order. The court will allow Gina to work for competitors, including WriteSmall. It will order her not to use or reveal any trade secrets belonging to Fission. She will, however, be permitted to use the general expertise she has acquired, and she may contact former customers, since anyone could get their names from the yellow pages.

More law in a minute, but first, how about something to eat?

CASE SUMMARY

LIAUTAUD v. LIAUTAUD

221 F.3d 981
United States Court of Appeals for the Seventh Circuit, 2000

FACTS: Jim Liautaud owned and operated a chain of gourmet submarine sandwich shops in Illinois called Jimmy John's, Inc. When his cousin, Michael, inquired about opening his own sandwich shop in Madison, Wisconsin, Jim agreed to provide his "secrets of success." Jim sent Michael this letter, outlining their agreement:

"I want to confirm at this time exactly what we agreed on so that it is clear and understood by both parties. The agreement:

1. Mike will open up a sub shop in Madison using Jimmy John's products and systems.

2. Mike can open up as many shops [as] he would like in Madison only.

3. If you want to expand the sub/club business beyond Madison you will do so using Jimmy John's sub shops as a partner or franchisee. This is subject to 100% agreement on both parties. If you don't use Jimmy John's Inc. you will not expand the sub/club business beyond Madison.

4. You will not disclose to anyone: recipes, products, or systems that are given to you. (Except your managers who run your store).

I believe thats [sic] what we agreed on. If I have made any misrepresentations of our agreement please correct them in the margin of this letter and return a copy to me. If I don't receive a copy I'll assume this letter to be the agreement."

Jim then helped Michael open the shop in Madison. A few years later, Michael opened a sandwich shop outside that city, in LaCrosse, Wisconsin. Jim sued to enforce their agreement. The district court found the agreement unreasonable and void, and Jim appealed.

ISSUE: Was the noncompetition agreement valid?

DECISION: The noncompetition agreement was void. Affirmed.

REASONING: For the contract to be valid, its terms may not restrict Michael more than necessary, and may not injure the public. Jim asserts that his trade secrets are the fundamental element of his success, and deserve protection. It does seem fair that he receive some compensation for sharing his methods. However, this agreement is far too broad to be enforced.

The noncompetition clause prevents Michael from expanding anywhere in the world outside of Madison. The prohibition lasts for the rest of his life, and applies even if Michael makes no use of Jim's secrets, even if he enters areas where Jim has no plans to do business. This is too harsh. The agreement permanently stifles Michael's development, and injures the public by limiting competition. Because the restrictions are unnecessary and oppressive, the agreement is void. ◢

EXCULPATORY CLAUSES

You decide to capitalize on your expert ability as a skier and open a ski school in Colorado, "Pike's Pique." But you realize that skiing sometimes causes injuries, so you require anyone signing up for lessons to sign this form:

I agree to hold Pike's Pique and its employees entirely harmless in the event that I am injured in any way or for any reason or cause, including but not limited to any acts, whether negligent or otherwise, of Pike's Pique or any employee or agent thereof.

The day your school opens, Sara Beth, an instructor, deliberately pushes Toby over a cliff because Toby criticized her color combinations. Eddie, a beginning student, "blows out" his knee attempting an advanced racing turn. And Maureen, another student, reaches the bottom of a steep run and slams into a snowmobile that Sara Beth parked there. Maureen, Eddie, and Toby's family all sue Pike's Pique. You defend based on the form you had them sign. Does it save the day?

The form on which you are relying is an **exculpatory clause,** that is, one that attempts to release you from liability in the event of injury to another party. Exculpatory clauses are common. Ski schools use them and so do parking lots, landlords, warehouses, and daycare centers. All manner of businesses hope to avoid large tort judgments by requiring their customers to give up any right to recover. Is such a clause valid? Sometimes. Courts frequently—but not always—ignore exculpatory clauses, finding that one party was forcing the other party to give up legal rights that no one should be forced to surrender.

An exculpatory clause is generally unenforceable when it attempts to exclude an intentional tort or gross negligence. When Sara Beth pushes Toby over a cliff, that is the intentional tort of battery. A court will not enforce the exculpatory clause. Sara Beth is clearly liable. As to the snowmobile at the bottom of the run, if a court determines that was gross negligence (carelessness far greater than ordinary negligence), then the exculpatory clause will again be ignored. If, however, it was ordinary negligence, then we must continue the analysis.

An exculpatory clause is generally unenforceable when the affected activity is in the public interest, such as medical care, public transportation, or some essential service. Suppose Eddie goes to a doctor for surgery on his damaged knee, and the doctor requires him to sign an exculpatory clause. The doctor negligently performs the surgery, accidentally leaving his cuff links in Eddie's left knee. The exculpatory clause will not protect the doctor. Medical care is an essential service, and the public cannot give up its right to demand reasonable work.

But what about Eddie's suit against Pike's Pique? Eddie claims that he should never have been allowed to attempt an advanced maneuver. His suit is for ordinary negligence, and the exculpatory clause probably *does* bar him from recovery. Skiing is a recreational activity. No one is obligated to do it, and there is no strong public interest in ensuring that we have access to ski slopes.

An exculpatory clause is generally unenforceable when the parties have greatly unequal bargaining power. When Maureen flies to Colorado, suppose that the airline requires her to sign a form contract with an exculpatory clause. Because the airline almost certainly has much greater bargaining power, it can afford to offer a "take-it-or-leave-it" contract. The bargaining power is so unequal, though, that the clause is probably unenforceable.

An exculpatory clause is generally unenforceable unless the clause is clearly written and readily visible. Thus, if Pike's Pique gave all ski students an eight-page contract, and the exculpatory clause was at the bottom of page seven in small print, the average customer would never notice it. The clause would be void.

Bailment Cases

Exculpatory clauses are very common in bailment cases. **Bailment means giving possession and control of personal property to another person.** The person giving up possession is the bailor, and the one accepting possession is the bailee. When you leave your laptop computer with a dealer to be repaired, you create a bailment. The same is true when you check your coat at a restaurant or lend your Matisse to a museum. Bailees often try to limit their liability for damage to property by using an exculpatory clause.

Judges are slightly more apt to enforce an exculpatory clause in a bailment case, because the harm is to property and not person. But courts will still look at many of the same criteria we have just examined to decide whether a bailment contract is enforceable. In particular, when the bailee is engaged in an important public service, a court is once again likely to ignore the exculpatory clause. The following contrasting cases illustrate this.

In *Weiss v. Freeman*,[2] Weiss stored personal goods in Freeman's self-storage facility. Freeman's contract included an exculpatory clause relieving it of any and all liability. Weiss's goods were damaged by mildew and she sued. The court held the exculpatory clause valid. The court considered self-storage to be a significant business, but not as vital as medical care or housing. It pointed out that a storage facility would not know what each customer stored and therefore could not anticipate the harm that might occur. Freedom of contract should prevail, the clause was enforceable, and Weiss got no money.

In *Gardner v. Downtown Porsche Audi*,[3] Gardner left his Porsche 911 at Downtown for repairs. He signed an exculpatory clause saying that Downtown was "Not Responsible for Loss or Damage to Cars or Articles Left in Cars in Case of Fire, Theft, or Any Other Cause Beyond Our Control." Due to Downtown's negligence, Gardner's Porsche was stolen. The court held the exculpatory clause void. It ruled that contemporary society is utterly dependent upon automobile transportation, and Downtown was therefore in a business of great public importance. No repair shop should be able to contract away liability, and Gardner won. (This case also illustrates that using 17 uppercase letters in one sentence does not guarantee legal victory.)

UNCONSCIONABLE CONTRACTS

Gail Waters was young, naive, and insecure. A serious injury when she was 12 years old left her with an annuity, that is, a guaranteed annual payment for many years. When Gail was 21, she became involved with Thomas Beauchemin, an ex-convict, who introduced her to drugs. Beauchemin suggested that Gail sell her annuity to some friends of his, and she agreed. Beauchemin arranged for a lawyer to draw up a contract, and Gail signed it. She received $50,000 for her annuity, which at that time had a cash value of $189,000 and was worth, over its remaining 25 years, $694,000. Gail later decided this was not a wise bargain. Was the contract enforceable? That depends on the law of unconscionability.

An unconscionable contract is one that a court refuses to enforce because of fundamental unfairness. Historically, a contract was considered unconscionable

---

[2] 1994 Tenn.App. LEXIS 393 (Tenn. Ct. App. 1993).
[3] 180 Cal. App. 3d, 713, 225 Cal. Rptr. 757 (Cal. Ct. App. 1986).

if it was "such as no man in his senses and not under delusion would make on the one hand, and as no honest and fair man would accept on the other." The two factors that most often led a court to find unconscionability were (1) oppression, meaning that one party used its superior power to force a contract on the weaker party; and (2) surprise, meaning that the weaker party did not fully understand the consequences of its agreement.

Gail Waters won her case. The Massachusetts high court ruled:

> "*Beauchemin introduced the plaintiff to drugs, exhausted her credit card accounts, unduly influenced her, suggested that the plaintiff sell her annuity contract, initiated the contract negotiations, and benefited from the contract between the plaintiff and the defendants. For payment of not more than $50,000 the defendants were to receive an asset that could be immediately exchanged for $189,000, or they could elect to hold it for its guaranteed term and receive $694,000. The defendants assumed no risk and the plaintiff gained no advantage. We are satisfied that the disparity of interests in this contract is so gross that the court cannot resist the inference that it was improperly obtained and is unconscionable.*"[4]

Adhesion Contracts

A related issue concerns **adhesion contracts, which are standard form contracts prepared by one party and given to the other on a "take-it-or-leave-it" basis.** We have all encountered them many times when purchasing goods or services. When a form contract is vigorously negotiated between equally powerful corporations, the resulting bargain is generally enforced. However, when the contract is simply presented to a consumer, who has no ability to bargain, it is an adhesion contract and subject to an unconscionability challenge.

CASE SUMMARY

WORLDWIDE INSURANCE v. KLOPP

603 A.2d 788, 1992 Del. LEXIS 13
Supreme Court of Delaware, 1992

FACTS: Ruth Klopp had auto insurance with Worldwide. She was injured in a serious accident that left her with permanent neck and back injuries. The other driver was uninsured, so Klopp filed a claim with Worldwide under her "uninsured motorist" coverage. Her policy required arbitration of such a claim, and the arbitrators awarded Klopp $90,000. But the policy also stated that if the arbitrators awarded more than the statutory minimum amount of insurance ($15,000), either side could appeal the award and request a full trial. Worldwide appealed and demanded a trial.

In the trial court, Klopp claimed that the appeal provision was unconscionable and void. The trial court agreed and entered judgment for the full $90,000. Worldwide appealed.

ISSUE: Is the provision that requires arbitration and then permits appeal by either party void as unconscionable?

---

[4] *Waters v. Min Ltd.*, 412 Mass. 64, 587 N.E.2d 231, 1992 Mass. LEXIS 66 (1992).

DECISION: The contract provision is unconscionable. Affirmed.

REASONING: Worldwide contends that the arbitration provision is clear and unambiguous, but Klopp argues that it is grossly unfair. This contract binds both parties to a low award, one that an insurance company would be unlikely to appeal anyway. Either party may appeal a high award, but common sense suggests that only the insurer would do so. The policy enables the insurer to avoid a high arbitration award that may have been perfectly fair. This "escape hatch" favors the insurance company. The provision is unconscionable and void. ◢

Chapter Conclusion

It is not enough to bargain effectively and obtain a contract that gives you exactly what you want. You must also be sure that the contract is legal. Accidentally forgetting to obtain a state license to perform a certain job could mean you will never be paid for it. Bargaining a contract with a noncompete or exculpatory clause that is too one-sided may lead a court to ignore it. Legality is many-faceted, sometimes subtle, and always important.

Chapter Review

Illegal contracts are void and unenforceable. Illegality most often arises in these settings:

1. *Wagering.* A purely speculative contract—whether for gambling or insurance—is likely to be unenforceable.

2. *Licensing.* When the licensing statute is designed to protect the public, a contract by an unlicensed plaintiff is generally unenforceable. When such a statute is designed merely to raise revenue, a contract by an unlicensed plaintiff is generally enforceable.

3. *Usury.* Excessive interest is generally unenforceable and may be fatal to the entire debt.

4. *Noncompete.* A noncompete clause in the sale of a business must be limited to a reasonable time, geographic area, and scope of activity. In an employment contract, such a clause is considered reasonable—and enforceable—only to protect trade secrets, confidential information, and customer lists.

5. *Exculpatory clauses.* These clauses are generally void if the activity involved is in the public interest, the parties are greatly unequal in bargaining power, or the clause is unclear. In other cases they are generally enforced.

6. *Unconscionability.* Oppression and surprise may create an unconscionable bargain. An adhesion contract is especially suspect when it is imposed by a corporation on a consumer.

PRACTICE TEST

Matching Questions

Match the following terms with their definitions:

___ **A.** Usury

___ **B.** Unconscionable

___ **C.** Exculpatory

1. A contract clause intended to relieve one party from potential tort liability.

2. A contract clause designed to prevent, among other things, an employee from working for a competitor.

___ **D.** Licensing statute

3. A contract provision that no one who understood it would sign.

___ **E.** Noncompete

4. Illegally high interest rates.

5. A law designed to protect the public from incompetent professionals and trades people.

True/False Questions

Circle true or false:

1. T F A merchant who fails to obtain a license to operate a retail store cannot enforce a commercial contract.

2. T F Noncompete clauses are suspect because they tend to restrain free trade.

3. T F An unconscionable contract clause is immoral but legal.

4. T F A court is unlikely to enforce an exculpatory clause included in a contract for surgery.

5. T F Giving possession and control of personal property is called personal domain.

Multiple-Choice Questions

6. Ernie attends a political rally where for the first time he meets Senator Smiles. Ernie thinks that Smiles looks unhealthy, and that same day purchases a $100,000 life insurance contract on Smiles, with himself as the beneficiary. A month later, Smiles dies of a heart attack. Ernie is entitled to

    (a) $33,333.

    (b) $50,000.

    (c) $66,666.

    (d) $100,000.

    (e) Nothing.

7. In which case is a court most likely to enforce an exculpatory clause?

    (a) Dentistry.

    (b) Hang gliding.

    (c) Parking lot.

    (d) Public transportation.

    (e) Accounting.

8. Molly is a graduate student in architecture. Her uncle, Shelby, asks her to design a lakefront cottage for him, and offers a fee of $20,000. Molly says, "I'd love to do it, but you have to understand I'm still just a student. I don't have a license." Shelby says, "I know that, but I've seen your work and you're far better than most of the professionals." Molly designs a splendid house, which is built to Shelby's satisfaction. He then refuses to pay and she sues. Molly wins

    (a) $10,000 because she is not licensed.

    (b) $20,000 because she did the work.

    (c) $20,000 because she told Shelby about her lack of license and he did not mind.

    (d) $20,000 because the work is finished and there is no risk of harm to anyone.

    (e) Nothing.

9. You drive up to a fancy restaurant and hand your car keys to the valet. You have created

    (a) An exculpatory clause.

    (b) A noncompete clause.

    (c) A bailment.

    (d) An illusory contract.

    (e) An adhesion contract.

10. One policy reason that courts dislike noncompete clauses is their desire to protect

    (a) Job mobility.

    (b) Employer satisfaction.

    (c) A valid contract.

    (d) Lower interest rates.

    (e) The public from unlicensed professionals.

Short-Answer Questions

11. For 20 years, Art's Flower Shop relied almost exclusively on advertising in the Yellow Pages to bring business to its shop in a small West Virginia town. One year the Yellow Pages printer accidentally omitted to print Art's ad, and Art's suffered an enormous drop in business. Art's sued for negligence and won a judgment of $50,000 from the jury, but the printing company appealed, claiming that under an exculpatory clause in the contract, the company could not be liable to Art's for more than the cost of the ad, about $910. Art's claimed that the exculpatory clause was unconscionable. Please rule.

12. Oasis Waterpark, located in Palm Springs, California, sought out Hydrotech Systems, Inc., a New York corporation, to design and construct a surfing pool. Hydrotech replied that it could design the pool and sell all the necessary equipment to Oasis, but could not build the pool because it was not licensed in California. Oasis insisted that Hydrotech do the construction work, because Hydrotech had unique expertise in these pools. Oasis promised to arrange for a licensed California contractor to "work with" Hydrotech on the construction; Oasis also assured Hydrotech that it would pay the full contract price of $850,000, regardless of any licensing issues. Hydrotech designed and installed the pool as ordered. But Oasis failed to make the final payment of $110,000. Hydrotech sued. Can Hydrotech sue for either breach of contract or fraud (trickery)?

13. Guyan Machinery, a West Virginia manufacturing corporation, hired Albert Voorhees as a salesman and required him to sign a contract stating that if he left Guyan he would not work for a competing corporation anywhere within 250 miles of West Virginia for a two-year period. Later, Voorhees left Guyan and began working at Polydeck Corp., another West Virginia manufacturer. The only product Polydeck made was urethane screens, which comprised half of 1% of Guyan's business. Is Guyan entitled to enforce its noncompete clause?

14. McElroy owned 104 acres worth about $230,000. He got into financial difficulties and approached Grisham, asking to borrow $100,000. Grisham refused, but ultimately the two reached this agreement: McElroy would sell Grisham his property for $80,000, and the contract would include a clause allowing McElroy to repurchase the land within two years for $120,000. McElroy later claimed the contract was void. Is he right?

15. ETHICS: Richard and Michelle Kommit traveled to New Jersey to have fun in the casinos. While in Atlantic City, they used their MasterCard to withdraw cash from an ATM conveniently located in the "pit," which is the gambling area of a casino. They ran up debts of $5,500 on the credit card and did not pay. The Connecticut National Bank sued for the money. What argument should the Kommits make? Which party, if any, has the moral high ground here? Should a casino offer ATM services in the gambling pit? If a credit card company allows customers to withdraw cash in a casino, is it encouraging them to lose money? Do the Kommits have any ethical right to use the ATM, attempt to win money by gambling, and then seek to avoid liability?

16. ROLE REVERSAL: Write one multiple-choice question with two noncompete clauses, one of which is valid and the other void.

Internet Research Problem

Go to **http://www.law.cornell.edu/topics/state_statutes.html#criminal_code** and choose any state, and then search for that state's law on Internet gambling. Is it legal in that state? Has the state attempted to regulate this activity in any way? Do you believe the state will succeed? Conduct the same search in a second state and compare the results of the two searches.

You can find further practice problems in the Online Quiz at **http://beatty.westbuslaw.com** or in the Study Guide that accompanies this text.

Capacity and Consent

For Kevin Green, it was love at first sight. She was sleek, as quick as a cat, and a beautiful deep blue. He paid $4,600 cash for the used Camaro. The car soon blew a gasket, and Kevin demanded his money back. But the Camaro came with no guarantee, and the dealer refused. Kevin repaired the car himself. Next, some unpleasantness on the highway left the car a worthless wreck. Kevin received the full value of the car from his insurance company. Then he sued the dealer, seeking a refund of his purchase price. The dealer pointed out that it was not responsible for the accident, and that the car had no warranty of any kind. Yet the trial court awarded Kevin the full $4,600.

Kevin Green was only 16 years old when he bought the car, and a minor, said the court, has the right to cancel any agreement he has made. We will see how the appellate court resolved the case, as we examine two related issues: capacity and consent.

Capacity

Capacity is the legal ability to enter into a contract. An adult of sound mind has the legal capacity to contract. Generally, any deal she enters into will be enforced if all elements we have seen—agreement, consideration, and so forth—are present. But two groups of people usually lack legal capacity: minors and those with a mental impairment.

MINORS

A minor is someone under the age of 18. Because a minor lacks legal capacity, she normally can create only a voidable contract. **A voidable contract may be canceled by the party who lacks capacity.** Notice that only the party lacking capacity may cancel the agreement. So a minor who enters into a contract generally may choose between enforcing the agreement or negating it. The other party, however, has no such right.

Disaffirmance

A minor who wishes to escape from a contract generally may **disaffirm** it; that is, he may notify the other party that he refuses to be bound by the agreement. He also may file a suit seeking to **rescind** the contract, that is, to have a court formally cancel it.

Kevin Green was 16 when he signed a contract with Star Chevrolet. Since he was a minor, the deal was voidable. When the Camaro blew a gasket and Kevin informed Star Chevrolet that he wanted his money back, he was disaffirming the contract. He happened to do it because the car suddenly seemed a poor buy, but notice that he could have disaffirmed for any reason at all, such as deciding that he no longer liked Camaros. When Kevin disaffirmed, he was entitled to his money back. If Star Chevrolet had understood the law of capacity, it would have towed the Camaro away and returned Kevin's $4,600. At least Star would have had a repairable automobile.

Restitution

A minor who disaffirms a contract must return the consideration he has received, to the extent he is able. Restoring the other party to its original position is called restitution. The consideration that Kevin Green received in the contract was, of course, the Camaro. If Star Chevrolet had delivered a check for $4,600, Kevin would have been obligated to return the car.

What happens if the minor is not able to return the consideration because he no longer has it or it has been destroyed? Most states hold that the minor is still entitled to his money back. Star Chevrolet hoped that Mississippi would prove to be an exception.

CASE SUMMARY

STAR CHEVROLET CO. v. GREEN

473 So. 2d 157, 1985 Miss. LEXIS 2141
Supreme Court of Mississippi, 1985

FACTS: The facts are summarized in the opening paragraph of this chapter.

ISSUE: Is Kevin Green entitled to disaffirm the contract with Star Chevrolet even though the Camaro has been destroyed?

DECISION: Green is entitled to disaffirm the contract. Affirmed.

REASONING: Sound public policy permits a minor to disaffirm a contract. The goal is to protect a young person from her own impetuous conduct and to discourage aggressive adults from taking advantage of youthful inexperience. The simple way for an adult to avoid the harsh consequences of this rule is to refrain from contracts with those under 18.

When a minor disaffirms an agreement, she must return any portion of the property still in her possession. However, the young person need not return or pay for anything she has sold, destroyed, or otherwise lost.

Kevin Green had the automobile when he notified Star Chevrolet that he was disaffirming the contract. If Star had offered Kevin the full purchase price, as the law required, the young man would have been obligated to return the vehicle. The car dealer failed to do that, though, and the auto was demolished. Kevin need not return the auto or pay for it.[1] ◢

As the Mississippi court tells us, the rule permitting a minor to disaffirm a contract is designed to discourage adults from making deals with innocent children. The rule is centuries old. But is this rule workable in our consumer society? There are entire industries devoted to (and dependent upon) minors. Think of children's films, and music, and sneakers, and toys. Does this rule imperil retailers? How should a retailer protect himself? An automobile dealer? ▪

Timing of Disaffirmance/Ratification

A minor may disaffirm a contract anytime before she reaches age 18. She also may disaffirm within a reasonable time after turning 18. Suppose that Betsy is 17 when she buys her stereo. Four months later she turns 18, and two months after that she disaffirms the contract. Her disaffirmance is effective. In most states, she gets 100% of her money back. In some cases, minors have been entitled to disaffirm a contract several years after turning 18.

Exception: Necessaries

There is one exception on which all states agree, and that is a contract for necessaries. Food, clothing, housing, and medical care are **necessaries.** On a contract for

---

[1] The court awarded Kevin $3,100, representing the $4,600 purchase price minus $1,500, which was the salvage value of the car when he delivered it to his insurance company. You may wonder why Kevin Green is permitted to keep the insurance money and his original purchase price, thus putting him in a better position than he was in before buying the Camaro. The reason is the collateral source rule, which states that a defendant (Star Chevrolet) that is found to owe the plaintiff (Green) money may not have its liability reduced because the plaintiff will be compensated by another source (the insurance company). The rule is routinely applied in tort cases. Many courts refuse to use it in contract cases, but the Mississippi court applied it, and as a result, Kevin was in the green.

necessaries, a minor must pay for the value of the benefit received. In other words, the minor may still disaffirm the contract and return whatever is unused. But he is liable to pay for whatever benefit he obtained from the goods while he had them. The Mississippi court followed the general rule and held that an automobile was not a necessary.

MENTALLY IMPAIRED PERSONS

A person suffers from a mental impairment if by reason of mental illness or defect he is unable to understand the nature and consequences of the transaction. The mental impairment can be insanity that has been formally declared by a court, or mental illness that has never been ruled on but is now evident. The impairment may also be due to other mental health problems, such as mental retardation or senility.

A party suffering a mental impairment generally creates only a voidable contract. The impaired person has the right to disaffirm the contract just as a minor does. But again, the contract is voidable, not void. The mentally impaired party generally has the right to full performance if she wishes.

The law presumes that an adult is mentally competent. As always, courts respect the freedom to contract. Anyone seeking to avoid a contract because of mental impairment has the burden of proving the infirmity, since "mental incompetence" could be a very handy way out of a deal gone sour. **A mentally infirm party who seeks to void a contract must make restitution.** If a party succeeds with a claim of mental impairment, the court will normally void the contract but will require the impaired party to give back whatever she got.

Intoxication

Similar rules apply in cases of drug or alcohol intoxication. When one party is so intoxicated that he cannot understand the nature and consequences of the transaction, the contract is voidable. Toby's father gives him a new Jaguar sports car for his birthday, and foolish Toby celebrates by getting drunk. Amy, realizing how intoxicated he is, induces Toby to promise in writing that he will sell his car to her the next day for $1,000. Toby may void the contract and keep his auto.

Reality of Consent

Smiley offers to sell you his house for $300,000, and you agree in writing to buy. After you move in, you discover that the house is sinking into the earth at the rate of 6 inches per week. In 12 months, your only access to the house will be through the chimney. You sue, asking to rescind. You argue that when you signed the contract you did not truly consent because you lacked essential information. In this section we look at claims parties make in an effort to rescind a contract based on lack of valid consent: (1) misrepresentation or fraud; (2) mistake; and (3) undue influence.

MISREPRESENTATION AND FRAUD

Misrepresentation occurs when a party to a contract says something that is factually wrong. "This house has no termites," says a homeowner to a prospective buyer. If the house is swarming with the nasty pests, the statement is a misrepresentation.

The misrepresentation might be innocent or fraudulent. If the owner believes the statement to be true and has a good reason for that belief, he has made an innocent misrepresentation. If the owner knows that it is false, the statement is **fraudulent misrepresentation.** To explain these concepts, we will assume that two people are discussing a possible deal. One is the "maker," that is, the person who makes the statement that is later disputed. The other is the "injured person," the one who eventually claims to have been injured by the statement. **In order to rescind the contract, the injured person must show that the maker's false statement was fraudulent or a material misrepresentation, and that she relied on it.**

Element One: False Statement of Fact

The injured party must show a false statement of fact. Notice that this does not mean the statement was a lie. If a homeowner says that the famous architect Stanford White designed his house, but Bozo Loco actually did the work, it is a false statement. The owner might have a good reason for the error. Perhaps a local history book identifies the house as a Stanford White. Or his words might be an intentional lie. In either case, it is a false statement of fact.

An opinion, though, is not a statement of fact. A realtor says, "I think land values around here will be going up 20% or 30% for the foreseeable future." That statement is pretty enticing to a buyer, but it is not a false statement of fact. The maker is clearly stating her own opinion, and the buyer who relies on it does so at his peril.

Puffery. **A statement is puffery when a reasonable person would realize that it is a sales pitch, representing the exaggerated opinion of the seller.** Puffery is not a statement of fact. Because puffery is not factual, it is never a basis for rescission.

Marie Rodio purchased auto insurance from Allstate and then, after she was involved in a serious accident, received from the company less money than she thought fair. She sued, arguing that the company had committed fraud by advertising that customers would be in "good hands." She lost when the state supreme court ruled that, even if she could prove the company did not treat her well, the ad was mere puffery and not fraud.

Element Two: Fraud or Materiality

This is the heart of the case. The injured party must demonstrate that the statement was fraudulent or material:

- The statement was *fraudulent* if the maker intended to induce the other party to contract, either knowing that her words were false or uncertain that they were true.

- The statement was *material* if the maker expected the other party to rely on her words in reaching an agreement.

Consider the examples in the following chart. In case 1, the homeowner tells a prospective buyer that the heating system works perfectly, when he knows that it barely functions, leaving some rooms suitable only for penguins. The words are fraudulent.

In case 2, the homeowner is not lying when he says his cliff house is built on solid bedrock, but he is making a statement without being certain of its truth. This is also fraud.

By contrast, in case 3 there is no fraud because the homeowner is acting in good faith. He says that the roof is six years old because half a dozen years ago the previous owner said it was new. In fact, the roof is 25 years old and will soon need replacement. The homeowner's statement is a *material misrepresentation* because it is incorrect and the owner expects the buyer to rely on it.

Finally, in case 4 the homeowner says that the swimming pool is 30 feet long because he measured it himself. But did the job incorrectly, and the pool is only 29 feet. This is another misrepresentation, but is it material? No. An error of a foot or so would not influence a reasonable purchaser, and this buyer has failed to prove her case.

The Difference between Fraud and Misrepresentation

Statement. In each case, the words are false.	Owner's Belief	Legal Result	Explanation
1. "The heating system is perfect."	Owner knows this is false.	Fraud.	Owner knew the statement was false and intended to induce the buyer to enter into a contract.
2. "The house is built on solid bedrock."	Owner has no idea what is under the surface.	Fraud.	Owner was not certain the statement was true and intended to induce the buyer to enter into a contract.
3. "The roof is only six years old."	Owner has a good reason to believe the statement is true.	Material misrepresentation.	Owner acted in good faith, but the statement is material because owner expects the buyer to rely on it.
4. "The pool is 30 feet long."	Owner has a good reason to believe the statement is true.	Not a material misrepresentation.	Although this is a misrepresentation, it is not material, since a reasonable buyer would not make a decision based on a one-foot error in the pool length.

Element Three: Justifiable Reliance

The injured party must also show that she reasonably relied on the false statement. Suppose the seller of a gas station lies through his teeth about the structural soundness of the building. The buyer believes what he hears but does not much care, because he plans to demolish the building and construct a daycare center. There was fraud but no reliance, and the buyer may not rescind.

Plaintiff's Remedy for Misrepresentation or Fraud

Both innocent and fraudulent misrepresentation permit the injured party to rescind the contract. In other words, the injured party who proves all three elements will get her money back. She will, of course, have to make restitution to the other party. If she bought land and now wants to rescind, she will get her money back but must return the property to the seller. She often has the option of simply suing for damages.

ETHICS

Lilly is a good person. She runs a nonprofit center in Los Angeles that teaches adoptive parents to care for troubled children. Yet major airlines believe that people such as Lilly routinely commit fraud. Here is why.

Lilly needs to fly to Chicago to attend a fundraising conference on Wednesday. She would like to travel on Tuesday and return two days later, but an economy-class ticket would cost her agency a crushing $1,650. So Lilly buys a pair of "back-to-back" tickets. The first is for a flight leaving Los Angeles on Tuesday, with a return date a week later. Because the travel includes a Saturday stayover, this ticket costs a mere $325. The second ticket, also for $325, allows travel leaving Chicago on Thursday and returning one week later. Lilly uses only the first half of each ticket. She flies to Chicago on Tuesday and returns to Los Angeles 48 hours later, having avoided a Saturday stayover while saving her agency $1,000. Clever? "No," respond the airlines, "fraud!"

What are the consequences of Lilly's behavior? What values are involved? ▪

Special Problem: Silence

We know that a party negotiating a contract may not misrepresent a material fact. What about silence? Suppose the seller knows the roof is in dreadful condition but the buyer never asks. Does the seller have an affirmative obligation to disclose what she knows?

A seller who knows something that the buyer does not know is often required to divulge it. The Restatement (Second) of Contracts offers guidance: **Nondisclosure of a fact is misrepresentation when disclosure is necessary to correct a** *previous assertion* **or a** *basic mistake*.

To Correct a Previous Assertion. During the course of negotiations, one party's perception of the facts may change. When an earlier statement later appears inaccurate, the change generally must be reported.

W. R. Grace & Company wanted to buy a natural-gas field in Mississippi. An engineer's report indicated large gas reserves. On the basis of the engineering report, the Continental Illinois National Bank committed to a $75 million nonrecourse production loan, meaning that Continental would be repaid only with revenues from the gas field. After Continental committed but before it had closed on the loan, Grace had an exploratory well drilled and struck it rich—with water. The land would never produce any gas. Without informing Continental of the news, Grace closed the $75 million loan. When Grace failed to repay, Continental sued and won. A party who learns new information indicating that a previous statement is inaccurate must disclose the bad news.

To Correct a Basic Mistake. When one party knows that the other is negotiating with a mistaken assumption about an important fact, the party who knows of the error must correct it. Jeffrey Stambovsky agreed to buy Helen Ackley's house in Nyack, New York for $650,000. Stambovsky signed a contract and made a $32,500 down payment. Before completing the deal, he learned that in several newspaper articles Ackley had publicized the house as being haunted. Ackley had also permitted the house to be featured in a walking tour of the neighborhood as "a riverfront Victorian (with ghost)." Stambovsky refused to go through with the deal and sued to rescind. He won. The court ruled that Ackley sold the house knowing Stambovsky was ignorant of the alleged ghosts. She also knew that a reasonable buyer might avoid a haunted house, fearing grisly events—or diminished resale value. Stambovsky could not have discovered the apparitions himself, and Ackley's failure to warn permitted him to rescind the deal.

A seller generally must report any latent defect he knows about that the buyer should not be expected to discover himself. The judge in the following case states the rule somewhat differently, but the outcome is the same.

CASE SUMMARY

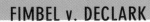

FIMBEL v. DECLARK

695 N.E.2d 125
Indiana Court of Appeals, 1998

FACTS: Ronald and Patricia Fimbel bought two lake-front lots on Lake Latonka in Indiana, intending to build a summer cottage. However, they discovered that the soil was not suitable for a septic system. They would have to hire an engineer at a substantial expense to determine if it was even possible to construct an alternative system. They decided to sell the land.

The Fimbels met with several interested buyers, including Thomas and Joan DeClark. The Fimbels said nothing about the septic problems. The DeClarks bought the property and, one week later, learned that the property was unbuildable. They sued, and the trial court granted them rescission. The Fimbels appealed.

ISSUE: Did the Fimbels have a duty to disclose the septic problems?

DECISION: Yes, the Fimbels had a duty to disclose. Affirmed.

REASONING: If a buyer questions the condition or quality of property, a seller is obligated to disclose what he knows. When asked if he had ever planned to construct a house on the lots, Fimbel replied that he had considered doing so but decided instead to build on land he owned in Minnesota, near a friend's residence. DeClark mentioned that he did in fact want to erect a house on the property. That conversation obligated Fimbel to inform DeClark about the septic problem.

Fimbel argues that he never misrepresented the soil's condition. Although that is technically accurate, Fimbel's statement as to why he preferred to build in Minnesota was only partially correct, at best. He concealed what he knew about the land he was selling. Creating a false impression by partially disclosing facts is misrepresentation. The Fimbels' silence, together with their misrepresentation, makes them liable for fraud. ◢

ETHICS

There are various disclosure rules that a state could adopt:

- Caveat emptor—let the buyer beware.

- Seller has a duty to disclose only if asked.

- Seller has a duty to disclose regardless of whether asked.

- Seller's only duty is to notify buyer of important considerations that buyer may wish to investigate (soil condition, building laws, problems with neighboring property, etc.).

Which rule do you prefer, and why? As you answer this question, apply these concepts from the Chapter 2 ethics checklist: What are the alternatives? What outcome does the Golden Rule require? ◼

MISTAKE

Most contract principles come from appellate courts, but in the area of "legal mistake" a cow wrote much of the law. The cow was Rose 2d of Aberlone, a gentle animal that lived in Michigan in 1886. Rose's owner, Hiram Walker & Sons, had bought her for $850. After a few years, the company concluded that Rose could have no calves. As a barren cow she was worth much less, so Walker contracted to sell her to T. C. Sherwood for $80. But when Sherwood came to collect Rose, the parties realized she was pregnant. Walker refused to part with the happy mother, and Sherwood sued. Walker defended, claiming that both parties had made a mistake and that the contract was voidable.

Mistake can occur in many ways. The first distinction is between bilateral and unilateral mistakes.

Bilateral Mistake

A **bilateral mistake** occurs when both parties negotiate based on the same factual error. Sherwood and Walker both thought Rose was barren, both negotiated accordingly, and both were wrong. The Michigan Supreme Court gave judgment for Walker, the seller, permitting him to rescind the contract because the parties were both wrong about the essence of what they were bargaining for.

If the parties contract based on an important factual error, the contract is voidable by the injured party. Sherwood and Walker were both wrong about Rose's reproductive ability, and the error was basic enough to cause a tenfold difference in price. Walker, the injured party, was entitled to rescind the contract. Note that the error must be *factual*. Suppose Walker sold Rose thinking that the price of beef was going to drop, when in fact the price rose 60% in five months. He made a mistake, but it was simply a business prediction that proved wrong. Walker would have no right to rescind.

Conscious Uncertainty. No rescission is permitted where one of the parties knows he is taking on a risk, that is, he realizes there is uncertainty about the quality of the thing being exchanged. Rufus offers 10 acres of mountainous land to Priscilla. "I can't promise you anything about this land," he says, "but they've found gold on every adjoining parcel." Priscilla, panting with gold lust, buys the land, digs long and hard, and discovers—mud. She may not rescind the contract because she understood the risk.

Unilateral Mistake

Sometimes only one party enters a contract under a mistaken assumption, a situation called **unilateral mistake.** In these cases it is more difficult for the injured party to rescind a contract. To rescind for unilateral mistake, a party must demonstrate that she entered the contract because of a basic factual error and that either (1) enforcing the contract would be unconscionable; or (2) the nonmistaken party knew of the error.

UNDUE INFLUENCE

She was single and pregnant. A shy young woman in a large city with no family nearby, she needed help and support. She went to the Methodist Mission Home of Texas, where she found room and board, support, and a lot of counseling. Her discussions with a minister and a private counselor stressed one point: that she should give up her baby for adoption. She signed the adoption papers, but days later she decided she wanted the baby after all. Was there any ground to rescind? She claimed undue influence, in other words, that the Mission Home so dominated her thinking that she never truly consented. Where one party has used undue influence, the contract is voidable at the option of the injured party. There are two elements to the plaintiff's case. **To prove undue influence, the injured party must demonstrate:**

- A relationship between the two parties either of trust or of domination, and

- Improper persuasion by the stronger party.

In other words, a party seeking to rescind based on undue influence must first show that the parties had some close bond, either because one would normally have trusted and relied on the other or because one was able to dominate the other. Second, the party seeking to rescind must show improper persuasion, which is an effort by the stronger party to coerce the weaker one into a decision that she otherwise would not have made.

Keeping those two factors in mind, what should be the outcome of the Methodist Mission case? The court held that the plaintiff had been young and extremely vulnerable during the emotional days following the birth of her child. The mission's counselor, to whom she turned for support, had spent day after day forcefully insisting that the young woman had no moral or legal right to keep her child. The harangue amounted to undue influence. The court voided the adoption agreement.[2]

Chapter Conclusion

An agreement between two parties may not be enough to make a contract enforceable. A minor or a mentally impaired person may generally disaffirm contracts. Even if both parties are adults of sound mind, courts will insist that consent be genuine. Misrepresentation, mistake, and undue influence all indicate that at least one party did not truly consent. As the law evolves, it imposes an increasingly greater burden of good-faith negotiating on the party in the stronger position. Do not bargain for a contract that is too good to be true.

Chapter Review

1. Capacity and consent are different contract issues that can lead to the same result: a voidable contract. A voidable agreement is one that can be canceled by a party who lacks legal capacity or who did not give true consent.

2. A minor (someone under the age of 18) generally may disaffirm any contract while she is still a minor or within a reasonable time after reaching age 18.

3. A minor who disaffirms must make restitution; that is, she must return to the other party whatever consideration she received, such as goods that she purchased. If she cannot make restitution because the goods are damaged or destroyed, in most states the minor is still entitled to disaffirm and receive her money.

---

[2] *Methodist Mission Home of Texas v. N A B*, 451 S.W.2nd 539, 1970 Tex. App. LEXIS 2055 (Tex. Civ. App. 1970).

4. A mentally impaired person may generally disaffirm a contract. In this case, though, he generally must make restitution.

5. Fraud and misrepresentation. Both fraud and material misrepresentation are grounds for disaffirming a contract. The injured party must prove:

    (a) A false statement of fact; and

    (b) Fraud *or* materiality; and

    (c) Justifiable reliance.

6. Silence amounts to misrepresentation when disclosure is necessary to correct a previous assertion or to correct a basic mistake.

7. *Mistake.* In a case of bilateral mistake, either party may rescind the contract. In a case of unilateral mistake, the injured party may rescind only upon a showing that enforcement would be unconscionable or that the other party knew of her mistake.

8. *Undue Influence.* Once again the injured party may rescind a contract, but only upon a showing of a special relationship and improper persuasion.

PRACTICE TEST

Matching Questions

Match the following terms with their definitions:

___ **A.** Undue influence

___ **B.** Disaffirm

___ **C.** Restitution

___ **D.** Fraud

___ **E.** Misrepresentation

1. Misstatement of fact.

2. The intention to deceive the other party.

3. One party to a contract notifies the other that he refuses to go through with the agreement.

4. Restoring the other party to its original position.

5. A dominant relationship together with improper persuasion.

True/False Questions

Circle true or false:

1. T   F   A minor may disaffirm a contract for any reason at all.

2. T   F   A mentally ill person may not disaffirm a contract, but may request restitution.

3. T   F   A contract may not be rescinded based on puffery.

4. T   F   A fraudulent statement permits rescission, regardless of whether there was reliance.

5. T   F   A seller of property must generally disclose latent defects that he knows about.

Multiple-Choice Questions

6. Sarah, age 17, uses $850 of her hard-earned, summer-job money to pay cash for a diamond pendant for the senior prom. She has a wonderful time at the dance but decides the pendant was an extravagance, returns it, and demands a refund. The store has a "no refund" policy that is clearly stated, on a sign on the wall. There was no defect in the pendent. The store refuses the refund. When Sarah sues, she will

    (a) Win $850.

    (b) Win $425.

    (c) Win, but only if she did not notice the "no refund" policy.

    (d) Win, but only if she did not think the "no refund" policy applied to her.

    (e) Lose.

7. Miles is selling his used Corvette for $35,000. "The brakes have less than 1,000 miles on them," he says, knowing that in fact the brakes are old and need replacement. Kody buys the car, takes it to his mechanic, and instructs the man to install new, larger racing brakes. When the mechanic informs Kody that the existing brakes had at least 40,000 miles on them, Kody sues Miles.

(a) Kody will win because Miles committed fraud.

(b) Kody will win because Miles committed misrepresentation.

(c) Kody will win because Miles expected him to rely on a false statement.

(d) Kody will win because Miles has shown deliberate bad faith.

(e) Kody will lose because he did not rely on the statement.

8. Tobias is selling a Surrealist painting. He tells Maud that the picture is by the famous French artist Magritte, although in fact Tobias has no idea whether that is true or not. Tobias's statement is

(a) Bilateral mistake.

(b) Unilateral mistake.

(c) Fraud.

(d) Misrepresentation.

(e) Legal, as long as he acted in good faith.

9. Beverly, a sales clerk, sells a $6,000 stereo to Samantha. The next day, Samantha's brother comes to the store and presents a doctor's letter indicating that Samantha is mentally disabled. The store refuses to refund the money.

(a) Samantha is not entitled to her money back unless the clerk suspected she had mental health problems.

(b) Samantha would only be entitled to her money if the clerk had seen the doctor's letter before selling the stereo.

(c) Samantha is entitled to her money back, but she must return the stereo.

(d) Samantha is entitled to her money back, and she does not have to return the stereo.

(e) Samantha is not entitled to her money back.

10. Marty, a college student, finds a pretty ring on the way to class. He shows it to Felicia. "Gorgeous," she says. "Is that a real emerald?" "I have no idea what it is," Marty answers truthfully. "I'll sell it to you for a hundred bucks." Felicia buys it. When she discovers that the colored stone is glass, she sues for her $100. Felicia

(a) Wins, based on fraud.

(b) Wins, based on misrepresentation.

(c) Wins, based on mutual mistake.

(d) Wins, based on unilateral mistake.

(e) Loses.

Short-Answer Questions

11. On television and in magazines, Maurine and Mamie Mason saw numerous advertisements for Chrysler Fifth Avenue automobiles. The ads described the car as "luxurious," "quality-engineered," and "reliable." When they went to inspect the car, the salesman told them the warranty was "the best . . . comparable to Cadillacs and Lincolns." After the Masons bought a Fifth Avenue, they began to have many problems with it. Even after numerous repairs, the car was unsatisfactory and required more work. The Masons sued, seeking to rescind the contract based on the ads and the dealer's statement. Will they win?

12. John Marshall and Kirsten Fletcher decided to live together. They leased an apartment, each agreeing to pay one half of the rent. When he signed the lease, Marshall was 17. Shortly after signing the lease, Marshall turned 18, and two weeks later he moved into the apartment. He paid his half of the rent for two months and then moved out because he and Fletcher were not getting along. Fletcher sued Marshall for one half of the monthly rent for the remainder of the lease. Who wins?

13. The McAllisters had several serious problems with their house, including leaks in the ceiling, a buckling wall, and dampness throughout. They repaired the buckling wall by installing I-beams to support it. They never resolved the leaks and the dampness. When they decided to sell the house, they said nothing to prospective buyers about the problems. They stated that the I-beam had been added for reinforcement.

The Silvas bought the house for $60,000. Soon afterwards, they began to have problems with leaks, mildew, and dampness. Are the Silvas entitled to any money damages? Why or why not?

14. ETHICS: Sixteen-year-old Travis Mitchell brought his 19-year-old Pontiac GTO into M&M Precision Body and Paint for body work and a paint job. M&M did the work and charged $1,900, which Travis paid. Travis later complained about the quality of the work and M&M did some touching up, but Travis was still dissatisfied. Travis demanded his $1,900 back, but M&M refused to give it back since all of the work was "in" the car and Travis could not return it to the shop. The state of Nebraska, where this occurred, follows the majority rule on this issue. Does Travis get his money? What is the common-law rule? Who ought to win? Is the common-law rule fair? What is the rationale for the rule?

15. Susan Gould was appointed to a three-year probationary position as a teacher at Sewanhaka High School. Normally, after three years, the school board either grants tenure or dismisses the teacher. The Sewanhaka school board notified Gould she would not be rehired. To keep the termination out of her file, Gould agreed to resign. In fact, because Gould had previously taught at a different New York school, state law required that she be given a tenure decision after only two years. If the board failed to do that, the teacher was automatically tenured. When she learned this, Gould sued to rescind her agreement to resign. Is Gould entitled to rescind the contract (i.e., her agreement to resign)?

16. ROLE REVERSAL: Write a short-essay question that includes one instance each of puffery, misrepresentation, and fraud.

Internet Research Problem

Visit **http://www.tobaccofreekids.org** and find the link that focuses on marketing to children. Use the ethics checklist from Chapter 9 to analyze the conduct described. Should society limit tobacco marketing? If not, why not? If so, should it be done by legislation, regulation, litigation, or some other means?

You can find further practice problems in the Online Quiz at **http://beatty.westbuslaw.com** or in the Study Guide that accompanies this text.

Written Contracts

Oliver and Perry were college roommates, two sophomores with contrasting personalities. They were sitting in the cafeteria with some friends. Oliver suggested that they buy a lottery ticket, as the prize for that week's drawing was $13 million. Perry muttered, "Nah. You never win if you buy just one ticket." Oliver bubbled up, "OK, we'll buy a ticket every week. We'll keep buying them from now until we graduate. This month, I'll buy the tickets. Next month, you will, and so on." Other students urged Perry to do it and, finally, grudgingly, he agreed. The two friends carefully reviewed their deal. Each party was providing consideration, namely, the responsibility for purchasing tickets during his month. The amount of each purchase was clearly defined at one dollar. They would start that week and continue until graduation day, two and a half years down the road. Finally, they would share equally any money won. As three witnesses looked on, they shook hands on the bargain. That month, Oliver bought a ticket every week, randomly choosing numbers, and won nothing. The next month, Perry bought a ticket with equally random numbers—and won $52 million. Perry moved out of their dorm room into a suite at the Ritz and refused to give Oliver one red cent. Oliver sued, seeking $26 million, and the return of an Eric Clapton compact disk that he had loaned Perry. If the former friends had understood the statute of frauds, they would never have slid into this mess.

The rule we examine in this chapter is not exactly news. The British Parliament passed the original statute of frauds in 1677. The purpose was to prevent lying (fraud) in contracts that historically were the most important. The law required that in six types of cases, a contract would be enforced only if it were in writing. Almost all states in this country later passed their own statutes making the same requirements. It is important to remember, as we examine the rules and exceptions, that Parliament and the state legislatures all wanted to provide a court with the best possible evidence of whether the parties intended to make a contract.

The statute of frauds: A plaintiff may not enforce any of the following agreements, unless the agreement, or some memorandum of it, is in writing and signed by the defendant. The agreements that must be in writing are those:

- For any interest in **land.**

- That cannot be performed within **one year.**

- To pay the **debt of another.**

- Made by an executor of an **estate.**

- Made in consideration of **marriage**; and

- For the sale of **goods worth $500 or more.**

Unenforceable

In other words, when two parties make an agreement covered by any one of these six topics, it must be in writing to be enforceable. Oliver and Perry agreed to share the cost—and proceeds—of lottery tickets for two and one half years. But a contract must be in writing if it cannot be performed within one year. The good news is, Oliver gets back his Eric Clapton disk. The bad news is he gets none of the lottery money. Perry the pessimist will walk away with all $52 million.

Contracts That Must Be in Writing

AGREEMENTS FOR AN INTEREST IN LAND

A contract for the sale of any interest in land must be in writing to be enforceable. Notice the phrase "interest in land." This means any legal right regarding land. A house on a lot is an interest in land. A mortgage, an easement, and a leased apartment are all interests in land.

Kary Presten and Ken Sailer were roommates in a rental apartment in New Jersey, with a view of the Manhattan skyline. The lease was in Sailer's name, but the two split all expenses. Then the building became a "cooperative," meaning that each tenant would have the option of buying the apartment. Sailer learned he could buy his unit for only $55,800 if he promptly paid a $1,000 fee to maintain his rights. He mentioned to Presten that he planned to buy the unit, and Presten asked if he could become half owner. Sailer agreed and borrowed the $1,000 from Presten to pay his initial fee. But as the time for closing on the purchase came nearer, Sailer realized that he could sell the apartment for a substantial profit. He placed an ad in a paper, and promptly received a firm offer for $125,000. Sailer then told Presten that their deal was off, and that he, Sailer, would be buying the unit alone. He did exactly that, and Presten filed suit. Regrettably, the outcome of Presten's suit was only too easy to predict.

A cooperative apartment is an interest in land, said the court. This agreement could be enforced only if put in writing and signed by Sailer. The parties had put nothing in writing, and therefore Presten was out of luck. He was entitled to his $1,000 back, but nothing more. The apartment belonged to Sailer, who could live in it or sell it for a large, quick profit.

Exception: Full Performance by the Seller

If the seller completely performs her side of a contract for an interest in land, a court is likely to enforce the agreement even if it was oral. Adam orally agrees to sell his condominium to Maggie for $150,000. Adam delivers the deed to Maggie and expects his money a week later, but Maggie fails to pay. Most courts will allow Adam to enforce the oral contract and collect the full purchase price from Maggie.

Exception: Part Performance by the Buyer

The buyer of land may be able to enforce an oral contract if she paid part of the purchase price and either entered upon the land *or* made improvements to it. Suppose that Eloise sues Grover to enforce an alleged oral contract to sell a lot in Happydale. She claims they struck a bargain in January. Grover defends based on the statute of frauds, saying that even if the two did reach an oral agreement, it is unenforceable. Eloise proves that she paid 10% of the purchase price and that in February she began excavating on the lot, to build a house, and that Grover knew of the work. Eloise has established part performance and will be allowed to enforce her contract.

This exception makes sense if we recall the purpose of the statute of frauds: to provide the best possible evidence of the parties' intentions. The fact that Grover permitted Eloise to enter upon the land and begin building on it is compelling evidence that the two parties had reached an agreement.

Exception: Promissory Estoppel

The other exception to the writing requirement is our old friend promissory estoppel. **If a promisor makes an oral promise that should reasonably cause the promisee to rely on it, and the promisee does rely, the promisee *may* be able to enforce the promise,** despite the statute of frauds, if that is the only way to avoid injustice. This exception potentially applies to any contract that must be written (not only to agreements concerning land).

Maureen Sullivan and James Rooney lived together for seven years, although they never married. They decided to buy a house. The parties agreed that they would be equal owners, but Rooney told Sullivan that in order to obtain Veterans Affairs financing he would have to be the sole owner on the deed. They each contributed to the purchase and maintenance of the house, and Rooney repeatedly told Sullivan that he would change the deed to joint ownership. He never did. When the couple split up, Sullivan sued, seeking a 50% interest in the house. She won. The agreement was for an interest in land and should have been in writing, said the court. But Rooney had clearly promised Sullivan that she would be a half owner, and she had relied by contributing to the purchase and maintenance. The statute of frauds was passed to prevent fraud, not to enable one person to mislead another and benefit at her expense.

In the following case, the plaintiffs make three valiant efforts to evade the piercing grasp of the statute of frauds.

CASE SUMMARY

HERSHON v. CANNON

1993 U.S. Dist. LEXIS 689
United States District Court, District of Maryland, 1993

FACTS: Mary Drysdale and her husband, Simon Hershon, wanted to buy Tulip Hill, an 18th-century mansion located on 54 acres in Anne Arundel County, Maryland. Drysdale and Hershon orally agreed with Cannon on a purchase price of $1.2 million. Cannon promised that while the lawyers were drafting the written purchase agreement, he would not seek offers from anyone else. Also, if he received an unsolicited offer, he agreed to give Drysdale and Hershon the opportunity to match it.

Drysdale and Hershon applied for a mortgage to buy Tulip Hill. They also met with the Maryland Historical Commission to discuss improvements to the property. Meanwhile, Cannon sold Tulip Hill to someone else. Drysdale and Hershon sued.

ISSUE: Did Drysdale and Hershon have an enforceable contract for Tulip Hill?

DECISION: No, the plaintiffs have no enforceable contract. Case dismissed.

REASONING: The buyers admit that they have no written contract but make three arguments for enforcement of an oral agreement. First, they claim that they are only trying to enforce Cannon's agreement not to sell elsewhere. Wrong. What they are really trying to do is enforce an oral contract for the sale of real estate, and they may not do it.

Next, they urge part performance. The buyers did meet with an historical commission, apply for mortgages, and liquidate assets. They might, however, have taken these steps in anticipation of an agreement; the actions are too ambiguous to demonstrate a contract.

Finally, the buyers suggest that promissory estoppel entitles them to complete the purchase. The problem is that even if they relied on Cannon's promises, the actions they took were very modest. They will suffer no great injustice if denied Tulip Hill. Their claims must be dismissed. ◢

AGREEMENTS THAT CANNOT BE PERFORMED WITHIN ONE YEAR

Contracts that cannot be performed within one year are unenforceable unless they are in writing. This one-year period begins on the date the parties make the agreement. The critical phrase here is "*cannot* be performed within one year." If a contract *could* be completed within one year, it need not be in writing. Betty gets a job at Burger Brain, throwing fries in oil. Her boss tells her she can have Fridays off for as long as she works there. That oral contract is enforceable, whether Betty stays one week or five years. It could have been performed within one year if, say, Betty quit the job after six months. Therefore it does not need to be in writing.

If the agreement will necessarily take longer than one year to finish, it must be in writing to be enforceable. If Betty is hired for three years as manager of Burger Brain, the agreement is unenforceable unless put in writing. She cannot perform three years of work in one year.

Type of Agreement	Enforceability
Cannot be performed within one year. *Example:* An offer of employment for three years.	Must be in writing to be enforceable.
Might be performed within one year, although could take many years to perform. *Example:* "As long as you work here at Burger Brain you may have Fridays off."	Enforceable whether it is oral or written, since the employee might quit working a month later.

PROMISE TO PAY THE DEBT OF ANOTHER

When one person agrees to pay the debt of another as a favor to that debtor, it is called a collateral promise, and it must be in writing to be enforceable. D. R. Kemp was a young entrepreneur who wanted to build housing in Tuscaloosa, Alabama. He needed $25,000 to complete a project he was working on, so he went to his old college professor, Jim Hanks, for help. Professor Hanks spoke with his good friend Travis Chandler, telling him that Kemp was highly responsible and would be certain to repay any money loaned. The professor assured Chandler that if for any reason Kemp did not repay the loan, he, Hanks, would pay in full. With that assurance, Chandler wrote out a check for $25,000, payable to Kemp, never having met the young man.

Kemp, of course, never repaid the loan. (Thank goodness he did not; this textbook has no use for people who do what they are supposed to.) Kemp exhausted the cash trying to sustain his business, which failed anyway, so he had nothing to give his creditor. Chandler approached Professor Hanks, who refused to pay (some professor!), and Chandler sued. The outcome was only too predictable. Chandler had nothing in writing, and that is exactly what he got from his lawsuit—nothing.

PROMISE MADE BY AN EXECUTOR OF AN ESTATE

This rule is merely a special application of the previous one, concerning the debt of another person. An executor is the person who is in charge of an estate after someone dies. The executor's job is to pay debts of the deceased, obtain money owed to him, and disburse the assets according to the will. In most cases, the executor will use only the estate's assets to pay those debts. The statute of frauds comes into play only when an executor promises to pay an estate's debts with her own funds. **An executor's promise to use her own funds to pay a debt of the deceased must be in writing to be enforceable.** Suppose Esmeralda dies penniless, owing Tina $35,000. Esmeralda's daughter, Sapphire, is the executor of her estate. Tina comes to Sapphire and demands her $35,000. Sapphire responds, "There is no money in mama's estate, but don't worry, I'll make it up to you with my own money." Sapphire's oral promise is unenforceable. Tina should get it in writing while Sapphire is feeling generous.

PROMISE MADE IN CONSIDERATION OF MARRIAGE

Barney is a multimillionaire with the integrity of a gangster and the charm of a tax collector. He proposes to Li-Tsing, who promptly rejects him. Barney then pleads that if Li-Tsing will be his bride, he will give her an island he owns off the coast of California. Li-Tsing begins to see his good qualities and accepts. After they are married, Barney refuses to deliver the deed. Li-Tsing will get nothing from a court either, since **a promise made in consideration of marriage must be in writing to be enforceable.**

What the Writing Must Contain

Each of the five types of contract described above must be in writing in order to be enforceable. What must the writing contain? It may be a carefully typed contract, using precise legal terminology, or an informal memorandum scrawled on the back of a paper napkin at a business lunch. The writing may consist of more than one document, written at different times, with each document making a piece of the puzzle. But there are some general requirements: **The contract or memorandum**

- **Must be signed by the defendant;** and

- **Must state with reasonable certainty the name of each party, the subject matter of the agreement, and all of the essential terms and promises.**

SIGNATURE

A statute of frauds typically states that the writing must be "signed by the party to be charged therewith," that is, the party who is resisting enforcement of the contract. Throughout this chapter we refer to that person as the defendant, since when these cases go to court, it is the defendant who is disputing the existence of a contract.

Judges define "signature" very broadly. Using a pen to write one's name, though sufficient, is not required. A secretary who stamps an executive's signature on a letter fulfills this requirement. Any other mark or logo placed on a document to indicate acceptance, even an "X," will likely satisfy the statute of frauds. Electronic commerce creates new methods of signing—and new controversies, discussed in the Cyberlaw feature later in the chapter.

REASONABLE CERTAINTY

Suppose Garfield and Hayes are having lunch, discussing the sale of Garfield's vacation condominium. They agree on a price and want to make some notation of the agreement even before their lawyers work out a detailed purchase and sales agreement. A perfectly adequate memorandum might say, "Garfield agrees to sell Hayes his condominium at 234 Baron Boulevard, apartment 18, for $350,000 cash, payable on June 18, 2005, and Hayes promises to pay the sum on that day." They should make two copies of their agreement and sign both. Notice that although Garfield's memo is short, it is certain and complete.

Sale of Goods

The UCC requires a writing for the sale of goods worth $500 or more. This is the sixth and final contract that must be in writing, although the Code's requirements are easier to meet than those of the common law.

UCC §2-201(1)—THE BASIC RULE

A contract for the sale of goods worth $500 or more is not enforceable unless there is some writing, signed by the defendant, indicating that the parties reached an agreement. The key difference between the common-law rule and the UCC rule is that the Code does not require all of the terms of the agreement to be in writing. The Code looks for something simpler: an indication that the parties reached an agreement. The two things that *are* essential are the signature of the defendant and the quantity of goods being sold. The quantity of goods is required because this is the one term for which there will be no objective evidence. Suppose a short memorandum between textile dealers indicates that Seller will sell to Buyer "grade AA 100% cotton, white athletic socks." If the writing does not state the price, the parties can testify at court about what the market price was at the time of the deal. But how many socks were to be delivered? One hundred pairs, or 100,000? The quantity must be written. (A basic sale-of-goods contract appears at **http://www.lectlaw.com/form.html**.)

Writing	Result
"Confirming phone conversation today, I will send you 1,000 reams of paper for laser printing, usual quality & price. [Signed,] Seller."	This memorandum satisfies UCC §2-201(1), and the contract may be enforced against the seller. The buyer may testify as to the "usual" quality and price between the two parties, and both sides may rely on normal trade usage.
"Confirming phone conversation today, I will send you best quality paper for laser printing, $3.25 per ream, delivery date next Thursday. [Signed,] Seller."	This memorandum is not enforceable because it states no quantity.

UCC §2-201(2)—THE MERCHANTS' EXCEPTION

When both parties are "merchants," that is, businesspeople who routinely deal in the goods being sold, the Code will accept an even more informal writing. **Within a reasonable time of making an oral contract, if one merchant sends a written confirmation to the other, and the confirmation is definite enough to bind the sender herself, then the merchant who receives the confirmation will also be bound by it unless he objects in writing within 10 days.**

Madge manufactures "beanies," that is, silly caps with plastic propellers on top. Rachel, a retailer, telephones her and they discuss the price of the beanies, shipping time, and other details. Madge then faxes Rachel a memo: "This confirms your order for 2,500 beanies at $12.25 per beanie. Colors: blue, green, black, orange, red. Delivery date: 10 days. [Signed] Madge." Rachel receives the fax and throws it in the wastebasket. She buys her beanies elsewhere and Madge sues. Rachel claims there is no written contract because she never signed anything. Madge wins, under UCC §2-201(2). Both parties were merchants, because they routinely dealt in these goods. Madge signed and sent a confirming memo that could have been used to hold her, Madge, to the deal. When Rachel received it, she was not free to disregard it. Obviously, the intelligent business practice would have been promptly to fax a reply saying, "I disagree. We do not have any deal for beanies." Since Rachel failed to respond within 10 days, Madge has an enforceable contract. In the following case, the merchant's confirmation contained a troubling ambiguity.

CASE SUMMARY

GPL TREATMENT, LTD. v. LOUISIANA-PACIFIC CORP.

323 Or. 116, 914 P.2d 682, 1996 Ore. LEXIS 34
Oregon Supreme Court, 1996

FACTS: GPL manufactures and sells cedar shakes, which are wooden shingles that many homeowners use for their roofs. Louisiana-Pacific (L-P) often purchased shakes from GPL. Executives of the two companies negotiated over the telephone and allegedly agreed that L-P would buy 88 truckloads of shakes. GPL sent an "Order Confirmation" form that included this language:

> "CONDITIONS OF SALES: GPL LTD.
> "All orders accepted subject to strikes, labor troubles, car shortages or other contingencies beyond our power to control. Any freight rate increases, sales, or use taxes is for buyers account.
> "SIGN CONFIRMATION COPY AND
> RETURN BY: _____ THANK YOU."

L-P neither signed nor rejected the form. The company accepted 13 truckloads of shakes but about that time the market price of shakes dropped, and L-P refused to accept any more. GPL sued. A jury awarded the company its lost profits, and the court of appeals affirmed. L-P appealed, arguing that, because GPL's form required the buyer to sign, no acceptance was valid without a signature.

ISSUE: Was GPL's form sufficient to satisfy the merchants' exception to the statute of frauds?

DECISION: Yes, GPL's form satisfied the merchant's exception. Affirmed.

REASONING: GPL's confirmation form clearly identified the parties, price, and quantity of goods. After GPL signed the document, L-P received it and did not object within 10 days. The order form would have been sufficient against GPL, the sender, if the price of shakes suddenly increased and the company tried to get out of the deal. Therefore, it would normally be valid against the buyer, too.

L-P argues that the phrase "sign confirmation copy and return" indicates that GPL did not expect either party to be bound by the agreement until L-P signed and returned a copy. That is not, however, what those words indicate. The phrase simply asks the recipient to acknowledge receipt of the form. This was nothing more than GPL's method of record keeping. The form satisfied the merchant exception of UCC §2-201 (2). ◢

AT RISK | Assume that you work for GPL. What change in the form should you make? ▪

CYBERLAW | **Electronic Contracts and Signatures.** E-commerce has grown at a dazzling rate, and U.S. enterprises buy and sell tens of billions of dollars worth of goods and services over the Internet. What happens to the writing requirement, though, when there is no paper? The present statute of frauds requires some sort of "signing" to ensure that the defendant committed to the deal. Today, an "electronic signature" could mean a name typed (or automatically included) at the bottom of an e-mail message, a retinal or vocal scan, or a name signed by electronic pen on a writing tablet, among others.

Are electronic signatures valid? Yes. State legislatures and Congress are struggling to craft a cohesive law, and the job is incomplete, but here are the rules so far:

- The **Uniform Electronic Transaction Act** (UETA). This proposed legislation was drafted by the National Conference of Commissioners on Uniform State Laws, who also draft the UCC. As this book goes to press, UETA is the law in about 48 states and territories, with more likely to adopt it soon. UETA declares that a contract or signature may not be denied enforceability simply because it is in electronic form. In other words, the normal rules of contract law apply, but one party may not avoid such a deal simply because it originated in cyberspace.

- The **Electronic Signatures in Global and National Commerce Act** (E-Sign). This federal statute, which applies in any state that has not adopted UETA, also states that contracts will not be denied enforcement simply because they are in electronic form, or signed electronically.

With cyberlaw in its early stages, how can an executive take advantage of the Internet's commercial opportunities while protecting his company against losses unique to the field?

First, acknowledge the risks, which include lost or intercepted communications, fraudulently altered documents, and difficulties authenticating the source of an offer or acceptance. Second, be cautious about "electronic signatures." Assume that any commitments you make electronically can be enforced against you. Paradoxically, if the contract is important, do not assume that the other party's promises, if made electronically, are enforceable unless your lawyer has given you assurance. ◾

Parol Evidence

Tyrone agrees to buy Martha's house for $800,000. The contract obligates Tyrone to make a 10% down payment immediately and pay the remaining $720,000 in 45 days. As the two parties sign the deal, Tyrone discusses his need for financing. Unfortunately, at the end of 45 days, he has failed to get a mortgage. He claims that the parties orally agreed that he would get his deposit back if he could not obtain financing. But the written agreement says no such thing, and Martha disputes the claim. Who will win? Martha, because of the parol evidence rule. To understand this rule, you need to know two terms. **Parol evidence** refers to anything (apart from the written contract itself) that was said, done, or written before the parties signed the agreement or as they signed it. Martha's conversation with Tyrone about financing the house was parol evidence. The other important term is **integrated contract,** which means a writing that the parties intend as the final, complete expression of their agreement. Now for the rule.

The parol evidence rule: When two parties make an integrated contract, neither one may use parol evidence to contradict, vary, or add to its terms. Negotiations may last for hours or years. Almost no contract includes everything that the parties said. When parties consider their agreement integrated, any statements they made before or while signing are irrelevant. If a court determines that Martha and Tyrone intended their agreement to be integrated, it will prohibit testimony about Martha's oral promises.

EXCEPTION: AN INCOMPLETE OR AMBIGUOUS CONTRACT

If a court determines that a written contract is incomplete or ambiguous, it will permit parol evidence. Suppose that an employment contract states that the company will provide "full health coverage for Robert Watson and his family." Three years later, Watson divorces and remarries, acquiring three stepchildren, and a year later his second wife has a baby. Watson now has two children by his first marriage, and four by the second. The company refuses to ensure Watson's first wife or his stepchildren. A court will probably find that the health care clause is ambiguous. A judge cannot determine exactly what the clause means from the contract itself, so the parties will be permitted to introduce parol evidence to prove whether or not the company must insure Watson's extended family.

One way to avoid parol evidence disputes is to include an **integration clause.** That is a statement clearly proclaiming that this writing is the full and final expression of the parties' agreement, and that anything said before signing or while signing is irrelevant.

Chapter Conclusion

Some contracts must be in writing to be enforceable. Drafting the contract need not be arduous. The disputes illustrated in this chapter could all have been prevented with a few carefully crafted sentences. It is worth the time and effort to write them.

Chapter Review

1. Contracts that must be in writing to be enforceable concern:
   - The sale of any interest in land.
   - Agreements that cannot be performed within one year.
   - Promises to pay the debt of another.
   - Promises made by an executor of an estate.
   - Promises made in consideration of marriage; and
   - The sale of goods for $500 or more.

2. The writing must be signed by the defendant and must state the names of all parties, the subject matter of the agreement, and all essential terms and promises.

3. A contract or memorandum for the sale of goods may be less complete than those required by the common law.

4. Between merchants, even less is required. If one merchant sends written confirmation of a contract, the merchant who receives the document must object within 10 days or be bound by the writing.

5. When an integrated contract exists, neither party may generally use parol evidence to contradict, vary, or add to its terms.

PRACTICE TEST

Matching Questions

Match the following terms with their definitions:

___ **A.** Executor

___ **B.** Parol evidence

___ **C.** Merchant exception

___ **D.** Integration clause

___ **E.** Part performance

1. Entry onto land, or improvements made to it, by a buyer who has no written contract.

2. A rule permitting enforcement of certain oral contracts for the sale of goods.

3. A provision limiting a contract to the writing alone.

4. The person in charge of a deceased's estate.

5. Anything said or written before the parties sign a contract or as they do so.

True/False Questions

Circle true or false:

1. T F An agreement for the sale of a house does not need to be in writing if the deal will be completed within one year.

2. T F An agreement for the sale of 600 plastic cups, worth $.50 each, does not need to be in writing to be enforceable.

3. T F An agreement to lease an apartment for two years must be in writing to be enforceable.

4. T F To create an enforceable contract, the signatures must appear on a "hard copy," i.e., a piece of paper.

5. T F On Monday, two parties sign a written contract for the sale of 600 athletic jerseys. On Tuesday, the parties orally modify the deliver date. The oral modification is barred by the parol evidence rule.

Multiple-Choice Questions

6. Louise e-mails Sonya, "I will sell you my house at 129 Brittle Blvd. for $88,000, payable in one month. Best, Louise." Sonya e-mails back, "Louise, I accept the offer to buy your house at that price. Sonya." Neither party prints a copy of the two e-mails.

(a) The parties have a binding contract for the sale of Louise's house.

(b) Louise is bound by the agreement but Sonya is not.

(c) Sonya is bound by the agreement but Louise is not.

(d) Neither party is bound because the agreement was never put in writing.

(e) Neither party is bound because the agreement was never signed.

7. Raul sends Barclay a fax: "Confirm our agreement; you buy 9,000 pounds of my Grade A peanuts; market price next September. Raul." Barclay spends two weeks negotiating with other peanut salesmen for a better price, but fails to find them cheaper. He e-mails Raul, "Accept.Barclay."

(a) The parties have a binding contract for peanuts.

(b) Raul is bound by his fax but Barclay is not bound.

(c) Barclay is bound by his email, but Raul is not bound.

(d) Neither party is bound because Barclay counteroffered.

(e) Neither party is bound because this contract must be in writing.

8. In February, Chuck orally agrees to sell his hunting cabin, with 15 acres, to Kyle for $35,000, with the deal to be completed in July, when Kyle will have the money. In March, while Chuck is vacationing on his land, he permits

Kyle to enter the land and dig the foundation for a new cottage. In July, Kyle arrives with the money but Chuck refuses to sell. Kyle sues.

(a) Chuck wins because the contract was never put in writing.

(b) Chuck wins because the contract terms were unclear.

(c) Kyle wins because a contract for vacation property does not need to be written.

(d) Kyle wins because Chuck allowed him to dig the foundation.

(e) Kyle wins because Chuck has committed fraud.

9. Cathy hires Molly to work in her shop. "You will start as a sales clerk. After 18 months, I promise to make you store manager, at a 50% pay raise." Molly works for 18 months, and several times Cathy renews the promise about manager. After 18 months, Cathy says, "The store isn't doing well. I can't afford to make you manager." Molly sues. Her best argument is

(a) Statute of frauds.

(b) Part performance.

(c) Parol evidence.

(d) Promissory estoppel.

(e) Reasonable certainty.

10. Barney sells a sophisticated computer system to a large warehouse, for $320,000. Both parties sign a written contract. A month later, when the warehouse complains about the system, Barney states that there were no warranties included. The warehouse replies that as they were negotiating the agreement, Barney promised to fix any glitches that arose during the first six months. Barney's best defense is

(a) UETA.

(b) Part performance.

(c) The contract's integration clause.

(d) The contract's price.

(e) Fraud by the warehouse.

Short-Answer Questions

11. Richard Griffin and three other men owned a grain company called Bearhouse, Inc., which needed to borrow money. First National Bank was willing to loan $490,000, but insisted that the four men sign personal guaranties on the loan, committing themselves to repaying up to 25% of the loan each if Bearhouse defaulted. Bearhouse went bankrupt. The bank was able to collect some of its money from Bearhouse's assets, but it sued Griffin for the balance. At trial, Griffin wanted to testify that before he signed his guaranty, a bank officer assured him that he would only owe 25% of whatever balance was unpaid, not 25% of the total loan. How will the court decide whether Griffin is entitled to testify about the conversation?

12. Donald Waide had a contracting business. He bought most of his supplies from Paul Bingham's supply center. Waide fell behind on his bills, and Bingham told Waide that he would extend no more credit to him. That same day, Donald's father, Elmer Waide, came to Bingham's store, and said to Bingham that he would "stand good" for any sales to Donald made on credit. Based on Elmer's statement, Bingham again gave Donald credit, and Donald ran

up $10,000 in goods before Bingham sued Donald and Elmer. What defense did Elmer make and what was the outcome?

13. Lonnie Hippen moved to Long Island, Kansas to work in an insurance company owned by Griffiths. After he moved there, Griffiths offered to sell Hippen a house he owned, and Hippen agreed in writing to buy it. He did buy the house and moved in, but two years later Hippen left the insurance company. He then claimed that at the time of the sale, Griffiths had orally promised to buy back his house at the selling price if Hippen should happen to leave the company. Griffiths defended based on the statute of frauds. Hippen argued that the statute of frauds did not apply because the repurchase of the house was essentially part of his employment with Griffiths. Comment.

14. ETHICS: Jacob Deutsch owned commercial property. He orally agreed to rent it for six years to Budget Rent-A-Car. Budget took possession, began paying monthly rent, and over a period of several months expended about $6,000 in upgrading the property. Deutsch was aware of the repairs. After a year,

Deutsch attempted to evict Budget. Budget claimed it had a six-year oral lease, but Deutsch claimed that such a lease was worthless. Please rule. Is it ethical for Deutsch to use the statute of frauds in attempting to defeat the lease? Assume that, as landlord, you had orally agreed to rent premises to a tenant, but then for business reasons preferred not to carry out the deal. Would you evict a tenant if you thought the statute of frauds would enable you to do so? How should you analyze the problem? What values are most important to you?

15. Landlord owned a clothing store and agreed in writing to lease the store's basement to another retailer. The written lease, which both parties signed, (1) described the premises exactly; (2) identified the parties; and (3) stated the monthly rent clearly. But an appeals court held that the lease did not satisfy the statute of frauds. Why not?

16. Mast Industries and Bazak International were two textile firms. Mast orally offered to sell certain textiles to Bazak for $103,000. Mast promised to send documents confirming the agreement, but never did. Finally, Bazak sent a memorandum to Mast confirming the agreement, describing the goods, and specifying their quantity and the price. Bazak's officer signed the memo. Mast received the memo but never agreed to it in writing. When Mast failed to deliver the goods, Bazak sued. Who won?

17. ROLE REVERSAL: Write a multiple-choice question that focuses on the merchants' exception to the statute of frauds.

Internet Research Problem

Examine the lease shown at **http://www.kinseylaw.com/freestuff/leaseten/ResLease.html**. Is it important for a lease to be in writing? Who probably drafted the lease, a landlord or a tenant? How can you tell? Should any other provisions be included?

You can find further practice problems in the Online Quiz at **http://beatty.westbuslaw.com** or in the Study Guide that accompanies this text.

Third Parties

During television's formative days, Howdy Doody was one of the medium's biggest stars. His acting was wooden—as were his head and body—but for 13 years Howdy and an assorted group of puppets starred in one of the most popular children's programs of all time. Rufus Rose maintained and repaired the puppets. When Howdy took his last double-jointed bow (to a chorus of toddler wails), NBC permitted Rose temporarily to keep the various puppets. Six years later, NBC became concerned that Rose was inadequately maintaining them. The network wanted Howdy and friends moved to a safe, public location. Rose claimed the puppets were in good shape and wanted payment for the maintenance he had provided. The two parties agreed in writing that Rose would give Howdy and the other stars of the show (including Dilly Dally and Flub-A-Dub) to a puppet museum at the Detroit Institute of Arts (DIA). NBC agreed to pay the puppeteer for his work. The company permitted Rose to keep some of the minor puppets from the program, provided they were not used for commercial purposes.

When Rose died, his son Christopher took possession of the famous puppet. At about that time, a copy of Howdy sold at auction for $113,000. Christopher then claimed ownership

of Howdy Doody and refused to give him to the museum. The DIA wanted its famous puppet, but the museum had never been a party to the agreement between NBC and Rose. Did the DIA have any rights to Howdy? The museum filed suit, making a third party claim. ◾

The basic pattern in third party law is quite simple. Two parties make a contract, and their rights and obligations are subject to the rules that we have already studied: offer and acceptance, consideration, and so forth. However, sometimes their contract affects a *third party*, one who had no role in forming the agreement itself. The two contracting parties may intend to benefit a third person. Those are cases of *third party beneficiary*. In other cases, one of the contracting parties may actually transfer his rights or responsibilities to a third party, raising issues of *assignment* or *delegation*. We consider the issues one at a time.

Third Party Beneficiary

The two parties who make a contract always intend to benefit themselves. Oftentimes their bargain will also benefit someone else. **A third party beneficiary is someone who was not a party to the contract but stands to benefit from it.** Many contracts create third party beneficiaries. In the chapter's introduction, NBC and Rufus Rose contracted to give Howdy Doody to the Detroit Institute of Arts. The museum stood to benefit from this agreement.

As another example, suppose a city contracts to purchase from Seller 20 acres of an abandoned industrial site in a rundown neighborhood, to be used for a new domed stadium. The owner of a pizza parlor on the edge of Seller's land might benefit enormously. A once marginal operation could become a gold mine of cheese and pepperoni.

When the two contracting parties fulfill their obligations and the third party receives her benefit, there is no dispute to analyze. If Christopher Rose had walked Howdy Doody into the puppet museum, and if the city completed the stadium, there would be no unhappy third parties. Problems arise when one of the parties fails to perform the contract as expected. The issue is this: May the third party beneficiary enforce the contract? The museum had no contract with the Rose family. Is the museum entitled to the puppet? The pizza parlor owner was not a party to the contract for the sale of the stadium land. If the city breaks its agreement to buy the property, should the owner recover profits for unsold sausage and green pepper?

The outcome in cases like these depends upon the intentions of the two contracting parties. If they intended to benefit the third party, she will probably be permitted to enforce their contract. If they did not intend to benefit her, she probably has no power to enforce the agreement. The Restatement (Second) of Contracts uses more detail to analyze these cases. We must first recall the terms "promisor" and "promisee." The **promisor** is the one who makes the promise that the third party beneficiary is seeking to enforce. The **promisee** is the other party to the contract.

According to the Restatement §302: **A beneficiary of a promise is an intended beneficiary and may enforce a contract if the parties intended her to benefit and if either (A) enforcing the promise will satisfy a duty of the promisee to the beneficiary, or (B) the promisee intended to make a gift to the beneficiary.**

Any beneficiary who is not an intended beneficiary is an **incidental beneficiary,** and may not enforce the contract. In other words, a third party beneficiary
must show two things. First, she must show that the two contracting parties were
aware of her situation and knew that she would receive something of value from
their deal. Second, she must show that the promisee wanted to benefit her for one
of two reasons: either to satisfy some duty owed or to make her a gift.

We will apply this rule to the dispute over Howdy Doody. Like most contracts,
the deal between NBC and Rufus Rose had two promises: Rose's agreement to
give the puppet to the museum, and NBC's promise to pay for the work done on
Howdy. The promise that interests us was the one concerning Howdy's destination in Detroit. Rose was the promisor and NBC was the promisee.

Did the two parties intend to benefit the museum? Yes, they did. NBC wanted
Howdy to be displayed to the general public, and in a noncommercial venue.
Rose, who wanted payment for work already done, was happy to go along with
the network's wishes. Did NBC owe a duty to the museum? No. Did the network
intend to make a gift to the museum? Yes. The museum wins! The Detroit Institute
of Arts was an intended third party beneficiary, and is entitled to Howdy Doody.
See Exhibit 15.1.

By contrast, the pizza parlor owner will surely lose. A stadium is a multimillion-
dollar investment, and it is most unlikely that the city and the seller of the land

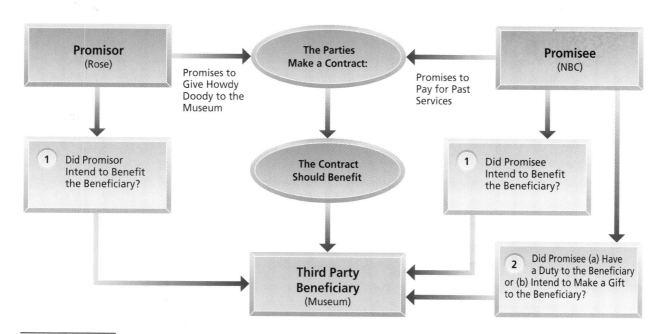

Exhibit 15.1
The issue: May a third party beneficiary enforce a contract to which it was not a party?
The answer: A third party beneficiary may enforce a contract if (1) the parties intended to benefit it *and
either* (2)(a) enforcing the promise will satisfy a duty of the promisee to the beneficiary or (2)(b) the
promisee intended to make a gift to the beneficiary.
In this case: Rose and NBC both intended to benefit the museum. The promisee (NBC) intended to make a *gift* to
the museum. The museum is therefore an intended third party beneficiary, entitled to the puppet.

were even aware of the owner's existence, let alone that they intended to benefit him. He probably cannot prove either the first element or the second element, and certainly not both.

AT **RISK**

Real Estate Support Services (RESS) performed house inspections for potential buyers. RESS contracted with a realtor, Coldwell Banker Relocation Services, Inc., to inspect houses and furnish reports to Coldwell. The agreement stated that the purpose of the reports was:

> *"To provide the client [Coldwell] with a report of a relocating employee's home, which the client may, at its discretion, disclose to other interested parties."*

RESS inspected a house in Greencastle, Indiana and gave its report to Coldwell, which passed the document on to Paul and Norma Nauman. The Naumans relied on the report and bought the house, but later discovered defects RESS had not mentioned. They sued RESS, claiming to be third party beneficiaries of the company's contract with Coldwell. The court ruled for the Naumans. Coldwell obviously intended to use the reports as a sales tool, and RESS knew it, making buyers such as the Naumans intended beneficiaries.

Coldwell presented RESS with a contract that invited claims from third party beneficiaries. That was the time for RESS to decide, "Can we tolerate liability to all buyers who might see the report?" If the company was unwilling to assume such extensive liability, it should have proposed appropriate contract language, such as:

> *"RESS is preparing these reports exclusively for Coldwell's use. Coldwell will not disclose any report to a house purchaser or any other person without first obtaining written permission from RESS."*

If Coldwell had accepted the language, there would have been no lawsuit. If Coldwell had rejected the wording, RESS would have had two options: sign the contract, acknowledging the company's exposure to third parties, or walk away from the negotiations. ◾

Although most third party cases arise in traditional business settings, contract law is a powerful tool that can be used in unexpected settings, as the criminal defendant in the following case demonstrates.

CASE SUMMARY

UNITED STATES v. EL-SADIG

133 F. Supp. 2d 600
Northern District of Ohio, 2001

FACTS: Prince Bander of Saudi Arabia came to the Cleveland Clinic, in Ohio, for medical treatment, accompanied by a large entourage that included his son, Prince Mansour. During their stay in Cleveland, the visitors employed Gabshawi El-Sadig, a lawful resident of the United States, as a driver and errand man. Two members of the Saudi entourage asked El-Sadig to buy guns for them. He bought more than 20 weapons for them at a local gun store, falsely indicating in the required forms that he himself was the true purchaser.

The Bureau of Alcohol, Tobacco and Firearms learned that the weapons had been purchased for the group and would be illegally exported when the

Saudi entourage left the country. In a series of rapid phone conversations among the Justice Department, the State Department, the Saudi Embassy, and others, it was agreed that if all of the weapons were turned over to the police chief of the Cleveland Clinic, the case would be dropped. The weapons were promptly delivered and the Saudi group left the United States.

The government prosecuted El-Sadig for illegally purchasing the weapons and assisting in an illegal attempt to export them, claiming that the agreement not to prosecute applied only to the Saudi nationals. El-Sadig moved to dismiss, arguing that he was a third party beneficiary of the agreement.

ISSUE: Was El-Sadig a third party beneficiary of the agreement to avoid prosecution?

DECISION: Motion to dismiss granted. El-Sadig was a third party beneficiary of the agreement. The government may not prosecute him.

REASONING: Prince Mansour was not involved in any of the illegal activity. He negotiated with the government on behalf of other people (third parties), hoping to protect the Saudi delegation and royal family from embarrassment. The Prince clearly wanted to benefit everybody associated with the Saudi group, because if anyone was prosecuted for the gun purchases, the full story would become public and the royal family implicated. The government, in turn, agreed that "the matter would be closed" if all weapons were given to the police.

If the parties to an agreement intend to benefit a third party, that person can enforce the contract. Although El-Sadig was never named by either party, he was a member of the group that the Prince intended to benefit, and the government consented to protect. He was a third party beneficiary of the contract not to prosecute. The government agreed to close the matter if all weapons were delivered, and it lost the right to prosecute El-Sadig the moment the guns were handed over. ◢

Assignment and Delegation

A contracting party may transfer his rights under the contract, which is called an **assignment of rights.** Or a party may transfer her duties pursuant to the contract, which is a **delegation of duties.** Frequently, a party will make an assignment and delegation simultaneously, transferring both rights and duties to a third party.

For our purposes, the Restatement (Second) of Contracts serves as a good summary of common-law provisions. (The UCC rules are similar but not identical.) Our first example is a sale-of-goods case, governed by the UCC, but the outcome would be the same under the Restatement.

Lydia needs 500 bottles of champagne. Bruno agrees to sell them to her for $10,000, payable 30 days after delivery. He transports the wine to her. Bruno happens to owe Doug $8,000 from a previous deal, so he says to Doug, "I don't have the money, but I'll give you my claim to Lydia's $10,000." Doug agrees. Bruno then assigns to Doug his rights to Lydia's money, and in exchange Doug gives up his claim for $8,000. Bruno is the **assignor, the one making an assignment,** and Doug is the **assignee, the one receiving an assignment.**

Why would Bruno offer $10,000 when he owed Doug only $8,000? Because all he has is a claim to Lydia's money. Cash in hand is often more valuable. Doug, however, is willing to assume some risk for a potential $2,000 gain.

Bruno notifies Lydia of the assignment. Lydia, who owes the money, is called the **obligor,** that is, the one obligated to do something. At the end of 30 days, Doug arrives at Lydia's doorstep, asks for his money, and gets it, since Lydia is obligated to him. Bruno has no claim to any payment. See Exhibit 15.2.

Lydia bought the champagne because she knew she could sell it at a profit. She promptly agrees to sell and deliver the 500 bottles to Coretta, at a mountaintop

Exhibit 15.2

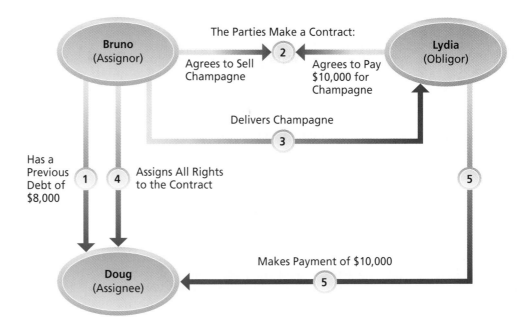

Exhibit 15.3

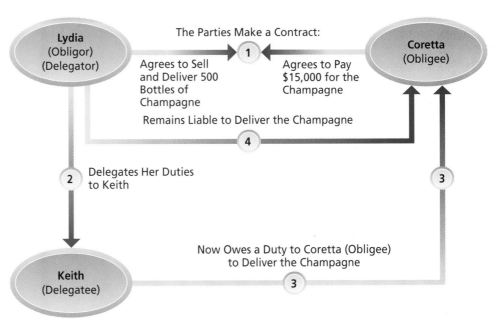

wilderness camp. Lydia has no four-wheel-drive cars, so she finds Keith, who is willing to deliver the bottles for $1,000. Lydia delegates her duty to Keith to deliver the bottles to Coretta. Keith is now obligated to deliver the bottles to Coretta, the obligee, that is, the one who has the obligation coming to her. As we see later, Lydia also remains obligated to Coretta, the **obligee,** to ensure that the bottles are delivered. See Exhibit 15.3.

Assignment and delegation can each create problems. We will examine the most common ones.

ASSIGNMENT

What Rights Are Assignable?

Any contractual right may be assigned unless assignment

(a) Would substantially change the obligor's rights or duties under the contract; or

(b) Is forbidden by law or public policy; or

(c) Is validly precluded by the contract itself.

Substantial Change. Subsection A prohibits an assignment if it would substantially change the obligor's situation. For example, Bruno is permitted to assign to Doug his rights to payment from Lydia because it makes no difference to Lydia whether she writes a check to one or the other. But suppose Erica, who lives on a quarter-acre lot in Hardscrabble, hires Keith to mow her lawn once per week for the summer, for a total fee of $700. Erica pays up front, before she leaves for the summer. May she assign her right to weekly lawn care to Lloyd, who enjoys a 3-acre estate in Halcyon, 60 miles distant? No. The extra travel and far larger yard would dramatically change Keith's obligations.

Public Policy. Some assignments are prohibited by public policy. For example, someone who has suffered a personal injury may not assign her claim to a third person.

Contract Prohibition. Finally, one of the contracting parties may try to prohibit assignment in the agreement itself. For example, most landlords include in the written lease a clause prohibiting the tenant from assigning the tenancy without the landlord's written permission. Such clauses are generally, but not always, enforced by a court.

The following case begins with everyone's dream come true: a winning lottery ticket.

CASE SUMMARY

PETERSON v. DISTRICT OF COLUMBIA LOTTERY AND CHARITABLE GAMES CONTROL BOARD

673 A.2d 664, 1996 D.C. App. LEXIS 54
District of Columbia Court of Appeals, 1996

FACTS: In 1986, Eugene Peterson won $1,050,000 in the District of Columbia Lucky Lotto Game, payable in 20 installments. In 1993, he assigned his future payments to Stone Street Capital, Inc., in exchange for a present-value lump sum. The District's Lottery and Charitable Games Control Board (the Board) refused to honor the assignment, based on its regulations. Peterson and Stone Street sued, but the court ruled that the assignment was illegal. Peterson and Stone Street appealed.

ISSUE: Was Peterson entitled to assign his lottery winnings?

DECISION: Peterson was entitled to assign his lottery winnings.

REASONING: Courts generally protect a party's right to assign unless the contract contains a clear prohibition. The District of Columbia acknowledges that its lottery regulations do not expressly forbid a prize winner from assigning her winnings. However, the District points to a regulation that discharges the Board of liability once it pays the person named on the ticket. The District argues that this regulation was intended to prohibit assignments. A simpler interpretation, though, is that payment need be made only to the named winner, relieving the Board of any obligation to pay others claiming a stake in the prize. The Board's regulation is too ambiguous to prevent an assignment. Peterson had a right to assign his winnings. ◢

How Rights Are Assigned

An assignment may be written or oral, and no particular formalities are required. However, when someone wants to assign rights governed by the statute of frauds, she must do it in writing. Suppose City contracts with Seller to buy Seller's land for a domed stadium and then brings in Investor to complete the project. If City wants to assign to Investor its rights to the land, it must do so in writing.

Rights of the Parties after Assignment

Once the assignment is made and the obligor notified, the assignee may enforce her contractual rights against the obligor. If Lydia fails to pay Doug for the champagne she gets from Bruno, Doug may sue to enforce the agreement. The law will treat Doug as though he had entered into the contract with Lydia.

But the reverse is also true. **The obligor may generally raise all defenses against the assignee that she could have raised against the assignor.** Suppose Lydia opens the first bottle of champagne—silently. "Where's the pop?" she wonders. There is no pop because all 500 bottles have gone flat. Bruno has failed to perform his part of the contract, and Lydia may use Bruno's nonperformance as a defense against Doug. If the champagne was indeed worthless, Lydia owes Doug nothing.

DELEGATION OF DUTIES

Garret has always dreamed of racing stock cars. He borrows $250,000 from his sister, Maybelle, in order to buy a car and begin racing. He signs a promissory note in that amount, in other words, a document guaranteeing that he will repay Maybelle the full amount, plus interest, on a monthly basis over 10 years. Regrettably, during his first race, on a Saturday night, Garret discovers that he has a speed phobia. He finishes the race at noon on Sunday and quits the business. Garret transfers the car and all of his equipment to Brady, who agrees in writing to pay all money owed to Maybelle. For a few months Brady sends a check, but he is killed while watching bumper cars at a local carnival. Maybelle sues Garret, who defends based on the transfer to Brady. Will his defense work?

Garret has assigned his rights in the car and business to Brady, and that is entirely legal. But more important, he has *delegated his duties* to Brady. Garret was the **delegator** and Brady was the **delegatee.** In other words, the promissory note he signed was a contract, and the agreement imposed certain duties on Garret, primarily the obligation to pay Maybelle $250,000 plus interest. Garret had a right to delegate his duties to Brady, but delegating those duties did not relieve Garret of his own obligation to perform them. When Maybelle sues, she will win. Garret, like many debtors, would have preferred to wash his hands of his debt, but the law is not so obliging.

Most duties are delegable. But delegation does not by itself relieve the delegator of his own liability to perform the contract. See Exhibit 15.4.

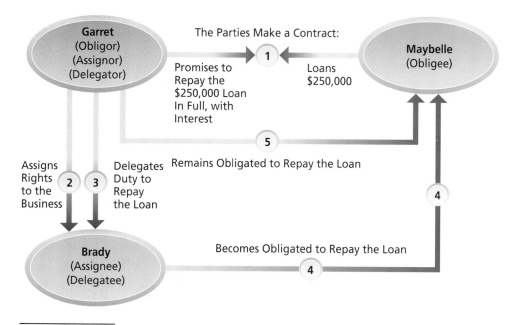

Exhibit 15.4

What Duties Are Delegable

The rules concerning what duties may be delegated mirror those about the assignment of rights.

An obligor may delegate his duties unless

1. Delegation would violate public policy; or

2. The contract prohibits delegation; or

3. The obligee has a substantial interest in personal performance by the obligor.

Public Policy. Delegation may violate public policy, for example, in a public works contract. If City hires Builder to construct a subway system, state law may prohibit Builder from delegating his duties to Beginner. The theory is that a public agency should not have to work with parties that it never agreed to hire.

Contract Prohibition. The parties may forbid almost any delegation, and the courts will enforce the agreement. Hammer, a contractor, is building a house and hires Spot as his painter, including in his contract a clause prohibiting delegation. Just before the house is ready for painting, Spot gets a better job elsewhere and wants to delegate his duties to Brush. Hammer may refuse the delegation even if Brush is equally qualified.

Substantial Interest in Personal Performance. Suppose Hammer had omitted the "nondelegation" clause from his contract with Spot. Could Hammer still refuse the delegation on the grounds that he has a substantial interest in having Spot do the work? No. Most duties are delegable. There is nothing so special about painting a house that one particular painter is required to do it. But some kinds of work do require personal performance, and obligors may not delegate these tasks. The services of lawyers, doctors, dentists, artists, and performers are considered too personal to be delegated. There is no single test that will perfectly define this group, but generally, when the work will test the character, skill, discretion, and good faith of the obligor, she may *not* delegate her job.

AT RISK

The law can be annoyingly vague, as it is with the test of "personal performance" contracts. But avoiding problems is not difficult. Before entering into a contract, briefly discuss delegation with the other party and decide what duties, if any, may be delegated. Then include an appropriate clause in the contract. As always, if there are differences over delegation, it is better to be aware of them early. ▪

Novation

As we have seen, a delegator does not get rid of his duties merely by delegating them. But there is one way a delegator can do so. **A novation is a three-way agreement in which the obligor transfers all rights and duties to a third party. The obligee agrees to look *only* to that third party for performance.**

Recall Garret, the forlorn race car driver. When he wanted to get out of his obligations to Maybelle, he should have proposed a novation. He would assign all rights and delegate all duties to Brady, and Maybelle would agree that *only Brady* was obligated by the promissory note, releasing Garret from his responsibility to repay. Why would Maybelle do this? She might conclude that Brady was a financially better bet than Garret and that this was the best way to get her money. Maybelle would prefer to have both people liable. But Garret might refuse to bring Brady into the deal until Maybelle permits a novation. In the example given, Garret failed to obtain a novation, and hence he and Brady (or Brady's estate) were *both* liable on the promissory note.

Since a novation has the critical effect of releasing the obligor from liability, you will not be surprised to learn that two parties to a contract sometimes fight over whether some event was a simple delegation of duties or a novation. In the following case, who pays for the ice cream?

YOU BE THE JUDGE

ROSENBERG v. SON, INC.
491 N.W.2d 71, 1992 N.D. LEXIS 202
Supreme Court of North Dakota, 1992

FACTS: The Rosenbergs owned a Dairy Queen in Grand Forks, North Dakota. They agreed in writing to sell the Dairy Queen to Mary Pratt. The contract required her to pay $10,000 down and $52,000 over 15 years, at 10% interest. Two years later, Pratt assigned her rights and delegated her duties under the sales contract to Son, Inc. The agreement between Pratt and Son contained a "Consent to Assignment" clause that the Rosenbergs signed. Pratt then moved to Arizona and had nothing further to do with the Dairy Queen. The Rosenbergs never received full payment for the Dairy Queen. They sued Mary Pratt.

The trial court gave summary judgment for Pratt, finding that she was no longer obligated on the original contract. The Rosenbergs appealed.

YOU BE THE JUDGE: Did Pratt obtain a novation relieving her of her duties under the original sales contract?

ARGUMENT FOR THE ROSENBERGS: Your honors, a party cannot escape contract liability merely by assigning its rights and delegating its duties to a third party. It is evident from the express language of the agreement between Pratt and Son, Inc. that the parties only intended an assignment, not a novation. The agreement made no mention of discharging Pratt from liability. It would be odd to write a novation and make no mention of discharge, which happens to be the primary point of a true novation. It is true that the Rosenbergs signed a consent to the assignment, but merely by permitting Son, Inc. to become involved they did not discharge their principal obligor—Pratt.

ARGUMENT FOR Ms. PRATT: Your honors, it is obvious from the contract that Ms. Pratt intended to rid herself entirely of this business. She planned to move out of state, and wanted to terminate all rights and responsibilities in the business. Why would she go to the trouble of assigning rights *and* delegating duties if she still expected to be involved in the business? If that weren't enough, she went one step further, by asking the Rosenbergs to acknowledge the new arrangement—which the Rosenbergs did. If Son, Inc. failed to keep its end of the bargain, then the Rosenbergs should sue that company—not an innocent woman who is long out of the business.

Chapter Conclusion

A moment's caution! That is what enables contracting parties to anticipate and realistically appraise any rights and responsibilities of third parties.

Chapter Review

1. A third party beneficiary is an intended beneficiary and may enforce a contract if the parties intended her to benefit from the agreement and if either (1) enforcing the promise will satisfy a debt of the promisee to the beneficiary; or (2) the promisee intended to make a gift to the beneficiary. Any beneficiary who meets neither description is an incidental beneficiary and has no right to enforce the contract.

2. An assignment transfers the assignor's contract rights to the assignee. A delegation transfers the delegator's duties to the delegatee.

3. A party generally may assign contract rights unless doing so would substantially change the obligor's rights or duties, is forbidden by law, or is validly precluded by the contract.

4. Once the assignment is made and the obligor notified, the assignee may enforce her contractual rights against the obligor. The obligor, in turn, may generally raise all defenses against the assignee that she could have raised against the assignor.

5. Duties are delegable unless delegation would violate public policy, the contract prohibits delegation, or the obligee has a substantial interest in personal performance by the obligor.

6. Unless the obligee agrees otherwise, delegation does not discharge the delegator's duty to perform.

7. A novation is a three-way agreement in which the obligor delegates all duties to the delegatee and the obligee agrees to hold only the delegatee responsible.

PRACTICE TEST

Matching Questions

Match the following terms:

___ **A.** Intended beneficiary

___ **B.** Personal performance

___ **C.** Novation

___ **D.** Lease

___ **E.** Rights to real property

1. One way in which an obligor can get rid of his contractual obligations.
2. A type of contract in which assignment is typically prohibited.
3. A third party who should be able to enforce a contract between two others.
4. A type of contractual obligation that generally cannot be delegated.
5. A type of assignment that must be in writing.

True/False Questions

Circle true or false:

1. T F All parties must normally agree before a contract can be assigned.

2. T F An incidental beneficiary has the same rights to enforce a contract as any other party.

3. T F A party who delegates duties remains liable for contract performance.

4. T F Assignment implies novation whereas delegation does not.

5. T F Once an assignment has been made, the obligor may raise all defenses against the assignee that she could have raised against the assignor.

Multiple-Choice Questions

6. Bob, a mechanic, claims that Cathy owes him $1,500 on a repair job. Bob wants to assign his claim to Hardknuckle Bank. The likeliest reason that Bob wants to do this is

   (a) Cathy also owes Hardknuckle Bank money.

   (b) Hardknuckle Bank owes Bob money on a consumer claim.

   (c) Hardknuckle Bank owes Bob money on a repair job.

   (d) Bob owes Hardknuckle Bank money.

   (e) Bob and Cathy are close friends.

7. The agreement between Bob and Cathy says nothing about assignment. May Bob assign his claim to Hardknuckle?

   (a) Bob may assign his claim but only with Cathy's agreement.

   (b) Bob may assign his claim, but only if Cathy and Hardknuckle agree.

   (c) Bob may assign his claim without Cathy's agreement.

   (d) Bob may assign his claim but Cathy may nullify the assignment.

   (e) Bob may not assign his claim because it violates public policy.

8. Assuming that Bob successfully assigns his claim to the Hardknuckle Bank, which statement is true?

   (a) Hardknuckle could sue Cathy for the money, with or without Bob's consent.

   (b) Hardknuckle could sue Cathy for the money, but only with Bob's consent.

   (c) Hardknuckle could sue Cathy for the money, but only with Bob *and* Cathy's consent.

   (d) Hardknuckle could sue Bob *and* Cathy for the money.

   (e) Hardknuckle could sue only Bob for the money.

9. Assuming that Bob successfully assigns his claim to the Hardknuckle Bank, which statement is true?

    (a) Cathy remains obligated only to Bob.

    (b) Cathy is now obligated to Bob and Hardknuckle.

    (c) Cathy could raise any defenses against Hardknuckle that she could have raised against Bob.

    (d) Cathy may assign her rights to any party she wishes.

    (e) Cathy may delegate her duties to any party she wishes.

10. Cathy believes that her friend, Stephanie, owes her more money than she, Cathy, owes to Bob. Cathy wants Stephanie to take over her obligation to pay Bob. Cathy wants no further dealings with Bob. Cathy's best approach is

    (a) Intended beneficiary.

    (b) Incidental beneficiary

    (c) Delegation.

    (d) Assignment.

    (e) Novation.

Short-Answer Questions

11. Intercontinental Metals Corp. (IMC) contracted with the accounting firm of Cherry, Bekaert & Holland to perform an audit. Cherry issued its opinion about IMC, giving all copies of its report directly to the company. IMC later permitted Dun & Bradstreet to examine the statements, and Raritan River Steel Company saw a report published by Dun & Bradstreet. Relying on the audit, Raritan sold IMC $2.2 million worth of steel on credit, but IMC promptly went bankrupt. Raritan sued Cherry, claiming that IMC was not as sound as Cherry had reported, and that the accounting firm had breached its contract with IMC. Comment on Raritan's suit.

12. Angelo Zavarella and Yvette Rodrigues were injured in an automobile accident allegedly caused by a vehicle belonging to Truck Equipment of Boston. Travelers Insurance Company paid insurance benefits to Zavarella and Rodrigues, who then assigned to Travelers their claims against Truck Equipment. Travelers sued Truck Equipment, which moved to dismiss. What is Truck Equipment's claim that the case should be dismissed, and how would you rule?

13. Woodson Walker and Associates leased computer equipment from Park Ryan Leasing. The lease said nothing about assignment. Park Ryan then assigned the lease to TCB as security for a loan. Park Ryan defaulted on its loan, and Walker failed to make several payments on the lease. TCB sued Walker for the lease payments. Please rule on two issues:

    (a) Was the assignment valid, given the fact that the original lease made no mention of it?

    (b) If the assignment was valid, may Walker raise defenses against TCB that it could have raised against Park Ryan?

14. ETHICS: A century and a half ago an English judge stated: "All painters do not paint portraits like Sir Joshua Reynolds, nor landscapes like Claude Lorraine, nor do all writers write dramas like Shakespeare or fiction like Dickens. Rare genius and extraordinary skill are not transferable." What legal doctrine is the judge describing? What is the ethical basis of this rule?

15. Pizza of Gaithersburg, Maryland owned five pizza shops. Pizza arranged with Virginia Coffee Service to install soft drink machines in each of its stores and maintain them. The contract made no mention of the rights of either party to delegate. Virginia Coffee delegated its duties to the Macke Co., leading to litigation between Pizza and Macke. Pizza claimed that Virginia Coffee was barred from delegating because Pizza had a close working relationship with the president of Virginia Coffee, who personally kept the machines in working order. Was the delegation legal?

16. Judith and John Brooks hired Wayne Hayes to build a house. The contract required Hayes to "provide all necessary labor and materials and perform all work of every nature whatsoever to be done in the erection of the residence." Hayes hired subcontractors to do all of the work. One of Hayes's employees checked on the work site daily, but neither Hayes nor any of his employees actively supervised the building. The Brookses were aware of this working arrangement and consented to it. The mason negligently installed

the fireplace, ultimately leading to a serious fire. The Brookses sued Hayes for breach of contract. Hayes contended that when the Brookses approved of his hiring of subcontractors to do all work, that created a novation, relieving him of any liability. Discuss.

17. ROLE REVERSAL: Write a short-answer question that highlights the difference between an assignment and a novation.

Internet Research Problem

Go to **http://www.kinseylaw.com/freestuff/leaseten/ResLease.html** and read clause 5(b) of the lease. What does the clause mean, in English? Do leases commonly include such clauses? Suppose you intend to rent an apartment next year, live there during the school year, and then sublet over the summer. What legal issue will probably arise concerning a sublet?

You can find further practice problems in the Online Quiz at **http://beatty.westbuslaw.com** or in the Study Guide that accompanies this text.

Performance and Discharge

Polly was elated. It was the grand opening of her new restaurant, Polly's Folly, and everything was bubbling. The wait staff hustled and Caesar, the chef, churned out succulent dishes. Polly was determined that her Folly would be a glorious one. Her three-year lease would cost $6,000 per month, and she had signed an advertising deal with Billboard Bonanza for the same period. Polly had also promised Eddie, a publicity agent, a substantial monthly fee, to begin as soon as the restaurant was 80% booked for one month. Tonight, with candles flickering at packed tables, Polly beamed.

After a week, Polly's smiles were a bit forced. The restaurant was only 60% full, and the publicity agent yelled at Caesar for costing him money. Then troubles gushed forth—literally. A water main burst in front of Polly's restaurant, flooding the street. The city embarked on a two-month repair job that ultimately took four times that long. The street was closed to traffic, and no one could park within blocks of the Folly. For several months Polly bravely served food, but patronage dropped steadily, as hungry customers refused to deal with the bad parking and construction noise. Finally, behind on the rent and in debt to everyone, Polly closed her doors for good. ▪

Discharge

Grimly, the court doors swung open, offering a full menu of litigation. Polly's landlord sued for three years' rent, and Billboard Bonanza demanded its money for the same period. Eddie, the agent, insisted on some money for his hard work.

Polly defended vigorously, seeking to be discharged from her various contracts. **A party is discharged when she has no more duties under a contract.** In each lawsuit, Polly asked a court to declare that her obligations were terminated and that she owed no money.

DEFENSES THAT DISCHARGE

Most contracts are discharged by full performance. In other words, the parties generally do what they promise. At times, though, a court may discharge a party who has not performed. When things have gone amiss, a judge must interpret the contract to determine who, in fairness, should suffer the loss. In the lawsuits brought by the landlord and Billboard Bonanza, Polly argued a defense called "commercial impracticability," claiming that she should not be forced to rent space that was useless to her or buy advertising for a restaurant that had closed. The claim was understandable, but we can also respect her opponents' argument, that they did not break the water main. Claims of commercial impracticability are difficult to win, and Polly lost against both of these opponents. Though she was making no money at all from the restaurant, the court found her liable in full for the lease and the advertising contract.

As to Eddie's suit, Polly raised a defense based on a "condition," meaning that some event had to occur before she was obligated to pay. Polly claimed that she owed Eddie money only if and when the restaurant was 80% full, and that had never happened. The court agreed and discharged Polly on Eddie's claim.

We will analyze each of these issues, and begin with a look at conditions.

Conditions

Parties often put conditions in a contract. **A condition is an event that must occur before a party becomes obligated under a contract.** Polly agreed to pay Eddie, the agent, a percentage of her profits, but with an important condition: 80% of the tables had to be booked for a month. Unless and until those tables were occupied, Polly owed Eddie nothing. That never happened, or, in contract language, the *condition failed,* and so Polly was discharged.

Conditions can take many forms. Alex would like to buy Kevin's empty lot and build a movie theater on it, but the city's zoning law will not permit such a business in that location. Alex signs a contract to buy Kevin's empty lot in 120 days, provided that within 100 days the city rezones the area to permit a movie theater. If the city fails to rezone the area by day 100, Alex is discharged and need not complete the deal.

HOW CONDITIONS ARE CREATED

No special language is necessary to create the condition. Contract phrases such as "provided that" frequently indicate a condition, but neither those nor any other words are essential. As long as the parties intended to create a condition, a court will enforce it.

AT RISK

Because informal language can create a condition, the parties may dispute whether they intended one or not. Sand Creek Country Club, in Indiana, was eager to expand its clubhouse and awarded the design work to CSO Architects. The club wanted the work done quickly but had not secured financing. The architects sent a letter confirming their agreement:

"It was our intent to allow Mr. Dan Moriarty of our office to start work on your project as early as possible in order to allow you to meet the goals that you have set. Also, it was the intent of CSO to begin work on your project and delay any billings to you until your financing is in place. As I explained to you earlier, we will continue on this course until we reach a point where we can no longer continue without receiving some payment."

The club gave CSO the go-ahead to begin design work, and the architects did their work and billed Sand Creek for $33,000. But the club, unable to obtain financing, refused to pay. Sand Creek claimed that CSO's letter created a condition in their agreement, namely, that the club would have to pay only if and when it obtained financing. The court was unpersuaded and ruled that the parties had never intended to create an express condition. The architects were merely delaying their billing as a convenience to the club. It would be absurd, said the court, to assume that CSO intended to perform $33,000 worth of work for free.

The Sand Creek case demonstrates the need for clarity in business dealings. The architect's letter should have emphasized that Sand Creek was obligated to pay the full amount, for example by saying: "CSO agrees to delay billing for a reasonable period but the Club remains liable for the full amount of the contract, whether or not it obtains financing." A one-sentence ambiguity meant that the firm could not obtain its money without a lawsuit and an appeal. ∎

Public Policy

At times a court will refuse to enforce an express condition on the grounds that it is unfair and harmful to the general public. In other words, a court might agree that the parties created a conditional clause but conclude that permitting its enforcement would hurt society. Did the insurance contract in the following case harm society? You be the judge.

YOU BE THE JUDGE

ANDERSON v. COUNTRY LIFE INS. CO.
180 Ariz. 625, 886 P.2d 1381, 1994 Ariz. App. LEXIS 240
Arizona Court of Appeals, 1994

FACTS: On November 26, a Country Life Insurance agent persuaded Donald and Anna Mae Anderson to buy a life insurance policy. He accepted a check for $1,600. The agent gave the Andersons a "conditional receipt for medical policy." The form stated that the Andersons would have a valid life insurance policy with Country Life, effective November 26, but only when all conditions were met. The most important of these conditions was that the Country Life home office accept the Andersons as medical risks. The Andersons were pleased with the new policy and glad it was effective that same day.

It was not. Donald Anderson died of a heart attack a few weeks later. Country Life declined the Andersons as medical risks and refused to issue a policy. Anna Mae Anderson sued. Country Life pointed out that medical approval was a contract condition. In other words, the policy would be effective as of November 26, but only if the company later gave medical approval. The trial court gave summary judgment for Country Life. Ms. Anderson appealed, claiming that the conditional clause was a violation of public policy.

YOU BE THE JUDGE: **Did the conditional clause violate public policy?**

ARGUMENT FOR Ms. ANDERSON: Your honors, this policy is a scam. This so-called "conditional receipt for medical policy" is designed to trick customers and steal their money. The company leads people to believe they are covered as of the day they write the check. But they aren't.

The company gets the customer's money right away and gives nothing in exchange. If the company, after taking its time, decides the applicant is not medically fit, it returns the money, having used it to earn interest. If the insurance company decides the applicant is a good bet, it then issues the policy effective for weeks or months in the *past*, when coverage is of no use. The company is being paid for a period during which it had no risk.

ARGUMENT FOR COUNTRY LIFE: Your honors, is Country Life supposed to issue life insurance policies without doing a medical check? Of course we do a medical inquiry, as quickly as possible. It's in our interest to get the policy decided one way or the other.

The policy clearly stated that coverage was effective only when approved by the home office, after all inquiries were made. The Andersons knew that as well as the agent. If they were covered immediately, why would the company do a medical check? Ms. Anderson is trying to profit from a tragedy that was not the company's fault.

Performance

Caitlin has an architect draw up plans for a monumental new house, and Daniel agrees to build it by September 1. Caitlin promises to pay $900,000 on that date. The house is ready on time but Caitlin has some complaints. The living room was supposed to be 18 feet high but it is only 17 feet; the pool was to be azure yet it is aquamarine; the maid's room was not supposed to be wired for cable television but it is. Caitlin refuses to pay anything for the house. Is she justified? Of course not, it would be absurd to give her a magnificent house for free when it has only tiny defects. And that is how a court would decide the case. But in this easy answer lurks a danger. Technically, Daniel did breach the contract, and yet the law allows him to recover the full contract price, or virtually all of it. Once that principle is established, how far will a court stretch it? Suppose the living room is only 14 feet high, or 10 feet, or 5 feet?

STRICT PERFORMANCE AND SUBSTANTIAL PERFORMANCE

Strict Performance

Caitlin argued that Daniel had not *strictly performed.* Caitlin was right, yet she lost anyway. Courts dislike strict performance because it enables one party to benefit without paying, and sends the other one home empty-handed. **A party is generally not required to give strict performance unless the contract expressly demands it *and* such a demand is reasonable.** Caitlin's contract never suggested that Daniel would forfeit all payment if there were minor problems.

There are cases where strict performance does make sense. Marshall agrees to deliver 500 sweaters to Leo's store, and Leo promises to pay $20,000 cash on delivery. If Leo has only $19,000 cash and a promissory note for $1,000, he has failed to perform, and Marshall need not give him the sweaters. Leo's payment represents 95% of what he promised, but there is a big difference between cash and a promissory note.

Substantial Performance

Daniel, the house builder, won his case against Caitlin because he fulfilled most of his obligations, even though he did an imperfect job. **In a contract for services, a party that substantially performs its obligations will receive the full contract price, minus the value of any defects.** Daniel receives $900,000, the contract price, minus the value of a ceiling that is one foot too low, a pool the wrong color, and so forth. It will be for the trial court to decide how much those defects are worth. If the court decides the low ceiling is a $10,000 damage, the pool color worth $5,000, and the cable television worth $500, then Daniel receives $884,500.

On the other hand, **a party that fails to give substantial performance receives nothing on the contract itself and will only recover the value of the work, if any.** If the foundation cracks in Caitlin's house and the walls collapse, Daniel will not receive his $900,000. In such a case he collects only the market value of the work he has done, which is probably zero.

To analyze substantial performance, courts look at these issues:

- How much benefit has the promisee received?

- If it is a construction contract, can the owner use the thing for its intended purpose?

- Can the promisee be compensated with money damages for any defects?

- Did the promisor act in good faith?

The following case deals with several of these issues.

CASE SUMMARY

FOLK v. CENTRAL NATIONAL BANK & TRUST CO.

210 Ill. App. 3d 43, 1991 Ill. App. LEXIS 308
Illinois Court of Appeals, 1991

FACTS: Byron Dragway, a drag strip located in Byron, Illinois, needed work, including concrete retaining walls and resurfacing of the racing strip. Leek hired Randy Folk to do all of the work. When Folk finished, Leek refused to pay, claiming that the work was shabby and would need to be entirely redone. Folk sued. The trial court gave judgment for Folk in the amount of $140,000, finding that, although there were problems, he had substantially performed. Byron Dragway appealed.

ISSUE: Did Folk substantially perform?

DECISION: Folk did not substantially perform. Reversed.

REASONING: The president of the nation's largest drag racing association testified that the new starting pads were too smooth and that the new concrete contained dangerous dips. One of the dips caused dragster tires to spin sideways. He observed hazardous puddles in both lanes. As he watched a meet, one car crashed and others struggled to negotiate the track. His organization refused to authorize events at Byron until the drag strip was resurfaced.

Other experts agreed that the problems were too severe for simple repairs, and that the surface would have to be ground off and replaced. Clearly, Folk did not substantially perform. The judgment is reversed in favor of Byron Dragway. ◢

PERSONAL SATISFACTION CONTRACTS

Sujata, president of a public relations firm, hires Ben to design a huge multimedia project for her company, involving computer software, music, and live actors, all designed to sell frozen bologna sandwiches to supermarkets. His contract guarantees him two years' employment, provided all of his work "is acceptable in the sole judgment of Sujata." Ben's immediate supervisor is delighted with his work and his colleagues are impressed—all but Sujata. Three months later she fires him, claiming that his work is "uninspired." Does she have the right to do that?

This is a **personal satisfaction contract, in which the promisee makes a personal, subjective evaluation of the promisor's performance.** Employment contracts may require personal satisfaction of the employer, and agreements for the sale of goods may demand that the buyer be personally satisfied with the product. Judges must decide: When is it fair for the promisee to claim that she is not satisfied? May she make that decision for any reason at all, even on a whim?

A court applies a **subjective standard** only if assessing the work involves personal feelings, taste, or judgment and the contract explicitly demanded personal satisfaction. A "subjective standard" means that the promisee's personal views will greatly influence her judgment, even if her decision is foolish and unfair. Artistic or creative work, or highly specialized tasks designed for a particular employer, may involve subtle issues of quality and personal preference. Ben's work combines several media and revolves around his judgment. Accordingly, the law applies a subjective standard to Sujata's decision. Since she concludes that his work is uninspired, she may legally fire him, even if her decision is irrational.

Note that the promisee, Sujata, has to show two things: that assessing Ben's work involves her personal judgment and that their contract explicitly demands personal satisfaction. If the contract were vague on this point, Sujata would lose. Had the agreement merely said, "Ben will at all times make his best efforts," Sujata could not fire him.

GOOD FAITH

The parties to a contract must carry out their obligations in good faith. The Restatement (Second) of Contracts §205 states: **"Every contract imposes upon each party a duty of good faith and fair dealing in its performance and its enforcement."** The difficulty, of course, is applying this general rule to the infinite problems that may arise when two people, or companies, do business. How far must one side go to meet its good-faith burden? The Restatement emphasizes that the parties must remain faithful to the "agreed common purpose and justified expectations of the other party." Good-faith cases frequently arise between insurance companies and their customers.

Suppose that Doug causes a car accident, seriously injuring Virginia. She sues Doug, who is defended by his insurance company. Insurer's maximum liability is $100,000 and the company knows Doug is liable. Virginia is willing to accept $100,000 in full settlement, but Insurer refuses, even though it considers the figure reasonable. The company has a policy of refusing all early offers, in the hope that the long litigation process will wear down the other side and force a cheaper settlement. There is no risk to the company, since it can never be forced to pay more than $100,000, even if a jury returns a much larger verdict. The case goes to trial, and Virginia is awarded $500,000, meaning that Doug now personally owes $400,000. This is bad faith on the part of Insurer. If Doug sues the company, he will win. The company was obligated to fairly analyze the initial settlement offer, and deal fairly with its customer, Doug.

UPDATE | The last decade has seen an increase in bad-faith lawsuits against insurers. Find a new case making this claim. What is the dispute? What is your view? ◼

TIME OF THE ESSENCE CLAUSES

"Go, sir, gallop, and don't forget that the world was made in six days. You can ask me for anything you like, except time."

—Napoleon, to an aide, 1803

Generals are not the only ones who place a premium on time. Ask Gene LaSalle. The Seabreeze Restaurant agreed to sell him all of its assets. The parties signed a contract stating the price and closing date. Seabreeze insisted on a clause saying, "Seabreeze considers that time is of the essence in consummating the proposed transaction." Such clauses are common in real estate transactions and in any other agreement where a delay would cause serious damage to one party. LaSalle was unable to close on the date specified and asked for an extension. Seabreeze refused and sold its assets elsewhere. A Florida court affirmed that Seabreeze acted legally.

A time of the essence clause will generally make contract dates strictly enforceable. Seabreeze regarded a timely sale as important, and LaSalle agreed to the provision. There was nothing unreasonable about the clause, and LaSalle suffered the consequences of his delay. Notice, though, that merely including a date for performance does *not* make time of the essence.

Breach

When one party breaches a contract, the other party is discharged. The discharged party has no obligation to perform and may sue for damages. Edwin promises that on July 1 he will deliver 20 tuxedos, tailored to fit male chimpanzees, to Bubba's circus for $300 per suit. After weeks of delay, Edwin concedes he hasn't a cummerbund to his name. Bubba is discharged and obviously owes nothing. In addition, he may sue Edwin for damages. If Bubba is forced to pay $350 elsewhere to obtain similar tuxedos, he will recover the difference in cost. Twenty tuxedos, at $50 extra per suit, means that Bubba will get $1,000 from Edwin.

MATERIAL BREACH

Courts only discharge a contract if a party committed a material breach. A material breach is one that substantially harms the innocent party and for which it would be hard to compensate without discharging the contract. Suppose Edwin fails to show up with the tuxedos on June 1, but calls to say they will arrive under the big top the next day. He has breached the agreement. Is his breach material? No. This is a trivial breach, and Bubba is not discharged. When the tuxedos arrive, he must pay.

ANTICIPATORY BREACH

Sally will receive her bachelor's degree in May and already has a job lined up for September, a two-year contract as window display designer for Surebet Department Store. The morning of graduation, she reads in the paper that Surebet is going out of business that very day. Surebet has told Sally nothing about her status. Sally need not wait until September to learn her fate. Surebet has committed an anticipatory breach by making it unmistakably clear that it will not honor the contract. Sometimes a promisor will actually inform the promisee that it will not perform its duties. At other times, as here, the promisor takes some step that makes the breach evident. Sally is discharged and may immediately seek other work. She is also entitled to file suit for breach of contract. The court will treat Surebet's anticipatory breach just as though the store had actually refused to perform on September 1.

STATUTE OF LIMITATIONS

A party injured by a breach of contract should act promptly. **A statute of limitations begins to run at the time of injury and will limit the time within which the injured party may file suit.** Statutes of limitation vary from state to state and even from issue to issue within a state. In some states, for example, an injured party must sue on oral contracts within three years, on a sale-of-goods contract within four years, and on some written contracts within five years. Failure to file suit within the time limits discharges the party who breached the contract.

Impossibility

If performing a contract is truly impossible, a court will discharge the agreement. But if honoring the deal merely imposes a financial burden, the law will generally enforce the contract.

True impossibility means that something has happened making it utterly impossible to do what the promisor said he would do. Françoise owns a vineyard that produces Beaujolais nouveau wine. She agrees to ship 1,000 cases of her wine to Tyrone, a New York importer, as soon as this year's vintage is ready. Tyrone will pay $50 per case. But a fungus wipes out her entire vineyard. Françoise is discharged. It is theoretically impossible for Françoise to deliver wine from her vineyard, and she owes Tyrone nothing.

Meanwhile, though, Tyrone has a contract with Jackson, a retailer, to sell 1,000 cases of any Beaujolais nouveau wine at $70 per case. Tyrone has no wine from Françoise, and the only other Beaujolais nouveau available will cost him $85 per case. Instead of earning $20 per case, Tyrone will lose $15. Does this discharge Tyrone's contract with Jackson? No. It is possible for him to perform, just undesirable. He must fulfill his agreement.

True impossibility is generally limited to these three causes:

- Destruction of the Subject Matter, as happened with Françoise's vineyard.

- Death of the Promisor in a personal services contract. When the promisor, say a portrait painter, agrees personally to render a service that cannot be transferred to someone else, her death discharges the contract.

- Illegality. If the purpose of a contract becomes illegal, that change discharges the contract. Kitty hires Kato to work in her new Keno Klub (a club with electronic gambling games), but a month later the state legislature KO's keno, declaring that "Keno korrupts." Kitty's contract is discharged.

COMMERCIAL IMPRACTICABILITY AND FRUSTRATION OF PURPOSE

It is rare for contract performance to be truly impossible, but common for it to become a financial burden to one party. Suppose Bradshaw Steel in Pittsburgh agrees to deliver 1,000 tons of steel beams to Rice Construction in Saudi Arabia at a given price, but a week later the cost of raw ore increases 30%. A contract once lucrative to the manufacturer is suddenly a major liability. Does that change discharge Bradshaw? Absolutely not. Rice signed the deal precisely to protect itself against price increases.

Yet there may be times when a change in circumstances is so extreme that it would be unfair to enforce a deal. What if a strike made it impossible for Bradshaw to ship the steel to Saudi Arabia, and the only way to deliver would be by air, at five times the sea cost? Must Bradshaw fulfill its deal? What if war in the Middle East meant that any ships or planes delivering the goods might be fired upon? Other changes could make the contract undesirable for Rice. Suppose the builder wanted steel for a major public building in Riyadh, but the Saudi government decided not to go forward with the construction. The steel would then be worthless to Rice. Must the company still accept it? Courts use the related doctrines of commercial impracticability and frustration of purpose to decide when a change in circumstances should permit one side to escape its duties.

Commercial impracticability means some event has occurred that neither party anticipated, and fulfilling the contract would now be extraordinarily difficult and unfair to one party. If a shipping strike forces Bradshaw to ship by air, the company will argue that neither side expected the strike and that Bradshaw should not suffer a fivefold increase in shipping cost. Bradshaw will probably win the argument.

Frustration of purpose means some event has occurred that neither party anticipated and the contract now has no value for one party. If Rice's building project is canceled, Rice will argue that the steel now is useless to the company. Frustration cases are hard to predict. Some states would agree with Rice, but others would hold that it was Rice's obligation to protect itself with a government guarantee that the project would be completed. Courts consider the following factors in deciding impracticability and frustration claims:

- Mere financial difficulties will never suffice to discharge a contract.

- The event must have been truly unexpected.

- If the promisor must use a different means (such as transportation) to accomplish her task, at a greatly increased cost, she probably does have a valid claim of impracticability.

- A *force majeure* clause may help. A typical *force majeure* clause might permit the seller of goods to delay or cancel delivery in the event of "acts of God, fire, labor disputes, accidents or transportation difficulties." A court will consider such a clause, but may not enforce it if one party is trying to escape from routine financial problems.

CASE SUMMARY

CAPE-FRANCE ENTERPRISES v. PEED

29 P.3d 1011
Montana Supreme Court, 2001

FACTS: Cape-France Enterprises owned a large tract of land in Montana. Lola Peed and her granddaughter Marthe Moore offered to buy 5 acres of the property to build a hotel, and the parties signed a written agreement. However, the Department of Environmental Quality (DEQ) warned the parties that there was an underground pollution plume of perchloroethylene (PCE) near the property. The DEQ would not permit the subdivision and sale unless the parties dug a well and tested the water. DEQ letters acknowledged that no one knew the contamination's extent, but cautioned that drilling a well could cause it to spread further, creating liability for whoever owned the land.

Cape-France sued to rescind the contract. The buyers counterclaimed, seeking specific performance of the agreement. The trial court ordered the contract rescinded, based on impracticability. The buyers appealed.

ISSUE: Did impracticability prevent enforcement of the contract?

DECISION: Yes, impracticability prevented enforcement. Affirmed.

REASONING: Peed and Moore argue that the contract should not be rescinded because it remains possible to drill the well. Because there is no proof that drilling would cause the contamination to spread, they conclude that this is not a case of commercial impracticability.

PCE is a dangerous substance that has been linked to cancer, nerve damage, and other major illnesses. The chemical is also toxic to aquatic life. Although a new well *might* not cause the PCE to spread, there is a substantial risk it would do so. Both seller and buyer could be exposed to major, unquantifiable liability. All parties refused to assume responsibility if the contamination broadened.

The Montana Constitution guarantees everyone within the state a clean, healthful environment. Enforcing this contract would expose our citizens to potentially major environmental damage, violating the state's Constitution and leaving the parties liable for untold sums. Public policy requires that the contract be rescinded. ◢

Chapter Conclusion

Negotiate carefully. A casually written letter may imply a condition that the author never intended. Never assume that mere inconvenience or financial loss will discharge contractual duties.

Chapter Review

1. A condition is an event that must occur before a party becomes obligated.

2. Strict performance, which requires one party to fulfill its duties perfectly, is unusual. In construction and service contracts, substantial performance is generally sufficient to entitle the promisor to the contract price, minus the cost of defects in the work.

3. Good-faith performance is required in all contracts.

4. Time of the essence clauses result in strict enforcement of contract deadlines.

5. A material breach is the only kind that will discharge a contract; a trivial breach will not.

6. True impossibility means that some event has made it impossible to perform an agreement.

7. Commercial impracticability means that some unexpected event has made it extraordinarily difficult and unfair for one party to perform its obligations.

8. Frustration of purpose may occur when an unexpected event renders a contract completely useless to one party.

PRACTICE TEST

Matching Questions

Match the following terms with their definitions:

___ **A.** Strict performance

___ **B.** Material

___ **C.** Discharged

___ **D.** Substantial performance

___ **E.** Condition

1. An event that must occur before a party becomes obligated under a contract.

2. Entitles a party to most or all of the contract price.

3. May be required in a personal services contract.

4. A type of breach that substantially harms the innocent party.

5. When a party has no more obligations under a contract.

True/False Questions

Circle true or false:

1. T   F   Frustration of purpose means that a contract has become a financial liability for one party.

2. T   F   A statute of limitations begins to run at the time of injury.

3. T F Contract dates and deadlines are strictly enforceable unless the parties agree otherwise.

4. T F Parties must use good faith in performing their contractual duties.

5. T F When one party breaches a contract the other party is still obligated to perform.

Multiple-Choice Questions

6. Jody is obligated under a contract to deliver 100,000 plastic bottles to a spring water company. Jody's supplier has just gone bankrupt; any other suppliers will charge her more than she expected to pay. This is

   (a) Frustration of purpose.

   (b) Impossibility.

   (c) Commercial impracticability.

   (d) Substantial performance

   (e) Legally irrelevant.

7. Strict performance

   (a) Is the norm in contract cases.

   (b) Is required in services contracts, but not sale of goods.

   (c) May be required concerning payment, in a sale-of-goods case.

   (d) Used to be the norm in contract cases but is now illegal.

   (e) Only applies when there has been a material breach.

8. Monica agrees to buy Kelly's house for $600,000 "on July 10, provided that by July 5 buyer has obtained financing of at least $500,000 at no more than 6% interest." Both parties sign the agreement. Monica is unable to obtain financing. Kelly sues to enforce the deal.

   (a) Monica wins, because the contract is impossible.

   (b) Monica wins, because the condition failed.

   (c) Monica wins, because of frustration of purpose.

   (d) Kelly wins, because the clause is against public policy.

   (e) Kelly wins, because there was no "time of the essence" clause.

9. Contracting parties are most commonly discharged by

   (a) Impracticability.

   (b) Full performance.

   (c) Part performance.

   (d) Public policy.

   (e) Strict performance.

10. An example of true impossibility is

    (a) Strict performance.

    (b) Failure of condition.

    (c) Illegality.

    (d) Material breach.

    (e) Novation.

Short-Answer Questions

11. Stephen Krogness was a real estate broker. He signed an agreement to act as an agent for Best Buy Co., which was interested in selling several of its stores. The contract provided that Best Buy would pay Krogness a commission of 2% for a sale to "any prospect submitted directly to Best Buy by Krogness." Krogness introduced Corporate Realty Capital (CRC) to Best Buy, and the parties negotiated a possible sale but could not reach agreement. CRC then introduced Best Buy to BB Properties (BB). Best Buy sold several properties to BB for a total of $46 million. CRC acted as the broker on the deal. After the sale, Krogness sought a commission of $528,000. Is he entitled to it?

12. Evans built a house for Sandra Dyer, but the house had some problems. The garage ceiling was too low. Load-bearing beams in the great room cracked and appeared to be steadily weakening. The patio did not drain properly. Pipes froze. Evans wanted the money promised for the job, but Dyer refused to pay. Comment.

13. ETHICS: Ken Ward was an Illinois farmer who worked land owned by his father-in-law, Frank Ruda. To finance his operation, he frequently borrowed money from Watseka First National Bank, paying back the loans with farming profits. But Ward fell deeper and deeper into debt, and Watseka became concerned. When Ward sought additional loans, Watseka insisted that Ruda become a guarantor on all of the outstanding debt, and the father-in-law agreed. The new loans had an acceleration clause, permitting the bank to demand payment of the entire debt if it believed itself "insecure," that is, at risk of a default. Unfortunately, just as Ward's debts reached more than $120,000, Illinois suffered a severe drought, and Ward's crops failed. Watseka asked Ruda to sell some of the land he owned to pay back part of the indebtedness. Ruda reluctantly agreed but never did so. Meanwhile, Ward decreased his payments to the bank because of the terrible crop. Watseka then "accelerated" the loan, demanding that Ruda pay off the entire debt. Ruda defended by claiming that Watseka's acceleration at such a difficult time was bad faith. Who wins the legal case? Analyze the ethical issues.

14. In August 1985, Colony Park Associates signed a contract to buy 44 acres of residential land from John Gall. The contract stated that "closing will take place August 20, 1986." The year's delay was to enable Colony Park to obtain building permits to develop condominiums. Colony Park worked diligently to obtain all permits and kept Gall abreast of its efforts. But delays in sewer permits forced Colony Park to notify Gall it could not close on the agreed date. Colony Park suggested a date exactly one month later. Gall refused the new date and declined to convey the property to Colony Park. Colony Park sued. Gall argued that since the parties specified a date, time was of the essence and Colony Park's failure to buy on time discharged Gall. Please rule.

15. Omega Concrete had a gravel pit and factory. Access was difficult, so Omega contracted with Union Pacific Railroad (UP) for the right to use a private road that crossed UP property and tracks. The contract stated that use of the road was solely for Omega employees and that Omega would be responsible for closing a gate that UP planned to build where the private road joined a public highway. In fact, UP never constructed the gate; Omega had no authority to construct the gate. Mathew Rogers, an Omega employee, was killed by a train while using the private road to reach Omega. Rogers's family sued Omega, claiming, among other things, that Omega failed to keep the gate closed as the contract required. Is Omega liable based on that failure?

16. Krug International, an Ohio corporation, had a contract with Iraqi Airways to build aeromedical equipment for training pilots. Krug then contracted for Power Engineering, an Iowa corporation, to build the specialized gearbox to be used in the training equipment, for $150,000. Power did not know that Krug planned to resell the gearbox to Iraqi Airways. When Power had almost completed the gearbox, the Gulf War broke out and the United Nations declared an embargo on all shipments to Iraq. Krug notified Power that it no longer wanted the gearbox. Power sued. Please rule.

17. ROLE REVERSAL: Write a multiple-choice question focusing on a contractor's claim to substantial performance. The answers should contain dollar amounts that the contractor could possibly recover, from zero to the full value of the contract.

Internet Research Problem

Using the Internet, find a contract that contains a "commercial impracticability" clause and/or a "frustration of purpose" clause. They often go together. A good place to look is at **http://www.findlaw.com**, although many other sites will contain such clauses. What is the subject of the contract generally? What did the drafters of the contract hope to achieve with the clause you have located? In your opinion, will a court enforce the clause? (Refer to the bulleted list of criteria on page 224) Why or why not? If the clause is valid, will it accomplish the purpose you have described?

You can find further practice problems in the Online Quiz at **http://beatty.westbuslaw.com** or in the Study Guide that accompanies this text.

Remedies

Anybody can wrestle an alligator. But Freddie could wrestle an alligator and a python simultaneously. Kira watched Freddie clamp the snake on the gator's back and pin them both to the hard red soil; and when the small roadside crowd screamed approval, she knew she was looking at profit. She immediately signed Freddie to a two-year contract, promising him $500 per week plus room and board. They agreed that Rasslin' Reptiles would start its tour in a month, as soon as Kira had everything ready. Kira then spent $20,000 on a used mobile home and paid $8,000 for two more alligators and another python. Next, she hustled out on the road, drumming up business. Country bars and suburban malls were intrigued by her promotional pitch, though slow with guarantees.

Some suggested they would pay her $500 to put on a show, if and when she arrived. Others promised to rent space to her, allowing her to charge admission. Everything was looking great, and Kira went back to collect her star performer. But Freddie had met the girl of his dreams. ▪

Breaching the Contract

The young woman had read Freddie one of her original sonnets, and the wrestler had fallen in love with poetry. He planned to enroll in State University's creative writing program. Kira hissed and thrashed to no avail, and finally sued. Freddie had certainly breached his contract. **Someone breaches a contract when he fails to perform a duty, without a valid excuse.** When the case gets to trial, a court will declare that Freddie is in breach of the agreement. But what will Kira's remedy be? **A remedy is the method a court uses to compensate an injured party.** How will a court help Kira? Should the court force Freddie to return to rasslin'? An order forcing someone to do something, or refrain from doing something, is an **injunction.** Courts seldom grant injunctions to compel a party to perform a job, since that would force two antagonistic people to work together. The court could prohibit Freddie from working elsewhere, and perhaps from going to school. Is that sensible?

The most common remedy, used in the great majority of lawsuits, is money damages. If the court decides to award Kira damages, how much money should she get? Kira may claim that she could have performed 8 to 10 shows a week, at $500 per show, for a total of $4,000 to $5,000 per week. Lost profits are considered *expectation* damages. Freddie will respond that all of the "shows" were hypothetical, since not one penny of income had been guaranteed. If Kira is not entitled to lost profits, should she receive the money spent on tour preparations? Such a remedy is called *reliance* **damages.**

How to help an injured party, without unfairly harming the other person, is the focus of remedies. Courts have struggled with remedies for centuries, but we will master them in one chapter. Kira will not obtain an injunction forcing Freddie to wrestle. An order barring him from college is also unlikely. And she will be hard pressed to prove lost profits, since she had no guarantee of earnings. She should win something for her reliance on Freddie's deal, since she spent $28,000 on major purchases. But she may not get that full amount because in losing Freddie's services she also shed the expense of an unproven road tour. The questions and issues created by Kira's broken road tour are typical remedy problems.

Though a court may have several alternative remedies available, it is important to note that almost all of them have one thing in common: The focus is on compensating the injured party, rather than punishing the party in breach. A court must decide whether to give Kira her lost profits or her expenses, but it will not consider sending Freddie to jail or assessing damages to punish him.

IDENTIFYING THE "INTEREST" TO BE PROTECTED

The first step that a court takes in choosing a remedy is to decide what interest it is trying to protect. An **interest** is a legal right in something. Someone can have an interest in property, for example, by owning it, or renting it to a tenant, or lending money to buy it. He can have an interest in a contract if the agreement gives him some benefit. There are four principal contract interests that a court may seek to protect:

• *Expectation interest.* This refers to what the injured party reasonably thought she would get from the contract. The goal is to put her in the position she would have been in if both parties had fully performed their obligations.

- *Reliance interest.* The injured party may be unable to demonstrate expectation damages, perhaps because it is unclear he would have profited. But he may still prove that he expended money in reliance on the agreement and that in fairness he should receive compensation.

- *Restitution interest.* The injured party may be unable to show an expectation interest or reliance. But perhaps she has conferred a benefit on the other party. Here, the objective is to restore to the injured party the benefit she has provided.

- *Equitable interest.* In some cases, money damages will not suffice to help the injured party. Something more is needed, such as an order to transfer property to the injured party (specific performance) or an order forcing one party to stop doing something (an injunction).

In this chapter, we look at all four interests.

Expectation Interest

This is the most common remedy that the law provides for a party injured by a breach of contract. **The expectation interest is designed to put the injured party in the position she would have been in had both sides fully performed their obligations.** A court tries to give the injured party the money she would have made from the contract. If accurately computed, this should take into account all the gains she reasonably expected and all the expenses and losses she would have incurred. The injured party should not end up better off than she would have been under the agreement, nor should she suffer serious loss.

William Colby was a former director of the CIA. He wanted to write a book about his 15 years of experiences in Vietnam. He paid James McCarger $5,000 for help in writing an early draft and promised McCarger another $5,000 if the book was published. Then he hired Alexander Burnham to coauthor the book. Colby's agent secured a contract with Contemporary Books, which included a $100,000 advance. But Burnham was hopelessly late with the manuscript, and Colby missed his publication date. Colby fired Burnham and finished the book without him. Contemporary published *Lost Victory* several years late, and the book flopped, earning no significant revenue. Because the book was so late, Contemporary paid Colby a total of only $17,000. Colby sued Burnham for his lost expectation interest. The court awarded him $23,000, calculated as follows:

	$100,000	Advance, the only money Colby was promised.
	−10,000	Agent's fee.
	= 90,000	Fee for the two authors combined.
Divided by 2 =	45,000	Colby's fee.
	5,000	Owed to McGarger under the earlier agreement.
	= 40,000	Colby's expectation interest.
	−17,000	Fee Colby received from Contemporary.
	= 23,000	Colby's expectation damages, that is, the amount he would have received had Burnham finished on time.

The Colby case presented an easy calculation of damages. Other contracts are complex. Courts typically divide the expectation damages into three parts: (1) compensatory (or "direct") damages, which represent harm that flowed directly from the contract's breach; (2) consequential (or "special") damages, which represent harm caused by the injured party's unique situation; and (3) incidental damages, which are minor costs such as storing or returning defective goods, advertising for alternative goods, and so forth. The first two, compensatory and consequential, are the important ones. We look at them one at a time.

COMPENSATORY DAMAGES

Compensatory damages are the most common monetary awards for the expectation interest. Courts also refer to these as "direct damages." **Compensatory damages are those that flow directly from the contract.** In other words, these are the damages that inevitably result from the breach. Suppose Ace Productions hires Reina to star in its new movie, *Inside Straight.* Ace promises Reina $3 million, providing she shows up June 1 and works until the film is finished. But in late May, Joker Entertainment offers Reina $6 million to star in its new feature, and on June 1 Reina informs Ace that she will not appear. Reina has breached her contract, and Ace should recover compensatory damages.

What are the damages that flow directly from the contract? Ace obviously has to replace Reina. If Ace hires Kween as its star and pays her a fee of $4 million, Ace is entitled to the difference between what it expected to pay ($3 million) and what the breach forced it to pay ($4 million), or $1 million in compensatory damages. Suppose the rest of the cast and crew are idle for two weeks because of the delay in hiring a substitute, and the lost time costs the producers an extra $2.5 million. Reina is also liable for those expenses. Both the new actress and the delay are inevitable.

Reasonable Certainty

The injured party must prove the breach of contract caused damages that can be quantified with reasonable certainty. What if *Inside Straight,* now starring Kween, bombs at the box office? Ace proves that each of Reina's last three movies grossed over $60 million, but *Inside Straight* grossed only $28 million. Is Reina liable for the lost profits? No. Ace cannot prove that it was Reina's absence that caused the film to fare poorly. The script may have been mediocre, or Kween's costars dull, or the publicity efforts inadequate. Mere "speculative damages" are worth nothing.

CONSEQUENTIAL DAMAGES

In addition to compensatory damages, the injured party may seek consequential damages or, as they are also known, "special damages." **Consequential damages are those resulting from the unique circumstances of *this injured party.*** The rule concerning this remedy comes from a famous 1854 case, which all American law students read. Now it is your turn.

CASE SUMMARY

HADLEY v. BAXENDALE

9 Ex. 341, 156 Eng. Rep. 145
Court of Exchequer, 1854

FACTS: The Hadleys operated a flour mill in Gloucester. The crankshaft broke, causing the mill to grind to a halt. The Hadleys employed Baxendale to cart the damaged part to a foundry in Greenwich, where a new one could be manufactured. Baxendale promised to make the delivery in one day, but he was late transporting the shaft, and as a result the Hadleys' mill was shut for five extra days. They sued, and the jury awarded damages based in part on their lost profits. Baxendale appealed.

ISSUE: Should the defendant be liable for profits lost because of his delay in delivering the shaft?

DECISION: The defendant is not liable for lost profits. Reversed.

REASONING: When one side breaches a contract, the other party's damages should be those that arise inevitably from the breach or those that *both* parties

reasonably anticipated when they made the agreement. If the contract involves special circumstances, and the plaintiff tells the defendant about them when they make the deal, then the defendant is liable for all injuries. On the other hand, if the plaintiff never informed the defendant about the unique situation, then the defendant should only be liable for harm that might occur in the normal course of events.

The Hadleys only told Baxendale that the article to be carried was a broken shaft from their mill. How could Baxendale have realized that a delay in delivery would prevent the mill from operating? He might have assumed very reasonably that the Hadleys owned a second shaft, and were sending this one for repairs while the mill ground on. It would be unfair to presume Baxendale realized that delay would halt the mill. The case should be retried, and the jury may *not* consider the Hadleys' lost profits.

The rule from Hadley v. Baxendale has been unchanged ever since: **the injured party may recover consequential damages only if the breaching party should have foreseen them.**

Let us return briefly to *Inside Straight*. Suppose that, long before shooting began, Ace had sold the film's soundtrack rights to Spinem Sound for $2 million. Spinem believed it would make a profit only if Reina appeared in the film, so it demanded the right to discharge the agreement if Reina dropped out. When Reina quit, Spinem terminated the contract. Now, when Ace sues Reina, it will also seek $2 million in consequential damages for the lost music revenue. If Reina knew about Ace's contract with Spinem when she signed to do the film, she is liable for $2 million. If she never realized she was an essential part of the music contract, she owes nothing for the lost profits.

INCIDENTAL DAMAGES

Incidental damages are the relatively minor costs that the injured party suffers when responding to the breach. When Reina, the actress, breaches the film contract, the producers may have to leave the set and fly back to Los Angeles to hire a new actress. The cost of travel, food, and audition-room rental are incidental damages.

SALE OF GOODS

Under the Uniform Commercial Code (UCC), remedies for breach of contract in the sale of goods are similar to the general rules discussed throughout this chapter. UCC §§2-703 through 2-715 govern the remedies available to buyers and sellers.

Seller's Remedies

If a buyer breaches a sale-of-goods contract, the seller generally has at least two remedies. She may resell the goods elsewhere. If she acts in good faith, she will be awarded **the difference between the original contract price and the price she was able to obtain in the open market.** Assume that Maud, the manufacturer, had a contract to sell her shoes to Foot the Bill for $55 per pair, and Foot the Bill's breach forces her to sell them on the open market, where she gets only $48 per pair. Maud will win $7 per pair times 5,000 pairs, or $35,000, from Foot the Bill.

Alternatively, the buyer may choose not to resell and settle for the difference between the contract price and the market value of the goods. Maud, in other words, may choose to keep the shoes. If she can prove that their market value is $48 per pair, for example, by showing what other retailers would have paid her for them, she will still get her $7 each, representing the difference between what the contract promised her and what the market would support. In either case, the money represents compensatory damages. Maud is also entitled to incidental damages, such as the storage and advertising expenses described above. But there is one significant difference **under the UCC: Most courts hold that the seller of goods is not entitled to consequential damages.** Suppose Maud hired two extra workers to inspect, pack, and ship the shoes for Foot the Bill. Those are consequential damages, but Maud will not recover them because she is the seller and the contract is for the sale of goods.

Buyer's Remedies

The buyer's remedies under the Code are similar to those we have already considered. She typically has two options. First, the buyer can "cover" by purchasing substitute goods. To **cover** means to make a good faith purchase of goods similar to those in the contract. The buyer may then obtain **the difference between the original contract price and her cover price.** Alternatively, if the buyer chooses not to cover, she is entitled to the difference between the original contract price and the market value of the goods.

Suppose Mary has contracted to buy 1,000 6-foot Christmas trees at $25 per tree from Elmo. The market suddenly rises, and in the spirit of the season Elmo breaches his deal and sells the trees elsewhere. If Mary makes a good-faith effort to cover but is forced to pay $40 per tree, she may recover the difference from Elmo, meaning $15 per tree times 1,000 trees, or $15,000. Similarly, if she chooses not to cover but can prove that $40 is now the market value of the trees, she is entitled to her $15 per tree.

Under the UCC, the buyer *is* entitled to consequential damages provided that the seller could reasonably have foreseen them. If Mary tells Elmo, when they sign their deal, that she has a dozen contracts to resell the trees, for an average price of $50 per tree, she may recover $25 per tree, representing the difference between her contract price with Elmo and the value of the tree to her, based on her other contracts. If she failed to inform Elmo of the other contracts, she would not receive any money based on them. The buyer is also entitled to whatever incidental damages may have accrued.

We turn now to cases where the injured party cannot prove expectation damages.

Reliance Interest

George plans to manufacture and sell silk scarves during the holiday season. In the summer, he contracts with Cecily, the owner of a shopping mall, to rent a high-visibility stall for $100 per day. George then buys hundreds of yards of costly silk and gets to work cutting and sewing. But in September, Cecily refuses to honor the contract. George sues and easily proves Cecily breached a valid contract. But what is his remedy?

George cannot establish an expectation interest in his scarf business. He hoped to sell each scarf for a $40 gross profit, and wanted to make $2,000 per day. But how much would he actually have earned? Enough to retire on? Enough to buy a salami sandwich for lunch? A court cannot give him an expectation interest, so George will ask for reliance damages. **The reliance interest is designed to put the injured party in the position he would have been in had the parties never entered into a contract.** This remedy focuses on the time and money the injured party spent performing his part of the agreement.

Assuming he is unable to sell the scarves to a retail store (which is probable since retailers will have made purchases long ago), George should be able to recover the cost of the silk fabric he bought and perhaps something for the hours of labor he spent cutting and sewing. However, reliance damages can be difficult to win because they are harder to *quantify*. Judges dislike vague calculations. How much was George's time worth in making the scarves? How good was his work? How likely were the scarves to sell? If George has a track record in the industry, he will be able to show a market price for his services. Without such a record, his reliance claim becomes a tough battle.

RELIANCE DAMAGES AND PROMISSORY ESTOPPEL

In one type of case, courts use reliance damages exclusively. Recall the doctrine of promissory estoppel, which sometimes permits a plaintiff to recover damages even without a valid contract. The plaintiff must show that the defendant made a promise knowing that the plaintiff would likely rely on it, that the plaintiff did rely, and that the only way to avoid injustice is to enforce the promise. **In promissory estoppel cases, a court will generally award *only* reliance damages.** It would be unfair to give expectation damages for the full benefit of the bargain when, legally, there has been no bargain. Lou says to Costas, who lives in Philadelphia, "You're a great chef. Come out to Los Angeles. My new restaurant needs you, and I can double your salary if not more." Costas quits his job and travels out west, but Lou has no job for him. There is no binding contract, because the terms were too vague; however, the chef will *probably* obtain some reliance damages based on lost income and moving costs.

AT **RISK** | Costas's reliance damages are uncertain. How should he have protected himself? ◢

Restitution Interest

Jim and Bonnie Hyler bought an expensive recreational vehicle (RV) from Autorama. The salesman promised the Hylers that a manufacturer's warranty covered the entire vehicle for a year. The Hylers had a succession of major problems with their RV, including windows that wouldn't shut, a door that fell off, a loose windshield, and defective walls. Then they learned that the manufacturer had gone bankrupt. In fact, the Autorama salesman knew of the bankruptcy when he made the sales pitch. The Hylers returned the RV to Autorama and demanded their money back. They wanted restitution.

The restitution interest is designed to return to the injured party a benefit that he has conferred on the other party, which it would be unjust to leave with that person. Restitution is a common remedy in contracts involving fraud, misrepresentation, mistake, and duress. In these cases, restitution often goes hand-in-hand with **rescission,** which means to "undo" a contract and put the parties where they were before they made the agreement. The court declared that Autorama had misrepresented the manufacturer's warranty by omitting the small fact that the manufacturer itself no longer existed. Autorama was forced to return to the Hylers the full purchase price plus the value of the automobile they had traded. The dealer, of course, was allowed to keep the defective RV and stare out the ill-fitting windows.

Courts also award restitution in cases of quasi-contract, which we examined in Chapter 9. In quasi-contract cases, the parties never made a contract, but one side did benefit the other. A court may choose to award restitution where one party has conferred a benefit on another and it would be unjust for the other party to retain the benefit. Suppose Owner asks Supplier to install a new furnace in her home. Supplier forgets to ask Owner to sign a contract. If the furnace works properly, it would be unfair to let Owner keep it for free, and a court might order full payment as restitution, even though there was no valid contract.

Other Equitable Interests

In addition to restitution, the other three equitable powers that concern us are specific performance, injunction, and reformation.

SPECIFIC PERFORMANCE

Leona Claussen owned Iowa farmland. She sold some of it to her sister-in-law, Evelyn Claussen, and, along with the land, granted Evelyn an option to buy additional property at $800 per acre. Evelyn could exercise her option anytime during Leona's lifetime or within six months of Leona's death. When Leona died, Evelyn informed the estate's executor that she was exercising her option. But other relatives wanted the property, and the executor refused to sell. Evelyn sued and asked for specific performance. She did not want an award of damages; she wanted the land itself. The remedy of specific performance forces the two parties to perform their contract.

A court will award specific performance, ordering the parties to perform the contract, only in cases involving the sale of land or some other asset that is unique. Courts use this equitable remedy when money damages would be inadequate to compensate the injured party. If the subject is unique and irreplaceable, money damages will not put the injured party in the same position she would have been in had the agreement been kept. So a court will order the seller to convey the rare object and the buyer to pay for it.

Historically, every parcel of land has been regarded as unique, and therefore specific performance is always available in real estate contracts. Evelyn Claussen won specific performance. The Iowa Supreme Court ordered Leona's estate to convey the land to Evelyn, for $800 per acre. Generally speaking, either the seller or the buyer may be granted specific performance.

Other unique items, for which a court will order specific performance, include such things as rare works of art, secret formulas, and patents. By contrast, a contract for a new Cadillac Escalade is not enforceable by specific performance. An injured buyer can use money damages to purchase a virtually identical auto.

INJUNCTION

You move into your new suburban house on two acres of land, and the fresh air is exhilarating. But the wind shifts to the west, and you find yourself thinking of farm animals, especially pigs. It turns out that your next-door neighbor just started an organic bacon ranch, and the first 15 porkers have checked in. You check out the town's zoning code, discover that it is illegal to raise livestock in the neighborhood, and sue. But money damages will not suffice, because you want the bouquet to disappear. You seek the equitable remedy of injunction. **An injunction is a court order that requires someone to do something or refrain from doing something.**

The court will order your neighbor immediately to cease and desist raising any pigs or other farm animals on his land. "Cease" means to stop, and "desist" means to refrain from doing it in the future. The injunction will not get you any money, but it will move the pigs out of town, and that was your goal. (The Web site **http://www.kinseylaw.com/ATTY%20SERV/civil/complaints/injunction.html** provides a sample complaint requesting an injunction.)

In the increasingly litigious world of professional sports, injunctions are commonplace. Brian Shaw was playing professional basketball in Italy when the Boston Celtics flipped him a contract offer. In January, Shaw inked a five-year deal with the Celtics, to begin playing the following October. The player grabbed a $450,000 bonus and a guaranteed salary of over $1 million per year. In June, Shaw reversed direction, informing the Celtics that he would remain with his Italian team. Boston ran a fast break into federal court, seeking an injunction. Shaw argued that when he signed the Celtics' contract he had been homesick for America, and depressed by criticism in the Italian press. He added that no agent had been available to assist. The court rejected his claims, noting that Shaw was a college graduate and the contract was a simple, standard-form agreement. The judge granted the injunction, blocking Shaw from playing anywhere except Boston.

REFORMATION

The final remedy, and perhaps the least common, is **reformation,** a process in which a court will partially "rewrite" a contract. Courts seldom do this, because the whole point of a contract is to enable the parties to control their own futures. But a court may reform a contract if it believes a written agreement includes a simple mistake. Suppose that Roger orally agrees to sell 35 acres to Hannah for $600,000. The parties then draw up a written agreement, accidentally describing the land as including 50 additional acres that neither party considered part of the deal. Roger refuses to sell. Hannah sues for specific performance, but asks the court to reform the written contract to reflect the true agreement. Most but not all courts would reform the agreement and enforce it.

A court may also reform a contract to save it. If Natasha sells her advertising business to Joseph and agrees not to open a competing agency in the same city anytime in the next 10 years, a court may decide that it is unfair to force her to wait a decade. It could reform the agreement and permit Natasha to compete, say, three years after the sale. But some courts are reluctant to reform contracts and would throw out the entire noncompetition agreement rather than reform it. Parties should never settle for a contract that is sloppy or overbroad, assuming that a court will later reform errors. They may find themselves stuck with a bargain they dislike or with no contract at all.

Special Issues of Damages

MITIGATION OF DAMAGES

There is one major limitation on *all* contract remedies: **A party injured by a breach of contract may not recover for damages that he could have avoided with reasonable efforts.** In other words, when one party perceives that the other has breached or will breach the contract, the injured party must try to prevent unnecessary loss. A party is expected to **mitigate** his damages, that is, to keep damages as low as he reasonably can. If you breach your lease by moving out of the apartment six months early, your landlord must make reasonable attempts to find a new tenant.

LIQUIDATED DAMAGES

It can be difficult or even impossible to prove how much damage the injured party has suffered. So lawyers and executives negotiating a deal may include in the contract a **liquidated damages clause, a provision stating in advance how much a party must pay if it breaches.** Is that fair? The answer depends on two factors: A court will generally enforce a liquidated damages clause if

- At the time of creating the contract it was very difficult to estimate actual damages; *and*

- The liquidated amount is reasonable. In any other case, the liquidated damage will be considered a penalty and will prove unenforceable.

In the following case, a private school provided special tutoring in liquidated damages—but not for free.

CASE SUMMARY

LAKE RIDGE ACADEMY v. CARNEY

66 Ohio St. 3d 376, 613 N.E.2d 183, 1993 Ohio LEXIS 1210
Supreme Court of Ohio, 1993

FACTS: In March, Mr. Carney reserved a spot in the 4th grade class at Lake Ridge Academy for his son, Michael. He paid a $630 deposit and agreed in writing to pay the balance of the tuition, $5,610, later that year. The contract permitted Carney to cancel the agreement and withdraw his son with no further obligation provided he did so before August 1. If he failed to notify the school before that date, he became liable for the full tuition.

Carney wrote a letter notifying Lake Ridge that Michael would not attend. He dated the letter August 1, mailed it August 7, and the school received it August 14. Lake Ridge demanded its full tuition, Carney refused, and the school sued. One of the disputed issues was whether the liquidated damages clause was a penalty. The trial court found for Carney, but the court of appeals reversed, finding that the clause was valid. Carney appealed to the state's highest court.

ISSUE: Is the liquidated damages clause enforceable?

DECISION: Yes, the liquidated damages clause is enforceable.

REASONING: The question in cases like this is whether the contract clause creates legitimate liquidated damages or unacceptable punitive damages. The answer depends on how easily the parties might have calculated the damages of a breach, and also on the size of the stipulated sum, compared to the value of the contract and the consequences of the breach.

When Carney and Lake Ridge entered into their contract, the damages that Lake Ridge might suffer from a breach were uncertain in amount and difficult to prove. Creating the school's budget is an uncertain science. The process begins in January and ends in the fall. The tuition money from all students is pooled and goes toward staff salaries, department budgets, maintenance, improvements, and utilities. Lake Ridge would be unable to calculate the precise damages caused by the loss of one student's tuition.

The school designated August 1 as the cutoff date so that it could meet its financial commitments. Carney had almost five months in which to cancel. By August 1, Lake Ridge reasonably relied on full tuition payment. This is a valid, enforceable liquidated damages clause. ◢

Chapter Conclusion

The powers of a court are broad and flexible and may suffice to give an injured party what it deserves. But problems of proof and the uncertainty of remedies demonstrate that the best solution is a carefully drafted contract and socially responsible behavior.

Chapter Review

1. Someone breaches a contract when he fails to perform a duty, without a valid excuse.

2. A remedy is the method a court uses to compensate an injured party.

3. An interest is a legal right in something, such as a contract. The first step that a court takes in choosing a remedy is to decide what interest it is protecting.

4. The expectation interest puts the injured party in the position she would have been in had both sides fully performed. It has three components:

   (a) Compensatory damages, which flow directly from the contract.

   (b) Consequential damages, which result from the unique circumstances of the particular injured party.

   (c) Incidental damages, which are the minor costs an injured party incurs responding to a breach.

5. The reliance interest puts the injured party in the position he would have been in had the parties never

entered into a contract. It focuses on the time and money that the injured party spent performing his part of the agreement. If there was no valid contract, a court might still award reliance damages under a theory of promissory estoppel.

6. The restitution interest returns to the injured party a benefit that she has conferred on the other party, which it would be unjust to leave with that person. Restitution can be awarded in the case of a contract created, for example, by fraud, or in a case of quasi-contract, where the parties never created a binding agreement.

7. Specific performance, ordered only in cases of land or a unique asset, requires both parties to perform the contract.

8. An injunction is a court order that requires someone to do something or refrain from doing something.

9. Reformation is the process by which a court will—occasionally—rewrite a contract to ensure that it accurately reflects the parties' agreement and/or to maintain the contract's viability.

10. The duty to mitigate means that a party injured by a breach of contract may not recover for damages that he could have avoided with reasonable efforts.

11. A liquidated damages clause will be enforced if and only if, at the time of creating the contract, it was very difficult to estimate actual damages and the liquidated amount is reasonable.

PRACTICE TEST

Matching Questions

Match the following terms with their definitions:

___ **A.** Liquidated

___ **B.** Specific performance

___ **C.** Restitution

___ **D.** Injunction

___ **E.** Consequential

1. A remedy that typically accompanies rescission.

2. Damages that can be recovered only if the breaching party should have foreseen them.

3. A court order to do (or refrain from doing) something.

4. Damages agreed upon in advance, in the contract.

5. A remedy that requires the parties to perform the contract.

True/False Questions

Circle true or false:

1. T F Courts award the expectation interest more often than any other remedy.

2. T F Consequential damages are those that arise whenever one party breaches a contract.

3. T F In a case of promissory estoppel, a court is most likely to award liquidated damages.

4. T F In a case of quasi-contract, a court is most likely to award restitution.

5. T F Where one party has clearly breached, the injured party must mitigate damages.

Multiple-Choice Questions

6. Rodney and Katerina enter into an agreement. Both parties know exactly what the damages will be if either party breaches. This contract

(a) Is appropriate for liquidated damages.

(b) Is not appropriate for liquidated damages.

(c) Is appropriate for restitution.

(d) Is not appropriate for rescission.

(e) Cannot include consequential damages.

7. Museum schedules a major fundraising dinner, devoted to a famous Botticelli picture, for September 15. Museum then hires Sue Ellen to restore the picture, her work to be done no later than September 14. Sue Ellen is late with the restoration, forcing the Museum to cancel the dinner and lose at least $500,000 in donations. Sue Ellen delivers the picture, in excellent condition, two weeks late. Museum sues.

   (a) Museum will win.

   (b) Museum will win if, when the parties made the deal, Sue Ellen knew the importance of the date.

   (c) Museum will win provided that it was Sue Ellen's fault she was late.

   (d) Museum will win provided that it was *not* Sue Ellen's fault she was late.

   (e) Museum will lose.

8. Which contract interest is designed to put the injured party in the position she would have been in had both sides fully performed?

   (a) Reliance.

   (b) Restitution.

   (c) Expectation.

   (d) Injunction.

   (e) Quasi-contract.

9. Max has developed "Sky Juice," a new sports power drink. He signs a contract with the Crushers, a professional hockey team, which allows Max to sell Sky Juice at all Crusher home games, from three booths located inside the stadium. The Crushers, however, run into financial trouble, and cancel their season. Max sues. His best remedy is going to be

   (a) Expectation interest.

   (b) Reliance interest.

   (c) Restitution.

   (d) Rescission.

   (e) Injunction.

10. Tara is building an artificial beach at her lakefront resort. She agrees in writing to buy 1,000 tons of sand from Frank for $20 per ton, with delivery on June 1, at her resort. Frank fails to deliver any sand, and Tara is forced to go elsewhere. She buys 1,000 tons from Maureen at $25 per ton, and then is forced to pay Walter $5,000 to haul the sand to her resort. Tara sues Frank. Tara will recover

   (a) Nothing.

   (b) $5,000.

   (c) $10,000.

   (d) $15,000.

   (e) $30,000.

Short-Answer Questions

11. Mr. and Ms. Beard contracted for S/E Joint Venture to build a house on property it owned, and then sell the completed house to the Beards for $785,000. S/E was late with construction and ultimately never finished the house or conveyed anything to the Beards, who sued. Evidence at trial demonstrated that S/E had clearly breached the contract and that the Beards had spent about $32,000 in rent because of the delay. There was testimony that the market value of the house as promised would have been about $100,000 more than the contract price, but this point was not clearly established because the trial judge considered it irrelevant. The judge awarded only the rental payments. Both sides appealed. Is the market value of the house, as it should have been built, relevant? How much money are the Beards entitled to?

12. Lewis signed a contract for the rights to all timber located on Nine Mile Mine. He agreed to pay $70 per thousand board feet ($70/mbf). As he began work, Nine Mile became convinced that Lewis lacked sufficient equipment to do the job well and forbade him to enter the land. Lewis sued. Nine Mile moved for summary judgment. The mine offered proof that the market value of the timber was exactly $70/mbf, and Lewis had no evidence to contradict Nine Mile. The evidence about market value proved decisive. Why? Please rule on the summary judgment motion.

13. Racicky was in the process of buying 320 acres of ranch land. While that sale was being negotiated, Racicky signed a contract to sell the land to Simon. Simon paid $144,000, the full price of the land. But

Racicky then went bankrupt, before he could complete the purchase of the land, let alone its sale. Which of these remedies should Simon seek: expectation, restitution, specific performance, or reformation?

14. Ambrose hires Bierce for $25,000 to supervise the production of Ambrose's crop, but then breaks the contract by firing Bierce at the beginning of the season. A nearby grower offers Bierce $23,000 for the same growing season, but Bierce refuses to take such a pay cut. He stays home and sues Ambrose. How much money, if any, will Bierce recover from Ambrose, and why?

15. ETHICS: The National Football League owns the copyright to the broadcasts of its games. It licenses local television stations to telecast certain games and maintains a "blackout rule," which prohibits stations from broadcasting home games that are not sold out 72 hours before the game starts. Certain home games of the Cleveland Browns team were not sold out, and the NFL blocked local broadcast. But several bars in the Cleveland area were able to pick up the game's signal by using special antennas. The NFL wanted the bars to stop showing the games. What did it do? Was it unethical of the bars to broadcast the games that they were able to pick up? Apart from the NFL's legal rights, do you think it had the moral right to stop the bars from broadcasting the games?

16. ROLE REVERSAL: Write a multiple-choice question involving a contract for the sale of goods. The seller breaches, and the buyer definitely has compensatory damages. The test taker must decide whether there are also consequential damages, and the total amount of damages to which the buyer is entitled.

Internet Research Problem

You represent a group of neighborhood residents in a large city who are protesting construction of a skyscraper that will violate building height limitations. Draft a complaint, requesting an appropriate injunction. You may use the sample injunction complaint found at **http://www.kinseylaw.com/ATTY%20SERV/civil/complaints/injunction.html**.

You can find further practice problems in the Online Quiz at **http://beatty.westbuslaw.com** or in the Study Guide that accompanies this text.

COMMERCIAL TRANSACTIONS

UNIT 3

Introduction to Sales

He Sued, she sued. Harold and Maude made a great couple because both were compulsive entrepreneurs. One evening they sat on their penthouse roof deck, overlooking the twinkling Chicago skyline. Harold sipped a decaf coffee while negotiating, over the phone, with a real estate developer in San Antonio. Maude puffed a cigar as she bargained on a different line with a toy manufacturer in Cleveland. They hung up at the same time. "I did it!" shrieked Maude, "I made an incredible deal for the robots—five bucks each!" "No, *I* did it!" triumphed Harold, "I sold the 50 acres in Texas for $300,000 more than it's worth." They dashed indoors.

Maude quickly scrawled a handwritten memo, which said, "Confirming our deal— 100,000 Psychopath Robots—you deliver Chicago—end of summer." She didn't mention a price, or an exact delivery date, or when payment would be made. She signed her memo and faxed it to the toy manufacturer. Harold took more time. He typed a thorough contract, describing precisely the land he was selling, the $2.3 million price, how and when each payment would be made and the deed conveyed. He signed the contract and faxed it, along with a plot plan showing the surveyed land. Then the couple placed a side bet on whose contract would prove more profitable. The loser would have to serve dinner for six months.

Neither Harold nor Maude ever heard from the other parties. The toy manufacturer sold the Psychopath Robots to another retailer at a higher price. Maude bought comparable toys elsewhere for $9 each. She sued. And the Texas property buyer changed his mind, deciding

to develop a Club Med in Greenland and refusing to pay Harold for his land. He sued. Only one of the two plaintiffs succeeded. Which one? ◾

The adventures of Harold and Maude illustrate the Uniform Commercial Code (UCC) in action. The Code is the single most important source of law for people engaged in commerce and controls the vast majority of contracts made every day in every state.

Development of Commercial Law

Throughout the first half of the 20th century, commercial transactions changed dramatically in this country, as advances in transportation and communication revolutionized trade. The nation needed a modernized business law to give uniformity and predictability in a faster world. In 1942, two groups of scholars, the American Law Institute (ALI) and the National Conference of Commissioners on Uniform State Laws (NCCUSL), began the effort to draft a modern, national law of commerce. Finally, in 1952, Professor Karl N. Llewellyn and his colleagues published their work—the Uniform Commercial Code. The entire Code is available online at **http://www.law.cornell.edu/ucc/ucc.table.html**.

Article 1: *General Provisions*	The purpose of the code, general guidance in applying it, and definitions.
Article 2: *Sale of Goods*	The sale of *goods,* such as a new car, 20,000 pairs of gloves, or 101 Dalmatians. This is one of the two most important articles in the UCC.
Article 2A: *Leases*	A temporary exchange of goods for money, such as renting a car.
Article 3: *Negotiable Instruments*	The use of checks, promissory notes, and other negotiable instruments.
Article 4: *Bank Deposits and Collections*	The rights and obligations of banks and their customers.
Article 4A: *Funds Transfers*	An instruction, given by a bank customer, to credit a sum of money to another's account.
Article 5: *Letters of Credit*	The use of credit, extended by two or more banks, to facilitate a contract between two parties who do not know each other and require guarantees by banks they trust.
Article 6: *Bulk Transfers*	The sale of a major part of a company's inventory or equipment. This article has been repealed in all but a few states.
Article 7: *Warehouse Receipts, Bills of Lading, and Other Documents of Title*	Documents proving ownership of goods that are being transported or stored. This article is being revised as we go to press.
Article 8: *Investment Securities*	Rights and liabilities concerning shares of stock or other ownership of an enterprise.
Article 9: *Secured Transactions*	A sale of goods in which the seller keeps a financial stake in the goods he has sold, such as a car dealer who may repossess the car if the buyer fails to make payments. This is one of the two most important articles in the Code.

THE CODE TODAY

The ALI and the NCCUSL have revised the Code several times since then, with important changes coming as recently as 2003. Remember, though, that in a sense the UCC is artificial because it is the creation of scholars. No section of the Code has any legal effect until a state legislature adopts it. In fact, all 50 states and the District of Columbia have adopted the UCC, but not all have adopted identical versions.

This book discusses and applies provisions of the Code that have been widely adopted. Article 9, on secured transactions, is one of the two most important in the Code. The commissioners completely rewrote Article 9 at the turn of this century, and this text reflects those changes. The commissioners have also revised Article 2, on sales, but as this book goes to press the changes have not been adopted by state legislatures, so we focus on existing law. The next four chapters highlight elements of the Code *that have changed the common-law rules of contract.*

HAROLD AND MAUDE, REVISITED

Harold and Maude each negotiated what they believed was an enforceable agreement, and both filed suit: Harold for the sale of his land, Maude for the purchase of toy robots. The difference in outcome demonstrates one of the changes that the UCC has wrought. As we revisit the couple, Harold scowls and clears the dinner dishes. Maude sits back in her chair, lights a cigar, and compliments her husband on the apple tart.

Harold's contract was for the sale of land and governed by the common law. The statute of frauds requires any agreement for the sale of land to be in writing and signed by the defendant, in this case the buyer in Texas. Harold signed it, but the buyer never did, so Harold's meticulously detailed document was worth less than a five-cent cigar.

Maude's quickly scribbled memorandum, concerning psychotic robot toys, was for the sale of goods and was governed by Article 2 of the UCC. The Code requires less detail in a writing. Because Maude and the seller were both merchants, the document she scribbled could be enforced *even against the defendant*, who had never signed anything. The fact that Maude left out the price and other significant terms was not fatal to a contract under the UCC.

UCC Basics

SCOPE OF ARTICLE 2

Because the UCC changes the common law, it is essential to know whether the Code applies in a given case. Negotiations may lead to an enforceable agreement when the UCC applies, even though the same bargaining would create no contract under the common law.

UCC §2-102: Article 2 applies to the sale of goods. Goods are things that are movable, other than money and investment securities. Hats are goods, and so are railroad cars and bottles of wine. Land is not a good, nor is a house. An agreement for the delivery of 10,000 hats is a contract for the sale of goods, but a contract for the sale of an office building is not.

Mixed Contracts

Sophocles University hires ClickOn Computer to design software for the university's computerized grading system, which must be capable of recording and storing all grades, computing averages, and printing transcripts. ClickOn agrees to design the software, install it, and train the staff in its use. This is a contract for the sale of goods (the software) and also services (design, installation, and training). If something goes wrong, what law governs? **In a mixed contract involving sales and services, the UCC will govern if the *predominant purpose* is the sale of goods,** but the common law will control if the predominant purpose is services.

In this case, the sale of the software predominated. ClickOn did its design work in order to sell an expensive software package to a customer. It was the software that generated the contract, not ClickOn's work in preparing it. Software is a good, so the UCC does govern. We discussed this issue in more detail in Chapter 9.

Merchants

The UCC, we know, attempts to meet the unique needs of contemporary business. But while the UCC offers a contract law that is more flexible than the common law, it also requires a higher level of responsibility from the merchants it serves. Many sections of the Code offer two rules: one for "merchants" and one for everybody else.

UCC §2-104: A merchant is someone who routinely deals in the particular goods involved. A used car dealer is a "merchant" when it comes to selling autos, because he routinely deals in them. He is not a merchant when he goes to a furniture store and purchases a new sofa.

The UCC frequently holds a merchant to a higher standard of conduct than a nonmerchant. For example, a merchant (such as Maude's robot-seller) may be held to an oral contract if he received written confirmation of it, even though the merchant himself never signed the confirmation. That same confirmation memo, arriving at the house of a nonmerchant, would not create a binding deal.

Good Faith

The UCC imposes a duty of good faith in the performance of all contracts. For nonmerchants, this means honesty in fact. When a student sells his used car, he may not lie about its mileage or accident history.

For a *merchant*, good faith means honesty in fact *plus* the exercise of reasonable commercial standards of fair dealing. Lee has agreed to buy 1,000 gallons of milk every month from a dairy for two years. Now she finds herself in financial difficulties. To get out of the milk contract she demands delivery at unreasonable, constantly changing times. When the supplier fails to comply, Lee tries to cancel their agreement. By ignoring the standards in her industry, Lee is acting in bad faith. The Code will not permit her to use this device to escape her obligations.

Unconscionability

The UCC employs a second principle to encourage fair play and just results: unconscionability. **UCC §2-302: A contract may be unconscionable if it is shockingly one-sided and fundamentally unfair.** Courts seldom find a contract unconscionable if the two parties are businesses, but they are quicker to apply the doctrine when one party is a consumer.

Suppose Bill's Builderia sells building equipment. For every sales contract Bill uses a preprinted form that says the buyer takes the item "as is," and that Bill is not liable for repairs or for compensatory or consequential damages. If Bill sells a $3,000 power mower to a landscape contractor and the machine falls to pieces, a court will probably enforce the limitation on liability. A professional contractor should have the sophistication to read and understand the contract, and can bargain for different terms if he is unhappy. But if the buyer is a consumer, such as a homeowner intent on mowing his own lawn, a court will probably declare the clause unconscionable. The homeowner is unlikely even to read the entire agreement, let alone understand phrases like "consequential damages." It would be unfair to enforce the clause against the consumer. We will look at this issue in more detail in Chapter 20, on warranties and products liability.

Contract Formation

The common law expected the parties to form a contract with an offer that included all important terms, and an acceptance of those precise terms. The drafters of the UCC recognized that business people frequently do not think or work that way.

FORMATION BASICS: SECTION 2-204

UCC §2-204 provides three important rules that enable parties to make a contract quickly and informally:

1. *Any Manner That Shows Agreement.* The parties may make a contract in any manner that shows they reached an agreement. They may show the agreement with words, writings, or even their conduct. Lisa negotiates with Ed to buy 300 barbecue grills. The parties agree on a price, but other business prevents them from finishing the deal. Then six months later Lisa writes, "Remember our deal for 300 grills? I still want to do it if you do." Ed doesn't respond, but a week later a truck shows up at Lisa's store with the 300 grills, and Lisa accepts them. The combination of their original discussion, Lisa's subsequent letter, Ed's delivery, and her acceptance all adds up to show that they reached an agreement. The court will enforce their deal, and Lisa must pay the agreed-upon price.

2. *Moment of Making Is Not Critical.* The UCC will enforce a deal even though it is difficult to say exactly when it was formed. Was Lisa's deal formed when they orally agreed? When he delivered? She accepted? The Code's answer: It does not matter. The contract is enforceable.

3. *One or More Terms May Be Left Open.* **Under the UCC, a court may enforce a bargain even though one or more terms were left open.** Lisa's letter never said when she required delivery of the barbecues or when she would pay. Under the UCC, the omission is not fatal. As long as there is some certain basis for giving damages to the injured party, the court will do just that. Suppose Lisa refused to pay, claiming that the agreement included no date for her payment. A court would rule that the parties assumed she would pay within a commercially reasonable time, such as 30 days.

In our UCC cases, the court typically uses two or more sections of the Code to determine the outcome. To help keep track of them, we outline the relevant provisions at the outset.

Code Provisions Discussed in This Case

Issue	Relevant Code Section
1. What law governs?	UCC §2-102: Article 2 applies to the sale of goods.
2. Did the parties form a contract?	UCC §2-204: The parties may make a contract in any manner sufficient to show agreement.

CASE SUMMARY

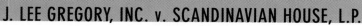

J. LEE GREGORY, INC. v. SCANDINAVIAN HOUSE, L.P.

209 Ga. App. 285, 433 S.E.2d 687, 1993 Ga. App. LEXIS 857
Georgia Court of Appeals, 1993

FACTS: Scandinavian House owned an apartment building that needed new windows. J. Lee Gregory, doing business as Perma Sash, sent a proposal to Scandinavian offering to remove all old windows and install new ones for $453,000. About two thirds of the price reflected material costs, and one third labor.

Scandinavian sent back a letter stating: "Please consider this letter an indication of our intent to purchase the windows contained in your proposal. This is your authorization to begin the measuring and the preparation of shop and installation drawings. We reserve the option to negotiate terms and conditions of the proposal which may impact or affect the operation of the building and the installation of the windows."

Perma Sash then spent three weeks measuring windows and preparing shop drawings, which it sent to Scandinavian House. The drawings were fine, but the parties, which had agreed on the price, could not agree on the method of payment. Perma Sash wanted certain guarantees of payment that Scandinavian House refused to make. Scandinavian notified Perma Sash that the deal was off and bought its windows elsewhere.

Perma Sash sued. The trial court gave summary judgment for Scandinavian, finding that the UCC did not govern and that the parties had never finalized an enforceable contract. Perma Sash appealed.

ISSUES: What law governs the case? Did the parties form a contract?

DECISION: The UCC governs, and the parties did form a contract.

REASONING: This was a hybrid contract, involving goods and services, and the first question is whether the UCC or the common law governs. The sale of the windows and their installation were both vital, and it is impossible to declare either component "more necessary." A court must decide what the parties considered to be the agreement's predominant purpose. Two thirds of the contract price was allocated to the windows; thus, the sale of goods was the predominant purpose. The UCC governs.

Did the parties form a contract? Under the Code, parties may create a binding agreement through conduct, rather than through a formal exchange of documents. Scandinavian House sent a letter awarding Gregory the contract and authorizing the company to take measurements and prepare drawings. Gregory responded by performing a substantial amount of work, with Scandinavian's cooperation. Even if the letter of intent was equivocal, the parties' conduct shows clear intent to create a binding agreement. The contract must be enforced.

J. Lee Gregory won a case that it would have lost under the common law. Next we look at changes the Code has made in the centuries-old requirement of a writing.

STATUTE OF FRAUDS

UCC §2-201 requires a writing for any sale of goods worth $500 or more. However, under the UCC, the writing need not completely summarize the agreement, and it need not even be entirely accurate. Once again, the Code permits parties to enforce deals with less formality. Here are the rules.

Writing Sufficient to Indicate a Contract

A simple memo is enough, or a letter or informal note, mentioning that the two sides reached an agreement. In general, the writing must be signed by the defendant, that is, whichever party is claiming there was no deal. Dick signs and sends to Shirley a letter saying, "This is to acknowledge your agreement to buy all 650 books in my rare book collection for $188,000." Shirley signs nothing. A day later, Louis offers Dick $250,000. Is Dick free to sell? No. He signed the memo, it indicates a contract, and Shirley can enforce it against him.

Incorrect or Omitted Terms

If the writing demonstrates the two sides reached an agreement, it satisfies §2-201 even if it omits important terms or states them incorrectly. Suppose Dick writes "$1888,000," indicating almost $2 million, when he meant to write "$188,000." The letter still shows that the parties made a deal, and the court will enforce it, relying on oral testimony to determine the correct price.

Enforceable Only to Quantity Stated

Since the writing only has to indicate that the parties agreed, it need not state every term of their deal. But one term is essential: quantity. The Code will enforce the contract only up to the quantity of goods stated in the writing. A court can surmise other terms, such as price or delivery time, based on the market, but will have no way of calculating the quantity.

Merchant Exception

This is a major change from the common law. When two merchants make an oral contract, and one sends a confirming memo to the other within a reasonable time, and the memo is sufficiently definite that it could be enforced against the sender herself, then **the memo is also valid against the merchant who receives it, unless he objects within 10 days.** Laura, a tire wholesaler, signs and sends a memo to Scott, a retailer, saying, "Confm yr order today—500 tires cat #886—cat price." Scott realizes he can get the tires cheaper elsewhere and ignores the memo. Big mistake. Both parties are merchants, and Laura's memo is sufficient to bind her. So it also satisfies the statute of frauds against Scott, unless he objects within 10 days.

ADDED TERMS: SECTION 2-207

Under the common law's mirror image rule, when one party makes an offer, the offeree must accept those exact terms. If the offeree adds or alters any terms, the acceptance is ineffective and the offeree's response becomes a counteroffer. In one of its most significant modifications of contract law, the UCC changes that result. **Under §2-207, an acceptance that adds or alters terms will often create a contract.** The Code has made this change in response to battles of the form. Every day, corporations buy and sell millions of dollars of goods using preprinted forms, with each form favorable to the side that sent it. The Code's drafters concluded that the law must cope with real practices.

Intention

The parties must still intend to create a contract. If the differing forms indicate that the parties never reached agreement, there is no contract.

Additional or Different Terms

An offeree may include a new term in his acceptance and still create a binding deal. Suppose Breeder writes to Pet Shop, offering to sell 100 guinea pigs at $2 each. Pet Shop faxes a memo saying, "We agree to buy 100 g.p. We get credit for any unhealthy pig." Pet Shop has added a new term, concerning unhealthy pigs, but the parties have created a binding contract because the writings show they intended an agreement. Now the court must decide what the terms of the contract are, since there is some discrepancy. The first step is to decide whether the new language is an additional term or a different term.

Additional Terms.   Additional terms are those that raise issues not covered in the offer.   The "unhealthy pig" issue is an additional term because the offer said nothing about it. **When both parties are merchants, additional terms generally become part of the bargain.** Pet Shop's insistence on credit for sick guinea pigs is binding on Breeder. In the following circumstances, however, additional terms do *not* become part of an agreement:

- If the original offer insisted on its own terms. If Breeder offered the pets for sale "on these and no other terms," Pet Shop's additional language would not become part of their deal.

- If the offeror promptly objects to the new terms. If Breeder received Pet Shop's fax and immediately called up to say, "no credit for unhealthy pigs," then Pet Shop's additional term is not part of their deal.

In other circumstances, additional terms generally become part of an agreement between merchants.

Different Terms.   **These are terms that contradict those in the offer.** Suppose Brilliant Corp. orders 1,500 cellular phones from Makem Co., for use by Brilliant's sales force. Brilliant places the order using a preprinted form stating that the product is fully warranted for normal use and that seller is liable for compensatory and consequential damages. This means, for example, that Makem would be liable for lost profits if a salesman's phone fails during a lucrative sales pitch. Makem responds with its own memo stating that in the event of defective phones, Makem is liable only to repair or replace, and is not liable for consequential damages, lost profits, or any other damages.

Makem's acceptance has included a different term because its language contradicts the offer. Almost all courts would agree that the parties intended to reach an agreement and therefore the contract is enforceable. The question is, what are its terms? **Different terms cancel each other out.** If there is no clear oral agreement, the Code supplies its own terms, called gap fillers, which cover prices, delivery dates and places, warranties, and other subjects. In the cellular phone case, the contradicting warranty provisions cancel each other out. A court would enforce the Code's gap-filler warranty, which *does* permit recovery of compensatory and consequential damages. Therefore, Makem would be liable for lost profits. We outline most of the gap-filler terms in Chapter 10, and analyze warranty provisions in greater detail in Chapter 20.

OPEN TERMS: SECTIONS 2-305 AND 2-306

Open Prices

Under §2-305, the parties may conclude a contract even though they have not settled the price. Again, this is a change from the common law, which required certainty of such an important contract term. **Under the Code, if the parties have not stated one, the price is a reasonable price at the time of delivery.** A court will use market value and other comparable sales to determine what a reasonable price would have been.

Output and Requirements Contracts

Under §2-306, an **output contract** obligates the seller to sell all of his output to the buyer, who agrees to accept it. Suppose Joel has a small plant in which he manufactures large plants, that is, handcrafted artificial flowers and trees, made of silk and other expensive materials. Joel isn't sure how many he can produce in a year, but wants a guaranteed market. He makes an output contract with Yolanda, in which he promises to sell the entire output of his plant and she agrees to buy it all.

A **requirements contract** is the reverse, obligating a buyer to purchase all of his needed goods from the seller. **The UCC requires that the parties in an output or requirements contract make their demands in good faith.** Neither party is free to make sudden, enormous changes in demand attempting to profit from market changes.

MODIFICATION

UCC §2-209: An agreement modifying a contract needs no additional consideration to be binding. Suppose Jeanette makes a deal to buy a used Mercedes "in good running order" from her sister, Valerie, for $29,000. Valerie writes to Jeanette confirming the agreement and promising to bring the car the following week. But before Valerie can deliver the car, a major transmission problem makes it inoperable. Valerie pays $1,200 to repair it. She telephones Jeanette and explains the extra cost. Jeanette faxes a note, promising to split the cost of the repair. Is Jeanette's promise enforceable? Valerie was already obligated to deliver a car in good running order. But under the UCC, contract modifications need no additional consideration to be valid.

The UCC also permits the parties to modify some contracts orally. Regrettably, the Code is not crystal clear about which changes may be oral and which must be written. The wise executive will insist that all parties sign any proposed modifications. For better or worse, though, §2-209 clearly implies that some alterations may be enforceable even with nothing in writing, so never orally agree to a contract change unless you are prepared to live with it.

Parties make a contract attempting to control their futures. One party's certainty can be undercut by the ease with which the other party may obtain a modification. Section 2-209 acknowledges this tension by enabling the parties to limit changes. **The parties may agree to prohibit oral modifications and insist that all modifications be in writing and signed.** Between merchants, such a clause is valid. But if either party is *not a merchant*, such a clause is valid only if the non-merchant separately signs it.

The following case looks at an oral modification and once again requires a decision as to whether a party is a merchant. You decide.

Code Provisions Discussed in This Case

Issue	Relevant Code Section
1. Was the tennis club a merchant?	UCC §2-104: A merchant is anyone who routinely deals in the goods involved.
2. Did the parties orally modify the contract?	UCC §2-209: The parties may prohibit oral modifications. If either party is *not* a merchant, such a clause is valid only if the nonmerchant separately signed it.

YOU BE THE JUDGE

CHESTNUT FORKS TENNIS CLUB v. T.J. INTERNATIONAL, INC.

1995 U.S. App. LEXIS 13279
United States Court of Appeals for the Fourth Circuit, 1995

FACTS: Chestnut Forks Tennis Club is an indoor tennis complex in Warrenton, Virginia. The club constructed a new indoor tennis arena and hired Trus Joist to build and install the roof truss system for $62,000. Trus Joist's contract contained express warranties guaranteeing that the trusses would be free of defects for a limited number of years. It also stated that no modifications of the contract were valid unless made in writing and signed by Trus Joist.

As Trus Joist was installing the roof, the partially completed system collapsed, damaging walls that had already been constructed and greatly delaying the opening of the new facility. The Chestnut Forks owners were furious. John Maloney, a general partner in the tennis club, spoke with William Walters, Trus Joist's national marketing manager, and threatened to terminate the agreement. Walters promised to give Chestnut Forks a $26,000 credit for the damage done, roughly 40% of the contract price. Walters also flatly guaranteed Maloney that the truss system would last from 80 to 100 years. Based on Walters's assurances, Maloney permitted Trus Joist to finish the job.

Eighteen years later, engineers discovered that the roof was dangerously weakened. Chestnut Forks was forced to replace it at a cost of over $400,000. All of the express warranties in the Trus Joist contract had long since expired, and Trus Joist refused to pay for the work. Chestnut Forks sued. The district court gave summary judgment for Trus Joist, and Chestnut Forks appealed, claiming that the conversation between Walters and Maloney, 18 years earlier, had modified the contract.

YOU BE THE JUDGE: **Did Walters's statements modify the contract?**

ARGUMENT FOR CHESTNUT FORKS: Mr. Walters explicitly guaranteed Chestnut Forks that the system would last 80 to 100 years. This was no casual conversation. Trus Joist's original installation was a disaster. The tennis club was prepared to terminate the deal and hire a competent company. Walters knew that and was determined to retain the job, so he reduced the price by 40% and guaranteed the product for 80 to 100 years. Walters's words were a valid oral modification of the contract. The contract language supposedly prohibiting oral modifications is irrelevant. Chestnut Forks is not a merchant because it does not routinely deal in the kind of goods at issue here, roof trusses.

ARGUMENT FOR TRUS JOIST: Your honors, warranties are one of the most important parts of any agreement, and Chestnut Forks was entirely satisfied with the warranty section. The club also agreed that no oral modifications would be binding on either side. And that, your honors, is it. The warranties have expired, and the plaintiffs have no case. Even if Mr. Walters made these alleged oral statements, they are irrelevant because no oral statements can modify this contract. Chestnut Forks is a business enterprise with experience and savvy. The "separate signing" provision in the Code is for the protection of the typical consumer buying something from a hardware store. The trial court correctly granted summary judgment for Trus Joist, and we ask you to affirm. ▮

The following table concludes this chapter with an illustration of the Code's impact on the common law.

Selected Code Provisions That Change the Common Law

Issue	Common Law Rule	UCC Section	UCC Rule	Example
Contract formation	Offer must be followed by acceptance that shows meeting of the minds on all important terms.	§2-204 and §2-305	Contract can be made in any manner sufficient to show agreement; moment of making not critical; one or more terms, including the price, may be left open.	Tilly writes Meg, "I need a new van for my delivery company." Meg delivers a van and Tilly starts to use it. Under the common law, there is no contract, because no price was ever mentioned; under the UCC, the writing plus the conduct show an intention to contract (2-204). The price is a *reasonable* one (2-305).
Writing requirement	All essential terms must be in writing.	§2-201	Any writing is sufficient if it indicates a contract; terms may be omitted or misstated; "merchant" exception can create a contract enforceable against a party who *receives* the writing and does nothing within 10 days.	Douglas, a car dealer, signs and sends to Michael, another dealer, a memo saying, "Confirming our deal for your blue Rolls." Michael reads it but ignores it; 10 days later Douglas has satisfied the statute of frauds under the UCC's merchant exception.
Added terms in acceptance	An acceptance that adds or changes any term is a counteroffer.	§2-207	Additional or different terms are not necessarily counteroffers; their presence does not prevent a contract from being formed, and in some cases the new terms will become a part of the bargain.	Roberts sends a pre-printed form to Julia, offering to buy 25 computers and stating a price; Julia responds with her own pre-printed form, accepting the offer but adding a term that balances unpaid after 30 days incur a finance charge. The additional term is *not* a counteroffer; there *is* a valid contract; and the finance charge is part of the bargain.
Modification	A modification is valid only if supported by new consideration.	§2-209	A modification needs no consideration to be binding.	Martin, a computer manufacturer, agrees to sell Steve, a retailer, 500 computers at a specified price, including delivery. The next day Martin learns that his delivery costs have gone up 20%; he calls Steve, who faxes a note agreeing to pay 15% extra. Under the common law, the modification would be void; under the Code, it is enforceable.

Chapter Conclusion

The Uniform Commercial Code enables parties to create a contract quickly. While this can be helpful in a fast-paced business world, it also places responsibility on executives. Informal conversations may cause at least one party to conclude that it has a binding agreement—and the law may agree.

Chapter Review

1. Article 2 applies to the sale of goods, which are movable things other than money and investment securities.

2. In a mixed contract involving goods and services, the UCC applies if the predominant purpose is the sale of goods.

3. A merchant is someone who routinely deals in the particular goods involved. The UCC frequently holds a merchant to a higher standard of conduct than a nonmerchant.

4. The UCC imposes a duty of good faith in the performance of all contracts.

5. UCC §2-204 permits the parties to form a contract in any manner that shows agreement.

6. For the sale of goods worth $500 or more, UCC §2-201 requires some writing that indicates an agreement. Terms may be omitted or misstated, but the contract will be enforced only to the extent of the quantity stated.

7. When two merchants make an oral contract, and one sends a confirming memo to the other within a reasonable time, and the memo is sufficiently definite that it could be enforced against the sender herself, then the merchant who receives it will also be bound unless he objects within 10 days.

8. UCC §2-207 governs an acceptance that does not "mirror" the offer. Additional terms usually, but not always, become part of the contract. Different terms contradict a term in the offer. When that happens, most courts reject both parties' proposals and rely on gap-filler terms.

9. UCC §2-209 permits contracts to be modified even if there is no consideration. The parties may prohibit oral modifications, but such a clause is ineffective against a nonmerchant unless she signed it.

PRACTICE TEST

Matching Questions

Match the following terms with their definitions:

___ A. Output

___ B. Additional terms

___ C. Predominant purpose

___ D. Different terms

___ E. Sale of goods worth $500 or more

1. Generally cancel each other out.

2. Determines whether the UCC or the common law governs.

3. Requires a written contract or memo.

4. A contract that limits the seller to one buyer.

5. Generally become part of a contract between merchants.

True/False Questions

Circle true or false:

1. T F A contract for the sale of goods may generally be modified without additional consideration.

2. T F In a contract for the sale of goods, the offer may include any terms the offeror wishes; the offeree must accept on exactly those terms or reject the deal.

3. T F A contract for the sale of $300 worth of decorative stone must be in writing to be enforceable.

4. T F If two parties agree in writing to the sale of 150 new Chevrolets of a particular model, the contract is enforceable even if they say nothing about price.

5. T F A merchant could become obligated on a contract for $15 million worth of oil, even though he never signed any agreement concerning it.

Multiple-Choice Questions

6. In a short memo, Maria agrees to sell Erin 100,000 pens, model #55. The contract says nothing about price. Both parties sign. Maria delivers the pens, but Erin refuses to say. The market value of the pens is $1. Maria sues.

   (a) Maria loses because the price was not specified, but she is entitled to the pens back.

   (b) Maria loses because the price was not specified, and she is not entitled to the pens back

   (c) Maria loses because there was no meeting of the minds.

   (d) Maria loses because neither party acted in good faith.

   (e) Maria wins $100,000.

7. Paul agrees to sell Rob 50 truckloads of bluestone. The total price is $50,000, which includes $40,000 for the stone, $5,000 for trucking, and $5,000 for stacking the stone on pallets and placing them as Rob directs. Does the UCC or the common law govern this contract?

   (a) The UCC governs.

   (b) The common law governs.

   (c) Both the UCC and the common law govern.

   (d) Neither the UCC nor the common law governs.

   (e) The parties must renegotiate the contract to specify which law governs.

8. Tuff sends a preprinted sales form, offering to sell Softee 5,000 watches, with Softee's logo on them, for $50,000. The form states that the watches are "novelty items and carry no warranty." Softee responds with its own form, agreeing to buy 5,000 watches at the stated price, "all watches warranted for one year." Softee pays, then discovers the watches do not work, and buys identical watches elsewhere for $60,000. Softee sues and wins

   (a) Nothing.

   (b) $25,000.

   (c) $50,000.

   (d) $60,000.

   (e) $110,000.

9. Marion orally agrees to sell Ashley her condominium in Philadelphia for $700,000. The parties have known each other for 20 years, and do not bother to put anything in writing. Based on the agreement, Marion hires a moving company to pack up all of her goods and move them to a storage warehouse. Ashley shows up with a cashier's check, and Marion says, "You're going to love it here." But at the last minute, Marion declines to take the check, and refuses to sell. Ashley sues and wins

   (a) Nothing.

   (b) The condominium.

   (c) $700,000.

   (d) The difference between $700,000 and the condominium's market value.

   (e) Damages for fraud.

10. Arthur signs a three-year requirements contract with Niles, for copper-based paint, at $40 per gallon. For the first year, Arthur averages 200 gallons per month. Then the price of copper skyrockets, and the cost of a gallon rises to $65. Arthur places an order for 1,000 gallons (at $40 per gallon) for the next month. Niles sends only 200 gallons, and Arthur sues.

(a) Arthur wins because Niles is obligated to sell Arthur whatever he requires.

(b) Arthur wins because the contract does not specify a maximum number of gallons.

(c) Arthur wins because a potential price rise is the only reason for the contract.

(d) Niles wins because Arthur is acting in bad faith.

(e) Niles wins because the contract is invalid from the start.

11. CPA QUESTION: Cookie Co. offered to sell Distrib Markets 20,000 pounds of cookies at $1.00 per pound, subject to certain specified terms for delivery. Distrib replied in writing as follows: "We accept your offer for 20,000 pounds of cookies at $1.00 per pound, weighing scale to have valid city certificate." Under the UCC:

(a) A contract was formed between the parties.

(b) A contract will be formed only if Cookie agrees to the weighing scale requirement.

(c) No contract was formed because Distrib included the weighing scale requirement in its reply.

(d) No contract was formed because Distrib's reply was a counteroffer.

Short-Answer Questions

12. ETHICS: Jim Dan, Inc. owned a golf course that had trouble with crabgrass. Jim Dan bought 20 bags of Scotts Pro Turf Goosegrass/Crabgrass Control for $835 and applied it to the greens. The Pro Turf harmed the greens, causing over $36,000 in damage. Jim Dan sued Scotts. Scotts defended by claiming that it sold the Pro Turf with a clearly written, easy-to-read disclaimer that stated that in the event of damage, the buyer's only remedy would be a refund of the purchase price. Jim Dan, Inc. argued that the clause was unconscionable. Please rule on the law, and comment on the ethics. *Should* a company be permitted to escape liability with such a clause? Which values are in conflict?

13. The Massachusetts Bay Transit Authority (MBTA) awarded the Perini Corp. a large contract to rehabilitate a section of railroad tracks. The work involved undercutting the existing track, removing the ballast and foundation, rebuilding the track, and disposing of the old material. Perini solicited an offer from Atlantic Track & Turnout Co. for Atlantic to buy whatever salvageable material Perini removed. Perini estimated the quantity of salvageable material that would be available. Atlantic offered to purchase "all available" material over the course of Perini's deal with the MBTA, and Perini accepted. But three months into the project, the MBTA ran short of money and told Perini to stop the undercutting part of the project. That was the work that made Perini its profit, so Perini requested that the

MBTA terminate the agreement, which the agency did. By that point Perini had delivered to Atlantic only about 15% of the salvageable material that it had estimated. Atlantic sued. What kind of contract do the parties have? Who should win and why?

14. Nina owns a used car lot. She signs and sends a fax to Seth, a used car wholesaler who has a huge lot of cars in the same city. The fax says, "Confirming our agrmt—I pick any 15 cars fr yr lot—30% below blue book." Seth reads the fax, laughs, and throws it away. Two weeks later, Nina arrives and demands to purchase 15 of Seth's cars. Is he obligated to sell?

15. The Brugger Corp. owned a farm, operated by Jason Weimer, who acted as the company's business agent. Tri-Circle, Inc. was a farm equipment company. On behalf of Brugger, Weimer offered to buy from Tri-Circle certain equipment for use on the farm. Tri-Circle accepted the offer, using a preprinted form. The form included a finance charge for late payment. Weimer's offer had said nothing about finance charges, but he made no objection to the new term. Tri-Circle supplied the farm equipment but later alleged that Brugger had refused to pay for $12,000 worth of the supplies. Tri-Circle sued. In deciding whether Tri-Circle was entitled to finance charges, the court first inquired whether Brugger, Weimer, and Tri-Circle were merchants. Why did it look into that issue? Were they merchants?

16. Are you the typical student who just cannot get enough questions and quizzes about the UCC? Type your way to **http://www.fullertonlaw.com** and click on the chapter concerning Sale of Goods. The Web site has a long discussion of the UCC, interspersed with contract hypotheticals and questions.

17. ROLE REVERSAL: Write a multiple-choice question that contrasts the common-law rules of contract formation with those of UCC §2-204.

Internet Research Problem

To find the latest legislation in your state regarding electronic contracts, go to **http://www.mbc.com/ecommerce.html**. Find the "Recent Updates" section and examine pending legislation. What is the goal of the legislation? Can you anticipate any problems that the proposed law might cause?

You can find further practice problems in the Online Quiz at **http://beatty.westbuslaw.com** or in the Study Guide that accompanies this text.

Ownership and Risk

He drove his truck fast along the rough country road, hurrying through the shadows of the Cascade Mountains. The door panel, freshly painted, read "Ernest Jenkins, Cattle Buyer." Spinning the wheel hard left, he passed under a wooden sign proclaiming "Double Q Ranch."

He introduced himself to Kate Vandermeer, the Double Q's business manager, and expressed an interest in buying 300 head of cattle. Vandermeer and the man mounted horses and rode out to inspect the herd. Vandermeer noticed that his boots were brand new and that he rode awkwardly.

He was satisfied with the cattle, so the two bargained, sitting on horseback. Vandermeer started at $310,000 and was surprised at how quickly they reached an agreement, at $285,000, a price she considered excellent. They agreed that Vandermeer would deliver the cattle by truck, in one week, in a nearby town. He would pay with a cashier's check and take possession of the cattle and all ownership documents, such as brand inspection certificates and veterinarian's certificates.

The next week he arrived on schedule and presented his cashier's check for the full amount.

The Double Q's bank sent the cashier's check for collection, but learned early the following week that it was forged. Three weeks later and 1,600 miles east, the FBI located the cattle, with the prominent "QQ" brand, in stockyards in Omaha. Ned Munson had purchased the cattle from the man for $225,000, which he considered a bargain. He had paid with a cashier's check. Ernest Jenkins, of course, had disappeared—literally. The truck's freshly painted door now read, "Ted J. Pringle, Grain Merchant," and it was parked a long, long way from Omaha. ◢

Legal Interest

Who owns the cows? The Double Q wanted its cattle back or $285,000. But Ned Munson claimed he had paid a fair price to a man who appeared to own them. If Vandermeer was so foolish as to give up the cattle to a con artist, let the ranch suffer the consequences. The Double Q sued. Both parties to this lawsuit are unhappy, but happily they have illustrated the theme for our chapter: When two parties claim a conflicting legal interest in particular goods, *who loses?*

An interest is a legal right in something. More than one party can have an interest in particular goods. In the cattle case, three parties had a legal interest. The Double Q ranch originally had valid **title** to the cattle, **meaning the normal rights of ownership.** Ernest Jenkins, the scam artist, acquired a lesser interest. His contract with Double Q was fraudulent because Jenkins intended to cheat the ranch. Nonetheless, he did have an agreement. He obtained **voidable title,** meaning limited rights in the goods, inferior to those of the owner. Finally, Ned Munson makes a claim to the cattle based on his payment and his possession of the cows and all documents.

The court will use various sections of the UCC to determine who keeps the cows and who bears the loss. Ned Munson should win the cattle. He was probably acting in good faith and a commercially reasonable manner when he bought the cows from a man who appeared to be a lawful cattle buyer. The Double Q must bear the loss. If, however, the Double Q can convince a court that Munson acted irresponsibly, because he had grounds for suspecting Jenkins, the court might order Munson to pay for the cattle.

Identification, Title, and Insurable Interest

Historically, courts settled disputes about legal interest by looking at one thing: title. The drafters of the UCC concluded that "title" was too abstract an answer for the assorted practical questions that arose. Today, title is only one of several issues that a court will use to resolve conflicting interests in goods. Identification and insurable interest have become more important as title has diminished in significance. We can begin to understand all three doctrines if we examine how title passes from seller to buyer.

EXISTENCE AND IDENTIFICATION

Title in goods can pass from one person to another only if the goods exist and have been identified to the contract.

Existence

Goods must exist before title can pass. Although most goods do exist when people buy and sell them, some have not yet come into being, such as crops to be grown later. A farmer may contract to sell corn even before it is planted, but title to the corn cannot pass until the corn exists.

Identification

Goods must be identified to the contract before title can pass. This means that the parties must have designated the specific goods being sold. Identification is an important concept that applies in other areas besides the passing of title. Often identification is obvious. If Dealer agrees to sell to Buyer a 60-foot motor yacht with identification number AKX472, the parties have identified the goods. But suppose Paintco agrees to sell Brushworks 1,000 gallons of white base paint at a specified price. Paintco has 25,000 gallons in its warehouse. Title cannot pass until Paintco identifies the specific gallons that will go to Brushworks.

The parties may agree in their contract how and when they will identify the goods. Paintco and Brushworks might agree, for example, that within one week of signing the sales agreement, Paintco will mark appropriate gallons. If the gallons are stored 50 to a crate, then Paintco will have a worker stick a "Brushworks" label on 20 crates. Once the label is on, the goods are identified to the contract.

PASSING OF TITLE

Once goods exist and are identified to the contract, title can pass from one person to another. **Title may pass in any manner the parties agree upon (UCC §2-401).** The parties can decide, for example, that title passes when the goods leave the manufacturer's factory, or when they reach the shipper who will transport them. If the parties do not agree on passing title, §2-401 decides. There are two possibilities:

- *When the goods are being moved,* title passes to the buyer when the seller completes whatever transportation it is obligated to do.

- *When the goods are not being moved,* title passes when the seller delivers ownership documents to the buyer. Suppose Seller, located in Louisville, has already manufactured 5,000 baseball bats, which are stored in a warehouse in San Diego. Under the terms of their contract, Buyer will take possession of the bats at the warehouse. When Seller gives Buyer ownership documents, title passes.

INSURABLE INTEREST

Anyone buying or selling expensive goods should make certain that the goods are insured. However, a party may insure something only when she has a legitimate interest in it. When does someone have an insurable interest in goods? The Code gives one answer for buyers and one for sellers. **A buyer obtains an insurable interest when the goods are identified to the contract (UCC §2-501).** Suppose, in January, Grain Broker contracts with Farmer to buy his entire wheat crop. Neither party mentions "identification." In January, the crop is not identified, and Broker has no insurable interest. In May, after weeks of breaking the soil, Farmer plants his wheat crop. Once he has planted it, the goods are identified. The Broker, who now has an insurable interest, purchases insurance. In July, a drought destroys the crop, and the Broker never gets one grain of wheat. The Broker need not worry: He is insured.

The seller's insurable interest is different. **The seller retains an insurable interest in goods as long as she has either title to the goods or a security interest in them (UCC §2-501).** "Security interest" refers to cases in which the buyer still owes the seller some money for the goods. Suppose Flyola Manufacturing sells a small aircraft to WingIt, a dealer, for $300,000. WingIt pays $30,000 cash and agrees to pay interest on the balance until it sells the plane. Flyola has an insurable interest even while the aircraft is in WingIt's showroom and may purchase insurance anytime until WingIt pays off the last dime. This means that a seller and buyer can have an insurable interest in the same goods simultaneously.

In the following case, a car accident leads several insurance companies to dispute who owned the damaged auto. Each company wants to claim that the car belonged to—someone else.

Code Provisions Discussed in This Case

Issue	Relevant Code Section
1. Which party had title to the car?	UCC §2-401: Title to goods may pass in any manner on which the parties agree.
2. Did the seller have an insurable interest in the car?	UCC §2-501: The seller retains an insurable interest in the goods as long as it holds title to a security interest in them.

CASE SUMMARY

VALLEY FORGE INSURANCE CO. v. GREAT AMERICAN INSURANCE CO.

1995 Ohio App. LEXIS 3939
Ohio Court of Appeals, 1995

FACTS: On a Friday afternoon, Karl and Linda Kennedy went to John Nolan Ford to buy a new Ford Mustang. The parties signed all necessary documents, including a New Vehicle Buyer's Order, an Agreement to Provide Insurance, and credit applications. The Kennedys made a down payment, but could not arrange financing before the dealership closed, so John Nolan Ford allowed them to take the car home for the weekend. That evening, Karl Kennedy permitted his brother-in-law, Cella, to take the car for a drive, along with a passenger named Campbell. Cella wrecked the car, injuring his passenger. Campbell sued, and the question was which insurance company was liable for all of the harm: John Nolan Ford's insurer (Milwaukee Mutual), Cella's insurer (Valley Forge), or Kennedy's insurer (Great American). The trial court ruled that title had never passed to Kennedy and found Milwaukee Mutual liable. The company appealed.

ISSUE: Had title passed to Kennedy at the time of the accident?

DECISION: Title had not yet passed to Kennedy. Affirmed.

REASONING: Milwaukee Mutual asserts that the risk of loss passed to the Kennedys when the car was delivered to them. However, the signed contract states that the buyer acquires "no right, title, or interest" in the automobile until it is delivered *and* either the full purchase price is paid in cash or satisfactory financing is arranged. At the time of the accident, the Kennedys had neither paid cash nor signed a financing agreement. Title never passed.

Milwaukee also argues that the Kennedys agreed to insure the automobile. The contract, though, does not state *when* the Kennedys were obligated to obtain insurance. It would be logical for them to do so after they had obtained title. Because the contract is ambiguous on this point, the agreement must be interpreted against the party who wrote it, namely the automobile dealer. John Nolan Ford still had the risk of loss when the accident occurred. ◢

When the Seller Has Imperfect Title

BONA FIDE PURCHASER

Some people are sleazy, and sales law must accommodate that reality. In the chapter opener we saw a scam artist purchase cattle from a respectable ranch and sell them to an honest dealer. The bad guy skipped town, leaving a dispute between two innocent companies. Either the original owner (the ranch) or the buyer (the cattle dealer) must bear the loss. Who loses?

The Question: Who must suffer the loss?

First we need to know what kind of title Bad Guy obtains: Is it void or voidable? If Bad Guy steals the goods from Owner, Bad Guy obtains **void title, which is no title at all.** When Bad Guy sells the goods to Buyer, she also gets no title at all. Abe steals Marvin's BMW and promptly sells it to Elaine for $35,000 cash. Two weeks later the police locate the car. Abe had no title to convey to Elaine and that is what she received—none. Elaine must return the car to Marvin and suffer the $35,000 loss for Abe's theft.

If Bad Guy purchases the goods from Owner, using fraud or deception, he obtains **voidable title, meaning limited rights in the goods, inferior to those of the Owner.** The owner should be able to recover the goods from the Bad Guy, but not from anyone else who ends up with them. Suppose Emily agrees to buy Marvin's other car, a Jeep. She gives him a check for $20,000 and he signs the vehicle over to her. Emily knows her check will bounce; she has used fraud to obtain the car. As a result, Emily obtains only voidable title. If Marvin learns of the deception before Emily sells the car to someone else, he will get his Jeep back.

Unfortunately, Emily is slippery, not stupid. She quickly sells the Jeep to Seth for cash. By the time Emily's check bounces, Emily is gone and Seth has the car. Who keeps the Jeep? Seth wins the car if he is a bona fide purchaser. **A person with voidable title has power to transfer valid title for value to a good-faith purchaser, generally called a bona fide purchaser or BFP.**

Seth can prove that he is a bona fide purchaser by showing two things:

• That he gave value for the goods; *and*

• That he acted in good faith.

It is generally easy for purchasers to show that they gave value, typically cash or a check. The real issue becomes whether the buyer acted in good faith. If Seth paid a reasonable purchase price and Emily showed him convincing identification and signed over to him all purchase documents, Seth acted in good faith. He keeps the Jeep and Marvin loses. If, though, Seth knew the car was stolen, he is not a BFP. Marvin receives the car back.

The Answer: Who loses?

Owner ⟶	Bad Guy ⟶	Buyer
The owner has good title.	1) Bad Guy STEALS the goods, obtaining *void* title (no title) and sells to the Buyer.	Buyer receives no title.
	2) Bad Guy uses fraud to PURCHASE the goods, obtaining *voidable* title, and sells to the Buyer.	If the Buyer gives value for the goods *and* acts in good faith, he is a BFP and receives good title.

ENTRUSTMENT

Your old Steinway grand piano needs a complete rebuilding. You hire Fred Showpan, Inc., a company that repairs and sells instruments. Showpan hauls your piano away work on it. Two months later, you are horrified to spot Showpan's showroom boarded up and pasted with bankruptcy notices. Worse still, you learn that Fred sold your beloved instrument to a customer, Frankie List. When you track down List, he howls that he paid $18,000 for the piano. Is he entitled to keep it?

Quite likely he is. Section 2-403(1), the BFP provision we just discussed, would not apply because Showpan did not purchase the piano from you. But §2-403(2) does apply. This is the "entrustment" section, and it covers cases in which the owner of goods voluntarily leaves them with a merchant, who then sells them without permission. According to **UCC §2-403(2), any entrusting to a merchant who deals in goods of that kind gives him power to transfer all rights of the entruster to a buyer in the ordinary course of business.** *Entrusting* means delivering goods to a merchant or permitting the merchant to retain them. In the piano example, you clearly entrusted goods to a merchant.

Deals in Goods of That Kind

The purpose of the section is to protect innocent buyers who enter a store, see the goods they expect to find, and purchase something, having no idea that the storekeeper is illegally selling the property of others. Buyers should not have to demand proof of title to everything in the store. But this protection does not extend to a buyer who arrives at a vacuum cleaner store and buys an $80,000 mobile home parked in the lot.

In the Ordinary Course of Business

This means that the buyer must act in good faith, without knowing that the sale violates the owner's rights. If Frank List buys your piano assuming that Showpan owns it, he has acted in good faith. If Frank was your neighbor and recognized your instrument, he is not buying in the ordinary course of business and must hand over the piano.

Of course, a merchant who violates the owner's rights is liable to that owner. If Showpan were still in business when you discovered your loss, you could sue and recover the value of the piano. The problems arise when the merchant is unable to reimburse the owner.

Code Provisions Discussed in This Case

Issue	Relevant Code Section
1. Did the buyer obtain the goods from a "merchant?"	UCC §2-104: A merchant is anyone who routinely deals in the goods involved.
2. Did the buyer obtain good title?	UCC §2-403: Any entrusting of goods to a merchant who deals in goods of that kind gives him power to transfer all rights of the entruster to a buyer in the ordinary course of business.

YOU BE THE JUDGE

PEREZ-MEDINA v. FIRST TEAM AUCTION, INC.

206 Ga. App. 719, 426 S.E.2d 397, 1992 Ga. App. LEXIS 1755
Georgia Court of Appeals, 1992

FACTS: At a farm auction, Juan Perez-Medina and Julio Lara bid against each other on a tractor, and Perez-Medina bought it for $66,500. At a second auction the same day, Perez-Medina bought some equipment that he wanted to add to his tractor. He again encountered Lara, and the two agreed that Lara would install the new equipment. Lara took the tractor to his place of business to work on it.

Later, Perez-Medina came to the shop and paid $10,000 for Lara to do the work. Lara in fact was a dealer in farm machinery. He regularly bought such equipment at auctions, then repaired and sold it. Perez-Medina testified, though, that Lara's shop appeared to him to be a repair shop rather than a sales shop.

First Team Auction had done business with Lara on a regular basis. Lara executed a standard pre-auction document declaring that he owned the tractor. Georgia law does not require ownership papers for a tractor. First Team then bought the tractor from Lara for $54,000. When Perez-Medina learned of this, he demanded the tractor back, but First Team refused. The trial court gave summary judgment in favor of First Team, and Perez-Medina appealed.

YOU BE THE JUDGE: Did First Team acquire good title to the tractor based on UCC §2-403(2)?

ARGUMENT FOR PEREZ-MEDINA: Your honors, UCC §2-403(2) does not apply, for several reasons. First, the section only protects a buyer who purchases from a merchant. Julio Lara was not a merchant. When Mr. Perez-Medina visited, it was clear to him that Lara operated a repair shop. A court should apply this section of the Code only when the owner realized he was entrusting goods to someone who might be tempted to sell them.

Second, Mr. Perez-Medina never entrusted the tractor to Lara. He simply asked Lara to repair the machine. First Team is arguing that a perfectly honest farmer should lose his hard-earned property simply because he took it to a repair shop for work. That means every time we take our car to a garage for an oil change, the garage is free to sell it.

Third, the auction company did not buy the tractor in the ordinary course of business because it lacked good faith. This is a $65,000 piece of equipment, not a pack of chewing gum. First Team should have inquired where Lara got the equipment and why he wanted to sell it so cheap.

ARGUMENT FOR FIRST TEAM: Your honors, we agree that the three issues mentioned resolve this case. First, Mr. Lara was and is a merchant. Perez-Medina met Lara at two farm auctions in one day. What did he think Lara was doing there, painting landscapes? Lara had to be a merchant: First he tried to buy the same tractor; then he offered to rebuild it for Perez-Medina. If he had been a farmer, he wouldn't have offered to make repairs; had he merely owned a repair shop, he wouldn't have attempted to buy the tractor himself.

Second, Perez-Medina did entrust the machine to Lara. Perez-Medina argues that he never intended Lara to sell it. We know that. The whole point of §2-403(2) is that buyers obtain good title even when the owner never authorized the sale.

Third, First Team acted entirely in good faith by buying in the ordinary course of business. It had done business with Lara before, and had no reason to suspect any wrongdoing here. ▮

Creditor's Rights

In the entrustment section, we considered the rights of the *owner* of goods and how her interests might conflict with those of a merchant and a buyer. A related issue concerns a *creditor*, specifically, one who has loaned money to a merchant and therefore has a financial stake in the goods the merchant is selling.

Article 9 of the Code controls the rights of parties with such credit interests. We look closely at the issues in Chapter 25. Briefly, UCC §9-320 governs the rights of a creditor, a merchant, and a buyer in the ordinary course of business. Suppose the Nickel & Dime Bank loans Yoyo's Yacht Sales $1,000,000 to purchase two yachts wholesale. The yachts arrive at Yoyo's and remain in the showroom, but Nickel & Dime retains a security interest in both. If Yoyo fails to repay its loan, the bank is entitled to seize the yachts. Further, Yoyo is obligated to notify the bank immediately of a sale and hold the money until the bank gets its share. Unaware of Nickel & Dime's security interest, Liz pays $400,000 for one of the yachts. Yoyo grabs the money and sails into the horizon, leaving the bank in his wake. May Nickel & Dime take Liz's new yacht? No. **UCC §9-320 generally permits a buyer in the ordinary course of business to take the goods free and clear of the security interest.** See Chapter 25 for details.

RETURNABLE GOODS

Sometimes the seller will allow the buyer to return goods even when he has no complaints about their quality. This, too, can create a problem for creditors. A bank may extend a loan to a business based on the inventory. The bank is willing to lend money because it can seize the goods if the merchant fails to pay on time. But what if the merchant does not own some of the goods, because he intends to return them to the original owner? If the merchant fails to pay his loan, who gets the goods—the creditor (bank) or the owner of the goods? The Code considers two types of contract that permit a buyer to return goods.

Sale on Approval

If a buyer takes goods intending to use them herself, but has the right to return the goods to the seller, it is a **"sale on approval."** Max manufactures bar code readers, the machines that scan magnetic bar codes on merchandise. He wants to sell half a dozen to Pinky's Superette, but Pinky isn't sure the machines are worth the price. To encourage Pinky, Max allows her to take the machines and try them out. At the end of 60 days she may return them or pay full price. There really is no sale until Pinky has formally accepted the goods.

Under UCC §2-326(2), in a sale on approval, the goods are not subject to the buyer's creditors until the buyer accepts them. Suppose Pinky has borrowed $200,000 from the bank and has given a security interest "in all goods in the store now or in the future." The bar code machines are "goods in the store," and if Pinky fails to pay her loans, the bank will try to seize the equipment. But this is a sale on approval, and the bank has no right to Max's machines.

 A finance company will often extend credit based on a merchant's inventory. A creditor considering such a loan must determine what goods, if any, are "sale on approval," since those goods give the creditor no security. ◾

Sale or Return

If a buyer takes goods intending to resell them, but has the right to return the goods to the seller, it is a **"sale or return."** This is generally the same as a consignment. The owner is called the consignor and the buyer is the consignee. Yvonne runs a used car lot. Trent offers to sell Yvonne his used Mustang auto, but Yvonne offers instead to place the car on her lot and try to sell it. She will pay Trent nothing for the car but will keep 20% of the price if she can sell it.

Under UCC §2-326, in a sale or return, the goods are subject to the claims of the buyer's creditors. Suppose Yvonne fails to pay back some loans. Her creditors will instantly round up the Mustang, and Trent will never get a dime for his car.

The issues we have looked at thus far involve someone doing something wrong, often a scoundrel selling goods that he never owned. Now we turn to cases where there may be no wrongdoer.

Risk of Loss

Accidents hurt businesses, and the law may again need to decide who suffers the loss. In the cases we have seen thus far, the parties were arguing, "It's mine!"— "Like heck, it's mine!" In risk of loss cases, the parties are generally shouting, "It was yours!"— "No way, chump, it was yours!"

Athena, a seafood wholesaler, is gearing up for the Super Bowl, which will bring 110,000 hungry visitors to her city for a week. Athena orders 25,000 lobsters from Poseidon's Fishfoods, 500 miles distant, and simultaneously contracts with a dozen local restaurants to resell them. Poseidon loads the lobsters, still kicking, into refrigerated rail cars owned by Demeter Trucking. But halfway to the city, the train collides with a prison van. The lobsters escape, hurtling into the swamps, from which they are never recaptured. Athena loses all of her profits and sues. As luck would have it, Demeter Trucking had foolishly economized by letting its insurance lapse. Poseidon claims the goods were out of its hands. Who loses?

The UCC permits the parties to agree on who bears the risk of loss. **UCC §2-509(4) states that the parties may allocate the risk of loss any way they wish.** Often the parties will do just that, avoiding arguments and litigation in the event of an accident. As part of her agreement with Poseidon, Athena should have included a one-sentence clause, such as "Seller bears all risk of loss until the lobsters are delivered to Athena's warehouse." As long as the parties make their risk allocation clear, the Code will enforce it.

SHIPPING TERMS

The parties can quickly and easily allocate the risk of loss by using common shipping terms that the Code defines. FOB means free on board; FAS indicates free alongside a ship; and CIF stands for cost, insurance, and freight. By combining these designations with other terms, the parties can specify risk in a few words:

- *FOB place of shipment.* The seller is obligated to put the goods into the possession of the carrier at the place named. The seller bears the expense *and risk* until they are in the carrier's possession. From that moment onward, the buyer bears the risk.

- *FOB place of destination.* The seller must deliver the goods at the place named and bears the expense *and risk* of shipping.

- *FAS a named vessel.* The seller at his expense *and risk* must deliver the goods alongside the named vessel and obtain proper receipts.

- *CIF.* The price includes in a lump sum the cost of the goods and the insurance and freight to the named destination.

- *C & F.* The price includes in a lump sum the cost of the goods and freight, but *not* insurance.

Thus, if Athena had put a clause in her contract saying, "FOB Athena's warehouse," Poseidon would have born the risk of any loss up to the time the lobsters were unloaded in Athena's possession. For an example of all shipping terms, as they actually appear in the statutes of one state (Maine), see **http://janus.state.me.us/legis/statutes**.

WHEN THE PARTIES FAIL TO ALLOCATE THE RISK

If the parties fail to specify when the risk passes from seller to buyer, the Code provides the answer. When neither party breached the contract, §2-509 determines the risk; when a party has breached the contract, §2-510 governs. The full analysis of risk is beyond the scope of this chapter, but we can supply you with a short version: **When neither party has breached, the risk of loss generally passes from seller to buyer when the seller has transported the goods as far as he is obligated to. When a party has breached, the risk of loss generally lies with that party.**

Chapter Conclusion

The Code enables the parties in most commercial transactions to control their own destiny. It reduces the importance of abstract terms like "title," and allows buyer and seller to specify when goods are identified and when risk shifts. Owners and creditors can anticipate problems and protect themselves. But the provisions only work if businesspeople understand the rules and apply them.

Chapter Review

1. An interest is a legal right in something. Title means the normal rights of ownership.

2. Goods must exist and be identified to the contract before title can pass. The parties may agree in their contract how and when they will identify goods; if they do not specify, the Code stipulates when it happens. The parties may also state when title passes, and once again, if they do not, the Code provides rules.

3. A buyer obtains an insurable interest when the goods are identified to the contract. A seller retains an insurable interest in goods as long as she has either title or a security interest in them.

4. Void title is no title at all. Voidable title means limited rights in the goods, inferior to those of the owner. A person with voidable title has power to transfer good title to a bona fide purchaser (BFP), that is, someone who purchases in good faith, for value.

5. Any entrusting of goods to a merchant who deals in goods of that kind gives him the power to transfer all rights of the entruster to a buyer in the ordinary course of business.

6. A buyer in the ordinary course of business generally takes goods free and clear of any security interest.

7. In a sale on approval, the goods are not subject to the buyer's creditors until the buyer accepts them; in a sale or return, the goods are subject to the buyer's creditors.

8. In their contract, the parties may allocate the risk of loss any way they wish. If they fail to do so, the Code provides several steps to determine who pays for any damage.

PRACTICE TEST

Matching Questions

Match the following terms with their definitions:

___ **A.** Voidable title

___ **B.** Sale or return

___ **C.** Identification

___ **D.** Seller's insurable interest

___ **E.** Sale on approval

1. Buyer takes goods intending to *use* them but with the right to return them.

2. The power to transfer valid title for value to a BFP.

3. Buyer takes goods intending to *resell* them, but with the right to return them.

4. A step that must be taken before title can pass.

5. Either title to goods or a security interest.

True/False Questions

Circle true or false:

1. T F In any sale of goods, title passes to the buyer when the seller completes their transportation.

2. T F A buyer obtains an insurable interest when the goods are identified to the contract.

3. T F A BFP who buys goods from a thief obtains voidable title.

4. T F Entrusting to a merchant who deals in those goods may give that merchant the power to sell the goods and give good title.

5. T F A buyer in the ordinary course of business normally takes goods free and clear of any security interest.

Multiple-Choice Questions

6. CPA QUESTION On Monday, Wolfe paid Aston Co., a furniture retailer, $500 for a table. On Thursday, Aston notified Wolfe that the table was ready to be picked up. On Saturday, while Aston was still in possession of the table, it was destroyed in a fire. Who bears the loss of the table?

(a) Wolfe, because Wolfe had title to the table at the time of loss.

(b) Aston, unless Wolfe is a merchant.

(c) Wolfe, unless Aston breached the contract.

(d) Aston, because Wolfe had not yet taken possession of the table.

7. CPA QUESTION Under UCC Article 9 on secured transactions, which of the following statements is correct concerning the disposition of goods by a secured creditor after a debtor defaults on a loan?

(a) A good-faith purchaser of the goods for value and without knowledge of any defects in the sale takes free of any security interest.

(b) The debtor may not redeem the goods after the default.

(c) Secured creditors retain the right to redeem the goods after they are sold to a third party.

(d) The goods may be disposed of only at a public sale.

8. CPA QUESTION: On September 10, Bell Corp. entered into a contract to purchase 50 lamps from Glow Manufacturing. Bell prepaid 40% of the purchase price. Glow became insolvent on September 19 before segregating, in its inventory, the lamps to be delivered to Bell. Bell will not be able to recover the lamps because:

(a) Bell is regarded as a merchant

(b) The lamps were not identified to the contract

(c) Glow became insolvent fewer than 10 days after receipt of Bell's prepayment

(d) Bell did not pay the full price at the time of purchase

9. CPA QUESTION: Quick Corp. agreed to purchase 200 typewriters from Union Suppliers, Inc. Union is a wholesaler of appliances and Quick is an appliance retailer. The contract required Union to ship the typewriters to Quick by common carrier, "FOB Union Suppliers, Inc. Loading Dock." Which of the parties bears the risk of loss during shipment?

(a) Union, because the risk of loss passes only when Quick receives the typewriters.

(b) Union, because both parties are merchants.

(c) Quick, because title to the typewriters passed to Quick at the time of shipment.

(d) Quick, because the risk of loss passes when the typewriters are delivered to the carrier.

10. In most European countries, a purchaser who has no reason to suspect she is buying stolen goods generally obtains good title. Compare this to the American rule.

(a) The European rule places primary responsibility on the seller to insure payment.

(b) The American rule places primary responsibility on the seller to insure payment.

(c) The European rule places more responsibility on the owner to prevent theft.

(d) The American rule places more responsibility on the buyer to investigate title.

(e) The American rule places more responsibility on the owner to prevent theft.

Short-Answer Questions

11. ETHICS: Myrna and James Brown ordered a $35,000 motor home from R. V. Kingdom, Inc. The manufacturer delivered the vehicle to R. V. Kingdom, with title in the dealer's name. The Browns agreed to accept the motor home, but soon regretted spending the money and asked R. V. Kingdom to resell it. The motor home stayed on R. V. Kingdom's lot for quite a few months, but when the Browns decided to come get it, they learned that R. V. Kingdom had illegally used the vehicle as collateral for a loan and that a bank had repossessed it. The Browns filed a claim with their insurance company, State Farm. The insurer agreed that the vehicle had been stolen and agreed that the Browns' policy covered newly acquired vehicles. But the company refused to pay, claiming that the Browns had not taken title or possession to the goods and therefore had no insurable interest. The Browns sued. Please rule on their case. Also, examine the ethics: Who are the stakeholders? How would each party's conduct look in the light of day? What are the consequences of the respective positions?

12. John C. Clark, using an alias, rented a Lexus from Alamo Rent-A-Car in San Diego, California. Clark never returned the car to Alamo and obtained a California "quick title" using forged signatures. He then advertised in the *Las Vegas Review Journal* newspaper and sold the car to Terry and Vyonne Mendenhall for $34,000 in cash. The Mendenhalls made improvements to the car, had it insured, smog and safety tested, registered, licensed, and titled in the state of Utah. When Alamo reported the car stolen, the Nevada Department of Motor Vehicles seized the auto and returned it to Alamo. The Mendenhalls sued Alamo. The trial court concluded that the Mendenhalls had purchased the car for value and without notice that it was stolen, and were bona fide purchasers entitled to the Lexus. Alamo appealed. Please rule.

13. Fay Witcher owned a Ford Bronco. Steve Risher operated a used car lot. (We know where this one's heading.) Witcher delivered his automobile to Risher, asking him to resell it if he could. Witcher specified that he wanted all cash for his car, not part cash plus a trade-in. Risher sold the car to Richard Parker for $12,800, but took a trade-in as part payment. Risher promised to deliver the Bronco's certificate of title to Parker within a few days, but never did. He was also obligated to deliver most of the proceeds of the sale to Witcher, the owner, but also failed to do that. Parker claimed that the car was rightfully his. Witcher argued that Parker owned nothing because he never got the title and because Witcher never got his money. Who loses?

14. Bradkeyne International, Ltd., an English company, bought a large quantity of batteries from Duracell, Inc. The contract specified delivery "FOB Jacksonville, Florida." Duracell supervised the loading of the batteries onto a ship in Jacksonville in early July, and they arrived in England in August. When loaded onto the ship, the batteries were conforming goods that could be used for normal purposes. But on board the ship, excessive heat damaged them. By the time they reached England, they were worth only a fraction of the original price. Bradkeyne sued Duracell. Who loses?

15. ROLE REVERSAL: Write a multiple-choice question concerning either insurable interest, bona fide purchaser, or entrustment.

Internet Research Problem

You own two powerful Clydesdale draft horses. A friend asks to borrow the horses for three months to give hayrides. You agree, provided your friend takes proper care of these valuable animals, providing good feed, adequate rest, and veterinary treatment. Examine the bailment contract at **http://www.gate.net/~legalsvc/autobail.html**; then draft a bailment agreement.

You can find further practice problems in the Online Quiz at **http://beatty.westbuslaw.com** or in the Study Guide that accompanies this text.

chapter 20

Warranties and Product Liability

You are sitting in a fast-food restaurant in Washington, D.C. Your friend Ben, who works for a member of Congress, is eating with one hand and gesturing with the other. "We want product liability reform and we want it now," he proclaims, stabbing the air with his free hand. "It's absurd, these multimillion-dollar verdicts, just because something has a *slight defect*." He waves angrily at the absurdity, takes a ferocious bite from his burger—and with a loud CRACK breaks a tooth. Ben howls in pain and throws down the bun, revealing a large piece of bone in the meat. As he tips back in misery, his defectively manufactured chair collapses, and Ben slams into the tile, knocking himself unconscious. Hours later, when he revives in the hospital, he refuses to speak to you until he talks with his lawyer. They will discuss **product liability,** which refers to goods that have caused an injury. The harm may be physical, as it was in Ben's case. Or it can be purely economic, as when a corporation buys a computer so defective it must be replaced, costing the buyer lost time and profits. The injured party may have a choice of possible remedies, including:

- *Warranty,* which is an assurance provided in a sales contract
- *Negligence,* which refers to unreasonable conduct by the defendant; and
- *Strict liability,* which prohibits defective products whether the defendant acted reasonably or not.

We discuss each of these remedies in this chapter. What all product liability cases have in common is that a person or business has been hurt by goods. We begin with warranties.

Express Warranties

A warranty is a contractual assurance that goods will meet certain standards. It is normally a manufacturer or a seller who gives a warranty, and a buyer who relies on it. A warranty might be explicit and written: "The manufacturer warrants that the light bulbs in this package will provide 100 watts of power for 2,000 hours." Or a warranty could be oral: "Don't worry, this machine can harvest any size of wheat crop ever planted in the state."

An express warranty is one that the seller creates with his words or actions.[1] Whenever a seller clearly indicates to a buyer that the goods being sold will meet certain standards, she has created an express warranty. For example, if the sales-clerk for a paint store tells a professional house painter that "this exterior paint will not fade for three years, even in direct sunlight," that is an express warranty and the store is bound by it. The store is also bound by express warranty if the clerk gives the painter a brochure making the same promise, or a sample that indicates the same thing.

Implied Warranties

Emily sells Sam a new jukebox for his restaurant, but the machine is so defective it never plays a note. When Sam demands a refund, Emily scoffs that she never made any promises. She is correct that she made no express warranties, but is liable nonetheless. Many sales are covered by implied warranties.

Implied warranties are those created by the Code itself, not by any act or statement of the seller.

IMPLIED WARRANTY OF MERCHANTABILITY

This is the most important warranty in the Code. **Unless excluded or modified, a warranty that the goods shall be merchantable is implied in a contract for their sale, if the seller is a merchant with respect to goods of that kind.**[2] Merchantable means that the goods are fit for the ordinary purposes for which they are used. This rule contains several important principles:

- *Unless excluded or modified* means that the seller does have a chance to escape this warranty.

- *Merchantability* requires that goods be fit for their normal purposes. A ladder, to be merchantable, must be able to rest securely against a building and support someone who is climbing it. The ladder need not be serviceable as a boat ramp.

---

[1] UCC §2-313.
[2] UCC §2-314.

- *Implied* means that the law itself imposes this liability on the seller.

- *A merchant with respect to goods of that kind* means that the seller is someone who routinely deals in these goods or holds himself out as having special knowledge about these goods.

Dacor Corp. manufactured and sold scuba diving equipment. Dacor ordered air hoses from Sierra Precision, specifying the exact size and couplings so that the hose would fit safely into Dacor's oxygen units. Within a year, customers returned a dozen Dacor units, complaining that the hose connections had cracked and were unusable. Dacor recalled 16,000 units and refit them at a cost of $136,000. Dacor sued Sierra and won its full costs. Sierra was a merchant with respect to scuba hoses, because it routinely manufactured and sold them. The defects were life-threatening to scuba divers, and the hoses could not be used for normal purposes.

The scuba equipment was not merchantable, because a properly made scuba hose should never crack under normal use. But what if the product being sold is food, and the food contains something that is harmful—yet quite normal?

CASE SUMMARY

GOODMAN v. WENCO FOODS, INC.

333 N.C. 1, 423 S.E.2d 444, 1992 N.C.LEXIS 671
Supreme Court of North Carolina, 1992

FACTS: Fred Goodman stopped for lunch at a Wendy's restaurant in Hillsborough, North Carolina. Goodman had eaten half of his double hamburger when he bit down and felt immediate pain in his lower jaw. He took from his mouth a triangular piece of cow bone, about one sixteenth to one quarter inch thick and one half inch long, along with several pieces of his teeth. Goodman's pain was intense and his dental repairs took months.

The restaurant purchased all of its meat from Greensboro Meat Supply Company (GMSC). Wendy's required its meat to be chopped and "free from bone or cartilage in excess of 1/8 inch in any dimension." GMSC beef was inspected continuously by state regulators and was certified by the United States Department of Agriculture (USDA). The USDA considered any bone fragment less than three quarters of an inch long to be "insignificant."

Goodman sued, claiming a breach of the implied warranty of merchantability. The trial court dismissed the claim, ruling that the bone was natural to the food and that the hamburger was therefore fit for its ordinary purpose. The appeals court reversed this, holding that a hamburger could be unfit even if the bone occurred naturally. Wendy's appealed to the state's highest court.

ISSUE: Was the hamburger unfit for its ordinary purpose because it contained a harmful but natural bone?

DECISION: Even if the harmful bone occurred naturally, the hamburger could be unfit for its ordinary purpose. Affirmed.

REASONING: When an object in food harms a consumer, the injured person may recover even if the substance occurred naturally, provided that a reasonable consumer would not expect to encounter it. A triangular, one half inch bone shaving may be inherent to a cut of beef, but whether a reasonable consumer would anticipate it is normally a question for the jury.

Wendy's hamburgers need not be perfect, but they must be fit for their intended purpose. It is difficult to imagine how a consumer could guard against bone particles, short of removing the hamburger from its bun, breaking it apart and inspecting its small components.

Wendy's argues that, since its meat complied with federal and state standards, the hamburgers were merchantable as a matter of law. However, compliance with legal standards does not ensure merchantability. A jury could still conclude that a bone this size was reasonably unforeseeable. ◢

IMPLIED WARRANTY OF FITNESS FOR A PARTICULAR PURPOSE

The other warranty that the law imposes on sellers is the implied warranty of fitness for a particular purpose. This cumbersome name is often shortened to the warranty of fitness. **Where the seller at the time of contracting knows about a particular purpose for which the buyer wants the goods, and knows that the buyer is relying on the seller's skill or judgment, there is an implied warranty that the goods shall be fit for such purpose.**[3]

Notice that the seller must know about some special use the buyer intends, and realize that the buyer is relying on the seller's judgment. Suppose a lumber salesclerk knows that a buyer is relying on his advice to choose the best wood for a house being built in a swamp. The Code implies a warranty that the wood sold will withstand those special conditions.

Warranties Compared

Express Warranty UCC §2-313	Implied Warranty of Merchantability UCC §2-314	Implied Warranty of Fitness for a Particular Purpose UCC §2-315
The Rule: Seller can create an express warranty with any affirmation or promise. *Example:* Manufacturer sends Retailer a brochure describing its children's bicycle: "These bikes will last for a minimum of eight years of normal use." If the handlebars snap off after six months, Manufacturer has breached its express warranty.	*The Rule:* With certain exceptions, the Code *implies a warranty* that the goods will be fit for their ordinary purpose. *Example:* Manufacturer sells Retailer 300 "children's bicycles," with no promise about quality. The UCC implies a warranty that the bikes will be fit for ordinary children's use.	*The Rule:* With some exceptions, the Code *implies* a warranty that the goods are fit for the buyer's special purpose, if the seller knows of it. *Example:* Retailer orders from Manufacturer "300 mountain bikes, for racing" and Manufacturer agrees. The UCC implies a warranty that the bikes will withstand the added stress of mountain racing.

Disclaimers

A disclaimer is a statement that a particular warranty *does not* apply. The Code permits the seller to disclaim most warranties.

ORAL EXPRESS WARRANTIES

Under the Code, a seller may disclaim an oral express warranty. Suppose Traffic Co. wants to buy a helicopter from HeliCorp. A salesman tells Traffic Co., "Don't

---

[3] UCC §2-315.

worry, you can fly this bird day and night for six months with nothing more than a fuel stop." HeliCorp's contract may disclaim the oral warranty. The contract could say, "HeliCorp's entire warranty is printed below. Any statements made by any agent or salesperson are disclaimed and form no part of this contract." That disclaimer is valid. If the helicopter requires routine servicing between flights, HeliCorp has not breached an oral warranty.

WRITTEN EXPRESS WARRANTIES

This is the one type of warranty that is difficult or impossible to disclaim. If a seller includes an express warranty in the sales contract, any disclaimer is invalid. Suppose HeliCorp sells an industrial helicopter for use in hauling building equipment. The sales contract describes the aircraft as "operable to 14,000 feet." Later, in the contract, a limited warranty disclaims "any other warranties or statements that appear in this document or in any other document." That disclaimer is invalid. The Code will not permit a seller to take contradictory positions in one document. The disclaimer will also be invalid if the warranty appeared in a separate document (such as a sales brochure) and a disclaimer would *unfairly surprise* the buyer.

IMPLIED WARRANTIES

A seller may disclaim the implied warranty of *merchantability* provided he actually mentions the word "merchantability" and makes the disclaimer conspicuous. Courts demand to see the word "merchantability" in the disclaimer to be sure the buyer realized she was giving up this fundamental protection. A seller may disclaim the implied warranty of *fitness* with any language that is clear and conspicuous.

GENERAL DISCLAIMERS

To make life easier, the Code permits a seller to disclaim all implied warranties by conspicuously stating that the goods are sold "as is" or "with all faults." So a seller who wants to disclaim only the warranty of merchantability must explicitly mention that term, but a seller may exclude *all* implied warranties with a short expression, such as "sold as is."

CONSUMER SALES

Protection is often stronger for consumers than for businesses. *Many states prohibit a seller from disclaiming implied warranties in the sale of consumer goods.* In these states, if a home furnishings store sells a bunk bed to a consumer, and the top bunk tips out the window on the first night, the seller is liable, regardless of any disclaimers.

REMEDY LIMITATIONS

Simon Aerials, Inc., manufactured boom lifts, the huge cranes used to construct multistoried buildings. Simon agreed to design and build eight unusually large machines for Logan Equipment Corp. Simon delivered the boom lifts late, and they functioned poorly. Logan requested dozens of repairs and modifications, which Simon attempted to accomplish over many months, but the equipment never worked well. Logan gave up and sued for $7.5 million, representing the profits it expected to make from renting the machines and the damage to its reputation. Logan clearly had suffered major losses, and it recovered—nothing. How could that be?

Simon had negotiated a **limitation of remedy clause,** by which **the parties may limit or exclude the normal remedies permitted under the Code.**[4] These important rights are entirely distinct from disclaimers. A disclaimer limits the seller's warranties and thus affects whether the seller has breached her contract. A remedy limitation, by contrast, states that if a party does breach its warranty, the injured party will not get all of the damages the Code normally allows.

In its contract, Simon had agreed to repair or replace any defective boom lifts, but that was all. The agreement said that if a boom lift was defective, and Logan lost business, profits, and reputation, Simon was not liable. The court upheld the remedy limitation. Since Simon had repeatedly attempted to repair and redesign the defective machines, it had done everything it promised to do. Logan got nothing.

Negligence

A buyer of goods may have remedies other than warranty claims. One is negligence. Negligence is notably different from contract law. In a contract case, the two parties have reached an agreement, and the terms of their bargain will usually determine how to settle any dispute. But in a negligence case, there has been no bargaining between the parties, who may never have met. A consumer injured by an exploding cola bottle is unlikely to have bargained for her beverage with the CEO of the cola company. Instead, the law imposes a standard of conduct on everyone in society, corporation and individual alike. The two key elements of this standard, for present purposes, are *duty* and *breach*. A plaintiff injured by goods she bought must show that the defendant, usually a manufacturer or seller of a product, had a duty to her and breached that duty. A defendant has a duty of due care to anyone who could foreseeably be injured by its misconduct. Generally, it is the duty to act as a reasonable person would in like circumstances; a defendant who acts unreasonably has breached his duty.

In negligence cases concerning the sale of goods, plaintiffs most often raise one or more of these claims:

- *Negligent Design.* The buyer claims that the product injured her because the manufacturer designed it poorly. Negligence law requires a manufacturer to design a product free of unreasonable risks. The product does not have to be absolutely safe. An automobile that guaranteed a driver's safety would be prohibitively expensive. Reasonable safety features must be built in if they can be included at a tolerable cost.

- *Negligent Manufacture.* The buyer claims that the design was adequate but that failure to inspect or some other sloppy conduct caused a dangerous product to leave the plant.

- *Failure to Warn.* A manufacturer is liable for failing to warn the purchaser or users about the dangers of normal use and also foreseeable misuse. However, there is no duty to warn about obvious dangers.

In the following case, the plaintiffs raise issues of negligent design and failure to warn, concerning a disposable lighter. You be the judge.

---

[4] UCC §2-719. A few states prohibit remedy limitations, but most permit them.

YOU BE THE JUDGE

BOUMELHEM v. BIC CORP.

211 Mich. App. 175, 535 N.W.2d 574, 1995 Mich. App. LEXIS 228
Michigan Court of Appeals, 1995

FACTS: Ibrahim Boumelhem, age four, began playing with a Bic disposable lighter that his parents had bought. He started a fire that burned his legs and severely burned his six-month-old brother over 85% of his body. Ibrahim's father sued Bic, claiming that the lighter was negligently designed because it could have been childproof. He also claimed failure to warn, because the lighter did not clearly warn of the danger to children.

The trial court found that consumers use over 500 million disposable lighters annually in the United States. Each lighter provides 1,000 to 2,000 lights. During one three-year period, children playing with disposable lighters started 8,100 fires annually, causing an average of 180 people to die every year, of whom 140 were children under five. Another 990 people were injured. The average annual cost of deaths, injuries, and property damage from child-play fires was estimated at $310 to $375 million, or 60 to 75 cents per lighter sold. Bic acknowledged it was foreseeable lighters would get into children's hands and injure them. Bic had also agreed that it was feasible to make a more child-resistant lighter.

The trial court followed precedent and dismissed Boumelhem's claims. He appealed.

YOU BE THE JUDGE: Did Bic negligently design its disposable lighter? Did Bic negligently fail to warn of the lighter's dangers?

ARGUMENT FOR BOUMELHEM: Your honors, Bic is killing hundreds of children every year. In its efforts to maximize corporate profits, it is literally burning these children to death and injuring hundreds more. That's wrong.

Bic has acknowledged that its disposable lighters can and will get into the hands of children and that its product will injure or kill a certain percentage of them. Bic has admitted that it could design a childproof lighter, and it knows perfectly well how to include effective warnings on its lighters. But rather than improve product design and give effective warnings, Bic prefers to do business as usual and litigate liability for injured and murdered children. We ask for a ruling that will keep our kids safe.

ARGUMENT FOR BIC: Your honors, the Bic Corp. is as horrified as anyone over the injuries to these children and the deaths of other kids. But Bic is not responsible. The children's parents are responsible. We sympathize with their grief but not with their attempt to pass parental responsibility onto the shoulders of a corporation.

Bic has no duty to design a different lighter. The test in design defect cases is whether the risks are unreasonable in light of the foreseeable injuries. Young children can hurt themselves in countless ways, from falls to poisonings to automobile injuries. There is one answer to these dangers, and it is called good parenting. The parents who bought this lighter purchased it because it could start a fire. The moment they purchased it, they assumed the obligation to keep it away from their children. These are useful products, which is why Bic sells hundreds of millions per year. Other consumers should not be forced to pay an outrageously high price for a simple tool, just because some parents fail to do their job.

The failure to warn argument is even weaker. The law imposes no failure to warn when the danger is obvious. ▌

UPDATE | The tragic deaths in cases like Boumelhem prompted a federal agency, the Consumer Product Safety Commission, to take action. What did the CPSC do, and with what results? You can search for news articles online, or go directly to the agency's website at **http://www.cpsc.gov**. ▪

Strict Liability

The other tort claim that an injured person can bring against the manufacturer or seller of a product is strict liability. Like negligence, strict liability is a burden created by the law rather than by the parties. And, as with all torts, strict liability concerns claims of physical harm. But there is a key distinction between negligence and strict liability: **In strict liability, the injured person need not prove that the defendant's conduct was unreasonable.**

The injured person must show only that the defendant manufactured or sold a product that was defective and that the defect caused harm. Almost all states permit such lawsuits, and most adopted the summary of strict liability provided by the Restatement (Second) of Torts **§402A**. Because §402A is the most frequently cited section in all of tort law, we quote it in full:

"**1.** One who sells any product in a defective condition unreasonably dangerous to the user or consumer or to his property is subject to liability for physical harm thereby caused to the ultimate user or consumer, or to his property, if

 (a) the seller is engaged in the business of selling such a product, and

 (b) it is expected to and does reach the user or consumer without substantial change in the condition in which it is sold.

 2. The rule stated in Subsection (1) applies although

 (a) the seller has exercised all possible care in the preparation and sale of his product, and

 (b) the user or consumer has not bought the product from or entered into any contractual relation with the seller."

These are the key terms in subsection (1):

- *Defective condition unreasonably dangerous to the user.* The defendant is liable only if the product is defective when it leaves his hands. If they are reasonably safe and the buyer's mishandling of the goods causes the harm, there is no strict liability. If you attempt to open a soda bottle by knocking the cap against a counter, and the glass shatters and cuts you, the manufacturer owes nothing.

 The article sold must be more dangerous than the ordinary consumer would expect. A carving knife can produce a lethal wound, but everyone knows that, and a sharp knife is not unreasonably dangerous. On the other hand, prescription drugs may harm in ways that neither a layperson nor a doctor would anticipate. The manufacturer must provide adequate warnings of any dangers that are not apparent.

- *In the business of selling.* The seller is liable only if she normally sells this kind of product. Suppose your roommate makes you a peanut butter sandwich and, while eating it, you cut your mouth on a sliver of glass that was in the jar. The peanut butter manufacturer faces strict liability, as does the grocery store where your roommate bought the goods. But your roommate is not strictly liable because he does not serve sandwiches as a business.

- *Reaches the user without substantial change.* Obviously, if your roommate put the glass in the peanut butter thinking it was funny, neither the manufacturer nor the store is liable.

And here are the important phrases in subsection (2).

- *Has exercised all possible care.* This is the heart of strict liability. It is *no defense* that the seller used reasonable care. If the product is dangerously defective and injures the user, the seller is liable even if it took every precaution to design and manufacture the product safely. Suppose the peanut butter jar did in fact contain a glass sliver when it left the factory. The manufacturer proves that it uses extraordinary care in keeping foreign particles out of the jars and thoroughly inspects each container before it is shipped. The evidence is irrelevant.

- *No contractual relation.* This means that the injured party need not have bought the goods directly from the party responsible for the defect. Suppose the manufacturer that made the peanut butter sold it to a distributor, which sold it to a wholesaler, which sold it to a grocery store, which sold it to your roommate. You may sue the manufacturer, distributor, wholesaler, and store, even though you never contracted with any of them.

RESTATEMENT (THIRD) AND CONTEMPORARY TRENDS

We saw that under traditional negligence law, a company could be found liable based on design, manufacture, or failure to warn. The same three activities can give rise to a claim of strict liability. It will normally be easier for a plaintiff to win a claim of strict liability, because she does not need to demonstrate that the manufacturer's conduct was unreasonable.

If the steering wheel on a brand new car falls off, and the driver is injured, that is a clear case of defective manufacturing, and the company will be strictly liable. Those are the easy cases. As courts have applied §402A, defective design cases have been more contentious. Suppose a vaccine that prevents serious childhood illnesses inevitably causes brain damage in a very small number of children, because of the nature of the drug. Is the manufacturer liable? What if a racing sailboat, designed only for speed, is dangerously unstable in the hands of a less experienced sailor? Is the boat's maker responsible for fatalities? How is a court to decide whether the design was defective? Often, these design cases also involve issues of warnings: Did drug designer diligently detail dangers to doctors? Should sailboat seller sell speedy sailboat solely to seasoned sailors?

Over the years, most courts have adopted one of two tests for design and warning cases. The first is consumer expectation. Here, a court finds the manufacturer liable for defective design if the product is less safe than a reasonable consumer would expect. If a smoke detector has a 3% failure rate, and the average consumer has no way of anticipating that danger, effective cautions must be included, though the design may be defective anyway. Many states have moved away from that test, and now use a risk-utility test. Here, a court must weigh the benefits for society against the dangers that the product poses. Principal factors in the risk-utility test include:

- The *value* of the product;
- The *gravity* of the danger (how bad will the harm be);

- The *likelihood* that such danger will occur (the odds); and

- The feasibility and cost of a *safer alternative design.*

Because of the conflicting court decisions, the American Law Institute drafted the Restatement (Third) of Torts: Product Liability, in an attempt to harmonize judicial opinions about product liability generally and design defects in particular. The new Restatement treats manufacturing cases differently from those involving design defects and failure to warn.

- In manufacturing cases, a product is defective whenever it departs from its intended design, regardless of how much care was taken. This is the traditional standard.

- In design and warnings cases, a product is defective only when the *foreseeable risks* could have been reduced by using a reasonable alternative design or warning. So-called "strict" liability in these cases is beginning to resemble plain old negligence. If courts adopt this new approach, it will become more difficult for plaintiffs to win a design or warning case, because they will need to prove that the manufacturer should have foreseen the danger and could have done something about it.

There is no strong trend in how judges examine these cases: courts tend to pick and choose the analytic tools they use. Most still regard §402A as the basic law for all strict liability lawsuits. In design cases, many courts use the risk-utility test, quite a few still examine consumer expectation, and some permit both analyses. As the following case indicates, some courts employ elements of the Restatement Third—with plenty of disagreement.

CASE SUMMARY

UNIROYAL GOODRICH TIRE COMPANY v. MARTINEZ

977 S.W.2d 328
Texas Supreme Court, 1998

FACTS: When Roberto Martinez, a mechanic, attempted to mount a 16-inch tire on a 16.5-inch rim (wheel), the tire exploded, causing him serious, permanent injuries. He sued Goodrich, the tire manufacturer; the Budd Company, which made the rim; and Ford Motor Company, which designed it. Budd and Ford settled out of court, and the case proceeded against Goodrich.

The tire had a conspicuous label, advising users never to mount a 16-inch tire on a 16.5-inch rim, warning of the danger of severe injury or death, and including a picture of a worker thrown into the air by an explosion. The label also urged the user never to lean or reach over the assembly while working. Martinez ignored the warnings.

Martinez admitted that the warnings were adequate, but claimed that Goodrich was strictly liable for failing to use a safer "bead" design. The bead, a rubber-encased steel wire, encircles the tire and holds it to the rim. Martinez's expert testified that an alternative design, used by other tire manufacturers, would have prevented his injury. The trial court gave judgment for Martinez in the amount of $10,308,792.45, the Court of Appeals affirmed, and Goodrich appealed to the state's highest court.

ISSUE: When warnings are adequate, is a manufacturer still obligated to use a safer alternative design?

DECISION: Affirmed. The manufacturer was obligated to use a safer design.

REASONING: The Restatement (Second) declared that a product was not defectively designed if it included adequate warnings. However, the Restatement (Third) has rejected this view. Under the new Restatement, the key question remains whether a safer alternative existed. To decide the issue, a court should look at a broad range of factors: the probability and magnitude of potential harm, instructions and warnings included, consumer expectations, cost of alternative design, and product longevity.

Goodrich urges this court to follow the old rule, from the Restatement (Second). We decline. People often ignore warnings. A redesigned tire would have prevented this accident. The company's competitors incorporated the safer bead design almost a decade before this accident occurred, and Goodrich itself followed suit a year after Martinez was hurt. A Goodrich expert acknowledged that if one of his loved ones were inflating a tire, he would prefer the tire to have a single-bead design.

DISSENT'S REASONING: Goodrich put a prominent, pictographic warning on the tire. Martinez saw it and ignored it. Thousands of these tires were sold, but only one other person ever claimed this type of injury. When the probability of harm is so low, and the warnings adequate, the company has done all that should be required. ◢

Chapter Conclusion

Both sellers and buyers of goods must understand the basic principles of product liability law. A seller must understand warranty, negligence, and strict liability law and consider all of those principles when designing, manufacturing, and marketing goods. A buyer, on the other hand, should be aware that each theory provides a possible basis for compensation and that consumers receive particularly strong protection.

Chapter Review

Products can injure. The harm may be economic or physical. The plaintiff might have a remedy in warranty, which is found in the UCC, or one in tort, either for negligence or strict liability. For ease of review, the following chart summarizes the different warranty and tort remedies.

	Contract or Tort	Source of Law	Summary of the Rule	Example	Potential Issue
Express Warranty	Contract	UCC §2-313	May be created by an affirmation of fact, a promise, a description of goods, or a sample.	Salesman says, "This helicopter will operate perfectly at 16,000 feet."	Written contract may disclaim any and all oral warranties.
Implied Warranty of Merchantability	Contract	UCC §2-314	The Code implies that the goods are fit for their ordinary purpose.	Buyer purchases a deep freezer. The Code implies a warranty that it will keep food frozen.	Seller may disclaim this warranty only disclaimer includes the word "merchantability."

(Continued)

Implied Warranty of Fitness	Contract	UCC §2-315	The Code implies that the goods are fit for buyer's special purpose that seller knows about.	Where seller knows (1) buyer wants pine trees to plant in sandy soil, and (2) buyer is relying on seller's judgment, the trees carry an implied warranty that they will grow in that soil.	Seller may disclaim this warranty with conspicuous writing. Note that some states will disregard a disclaimer of *any* implied warranty in a consumer sale.
Negligence	Tort	Common law	Seller is liable if she fails to show level of conduct that a *reasonable person* would use.	Manufacturer sells bathing suit made of miracle fabric; buyer swims in ocean where saltwater makes garment transparent; seller's failure to test suit in saltwater was unreasonable and leaves seller liable.	No duty to warn if the danger is obvious.
Strict Liability	Tort	Restatement section 402A (subject to new revisions) and common law.	Seller liable if the product leaves in a dangerously defective condition.	Can of barbecue lighter fluid explodes in user's hand because the can's metal was defective; manufacturer's reasonable precautions are irrelevant; seller liable.	Injured buyer need not prove negligence but must prove that the product was defective.

PRACTICE TEST

Matching Questions

Match the following terms with their definitions:

___ **A.** Negligence

___ **B.** Strict liability

___ **C.** Merchantability

___ **D.** Disclaimer

___ **E.** Fitness

1. Determined by the reasonableness of defendant's conduct.

2. An implied warranty that goods are fit for their ordinary purpose.

3. An implied warranty that goods are fit for any particular purpose that the seller knows the buyer intends.

4. The reasonableness of defendant's conduct is irrelevant.

5. Written statement that certain warranties do not apply.

True/False Questions

Circle true or false:

1. T F A statement that goods are sold "as is" may disclaim all implied warranties.

2. T F Seller cannot be found strictly liable if its conduct met or exceeded generally accepted industry standards.

3. T F Seller can be liable under the implied warranty of fitness regardless of whether Seller knows what Buyer is planning to do with the goods.

4. T F Seller can be bound by written warranties but not by oral statements.

5. T F Under strict liability, an injured consumer could potentially recover damages from the product's manufacturer *and* the retailer who sold the goods.

Multiple-Choice Questions

6. For which of these could a manufacturer *not* be found negligent?
   (a) Design.
   (b) Manufacture.
   (c) Failure to warn.
   (d) Failure to monitor buyer's use.
   (e) Unreasonable product risks.

7. Seller's sales contract states that "The model 8J flagpole will withstand winds up to 150 mph, for a minimum of 35 years." The same contract includes this: "This contract makes no warranties, and any implied warranties are hereby disclaimed." School buys the flagpole, which blows down six months later, in a 105 mph wind.
   (a) Seller is not liable because it never made any express warranties.
   (b) Seller is not liable because it disclaimed any warranties.
   (c) Seller is liable because the disclaimer was invalid.
   (d) Seller is liable because implied warranties may not be disclaimed.
   (e) Seller is liable because express warranties may not be disclaimed.

8. Manufacturer sells a brand new, solar-powered refrigerator. Because the technology is new, Manufacturer sells the product "as is." Plaintiff later sues Manufacturer for breach of warranty, and wins. Plaintiff is probably
   (a) A distributor with no understanding of legal terminology.
   (b) A retailer who had previously relied on manufacturer.
   (c) A retailer who had never done business before with manufacturer.
   (d) A retailer who failed to notice the "as is" label.
   (e) A consumer.

9. CPA QUESTION: To establish a cause of action based on strict liability in tort for personal injuries resulting from using a defective product, one of the elements the plaintiff must prove is that the seller (defendant):
   (a) Failed to exercise due care.
   (b) Was in privity of contract with the plaintiff.
   (c) Defectively designed the product.
   (d) Was engaged in the business of selling the product.

10. CPA QUESTION: Which of the following conditions must be met for an implied warranty of fitness for a particular purpose to arise? I. The warranty must be in writing. II. The seller must know that the buyer was relying on the seller in selecting the goods.
    (a) I only.
    (b) II only.
    (c) Both I and II.
    (d) Neither I nor II.

Short-Answer Questions

11. Leighton Industries needed steel pipe to build furnaces for a customer. Leighton sent Callier Steel an order for a certain quantity of "A 106 Grade B" steel. Callier confirmed the order and created a contract by sending an invoice to Leighton, stating that it would send "A 106 Grade B" steel, as ordered. Callier delivered the steel and Leighton built the furnaces, but they leaked badly and required rebuilding. Tests demonstrated that the steel was not, in fact, "A 106 Grade B," but an inferior steel. Leighton sued. Who wins?

12. United Technologies advertised a used Beechcraft Baron airplane for sale in an aviation journal. Attorney Thompson Comerford was interested and spoke with a United agent, who described the plane as "excellently maintained" and said it had been operated "under §135 flight regulations," meaning the plane had been subject to airworthiness inspections every 100 hours. Comerford arrived at a Dallas airport to pick up the plane, where he paid $80,000 for it. He signed a sales agreement stating that the plane was sold "as is" and that there were "no representations or warranties, express or implied, including the condition of the aircraft, its merchantability or its fitness for any particular purpose." Comerford attempted to fly the plane home, but immediately experienced problems with its brakes, steering, ability to climb, and performance while cruising. (Otherwise it was fine.) He sued, claiming breach of express and implied warranties. Did United Technologies breach express or implied warranties?

13. ETHICS: Texaco, Inc., and other oil companies sold mineral spirits in bulk to distributors, which then resold to retailers. Mineral spirits are used for cleaning. Texaco allegedly knew that the retailers, such as hardware stores, frequently packaged the mineral spirits (illegally) in used half-gallon milk containers and sold them to consumers, often with no warnings on the packages. Mineral spirits are harmful or fatal if swallowed. David Hunnings, aged 21 months, found a milk container in his home, swallowed the mineral spirits, and died. The Hunnings sued Texaco in negligence. The trial court dismissed the complaint and the Hunnings appealed. What is the legal standard in a negligence case? Have the plaintiffs made out a valid case of negligence? Remember that at this stage a court is not deciding who wins, but what standard a plaintiff must meet in order to take its case to a jury. Assume that Texaco knew about the repackaging and the grave risk, but continued to sell in bulk because doing so was profitable. (If the plaintiffs cannot prove those facts, they will lose even if they do get to a jury.) Would that make you angry? Does that mean such a case should go to a jury? Or would you conclude that the fault still lies with the retailer and/or the parents? In that case, the court should dismiss the suit against Texaco.

14. Boboli Co. wanted to promote its "California style" pizza, which it sold in supermarkets. The company contracted with Highland Group, Inc., to produce two million recipe brochures, which would be inserted in the carton when the freshly baked pizza was still very hot. Highland contracted with Comark Merchandising to print the brochures. But when Comark asked for details concerning the pizza, the carton, and so forth, Highland refused to supply the information. Comark printed the first lot of 72,000 brochures, which Highland delivered to Boboli. Unfortunately, the hot bread caused the ink to run, and customers opening the carton often found red or blue splotches on their pizzas. Highland refused to accept additional brochures, and Comark sued for breach of contract. Highland defended by claiming that Comark had breached its warranty of merchantability. Please comment.

15. ROLE REVERSAL: Write an essay question concerning a household product that injures a buyer. The buyer sues under theories of warranty and strict liability. The buyer should have a strong claim based on one theory but no reasonable claim based on the other.

Internet Research Problem

Go to **http://www.nhtsa.dot.gov** and find the crash test results. Which cars are safer than average? Less safe? How important is auto safety to you? Are you willing to pay more for a safe car? Who should be the final judge of auto safety: auto companies, insurance companies, juries, government regulators, or consumers?

You can find further practice problems in the Online Quiz at **http://beatty.westbuslaw.com** or in the Study Guide that accompanies this text.

Performance and Remedies

Patrick runs his own business, making hand-printed silk neckties, each depicting a famous work of art. Sales are booming and he has hired Hannah as a helper. Alden, who runs a chain of upmarket clothing stores, contracts to buy 1,000 of Patrick's ties for $50 each, to be delivered by September 1. In mid-July, Hannah leaves—to open her own business. Patrick manages to finish the ties and delivers them August 15. But Alden claims that the colors are not as subtle as the samples he had seen. Patrick promises to deliver 1,000 new ties on time. Alden snaps, "Deal's off. I'll get my merchandise elsewhere." In September, Alden's shops are filled with ties made by Hannah, which Alden bought at $35 per item. Is that just? No.

Alden has violated at least one and possibly two provisions of the Uniform Commercial Code (UCC). The Code requires that Patrick have a chance to cure, meaning to deliver a new shipment of satisfactory goods. It also looks as though Alden acted in bad faith, weaseling out of his contract with Patrick so that he could purchase cheaper goods. These are typical issues of contract performance under the Code, which we look at in this chapter along with principles of remedy. By all means, let us begin in good faith.

Good Faith

The Code requires good faith in the performance and enforcement of every contract. Good faith means honesty in fact. Between merchants, it also means the use of reasonable commercial standards of fair dealing. In the opening scenario, if Alden claimed the ties were defective in order to escape his contract with Patrick, and save money, he has acted in bad faith. A court will hear testimony about why Alden would not permit Patrick to furnish new ties, and will in all likelihood award Patrick damages.

With this good-faith requirement in mind, we look first at the seller's obligations, and then at those of the buyer.

Seller's Obligations (and a Few Rights)

The seller's primary obligation is to deliver conforming goods to the buyer. **Conforming goods satisfy the contract terms.** Nonconforming goods do not. The seller must **tender** the goods, which means to make conforming goods available to the buyer. Normally, the contract will state where and when the seller is obligated to tender delivery. For example, the parties may agree that Manufacturer is to tender 1,000 computer printers at a certain warehouse on July 3. If Manufacturer makes the printers available on that date, Buyer is obligated to pick them up then and there, and is in breach if it fails to do so.

PERFECT TENDER RULE

Under the **perfect tender rule,** the buyer may reject the goods if they fail in any respect to conform to the contract.[1] Under the common law, before the Code was drafted, the perfect tender rule required that the seller deliver goods that conformed absolutely to the contract specifications. The buyer had the right to reject goods with even minor deviations. Although commentators had criticized the rule for decades and courts had carved many exceptions into the rule, the drafters of the UCC retained it.

RESTRICTIONS ON THE PERFECT TENDER RULE

The Code includes sections that limit the perfect tender rule's effect. Indeed, courts often apply the limitations more enthusiastically than the rule itself, and so while perfect tender is the law, it must be understood in the context of other provisions.

---

[1] UCC §2-601

We will look at the most common ways that the law—or the parties themselves—undercut the perfect tender rule.

Usage of Trade and Course of Dealing

The Code takes the commonsense view that a contract for the sale of goods does not exist in a vacuum. **"Usage of trade"** means any practice that members of an industry expect to be part of their dealings. The Code requires that courts consider trade usage when they interpret contracts, which means that the perfect tender rule may not permit a buyer to reject goods with minor flaws. For example, the textile industry interprets the phrase "first-quality fabric" to permit a limited number of flaws in most materials. If a seller delivers 1,000 bolts of fabric and five of them have minor defects, the seller has not violated the perfect tender rule; in the textile industry, such a minor nonconformity is perfect tender.

The **course of dealing** between the two parties may also limit the rule. "Course of dealing" refers to previous commercial transactions between the same parties. The Code requires that the current contract be interpreted in the light of any past dealings that have created reasonable expectations. Suppose a buyer orders 20,000 board feet of "highest-grade pine" from a lumber company, just as it has in each of the three previous years. In the earlier deliveries, the buyer accepted the lumber even though 1 or 2% was not the highest grade. That course of dealing will probably control the present contract, and the buyer will not be permitted suddenly to reject an entire shipment because 1% is a lower grade of pine.

Parties' Agreement

The parties may limit the effect of the perfect tender rule by drafting a contract that permits imperfection in the goods. In some industries this is routine practice. For example, contracts requiring the seller to design or engineer goods specially for the buyer will generally state a level of performance that the equipment must meet. If the goods meet the level described, the buyer has no right to reject, even if the product has some flaws.

Cure

A basic goal of the UCC is a fully performed contract that leaves both parties satisfied. The seller's right to cure helps achieve this goal. **When the buyer rejects nonconforming goods, the seller has the right to cure,** by delivering conforming goods before the contract deadline.[2] LightCo is obligated to deliver 10,000 specially manufactured bulbs to Burnout Corp. by September 15. LightCo delivers the bulbs on August 20, and on August 25 Burnout notifies the seller that the bulbs do not meet contract specifications. If LightCo promptly notifies Burnout that it intends to cure and then delivers conforming light bulbs on September 15, it has fulfilled its contract obligations, and Burnout must accept the goods. A contract should not fail when a seller shows every willingness to cure the problem.

Destruction of the Goods

A farmer contracts to sell 250,000 pounds of sunflowers to a broker. The contract describes the 250 acres that the farmer will plant to grow the flowers. He plants his crop on time but a drought destroys most of the plants, and he is able to deliver

---

[2] UCC §2-508

only 75,000 pounds. Is the farmer liable for the flowers he could not deliver? No. Is the broker required to accept the smaller crop? No. **If identified goods are totally destroyed before risk passes to the buyer, the contract is void.** If identified goods are partially destroyed, the buyer may choose whether to accept the goods at a reduced price or void the contract.

Commercial Impracticability

Commercial impracticability means that a supervening event excuses performance of a contract, if the event was not within the parties' contemplation when they made the agreement.[3] An event is "supervening" if it interrupts the normal course of business and dominates performance of the contract. But a supervening event will excuse performance only if neither party had thought there was any serious chance it would happen.

NiteVision makes military equipment for nocturnal missions. The company contracts to sell $3 million worth of its goods to Exporter, who promptly contracts to resell the products to various countries around the world. Before the equipment can be delivered, the United States Department of Defense bans the export of all night vision systems. Exporter, losing money on its various agreements, sues NiteVision for failure to deliver. Exporter loses. Neither side anticipated the Defense Department order, and it had become legally impossible for NiteVision to perform.

In the following case, you decide whether the seller's unexpected problem created true impossibility.

YOU BE THE JUDGE

SPECIALTY TIRES OF AMERICA, INC. v. THE CIT GROUP/EQUIPMENT FINANCING, INC.

82 F. Supp. 2d 434
United States District Court for the Western District of Pennsylvania, 2000

FACTS: CIT Group leased 11 tire press machines to Condere Corporation, in Natchez, Mississippi, maintaining the right to repossess the goods if Condere defaulted on its payments. After making some payments, Condere (did you guess?) stopped making payments and filed for bankruptcy. Specialty Tires was interested in purchasing the machines. CIT and Specialty executives toured the Condere factory to examine the tire presses and discuss the logistics of their removal. Condere officials cooperated, acknowledging that CIT had the right to immediate possession and assisting in the transportation plans. CIT then agreed to sell the goods to Specialty for $250,000.

When CIT attempted to ship the presses to Specialty, Condere surprised everyone by refusing access to the equipment. CIT filed a complaint in the bankruptcy case, asking the court to award it the goods. Meanwhile, Specialty filed suit against CIT, in Pennsylvania, for breach of contract. In the Pennsylvania court, CIT moved for summary judgment, claiming commercial impracticability.

YOU BE THE JUDGE: Should CIT be discharged based on commercial impracticability?

ARGUMENT FOR CIT: Your honor, CIT cannot deliver goods that it cannot even get its hands on.

---

[3] UCC §2-615

Specialty bargained for these 11 tire presses, not for just any machines. The parties toured Condere's factory, identified all the equipment, and negotiated terms based on delivery of these goods. Condere assured everyone that the presses would be ready for delivery. CIT could not have foreseen Condere's bizarre turnabout or made provisions to protect itself. This is not a case where a seller, unable to deliver 1,000 bushels of apples, can supply identical goods from another source. There was nothing CIT could do to remedy the situation.

ARGUMENT FOR SPECIALTY: Your honor, companies enter into contracts to control future events and protect against risks. When CIT agreed to this contract, the company was promising either to deliver the goods or suffer the consequences. We realize it is Condere's irresponsible behavior that has induced this logjam. The question, though, is not who caused the snafu, but who must suffer the consequences. Specialty planned a major expansion in the area using these tire presses, and now is losing money based on factory space rented, other overhead incurred, and lost profits. CIT chose to lease the goods to Condere. Perhaps CIT should select its business partners more scrupulously. ▮

The following chart outlines the seller's obligations.

Seller's Basic Obligation: to deliver conforming goods. The **perfect tender rule** permits the buyer to reject the goods if they are in any way nonconforming. But many Code provisions limit the harshness of the perfect tender rule.

Limitation on Seller's Obligation	Code Provision	Effect on Seller's Obligations
Good faith	Sections 1-201 (19) and 2-103(1)(b)	Prohibits the buyer from using the perfect tender rule as a way out of a contract that has become unprofitable.
Course of dealing and usage of trade	Section 1-205	If applicable, will limit the buyer's right to reject for relatively routine defects.
The parties' agreement	Section 2-601	May describe tolerances for imperfections in the goods.
Cure	Section 2-508	Allows the seller to replace defective goods with conforming goods, if time permits.
Destruction of goods	Section 2-613	If goods identified to the contract are destroyed, the contract is void.
Commercial impracticability	Section 2-615	A supervening event excuses performance of a contract, if the event was not within the parties' contemplation when they made the agreement.

Buyer's Obligations (and a Few Rights)

The buyer's primary obligation is to accept conforming goods and pay for them. The buyer must also provide adequate facilities to receive the goods. For example, if the contract requires the seller to deliver to the buyer's warehouse, and the parties anticipate that delivery will be by rail, then the buyer must have facilities for unloading railcars at its warehouse.

INSPECTION AND ACCEPTANCE

The buyer generally has the right to inspect the goods before paying or accepting.[4] If the contract is silent on this issue, the buyer may inspect. Typically, a buyer will insist on this right. An exception is contracts in which the parties agree there is no right to inspect—for example, a contract allowing shipment COD, which means "cash on delivery." In that case, the buyer must pay upon receipt and do her inspecting later.

Along with the right of inspection comes the obligation to do it within a reasonable time and to notify the seller promptly if the buyer intends to reject the goods. **The buyer accepts goods** if (1) after a reasonable opportunity to inspect, she indicates to the seller that the goods are conforming or that she will accept them in spite of nonconformity; or (2) she has had a reasonable opportunity to inspect the goods and has not rejected them; or (3) she performs some act indicating that she now owns the goods, such as altering or reselling them.

Partial Acceptance

A buyer has the right to accept some goods while rejecting others, if the goods can be divided into commercial units. Such a unit is any grouping of goods that the industry normally treats as a whole. For example, one truckload of gravel would be a commercial unit. If the contract called for 100 truckloads of gravel, a buyer could accept the 10 that conformed to contract specifications while rejecting the 90 that did not.

Revocation

A buyer who has accepted goods has a limited right to revoke that acceptance. **A buyer may revoke acceptance, but only if the nonconformity substantially impairs the value of the goods and only if she had a legitimate reason for the initial acceptance.** This means the perfect tender rule does not apply: A buyer in this situation may not revoke because of minor defects. Further, the buyer must show that she had a good reason for accepting the goods originally. Acceptable reasons would include defects that were not visible on inspection or defects that the seller promised but failed to cure.

Rejection

The buyer may reject nonconforming goods by notifying the seller within a reasonable time.[5] Huntsville Hospital purchased electrocardiogram equipment from Mortara Instrument for $155,000. The equipment failed to work properly and caused continual problems for the hospital, which notified Mortara within a reasonable time that it was rejecting. The hospital asked Mortara to pick up the equipment and refund the full purchase price, but Mortara did neither. When the hospital sued, Mortara claimed that the hospital should have returned the equipment to Mortara and that its failure left it liable for the full cost. The court of appeals was unpersuaded and gave judgment for the hospital, declaring that the hospital's only obligation was to notify the seller of a rejection and hold the goods for the seller to collect.

---

[4] UCC §2-513

[5] UCC §2-601, 602

Remedies: Assurance and Repudiation

We have looked at the rights and obligations of the two parties. Now we turn our attention to the remedies they may employ. The first two, assurance and repudiation, are available to both buyer and seller.

ASSURANCE

One party to a contract may begin to fear that the other is not going to perform its obligations. When there are reasonable grounds for insecurity, **a party may demand written assurance of performance from the other party,** and until he receives it, generally may suspend his own performance. Suppose Auto Co. plans to give away 50,000 videos as a promotion for its new car, to be introduced October 1. VidKids has promised to copy, package, and deliver the tapes no later than September 20. On September 1, Auto learns that VidKids has not yet begun to package the video. Auto may demand written assurance that VidKids will meet the deadline. VidKids is obligated to respond promptly and assure Auto that it will perform.

REPUDIATION

A party **repudiates** a contract by indicating that it will not perform. A party may repudiate by notifying the other party that it will not perform, by making it clear from its conduct, or by failing to answer a demand for assurance. Suppose VidKids' president calls Auto and admits, "We're having a lot of staff problems. The earliest we're going to get you that video is mid- or late October." VidKids has repudiated the contract.

When either party repudiates the contract, the other party may (1) for a reasonable time, await performance; or (2) resort to any remedy for breach of contract. In either case it may suspend its own performance. In the VidKids case, it would be unreasonable for Auto to wait, because time is of the essence. So once VidKids has repudiated, Auto should protect itself by pursuing a remedy for breach, such as arranging for another company to produce the goods. (We discuss the buyer's remedies for breach later in this chapter.)

We turn now to remedies intended exclusively for the seller.

Seller's Remedies

When a buyer breaches a contract, the Code provides the seller with a variety of potential remedies. Exactly which ones are available depends upon who has the goods (buyer or seller) and what steps the seller took after the buyer breached. The seller can always cancel the contract. She may also be able to:

- Stop delivery of the goods.

- Identify goods to the contract.

- Resell and recover damages.

- Obtain damages for nonacceptance; or

- Obtain the contract price.

STOP DELIVERY

Sometimes a buyer breaches before the seller has delivered the goods, for example, by failing to make a payment due under the contract or perhaps by repudiating the contract. If that happens, the seller may refuse to deliver the goods.

IDENTIFY GOODS TO THE CONTRACT

If the seller has not yet **identified goods** to the contract when the buyer breaches, he may do so as soon as he learns of the breach. Suppose an electronics manufacturer, with 5,000 compact disk players in its warehouse, learns that a retailer refuses to pay for the 800 units it contracted to buy. The manufacturer may now attach a label to 800 units in its warehouse, identifying them to the contract. This will help it recover damages when it resells the identified goods or uses one of the other remedies described below.

RESALE

A seller may **resell goods** that the buyer has refused to accept, provided she does it reasonably. If the resale is commercially reasonable, the seller may recover the difference between the resale price and contract price, plus incidental damages, minus expenses saved.[6]

A seller who acts in a commercially reasonable manner is entitled to the following damages:

- Contract price (the price Seller expected from the original contract).

- The resale price (the money Seller got at resale).

- Incidental damages (storage, advertising, etc.).

- Expenses saved.

- Seller's damages.

DAMAGES FOR NONACCEPTANCE

A seller who does not resell, or who resells unreasonably, may recover the difference between the original contract price and the market value of the goods at the time of delivery.[7] Oilko agrees to sell Retailer 100,000 barrels of a certain grade of gasoline for $60 per barrel, to be delivered in Long Beach, California, on November 1. Oilko tenders the gasoline on November 1, but Retailer refuses to accept it. On February 20, Oilko resells the gasoline to another purchaser for $52 per barrel and sues Retailer for $800,000 (the difference between its contract price and what it finally obtained), plus the cost of storage. Will Oilko win? No. Oilko's resale was unreasonable. Because there is a ready market for gasoline, Oilko should have resold immediately. Because Oilko acted unreasonably, it will not obtain damages under the Code's resale provision. Oilko will be forced to base its damages on market value.

Often this remedy will be less valuable to the seller than resale damages. Suppose that on November 1 the market value of Oilko's gasoline was $59 per barrel.

---

[6] UCC §2-706

[7] UCC §2-708

Oilko's contract with Retailer was actually worth only one dollar per barrel to Oilko, the amount by which its contract price exceeded the market value. That is all that Oilko will get in court.

ACTION FOR THE PRICE

The seller may recover the contract price if (1) the buyer has accepted the goods; or (2) the seller's goods are conforming and the seller is unable to resell after a reasonable effort.[8] Engine Company orders 200 specially fitted carburetors that will work only in its engines, but then fails to pay for them. Supplier cannot resell the carburetors elsewhere because they will not fit in other engines. Supplier will sue successfully for the price.

Buyer's Remedies

The buyer, too, has a variety of potential remedies. If a seller fails to deliver goods or if the buyer rightfully rejects the goods, the buyer is entitled to cancel the contract. She may also recover money paid to the seller, assuming she has not received the goods. In addition, she may be able to:

- Cover.
- Obtain damages for nondelivery.
- Obtain incidental and consequential damages.
- Recover the goods themselves by an order for specific performance; or
- Recover liquidated damages.

COVER

If the seller breaches, **the buyer may "cover" by reasonably obtaining substitute goods;** it may then obtain the difference between the contract price and its cover price, plus incidental and consequential damages, minus expenses saved.[9] Opera House orders 1,000 yards of fabric for its curtain, agreeing to pay $100,000. When Fabric Company fails to deliver, Opera House promptly buys similar fabric elsewhere for $120,000. The Opera House has reasonably covered, and is entitled to $20,000.

Note that an injured buyer may also be awarded consequential damages, which we discuss below. Finally, if covering saves expense, the savings are deducted from any damages.

NONDELIVERY

In some cases the buyer does not cover, or fails to cover reasonably, leaving it with damages for nondelivery. The measure of damages for nondelivery is the difference between the market price at the time the buyer learns of the breach and the contract price, plus incidental and consequential damages, minus expenses saved.

---

[8] UCC §2-709
[9] UCC §2-712

ACCEPTANCE OF NONCONFORMING GOODS

A buyer will sometimes accept nonconforming goods from the seller, either because no alternative is available or because the buyer expects to obtain some compensation for the defects. Where the buyer has accepted goods but notified the seller that they are nonconforming, he may recover damages for the difference between the goods as promised and as delivered, plus incidental and consequential damages.

INCIDENTAL AND CONSEQUENTIAL DAMAGES

An injured buyer is generally entitled to incidental and consequential damages. Incidental damages cover such costs as advertising for replacements, sending buyers to obtain new goods, and shipping the replacement goods. Consequential damages can be much more extensive and may include lost profits. **A buyer expecting to resell goods may obtain the loss of profit caused by the seller's failure to deliver.**

In the following case, the court decides whether future profits may be too speculative to award as consequential damages.

CASE SUMMARY

SMITH v. PENBRIDGE ASSOCIATES, INC.

440 Pa. Super. 410, 655 A.2d 1015, 1995 Pa. Super. LEXIS 574
Superior Court of Pennsylvania, 1995

FACTS: Donna and Alan Smith wanted to raise emus, which are flightless Australian birds that look like ostriches. The creatures reproduce rapidly in almost any terrain and are sold for their meat, which is high in protein and low in fat, and for their oil, leather, and feathers. The Smiths paid Tomie Clark, the manager of Penbridge Farms, $4,000 as a down payment for "Andrew" and "Rachel," which the farm called a "proven breeder pair." Since it is impossible to discern an emu's gender by looking, the Smiths asked Clark several times if the two birds were male and female, and he assured them that the pair had successfully produced chicks the previous breeding season.

The Smiths placed the prospective lovebirds in the same pen, but the breeding season passed without a hint of romance. Donna Smith noticed that both birds were grunting, something that only male emus do. Indeed, it developed, Andrew and Rachel were both gentlemen. The would-be breeders asked for their money back but Penbridge refused, so the Smiths flew into court. The trial judge awarded the couple $105,215, representing lost profits from their anticipated chicks. Penbridge appealed, arguing

that a buyer cannot count her chicks before they have hatched.

ISSUE: Did the trial court err by awarding lost profits?

DECISION: The Smiths were entitled to lost profits. Affirmed.

REASONING: Penbridge argued that the evidence was too speculative to award consequential damages for lost profits. The company claimed that since breeding emus is a new business, there is no reliable data from which to project profits. However, section 2-715 (2) of the UCC permits consequential damages for any loss resulting from requirements that the seller knew about at the time of contracting, if the loss could not be prevented by cover.

The "proven breeder pair" had supposedly produced 16 chicks the previous season. The trial court found that the value of a three-month-old emu chick produced that year was $5,000. The court then calculated incidental and consequential damages at $90,000, based on conservative estimates of chick production. This was a reasonable approach. Although the amount is not absolutely certain, the breaching party should not escape liability merely because damages cannot be calculated with perfect accuracy. ◢

SPECIFIC PERFORMANCE

If the contract goods are unique, or the buyer is unable to obtain cover, the buyer may be allowed **specific performance, which means a court order requiring the seller to deliver those particular goods.** This remedy is most common when the goods are one-of-a-kind. Suppose Gallery agreed to sell to Trisha an original Corot painting for $120,000, but then refused to perform (because another buyer offered more money). Trisha can obtain specific performance because the painting cannot be replaced: The court will order Gallery to deliver the work. If Trisha also sued a bicycle store, claiming it failed to deliver her racing bike on time, she would not receive specific performance, because a substitute bicycle can easily be purchased.

LIQUIDATED DAMAGES

Liquidated damages are those that the parties agree, at the time of contracting, will compensate the injured party. They are enforceable, but only in an amount that is reasonable in light of the harm, the difficulties of proving actual loss, and the absence of other remedies. A clause that establishes unreasonably large or unreasonably small liquidated damages is void. Courts only enforce a liquidated damages clause if it would have been difficult to estimate actual damages when the parties reached the agreement.

Chapter Conclusion

The drafters of the Code intended the law to reflect contemporary commercial practices, but also to require a satisfactory level of sensible, ethical behavior. For example, the Code allows numerous exceptions to the perfect tender rule so that a buyer may not pounce on minor defects in goods to avoid a contract that has become financially burdensome. Good faith and common sense are the hallmarks of contract performance and remedies.

Chapter Review

1. Conforming goods are those that satisfy the contract terms; nonconforming goods fail to do so.

2. The Code requires good faith in the performance and enforcement of every contract.

3. The seller must tender the goods, which means make conforming goods available to the buyer. The perfect tender rule permits a buyer to reject goods that are nonconforming in any respect, although there are numerous exceptions.

4. Usage of trade and course of dealing may enable a seller to satisfy the perfect tender rule, even though there are some defects in the goods.

5. When the buyer rejects nonconforming goods, the seller has the right to cure by delivering conforming goods before the contract deadline.

6. If identified goods are destroyed before risk passes to the buyer, the contract is void.

7. Under commercial impracticability, a supervening event excuses performance if it was not within the parties' contemplation when they made the contract.

8. The buyer generally has the right to inspect goods before paying or accepting.

9. A buyer may reject nonconforming goods by notifying the seller within a reasonable time.

The following chart summarizes the contrasting remedies available to the two parties.

Seller's Remedies	Issue	Buyer's Remedies
§2-705: The seller generally may stop delivery, whether it was to be done by the seller herself or a carrier.	DELIVERY	§2-716: Specific performance: buyer may obtain specific per formance only if the goods are unique.
§2-706: Resale: If the resale is made in good faith and a commercially reasonable manner, the seller may recover the difference between the resale price and the contract price, plus incidental costs, minus savings.	WHEN THE INJURED PARTY MAKES AN ALTERNATE CONTRACT	§2-712: Cover: The buyer may purchase alternate goods and obtain the difference in price, plus incidental and consequential damages, minus expenses saved.
§2-708: Non-acceptance: The measure of damages for non-acceptance is the difference between the market price at the time and place of tender and and the contract price (plus incidental damages minus expenses saved).	WHEN THE GOODS HAVE NOT CHANGED HANDS	§2-713: Non-delivery: If the seller fails to deliver, the buyer's damages are the difference between the market price at the time he learned of the breach and the contract price (plus incidental and consequential damages, minus expenses saved).
§2-709: The seller may sue for the price.	WHEN THE BUYER HAS ACCEPTED THE GOODS	§2-714: A buyer who has accepted non-conforming goods and notified the seller may recover damages for resulting losses.
§§2-706, 2-708, 2-709, 2-710: The seller is entitled to incidental damages but *not* consequential damages.	INCIDENTAL AND CONSEQUENTIAL DAMAGES	§2-715: The buyer is entitled to incidental and consequential damages.

LIQUIDATED DAMAGES
§2-718: Either party may obtain liquidated damages but only in an amount that is reasonable at the time of the contract.

REMEDY LIMITATION
§2-719: The parties may add or exclude remedies, but no remedy limitation will be allowed if it results in the injured party obtaining no relief at all; consequential damages may not be limited in cases where doing so would be unconscionable.

PRACTICE TEST

Matching Questions

Match the following terms with their definitions:

___ **A.** Tender
___ **B.** Cure
___ **C.** Course of dealing
___ **D.** Cover
___ **E.** Usage of trade

1. Industry practices and expectations
2. Buyer's right when goods are nonconforming.
3. Previous transactions between the same parties.
4. Seller's right to correct for nonconforming goods.
5. To make conforming goods available to the buyer.

True/False Questions

Circle true or false:

1. T   F   Between merchants, bargaining and contract performance are both done at "arm's length," with no expectations of fair play.

2. T   F   Under the perfect tender rule, a buyer may reject goods if they fail to conform in any respect at all.

3. T   F   A seller has a right to cure nonconforming goods.

4. T   F   Under the Code, either party may void a contract that has become financially ruinous, based on commercial impracticability.

5. T   F   A buyer who has had an opportunity to examine goods, and has not rejected them, is deemed to have accepted them, whether or not she actually performed the inspection.

Multiple-Choice Questions

6. CPA QUESTION: Smith contracted in writing to sell Peters a used personal computer for $600. The contract did not specifically address the time for payment, place of delivery, or Peters's right to inspect the computer. Which of the following statements is correct?

   (a) Smith is obligated to deliver the computer to Peters's home.

   (b) Peters is entitled to inspect the computer before paying for it.

   (c) Peters may not pay for the computer using a personal check unless Smith agrees.

   (d) Smith is not entitled to payment until 30 days after Peters receives the computer.

7. CPA QUESTION: Cara Fabricating Co. and Taso Corp. agreed orally that Taso would custom-manufacture a compressor for Cara at a price of $120,000. After Taso completed the work at a cost of $90,000, Cara notified Taso that the compressor was no longer needed. Taso is holding the compressor and has requested payment from Cara. Taso has been unable to resell the compressor for any price. Taso incurred storage fees of $2,000. If Cara refuses to pay Taso and Taso sues Cara, the most Taso will be entitled to recover is:

   (a) $92,000.

   (b) $105,000.

   (c) $120,000.

   (d) $122,000.

8. CPA QUESTION: On February 15, Mazur Corp. contracted to sell 1,000 bushels of wheat to Good Bread, Inc., at $6 per bushel, with delivery to be made on June 23. On June 1, Good advised Mazur that it would not accept or pay for the wheat. On June 2, Mazur sold the wheat to another customer at the market price of $5 per bushel. Mazur had advised Good that it intended to resell the wheat. Which of the following statements is correct?

   (a) Mazur can successfully sue Good for the difference between the resale price and the contract price.

   (b) Mazur can resell the wheat only after June 23.

   (c) Good can retract its anticipatory breach at any time before June 23.

   (d) Good can successfully sue Mazur for specific performance.

9. CPA QUESTION: Under a contract governed by the UCC sales article, which of the following statements is correct?

   (a) Unless both the seller and the buyer are merchants, neither party is obligated to perform the contract in good faith.

   (b) The contract will not be enforceable if it fails to expressly specify a time and a place for delivery of the goods.

   (c) The seller may be excused from performance if the goods are accidentally destroyed before the risk of loss passes to the buyer.

   (d) If the price of the goods is less than $500, the goods need not be identified to the contract for title to pass to the buyer.

10. Louise and Phil signed a valid contract, in which Phil agreed to sell a cello for $800,000. Phil never delivered the instrument and Louise sued. At trial, she proves that she had a binding contract with another party to resell the

cello for $950,000. Insuring and transporting the cello to the new buyer would have cost Louise $10,000. Louise wins

(a) Nothing.

(b) $140,000.

(c) $150,000.

(d) $800,000.

(e) $950,000.

Short-Answer Questions

11. Jewell-Rung was a Canadian corporation that imported and sold men's clothing at wholesale. Haddad was a New York corporation that manufactured and sold men's clothing under the "Lakeland" label. The companies agreed that Haddad would sell 2,325 Lakeland garments to Jewell-Rung, for $250,000. Jewell-Rung began to take orders for the garments from its Canadian customers. Jewell-Rung had orders for about 372 garments when it learned that Haddad planned to allow another company, Olympic, the exclusive Canadian right to manufacture and sell Lakeland garments. Jewell-Rung sued Haddad for its lost profits. Haddad moved for summary judgment, claiming that Jewell-Rung could not recover lost profits because it had not "covered." Is Haddad right? Why might Jewell-Rung not have covered?

12. Cargill, Inc., sold cottonseed, which is used in feed for dairy cattle. Bill Storms, a dairy farmer, agreed to buy 17 truckloads of cottonseed from Cargill for $176 per ton, to be delivered at Storms's farm. Storms had the option of accepting the seed at any time during the next nine months. Over the first two months, Storms ordered three truckloads of seed and paid Cargill, but Storms then informed Cargill that he would accept no more cottonseed. What rights does Cargill have?

13. Mastercraft Boat manufactured boats and often used instrument panels and electrical systems assembled and/or manufactured by Ace Industries. Typically, Ace would order electrical instruments and other parts and assemble them to specifications that Mastercraft provided. Mastercraft decided to work with a different assembler, M & G Electronics, so it terminated its relationship with Ace. Mastercraft then requested that Ace deliver all of the remaining instruments and other parts that it had purchased for use in Mastercraft boats. Ace delivered the inventory to Mastercraft, which inspected it and kept some of the items, but returned others to Ace, stating that the shipment had been unauthorized. Later, Mastercraft requested that Ace deliver the remaining parts (which Mastercraft had sent back to Ace) to M & G, which Ace did. Mastercraft then refused to pay for these parts, claiming that they were nonconforming. Is Ace entitled to its money for the parts?

14. Allied Semi-Conductors International agreed to buy 50,000 computer chips from Pulsar, for a total price of $365,750. Pulsar delivered the chips, which Allied then sold to Apple Computer. But at least 35,000 of the chips proved defective, so Apple returned them to Allied, which sent them back to Pulsar. Pulsar agreed to replace any defective chips, but only after Allied, at its expense, tested each chip and established the defect. Allied rejected this procedure and sued. Who wins?

15. ETHICS: The AM/PM Franchise Association was a group of 150 owners of ARCO Mini-Market franchises in Pennsylvania and New York. Each owner had an agreement to operate a gas station and mini-market, obtaining all gasoline, food, and other products, from ARCO. The Association sued, claiming that ARCO had experimented with its formula for unleaded gasoline, using oxinol, and that the poor-quality gas had caused serious engine problems and a steep drop in customers. The Association demanded (1) lost profits for gasoline sales; (2) lost profits for food and other items; and (3) loss of goodwill. The trial court dismissed the case, ruling that the plaintiff's claims were too speculative, and the Association appealed. Please rule on the law, and comment on the ethics.

16. ROLE REVERSAL: Write a multiple-choice question that involves a buyer's rejection of goods, the perfect tender rule, and either usage of trade or course of dealing.

Internet Research Problem

Go to **http://www.law.cornell.edu/ucc/ucc.table.html**, click on Article 2, and find your way to §2-615. You represent a buyer of goods who insists that the goods be delivered on time, regardless of any natural disasters. Read the opening sentence, as well as subsection (a). Draft a provision that requires the seller to deliver on time, period.

Creating a Negotiable Instrument

As a freshman in college, Bemis was having lots of new experiences: For the first time in his life he was living away from home and also had his own bank account and checkbook. He was discovering, however, that being on his own offered new freedom, but it also imposed new responsibilities.

As an experiment, Bemis's college distributed free iPods to all freshman. So Bemis decided to sell his old iPod to an upperclassman. When Vanessa offered to pay for the iPod with a personal check, Bemis had enough sense to make her show him online that her account had sufficient money to cover the check. Unfortunately, Bemis waited a couple of weeks to deposit the check and by then Vanessa had dropped out of school and emptied her bank account. Bemis was out of luck. A bank officer explained to him that he should have insisted that Vanessa give him a cashier's check.

Bemis bought a combination refrigerator and microwave from a fellow selling them out on the sidewalk in front of the dorm. Since Bemis could not afford the entire $300 purchase price, he put down $100 in cash and signed a promissory note for the balance. When the microwave burst into flames, Bemis was relieved to think that at least he was only out $100. That was until Samantha showed up at his door demanding payment on the note. It turns out that the seller had sold the note to Samantha, and Bemis was liable to her for the full amount.

During fraternity rush week, the president of Freaks House insisted that all the potential pledgers write a substantial check to the fraternity. Bemis wasn't sure that fraternity life was for him, so he stalled by saying that he did not have a check with him. The president suggested that Bemis write a check on the bottom of a beer carton. He was unpleasantly surprised when the bank actually cashed his handwritten "check." Especially since by then, he was a member of Geeks House. ◾▪

Commercial Paper

The law of commercial paper is important to anyone who writes checks or borrows money. Historically speaking, however, commercial paper is a relatively new development. In early human history, people lived on whatever they could hunt, grow, or make for themselves. Imagine what your life would be like if you had to subsist only on what you could make yourself. Over time, people improved their standard of living by bartering for goods and services they could not make themselves. But traders needed a method for keeping account of who owed how much to whom. That was the role of currency. Many items have been used for currency over the years, including silver, gold, copper, and cowrie shells. Even cigarettes were used briefly in Greece at the end of World War II, after Hitler's troops left. These currencies have two disadvantages—they are easy to steal and difficult to carry.

In 1661, Sweden became the first country in Europe to try paper currency. This effort was not a success because too much paper money was printed, and the president of the bank went to prison. Ultimately paper currency did catch on, but it created new problems—it was even easier to steal than gold. As a result, money had to be kept in a safe place, and banks developed to meet that need. However, money in a vault is not very useful unless it can be readily spent. Society needed a system for transferring paper funds easily. Commercial paper is that system. Electronic alternatives may ultimately dominate the marketplace, but for now paper is still king. (For more on the history of money, see **http://www.ex.ac.uk/~RDavies/arian/llyfr.html**.)

Commercial paper is a contract to pay money. It is used as:

- **A substitute for money.** When Darla stops at the Drive-In-Convenience Store to buy food for dinner, she has only 32 cents in her wallet. Not a problem, she can pay by check. Darla's check is a promise that she has money in the bank. It is also an order to the bank to transfer funds to Drive-In-Convenience. Darla is going to eat immediately (in the car on the way home), and the store would also like to be paid quickly. For commercial paper to be a substitute for money, it must be payable on demand.

- **A loan of money.** This type of commercial paper is a contract to pay what is owed sometime in the future. Darla buys a beautiful concert grand piano that costs more than her parents paid for their first house. She does not have enough money in the bank to write a check for the full amount, so she signs a **promissory note,** that is, an assurance that she will pay for the piano in five years. The manager at the House of Music does not expect to take the note to Darla's bank and be paid right away; he understands that he will have to wait.

The four previous chapters covered the Uniform Commercial Code (UCC) and the sale of goods. This chapter and the following three focus on Articles 3 and 4 of the UCC as they regulate commercial paper.

The purpose of the UCC articles on negotiable instruments is to facilitate commerce. When the United States Treasury issues money, it is consistent—all dollar bills look alike. But when practically the entire population of the United States issues commercial paper, creativity takes over and consistency disappears. The purpose of Articles 3 and 4 is to transform these pieces of paper into something almost as easily transferable and reliable as money.

The fundamental "rule" of commercial paper can be stated this way:

The possessor of a piece of commercial paper has an unconditional right to be paid, as long as (1) the paper is *negotiable*; (2) it has been *negotiated* to the possessor; (3) the possessor is a *holder in due course*; and (4) the issuer cannot claim any of a limited number of "real" *defenses*.

This rule is the backbone of this chapter and the next. You will want to keep this rule in mind throughout these two chapters.

Types of Negotiable Instruments

There are two kinds of commercial paper: negotiable and nonnegotiable instruments. Article 3 of the Code covers only negotiable instruments; nonnegotiable instruments are governed by ordinary contract law. There are also two categories of negotiable instruments: notes and drafts. The essential difference between the two is that a note is a *promise* to do something, while a draft is an *order* to someone else to do it. This is an overview; now for the details.

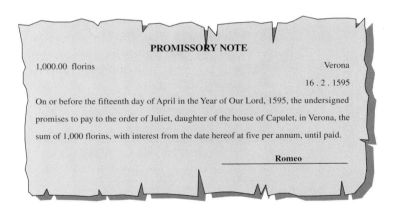

PROMISSORY NOTE

1,000.00 florins

Verona

16 . 2 . 1595

On or before the fifteenth day of April in the Year of Our Lord, 1595, the undersigned promises to pay to the order of Juliet, daughter of the house of Capulet, in Verona, the sum of 1,000 florins, with interest from the date hereof at five per annum, until paid.

_____ **Romeo**

In this note, Romeo is the maker and Juliet is the payee.

A **note** (also called a **promissory note**) is your promise that you will pay money. A promissory note is used in virtually every loan transaction, whether the borrower is buying a multimillion dollar company, a house, or a TV set. For example, the National Basketball Association permits players to borrow money from their teams. If Kobe Bryant borrows $5 million from the Los Angeles Lakers, he must sign a note promising to repay the money. Bryant is the **maker** because he is the one who has made the promise. His team is called the **payee** because it expects to be paid. Remember that only two parties are involved in a note: the maker and the payee.

Some notes are due at a definite date in the future. Others are payable on demand, which means that the maker must pay whenever he is asked. Thus, Bryant's note could be payable, say, in three years when his contract expires, or it could be **payable on demand** (which means that, if his team is ever annoyed at him, it could insist on immediate payment). The Web site **http://www.legaldocs.com/** provides a sample promissory note with fill-in blanks.

If the note is made by a bank, it is called a **certificate of deposit** (also known as a CD). When investors loan money to a bank, the bank gives them a note promising to repay the loan at a specific date in the future. The bank is the maker and the investor is the payee. The bank pays a higher rate of interest on CDs than it does on regular savings accounts because the investor cannot demand payment on the CD until its due date. In return for the lower rate on a savings account, the depositor can withdraw that money anytime.

A **draft** is an order directing someone else to pay money for you. A **check** is the most common form of a draft—it is an order telling a bank to pay money. In a draft, three people are involved: The **drawer** orders the **drawee** to pay money to the **payee**. Now before you slam the book shut in despair, let us sort out the players. Suppose that Tiger Woods wins a golf tournament. The Angel Pet Shelter, which is sponsoring the tournament, writes him a check for $500,000. This check is an order by the Pet Shelter (the drawer) to its bank (the drawee) to pay money to Tiger Woods (the payee). The terms make sense if you remember that, when you take money out of your account, you draw it out. Therefore, when you write a check, you are the drawer and the bank is the drawee. The person to whom you make out the check is being paid, so he is called the payee.

The following table illustrates the difference between notes and drafts. Even courts sometimes confuse the terms drawer (the person who signs a check) and maker (someone who signs a promissory note). But the UCC is a very precise set of rules, so it is important to get the details right. Issuer is an all-purpose term that means both maker and drawer.

	Who Pays	Who Plays
Note	You make a promise that you will pay.	Two people are involved: maker and payee.
Draft	You order someone else to pay.	Three people are involved: drawer, drawee, and payee.

Tiger Woods presumably feels confident that the Angel Pet Shelter has enough money in its account to cover the check. When Stewart Student goes to the MegaLoud store to buy a $3,000 sound system, MegaLoud has no way of knowing if his check is good. Even if MegaLoud calls the bank to confirm Stewart's balance, he could withdraw it all by the time the check is deposited that evening. To protect itself, MegaLoud insists upon a cashier's check. A **cashier's check** is drawn by a bank on itself. When Stewart asks for a cashier's check, the bank takes the money out of his account on the spot and then issues a check itself, payable out of its own funds. When MegaLoud gets the cashier's check from Stewart, it knows that the check is good as long as the bank itself is solvent.

Negotiability

To work as a substitute for money, commercial paper must be freely transferable in the marketplace. In other words, it must be *negotiable*. Suppose that Krystal buys a used car from the Trustie Car Lot for her business, Krystal Rocks. She cannot afford to pay the full $15,000 right now, but she is willing to sign a note promising to pay later. As long as Trustie keeps the note, Krystal's obligation to pay is contingent upon the validity of the underlying contract. If, for instance, the car is defective, then Krystal might not be liable to Trustie for the full amount of the note. Trustie, however, does not want to keep the note. He needs the cash *now* so that he can buy more cars to sell to other customers. Reggie's Finance Co. is happy to buy Krystal's promissory note from Trustie, but the price Reggie is willing to pay depends upon whether her note is negotiable.

The possessor of *non*negotiable commercial paper has the same rights—no more, no less—as the person who made the original contract. With nonnegotiable commercial paper, the transferee's rights are *conditional* because they depend upon the rights of the original party to the contract. If, for some reason, the original party loses his right to be paid, so does the transferee. The value of nonnegotiable commercial paper is greatly reduced because the transferee cannot be absolutely sure what his rights are or whether he will be paid at all.

If Krystal's promissory note is nonnegotiable, Reggie gets exactly the same rights that Trustie had. As the saying goes, he steps into Trustie's shoes. Other people's shoes may not be a good fit. Suppose that Trustie tampered with the odometer and, as a result, Krystal's car is worth only $12,000 instead of the $15,000 she paid for it. If, under contract law, she owes Trustie only $12,000, then that is all she has to pay Reggie, even though the note *says* $15,000.

The possessor of *negotiable* commercial paper has *more* rights than the person who made the original contract. With negotiable commercial paper, the transferee's rights are *unconditional* and generally do not depend upon the rights of the original party to the contract. As long as the transferee is a *holder in due course* (discussed in the next chapter), he is entitled to be paid the full amount of the note, regardless of the relationship between the original parties (with a few limited exceptions). If Krystal's promissory note is a negotiable instrument, she must pay the full amount to whoever has possession of it, no matter what complaints she might have against Trustie. Even if the car explodes within the month, Krystal must still pay Reggie the full $15,000. If, however, Trustie keeps the note, Krystal can subtract from what she owes *him* any claims she has against him for breach of contract because, as the original party to the note, Trustie cannot be a holder in due course. Therefore, Reggie (and any subsequent holder in due course) is in a better position than Trustie.

Exhibit 22.1 illustrates the difference between negotiable and nonnegotiable commercial paper.

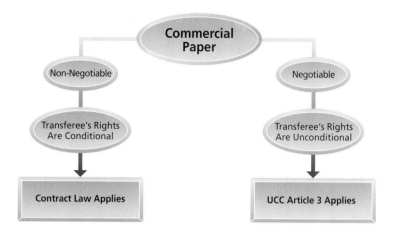

Exhibit 22.1

REQUIREMENTS FOR NEGOTIABILITY

Because negotiable instruments are more valuable than nonnegotiable ones, it is important for buyers and sellers to be able to tell, easily and accurately, if an instrument is indeed negotiable. An instrument is negotiable if it meets the six standards set out in UCC §3-104(a).

1. **The instrument must be in** *writing.* Trustie cannot negotiate Krystal's *oral* promise to pay $15,000. However, the writing need not be on any official form or even on paper. To protest a speeding ticket, Barry Lee Brown of Missoula, Montana wrote a check for the $35 fine on a pair of old (but clean!) underpants. The bank cashed it.

2. **The instrument must be** *signed* **by the maker or drawer.** Any signature counts—initials, an "X," a stamp—as long as the issuer intends to indicate her signature.

3. **The instrument must contain an** *unconditional promise* or *order* **to pay.** The whole point of a negotiable instrument is that the holder can sleep soundly at night, confident that he will be paid *without conditions.* If Krystal's promissory note says, "I will pay $15,000 as long as the car is still in working order," it is not negotiable.

   The instrument must also contain a promise or order to pay. It is not enough simply to say, "Krystal owes Trustie $15,000." She has to indicate that she owes the money and also that she intends to pay it. "Krystal promises to pay Trustie $15,000" would work.

4. **The instrument must state a** *definite amount* **of money.** It is not easy to sell an instrument if the buyer cannot tell how much it is worth; to be negotiable, therefore, the document must clearly state how much money is owed. Suppose Krystal's note says, "$15,000 with annual interest of 10%". It is negotiable even though Reggie needs to calculate the interest to know exactly what the note is worth. But if Krystal's note says, "I promise to pay $15,000 worth of diamonds," it is not negotiable because it does not state a definite amount of money.

5. **The instrument must be payable on** *demand* **or at a** *definite time.* To determine what an instrument is worth, the holder must know when he will be paid. Ten thousand dollars today is worth more than $10,000 the day the earth stands still.

A demand instrument must be paid whenever the holder requests payment. If an instrument is undated, it is treated as a demand instrument and is negotiable.

An instrument can be negotiable even if it will not be paid until sometime in the future, provided that the payment date can be determined *when the document is made*. A prep school graduate wrote a generous check to his alma mater, but for payment date he put, "The day the headmaster is fired." This check is not negotiable because it is neither payable on demand nor at a definite time. When the check was written, no one knew when (or whether) the headmaster would be fired. If the headmaster is finally fired, the checks do not suddenly become negotiable.

6. **The instrument must be payable to *order* or to *bearer*.** To be negotiable, an instrument must be either order paper or bearer paper. Order paper must include the words "Pay to the order of" Trustie (or an equivalent, such as "Pay to Trustie, or order"). If the note simply says "Pay to Trustie," it is not negotiable. By including the word "order," the maker is indicating that the instrument is not limited to only one person. "Pay to the order of Trustie Car Lot" means that the money will be paid to Trustie *or to anyone Trustie designates.*

If the note is made out "To bearer," it is bearer paper and can be redeemed by any holder in due course. The good news is that bearer paper is easily and freely transferable, but the bad news is that it may be too easily redeemed. Suppose that Krystal's note is payable to bearer and Reggie mails it to his sweetheart Sue as a birthday present. If dastardly Dan steals the note from Sue's mailbox and sells it to unknowing Neal, Krystal will have to pay Neal when he presents the note.

A note is bearer paper if it is made out to "bearer" or it is not made out to any specific person. If Krystal's note says, "Pay to the order of cash," or "Pay to the order of a Happy Birthday," it is bearer paper. If Krystal signs a note but leaves blank the space after "Pay to the order of," that note is bearer paper, and any holder in due course can redeem it.

The rules for checks are different from other negotiable instruments. All checks are, by definition, negotiable. Most checks are preprinted with the words, "Pay to the order of," but sometimes people inadvertently cross out "order of." Even so, the check is still negotiable. Checks are frequently received by consumers who, sadly, have not completed a course on business law. The drafters of the UCC did not think it fair to penalize them when the drawer of the check was the one who made the mistake. If a check is made out to "Reggie *and* Sue," both payees must sign it before it can be transferred. If the check is made out to "Reggie *or* Sue," the signature of either is sufficient.

CYBERLAW

An instrument must be *signed* by the maker or drawer. This sounds straightforward, but what does it mean to sign a note or draft? Many people, for example, pay bills online. How do they sign an online check? How does their bank know the signature is valid? Many states now grant digital signatures the same legal status under the UCC as a traditional paper signature (which is called a "wet" signature).[1] A computer signature does not look like handwriting; instead, it is a unique series

---

[1] The federal Electronic Signatures in Global and National Commerce Act expanded the definition of electronic signature to include "biometric" identifications such as fingerprints, retina scans, and voiceprints. However, the federal statute does not apply to UCC Articles 3 and 4.

of letters and numbers in code. A digital signature can actually be safer than the traditional wet signature. If the digital document is dishonestly altered, the sender and recipient can tell. ◾

INTERPRETATION OF AMBIGUITIES

Perhaps you have noticed that people sometimes make mistakes. Although the UCC establishes simple and precise rules for creating negotiable instruments, people do not always follow these rules to the letter. It might be tempting simply to invalidate defective documents (after all, money is at stake here). But instead, the UCC favors negotiability and has rules to resolve uncertainty and supply missing terms.

Notice anything odd about the check pictured below? Is it for $1,500 or $15,000? When the terms in a negotiable instrument contradict each other, three rules apply:

- Words take precedence over numbers.

- Handwritten terms prevail over typed and printed terms.

- Typed terms win over printed terms.

According to these rules, Krystal's check is for $15,000 because, in a conflict between words and numbers, words win.

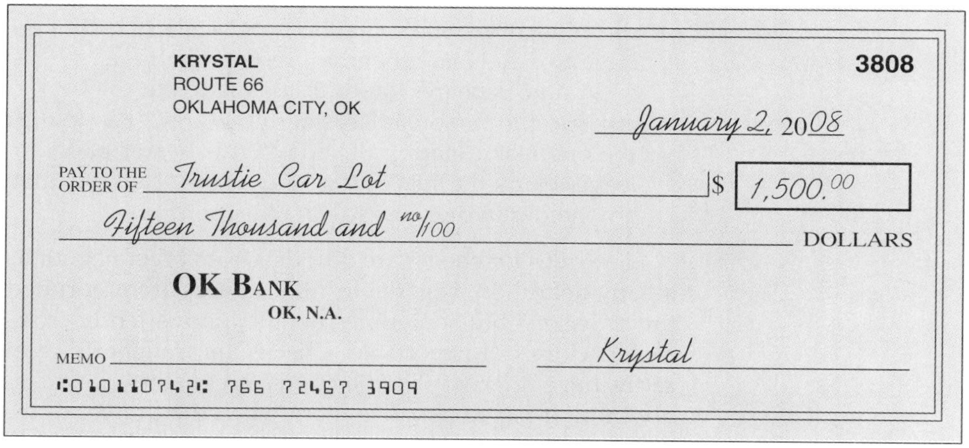

KRYSTAL
ROUTE 66
OKLAHOMA CITY, OK

3808

January 2, 2008

PAY TO THE
ORDER OF _Trustie Car Lot_ $ | 1,500.00

Fifteen Thousand and no/100 _____ DOLLARS

OK BANK
OK, N.A.

MEMO _____

Krystal

⑆010110742⑆ 766 72467 3909

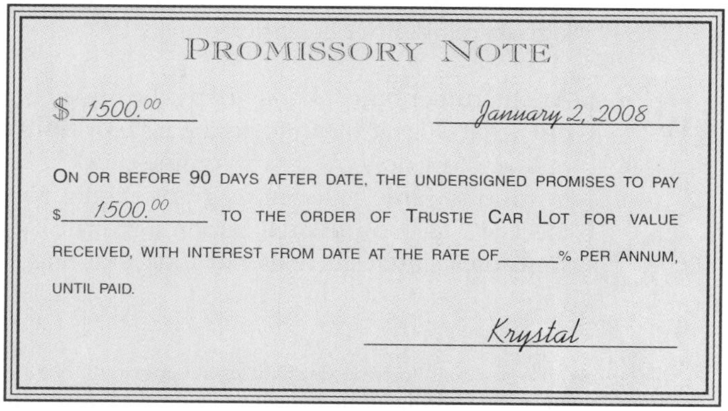

PROMISSORY NOTE

$ _1500.00_   _January 2, 2008_

ON OR BEFORE 90 DAYS AFTER DATE, THE UNDERSIGNED PROMISES TO PAY
$___1500.00___ TO THE ORDER OF TRUSTIE CAR LOT FOR VALUE
RECEIVED, WITH INTEREST FROM DATE AT THE RATE OF_____% PER ANNUM,
UNTIL PAID.

_____ _Krystal_ _____

What is wrong with the promissory note on the previous page? The interest rate is left blank. When this happens, UCC §3-112 directs that the judgment rate applies. The judgment rate is simply the rate that courts use on court-ordered judgments.

AT RISK | Careful proofreading will avoid many of these problems with negotiable instruments. Always read an instrument (or any other document) before signing it, and never sign an instrument that has contradictory or blank terms. ◼

In the following case, a set of notes deviated slightly from the requirements of the UCC. Are the notes negotiable despite the errors?

CASE SUMMARY

In Re BOARDWALK MARKETPLACE SECURITIES LITIGATION

688 F. Supp. 115, 1987 U.S. Dist. LEXIS 15122
United States District Court, District of Connecticut, 1987

FACTS: Investors purchased interests in limited partnerships that were organized to redevelop property in Atlantic City, New Jersey. To finance their purchases, the investors executed promissory notes payable to American Funding Limited. The notes stated, in part:

> "I will pay___monthly installments of principal and interest, each in the amount of $___, commencing on the___day of___19___ (estimated first payment date). Lender will notify me in writing of the first payment due date, the amount of the first payment, the date of the first payment, the date of the final payment and the amount of the final payment."

In the blanks, someone had handwritten figures representing the number of monthly payments, the amount of each payment, and an estimated date on which the payments were to begin.

American Funding Limited sold these notes to various banks. When the redevelopment plan collapsed, many of the investors ceased making payments on their notes. The investors asserted that the notes were nonnegotiable because the payment date was not definite. The banks argued that, whether or not the payment date was definite, equity demanded that the notes be treated as if they were negotiable so that the banks, which were innocent of all wrongdoing, could collect the money

owed them. If the notes were nonnegotiable, the banks' right to collect might be defeated by claims the investors had against American Funding.

ISSUES: Did these notes comply with UCC requirements for negotiability? If not, should the notes be treated as if they were negotiable?

DECISION: These notes did not meet the UCC requirements for negotiability. They should not be treated as if they were negotiable.

REASONING: For notes to be negotiable, they must be payable either on demand or at a definite time. Since these notes are not payable on demand, they must be payable at a definite time to be negotiable. But these notes had *estimated*, not definite, payment dates. At some point after they were signed, the lender was to notify the investors of the *actual* payment dates. Because these dates were not definite at the time the notes were signed, the notes are not negotiable.

It may, in some sense, be unfair if the banks are not paid, but one important goal of the UCC is to create certainty. In the long run, commerce is much better served if the UCC is interpreted predictably. It is both simple and necessary to comply strictly with the rules of negotiability. ◢

ETHICS

Was the result in this case fair? These investors were using a technicality of Article 3 to avoid paying legitimate debt. Why should the banks (and their shareholders or depositors) suffer when they had absolutely no involvement in the investment scheme?

Which of the questions from the Chapter 2 ethics checklist does the court rely on in reaching its decision? Can you argue that this decision violates some of the guidelines on the ethics checklist? ◾

Negotiation

Remember the fundamental rule that underlies this chapter: The possessor of a piece of commercial paper has an unconditional right to be paid, as long as (1) the paper is negotiable; (2) it has been negotiated to the possessor; (3) the possessor is a holder in due course; and (4) the issuer cannot claim any of a limited number of "real" defenses.

Negotiation means that an instrument has been transferred to the holder by someone *other than the issuer.* If the issuer has transferred the instrument to the holder, then it has not been negotiated and the issuer can refuse to pay the holder if there was some flaw in the underlying contract. Thus, if Jake gives Madison a promissory note for $2,000 in payment for a new computer, but the computer crashes and burns the first week, Jake has the right to refuse to pay the note. Jake was the issuer and the note was not negotiated. But if, before the computer self-destructs, Madison indorses and transfers the note to Kayla, then Jake is liable to Kayla for the full amount of the note, regardless of his claims against Madison.

To be negotiable, an instrument must be order paper (payable to the order of someone) or bearer paper (payable to anyone in possession). These two types of instrument have different rules for negotiation: **To be negotiated, order paper must first be** *indorsed* **and then** *delivered* **to the transferee. Bearer paper must simply be** *delivered* **to the transferee; no indorsement is required.**[2]

In its simplest form, **an indorsement is the signature of the payee.** Tess writes a rent check for $475 to her landlord, Larnell. He would like to use this money to pay Patty for painting the building. If Larnell signs the back of the check and delivers it to Patty, he has met the two requirements for negotiating order paper: indorsement and delivery. If Larnell delivers the check to Patty but forgets to sign it, the check has not been indorsed and therefore cannot be negotiated—it has no value to Patty. Similarly, the check is no use to Patty if Larnell signs it but never gives it to her. If someone forges Larnell's name, the indorsement is invalid and no subsequent transfer counts as a negotiation.

There are three different types of indorsements:

- **Blank Indorsement.** A blank indorsement occurs when Larnell simply signs the check on the back without designating any particular payee. A blank indorsement turns the check into bearer paper. Larnell can give the check to

---

[2] §3-201. The UCC spells the word "indorsed." Outside the UCC, the word is more commonly spelled "endorsed."

Patty the painter or Ellen the electrician. In either case, he has properly negotiated the check.

- **Special Indorsement.** A special indorsement limits an instrument to one particular person. If Larnell writes on the back of the check, "Pay Ellen Wilson" or "Pay to the order of Ellen Wilson," then only Ellen can cash the check.

- **Restrictive Indorsement.** A restrictive indorsement limits the check to one particular use. When Ellen receives the check from Larnell, she writes on the back, "For deposit only," and then signs her name. The check can only be deposited in Ellen's account. If Conrad finds the check, he cannot cash it or deposit it in his own account. This type of indorsement is the safest.

Note that indorsements can be used to change an instrument from order paper to bearer paper or vice versa. If Tess makes a check out to cash, it is bearer paper. When Larnell writes on the back, "Pay to the order of Patty," it becomes order paper. If Patty simply signs her name, the check becomes bearer paper again. And so on it could go forever.[3]

Chapter Conclusion

Commercial paper provides essential grease to the wheels of commerce. We could scarcely imagine our lives without it. This is, however, one area of the law where "close enough" is not good enough. For commercial paper to be valid, all the participants must follow the law precisely. In some ways, Article 3 is like a marine drill instructor: rigid, but predictable if you obey the rules.

Chapter Review

1. Commercial paper is a contract to pay money. It can be used either as a substitute for money or as a loan of money.

2. The possessor of a piece of commercial paper has an unconditional right to be paid, as long as:

    - The paper is negotiable.

    - It has been negotiated to the possessor.

    - The possessor is a holder in due course; and

    - The issuer cannot claim any of the few "real" defenses.

3. The possessor of nonnegotiable commercial paper has the same rights—no more, no less—as the person who made the original contract. The possessor of negotiable commercial paper has more rights than the person who made the original contract.

4. To be negotiable, an instrument must:

    - Be in writing.

    - Be signed by the maker or drawer.

    - Contain an unconditional promise or order to pay.

---

[3] Even when all the space on the back of the check is filled, the holder can attach a separate paper for indorsements, called an **allonge.**

- State a definite amount of money.
- Be payable on demand or at a definite time; and
- Be payable to order or to bearer.

5. When the terms in a negotiable instrument contradict each other, three rules apply:

- Words take precedence over numbers.

- Handwritten terms prevail over typed and printed terms.
- Typed terms win over printed terms.

6. To be negotiated, order paper must first be indorsed and then delivered to the transferee. Bearer paper must simply be delivered to the transferee; no indorsement is required.

PRACTICE TEST

Matching Questions

Match the following terms with their definitions:

___ **A.** Note.

___ **B.** Certificate of deposit.

___ **C.** Draft.

___ **D.** Special indorsement.

___ **E.** Restrictive indorsement.

1. Limits an instrument to one particular use.

2. An order to someone else to pay money.

3. Limits an instrument to one particular person.

4. A promise to pay money.

5. A promise by a bank to pay money.

True/False Questions

Circle true or false:

1. T F The possessor of a piece of commercial paper always has an unconditional right to be paid.

2. T F Three parties are involved in a draft.

3. T F To be negotiable, bearer paper must be indorsed and delivered to the transferee.

4. T F Negotiation means that an instrument has been transferred to the holder by the issuer.

5. T F A promissory note may be valid even if it does not have a specific due date.

Multiple-Choice Questions

6. CPA QUESTION: In order to negotiate bearer paper, one must:

   (a) Indorse the paper.

   (b) Indorse and deliver the paper with consideration.

   (c) Deliver the paper.

   (d) Deliver and indorse the paper.

7. The possessor of a piece of order paper has an unconditional right to be paid unless:

   (a) The paper is negotiable.

   (b) The possessor is the payee.

   (c) The paper has been indorsed to the possessor.

   (d) The possessor is a holder in due course.

   (e) The issuer cannot claim a "real" defense.

8. An instrument is negotiable unless:

   (a) It is in writing.

   (b) It is signed only by the drawee.

   (c) It contains an order to pay.

   (d) It is payable on demand.

   (e) It is payable only to bearer.

9. Chloe buys a motorcycle on eBay from Junior. In payment she gives him a promissory note for $7,000. He immediately negotiates the note to Terry. After the motorcycle arrives, Chloe discovers that it is not as advertised. One week later, she notifies Junior. She still has to pay Terry because:

(a) On eBay the rule is "buyer beware."

(b) Terry's rights are not affected by Junior's misdeeds.

(c) Terry indorsed the note.

(d) Chloe is the drawee.

(e) Chloe waited too long to complain.

10. Donna gives a promissory note to C. J. Which of the following errors would make the note invalid?

(a) It did not state the interest rate.

(b) Donna indicated her signature by writing an "X."

(c) The due date was specified as "three months after Donna graduates from college."

(d) The note stated that Donna owed C. J. "$1,500: One thousand and five dollars."

(e) Donna signed the note without reading it.

Short-Answer Questions

11. Shelby wrote the below check to Dana. When is it payable and for how much?

12. In the prior question, who are the drawer, drawee, and payee of this check?

13. A columnist for the *Arizona Republic/Phoenix Gazette* received the following problem from a reader. How would you answer it?

A check-cashing company was suing a local businessman. The check-cashing company said they accepted a check this businessman had given an ex-employee and later found out he had stopped payment. "We cannot locate the ex-employee so we opted to sue the issuing company," they said. The businessman said that he found out after he had given this ex-employee a check that he had made a mistake. He had the bank issue a stop payment. "I have a right to tell our bank not to pay a check. The check is null and void," the businessman said. "It is a worthless piece of paper. Go after the person who gave you the check." The check company argued that a check is a negotiable instrument. The stop payment only stopped the bank from paying the check. The company that issued the check placed it in interstate commerce and is legally bound to pay the face amount of the check, the check company argued. "We are the holder and have a right to be paid." Who is right?[4]

SHELBY CASE
3020 CREST DRIVE
ALVIN, TX

4201

July 27, 2002

August 3, 20*02*

PAY TO THE ORDER OF *Dana Locke* | $ | 352.00

Three Hundred Eighty-Two ——— DOLLARS

LAST NATIONAL BANK OF ALVIN
ALVIN, TX 77511
5-14/111

Shelby Case

MEMO ———

⑈010110456⑈ 286 72566 4201

---

[4] Quentin V. Tolby, "Stopping Payment Not Always Enough," *Arizona Republic/Phoenix Gazette*, July 4, 1995, p. 3.

14. Catherine Wagner suffered serious physical injuries in an automobile accident and became acutely depressed as a result. One morning, she received a check for $17,400 in settlement of her claims arising out of the accident. She indorsed the check and placed it on the kitchen table. She then called Robert Scherer, her long-time roommate, to tell him the check had arrived. That afternoon, she jumped from the roof of her apartment building, killing herself. The police found the check and a note from her, stating that she was giving it to Scherer. Had Wagner negotiated the check to Scherer?

15. ROLE REVERSAL: Write a multiple-choice question that raises the issue of an instrument's negotiability.

Internet Research Problem

Go to **http://www.legaldocs.com** and fill in the blanks of a promissory note. Who is the maker, and who is the payee of your note? Did you create a demand note?

You can find further practice problems in the Online Quiz at **http://beatty.westbuslaw.com** or in the Study Guide that accompanies this text.

chapter 23

Negotiable Instruments: Holder in Due Course

The figure lay on the couch by the fireplace. No signs of violence were visible, and a casual observer would have thought the man was napping. But Detective Waterston's trained eye immediately recognized the unnatural stiffness and pallor of a corpse. Walking behind the body, she saw matted blood against black hair and a heavy brass fireplace iron on the floor. She also noticed the crumpled document clutched in the victim's hand.

As the coroner was removing the body, Waterston slipped the crumpled paper out of the corpse's grasp. Sergeant Malloy asked whether she was ready to interview witnesses. "No," she said thoughtfully, looking at the document, "I believe I have everything I need right here." An hour later, the police arrested Tony Jenkins, the dead man's business partner. Jenkins immediately confessed.

"How did you know?" Malloy demanded.

"Simple," Waterston responded, "The answer is right here on this promissory note." She spread the crumpled page on the table. "On the front, it's a straightforward note for $1 million, payable by Tony Jenkins, the accused, to Letitia Lamour on August 1. You remember—she was recently arrested for selling fraudulent securities. Jenkins must have invested in one

of her enterprises. It gets even more interesting on the back, though," she said, turning the paper over. "Lamour held onto the note for some time. But you see, on August 15th, she wrote on the back 'Pay to the order of Sebastian Haverstock.'"

"The dead man," Malloy whistled through his teeth.

"Precisely. Haverstock and Jenkins were planning to take their computer software company public in a month or two. The sale would have made them both wealthy men. But Haverstock called Jenkins to demand payment on the note. Jenkins did not have a million dollars; he had lost everything in a series of unfortunate investments. Haverstock demanded that Jenkins turn over his shares in the company as payment for the note. In his rage and frustration, Jenkins picked up the first thing that came to hand and struck Haverstock with the brass iron. An antique instrument, and very heavy.

"It's a shame, really," Detective Waterston continued. "If Jenkins had understood Article 3 of the Uniform Commercial Code, he would not have been tempted to murder. In fact, he owed Haverstock nothing. You see, the note was overdue—it should have been paid on August 1st, but today is the 31st. You can't be a holder in due course on an overdue note. Since Haverstock was not a holder in due course, Jenkins could have used the fraud claim he had against Lamour as a defense to Haverstock's demand for payment. In any event, Haverstock was well aware that Lamour had committed fraud—he was the one who set her up in business in the first place. Jenkins could have used Haverstock's knowledge of the fraud as another weapon against any demands for payment. That legal weapon would have been a better choice than a fireplace iron," Waterston concluded wryly.

Holder in Due Course

As we saw in the prior chapter, the fundamental "rule" of commercial paper is that:

> **The possessor of a piece of commercial paper has an unconditional right to be paid, as long as (1) the paper is *negotiable*; (2) it has been *negotiated* to the possessor; (3) the possessor is a *holder in due course*; and (4) the issuer cannot claim any of a limited number of "real" *defenses*.**

This statement begs the question: What is a holder in due course?

It is important to know the answer to this question **because a holder in due course has an automatic right to receive payment for a negotiable instrument (unless the issuer can claim a limited number of "real" defenses).** If the possessor of an instrument is not a holder in due course, then his right to payment depends upon the relationship between the issuer and payee. He inherits whatever claims and defenses arise out of that contract. Clearly, then, holder in due course status dramatically increases the value of an instrument because it enhances the probability of being paid.

REQUIREMENTS FOR BEING A HOLDER IN DUE COURSE

Under §3-302 of the UCC, a holder in due course is a *holder* who has given *value* for the instrument, in *good faith*, *without notice* of outstanding claims or other defects.

Holder

A holder in due course must, first of all, be a holder. For order paper, a **holder** is anyone in possession of the instrument if it is payable to or indorsed to her. For bearer paper, a **holder** is anyone in possession. When Felix borrows money from his mother, she insists that he sign a promissory note for the loan. He promptly writes, "I hereby promise to pay to the order of Imogene $5,000." He signs his name and gives the note to her. She is a holder because she has possession of the instrument and it is payable to her. She would like to give the note to her lawyer, Lance, to pay the legal bill she incurred when Felix smashed up a nightclub. If she simply hands the note to Lance, he is not a holder because the note is not payable to him. If she writes on the back of the note, "Pay to the order of Lance," but does not give it to him, he is not a holder either.

Value

A holder in due course must give value for an instrument. Thus, someone who receives a negotiable instrument as a gift is not a holder in due course because he has not given value.

Value means that the holder has *already* done something in exchange for the instrument. Lance has already represented Felix, so he has given value. Once Imogene indorses and delivers the note to Lance, he is a holder in due course. Although a promise to do something in the future is *consideration* under contract law, such a promise does not count as value under Article 3. If the holder receives an instrument in return for a promise, he does not deserve to be paid unless he performs the promise. But if he were a holder in due course, he would be entitled to payment whether he performed or not. For example, suppose that Imogene gave Lance the promissory note in exchange for his promise to represent Felix in an upcoming arson trial. Lance would not be a holder in due course because he has not yet performed the service. It would be unfair for him to be a holder in due course, with an unconditional right to be paid, if he, in fact, does not represent Felix.

Good Faith

There are two tests to determine if a holder acquired an instrument in good faith. The holder must meet *both* of these tests:

- **Subjective Test.** Did the holder *believe* the transaction was honest in fact?

- **Objective Test.** Did the transaction *appear* to be commercially reasonable?

Felix persuades his elderly neighbor, Serena, that he has invented a fabulous beauty cream guaranteed to remove wrinkles. She gives him a $10,000 promissory note, payable in 90 days, in return for exclusive sales rights in Pittsburgh. Felix sells the note to his old friend Dick for $2,000. Felix never delivers the sales samples to Serena. When Dick presents the note to Serena, she refuses to pay on the grounds that Dick is not a holder in due course. She contends that he did not buy the note in good faith.

Dick fails both tests. Any friend of Felix knows he is not trustworthy, especially when presenting a promissory note signed by an elderly neighbor. Dick did not believe the transaction was honest in fact. Also, $10,000 notes are not usually discounted to $2,000; $9,000 would be more normal. This transaction is not commercially reasonable, and Dick should have realized immediately that Felix was up to no good.

In the following case, the plaintiff also failed two tests: He neither gave value nor acted in good faith.

CASE SUMMARY

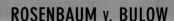

ROSENBAUM v. BULOW

1997 Bankr. LEXIS 555
United States Bankruptcy Court for the Eastern District of North Carolina, 1997

FACTS: Maude Rosenbaum was convicted of "obtaining property by false pretenses" (more commonly referred to as "fraud"). Pending the outcome of her appeal, she was sent to Women's Prison in Raleigh, North Carolina. Prison was not to her liking, but she could not raise bail of $50,000. Nor could she find a bondsman willing to post bail for her.[1]

Finally, Harvey Bowen, a local used car dealer, agreed to post the $7,500 bond in exchange for a $7,500 promissory note secured by Rosenbaum's house. In other words, Bowen demanded payment of $7,500 (instead of the more typical $750) even though he was entitled to a refund of his entire bond if Rosenbaum returned to prison as required. There was only one problem with this arrangement: Bowen was not a licensed bondsman. Thus, under state law, Rosenbaum had no obligation to pay him for posting bail.

Shortly after obtaining the note from Rosenbaum, Bowen attempted to solve this problem by asking her to sign a second note that was identical to the first, except this time W. F. Bulow was the payee.

(Bulow was married to Bowen's niece, but he was not a licensed bondsman either.) When Bulow tried to collect on the note, Rosenbaum argued that he was not entitled to be paid because he neither gave value nor acted in good faith.

ISSUES: Did Bulow give value for the promissory note? Did he act in good faith?

DECISION: Bulow did not give value for the promissory note, nor did he act in good faith. The note is void and unenforceable.

REASONING: *Bowen* gave value to Rosenbaum for the note, but *Bulow* did not give value either to Bowen or Rosenbaum. Bulow was simply part of a scheme by Bowen to mask his own illegal activity.

Nor was Bulow acting in good faith. He did not know Rosenbaum before receiving the note and he gave her nothing of value in return. Even if Bulow did not know about Bowen's unsavory activity, he had an obligation to ask questions before accepting a $7,500 note from a perfect stranger. ◢

---

[1] Typically, a prisoner will be released if a licensed bail bondsman is willing to post a cash bond equal to 15% of bail (in this case $7,500). The prisoner pays the bondsman a fee equal to 10% of the bond (here it would be $750). If the prisoner fails to return to prison when ordered by the court, the bondsman must pay the balance owing (that is, $42,500). Naturally, a licensed bondsman will post bail only if he is quite sure the defendant will return as promised. When the defendant does return, the bondsman gets back the bond of $7,500 and keeps the $750 fee as well.

Notice of Outstanding Claims or Other Defects

In certain circumstances, a holder is on notice that an instrument has an outstanding claim or other defect.

1. **The Instrument Is Overdue.** An instrument is overdue the day after its due date. At that point, the recipient is on notice that it may have a defect. He ought to wonder why no one has bothered to collect the money owed.

   A check is overdue 90 days after its date. Any other demand instrument is overdue (1) the day after a request for payment is made; or (2) a reasonable time after the instrument was issued.

The holder of this note should realize that there may be a problem.

PROMISSORY NOTE

$500.00   September 5, 1950

On or before 60 days after date, I promise to pay $500 to

the order of Soames for value received.

Irene

2. **The Instrument Is Dishonored.** To dishonor an instrument is to refuse to pay it. If Dick knows that Serena has refused to pay her note, then Dick cannot be a holder in due course. Likewise, once a check has been stamped, "Insufficient Funds" by the bank, it has been dishonored, and no one who obtains it afterward can be a holder in due course.

3. **The Instrument Is Altered, Forged, or Incomplete.** Anyone who knows that an instrument has been altered or forged cannot be a holder in due course. Suppose Joe wrote a check to Tony for $200. While showing the check to Liza, Tony cackles to himself and says, "Can you believe what that goof did? Look, he left the line blank after the words 'two hundred.'" Taking his pen out with a flourish, Tony changes the zeroes to nines and adds the words, "ninety-nine." He then indorses the check over to Liza, who is definitely not a holder in due course. However, if, instead of giving the check to Liza, Tony sells it to Kate, she is a holder in due course because she had no idea the check had been altered.

   Sometimes people (foolishly) sign blank promissory notes or checks. These issuers are liable for any amount subsequently filled in unless the holder was aware that a material term had been added later.

4. **The Holder Has Notice of Certain Claims or Disputes.** No one can qualify as a holder in due course if she is on notice that (1) someone else has a claim to the instrument; or (2) there is a dispute between the original parties to the instrument. Matt hires Sheila to put aluminum siding on his house. In payment, he gives her a $15,000 promissory note with the due date left blank. They agree that the note will not be due until 60 days after completion of the work. Despite the agreement, Sheila fills in the date immediately and sells the note to Rupert at American Finance Corp., who has bought many similar notes from Sheila. Rupert knows that the note is not supposed to be due until after the work is finished. Usually, before he buys a note from her, he demands a signed document from the homeowner certifying that the work is complete. Also, he lives near Matt and can see that Matt's house is only half finished. Rupert is not a holder in due course because he has reason to suspect there is a dispute between Sheila and Matt.

Holder in due course status is determined *when the holder receives the instrument.* If, at the very moment when he takes possession, the holder has no notice of outstanding claims or other defects, then he is a holder in due course, no matter what else happens afterward.

In the following case, Avon thought that American Express should have realized something fishy was going on.

CASE SUMMARY

HARTFORD ACCIDENT & INDEMNITY CO. v. AMERICAN EXPRESS CO.

74 N.Y.2d 153, 542 N.E.2d 1090, 1989 N.Y. LEXIS 881
New York Court of Appeals, 1989

FACTS: As manager of the import/export department at Avon Products, Stratford Skalkos had authority to requisition checks up to $25,000 on his signature alone. For nearly three years, Skalkos used that authority to steal $162,538.65 from Avon. Skalkos followed a simple pattern: He altered the names of the payees so that, although they still sounded like company suppliers, the checks could be cashed by businesses to which he owed money personally. For example, he paid his personal American Express bills with Avon checks that were payable to "Amerex Corp." Similarly, he purchased his Metropolitan Opera tickets with an Avon check to "Metropolitan Opng. Co."

Avon sued the recipients of the checks, demanding that the funds be returned. The trial court ruled against Avon and granted defendants' motion for summary judgment, concluding that defendants were holders in due course and thus took the checks free of any claims or defenses. The appellate division affirmed. Avon appealed.

ISSUE: Must the defendants return to Avon the funds they received from Skalkos?

DECISION: The defendants may keep the funds they received from Skalkos. The order dismissing the complaint is affirmed.

REASONING: According to UCC §3-304(1)(a), defendants must repay Avon if the checks were "so irregular as to call into question [their] validity." Avon argued that the misspelled names on the checks should have alerted the defendants that something was wrong. However, these misspellings were so minor that a recipient would not necessarily know the checks had been wrongly issued. Nor should a credit card company or an opera house be surprised to receive corporate checks. Businesses often pay their employees' personal expenses—to maintain a residence in a high-rent district, to entertain customers, or to travel.

Of all the parties involved in this case, Avon was clearly most at fault. Its misplaced trust or inattention permitted an employee to steal money for several years. Avon was in the best position to prevent the losses or to protect itself with insurance. ◢

SHELTER RULE

Under the shelter rule, the transferor of an instrument passes on all of his rights. When a holder in due course transfers an instrument, the recipient acquires all the same rights *even if she is not a holder in due course herself.*[2]

Cigna Insurance Company sent James Mills a check for $484.12 in payment for his insurance claim. Dishonest fellow that he was, Mills told Cigna that he had never received the check because it had been sent to the wrong address. Cigna stopped payment and issued a new check. Mills took the old check to Sun's Market and used it to buy goods there. When Sun deposited the check at its bank, the bank refused to pay and stamped the check "Stop Payment." At this point, Sun was a holder in due course and was entitled to payment from Cigna. Instead of presenting the check itself, Sun sold it to Robert Triffin, who was in the business of buying dishonored instruments. Triffin then sued Cigna for payment. Triffin acknowledged that he was not a holder in due course because he knew the check had been dishonored. However, under the shelter rule, he acquired Sun's rights as a holder in due course and he was entitled to payment.[3]

The point of the shelter rule is not to benefit Mills or Triffin—it is to protect Sun. It would not do Sun much good to be a holder in due course if it were unable to sell the instrument to anyone.

There is one small exception to the shelter rule. If a holder in due course transfers the instrument back to a prior holder who was a party to fraud involving the instrument, that prior holder does not acquire the rights of a holder in due course. Thus, if Triffin transferred the check back to Mills, then Mills would not be entitled to payment from Cigna (even if he had the nerve to ask).

DEFENSES AGAINST A HOLDER IN DUE COURSE

Negotiable instruments are meant to be a close substitute for money, and, as a general rule, holders expect to be paid. However, an issuer may legitimately refuse to pay an instrument under certain circumstances. Section 3-305 of the UCC lists so-called *real* defenses that an issuer may legitimately use even against a holder in due course. If the holder is not in due course but is simply a plain ordinary holder, the issuer may use both real defenses and *personal* defenses. **Real and personal defenses are valid against an ordinary holder; only real defenses can be used against a holder in due course.**

---

[2] §3-203(b).

[3] *Triffin v. Cigna*, 297 N.J. Super. 199; 687 A.2d 1045; 1997 N.J. Super. LEXIS 50 (Sup. Ct. N.J., App. Div., 1997).

REAL DEFENSES

The following real defenses are valid against both a holder and a holder in due course:

Forgery. If Sharon forges Jared's name to a promissory note and sells it to Jennifer, Jared does not have to pay Jennifer, even if she is a holder in due course.

Bankruptcy. If Jared's debts are discharged in a bankruptcy proceeding after he has signed a promissory note, he does not have to pay the note, even to a holder in due course.

Minority. If a minor has the right to void a contract under state law, then he also has the right not to pay a negotiable instrument, even to a holder in due course.

Alteration. If the amount of an instrument is wrongfully changed, the holder in due course can collect only the original (correct) amount. If the instrument was incomplete, the holder in due course can collect the full face amount, even if the instrument was incorrectly filled in. Suppose that Jared gives a $2,000 promissory note to Rose. As soon as he leaves, she whips out her pen and adds a zero to the note. She then takes it to the auto showroom to pay for her new car. If the showroom is a holder in due course, it is entitled to be paid the original amount of the note ($2,000), not the altered amount ($20,000). But, if Jared had accidentally forgotten to fill out the amount of the note, and Rose wrote in $20,000, the showroom could recover the full $20,000. Although the two notes look the same, they have a different result. In the case where Rose changed the amount, Jared was not to blame; but he was at fault for signing a blank note.

Duress, Mental Incapacity, or Illegality. These are customary contract defenses that you remember well from your study of contracts. They are a defense against a holder in due course if they are severe enough to make the underlying transaction void (not simply voidable) under state law. An instrument is not valid even in the hands of a holder in due course if, for example, Rose holds a gun to Jared's head to force him to sign it; or Jared has been declared mentally incompetent at the time he signs it; or Jared is using the instrument to pay for something illegal (cocaine, say).

Fraud in the Execution. In cases of fraud in the execution, the issuer has been tricked into signing an instrument without knowing what it is and without any reasonable way of finding out. In such instances, even a holder in due course cannot recover. Jared cannot read English. Helen, his boss, tells him that he must sign a document required by the company's health insurance plan. In fact, the document is a promissory note, payable to Helen. Jared does not have to pay the note, even to a holder in due course, because of fraud in the execution.

Personal Defenses

Personal defenses are valid against a holder, but not against a holder in due course. Typically, personal defenses have some connection to the initial transaction in which the instrument was issued.

Breach of Contract. Ross signs a contract to sell a new airplane to Paige in return for a $1 million promissory note. If Paige discovers that the plane is defective and that Ross has breached the contract, she can refuse to pay him because he is a mere holder. If, however, Ross sells the note to Helga, a holder in due course, Paige must pay her.

Lack of Consideration.   Ross gives his mother, Gertrude, a $1,000 check for her birthday. Then they have a disagreement over where to spend Thanksgiving, so Ross stops payment on Gertrude's check. Gertrude has no right to the $1,000 because she is a mere holder who did not give value for the check. But if Gertrude has already cashed the check at her bank, Ross must pay the bank because it is a holder in due course. Even though the check was a gift, and therefore lacking in value, the bank is a holder in due course because it has given value for the check, even if Gertrude has not.

Prior Payment.   Two years before, Gertrude had loaned Ross money to start his airplane business. When he paid off the note to Gertrude, he forgot to retrieve the original from her. Angry at him over the check, she sells the note to Carla. Of course, Ross would not have to pay Gertrude again, but he cannot refuse to pay Carla, who is a holder in due course. The moral is: When you pay off a note, be sure to retrieve it or mark it canceled.

Unauthorized Completion.   Ross writes a check to Carla to pay the note. He forgets to fill in the amount of the check, but Carla very helpfully does, for $5,000 more than he actually owes. If she uses that check to pay her debt at the bank, the bank is a holder in due course, and Ross must honor the check. Remember, however, that if the bank knew Carla had filled in the amount, it would not be a holder in due course and could not recover on the check.

Fraud in the Inducement.   Suppose that Carla gives Sean a promissory note to buy stock in his company. It turns out that the company is a fraud. Carla would not have to pay Sean (a holder), but, if Sean transfers the note to Peter, a holder in due course, Carla must pay Peter even though the underlying contract was fraudulent. Note that fraud in the execution (real defense) has a different result from fraud in the inducement (personal defense).

Nondelivery.   The note that Carla issued to Sean was bearer paper. When Oliver steals it and sells it to a holder in due course, Carla must pay the note even though neither she nor Sean had ever delivered it to the holder. Carla would not have to pay Oliver because he is a mere holder and she did not deliver it to him.

The following table lists, for quick reference, real and personal defenses.

Real Defenses	Personal Defenses
Forgery	Breach of contract
Bankruptcy	Lack of consideration
Minority	Prior payment
Alteration	Unauthorized completion
Duress	Fraud in the inducement
Mental incapacity	Non-delivery
Illegality	
Fraud in the execution	

In the following case, the defendant alleged that he was not liable on a promissory note. You be the judge.

YOU BE THE JUDGE

GRANITE MANAGEMENT CORPORATION v. GAAR

1997 U.S. App. LEXIS 27263
United States Court of Appeals for the Second Circuit, 1997

FACTS: Pay Tel Management, Inc., owned pay telephones. An agent of the company convinced Norman Gaar to borrow $275,000 from Citytrust and invest it in Pay Tel. Gaar was to receive dividends from Pay Tel that were sufficient to repay the Citytrust loan. The Pay Tel agent assured Gaar that he would not have to pay any money out of his own pocket. In reliance on this promise, Gaar signed a promissory note for $275,000, payable to Citytrust. The sums Gaar owed on the note were due on the same dates and in the same amounts as the payments Pay Tel had promised to make to Gaar.

Although Gaar did not know it, Citytrust sold his note to First National Bank (FNB). FNB and Citytrust had been involved in other deals together but FNB did not participate in the negotiations between Gaar and Citytrust.

You will not be surprised to learn that Pay Tel failed to make the payments that it had promised Gaar (and its other investors). Gaar then stopped paying what he owed on his promissory note to Citytrust.

YOU BE THE JUDGE: Is Gaar liable to FNB for the promissory note he signed?

ARGUMENT FOR GAAR: Pay Tel promised Gaar that this investment would not require him to make any payments out of pocket. The company's payments to him were supposed to equal (in timing and amount) what he owed on the note. Pay Tel has not met these commitments and, therefore, Gaar is not liable. FNB should seek payment from Pay Tel.

FNB had engaged in many deals with Citytrust, and therefore had reason to know that the Gaar transaction was fraudulent. In that case, FNB was not acting in good faith and therefore is not a holder in due course. FNB is merely a holder and as such cannot enforce a note in which there was fraud in the inducement.

ARGUMENT FOR FNB: Even if Pay Tel committed fraud, even if Citytrust knew of the fraud, Gaar is still liable on the note unless he can show that FNB also knew of Pay Tel's alleged fraud. Gaar has presented no evidence that FNB knew of any fraud. Therefore, FNB is a holder in due course and can enforce the note. Fraud in the inducement is a valid defense only against a holder, not against a holder in due course. ◢

CONSUMER EXCEPTION

Currently, the most common use for negotiable instruments is in consumer transactions. A consumer pays for a refrigerator by giving the store a promissory note. The store promptly sells the note to a finance company. Even if the refrigerator is defective, under Article 3 the consumer must pay full value on the note because the finance company is a holder in due course.

Some commentators have argued that the concept of holder in due course no longer serves a useful purpose and that it should be eliminated once and for all (and with it Article 3 of the UCC). No state has yet taken such a dramatic step. Instead, some states require promissory notes given by a consumer to carry the words "consumer paper." Notes with this legend are nonnegotiable. As you remember from the last chapter, that means that the holder has the same rights—no more, no less—as the person who made the original contract.

Meanwhile, under Federal Trade Commission rules, the holder of a consumer credit contract is not a holder in due course. Thus, both real and personal defenses are valid against such a holder. A **consumer credit contract** is one in which a consumer borrows money from a lender to purchase goods and services from a seller who is affiliated with the lender. If Sears loans money to Gerald to buy a big-screen TV at Sears, that is a consumer credit contract.

Chapter Conclusion

Whenever someone acquires commercial paper, the first question he ought to ask is, "How certain is it that I will be paid the face value of this document?" Article 3 of the UCC contains the answer to this question: If a negotiable instrument is negotiated to a holder in due course, then that holder knows he has an unconditional right (subject to a few real defenses) to be paid the value of the note.

Chapter Review

1. A holder in due course is a holder who has given value for the instrument, in good faith, without notice of outstanding claims or other defects.

2. These real defenses are valid against both a holder and a holder in due course:
   - Forgery.
   - Bankruptcy.
   - Minority.
   - Alteration.
   - Duress, mental incapacity, or illegality.
   - Fraud in the execution.

3. These personal defenses are valid against any holder except a holder in due course:
   - Breach of contract.
   - Lack of consideration.
   - Prior payment.
   - Unauthorized completion.
   - Fraud in the inducement.
   - Nondelivery.

4. Under Federal Trade Commission rules, both real and personal defenses are valid against the holder of a consumer credit contract.

PRACTICE TEST

Matching Questions

Match the following terms with their definitions:

___ **A.** Subjective test.

___ **B.** Real defense.

___ **C.** Personal defense.

___ **D.** Objective test.

___ **E.** Real defense.

1. Bankruptcy.

2. Nondelivery.

3. The transaction appeared to be commercially reasonable.

4. The holder believed the transaction was honest in fact.

5. Duress.

True/False Questions

Circle true or false:

1. T   F   A holder in due course has an automatic right to receive payment for a negotiable instrument.

2. T   F   If the possessor of an instrument is not a holder in due course, then his right to payment depends upon the relationship between the issuer and payee.

3. T   F   Someone who receives a negotiable instrument as a gift is a holder in due course because he has the same rights as the person who transferred the instrument to him.

4. T   F   A holder has acquired an instrument in good faith if she meets either the subjective or objective test.

5. T   F   A check is overdue 90 days after its date.

6. T   F   Holder in due course status is determined at any point while the holder has possession of the instrument.

Multiple-Choice Questions

7. CPA QUESTION: Bond fraudulently induced Teal to make a note payable to Wilk, to whom Bond was indebted. Bond delivered the note to Wilk. Wilk negotiated the instrument to Monk, who purchased it with knowledge of the fraud and after it was overdue. If Wilk qualifies as a holder in due course, which of the following statements is correct?

    (a) Monk has the standing of a holder in due course through Wilk.

    (b) Teal can successfully assert the defense of fraud in the inducement against Monk.

    (c) Monk personally qualifies as a holder in due course.

    (d) Teal can successfully assert the defense of fraud in the inducement against Wilk.

8. A possessor of an instrument does not need one of the following elements in order to be a holder in due course:

    (a) To be a holder.

    (b) To promise to pay money for the instrument.

    (c) To act in good faith.

    (d) To believe that the instrument is without defects.

9. Which of the following items is not considered notice of an outstanding claim or defect?

    (a) The issuer has refused to pay it.

    (b) The instrument is incomplete.

    (c) The instrument is handwritten.

    (d) The holder knows of a dispute between the original parties to the instrument.

    (e) The issuer's signature has been forged.

10. The possessor of a piece of commercial paper does not have an unconditional right to be paid, if:

    (a) The paper is negotiable.

    (b) The issuer has a personal defense.

    (c) The paper has been negotiated to the possessor.

    (d) The possessor is a holder in due course.

    (e) The issuer has a real defense.

11. The following is not a real defense:

    (a) Fraud in the execution.

    (b) Fraud in the inducement.

    (c) Mental incapacity.

    (d) Duress.

    (e) Minority.

Short-Answer Questions

12. Gary Culver, a farmer in Missouri, was having financial problems. He agreed to let Nasib Ed Kalliel assume control of the farm's finances. After a few months, Culver urgently asked Kalliel for money. One week later, $30,000 was wire-transferred to Culver from the Rexford State Bank. Culver thought that Kalliel would be responsible for repaying this sum. A man who worked for Kalliel stopped Culver on the street and asked him to sign a receipt for the $30,000. Culver signed without intending to commit himself to repaying the money. In fact, the document Culver signed was a blank promissory note, payable to Rexford. Someone later filled in the blanks, putting in $50,000 instead of $30,000. Kalliel had received $50,000 before transferring $30,000 to Culver. When Rexford sued Culver to enforce the note, Culver asserted the defense of fraud. Is Culver liable on the note?

13. On June 30, John N. Willis signed a demand promissory note for $1,620 to the Camelot Country Club in Carrollton, Texas. The note stated that it was being given in payment for a membership in the country club, but, in fact, the club was insolvent, its memberships had no value, and Willis was already a member. He was also the club's golf pro. Willis signed the note at the request of the club's manager to enable the club to borrow money from the Commonwealth National Bank to meet its payroll. The Bank of Dallas purchased the note on July 14 and immediately made demand. Willis alleged the note was overdue and therefore the bank could not be a holder in due course. Do you agree?

14. How would you advise this troubled newspaper reader?

    Q: I have paid off a loan and have a receipt from the lender for payment, but the lender will not give me the original promissory note. Do I need the original promissory note?

15. Gina and Douglas Felde purchased a Dodge Daytona with a 70,000-mile warranty. They signed a loan contract with the dealer to pay for the car in 48 monthly installments. The dealer sold the contract to the Chrysler Credit Corp. Soon, the Feldes complained that the car had developed a tendency to accelerate abruptly and without warning. Neither of two Dodge dealers was able to correct the problem. The Feldes filed suit against Chrysler Credit Corp., but the company refused to rescind the loan contract. The company argued that, as a holder in due course on the note, it was entitled to be paid regardless of any defects in the car. How would you decide this case if you were the judge?

16. ETHICS: S. J. Littlegreen owned the Lookout Mountain Hotel. In financial trouble, he put the hotel on the market at a price of $850,000. C. Abbott Gardner was his real estate agent. To obtain more time to sell, Littlegreen decided to refinance his debt. Mr. Rupe agreed to lend Littlegreen $300,000. When this loan was ready for closing, Gardner informed Littlegreen that he expected a commission of 5% of the amount of the loan, or $15,000. Gardner threatened to block the loan if his demands were not met. Littlegreen needed the proceeds of the loan badly, so he agreed to give Gardner $4,000 in cash and a promissory note for $11,000. On what grounds might Littlegreen claim that the note is invalid? Would this be a valid defense? Even if Gardner was in the right legally, was he in the right ethically? Would he like everyone in town to know that he had squeezed Littlegreen in this way? How would he have felt if he had been in Littlegreen's position? Does might make right?

17. ROLE REVERSAL: Write a multiple-choice question dealing with a holder in due course.

Internet Research Problem

Find two state statutes that make consumer paper nonnegotiable. Is the language in the two statutes the same? If not, what is the impact of any differences? Do these statutes make sense? Why or why not?

Liability for Negotiable Instruments

Willie groaned under his breath. How had he ever gotten into this mess? Producing a rock video for the Hot Tamales had seemed a golden opportunity. He loved the music, and he didn't even mind living in a trailer on location, but the business end was driving him to despair. That morning, he had glanced out his trailer window and seen Vidalia slinking across the set. How could he have been so stupid as to let her finance the video? "Willie, darling," she had purred, as a circle of smoke from her cigarette caught in his throat, "I know that your promissory note for $50,000 isn't due 'til next month, but I simply do not like the music in this video, and I cannot support what I do not like. But, take your time, dearest one, my driver will be back this afternoon to collect what you owe me."

Sitting in his trailer holding his head in his hands, Willie heard a timid knock. Opening the door, he saw a teenage girl smiling at him. "Hi, Mister Willie," she beamed. "I'm Vera Brown. My mom sent me over to collect the rent check for the trailer. And could I please, please have your autograph? Your work is so awesome."

Willie smiled. "Sure, kiddo, here's my autograph and here's the rent check."

Seeing a helpful, enthusiastic kid like Vera helped brighten an otherwise dark day. But his spirits took a blow later that afternoon when the landlady came by for her check and Willie discovered she had no daughter. He immediately called his bank to stop payment on the check, only to discover that his balance was zero dollars and zero cents. Vera had used her computer to create a second check drawn on Willie's account. She had then forged his signature and cashed both checks before skipping town. ◾

To understand the full impact of the day's catastrophes, Willie needs a crash course on liability for negotiable instruments:

- *The promissory note to Vidalia.* When Willie gave a promissory note in payment for the debt, the debt was *suspended* until the note comes due. *Verdict:* Vidalia cannot collect her money until next month when the note is due.

- *The rent check to the landlady.* Vera was not Mrs. Brown's lovely daughter; she was an impostor. Banks are not liable on checks that the issuer voluntarily gives to an impostor.[1] *Verdict:* The bank will not reimburse Willie for the rent check. Of course, Willie must still pay the landlady.

- *The check that vera forged.* A bank is liable if it pays a check on which the issuer's name is forged. *Verdict:* The bank must reimburse Willie for the second check.

Introduction

In the two prior chapters, you learned that the issuer of a negotiable instrument is liable to a holder in due course, unless the issuer can assert one of a limited number of real defenses. Against a mere holder, an issuer can assert both personal and real defenses. The life of a negotiable instrument, however, is more complicated than these simple statements indicate. Not everyone who signs a negotiable instrument is an issuer, and not everyone who presents an instrument for payment is a holder in due course, or even a holder. This chapter focuses on the liability of these extra players: non-issuers who sign an instrument and non-holders who receive payment. The liability of someone who has signed an instrument is called **signature liability.** The liability of someone who receives payment is called **warranty liability.**

---

[1] You remember from Chapter 22 that *issuer* means the *drawer* of a check or the *maker* of a note.

THE CONTRACT VERSUS THE INSTRUMENT

People generally do not hand out promissory notes or checks to random strangers. Negotiable instruments are issued to fulfill a contract. The instruments create a *second* contract to pay the debt created by the *first* agreement. When Beverly agrees to buy a house from John, that is Contract Number 1. When she gives him a promissory note in payment, that is Contract Number 2.

Once an instrument has been accepted in payment for a debt, the debt is suspended until the instrument is paid or dishonored. When Beverly buys a house from John, she pays with a promissory note that is not due for five years. Until she defaults on the note, he cannot sue her for payment even if, after a year, he decides he wants all the money right away.

ENFORCING AN INSTRUMENT

The following people have the right to demand payment on an instrument:

- A holder of the instrument.

- Anyone to whom the shelter rule applies (this rule was defined in Chapter 22).

- A holder who has lost the instrument.[2]

PRIMARY VERSUS SECONDARY LIABILITY

A number of different people may be liable on the same negotiable instrument, but some are *primarily* liable; others are only *secondarily* liable. Someone with **primary liability** is unconditionally liable—he must pay unless he has a valid defense. Those with **secondary liability** pay only if the person with primary liability does not. The holder of an instrument must first ask for payment from those who are primarily liable before making demand against anyone who is only secondarily liable.

THE PAYMENT PROCESS

The payment process comprises as many as three steps:

- **Presentment.** Presentment means that the holder of the instrument demands payment from someone who is obligated to pay it (such as the maker or drawee).[3] To present, the holder must (1) exhibit the instrument; (2) show identification; and (3) surrender the instrument (if paid in full) or give a receipt (if only partially paid).

- **Dishonor.** The instrument is due, but the maker (of a note) or the drawee (of a draft) refuses to pay.[4]

- **Notice of Dishonor.** The holder of the instrument notifies those who are secondarily liable that the instrument has been dishonored.[5] This notice must be given within 30 days of the dishonor (except in the case of banks, which must give notice by midnight of the next banking day). Anyone who has ever

---

[2] UCC §3-301.
[3] UCC §3-501.
[4] UCC §3-502.
[5] UCC §3-503.

bounced a check has received a notice of dishonor—a check stamped "Insufficient Funds."

This check has been dishonored.

Charles Bingley Netherfield Park	**1200**
	Insufficient Funds _June 10,_ 20_04_
PAY TO THE ORDER OF _Jane Bennet_	$ _5,000.⁰⁰_
Five Thousand and ⁿᵒ/₁₀₀	DOLLARS
Somerset Bank and Trust	
MEMO _for a loan_	_Charles Bingley_
010110562 766 72467 3967	

Signature Liability

Virtually everyone who signs an instrument is potentially liable for it, but the liability depends upon the capacity in which it was signed. The maker of a note, for example, has different liability from an indorser.

MAKER

As you remember from Chapter 21, the issuer of a note is called the **maker. The maker is primarily liable.**[6] He has promised to pay, and pay he must, unless he has a valid defense.[7]

Anne Elliot is only secondarily liable, but no one is primarily liable until the bank accepts the check.

Anne Elliot Kellynch, N.Y.	**0912**
	August 27, 20_04_
PAY TO THE ORDER OF _Frederick Wentworth_	$ _15,000.⁰⁰_
Fifteen Thousand and ⁿᵒ/₁₀₀	DOLLARS
TSN Savings Bank	
MEMO _real estate_	_Anne Elliot_
010110562 766 72467 3967	

---

[6] UCC §3-412.

[7] For example, if the maker goes bankrupt, he does not have to pay the note because bankruptcy is a defense even against a holder in due course.

DRAWER

The drawer is the person who writes a check. **The drawer of a check has *secondary* liability.** He is not liable until he has received notice that the bank has dishonored the check.[8] Although the bank pays the check with the drawer's funds, the drawer is secondarily liable in the sense that he does not have to write a new check or give cash to the holder unless the bank dishonors the original check. Suppose that Shane writes a $10,000 check to pay Casey for new inventory. Casey is nervous and, before he can get to the bank to deposit the check, he calls Shane seven times to ask whether the check is good. He even asks Shane for payment in cash instead of by check. Shane finally snarls at Casey, "Just go cash the check and get off my back, will you?" At this point, Casey has no recourse against Shane because Shane is only secondarily liable.

Sadly, however, Casey's fears are realized. When he presents the check to the bank teller, she informs him that Shane's account is overdrawn. Once Shane learns that his check has been dishonored, he must pay Casey the $10,000.

DRAWEE

The **drawee** is the bank on which a check is drawn. Since the draw*er* of a check is only secondarily liable, logically you might expect the drawee bank to be primarily liable. That is not the case, however. When a drawer signs a check, the instrument enters a kind of limbo. **The bank is not liable to the holder and owes no damages to the holder for refusing to pay the check.**[9] The bank may be liable to the drawer for violating their checking account agreement, but this contract does not extend to the holder of the check.

When a holder presents a check, the bank can do one of the following:

- Pay the check.
- Dishonor the check. In this case, the holder must pursue remedies against the drawer.

In the following case, a bank refused to pay three checks even though the drawer had sufficient funds in his account. Should the bank be liable to the holder of these checks?

CASE SUMMARY

FOUR CIRCLE CO-OP v. KANSAS STATE BANK & TRUST

771 F. Supp. 1144, 1991 U.S. Dist. LEXIS 10648
United States District Court, District of Kansas, 1991

FACTS: John Fleming was a grain dealer who maintained a checking account at Kansas State Bank and Trust Co. (KSBT). He also borrowed money from KSBT. On July 25, Fleming informed the bank that he had lost over $1 million speculating in the commodity futures market and would be unable to pay his loan. On July 26, KSBT seized the funds in Fleming's checking account to pay part of his debt to the bank. The plaintiffs are farmers who sold grain to Fleming before July 25. He had issued checks to them at a time when he had sufficient funds in his account to cover the checks. By the time these checks were presented for payment, however, his account no longer had funds to pay the checks because the bank

---

[8] UCC §3-414.

[9] UCC §3-408.

had seized all his money. Accordingly, the checks were dishonored. In their suit, plaintiffs allege that KSBT wrongfully dishonored the checks.

ISSUE: **Does a bank have an obligation to honor a check if the account has sufficient funds?**

DECISION: The farmers had no claim against the bank, only against Fleming, who was the issuer of the check.

REASONING: Under the Uniform Commercial Code (UCC), a bank is not liable on a check until it has accepted the check for payment. If a bank refuses to accept a check when the account has sufficient funds, the holder of the check has no claim against the bank because there is not one ounce of privity between these two parties. The holder's only claim is against the issuer of the check. The issuer may then have a valid claim against his bank.

In this case, the farmers had no claim against the bank that refused to honor the checks. They could only recover from Fleming, who had issued the checks. Then Fleming might have a claim against the bank. ◢

INDORSER

An **indorser** is anyone, other than an issuer, who signs an instrument. Shane gives Hannah a check to pay her for installing new shelves in his bookstore. On the back of Shane's check, Hannah writes, "Pay to Christian," signs her name, and then gives the check to Christian in payment for back rent. Hannah is an indorser.

Indorsers are *secondarily* liable. Indorsers must pay if the issuer or drawee does not, except in the following circumstances:

- The indorser writes the words "without recourse" next to his signature.

- A bank certifies the check.

- The check is presented for payment more than 30 days after the indorsement; or

- The check is dishonored and the indorser is not notified within 30 days.[10]

Hannah has doubts about Shane's creditworthiness, so she writes the words "without recourse" when she indorses the check to Christian. However, if Christian is familiar with the UCC, he will not accept an instrument that has been indorsed without recourse, because he wants to make sure that Hannah is also liable, not just Shane. After all, Hannah is the person he knows.

ACCOMMODATION PARTY

An **accommodation party** is someone—other than an issuer or indorser—who adds her signature to an instrument for the purpose of being liable on it.[11] The accommodation party typically receives no direct benefit from the instrument but is acting for the benefit of the accommodated party. Shane wants to buy a truck from the Trustie Car Lot. Trustie, however, will not accept a promissory note from Shane unless his father, Walter, also signs it. Shane has no assets, but Walter is wealthy. When Walter signs, he becomes an accommodation party to Shane, who is the accommodated party.

An accommodation party has the same liability to the holder as the person for whom he signed. The holder can make a claim directly against the accommodation party without first demanding payment from the accommodated party.

---

[10] UCC §3-415.

[11] UCC §3-419.

Walter is liable to Trustie, whether or not Trustie first demands payment from Shane. If forced to pay Trustie, Walter can try to recover from Shane.

AT RISK

People sign for the debts of their friends and relatives with such abandon that one can only assume they do not fully understand the situation. As the saying goes, nothing is more dangerous than a fool with a pen. Certainly, Yeung Sau-lin caused some serious damage with her pen. The 53-year-old mother of four was jailed for two years when her decision to guarantee a friend's $300,000 loan went horribly wrong. The friend defaulted and disappeared, leaving Yeung to face loan sharks who pressured her into taking part in a bad-check scheme. Yeung pleaded guilty to charges that she had written $4.1 million in bad checks.[12] ◼

In the following case, an accommodation party argued that she was not liable because she did not receive the proceeds from the loan. Was she correct in her interpretation of the UCC?

CASE SUMMARY

In Re COUCHOT

169 B.R. 40, 1994 Bankr. LEXIS 899
United States Bankruptcy Court, Southern District of Ohio, 1994

FACTS: Kathy J. Couchot and her mother-in-law, Jean Couchot, borrowed $6,317.48 from Star Bank to pay the funeral expenses of Kathy's husband. Jean executed a note to the bank, and Kathy signed as an accommodation party. To disburse the proceeds of the loan, Star Bank issued a check payable to "Kathy and Jean Couchot." Somehow this check was altered to read "Kathy or Jean Couchot." Jean cashed the check and used the loan proceeds to pay her son's funeral expenses and some of Kathy's back taxes and insurance premiums. Jean did not repay the loan to the bank; Kathy made six payments before defaulting.

ISSUES: Is an accommodation party liable for the full amount of a note when she received only a small portion of the proceeds? Is an accommodation party liable even though the check was altered?

DECISION: Kathy Couchot is liable for the full amount of the note.

REASONING: Accommodation parties often say, "I'm not liable because I did not receive any consideration for the loan." This is a losing argument. The accommodation party is liable, whether or not she obtained *any* of the proceeds. Her consideration is whatever the original debtor received. Although Kathy Couchot got only a small part of the proceeds of the loan, she is liable for the full amount and would be even if she had received nothing. Her consideration is whatever her mother-in-law obtained.

The fact that the check was altered makes no difference either. The proceeds of the check were used exactly as Kathy and Jean had intended. There was no fraud here, and Kathy is liable. ◢

Warranty Liability

Warranty liability rules apply when someone receives payment on an instrument that is invalid because it has been forged, altered, or stolen.

---

[12] "Loan Decision Leads to Prison," *South China Morning Post*, Aug. 6, 1994, p. 5.

BASIC RULES OF WARRANTY LIABILITY

1. **The culprit is always liable.** If a forger signs someone else's name to an instrument, that signature counts as the *forger's*, not as that of the person whose name she signed. The forger is liable for the value of the instrument. If Hope signs David's name on one of his checks, Hope is liable, but not David. (For everything you ever wanted to know about forgery, sneak over to **http://www.bham.ac.uk/english/bibliography/handwriting/hwbiblio/hwbiblio.htm**.)

2. **The drawee bank is liable if it pays a check on which the drawer's name is forged.** If a bank cashes David's forged check, it must reimburse him whether or not it ever recovers from Hope.

3. **In any other case of wrongdoing, a person who first acquires an instrument from a culprit is ultimately liable to anyone else who pays value for it.**

TRANSFER WARRANTIES

When someone transfers an instrument, she warrants that:

- She is a holder of the instrument.

- All signatures are authentic and authorized.

- The instrument has not been altered.

- No defense can be asserted against her; and

- As far as she knows, the issuer is solvent.[13]

When someone transfers an instrument, she promises that it is valid. The culprit—the person who created the defective instrument in the first place—is always liable, but if he does not pay what he owes, the person who took it from him is liable in his place. She may not be that much at fault, but she is more at fault than any of the other innocent people who paid good value for the instrument.

Suppose that Annie writes a check for $100 to pay for a fancy dinner at Barbara's Bistro. Cecelia steals the check from Barbara's cash register, indorses Barbara's name, and uses the check to buy a leather jacket from Deirdre. In her turn, Deirdre takes the check home and indorses it over to her condominium association to pay her monthly service fee. Barbara notices the check is gone and asks Annie to stop payment on it. Once payment is stopped, the condominium association cannot cash the check. Who is liable to whom? The chain of ownership looks like this:

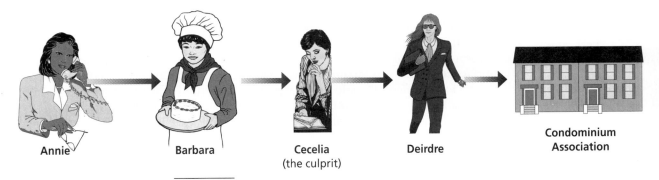

| Annie | Barbara | Cecelia (the culprit) | Deirdre | Condominium Association |

---

13 UCC §3-416.

Cecelia is the culprit and, of course, she is liable. Unfortunately, she is currently studying at the University of the Azores and refuses to return to the United States. The condominium association makes a claim against Deirdre. When she transferred the check, she warranted that all the signatures were authentic and authorized, but that was not true because Barbara's signature was forged. Deirdre cannot make a claim against Annie or Barbara because neither of them violated their transfer warranties—all the signatures at that point were authentic and authorized.

PRESENTMENT WARRANTIES

Transfer warranties impose liability on anyone who sells a negotiable instrument, such as Deirdre. **Presentment warranties** apply to someone who demands payment for an instrument from the maker, drawee, or anyone else liable on it. Thus, if the condominium association cashes Annie's check, it is subject to presentment warranties because it is demanding payment from her bank, the drawee. In a sense, transfer warranties apply to all transfers *away* from the issuer; presentment warranties apply when the instrument *returns* to the maker or drawee for payment. As a general rule, payment on an instrument is final, and the payer has no right to a refund, unless the presentment warranties are violated.

Anyone who presents a *check* for payment warrants that:

- She is a holder.

- The check has not been altered; and

- She has no reason to believe the drawer's signature is forged.[14]

If any of these promises is untrue, the bank has a right to demand a refund from the presenter. Suppose that Adam writes a $500 check to pay Bruce for repairing his motorcycle. Bruce changes the amount of the check to $1,500 and indorses it over to Chip as payment for an oil bill. When Chip deposits the check, the bank credits his account for $1,500 and deducts the same amount from Adam's account. When Adam discovers the alteration, the bank is forced (for reasons discussed in Chapter 24) to credit his account for $1,000. Chip violated his *presentment* warranties when he deposited an altered check (even though he did not know it was altered). Although Chip was not at fault, he must still reimburse the bank for $1,000. But Chip is not without recourse—Bruce violated his *transfer* warranties to Chip (by transferring an altered check). Bruce must repay the $1,000. Chip loses out only if he cannot make Bruce pay.

The presentment warranty rules for a promissory note are different from those for a check. **Anyone who presents a *promissory note* for payment makes only one warranty—that he is a holder of the instrument.** Anyone who presents a note with a forged signature is violating the presentment warranties, because a forged signature prevents subsequent owners from being holders. Suppose that Adam gives a promissory note to Bruce to pay for a new motorcycle. Chip steals the note and forges Bruce's indorsement before passing it on to Donald, who presents it to Adam for payment. Donald has violated his presentment warranties because he is not a holder. Adam can refuse to pay him. For his part, Donald can claim repayment from Chip, who violated his transfer warranties by passing on a note with a forged signature.

---

[14] UCC §3-417.

The person who first takes a forged or altered instrument from the culprit is liable to everyone thereafter who gives value for the instrument. Therefore, before accepting an instrument, it is absolutely essential to obtain foolproof identification and to examine the instrument carefully for any signs of alteration. For advice on how to avoid check fraud, see **http://www.bizcashflow.com/faqs/checkfraud.htm** and also **http://www.treas.gov/usss/faq.html#check_fraud**. ▪

Other Liability Rules

This section contains other UCC rules that establish liability for wrongdoing on instruments.

IMPOSTOR RULE

If someone issues an instrument to an impostor, then any indorsement in the name of the payee is valid as long as the person (a bank, say) who pays the instrument does not know of the fraud.[15] A teenager knocks on your door one afternoon. He tells you he is selling magazine subscriptions to pay for a school trip to Washington, D.C. After signing up for *Career* and *Popular Accounting*, you make out a check to "Family Magazine Subscriptions." Unfortunately, the boy does not represent Family Magazine at all. He does cash the check, however, by forging an indorsement for the magazine company. Is the bank liable for cashing the fraudulent check?

No. The teenager was an impostor—he said he represented the magazine company, but he did not. If anyone indorses the check in the name of the payee (Family Magazine Subscriptions), you must pay the check and the bank is not liable. Does this rule seem harsh? Maybe, but you were in the best position to determine if the teenager really worked for the magazine company. You were more at fault than the bank, and you must pay. Of course, the teenager would be liable to you, if you could ever find him.

FICTITIOUS PAYEE RULE

If someone issues an instrument to a person who does not exist, then any indorsement in the name of the payee is valid as long as the person (a bank, say) who pays the instrument does not know of the fraud.[16] For example, if a manager in the payroll department issues salary checks to employees who do not exist, and then cashes these checks himself, the company can recover only from the crooked employee, not from the bank.

EMPLOYEE INDORSEMENT RULE

If an employee with responsibility for issuing instruments forges a check or other instrument, then any indorsement in the name of the payee, or a similar name, is valid as long as the person (a bank, say) who pays the instrument does not know of the fraud.[17] For example, Dennis M. Hartotunian had a major

---

[15] UCC §3-404(a).

[16] UCC §3-404(b).

[17] UCC §3-405.

gambling problem—he owed nearly $10 million. Unfortunately, he was also the controller and accountant for the Aesar Group. Over the course of three years, he wrote himself 154 checks worth $9.24 million. Any check for more than $500 required the signature of Aesar's general manager, but Hartotunian forged it. When Hartotunian heard that company officers were coming to talk with him, he walked out and never came back.

It is always a bad sign when the company controller disappears. If an employee is generally authorized to prepare or sign checks, then the bank is not liable on checks that the employee forges. Hartotunian was clearly covered by this rule because he was the company controller. If he had been a mailroom employee without authority to sign checks, the bank would have been liable.

NEGLIGENCE

Regardless of the impostor rule, the fictitious payee rule, and the employee indorsement rule, **anyone who behaves negligently in creating or paying an unauthorized instrument is liable to an innocent third party.** For example, a bank teller should have been suspicious when she noticed that an employee of a local company kept depositing paychecks made out to someone who did not work at the company. But the teller kept quiet, and the bank was liable for having paid the checks that were deposited into this fictitious person's account.

In the following case, the Professional Golfers' Association had a bad lie. Who must take penalty strokes—the PGA or its bank?

YOU BE THE JUDGE

GULF STATES SECTION, PGA, INC. v. WHITNEY NATIONAL BANK OF NEW ORLEANS

689 So. 2d 638, 1997 La. App. LEXIS 167
Court of Appeal of Louisiana, Fourth Circuit, 1997

FACTS: Robert Brown was the executive director of the Gulf States Section of the Professional Golfers' Association (PGA). He was responsible for paying bills and handling the bank account. Blank checks were kept in a box beneath the printer stand in his office.

Adrenetti Collins was a secretary who worked in the PGA office with Brown. During a four-month period, she forged 18 PGA checks totaling $22,699.81. To avoid detection, she intercepted two of the bank statements sent by Whitney National Bank and replaced them with forged statements that left out the numbers of the checks she had stolen. The forged statements did contain the Whitney logo, but they were on paper that was a different color and size from the real ones. After receiving the two forged statements, Brown received no statements at all for two months.

The bank's policy was to verify signatures on checks equal to or greater than $5,000. One of the forged checks was in the amount of $5,000, but Whitney did not verify Brown's signature before paying it. The forged signature on the check looked very similar to the real one.

YOU BE THE JUDGE: Is Whitney liable to the PGA for the forged checks it paid?

ARGUMENT FOR THE PGA: The general rule is that a person is not liable on an instrument unless his signature appears on it. Brown's signature did not appear on these checks, so only the bank is liable on them.

Brown traveled extensively and was not available to supervise the office staff carefully. If this is negligence, then half the companies in America are negligent, too. After all, Brown stored the checks in his private office. Whitney admits that it did not verify the signatures on any of the checks, even the one for $5,000. This is in direct violation of its own policies. If Whitney had simply followed its policies, the forgeries would have been detected months earlier.

ARGUMENT FOR WHITNEY: The PGA was clearly negligent in this case. The checks should have been locked up, not sitting under the printer in an open box. Brown should have realized that checks were missing, and he should have noticed that the bank statements were forged. Without his negligence, Collins could never have committed the forgeries. In any event, she would have been caught much earlier—when the first bank statement was received, not four months later. As for the bank's failure to verify Brown's signature, the forgery was close enough to his writing that no one could have realized the signature was a fake.

Discharge

DISCHARGE OF THE OBLIGOR

Discharge means that liability on an instrument terminates. The UCC establishes five different ways to discharge an instrument:

- **By proper payment.**

- **By agreement.** The parties to the instrument can agree to a discharge, even if the instrument is not paid.

- **By cancellation.** Cancellation means the intentional, voluntary surrender, destruction, or disfigurement of an instrument. If Ted accidentally forgets to take a check out of his pocket before throwing his shirt in the wash, he has not canceled the check (even though it was destroyed) because the destruction was unintentional. If, while arguing with his business partner, he takes her promissory note and tears it into a thousand pieces while screaming, "This is what I think of you and your business skills," he has canceled the note. He could achieve the same result less dramatically by simply writing "canceled" on it or by giving it back to her.

- **By certification.** When a bank certifies or accepts a check, the drawer and all indorsers of the check are discharged, and only the bank is liable.

- **By alteration.** An instrument is discharged if its terms are intentionally changed. Laura gives Todd a promissory note. Thinking he is being very clever, Todd changes the amount of her note from $200 to $2,000. He has actually done Laura a favor because he has discharged the note.

DISCHARGE OF AN INDORSER OR ACCOMMODATION PARTY

Virtually any change in an instrument that harms an indorser or accommodation party also discharges them unless they consent to the change. These fatal changes include an extension of the due date on the instrument, a material modification of the instrument, or any impairment of the collateral that secures the instrument. When Chelsea borrows money from Jordan, she signs a promissory note due on December 24. Helena agrees to serve as an accommodation party on the note. Chelsea cannot pay, but Jordan does not have the stomach for declaring Chelsea in default on Christmas Eve. He generously extends the due date for another week. Helena is no longer liable, even secondarily, because Jordan has granted an extension of the due date.

Chapter Conclusion

It is never wise to play an important game without understanding the rules. Virtually everyone uses negotiable instruments regularly to pay bills or borrow money. Although the rules sometimes seem complex, it is important to know them well.

Chapter Review

1. Someone who is primarily liable on a negotiable instrument must pay unless he has a valid defense. Those with secondary liability only pay if the person with primary liability does not.

2. The payment process for a negotiable instrument comprises as many as three steps:

    • *Presentment.* The holder makes a demand for payment to the issuer.

    • *Dishonor.* The instrument is due, but the issuer does not pay.

    • *Notice of dishonor.* The holder of the instrument notifies those who are secondarily liable that the instrument has been dishonored.

3. The maker of a note is primarily liable.

4. The drawer of a check has secondary liability: He is not liable until he has received notice that the bank has dishonored the check.

5. Indorsers are secondarily liable; they must pay if the issuer does not.

6. By signing the instrument, an accommodation party agrees to be liable on it, whether or not she directly benefits from it.

7. The basic rules of warranty liability are as follows:

    • The culprit is always liable.

    • The drawee bank is responsible if it pays a check on which the drawer's name is forged.

    • In any other case of wrongdoing, a person who initially acquires an instrument from a culprit is ultimately liable to anyone else who pays value for it.

8. When someone transfers an instrument, she warrants that:

    • She is a holder of the instrument.

    • All signatures are authentic and authorized.

- The instrument has not been altered.
- No defense can be asserted against her; and
- As far as she knows the issuer is solvent.

9. Anyone who presents a check for payment warrants that:
   - She is a holder.
   - The check has not been altered; and
   - She has no reason to believe the drawer's signature is forged.

10. The presenter of a note only warrants that he is a holder.

11. *Impostor rule.* If someone issues an instrument to an impostor, then any indorsement in the name of the payee is valid as long as the person who pays the instrument is ignorant of the fraud.

12. *Fictitious payee rule.* If someone issues an instrument to a person who does not exist, then any indorsement in the name of the payee is valid as long as the person who pays the instrument does not know of the fraud.

13. *Employee indorsement rule.* If an employee with responsibility for issuing instruments forges a check or other instrument, then any indorsement in the name of the payee is valid as long as the person who pays the instrument is ignorant of the fraud.

14. Anyone who behaves negligently in creating or paying an unauthorized instrument is liable to an innocent third party.

15. Discharge means that liability on an instrument terminates. An instrument may be discharged by payment, agreement, cancellation, certification, or alteration.

PRACTICE TEST

Matching Questions

Match the following terms with their definitions:

___ **A.** Warranty liability.

___ **B.** Maker.

___ **C.** Accommodation party.

___ **D.** Indorser.

___ **E.** Presentment.

1. Holder demands payment.

2. Applies to someone who receives payment.

3. Has secondary liability.

4. Has the same liability to the holder as the person for whom he signed.

5. Has primary liability.

True/False Questions

Circle true or false:

1. T F Once a promissory note has been accepted in payment for a debt, the payee cannot recover the money owed him until the note is paid or dishonored.

2. T F When a note becomes due, the holder of an instrument may ask for payment from anyone who is primarily or secondarily liable.

3. T F If an employee forges a company check, the bank that pays the check is not liable.

4. T F To be valid, a notice of dishonor must be given within 90 days of the dishonor.

5. T F To be paid on an instrument, the holder must show identification.

Multiple-Choice Questions

6. CPA QUESTION: Vex Corp. executed a negotiable promissory note payable to Tamp, Inc. The note was collaterized by some of Vex's business assets. Tamp negotiated the note to Miller for value. Miller indorsed the note in blank and negotiated it to Bilco for value. Before the note became due, Bilco agreed to release Vex's collateral. Vex

refused to pay Bilco when the note became due. Bilco promptly notified Miller and Tamp of Vex's default. Which of the following statements is correct?

(a) Bilco will be unable to collect from Miller because Miller's indorsement was in blank.

(b) Bilco will be able to collect from either Tamp or Miller because Bilco was a holder in due course.

(c) Bilco will be unable to collect from either Tamp or Miller because of Bilco's release of the collateral.

(d) Bilco will be able to collect from Tamp because Tamp was the original payee.

7. CPA QUESTION: A check has the following indorsements on the back:

Paul Frank

without recourse

George Hopkins

payment guaranteed

Ann Quarry

Collection guaranteed

Rachel Ott

Which of the following conditions occurring subsequent to the indorsements would discharge all of the indorsers?

(a) Lack of notice of dishonor.

(b) Late presentment.

(c) Insolvency of maker.

(d) Certification of check.

8. CPA QUESTION: Which of the following actions does not discharge a prior party to a commercial instrument?

(a) Good-faith payment or satisfaction of the instrument.

(b) Cancellation of that prior party's indorsement.

(c) The holder's oral renunciation of that prior party's liability.

(d) The holder's intentional destruction of the instrument.

9. Which of the following people does *not* have the right to demand payment on an instrument:

(a) A holder of the instrument.

(b) Anyone to whom the shelter rule applies.

(c) An accommodation party.

(d) A holder who has lost the instrument.

10. When someone transfers an instrument, she warrants that:

(a) She is a holder of the instrument.

(b) All signatures are authentic and authorized.

(c) The instrument has not been altered.

(d) No defense can be asserted against her.

(e) The issuer is solvent.

Short-Answer Questions

11. Phariss filed a claim in bankruptcy court against the Chicago, Rock Island and Pacific Railroad. Phariss then left Iowa and closed his bank account with the Security State Bank in Independence. Somehow, Carl Eddy obtained possession of the check that the railroad issued in payment of Phariss's claim. Eddy indorsed the check in Eddy's name and deposited it in his own account at Security State Bank. Phariss sued the bank, alleging that it was liable to him for having paid the check over an unauthorized indorsement. Is Security State Bank liable to Phariss? On what theory?

12. Sidney Knopf entered into a contract for $35,000 with MacDonald Roofing Co., Inc., to reroof Knopf's building. Knopf made his initial payment by writing a check for $17,500 payable to "MacDonald Roofing Company, Inc., and D-FW Supply Company." MacDonald took the check to D-FW and requested an indorsement. MacDonald Roofing was a customer of D-FW, so D-FW indorsed the check. When MacDonald failed to complete the roofing work, Knopf filed suit for damages against D-FW. Knopf argues that D-FW was liable as an indorser. Do you agree?

13. ETHICS: Steven was killed in an automobile accident. His wife, Debra, was the beneficiary of a life insurance policy for $60,000. She decided to move from Bunkie to Sulphur, Louisiana. Before she could leave, however, arrangements had to be made to settle outstanding debts. Debra executed a document authorizing her mother-in-law, Helen, to sign checks on Debra's account at the bank. Debra also signed several blank checks and gave them to Helen with instructions to use them to pay off the remaining debt on Debra's trailer. When Helen received the life insurance checks, she deposited them in Debra's account. So far so good. But then she immediately withdrew $50,000 from the account by using one of the blank checks Debra had left her. She did not use these funds to pay off the trailer debt. When Debra discovered the theft, she sued the bank for having paid an unauthorized check. How would you rule in this case? Debra has suffered a grievous loss—her husband died tragically in an automobile accident. She trusted her mother-in-law and counted on her help. Should the bank show compassion? If the bank made good on the forged checks, how great would be the injury to the bank's shareholders compared with the harm to Debra if she loses this entire sum?

14. Merlyn Yagow borrowed money from P.C.A. to finance his farming expenses. Fearing that Yagow would not be able to pay his debt, P.C.A. required him to accept payment for his crops with checks that named him and P.C.A. as co-payees. This way, Yagow could not cash the checks without P.C.A.'s indorsement. Yagow sold corn to Farmer's Co-op Elevator, which paid $5,698.71 by check made out to "Merlyn Yagow, Alvin Yagow, P.C.A." When Yagow deposited this check, the comma between Alvin Yagow and P.C.A. appeared as "or." The check was indorsed by Merlin Yagow alone, not by P.C.A. When P.C.A. sued the bank for having paid this check, the bank in turn filed suit against Yagow, demanding indemnification for the P.C.A. claims. What claim did the bank make against Yagow?

15. Using the company's check-signing machine, Doris Britton forged $148,171.30 of checks on the account of her employer, Winkie, Inc. One of Britton's jobs at the company was to prepare checks for the company president, W. J. Winkie, Jr., to sign. He did not (1) look at the sequence of check numbers; (2) examine the monthly account statements; or (3) reconcile company records with bank statements. Winkie's bank, as a matter of policy, did not check indorsements on checks with a face value of less than $1,000. By accident, it paid a forged check that had not even been indorsed. Is the bank liable to Winkie, Inc., for the forged checks?

16. ROLE REVERSAL: Write a short-answer question that tests the reader's knowledge of at least one of the transfer warranties.

Internet Research Problem

At **http://www.treas.gov/usss/faq.html#check_fraud** the United States Secret Service offers advice on how to avoid check fraud. Click on FAQs and then "How can I protect myself against check fraud?" Have you ever violated this advice and left yourself vulnerable to fraud?

You can find further practice problems in the Online Quiz at **http://beatty.westbuslaw.com** or in the Study Guide that accompanies this text.

Liability for Negotiable Instruments: Banks and Their Customers

For Jeffrey, it was the best of times and it was the worst of times—he had started his own computer business. There were days when he could not believe the utter bliss of being on his own. Then there were days when absolutely everything went wrong and he looked longingly out his window at the McDonald's across the street, wondering if he could get a job there.

At the moment, Jeffrey was pretty miserable. He and his chief financial officer, Marnie, were meeting with their banker to sort out the company account. Although he thought he had thousands of dollars in the bank, a supplier had called the day before to complain about a bounced check. Jeffrey was very good at numbers that had "CPU" or "megabyte" after them, but he never had time for finances.

"Hmmm, now let's see," said Leena, the banker, as she peered at her computer screen. "Your account is deep into the red."

"What a dog," Jeffrey thought, looking at Leena's computer. "Must be five years old." He was imagining what one of his sleek new machines would look like on Leena's desk when her shocking statement forced him to pull his attention back to finances. "I couldn't possibly be overdrawn," he insisted, "I haven't written a check in weeks."

Leena countered, "Maybe not, but you have been withdrawing $500 a day from the automatic teller machine."

"Not a chance," said Jeffrey, "I don't have an ATM card."

"Indeed you do," Leena insisted, "We sent them to all our customers last fall."

"Hold on," Marnie interrupted. "Jeffrey never asked the bank to validate his ATM card, so the bank is liable for all unauthorized withdrawals."

Leena smiled grimly. "How nice to be an authority on the UCC. But, Jeffrey, I see that last month you wrote a check to your landlord for $18,000."

Jeffrey turned pale. "That was for 18 hundred dollars, not 18 thousand."

"I have an electronic copy of your canceled checks right here on the screen. Let's take a look. Yes, this check is definitely for $18,000. Here, you can see." She swiveled her monitor so Jeffrey could look at the screen.

He tugged at his hair. "Someone added extra zeros and the word 'thousand.' If you look carefully, you can see that the writing is slightly different."

"That's too bad," said Leena, with insincere sympathy. "But perhaps you can recover from the landlord."

"No way," Marnie interrupted again. "When a check is altered, the customer is only required to pay the *original* amount. Jeffrey is liable for $1,800, the bank is liable for the rest."

For Jeffrey, it was the spring of hope, not the winter of despair. ◼

Introduction

Americans write over 68 billion checks each year. They also execute 11 billion transactions at the more than 227,000 automatic teller machines (ATMs) located everyplace from banks to grocery stores, gas stations, and airports. This chapter is about the laws that govern the relationship between banks and their customers.

Checking Accounts

When a customer deposits money in a checking account, the bank becomes a debtor to the customer—the bank owes the customer money. At the same time, the bank serves as an agent for the customer. As such, the bank has certain duties to its depositors.

THE BANK'S DUTY TO PROVIDE INFORMATION

The Uniform Commercial Code (UCC) does not require banks to provide customers with a monthly statement that lists transactions. Virtually every bank does so, however, because customers expect it. If a bank provides a statement, it must include either a copy of all checks or a list of check numbers, amounts, and dates of payment.

THE BANK'S DUTY TO PAY

A bank must pay a check if the check is authorized by the customer and complies with the terms of the checking account agreement. A bank may, however, choose the order in which it pays authorized checks. Suppose that Elizabeth writes a check to each of her four sisters: Jane ($100), Mary ($50), Lydia ($40), and Kitty ($10). When the sisters appear at the bank the next morning to cash the checks, they discover Elizabeth has only $100 in her account. The bank is free to choose which sisters it pays. It is not forced to pay the sister who appears first, nor must it pay Mary, Lydia, and Kitty together, instead of Jane by herself.

WRONGFUL DISHONOR

If a bank violates its duty and wrongfully dishonors an authorized check, it is liable to the customer for all *actual* **and** *consequential* **damages.** Bouncing a check is not only embarrassing, it can cost real money—a retailer may charge for a returned check, the customer's credit rating may suffer, or the customer may even be arrested. When it has wrongfully dishonored a check, the bank is liable for these damages. What should the bank's liability be in the following case?

CASE SUMMARY

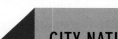

CITY NATIONAL BANK OF FORT SMITH v. GOODWIN

301 Ark. 182, 783 S.W.2d 335, 1990 Ark. LEXIS 49
Supreme Court of Arkansas, 1990

FACTS: City National Bank of Fort Smith (CNB) had two customers with similar names: Larry J. Goodwin and Larry K. Goodwin. Larry K. defaulted on two loans from CNB. Jim Geels, a collection officer at the bank, sought to take money from Larry K.'s checking account and credit it to the loan (which he had the right to do). On November 26, he pulled Larry K.'s loan file to check his Social Security number, but the file had Larry J.'s number instead. Geels took $3,229.07 from the checking account of Larry J. and his wife, Sandra.

On November 30, Sandra Goodwin received written notice from CNB that four checks she had written between November 21 and 26 had not been paid because of insufficient funds and that the Goodwins' joint checking account had a zero balance. Ms. Goodwin knew the bank was in error and requested that CNB both call and send certified letters of apology to the merchants involved. On December 2, she called three of the businesses to which she had written the checks. None of them had received a call or letter. Later in the day, Geels

promised Ms. Goodwin that letters would be sent to the merchants stating that the bank was at fault. On the next day, December 3, he did mail the letters.

It turned out that other checks written to merchants on November 12 and 21 had also bounced. CNB wrote a letter to one merchant and called the other, stating that it was the bank's fault that the checks were returned. On February 6, the Goodwins filed suit against CNB. The jury found for the Goodwins and awarded compensatory damages of $10,000 and punitive damages of $30,000. The bank appealed.

ISSUE: Is a bank liable for punitive damages when it wrongfully dishonors a customer's check?

DECISION: Reversed and remanded. CNB is not liable for punitive damages.

REASONING: Under UCC §4-402, a bank that wrongfully dishonors a check is liable for punitive damages only if it acted intentionally or in bad faith.

If the bank acted in good faith or by accident, then it is liable only for compensatory damages. In this case, there was no evidence that CNB deliberately dishonored the Goodwins' checks. It simply mixed up the names of Larry K. and Larry J. Goodwin. Accordingly, the case is reversed and remanded. ◢

Banks are in a difficult position. If they refuse to pay an authorized check, they are liable for damages. On the other hand, if they pay an unauthorized check, they must bear the liability and recredit the customer's account. Following are the most common problems banks face in determining which checks to pay and which to dishonor.

The Death of a Customer

If a customer dies, the bank may continue to pay checks *for 10 days* after it learns of the death, unless it receives a stop payment order from someone claiming an interest in the account. After all, the customer was alive when he wrote the checks. Refusing to pay may cause hardship for innocent merchants who accepted checks in return for goods. A refusal to pay may also complicate matters for his family when they sort out his financial affairs. Certainly, the last thing his widow wants is for all his checks to bounce.

In reality, however, banks typically do freeze an account after the holder dies. First, a bank must stop payment on checks if someone else makes a claim to the funds in the account, no matter how weak that claim is. If Mildred, a seventh cousin twice removed, makes a claim, the bank must stop payment. Second, although the UCC permits banks to pay checks even after the customer has died, most states require banks to freeze enough money to cover the decedent's taxes. Since the bank does not know what the decedent will ultimately owe, it typically freezes the entire account.

Incompetent Customers

Once a bank is notified that a court has found a customer to be incompetent, it is liable if it pays the customer's checks.

Forgery

If a bank pays a check on which the issuer's name is forged, it must recredit the issuer's account. When a bank pays a forged check, either the bank or the customer will lose money, except in the unlikely event that the forger repays what he has stolen. As a matter of policy, the drafters of the UCC decided that the bank should bear the risk of forgery, rather than the customer.

Alteration

If a bank pays a check that has been altered, the customer is liable only for the original amount of the check, and the bank is liable for the balance. There is one exception to this rule: If the alteration is obvious, the bank is liable for the full amount of the check because it should have known better than to pay it in the first place. Exhibit 25.1 illustrates this rule.

Exhibit 25.1

If the bank pays this check, it is liable for the full amount because the check has obviously been altered.

Anna Karenina originally wrote this check for $9.60. Because the check looks unaltered, she is liable for $9.60, and the bank is liable for the balance.

Completion

If an incomplete check is later filled in by someone other than the original issuer, the bank is not liable unless it was on notice that the completion was improper. Joey and Lisa want to buy a house. Negotiations are still incomplete when Joey goes out of town for a few days. He signs a blank check and leaves it with Lisa to pay his half of the deposit, if their offer is accepted. Lisa absentmindedly uses the check as a bookmark and forgets to remove it before she returns the book to the library. Marian the librarian finds the check and, glorying in the thought of hundreds of new books, fills in the library's name and the amount of $10,000. If Lisa realizes the check is missing and notifies the bank, then the bank is liable to Joey if it later pays the check. Otherwise, the bank owes Joey nothing.

Comparative Negligence and Bank Statements

Customers must use reasonable care in examining their bank statements to look for forged or altered checks. In any case, a customer cannot recover for a forgery or alteration if it is reported more than one year after receiving the statement that first revealed the problem. Moreover, if a customer fails to notify the bank of a forgery or alteration within 30 days of receiving a statement, then the bank is not liable for any subsequent bad checks by the same wrongdoer.

Tom likes to brag at family gatherings that he is too busy making money to waste time balancing his checkbook. "My time is so valuable," he says, "it would cost me thousands of dollars just to open the envelope." His careful brother, David, gets a certain amount of secret satisfaction when Tom discovers that, over the course of six months, a disgruntled employee had forged Tom's name to six different checks amounting to $30,000. The bank is not liable for the last five checks because Tom did not report the forgeries within 30 days of receiving his bank statement.

Stale Checks

A bank is not required to pay checks that are presented more than six months after their date, but it is not liable if it does pay. In 1962, John Glenn became the first person to orbit the earth. Many people were so eager to have his autograph that they did not cash checks he gave them. In 1974, Glenn was elected senator from Ohio. Suppose that one of his admirers became so disgusted with his political views that she no longer treasured his autograph and tried, in 1974, to cash a check from 1962. Would she be successful? Although Glenn's bank, as a matter of policy, would probably reject the 12-year-old check, it would not be liable to Glenn if it paid.

Post-Dated Checks

A post-dated check is one that is presented for payment before its date. **A bank is not liable for paying a post-dated check unless the customer has notified the bank in advance that a post-dated check is coming.** Because most banks use machines to process checks, it is impractical to expect them to review the date on each check.

Stop Payment Orders

Even if a check is authorized when issued, the customer has the right to stop payment later. **As a general rule, if a bank pays a check over a stop payment order, it is liable to the customer for any loss he suffers.** However, a bank customer must be aware of these additional rules:

- A stop payment order is valid only if it describes the check with reasonable certainty and the bank receives the order before paying the check.

- An oral stop payment order is valid for only 14 days; a written order expires in six months. This is an important point. Many people think that, once they have stopped payment on a check, they can relax and forget about it. Not true. One woman, for example, wrote a $1,000 check to a contractor. When he told her he had lost the check, she stopped payment and gave him a new one, which he promptly cashed. Ten months later, he cashed the old check, too. The customer could have continued to renew the stop payment order every six months (at a cost of about $20 each time), but that would have been a hassle. The only surefire method for stopping a check permanently is to close the old account and open a new one.

In the following case, the bank did not stop payment because the customer slightly misidentified the check. Who should be liable—the customer or the bank? You be the judge.

YOU BE THE JUDGE

PARR v. SECURITY NATIONAL BANK

680 P.2d 648, 1984 OK CIV APP 16, 1984 Okla. Civ. App. LEXIS 99
Court of Appeals of Oklahoma, 1984

FACTS: Joan Parr sent Champlin Oil a check for $972.96. The next day, she called Security National Bank (Bank) to stop payment. She gave the Bank her account number, the check number, the date, the payee, and the amount of the check. Unfortunately, she told the Bank that the check had been for $972.46, instead of $972.96. The next day, the Bank paid the check.

Parr brought suit against the Bank. In its defense, the Bank explained that its computers were programmed to stop payment only if the reported amount of the check was correct. It argued that Parr's 50-cent error relieved the Bank of liability.

YOU BE THE JUDGE: Did Parr describe the check with reasonable certainty?

ARGUMENT FOR PARR: Banks are required by law to obey stop payment orders. The Bank argues that it is not at fault because its computer failed to find this check. The Bank made two choices: (1) It used a computer to sort checks; and (2) it programmed the computer to search for stopped checks by amount alone. The Bank evidently found benefits to this system that outweighed the risk that it might pay an item on which a stop payment order had been issued. The bank made a decision to accept that risk; it cannot now shirk its responsibility.

Furthermore, the Bank could have avoided this whole problem if it had simply informed Ms. Parr that the amount listed in the stop order had to be exact. It would never occur to a reasonable person that, having given the date, number, and payee of this check, the amount also had to be accurate to the last penny.

ARGUMENT FOR THE BANK: The law generally provides that whoever makes a mistake pays for it.

Who made the mistakes here? Parr did. First, she wrote a check that, in fact, she did not want paid. Under the UCC her bank must stop payment on a check that has been received "in such manner as to afford the bank a reasonable opportunity to act." But then Parr made a second mistake—she gave the Bank the wrong amount for the check. Parr argues that, if the Bank uses check processing machines, it must bear the risk of loss. Every bank uses check processing machines. We do it to keep our expenses low. And that benefits our customers. Parr cannot have it both ways. She cannot take the benefit of lower fees and then complain that her bank uses machines to process checks.

Parr also argues that, if she had known that the Bank's machines look for the amount of a check, she would have taken more care to provide the right number. In short, Parr admits she was careless, but she expects the Bank to pay the price for her carelessness. ▮

AT RISK

Consumer advocates suggest that bank customers should follow these safeguards:

- *Read bank statements.* Many financial advisers now say that it is not crucial to *balance* a checkbook, but it is important to *look* at bank statements to detect anything out of the ordinary.

- *Keep bank statements and copies of canceled checks.* Without this documentation, it is difficult to prove the bank has made an error.

- *Look at receipts from ATMs to make sure they are correct.*

- *Write immediately to the bank if there is an error in a statement or ATM receipt.* Mail the information to a specific person who handles consumer complaints; then keep a record of when you contacted the bank, the names of any people you spoke to, and what they said. Be persistent. If you do not hear from the bank, or the answer is unsatisfactory, take your complaint to a higher level in the bank.

- *If you cannot resolve your dispute directly with the bank, write to the agency that regulates it.* Ask someone at your bank for the name of its primary regulator, or call your state banking department and ask for help.[1] ▮

---

[1] Christine Dugas, "Fighting the Bank," *Newsday,* Nov. 13, 1994, p. 3.

Customer's Right to Withdraw Funds

Before the Expedited Funds Availability Act (EFAA) was passed, scenarios such as the following were common: On August 7, a Los Angeles woman deposited a $7,500 check drawn on a bank in New York. Her bank told her that she could not withdraw these funds for 10 working days, that is, until August 21. On August 19, when her bank still would not let her withdraw the money, she called the issuer of the check and discovered that the funds had been paid out on August 9. She was aghast to realize that her bank had had good funds for over a week, but would still not let her withdraw them.

The EFAA was passed to avoid problems such as this. It specifies the maximum time a bank may hold funds before allowing a customer to withdraw them. Exhibit 25.2 lists rules that establish how quickly you can write a check against funds in your account.

Customers must, however, wait longer to withdraw cash than they do to write a check. Banks are at greater risk when customers withdraw cash than when they write a check: The bank still has a number of days before a check must be paid; the cash is gone immediately. Thus, under the EFAA, a customer can only withdraw the first $100 in cash on the next business day after depositing a check. He can withdraw $400 more in cash by 5 p.m. on the same day that the funds are available for check writing. The rest of the deposit can be withdrawn the day after funds are available for check writing.

Electronic Banking

The Electronic Fund Transfer Act (EFTA) protects *consumers* in their dealings with banks. A consumer is "any natural person," that is, not a corporation or business. Following are the major provisions of the EFTA.

Item Deposited	When Funds May Be Withdrawn by Check:
Cash Cashier's check Certified check Government check Check drawn on same bank Wire transfer	• Next business day, if deposited with a teller • Second business day, if deposited in an ATM
Local check (both the depositary bank and the payor bank are in the same region)	• Next business day, for the first $100 • Second business day, for the balance up to $5,000 • Ninth business day, for the balance over $5,000
Nonlocal check	• Next business day, for the first $100 • Fifth business day, for the balance up to $5,000 • Ninth business day, for the balance over $5,000

Exhibit 25.2

REQUIRED ELECTRONIC FUND TRANSFERS

Employers may not require their employees to receive paychecks via an electronic fund transfer *at a particular bank.* Suppose the Dawes Bank offers to give MegaCorp. favorable financing on a major loan if the company pays all employees by electronic fund transfer to Dawes. Under the EFTA, MegaCorp. can require all employees to receive their pay via an electronic fund transfer, but the company cannot require employees to be paid at Dawes.

Cards

If a bank sends an electronic fund transfer card (for example, an ATM card) to a consumer who has not requested it, the card must be invalid until the consumer requests validation. Otherwise, if banks sent valid ATM cards to consumers who were not expecting them, the cards could be stolen and used without the consumer ever knowing.

Debit, Credit, and ATM Cards

Although debit, credit, and ATM cards have become very popular, many Americans are still confused about all those pieces of plastic in their wallets:

- *Debit cards versus ATM cards.* The very same piece of plastic can be both an ATM card and a debit card, depending on where you use it. If you want to buy dinner, you can put your card in an ATM, punch in your personal identification number (PIN), and withdraw cash on the spot. Or you can take your card to a restaurant that has a point-of-sale (POS) terminal. At the end of the meal, you present the card and your meal is paid for. What is the difference? Your money from the ATM disappears from your account immediately; the debit card transaction takes a day or two to register (especially on the weekend). If you lose your wallet on the way to the restaurant, the cash is gone for good, but your losses on the debit card are limited.

- *Debit cards versus credit cards.* At the restaurant, you might have a choice between using your debit card or a credit card. What is the difference here? If you pay with a credit card, the money stays firmly in your account until you pay your credit card bill. With a debit card, the funds disappear from your account much sooner. Also, many credit cards now offer perks such as frequent flyer mileage.

- *Debit cards versus checks.* Many restaurants accept checks reluctantly or not at all. Debit cards are easier, and in both cases, your funds disappear from your account within days. At the end of the month, however, most banks will send you copies of canceled checks. With debit cards you get only a bank statement.

Documentation

A bank must provide consumers with (1) a transaction statement each time an electronic fund transfer is made at an ATM; and (2) a monthly (or, in the case of infrequent transactions, quarterly) statement reporting all electronic fund transfers for the period.

Errors

If, within 60 days of receiving a bank statement, a consumer tells the bank (either orally or in writing) that the account is in error, the bank must investigate and

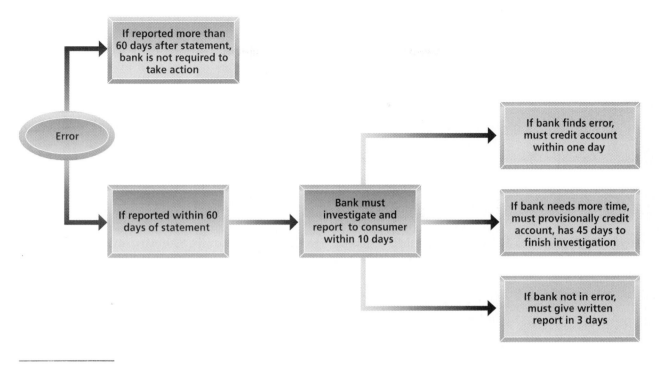

Exhibit 25.3

report the result of its investigation to the consumer within 10 *business* days. If the bank discovers an error, it must recredit the consumer's account (including interest) within one business day. If the bank cannot complete its investigation within 10 *business* days, it must provisionally recredit the consumer's account (including interest) pending the termination of its investigation, which must be completed within 45 *calendar* days. If the bank finds there was no error, it must give the consumer a full explanation in writing within three *business* days of so finding. When a bank violates this provision, it must pay the consumer treble damages (three times the amount in dispute). Exhibit 25.3 illustrates these rules.

Consumer Liability for Unauthorized Transactions

When a thief steals an ATM or debit card, it is important for the consumer to report the theft to the bank as quickly as possible.[2] If she reports the loss within two days of discovering it, she is liable only for the first $50 stolen. If she reports the loss after two days, but within 60 days of receiving her bank statement that shows the unauthorized withdrawal, she is liable for a maximum of $500. After 60 days, she is liable for the full amount.

If an unauthorized transfer takes place without the use of a stolen card, then the consumer is not liable at all, as long as she reports the loss within 60 days of receiving a bank statement that shows the loss. After 60 days, however, she is liable for the full amount. (Clever thieves can, for example, make cards that will work in someone else's account.)

---

[2] The Web site **http://www.ftc.gov/bcp/menu-credit.htm** tells you what to do if you lose a credit card.

The goal of the EFTA is to protect consumers. But that protection goes only so far. It is important for consumers to pay careful attention to the EFTA time limits. For example, Mr. Kruser thought that his ATM card was destroyed in September. It turned out, however, that someone used it to make an unauthorized withdrawal of $20 from the account in December (evidently, a very slow and patient thief). Then Mrs. Kruser had surgery, and during her six-month recuperation, did not check the bank statements. In August, someone illegally withdrew $9,020 from the account, which she did not discover until September. When the bank refused to refund the money, the Krusers sued on the grounds that a reasonable person would not have noticed the initial $20 theft. But the court found for the bank because, if the Krusers had reported the first theft, the bank would have canceled their ATM card and the larger sum would not have been stolen.

ETHICS

Someone uses Mr. Kruser's ATM card to withdraw $20. Mrs. Kruser undergoes major surgery and fails to notice the unauthorized withdrawal. (How many *healthy* people would notice one unauthorized $20 withdrawal?) Six months later, someone steals more than $9,000 from the Krusers' account and the bank refuses to pay. It litigates the case to the appeals court, undoubtedly incurring well more than $9,000 in legal fees. Why did the bank do this? Was it the right thing to do? What are the consequences of the bank's decision? ◾

Privacy

Think about how much information your bank knows about you. Add to that what your insurance company, stock brokerage, and acredit card companies know. Imagine that they can sell that information to anyone they wish, without telling you. Are you nervous yet?

This is the problem that the Gramm-Leach-Bliley Act of 1999 (GLB) sought to solve. Under this statute, banks and other financial institutions must disclose to consumers any nonpublic information they wish to reveal to third parties. A financial institution cannot disclose this private information if the consumer opts out (that is, denies permission). Note that GLB permits financial institutions to provide information to third parties unless the consumer affirmatively requests privacy.

Chapter Conclusion

This area of law is important to anyone who has ever written a check or used an ATM, which is to say, virtually everyone. Knowing your rights and obligations can make all the difference in your financial future.

Chapter Review

1. If a bank wrongfully dishonors an authorized check, it is liable to the customer for all actual and consequential damages.

2. A bank is not liable for paying the checks of an incompetent customer until it knows that the customer has been adjudicated incompetent.

3. If a customer dies, the bank may continue to pay checks for 10 days after it learns of the death, unless it receives a stop payment order from someone claiming an interest in the account.

4. If a bank pays a check on which the issuer's name is forged, it must recredit the issuer's account.

5. If a bank pays a check that has been altered, the customer is liable only for the original amount of the check, and the bank is liable for the balance.

6. If a bank pays an incomplete check that was filled in by someone other than the original issuer, the bank is not liable unless it was on notice that the completion was improper.

7. A bank is not required to pay checks that are presented more than six months after their date, but it is not liable if it does pay.

8. A bank has no liability for paying a post-dated check unless the customer notifies the bank in advance that the check is coming.

9. If a bank pays a check over a stop payment order, it is liable to the customer for any loss he suffers as a result.

10. If a bank sends an electronic fund transfer card (for example, an ATM card) to a consumer who has not requested it, the card must be invalid until the consumer requests validation.

11. If, within 60 days of receiving a bank statement, a consumer tells the bank (either orally or in writing) that the account is in error, the bank must investigate and report the result of its investigation to the consumer within 10 business days.

12. When a thief uses a stolen ATM or debit card to withdraw money from a bank, the consumer is not liable for more than $50, provided she notifies the bank within two business days that the card has been stolen.

13. Banks and other financial institutions must disclose to consumers any nonpublic information they wish to reveal to third parties. A financial institution cannot disclose this private information if the consumer opts out (that is, denies permission).

PRACTICE TEST

Matching Questions

Match the following:

___ **A.** A consumer is liable only for $50 if she reports the loss of her ATM card within

___ **B.** A written stop payment order expires in

___ **C.** To recover on a forged or altered check, the customer must report it to the bank within

___ **D.** A consumer is liable for the full amount of the loss if she reports a stolen ATM card after

___ **E.** A bank must provide consumers with a statement of electronic fund transfers

1. Two days.
2. Monthly.
3. 60 days of receiving the bank statement.
4. Six months.
5. One year of receiving the bank statement.

True/False Questions

Circle true or false:

1. T   F   Under the UCC, banks are required to provide customers with a monthly statement.

2. T   F   If an incomplete check is later filled in by someone other than the original issuer, the bank is never liable.

3. T   F   Banks are never liable for paying a post-dated check.

4. T   F   For a stop payment order to be valid, it must describe the check with reasonable certainty, and the bank must receive the order before paying the check.

5. T   F   An oral stop payment order is never valid.

Multiple-Choice Questions

6. CPA QUESTION: In general, which of the following statements is correct concerning the priority among checks drawn on a particular account and presented to the drawee bank on a particular day?

    (a) The checks may be charged to the account in any order convenient to the bank.

    (b) The checks may be charged to the account in any order provided no charge creates an overdraft.

    (c) The checks must be charged to the account in the order in which the checks were dated.

    (d) The checks must be charged to the account in the order of lowest amount to highest amount to minimize the number of dishonored checks.

7. Harriet goes to the teller window and deposits a $1,000 tax refund check from the United States Treasury into her checking account. Two business days later, she sees the apartment of her dreams and wants to withdraw the entire $1,000 in cash to put down as a security deposit and first month's rent on the apartment before anyone else sees it. She:

    (a) Can withdraw only $100.

    (b) Can withdraw only $400.

    (c) Can withdraw only $500.

    (d) Can withdraw the whole amount.

    (e) Cannot withdraw anything.

8. By mistake, Brendan's bank withdrew money from his account instead of from Brandon's. As a result, Brendan's check to pay his mortgage bounced. The bank is liable to Brendan for:

    (a) The amount of money it mistakenly took out of his account.

    (b) The amount of money it mistakenly took out of his account plus the amount of his mortgage payment.

    (c) The amount of money it mistakenly took out of his account plus the penalties he incurred because his mortgage payment was late.

    (d) The amount of money it mistakenly took out of his account plus the penalties he incurred because his mortgage payment was late plus punitive damages.

    (e) Nothing, because it acted in good faith.

9. If a customer dies, the bank:

    (a) May continue to pay checks for 10 days after it learns of the death.

    (b) May continue to pay checks until it receives a stop payment order from a court.

    (c) May continue to pay checks for 10 days after it learns of the death, unless it receives a stop payment order from someone claiming an interest in the account.

    (d) May continue to pay checks unless it receives a stop payment order from someone claiming an interest in the account.

    (e) Must stop payment on all checks immediately.

10. If a bank pays a check that has been altered:

    (a) The customer is liable only for the original amount of the check, and the bank is liable for the balance.

    (b) The bank is liable for the full amount of the check.

    (c) The customer is liable for the full amount of the check.

    (d) The bank is liable for the original amount of the check, the customer is liable for the balance.

    (e) The check is void and no one is liable on it.

Short-Answer Questions

11. Hassan Qassemzadeh had an account at the IBM Poughkeepsie Employees Federal Credit Union. On December 1, he wrote a check for $9.60, which was altered and subsequently cashed for $9,000.60. In January, the credit union mailed his statement to his niece, as he had directed. This statement indicated that the check had been paid on January 6 for $9,000.60. Qassemzadeh notified the credit union of the alteration the following January. Is the credit union liable to Qassemzadeh for the amount of the altered check?

12. Begg & Daigle, Inc., wrote a check for $31,989.80 to Newwall Interior Partitions, Inc. Begg then asked Chemical Bank to stop payment on the check. In November, the bank accidentally paid the check. This payment was reflected in Begg's November statement, but Begg did not discover the mistaken payment until the following February. In the meantime, Begg sent a second check to Newwall in payment of the full amount. Begg demanded that the bank re-credit its account for the amount of the stopped check. Is the bank liable for paying this check over the stop payment order?

13. This question appeared in the *Minneapolis Star Tribune*. How would you answer it?

    Q.—I have a payroll check issued to me that was misplaced and recently found. The check is from 1974 but nothing on the check says it must be cashed within a certain amount of time. Will a bank accept this check?

14. Rev. Janet Hooper Ritchie knew that the shoe store at Buckland Hills Mall in Manchester, Connecticut would not accept a Discover credit card, so she stopped at the ATM for a $100 cash advance. Ritchie, a Congregational minister, inserted her card, only to have it returned with a slip that said her withdrawal had been rejected. Ritchie thought that it was odd the slip did not bear the name of a bank. A few days later, she learned she was one of more than 100 customers bilked of confidential code information through the phony ATM. The crooks made off with a total of $100,000 after using the code information obtained by the ATM to make counterfeit bank cards. They used these fake cards to hit ATMs up and down the east coast and pillage customer accounts. Who is liable for these losses—the banks or the customers whose accounts were looted?

15. The following article appeared in the *Los Angeles Times*. Is there anything Elowsky could have done to reduce Prudential Bache's losses?

    A former Prudential Bache Finance vice president testified Friday that she accepted a $2-million postdated check from ZZZZ Best carpet cleaning kingpin Barry Minkow after he flew her to Los Angeles, showered her with flowers and took her out for an intimate seaside dinner in Malibu. After a "lark" of a weekend, Sheri Elowsky called Minkow to tell him she had approved a $225,000 extension on the young entrepreneur's $5 million credit line with Prudential Bache. Two days later, ZZZZ Best's stock dropped by nearly 25 percent. Minkow failed to return [Elowsky's] frantic phone calls. A day later, she reached two members of ZZZZ Best's board of directors, who told her that Minkow had resigned "for health reasons" and that the $2 million postdated check "would not be honored."[3]

16. ROLE REVERSAL: Write a multiple-choice question that involves consumer liability for unauthorized transactions.

Internet Research Problem

Visit the Federal Reserve Board's Web site at **http://www.federalreserve.gov//otherfrb.htm** to find out where the Federal Reserve Bank for your region is located. Where did you send the last check you mailed? Was it in the same region? What difference does it make if you sent a check out of the region?

You can find further practice problems in the Online Quiz at **http://beatty.westbuslaw.com** or in the Study Guide that accompanies this text.

---

[3] Kim Murphy, "Minkow Wooed and Swindled Her, Loan Officer Says," *Los Angeles Times*, Oct. 22, 1988, Part 2, p.1.

Secured Transactions

Dear Help-for-All:

Somebody must be crazy. When I got out of school, I paid $18,000 for a used Lexus. I made every payment for over two years. I shelled out over 9,000 bucks for that car. Then I got laid off through no fault of my own. I missed a few payments, and the bank repossessed the car. They auctioned off the Lexus. Now the bank's lawyer phones and says I'm still liable for over $5,000. They take my car away, they sell it—and I still I owe money?

Signed,

Still Sane, I Hope

Dear Still Sane,

I am sympathetic, but unfortunately the bank is entitled to its money. When you bought the car, you signed two documents: a note, in which you promised to pay the full balance owed, and a security agreement, which said that if you stopped making payments, the bank could repossess the vehicle and sell it.

There are two problems. First, even after two years of writing checks, you might still have owed about $10,000 (because of interest). Second, cars depreciate quickly. Your $18,000 vehicle probably had a market value of about $8,000 30 months later. The security agreement allowed the bank to sell the Lexus at auction, where prices are still lower. Your car evidently fetched about $5,000. That leaves a deficiency of $5,000—for which you are legally responsible, regardless of who is driving the car.

Sorry,

Help-for-Almost-All ◾

Secured Transactions

We can sympathize with "Still Sane," but the bank is entitled to its money. The buyer and the bank had entered into a secured transaction, meaning that one party gave credit to another, insisting on full repayment and the right to seize certain property if the debt went unpaid. It is essential to understand the basics of this law, because we live and work in a world economy based solidly—or shakily—on credit.

Article 9 of the Uniform Commercial Code (UCC) governs secured transactions in personal property. Article 9 employs terms not used elsewhere, so we must lead off with some definitions:

- **Fixtures** are goods that have become attached to real estate. For example, heating ducts are goods when a company manufactures them, but they become fixtures when installed in a house.

- **Security interest** means an interest in personal property or fixtures that secures the performance of some obligation. If an automobile dealer sells you a new car on credit and retains a security interest, it means she is keeping legal rights in your car, including the right to drive it away if you fall behind in your payments.

- **Secured party** is the person or company that holds the security interest. The automobile dealer who sells you a car on credit is the secured party.

- **Collateral** is the property subject to a security interest. When a dealer sells you a new car and keeps a security interest, the vehicle is the collateral.

- **Debtor.** For our purposes, debtor refers to a person who has some original ownership interest in the collateral. If Alice borrows money from a bank and uses her Mercedes as collateral, she is the debtor because she owns the car.

- **Security agreement** is the contract in which the debtor gives a security interest to the secured party. This agreement protects the secured party's rights in the collateral.

- **Perfection** is a series of steps the secured party must take to protect its rights in the collateral against people other than the debtor.

- **Financing statement** is a record intended to notify the general public that the secured party has a security interest in the collateral.

- **Record** refers to information written on paper or stored in an electronic or other medium.

- **Authenticate** means to sign a document or to use any symbol or encryption method that identifies the person and clearly indicates she is adopting the record as her own. You authenticate a security agreement when you sign the papers at an auto dealership. A company may authenticate by using the Internet to transmit an electronic signature.

Here is an example using the terms just discussed. A medical equipment company manufactures a CT scanner and sells it to a clinic for $2 million, taking $500,000 cash and the clinic's promise to pay the rest over five years. The clinic simultaneously authenticates a security agreement, giving the manufacturer a security interest in the CT scanner. The manufacturer then electronically files a financing statement in an appropriate state agency. This perfects the manufacturer's rights, meaning that its security interest in the CT scanner is now valid against all the world. Exhibit 26.1 illustrates this transaction.

If the clinic goes bankrupt and many creditors try to seize its assets, the manufacturer has first claim to the CT scanner. The clinic's bankruptcy is of great importance. When a debtor has money to pay all of its debts, there are no concerns

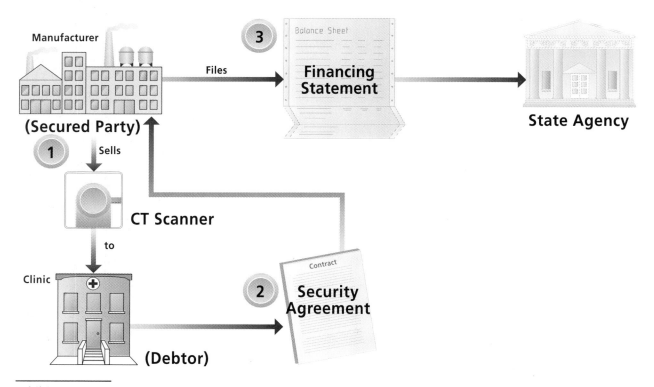

Exhibit 26.1
A simple security agreement:
(1) The manufacturer sells a CT scan machine to a clinic, taking $500,000 and the clinic's promise to pay the balance over five years.
(2) The clinic simultaneously authenticates a security agreement.
(3) The manufacturer perfects by electronically filing a financing statement.

about security interests. A creditor insists on a security interest to protect itself in the event the debtor cannot pay all of its debts.

Revised Article 9

The American Law Institute and the National Conference of Commissioners on Uniform State Laws rewrote Article 9 early in this millenium, and the revisions are now the law in all states. All citations in this chapter are to the revised Article 9. The Uniform Commercial Code is available online at **http://www.law.cornell.edu/ ucc/ucc.table.html**.

Article 9 applies to any transaction intended to create a security interest in personal property or fixtures. The personal property that may be used as collateral includes:

- **Goods,** which are things that are movable.

- **Inventory,** meaning goods held by someone for sale or lease, such as all the beds and chairs in a furniture store.

- **Instruments,** such as drafts, checks, certificates of deposit, and notes.

- **Investment Property**, which refers primarily to securities and related rights.

- **Other property,** including documents of title, accounts, general intangibles (copyrights, patents, goodwill, and so forth), and chattel paper (for example, a sales document indicating that a retailer has a security interest in goods sold to a consumer). Slightly different rules apply to some of these forms of property, but the details are less important than the general principles on which we shall focus.

Article 9 applies anytime the parties intended to create a security interest in any of the items listed above.

Attachment of a Security Interest

Attachment is a vital step in a secured transaction. This means that the secured party has taken three steps to create an enforceable security interest:

- The two parties made a security agreement and either the debtor has authenticated a security agreement describing the collateral, or the secured party has obtained possession.

- The secured party has given value to obtain the security agreement; and

- The debtor has rights in the collateral.[1]

AGREEMENT

Without an agreement there can be no security interest. Generally, the agreement either must be written on paper and signed by the debtor, or electronically

---

[1] UCC §9-203.

recorded and authenticated by the debtor. The agreement must reasonably identify the collateral. For example, a security agreement may properly describe the collateral as "all equipment in the store at 123 Periwinkle Street."

A security agreement at a minimum might:

- State that Happy Homes, Inc. and Martha agree that Martha is buying an Arctic Co. refrigerator, and identify the exact unit by its serial number.

- Give the price, the down payment, the monthly payments, and interest rate.

- State that because Happy Homes is selling Martha the refrigerator on credit, it has a security interest in the refrigerator; and

- Provide that if Martha **defaults** (fails to make payments when due), Happy Homes is entitled to repossess the refrigerator.

Possession

In certain cases, the security agreement need not be in writing if the parties have an oral agreement and the secured party has **possession.** For some kinds of collateral, for example stock certificates, it is safer for the secured party actually to take the item than to rely upon a security agreement.

The court decided the following case based on former Article 9, but the outcome would be the same under the revised Code.

CASE SUMMARY

In Re CFLC, INC.

209 B.R. 508, 1997 Bankr. LEXIS 821
United States Bankruptcy Appellate Panel of the Ninth Circuit, 1997

FACTS: Expeditors was a freight company that supervised importing and exporting for Everex Systems, Inc. Expeditors negotiated rates and services for its client and frequently had possession of Everex's goods. During a 17-month period, Expeditors sent over 300 invoices to Everex. Each invoice stated that the customer either had to accept all the invoice's terms or to pay cash, receiving no work on credit. One of those terms gave Expeditors a security interest in all of the customer's property in its possession. In other words, if the customer failed to pay a bill, Expeditors asserted a right to keep the goods.

Everex filed for bankruptcy, and Expeditors claimed the right to sell Everex's goods, worth about $81,000. The trial judge rejected the claim, ruling that Expeditors lacked a valid security interest. Expeditors appealed.

ISSUE: Did Expeditors have a security interest in Everex's goods?

DECISION: Expeditors had no security interest in the goods. Affirmed.

REASONING: Expeditors and Everex never explicitly agreed to create a security interest. Expeditor did send many invoices with terms that the company *wished* to be part of a general agreement. However, repetitively mailing such documents does not make a security agreement. Everex said nothing about the invoice terms and did nothing to indicate that it agreed to a lien on its goods. All Everex did was pay the invoices.

If the parties had reached an initial agreement, then the invoices might be evidence of a continuing security interest. Without such a clear agreement, though, there is no security interest. ◢

AT RISK | Expeditors thought—or hoped—that it had a security interest, but the invoices failed to achieve that goal, so the company failed to obtain the money it was owed. How should Expeditors have protected itself? ◾

VALUE

For the security interest to attach, the secured party must give value. Usually, the value will be apparent. If a bank loans $400 million to an airline, that money is the value, and the bank may therefore obtain a security interest in the planes that the airline is buying.

DEBTOR RIGHTS IN THE COLLATERAL

The debtor can only grant a security interest in goods if he has some legal right to those goods himself. Typically, the debtor owns the goods. But a debtor may also give a security interest if he is leasing the goods or even if he is a bailee, meaning that he is lawfully holding them for someone else.

Result

Once the security interest has attached to the collateral, the secured party is protected against the debtor. If the debtor fails to pay, the secured party may **repossess** the collateral, meaning take it away.

ATTACHMENT TO FUTURE PROPERTY

After-acquired property refers to items that the debtor obtains after the parties have made their security agreement. The parties may agree that the security interest attaches to after-acquired property. Basil is starting a catering business, but owns only a beat-up car. He borrows $55,000 from the Pesto Bank, which takes a security interest in the car. But Pesto also insists on an after-acquired clause. When Basil purchases a commercial stove, cooking equipment, and freezer, Pesto's security interest attaches to each item as Basil acquires it.

A security agreement automatically applies to **proceeds**—whatever a debtor obtains who sells the collateral or otherwise disposes of it. The secured party obtains a security interest in the proceeds of the collateral, unless the security agreement states otherwise.[2]

Perfection

NOTHING LESS THAN PERFECTION

Once the security interest has attached to the collateral, the secured party is protected against the debtor. Pesto Bank loaned money to Basil and has a security interest in all of his property. If Basil defaults on his loan, Pesto may insist he deliver the goods to the bank. If he fails to do that, the bank can seize the collateral. But Pesto's security interest is valid only against Basil; if a third person claims

---

[2] UCC §9-204 and §9-203.

some interest in the goods, the bank may never get them. For example, Basil might have taken out another loan, from his friend Olive, and used the same property as collateral. Olive knew nothing about the bank's original loan. To protect itself against Olive, and all other parties, the bank must perfect its interest.

There are several kinds of perfection, including:

- Perfection by filing.

- Perfection by possession.

- Perfection of consumer goods.

In some cases the secured party will have a choice of which method to use; in other cases only one method works.

PERFECTION BY FILING

The most common way to perfect is by filing a financing statement with the appropriate state agency. A **financing statement** gives the names of all parties, describes the collateral, and outlines the security interest, enabling any interested person to learn about it. Suppose the Pesto Bank obtains a security interest in Basil's catering equipment and then perfects by filing with the secretary of state in the state capital. When Basil asks his friend Olive for a loan, she will check the records to see if anyone has a security interest in the catering equipment. Olive's search uncovers Basil's previous security agreement, and she realizes it would be unwise to make the loan. If Basil were to default, the collateral would go straight to Pesto Bank, leaving Olive empty-handed. See Exhibit 26.2.

Article 9 prescribes one form, to be used nationwide for financing statements. The financing form is available online at **http://www.ss.ca.gov/business/ucc/ra_9_ UCC-1page.htm**. Remember that the filing may be done on paper or electronically.

The most common problems that arise in filing cases are (1) whether the financing statement contained enough information to put other people on notice of the security interest; and (2) whether the secured party filed the papers in the right place.

Contents of the Financing Statement

A financing statement is sufficient if it provides the name of the debtor, the name of the secured party, and an indication of the collateral.[3] The name of the debtor is critical because that is what an interested person will use to search among the millions of other financing statements on file. The collateral must be described reasonably so that another party contemplating a loan to the debtor will understand which property is already secured. A financing statement could properly state that it applies to "all inventory in the debtor's Houston warehouse." If the debtor has given a security interest in everything he owns, then it is sufficient to state simply that the financing statement covers "all assets" or "all personal property."

The following case was decided under former Article 9, but the outcome would be the same under the revised Code.

---

[3] UCC §9-502.

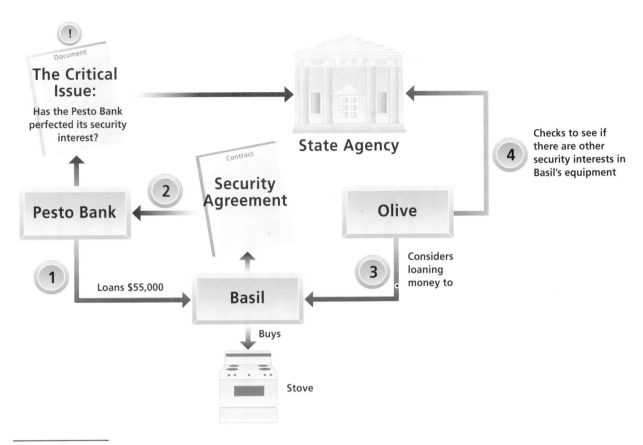

Exhibit 26.2
The Pesto Bank:
(1) Loans money to Basil and
(2) Takes a security interest in his equipment.
Later, when Olive:
(3) Considers loaning Basil money, she will
(4) Check to see if any other creditors already have a security interest in his goods.

YOU BE THE JUDGE

THE FIRST NATIONAL BANK OF LACON v. STRONG

278 Ill. App. 3d 762, 633 N.E.2d 432, 1996 Ill. App. LEXIS 169
Illinois Court of Appeal, 1996

FACTS: Elmer and Pam Strong leased and oper-
ated service stations. They were incorporated as
"E. Strong Oil Co.," although they used "Strong Oil
Co." as their trade name. The First National Bank of

Lacon loaned the couple $75,000. The promissory
note named "Strong Oil Co." as the borrower. Both
Elmer and Pam signed the note, along with an
agreement that gave the bank a security interest in

the company's inventory, equipment, accounts, and other assets. The bank filed a financing statement, listing the debtor as "Strong Oil Co."

The Illinois Department of Revenue seized all of the company's assets, claiming $229,000 in unpaid motor fuel taxes. The bank sued, claiming that it was entitled to all of the property, based on its security interest. The issue was whether the bank had perfected its interest. If the bank had perfected, it was entitled to the property. If the bank had failed to do so, because it filed under the name Strong rather than "E. Strong," the Department could take everything. The trial court found that the bank had validly perfected its interest, and the Department appealed.

YOU BE THE JUDGE: Did the bank have a perfected security interest in the property?

ARGUMENT FOR THE DEPARTMENT OF REVENUE: Financing statements are designed to permit interested parties to search an index and determine quickly if a debtor has other creditors. Accuracy is essential because the statements are indexed alphabetically by debtor. There are millions of secured transactions annually, and many companies and organizations have similar names. A creditor looking under "E. Strong" would be far from "Strong Oil," where the bank chose to file. Must a searcher also look under "Elmer Strong," "E & P Strong," "Strong Oil," "Strong Gasoline," "Strong Service Stations," and a hundred other permutations? Because the bank could not be bothered to verify the name of its debtor, it failed to perfect and must suffer the loss.

ARGUMENT FOR THE BANK: The Department's greed exceeds its common sense. The purpose of filing is to give a reasonably prudent creditor the chance to check on the credit of its prospective debtor. The company was most widely known as the Strong Oil Co. Any prudent company that considered extending credit to the Strongs would have looked under Strong Oil—exactly where the bank filed. The Code was never intended to elevate nitpicking to the status of policy. ▮

PLACE AND DURATION OF FILING

Article 9 specifies where a secured party must file. These provisions may vary from state to state, so it is essential to check local law: A misfiled record accomplishes nothing. Generally speaking, a party must file in a central filing office located in the state where an individual debtor lives or where an organization has its executive office.[4]

Once a financing statement has been filed, it is effective for five years (except for a manufactured home, where it lasts 30 years). After five years the statement will expire and leave the secured party unprotected, unless she files a continuation statement within six months prior to expiration. The continuation statement is valid for an additional five years, and a secured party may file one periodically, forever.

PERFECTION BY POSSESSION

For most types of collateral, in addition to filing, a secured party generally may perfect by possession. So if the collateral is a diamond brooch or 1,000 shares of stock, a bank may perfect its security interest by holding the items until the loan is paid off. However, possession imposes one important duty: **A secured party must use reasonable care in the custody and preservation of collateral in her**

---

[4] UCC §9-307.

possession.[5] Reliable Bank holds 1,000 shares of stock as collateral for a loan it made to Grady. Grady instructs the bank to sell the shares, and use the proceeds to pay off his debt in full. If Reliable neglects to sell the stock for five days, and the share price drops by 40% during that period, the bank will suffer the loss, not Grady.

PERFECTION OF CONSUMER GOODS

The Code gives special treatment to security interests in most consumer goods. Merchants cannot file a financing statement for every bed, television, and stereo for which a consumer owes money. To understand the UCC's treatment of these transactions, we need to know two terms. The first is **consumer goods,** which are those used primarily for personal, family, or household purposes. The second term is purchase money security interest.

A purchase money security interest (PMSI) is one taken by the person who sells the collateral or by the person who advances money so the debtor can buy the collateral.[6] Assume the Gobroke Home Center sells Marion a $5,000 stereo system. The sales document requires a payment of $500 down and $50 per month for the next 300 years, and gives Gobroke a security interest in the system. Because the security interest was "taken by the seller," the document is a PMSI. It would also be a PMSI if a bank had loaned Marion the money to buy the system and the document gave the bank a security interest. See Exhibit 26.3.

But aren't all security interests PMSIs? No, many are not. Suppose a bank loans a retail company $800,000 and takes a security interest in the store's present inventory. That is not a PMSI, since the store did not use the money to purchase the collateral.

What must Gobroke Home Center do to perfect its security interest? Nothing. **A PMSI in consumer goods perfects automatically, without filing.**[7] Marion's new stereo is clearly consumer goods, because she will use it only in her home. Gobroke's security interest is a PMSI, so the interest has perfected automatically.

The Code provisions about perfecting generally do not apply to motor vehicles, trailers, mobile homes, boats, or farm tractors. These types of secured interests are governed by state law, which frequently require a security interest to be noted directly on the vehicle's certificate of title.

Protection of Buyers

Generally, **once a security interest is perfected, it remains effective regardless of whether the collateral is sold, exchanged, or transferred** in some other way. Bubba's Bus Co. needs money to meet its payroll, so it borrows $150,000 from Francine's Finance Co., which takes a security interest in Bubba's 180 buses and perfects its interest. Bubba, still short of cash, sells 30 of his buses to Antelope Transit. But even that money is not enough to keep Bubba solvent: He defaults on his loan to Francine and goes into bankruptcy. Francine pounces on Bubba's buses. May she repossess the 30 that Antelope now operates? Yes. The security interest continued in the buses even after Antelope purchased them, and Francine can whisk them away.

---

[5] UCC §9-207.

[6] UCC §9-103.

[7] UCC §9-309.

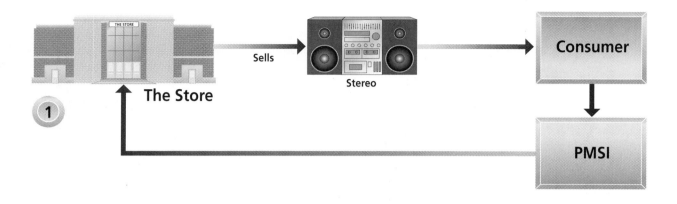

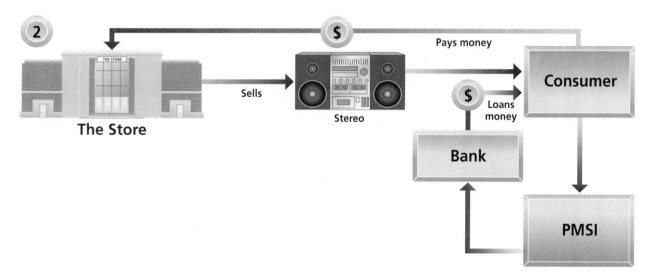

Exhibit 26.3
A purchase money security interest can arise in either of two ways. In the first example, a store sells a stereo to a consumer on credit; the consumer in turn signs a PMSI, giving the store a security interest in the stereo. In the second example, the consumer buys the stereo with money loaned from a bank; the consumer signs a PMSI giving the *bank* a security interest in the stereo.

There are some exceptions to this rule. The Code gives a few buyers special protection.

BUYERS IN ORDINARY COURSE OF BUSINESS

A buyer in ordinary course of business (BIOC) is someone who buys goods in good faith from a seller who routinely deals in such goods. For example, Plato's Garden Supply purchases 500 hemlocks from Socrates' Farm, a grower. Plato is a BIOC: He is buying in good faith and Socrates routinely deals in hemlocks. This is an important status, because a BIOC is generally not affected by security interests in the goods. However, if Plato realized that the sale violated another party's rights in the goods, there would be no good faith. If Plato knew that Socrates was bankrupt and had agreed with a creditor not to sell any of his inventory, Plato would not achieve BIOC status.

A buyer in ordinary course of business takes the goods free of a security interest created by his seller, even though the security interest is perfected.[8] Suppose that, a month before Plato made his purchase, Socrates borrowed $200,000 from the Athenian Bank. Athenian took a security interest in all of Socrates' trees and perfected by filing. Then Plato purchased his 500 hemlocks. If Socrates defaults on the loan, Athenian will have no right to repossess the 500 trees that are now at the Garden Supply. Plato took them free and clear. (Of course, Athenian can still attempt to repossess other trees from Socrates.) The BIOC exception is designed to encourage ordinary commerce. A buyer making routine purchases should not be forced to perform a financing check before buying.

Priorities Among Creditors

What happens when two creditors have a security interest in the same collateral? The party who has priority in the collateral gets it. Typically, the debtor lacks assets to pay everyone, so all creditors struggle to be the first in line. After the first creditor has repossessed the collateral, sold it, and taken enough of the proceeds to pay off his debt, there may be nothing left for anyone else. (There may not even be enough to pay the first creditor all that he is due, in which case that creditor will sue for the deficiency.) Who gets priority? There are three principal rules.[9]

The first rule is easy: **A party with a perfected security interest takes priority over a party with an unperfected interest.** This is the whole point of perfecting: to ensure that your security interest gets priority over everyone else's. On August 15, Meredith's Market, an antique store, borrows $100,000 from the Happy Bank, which takes a security interest in all of Meredith's inventory. Happy Bank does not perfect. On September 15, Meredith uses the same collateral to borrow $50,000 from the Suspicion Bank, which files a financing statement the same day. On October 15, as if on cue, Meredith files for bankruptcy and stops paying both creditors. Suspicion wins because it holds a perfected interest, whereas the Happy Bank holds merely an unperfected interest.

The second rule: **If neither secured party has perfected, the first interest to attach gets priority.** Suppose that Suspicion Bank and Happy Bank had both failed to perfect. In that case, Happy Bank would have the first claim to Meredith's inventory, since Happy's interest attached first.

And the third rule follows logically: **Between perfected security interests, the first to file or perfect wins.** Diminishing Perspective, a railroad, borrows $75 million from the First Bank, which takes a security interest in Diminishing's rolling stock (railroad cars) and immediately perfects by filing. Two months later, Diminishing borrows $100 million from Second Bank, which takes a security interest in the same collateral and also files. When Diminishing arrives, on schedule, in bankruptcy

---

[8] UCC §9-320(a).
[9] UCC §9-322.

court, both banks will race to seize the rolling stock. First Bank gets the railcars because it perfected first.[10]

March 1	April 2	May 3	The Winner:
First Bank lends money and perfects its security interest by filing a financing statement.	Second Bank lends money and perfects its security interest by filing a financing statement.	Diminishing goes bankrupt, and both banks attempt to take the rolling stock.	First Bank, because it perfected first.

Default and Termination

We have reached the end of the line. Either the debtor has defaulted, or it has performed its obligations and may terminate the security agreement.

DEFAULT

The parties define "default" in their security agreement. Generally, a debtor defaults when he fails to make payments due or enters bankruptcy proceedings. The parties can agree that other acts will constitute default, such as the debtor's failure to maintain insurance on the collateral. When a debtor defaults, the secured party has two principal options: (1) It may take possession of the collateral; or (2) it may file suit against the debtor for the money owed. The secured party does not have to choose between these two remedies; it may try one after the other, or both simultaneously.

TAKING POSSESSION OF THE COLLATERAL

When the debtor defaults, the secured party may take possession of the collateral.[11] The secured party may act on its own, without any court order, and simply take the collateral, provided this can be done without a breach of the peace. Otherwise, the secured party must file suit against the debtor and request that the court order the debtor to deliver the collateral.

Disposition of the Collateral

Once the secured party has obtained possession of the collateral, it has two choices. The secured party may (1) dispose of the collateral; or (2) retain the collateral as full satisfaction of the debt. Notice that until the secured party disposes of the collateral, the debtor has the right to redeem it, that is, to pay the full value of the debt and retrieve her property.

A secured party may sell, lease, or otherwise dispose of the collateral in any commercially reasonable manner.[12] Typically, the secured party will sell the collateral in either a private or a public sale. First, however, the debtor must receive

---

[10] Inevitably there are some exceptions to the basic priority rules, regarding purchase money security interests as well as interests perfected by possession. Readers with a particular interest in those exceptions should consult sections 9-330 and 9-324.

[11] UCC §9-609.

[12] UCC §9-610.

reasonable notice of the time and place of the sale, so that she may bid on the collateral.

When the secured party has sold the collateral, it applies the proceeds of the sale: first, to its expenses in repossessing and selling the collateral, and second, to the debt. Sometimes the sale leaves a **deficiency,** that is, insufficient funds to pay off the debt. The debtor remains liable for the deficiency, and the creditor will sue for it. On the other hand, the sale of the collateral may yield a **surplus,** that is, a sum greater than the debt. The secured party must pay the surplus to the debtor.

TERMINATION

Finally, we need to look at what happens when a debtor does not default, but pays the full debt. (You are forgiven if you lost track of the fact that things sometimes work out smoothly.) Once that happens, the secured party must complete a termination statement, a document indicating that it no longer claims a security interest in the collateral.[13]

Chapter Conclusion

Borrowed money is the lubricant that keeps a modern economy motoring smoothly. Without it many consumers would never own a car or stereo, and many businesses would be unable to grow. But unless these debts are repaid, the economy will falter. Secured transactions are one method for ensuring that creditors are paid.

Chapter Review

1. Article 9 applies to any transaction intended to create a security interest in personal property or fixtures.

2. Attachment means that (1) the two parties made a security agreement and either the debtor has authenticated a security agreement describing the collateral or the secured party has obtained possession; and (2) the secured party gave value in order to get the security agreement; and (3) the debtor has rights in the collateral.

3. Attachment protects against the debtor. Perfection of a security interest protects the secured party against parties other than the debtor.

4. Filing is the most common way to perfect. For many forms of collateral, the secured party may also perfect by obtaining either possession or control.

5. A purchase money security interest (PMSI) is one taken by the person who sells the collateral or advances money so the debtor can buy the collateral.

6. A buyer in ordinary course of business (BIOC) takes the goods free of a security interest created by his seller even though the security interest is perfected.

7. Priority among secured parties is generally as follows:

    (a) A party with a perfected security interest takes priority over a party with an unperfected interest.

    (b) If neither secured party has perfected, the first interest to attach gets priority.

    (c) Between perfected security interests, the first to file or perfect wins.

---

[13] UCC §9-513.

8. When the debtor defaults, the secured party may take possession of the collateral and then sell, lease, or otherwise dispose of the collateral in any commercially reasonable way, or it may ignore the collateral and sue the debtor for the full debt.

Note to the student: The following cases and problems were decided under the former Article 9. In each instance, the outcome would be the same under the revised laws.

PRACTICE TEST

Matching Questions

Match the following terms with their definitions:

___ **A.** Attachment.

___ **B.** BIOC.

___ **C.** Perfection.

___ **D.** PMSI.

___ **E.** Priority.

1. Someone who buys goods in good faith from a seller who deals in such goods.

2. Steps necessary to make a security interest valid against the whole world.

3. A security interest taken by the person who sells the collateral or advances money so the debtor can buy it.

4. The order in which creditors will be permitted to seize the property of a bankrupt debtor.

5. Steps necessary to make a security interest valid against the debtor, but not against third parties.

True/False Questions

Circle true or false:

1. T F A party with a perfected security interest takes priority over a party with an unperfected interest.

2. T F A buyer in ordinary course of business takes goods free of an unperfected security interest, but does not take them free of a perfected security interest.

3. T F When a debtor defaults, a secured party may seize the collateral and hold it, using reasonable care, but may not sell or lease it.

4. T F A party may take a security interest in tangible things, such as goods, but not in intangible things, such as bank accounts.

5. T F Without an agreement of the parties there can be no security interest.

Multiple-Choice Questions

6. CPA QUESTION: Under the UCC Secured Transactions Article, perfection of a security interest by a creditor provides added protection against other parties in the event the debtor does not pay its debts. Which of the following parties is not affected by perfection of a security interest?

   (a) Other prospective creditors of the debtor.

   (b) The trustee in a bankruptcy case.

   (c) A buyer in the ordinary course of business.

   (d) A subsequent personal injury judgment creditor.

7. CPA QUESTION: Mars, Inc., manufactures and sells VCRs on credit directly to wholesalers, retailers, and consumers. Mars can perfect its security interest in the VCRs it sells without having to file a financing statement or take possession of the VCRs if the sale is made to which of the following:

   (a) Retailers.

   (b) Wholesalers that sell to distributors for resale.

   (c) Consumers.

   (d) Wholesalers that sell to buyers in ordinary course of business.

8. Bank has loaned unsecured money to Retailer, which still owes $700,000. Bank becomes nervous that Retailer is on the verge of bankruptcy, and sends a "notice of security interest" to Retailer, claiming a security interest in all inventory and real estate of Retailer. Retailer does not respond. Bank files its notice in the state's central filing office. When Retailer goes bankrupt, Bank

(a) Has a perfected security interest in the inventory but not the real estate.

(b) Has a perfected security interest in the real estate but not the inventory.

(c) Has a perfected security interest in both the real estate and the inventory.

(d) Has no security interest in either the real estate or the inventory.

(e) Has an unperfected security interest in both the real estate and the inventory.

9. Which case does *not* represent a purchase money security interest?

(a) Auto dealer sells consumer a car on credit.

(b) Wholesaler sells retailer 5,000 pounds of candy on credit.

(c) Bank lends money to Retailer, using Retailer's existing inventory as collateral.

(d) Bank lends money to auto dealer to purchase 150 new cars, which are the collateral.

(e) Consumer applies to credit agency for loan with which to buy a yacht.

10. Millie lends Arthur, her next-door neighbor, $25,000. He gives her his diamond ring as collateral for the loan. Which statement is true?

(a) Millie has no valid security interest in the ring because the parties did not enter into a security agreement.

(b) Millie has no valid security interest in the ring because she has not filed appropriate papers.

(c) Millie has an attached, unperfected security interest in the ring.

(d) Millie has an attached, unperfected security interest in the ring but can perfect her interest by filing.

(e) Millie has an attached, perfected security interest in the ring.

Short-Answer Questions

11. John and Clara Lockovich bought a 22-foot Chaparral Villain II boat from Greene County Yacht Club for $32,500. They paid $6,000 cash and borrowed the rest of the purchase money from Gallatin National Bank, which took a security interest in the boat. Gallatin filed a financing statement in Greene County, Pennsylvania, where the bank was located. But Pennsylvania law requires financing statements to be filed in the county of the debtor's residence, and the Lockoviches lived in Allegheny County. The Lockoviches soon washed up in Bankruptcy Court. Other creditors demanded that the boat be sold, claiming that Gallatin's security interest had been filed in the wrong place. Who wins? (Please be advised: This is a trick question.)

12. The Copper King Inn, Inc., had money problems. It borrowed $62,500 from two of its officers, Noonan and Patterson, but that did not suffice to keep the inn going. So Noonan, on behalf of Copper King, arranged for the inn to borrow $100,000 from North-

west Capital, an investment company that worked closely with Noonan in other ventures. Copper King signed an agreement giving Patterson, Noonan, and Northwest a security interest in the inn's furniture and equipment. But the financing statement that the parties filed made no mention of Northwest. Copper King went bankrupt. Northwest attempted to seize assets, but other creditors objected. Is Northwest entitled to Copper King's furniture and equipment?

13. McMann Golf Ball Co. manufactured, as you might suppose, golf balls. Barwell, Inc., sold McMann a "preformer," a machine that makes golf balls, for $55,000. Barwell delivered the machine on February 20. McMann paid $3,000 down, the remainder to be paid over several years, and signed an agreement giving Barwell a security interest in the preformer. Barwell did not perfect its interest. On March 1, McMann borrowed $350,000 from First of America Bank, giving the bank a security interest in McMann's present and after-acquired property. First

of America perfected by filing on March 2. McMann, of course, became insolvent, and both Barwell and the bank attempted to repossess the preformer. Who gets it?

14. Sears sold a lawn tractor to Cosmo Fiscante for $1,481. Fiscante paid with his personal credit card. Sears kept a valid security interest in the lawnmower but did not perfect. Fiscante had the machine delivered to his business, Trackers Raceway Park, the only place he ever used the machine. When Fiscante was unable to meet his obligations, various creditors attempted to seize the lawnmower. Sears argued that because it had a purchase money security interest (PMSI) in the lawnmower, its interest had perfected automatically. Is Sears correct?

15. ETHICS: The Dannemans bought a Kodak copier worth over $40,000. Kodak arranged financing by GECC and assigned its rights to that company.

Although the Dannemans thought they had purchased the copier on credit, the papers described the deal as a lease. The Dannemans had constant problems with the machine and stopped making payments. GECC repossessed the machine and, without notifying the Dannemans, sold it back to Kodak for $12,500, leaving a deficiency of $39,927. GECC sued the Dannemans for that amount. The Dannemans argued that the deal was not a lease but a sale on credit. Why does it matter whether the parties had a sale or a lease? Is GECC entitled to its money? Finally, comment on the ethics. Why did the Dannemans not understand the papers they had signed? Who is responsible for that? Are you satisfied with the ethical conduct of the Dannemans? Kodak? GECC?

16. ROLE REVERSAL: Write a multiple-choice question with a conflict between a secured party and a buyer in ordinary course of business.

Internet Research Problem

Draft a security agreement in which your friend gives you a security interest in her $20,000 home entertainment system, in exchange for a loan of $12,000. Because the collateral is something that she uses daily, what special concerns do you have? How will you protect yourself? Next, find the UCC1 financing form at **http://www.dos.state.ny.us/corp/pdfs/ucc1.pdf**. Print the form, then complete it. In what office of your state should you file in order to perfect?

You can find further practice problems in the Online Quiz at **http://beatty.westbuslaw.com** or in the Study Guide that accompanies this text.

Bankruptcy

George Bryan Brummell, known as Beau Brummell, was a celebrity in nineteenth-century England. Known for his impeccable sense of style, he was the leading arbiter of taste and fashion for more than 20 years. This role was demanding—he routinely spent five hours a day simply getting dressed. After bathing in eau de cologne and water, he would spend an hour with his hairdresser and another two hours tying his cravat (a fancy necktie). Although he had inherited modest wealth, his extravagant lifestyle brought him to ruin. He fled to France to escape his creditors, taking his lavish tastes with him. After 14 years in France, he was thrown in debtors' prison.

For actor Kim Basinger, a modern celebrity, bankruptcy had a different outcome. A Los Angeles jury ordered her to pay $8.1 million to Main Line Pictures, Inc., because she broke her promise to appear in *Boxing Helena*, a film about a doctor who cuts off his lover's arms and legs. Five days after the verdict, she filed for bankruptcy protection, claiming $5 million in assets and $11 million in liabilities.

Despite filing for bankruptcy, Basinger spent $43,000 per month, including $6,100 for clothes; $4,000 for recreation, clubs, and entertainment; $7,000 for pet care and other personal expenses; as well as $9,000 in alimony to her ex-husband. She also reported owning

$592,000 in furniture and clothing and $192,000 in jewelry. In the meantime, she made no payments to creditors—those who had arranged her travel, repaired her home, or cut her grass.[1] ▪■

Overview of Bankruptcy

The U.S. Bankruptcy Code (Code) has three primary goals:

- To preserve as much of the debtor's property as possible.
- To divide the debtor's assets fairly between the debtor and creditors.
- To divide the debtor's assets fairly among creditors.

The following options are available under the Bankruptcy Code:

Number	Topic	Description
Chapter 7	Liquidation	The bankrupt's assets are sold to pay creditors. If the debtor owns a business, it terminates. The creditors have no right to the debtor's future earnings.
Chapter 9	Municipal bankruptcies	This chapter is not covered in this book.
Chapter 11	Reorganization	This chapter is designed for businesses and wealthy individuals. Businesses continue in operation, and creditors receive a portion of both current assets and future earnings.
Chapter 12	Family farmers	This chapter is not covered in this book.
Chapter 13	Consumer reorganizations	Chapter 13 offers reorganizations for the typical consumer. Creditors usually receive a portion of the individual's current assets and future earnings.

All of the Code's chapters have one of two objectives—rehabilitation or liquidation. Chapters 11 and 13, for example, focus on rehabilitation. These chapters hold creditors at bay while the debtor develops a payment plan. In return for retaining some of their assets, debtors typically promise to pay creditors a portion of their future earnings. However, when debtors are unable to develop a feasible plan for rehabilitation under Chapter 11 or 13, Chapter 7 provides for liquidation (also known as a straight bankruptcy). Most of the debtor's assets are distributed to creditors, but the debtor has no obligation to share future earnings.

Debtors are sometimes eligible to file under more than one chapter. No choice is irrevocable because both debtors and creditors have the right to ask the court to convert a case from one chapter to another at any time during the proceedings.

---

[1] Carol Marie Cropper, "The Basinger Bankruptcy Bomb," *The New York Times,* Jan. 1, 1995, §3, p. 1. A California appeals court overturned the judgment against Basinger in the Main Line suit and ordered a new trial. On the eve of retrial, Basinger settled for $3.8 million.

Chapter 7 Liquidation

All bankruptcy cases proceed in a roughly similar pattern, regardless of chapter. We use Chapter 7 as a template to illustrate common features of all bankruptcy cases. Later on, the discussions of the other chapters will indicate how they differ from Chapter 7.

FILING A PETITION

Any individual, partnership, corporation, or other business organization that lives, conducts business, or owns property in the United States can file under the Code. (Chapter 13, however, is available only to individuals.) The traditional term for someone who could not pay his debts was "**bankrupt**," but the Code uses the term "**debtor**" instead. We use both terms interchangeably.

A case begins with the filing of a bankruptcy petition in federal district court. Debtors may go willingly into the bankruptcy process by filing a **voluntary petition**, or they may be dragged into court by creditors who file an **involuntary petition**.

Voluntary Petition

Any debtor may file for bankruptcy. It is not necessary that the debtor's liabilities exceed assets. Debtors sometimes file a bankruptcy petition because cash flow is so tight they cannot pay their debts, even though they are not technically insolvent. However, debtors must meet these two criteria for a bankruptcy filing:

- Within 180 days before filing, a debtor must undergo credit counseling with an approved agency.

- Debtors may file under Chapter 7 if they earn less than the median income in their state *or* they cannot afford to pay back at least $6,000 over five years.[2] Generally, all other debtors must file under Chapters 11 or 13. (These Chapters require the bankrupt to repay some debt.) A table showing the median income in each state is available at **http://www.census.gov/hhes/income/4person.html.**

The voluntary petition must include the following documents:

Document	Description
Petition	Begins the case. Easy to fill out, it requires checking a few boxes and typing in little more than name, address, and Social Security number.
List of Creditors	The names and addresses of all creditors.
Schedule of Assets and Liabilities	A list of the debtor's assets and debts.
Claim of Exemptions	A list of all assets that the debtor is entitled to keep.
Schedule of Income and Expenditures	The debtor's job, income, and expenses.
Statement of Financial Affairs	A summary of the debtor's financial history and current financial condition. In particular, the debtor must list any recent payments to creditors and any other property held by someone else for the debtor.

---

[2] In some circumstances, debtors with income higher than $6,000 may still be eligible to file under Chapter 7, but the formula is highly complex and more than most readers want to know. The formula is available at 11 USC §707(b)(2)(A).

Involuntary Petition

Creditors may force a debtor into bankruptcy by filing an involuntary petition. The creditors' goals are to preserve as much of the debtor's assets as possible and to ensure that all creditors receive a fair share. Naturally, the Code sets strict limits—debtors cannot be forced into bankruptcy every time they miss a credit card payment. **An involuntary petition must meet all of the following requirements:**

- The debtor must owe at least $12,300 in unsecured claims to the creditors who file.

- If the debtor has at least 12 creditors, three or more must sign the petition. If the debtor has fewer than 12 creditors, any one of them can file a petition.

- The creditors must allege either that a custodian for the debtor's property has been appointed in the prior 120 days or that the debtor has generally not been paying debts that are due.

What does "a custodian for the debtor's property" mean? *State* laws sometimes permit the appointment of a custodian to protect a debtor's assets. The Code allows creditors to pull a case out from under state law and into federal bankruptcy court by filing an involuntary petition.

Once a voluntary petition is filed or an involuntary petition approved, the bankruptcy court issues an **order for relief.** This order is an official acknowledgment that the debtor is under the jurisdiction of the court, and it is, in a sense, the start of the bankruptcy process. An involuntary debtor must now make all the filings that accompany a voluntary petition. Official bankruptcy forms are available at **http://www.uscourts.gov/bkforms/index.html.**

TRUSTEE

The trustee is responsible for gathering the bankrupt's assets and dividing them among creditors. Creditors have the right to elect the trustee, but often they do not bother. In this case, the U.S. Trustee makes the selection. The U.S. Attorney General appoints a U.S. Trustee for each region of the country to administer the bankruptcy law. More information about the U.S. Trustee program is available at **http://www.usdoj.gov/ust/about_ustp.htm.**

Creditors

After the order for relief, the U.S. Trustee calls a meeting of creditors. At the meeting the bankrupt must answer (under oath) any question the creditors pose about his financial situation. If the creditors want to elect a trustee, they do so at this meeting.

After the meeting of creditors, unsecured creditors must submit a *proof of claim.* The proof of claim is a simple form stating the name of the creditor and the amount of the claim. Secured creditors do not file proofs of claim.

Automatic Stay

A fox chased by hounds has no time to make rational long-term decisions. What that fox needs is a safe burrow. Similarly, it is difficult for debtors to make sound financial decisions when hounded night and day by creditors shouting, "Pay me! Pay me!" The Code is designed to give debtors enough breathing space to sort out their affairs sensibly. An automatic stay is a safe burrow for the bankrupt. It goes into effect as soon as the petition is filed. An automatic stay prohibits creditors from collecting debts that the bankrupt incurred before the petition was filed. Creditors may not sue a bankrupt to obtain payment nor may they take other steps, outside of court, to pressure the debtor for payment. In the following case, the landlord ate crow instead of Chinese food.

CASE SUMMARY

In Re SECHUAN CITY INC.

96 B.R. 37, 1989 Bankr. LEXIS 103
United States Bankruptcy Court, Eastern District of Pennsylvania, 1989

FACTS: The Sechuan Garden restaurant leased space from North American Motor Inns, Inc. (Hotel). The entrance to the restaurant was in the Hotel lobby. The restaurant did not have a liquor license, but the Hotel bar would deliver drinks to restaurant guests at their tables. Sechuan Garden filed a voluntary petition in bankruptcy. Although the Hotel manager, Jose Garcia, knew that the bankruptcy court had entered an automatic stay, he posted the signs below at all Hotel entrances, in the

---

> **NOTICE**
>
> PLEASE DON'T PATRONIZE THE SECHUAN GARDEN
>
> THIS RESTAURANT UNFAIR TO MANAGEMENT
>
> IT DOES NOT PAY IT'S (sic) BILLS
>
> THANK YOU

> **THE TENANT HAS DISHONORED ITS**
>
> **OBLIGATION FOR PAYMENT**
>
> **TO THE LANDLORD**

> **NOTICE**
>
> NO ALCOHOLIC BEVERAGES ARE ALLOWED
>
> TO BE CONSUMED IN THE RESTAURANT AREA
>
> UNDER PENALTY OF LAW
>
> THANKS
>
> N.A.M.I. MGMT

Hotel lobby, and immediately outside the restaurant doors located in the lobby.

The restaurant's revenues dropped $1,000 a week for three weeks until Garcia finally removed the signs. Garcia testified that he had posted the signs to "shame" and "embarrass" the restaurant's owners into paying their bills.

ISSUE: Did the Hotel violate Sechuan Garden's automatic stay?

DECISION: Yes, the restaurant's automatic stay was violated.

REASONING: The automatic stay is a fundamental protection under the bankruptcy laws. By stopping all collection efforts and all harassment, the automatic stay gives the debtor a breathing spell from the financial pressures that drove him into bankruptcy. The automatic stay also protects creditors, by ensuring that all receive a fair share. Without it, creditors who acted first would receive more than those who came along later.

The language of the statute is very broad and is designed to prevent all forms of coercion and harassment, from telephone calls to judicial proceedings. Here, the Hotel undertook a serious attempt to coerce payment. The debtor either had to pay the Hotel or lose business. These actions were prohibited by the automatic stay and clearly harmed the debtor. The Hotel must pay the bankruptcy trustee $3,000 in damages and $600 in attorney's fees. ◀

BANKRUPTCY ESTATE

The filing of the bankruptcy petition creates a new legal entity separate from the debtor—the bankruptcy estate. All of the bankrupt's assets pass to the estate, except exempt property and new property that the debtor acquires after the petition is filed.

Exempt Property

The Code permits *individual* debtors (but not organizations) to keep some property for themselves. This exempt property saves the debtor from destitution during the bankruptcy process and provides the foundation for a new life once the process is over.

In this one area of bankruptcy law, the Code defers to state law. Although the Code lists various types of exempt property, it permits states to opt out of the federal system and define a different set of exemptions. However, debtors can take advantage of state exemptions only if they have lived in that state for two years prior to the bankruptcy.

Under the *federal* Code, a debtor is allowed to exempt only $18,450 of the value of her home. Most *states* exempt items such as the debtor's home, household goods, cars, work tools, disability and pension benefits, alimony, and health aids. Indeed, some states set no limit on the value of exempt property. Both Florida and Texas, for example, permit debtors to keep homes of unlimited value and a certain amount of land. But the federal statute limits this state exemption to $125,000 for any house that was acquired during the 40 months before the bankruptcy.

Voidable Preferences

A major goal of the bankruptcy system is to divide the debtor's assets fairly among creditors. It would not be fair if debtors were permitted to pay off some of their creditors immediately before filing a bankruptcy petition. Such a payment is called a **preference** because it gives unfair preferential treatment to a creditor. **The trustee can void any transfer to a creditor that took place in the 90-day period before the filing of a petition.**

Fraudulent Transfers

Suppose that a debtor sees bankruptcy inexorably approaching across the horizon like a tornado. He knows that, once the storm hits and he files a petition, everything he owns except a few items of exempt property will become part of the bankruptcy estate. Before that happens, he may be tempted to give some of his property to friends or family to shelter it from the tornado. If he succumbs to temptation, however, he is committing a fraudulent transfer.

A transfer is fraudulent if it is made within the year before a petition is filed and its purpose is to hinder or defraud creditors. The trustee can void any fraudulent transfer. Fraudulent transfers sound similar to voidable preferences, but there is an important distinction: voidable preferences pay legitimate debts, whereas fraudulent transfers protect the debtor's assets from legitimate creditors. For example, Lawrence Williams and his wife, Diana, enjoyed a luxurious lifestyle while his investment bank flourished. But when the bank failed, Lawrence was faced with debts of $6 million. On the eve of the bankruptcy filing, Diana suddenly announced that she wanted a divorce. In what had to be the most amicable breakup ever, Lawrence willingly transferred all of his assets to her. The court found that the transfer had been fraudulent.[3]

PAYMENT OF CLAIMS

Imagine a crowded delicatessen on Saturday evening. People are pushing and shoving because they know there is not enough food for everyone; some customers will go home hungry. The delicatessen could simply serve whoever pushes to the front of the line, or it could establish a number system to ensure that the most deserving customers are served first. The Code has, in essence, adopted a number system to prevent a free-for-all fight over the bankrupt's assets. Indeed, one of the Code's primary goals is to ensure that creditors are paid in the proper order, not according to who pushes to the front of the line.

All claims are placed in one of three classes: (1) secured claims, (2) priority claims, and (3) unsecured claims. **The trustee pays the bankruptcy estate to the various classes of claims in order of rank.** A higher class is paid in full before the next class receives any payment at all. The debtor is entitled to any funds remaining after all claims have been paid. The payment order is shown in Exhibit 27.1.

Secured Claims

Creditors whose loans are secured by specific collateral are paid first. Secured claims are fundamentally different from all other claims because they are paid not out of the general funds of the estate, but by selling a specific asset.

Priority Claims

Each category of priority claims is paid in order, with the first group receiving full payment before the next group receives anything. Priority claims include:

- Alimony and child support.

- Administrative expenses (such as fees to the trustee, lawyers, and accountants).

- Back wages to the debtor's employees for work performed during the 180 days prior to the date of the petition.

- Income and property taxes.

Exhibit 27.1

---

[3] *In re Williams*, 159 B.R. 648, 1993 Bankr. LEXIS 1482 (Bankr. D.R.I. 1993), remanded, 190 B.R. 728, 1996 U.S. Dist. LEXIS 539.

Unsecured Claims

Last, and frequently very much least, unsecured creditors have now reached the delicatessen counter. They can only hope that some food remains (and that they will be paid).

DISCHARGE

Filing a bankruptcy petition is embarrassing and time consuming. It can affect the debtor's credit rating for years, making the simplest car loan a challenge. To encourage debtors to file for bankruptcy despite the pain involved, the Code offers a powerful incentive: the **fresh start.** Once a bankruptcy estate has been distributed to creditors, they cannot make a claim against the debtor for money owed before the filing, *whether or not they actually received any payment.* These prepetition debts are **discharged.** All is forgiven, if not forgotten.

Discharge is an essential part of bankruptcy law. Without it, debtors would have little incentive to take part. To avoid abuses, however, the Code limits both the type of debts that can be discharged and the circumstances under which discharge can take place. In addition, a debtor must complete a course on financial management before receiving a discharge.

Debts That Cannot Be Discharged

The following debts are among those that can never be discharged. The debtor remains liable in full until they are paid:

- Recent income and property taxes.

- Money obtained by fraud.

- Cash advances on a credit card totaling more than $750 that an individual debtor takes out within 70 days before the order of relief.

- Debts omitted from the Schedule of Assets and Liabilities.

- Money owed for alimony, maintenance, or child support.

- Debts stemming from intentional and malicious injury.

- Student loans made or guaranteed by the government can be discharged only if repayment would cause undue hardship to the debtor.

Circumstances That Prevent Debts from Being Discharged

The Code also prohibits the discharge of debts under the following circumstances:

- *Business organizations.* Under Chapter 7 (but not the other chapters), only the debts of individuals can be discharged, not those of business organizations. Once its assets have been distributed, an organization must cease operation. If the company resumes business again, it becomes responsible for all its prefiling debts.

- *Repeated filings for bankruptcy.* A debtor who has received a discharge under Chapter 7 or 11 cannot receive another discharge under Chapter 7 for at least eight years after the prior filing.

- *Revocation.* A court can revoke a discharge within one year if it discovers the debtor engaged in fraud or concealment.

- *Dishonesty or bad-faith behavior.* The court may deny discharge altogether if the debtor has made fraudulent transfers, hidden assets, or otherwise acted in bad faith.

Reaffirmation

Sometimes debtors are willing to **reaffirm** a debt, meaning they promise to pay even after discharge. They may want to reaffirm a secured debt to avoid losing the collateral. For example, a debtor who has taken out a loan secured by a car may reaffirm that debt so that the finance company will agree not to repossess it. Sometimes debtors reaffirm because they feel guilty, or they want to maintain a good relationship with the creditor. They may have borrowed from a family member or an important supplier.

Because discharge is a fundamental pillar of the bankruptcy process, courts look closely at each reaffirmation to ensure that the creditor has not unfairly pressured the bankrupt. To be valid, either the court must determine that the reaffirmation is in the debtor's best interest and does not impose undue hardship, or the attorney representing the debtor must file an affidavit in court stating that the debtor's consent was informed and voluntary and the agreement does not create a hardship.

ETHICS

At some point in your life, you will borrow money. What *moral* obligation do you have to repay legitimate debts? Should you take the view that, if bankruptcy laws permit you to default on debts, then why not do so? Alternatively, if you get over your head in debt, should you struggle to pay even though you legitimately qualify for bankruptcy protection? How would the ethics checklist in Chapter 2 help you answer these questions? What are the consequences of filing for bankruptcy? Who are the stakeholders?

Chapter 11 Reorganization

For a business, the goal of a Chapter 7 bankruptcy is euthanasia—putting it out of its misery by shutting it down and distributing its assets to creditors. Chapter 11 has a much more complicated and ambitious goal—resuscitating a business so that it can ultimately emerge as a viable economic concern.

Both individuals and businesses can use Chapter 11. Businesses usually prefer Chapter 11 over Chapter 7 because Chapter 11 does not require them to dissolve at the end as Chapter 7 does. The threat of death creates a powerful incentive to try rehabilitation under Chapter 11. Individuals, however, tend to prefer Chapter 13 because it is specifically designed for them.

A Chapter 11 proceeding follows many of the same steps as Chapter 7: a petition (either voluntary or involuntary), an order for relief, a meeting of creditors, proofs of claim, and an automatic stay. There are, however, some significant differences.

Debtor in Possession

Chapter 11 does not require a trustee. The bankrupt is called the **debtor in possession** and, in essence, serves as trustee. The debtor in possession has two jobs: to operate the business and to develop a plan of reorganization. A trustee is chosen only if the debtor is incompetent or uncooperative. In that case, the creditors can elect the trustee, but if they do not choose to do so, the U.S. Trustee appoints one.

CREDITORS' COMMITTEE

In a Chapter 11 case, the creditors' committee plays a particularly important role because typically there is no neutral trustee to watch over the committee's interests. The committee has the right to help develop the plan of reorganization. The U.S. Trustee typically appoints the seven largest *un*secured creditors to the committee, although the court has the right to require the appointment of some small business creditors as well.

PLAN OF REORGANIZATION

Once the bankruptcy petition is filed, an automatic stay goes into effect to provide the debtor with temporary relief from creditors. The next stage is to develop a plan of reorganization that provides for the payment of debts and the continuation of the business. For the first 120 days after the order for relief, the debtor has the exclusive right to propose a plan. If the shareholders and creditors accept it, then the bankruptcy case terminates. If the creditors or shareholders reject the debtor's plan, they may file their own version.

CONFIRMATION OF THE PLAN

All the creditors and shareholders have the right to vote on the plan of reorganization. In preparation for the vote, each creditor and shareholder is assigned to a class. Chapter 11 classifies claims in the same way as Chapter 7: (1) secured claims, (2) priority claims, and (3) unsecured claims.

    The bankruptcy court will approve a plan if a majority of *each* **class votes in favor of it.** Even if some classes vote against the plan, the court can still confirm it under what is called a **cramdown** (as in, "the plan is crammed down the creditors' throats"). If the court rejects the plan of reorganization, the creditors must develop a new one.

DISCHARGE

A confirmed plan of reorganization is binding on the debtor and creditors. **The debtor now owns the assets in the bankrupt estate, free of all obligations except those listed in the plan.** Under a typical plan of reorganization, the debtor gives some current assets to creditors and also promises to pay them a portion of future earnings. In contrast, the Chapter 7 debtor typically relinquishes all assets (except exempt property) to creditors but then has no obligation to turn over future income. Exhibit 27.2 illustrates the steps in a Chapter 11 bankruptcy.

SMALL-BUSINESS BANKRUPTCY

Out of concern that the lengthy procedure in Chapter 11 was harming the creditors of small businesses, Congress decided to speed up the bankruptcy process for businesses with less than $2 million in debt. After the order of relief, the bankrupt has the exclusive right to file a plan for 180 days. Both a plan and a disclosure statement must be filed within 300 days. The court must confirm or reject the plan within 45 days after its filing. If these deadlines are not met, the case can be converted to Chapter 7 or dismissed. This provision may well cause more small companies to go out of business.

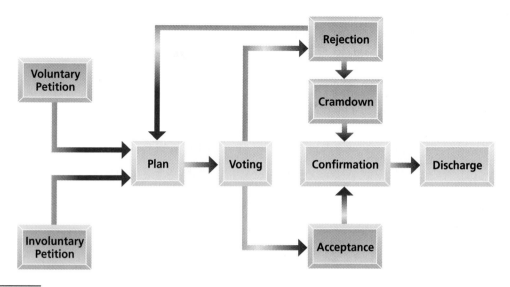

Exhibit 27.2

Chapter 13 Consumer Reorganizations

The purpose of Chapter 13 is to rehabilitate an individual debtor. It is not available at all to businesses or to individuals with more than $307,675 in unsecured debts or $922,975 in secured debts. Under Chapter 13, the bankrupt consumer typically keeps most of her assets in exchange for a promise to repay some of her debts using future income. Therefore, to be eligible, the debtor must have a regular source of income. Individuals usually choose this chapter because it is easier and cheaper than Chapters 7 and 11.

A bankruptcy under Chapter 13 generally follows the same course as Chapter 11: the debtor files a petition, creditors submit proofs of claim, the court imposes an automatic stay, the debtor files a plan, and the court confirms the plan. But there are some differences.

BEGINNING A CHAPTER 13 CASE

To initiate a Chapter 13 case, the debtor must file a voluntary petition. Creditors cannot use an involuntary petition to force a debtor into Chapter 13. In all Chapter 13 cases, the U.S. Trustee appoints a trustee to supervise the debtor. The trustee also serves as a central clearinghouse for the debtor's payments to creditors. The debtor pays the trustee who, in turn, transmits these funds to creditors. For this service the trustee is allowed to keep 10 percent of the payments.

PLAN OF PAYMENT

The debtor must file a plan of payment within 15 days after filing the voluntary petition. Only the bankruptcy court has the authority to confirm or reject a plan of payment. Creditors have no right to vote on it. However, to confirm a plan, the court must ensure that:

- The plan is feasible and the bankrupt will be able to make the promised payments;

- The plan does not extend beyond three years without good reason and in no event lasts longer than five years;

- If the plan does not provide for the debtor to pay off creditors in full, then all of the debtor's disposable income for the next five years must go to creditors; and

- The debtor is acting in good faith, making a reasonable effort to pay obligations.

In the following case, a creditor argued that the debtor's plan was not made in good faith.

CASE SUMMARY

In Re LeMAIRE

898 F.2d 1346, 1990 U.S. App. LEXIS 4374
United States Court of Appeals for the Eighth Circuit, 1990

FACTS: As Paul Handeen got out of his car one Sunday morning, Gregory LeMaire shot at him nine times with a rifle. Bullets struck Handeen in the mouth, neck, spine, arm, knee, and ankle. LeMaire pleaded guilty to a charge of aggravated assault and served 27 months in prison. After his release he earned a doctorate from the University of Minnesota.

Handeen sued LeMaire and received a judgment of $50,000. To avoid paying this judgment, LeMaire filed a bankruptcy petition under Chapter 13. He proposed a plan under which he would pay his creditors 42 percent of their claims. The bankruptcy court confirmed the plan over Handeen's objection. Handeen appealed, arguing that LeMaire had not filed his plan in good faith.

ISSUE: Did LeMaire file his plan in good faith?

DECISION: LeMaire did not file his plan in good faith.

REASONING: The bankruptcy court found that LeMaire's desire for a fresh start outweighed Handeen's desire to be compensated for his injuries. The court noted that, while LeMaire had not been able to pay his debt to the victim, he had paid his debt to society by serving a prison sentence. The court further concluded that LeMaire had made a wholehearted and sincere attempt to pay Handeen.

However, the bankruptcy court's analysis did not consider the strong public policy factors in the Bankruptcy Code. LeMaire shot at Handeen nine times, clearly intending to kill him. While prefiling conduct is not the only factor to consider in determining good faith, it is nevertheless relevant. The maliciousness of LeMaire's actions, absent any other mitigating factors, supports the view that he did not propose his plan in good faith. ◢

DISCHARGE

Once confirmed, a plan is binding on all creditors, whether they like it or not. **The debtor is washed clean of all prepetition debts except those provided for in the**

plan. But if the debtor violates the plan, all of the debts are revived, and the creditors have a right to recover them under Chapter 7. The debts become permanently discharged only when the bankrupt fully complies with the plan.

If the debtor's circumstances change, the debtor, the trustee, or unsecured creditors can ask the court to modify the plan. Most such requests come from debtors whose income has declined. However, if the debtor's income rises, the creditors or the trustee can ask that payments increase, too.

Chapter Conclusion

Bankruptcy law is the safety net that catches those who are not able to meet their financial obligations. Bankruptcy laws cannot create assets where there are none (or not enough), but they can ensure that the debtor's assets, however limited, are fairly divided between the debtor and creditors. Any bankruptcy system that accomplishes this goal must be deemed a success.

Chapter Review

The following chart sets out the important elements of each bankruptcy chapter.

	Chapter 7	Chapter 11	Chapter 13
Objective	Liquidation	Reorganization	Consumer reorganization
Who May Use It	Individual or organization	Individual or organization	Individual
Type of Petition	Voluntary or involuntary	Voluntary or involuntary	Only voluntary
Administration of Bankruptcy Estate	Trustee	Debtor in possession (trustee selected only if debtor is unable to serve)	Trustee
Selection of Trustee	Creditors have right to elect trustee; otherwise, U.S. Trustee makes appointment.	Usually no trustee	Appointed by U.S. Trustee
Participation in Formulation of Plan	No plan is filed	Both creditors and debtor can propose plans.	Only debtor can propose a plan.
Creditor Approval of Plan	Creditors do not vote.	Creditors vote on plan, but court may approve plan without the creditors' support.	Creditors do not vote on plan.
Impact on Debtor's Post-petition Income	Not affected; debtor keeps all future earnings.	Must contribute toward payment of pre-petition debts.	Must contribute toward payment of pre-petition debts.

Practice Test

Matching Questions

Match the following terms with the correct description:

___ **A.** Fresh start.

___ **B.** Fraudulent transfer.

___ **C.** Exempt property.

___ **D.** Reaffirmation.

___ **E.** Voidable preference.

1. Property individual debtors can keep for themselves.

2. Debtors are not liable for money owed before the filing.

3. Debtor's promise to pay a debt after discharge.

4. Payment to a creditor immediately before filing.

5. Payment made within the year before a petition is filed with the goal of hindering creditors.

True/False Questions

Circle true or false:

1. T F One of the primary goals of the Code is to punish the debtor.

2. T F Each of the Code's chapters has one of two objectives—rehabilitation or liquidation.

3. T F A creditor is not permitted to force a debtor into bankruptcy.

4. T F The bankruptcy court issues an order for relief to give the debtor a chance to file a petition.

5. T F The Code permits *individual* debtors (but not organizations) to keep some property for themselves.

Multiple Choice Questions

6. CPA QUESTION: Decal Corp. incurred substantial operating losses for the past three years. Unable to meet its current obligations, Decal filed a petition of reorganization under Chapter 11 of the federal Bankruptcy Code. Which of the following statements is correct?

(a) A creditors' committee, if appointed, will consist of unsecured creditors.

(b) The court must appoint a trustee to manage Decal's affairs.

(c) Decal may continue in business only with the approval of a trustee.

(d) The creditors' committee must select a trustee to manage Decal's affairs.

7. CPA QUESTION: A voluntary petition filed under the liquidation provisions of Chapter 7 of the federal Bankruptcy Code:

(a) Is not available to a corporation unless it has previously filed a petition under the reorganization provisions of Chapter 11 of the Code.

(b) Automatically stays collection actions against the debtor except by secured creditors.

(c) Will be dismissed unless the debtor has 12 or more unsecured creditors whose claims total at least $5,000.

(d) Does not require the debtor to show that the debtor's liabilities exceed the fair market value of assets.

8. CPA QUESTION: Unger owes a total of $50,000 to eight unsecured creditors and one fully secured creditor. Quincy is one of the unsecured creditors and is owed $6,000. Quincy has filed a petition against Unger under the liquidation provisions of Chapter 7 of the federal Bankruptcy Code. Unger has been unable to pay debts as they become due. Unger's liabilities exceed Unger's assets. Unger has filed papers opposing the bankruptcy petition. Which of the following statements regarding Quincy's petition is correct?

(a) It will be dismissed because the secured creditor failed to join in the filing of the petition.

(b) It will be dismissed because three unsecured creditors must join in the filing of the petition.

(c) It will be granted because Unger's liabilities exceed Unger's assets.

(d) It will be granted because Unger is unable to pay Unger's debts as they become due.

9. Why did Kim Basinger (see the chapter introduction) file under Chapter 11 rather than Chapter 13?

(a) Basinger's debts were too low to meet the requirements of Chapter 13.

(b) Basinger had committed fraud.

(c) Basinger had acted in bad faith.

(d) All individuals must file under Chapter 11.

(e) Basinger's debts exceeded the limits permitted by Chapter 13.

10. A debtor is not required to file the following document with his voluntary petition:

(a) Budget statement for the following three years.

(b) Statement of financial affairs.

(c) List of creditors.

(d) Claim of exemptions.

(e) Schedule of income and expenditures.

Short-Answer Questions

11. ETHICS: On November 5, The Fred Hawes Organization, Inc., a small subcontractor, opened an account with Basic Distribution Corp., a supplier of construction materials. Hawes promised to pay its bills within 30 days of purchase. Although Hawes purchased a substantial quantity of goods on credit from Basic, it made few payments on the accounts until the following March when it paid Basic over $21,000. On May 14, Hawes filed a voluntary petition under Chapter 7. Does the bankruptcy trustee have a right to recover this payment? Is it fair to Hawes's other creditors if Basic is allowed to keep the $21,000 payment?

12. Mark Milbank built custom furniture in Port Chester, New York. His business was unsuccessful, and he repeatedly borrowed money from his wife and her father. He promised that the loans would enable him to spend more time with his family. Instead, he spent more time in bed with his next-door neighbor. After the divorce, his ex-wife and her father demanded repayment of the loans. When Milbank filed under Chapter 13, his ex-wife and her father asked the court not to discharge Milbank's debts on the grounds that he had acted in bad faith toward them. Should the bankruptcy court discharge Milbank's loans?

13. Lydia D'Ettore received a degree in computer programming at DeVry Institute of Technology, with a grade point average of 2.51. To finance her education, she borrowed $20,516.52 from a federal student loan program. After graduation she could not find a job in her field, so she went to work as a clerk at a salary of $12,500. D'Ettore and her daughter lived with her parents free of charge. After setting aside $50 a month in savings and paying bills that included $233 for a new car (a Suzuki Samurai) and $50 for jewelry from Zales, her disposable income was $125 per month. D'Ettore asked the bankruptcy court to discharge the debts she owed for her DeVry education. Should the court discharge these debts?

14. After filing for bankruptcy, Yvonne Brown sought permission of the court to reaffirm a $6,000 debt to her credit union. The debt was unsecured and she was under no obligation to pay it. The credit union had published the following notice in its newsletter:

> If you are thinking about filing bankruptcy THINK about the long-term implications. This action, filing bankruptcy, closes the door on TOMORROW. Having no credit means no ability to purchase cars, houses, credit cards. Look into the future—no loans for the education of your children.

Should the court approve Brown's reaffirmation?

15. Robert Britton was an office manager at the Academy of Cosmetic Surgery Medical Group. Mary Price made an appointment for a consultation about a lipectomy (removal of abdominal fat). Britton wore a name tag that identified him as a doctor, and was addressed as "doctor" by the nurse. Britton and the

nurse then examined Price. Britton touched the area of her stomach where there was excess fat and showed her where the incision would be made. A doctor who worked for the Academy actually performed the surgical procedure on Price at the Academy's offices, with Britton present. After the procedure, Price went to a hospital suffering from severe pain. The hospital staff found that a tube had been left in her body at the site of the incision. The jury awarded her $275,000 in damages in a fraud suit against Britton. He subsequently filed a Chapter 7 bankruptcy petition. Is this judgment dischargeable in bankruptcy court?

16. ROLE REVERSAL: Write a multiple-choice question that highlights the difference between Chapters 7 and 11.

Internet Research Problem

The exemption rules for your state are listed at **http://www.bankruptcyaction.com/bankruptcyexemptions.htm.** Compared with other jurisdictions, is your state generous or stingy with exemptions? What do you think is a fair exemption?

You can find further practice problems in the Online Quiz at **http://beatty.westbuslaw.com** or in the Study Guide that accompanies this text.

AGENCY AND EMPLOYMENT LAW

UNIT 4

chapter 28

Agency: The Inside Relationship

It was a perfect spring day in Ashland, Ohio. Roger was having a great game as his Ohio State lacrosse team played a close match against Ashland University. Carefully gauging an Ashland pass, Roger stuck his stick out, intercepted the ball, whipped around, and launched a shot on goal. Score! His hands went up in the air. He never saw the Ashland player jump him from behind and knock him to the ground. But he did see the player stand over him, yelling obscenities. He also saw his teammate Brian grab the opponent in a bear hug. And he saw the Ashland player twist violently, throwing Brian to the ground, where he lay motionless. Brian never walked again—the blow to his head as he hit the ground left him a paraplegic. Brian sued Ashland, alleging that the university was responsible for his injury.[1]

Brian's parents hired a real estate broker to find a new house that was handicapped accessible. They were so delighted with the one-story bungalow she located that they did not begrudge paying her an $18,000 commission. But after the sale they discovered that the seller of the house had also paid her a commission. They sued for the return of their $18,000.

---

[1] Based on *Hanson v. Kynast*, 24 Ohio St. 3d 171, 494 N.E.2d 1091, 1986 Ohio LEXIS 667 (Ohio 1986).

Nonetheless, the house was perfect for their needs, and they stocked it with all the custom-made items that Brian required. Because these medical devices were so expensive, they asked their insurance agent to increase their house coverage from $400,000 to $800,000. Brian and his parents suffered a terrible blow a few months later when they returned home from an exhausting visit to the hospital to find their new house burned to the ground. They were even more distressed when they discovered that the insurance agent had misread his notes and only increased their policy to $480,000. They sued him for $320,000. ▪◆

This example raises several questions of agency law. Thus far, this book has primarily dealt with issues of individual responsibility: What happens if *you* knock someone down or *you* sign an agreement? Agency law, on the other hand, is concerned with your responsibility for the actions of others. What happens if your *agent* assaults someone or enters into an agreement? Agency law presents a significant trade-off: If you do everything yourself, you have control over the result. But the size and scope of your business (and your life) will be severely limited. Once you hire other people, you can accomplish a great deal more, but your risk of legal liability increases immensely.

Was Ashland University liable for Brian's injuries? It would have been if the Ashland player had been an agent of the university. But, on a similar set of facts, the Ohio Supreme Court held that the Ashland player was not an agent because Ashland had no *control* over him and he was not playing for the school's *benefit*. However, the real estate broker was an agent for Brian's parents. She violated her *duty of loyalty* to them when she acted for both buyer and seller in the same transaction, without disclosing her dual role to both parties. An agent who violates this important duty must forfeit her commission. And the insurance agent violated his *duty of care* when he bought a policy in the wrong amount for Brian's parents. An agent who violates this duty is liable for the harm his carelessness has caused—in this case $320,000.

Creating an Agency Relationship

Principals have substantial liability for the actions of their agents.[2] Therefore, it is important to know if an agency relationship exists. **To create an agency relationship, there must be:**

- A principal and;

- An **agent**

- Who mutually **consent** that the agent will act on behalf of the principal and

- Be subject to the principal's **control,**

- Thereby creating a **fiduciary relationship.**

---

[2] The word "principal" is always used when referring to a person. It is not to be confused with the word "principle," which refers to a fundamental idea.

CONSENT

To establish consent, the principal must ask the agent to do something, and the agent must agree. In the most straightforward example, Brian's parents asked their insurance agent to buy a policy on their house, and he agreed. Matters were more complicated, however, when Steven James met some friends one evening at a restaurant. During the two hours he was there, he drank four to six beers. (It is probably a bad sign that he cannot remember how many.) From then on, one misfortune piled upon another. After leaving the restaurant at about 7 p.m., James sped down a highway and crashed into a car that had stalled on the roadway, thereby killing the driver. James told the police at the scene that he had not seen the parked car (another bad sign). In a misguided attempt to help his client, James's lawyer took him to the local hospital for a blood test. Unfortunately, the test confirmed that James had indeed been drunk at the time of the accident.

The attorney knew that if this evidence was admitted at trial, his client would soon be receiving free room and board from the Massachusetts Department of Corrections. So at trial the lawyer argued that the blood test was protected by the client-attorney privilege because the hospital had been his agent and therefore a member of the defense team. The court disagreed, however, holding that the hospital employees were not agents for the lawyer because they had not consented to act in the role. The court upheld James's conviction of murder in the first degree by reason of extreme atrocity or cruelty.[3]

CONTROL

Principals are liable for the acts of their agents because they exercise control over the agents. If principals direct their agents to commit an act, it seems fair to hold the principal liable when that act causes harm.

William Stanford was murdered in Iran by terrorists who hijacked his Kuwait Airways (KA) flight. His widow sued Northwest Airlines because Stanford had originally purchased a ticket on that carrier. But Northwest had an agreement with KA permitting passengers to exchange tickets from one to another, so Stanford had switched to the KA flight. The court held that no agency relationship existed between the two airlines because Northwest had no *control* over KA.[4] Northwest did not tell KA how to fly planes or handle terrorists; therefore it should not be liable when KA made fatal errors.

FIDUCIARY RELATIONSHIP

A fiduciary relationship is a special relationship, with high standards. The beneficiary places special confidence in the fiduciary who, in turn, is obligated to act in good faith and candor, putting his own needs second. **Agents have a fiduciary duty to their principals.** When, in this chapter's opening scenario, Brian's parents hired a real estate broker to find a house for them, she was a fiduciary, obligated to act in their best interest alone. She violated this duty when she also acted for the seller of the house, without telling Brian's parents.

---

[3] *Commonwealth v. James*, 427 Mass. 312, 693 N.E.2d 148, 1998 Mass. LEXIS 175.
[4] *Stanford v. Kuwait Airways Corp.*, 648 F. Supp. 1158, 1986 U.S. Dist. LEXIS 18880 (S.D.N.Y. 1986).

ELEMENTS NOT REQUIRED FOR AN AGENCY RELATIONSHIP

The following elements are not necessary to establish an agency relationship:

A written agreement.

A formal agreement. The principal and agent need not agree formally that they have an agency relationship. As long as they act like an agent and a principal, the law will treat them as such.

Consideration. An agency agreement is valid even if the agent is not paid.

Duties of Agents to Principals

DUTY OF LOYALTY

The agent must act solely for the benefit of the principal in all matters connected with the agency. Thus, for example, while David is working for a sports agency, he cannot recruit clients for the new agency he is planning to start. If he does, he is in violation of his duty of loyalty. The various components of the duty of loyalty follow.

Outside Benefits

An agent may not receive profits unless the principal knows and approves. Suppose that Hope is an employee of the agency Big Egos and Talents, Inc. (BEAT). She has been representing Steven Seagal in his latest movie negotiations.[5] He often drives her to meetings in his new Hummer military vehicle. He is so thrilled that she has arranged for him to star in the new movie, *Little Men,* that he buys her a Hummer. Can Hope keep this generous gift? Only with BEAT's permission. She must tell BEAT about the Hummer; the company may then take the vehicle itself or allow her to keep it.

Confidential Information

Agents can neither disclose nor use for their own benefit any confidential information they acquire during their agency. As the following case shows, this duty continues even after the agency relationship ends.

CASE SUMMARY

ABKCO MUSIC, INC. v. HARRISONGS MUSIC, LTD.

722 F.2d 988, 1983 U.S. App. LEXIS 15562
United States Court of Appeals for the Second Circuit, 1983

FACTS: Bright Tunes Music Corp. (Bright Tunes) owned the copyright to the song "He's So Fine." The company sued George Harrison, a Beatle, alleging that the Harrison composition "My Sweet Lord" copied "He's So Fine." At the time the suit was filed, Allen B. Klein handled the business affairs of the Beatles.

After Klein's management contract with the Beatles expired, he began negotiating with Bright

---

[5] Do not be confused by the fact that Hope works as an agent for movie stars. As an employee of BEAT, her duty is to the company. She is an agent of BEAT, and BEAT works for the celebrities.

Tunes to purchase the copyright to "He's So Fine" for himself. To advance these negotiations, Klein gave Bright Tunes information about royalty income for "My Sweet Lord"—information that he had gained as Harrison's agent.

The court in the copyright case ultimately found that Harrison had infringed the copyright on "He's So Fine" and assessed damages of $1,599,987. After the trial, Klein purchased the "He's So Fine" copyright from Bright Tunes and with it, the right to recover from Harrison for the breach of copyright.

ISSUE: Did Klein violate his fiduciary duty to Harrison by using confidential information after the agency relationship terminated?

DECISION: Klein did violate his fiduciary duty to Harrison.

REASONING: While serving as Harrison's agent, Klein learned confidential information about royalty income for "My Sweet Lord." An agent has a duty not to use confidential information to compete against his principal. This duty continues even after the agency relationship ends. A former agent *does* have the right to compete against his principal using general business knowledge or publicly available information. However, the information that Klein passed on to Bright Tunes was not publicly available. ◢

To listen to the two songs involved in this case, tune in to **http://www.illegal-art.org/audio/historic.html**.

ETHICS | Klein was angry that the Beatles had failed to renew his management contract. Should his sense of ethics have told him that his behavior was wrong? Would the ethics checklist in Chapter 2 have helped Klein to make a better decision? ◾

Competition with the Principal

Agents are not allowed to compete with their principal in any matter within the scope of the agency business. If Allen Klein had purchased the "He's So Fine" copyright while he was George Harrison's agent, he would have committed an additional sin against the agency relationship. Owning song rights was clearly part of the agency business, so Klein could not make such purchases without Harrison's consent. Once the agency relationship ends, however, so does the rule against competition. Klein was entitled to buy the "He's So Fine" copyright after the agency relationship ended (as long as he did not use confidential information).

Conflict of Interest between Two Principals

Unless otherwise agreed, an agent may not act for two principals whose interests conflict. Suppose Travis represents both director Steven Spielberg and actress Julia Roberts. Spielberg is casting the title role in his new movie, *Nancy Drew: Girl Detective*, a role that Roberts covets. Travis cannot represent these two clients when they are negotiating with each other, unless they both know about the conflict and agree to ignore it.

Secretly Dealing with the Principal

If a principal hires an agent to arrange a transaction, the agent may not become a party to the transaction without the principal's permission. Suppose that Matt Damon hired Trang to read movie scripts for him. Unbeknownst to Damon, Trang had written her own script, which she thought would be ideal for him. She may not sell it to him without revealing that she wrote it herself. Damon may be perfectly happy to buy Trang's script, but he has the right, as her principal, to know that she is the person selling it.

Appropriate Behavior

An agent may not engage in inappropriate behavior that reflects badly on the principal. This rule applies even to *off-duty* conduct. For example, British Airways fired flight attendants for their off-duty behavior in a hotel bar. One of the attendants raised her shirt so that her female colleague could caress her breasts while kissing her on the mouth. She then lowered her trousers, revealing her underwear. Another crew member took off his shirt and poured wine down his trousers.

OTHER DUTIES OF AN AGENT

Before Taylor left for a five-week trip to England, he hired Angie to rent his vacation house. Angie never got around to listing his house on the regional rental list used by all the area brokers, but when the Fords contacted her looking for rental housing, she did show them Taylor's place. They offered to rent it for $750 per month.

Angie called Taylor in England to tell him. He responded that he would not accept less than $850 a month, which Angie thought the Fords would be willing to pay. He told Angie to call back if there was any problem. The Fords decided that they would go no higher than $800 a month. Instead of calling Taylor in England, Angie left a message on his home answering machine. When the Fords pressed her for an answer, she said she could not get in touch with Taylor. Not until Taylor returned home did he learn that the Fords had rented another house. Did Angie violate any of the duties that agents owe to their principals?

Duty to Obey Instructions

An agent must obey her principal's instructions, unless the principal directs her to behave illegally or unethically. Taylor instructed Angie to call him if the Fords rejected the offer. When Angie failed to do so, she violated her duty to obey instructions. If, however, Taylor had asked her to say that the house's basement was dry, when in fact it looked like a rice paddy every spring, Angie would be under no obligation to follow those illegal instructions.

Duty of Care

An agent has a duty to act with reasonable care. In other words, an agent must act as a reasonable person would, under the circumstances. A reasonable person would not have left a message on Taylor's home answering machine when she knew he was in Europe.

Duty to Provide Information

An agent has a duty to provide the principal with all information in her possession that she has reason to believe the principal wants to know. She also has a duty to provide accurate information. For example, Oma Grigsby signed up with O.K. Travel for a tour of Israel. O.K. purchased the tour from Trinity Tours. Under state law, tour promoters were required to register and post a financial bond. Although Trinity had not done so, O.K. never warned Grigsby. Matters were far from OK when Grigsby learned a week before her trip that Trinity had gone out of business. In the end, however, she was able to obtain a refund from O.K. because it had violated its duty to tell her that Trinity was unregistered and unbonded.[6] Did Angie violate her duty to provide information to Taylor?

Principal's Remedies When the Agent Breaches a Duty

A principal has three potential remedies when an agent breaches her duty:

- The principal can recover from the agent any **damages** the breach has caused. Thus, if Taylor can only rent his house for $600 a month instead of the $800 the Fords offered, Angie would be liable for the difference.

- If an agent breaches the duty of loyalty, he must turn over to the principal any **profits** he has earned as a result of his wrongdoing. Thus, after Klein violated his duty of loyalty to Harrison, he forfeited profits he would have earned from the copyright of "He's So Fine."

- If the agent has violated her duty of loyalty, the principal may **rescind** the transaction. When Trang sold a script to her principal, Matt Damon, without telling him that she was the author, she violated her duty of loyalty. Damon could rescind the contract to buy the script.

CYBERLAW

All the agents thus far in this chapter have been people. But do agents have to be human? Or can a *bot* can be your agent? A bot is software that performs automatic tasks. Suppose, for example, you want to buy a vintage lava lamp on eBay. The company has developed a system called "proxy bidding" which permits it to place automatic bids for you. Here is how the company describes this system on its Web site:

> Proxy bidding means that a bidder can submit a maximum bid amount and our system will bid in their absence, executing their bid for them and trying to keep the bid price as low as possible.
>
> An easier way to think of this would be to think of the bidding system standing in for you as a bidder at a live auction. Let's say you need to be somewhere and can't be present to bid and you ask a friend to go to the auction and bid for you. You tell your friend that you are willing to pay $25 for an item you saw.
>
> The auctioneer starts the bidding at $5 and your friend bids the $5. Then another bidder bids $6 and your friend then bids $7 on your behalf. Then another bidder bids $12 and your friend bids $13 for you. This would keep going until either your friend wins the item for you at or below $25 or the bidding exceeds the $25 you were willing to pay.

If your friend bid for you, he would be your agent. For that reason, legal commentators argue that this eBay bot is also an agent. However, the eBay User Agreement states: "You and eBay are independent contractors, and no agency . . . relationship is intended or created by this Agreement." So is eBay your agent or not? No cases have yet addressed this issue—what would you decide if you were the judge? ◪

---

[6] *Grigsby v. O.K. Travel*, 118 Ohio App. 3d 671, 693 N.E.2d 1142, 1997 Ohio App. LEXIS 875 (1997).

Duties of Principals to Agents

Typically, the role of the principal is limited to reimbursing the agent for reasonable expenses and cooperating with the agent in performing agency tasks. The respective duties of agents and principals can be summarized as follows:

Duties of Agents to Principals	Duty of Principals to Agents
Duty of loyalty	Duty to reimburse
Duty to obey instructions	Duty to cooperate
Duty of care	
Duty to provide information	

DUTY TO REIMBURSE THE AGENT

As a general rule, the principal must **indemnify** (i.e., reimburse) the agent for any expenses she has reasonably incurred. These reimbursable expenses fall into three categories:

- A principal must indemnify an agent for any expenses or damages reasonably incurred in carrying out his agency responsibilities. For example, Peace Baptist Church of Birmingham, Alabama asked its pastor to buy land for a new church. He paid part of the purchase price out of his own pocket, but the church refused to reimburse him. Although the pastor lost in church, he won in court.[7]

- A principal must indemnify an agent for tort claims brought by a third party if the principal authorized the agent's behavior and the agent did not realize he was committing a tort. Marisa owns all the apartment buildings on Elm Street, except one. She hires Rajiv to manage the units and tells him that, under the terms of the leases, she has the right to ask guests to leave if a party becomes too rowdy. But she forgets to tell Rajiv that she does not own one of the buildings, which happens to house a college sorority. One night, when the sorority is having a rambunctious party, Rajiv hustles over and starts ejecting the noisy guests. The sorority is furious and sues Rajiv for trespass. If the sorority wins its suit against Rajiv, Marisa would have to pay the judgment, plus Rajiv's attorney's fees, because she had told him to quell noisy parties, and he did not realize he was trespassing.

- The principal must indemnify the agent for any liability she incurs from third parties as a result of entering into a contract on the principal's behalf, including attorney's fees and reasonable settlements. An agent signed a contract to buy cucumbers for Vlasic Food Products Co. to use in making pickles. When the first shipment of cucumbers arrived, Vlasic inspectors found them unsuitable and directed the agent to refuse the shipment. The agent found himself in a pickle when the cucumber farmer sued. He notified Vlasic, which refused to

---

[7] *Lauderdale v. Peace Baptist Church of Birmingham*, 246 Ala. 178, 19 So. 2d 538, 1944 Ala. LEXIS 508 (1944).

defend him, so he settled the claim himself for $29,000. A court ordered Vlasic to reimburse the agent because he had notified them of the suit and had acted reasonably and in good faith.[8]

DUTY TO COOPERATE

Principals have a duty to cooperate with their agent:

- **The principal must furnish the agent with the opportunity to work.** If Lewis agrees to serve as Ida's real estate agent, Ida must allow Lewis access to the house.

- **The principal cannot unreasonably interfere with the agent's ability to accomplish his task.** Ida allows Lewis to show the house, but she refuses to clean it and then makes disparaging comments to prospective purchasers. "I really get tired of living in such a dank, dreary house," she says. This behavior would constitute unreasonable interference with an agent.

- **The principal must perform her part of the contract.** Once the agent has successfully completed the task, the principal must pay him, even if the principal has changed her mind and no longer wants the agent to perform. Ida is a 78-year-old widow who has lived alone for many years in a house that she loves. Her asking price is outrageously high. But, lo and behold, Lewis finds a couple who are happy to pay Ida's price. There is only one problem: Ida does not really want to sell. She put her house on the market because she enjoys showing it to all the folks who move to town. She rejects the offer. Now there is a second problem. The contract provided that Lewis would find a willing buyer at the asking price. Since he has done so, Ida must pay his real estate commission, even if she does not want to sell her house.

Terminating an Agency Relationship

Either the agent or the principal can terminate the agency relationship at any time. In addition, the relationship terminates automatically if the principal or agent can no longer perform their required duties, or a change in circumstances renders the agency relationship pointless.

TERMINATION BY AGENT OR PRINCIPAL

The two parties—principal and agent—have five choices in terminating their relationship:

- *Term agreement.* The principal and agent can agree in advance how long their relationship will last. Alexandra hires Boris to help her purchase exquisite enameled Easter eggs made for the Russian czars by Fabergé. If they agree that the relationship will last five years, they have a term agreement.

---

[8] *Long v. Vlasic Food Products Co.*, 439 F.2d 229, 1971 U.S. App. LEXIS 11455 (4th Cir. 1971).

- *Achieving a purpose.* The principal and agent can agree that the agency relationship will terminate when the principal's goals have been achieved. Alexandra and Boris might agree that their relationship will end when Alexandra has purchased 10 eggs.

- *Mutual agreement.* The principal and agent can always change their minds later on, as long as the change is mutual. If Boris and Alexandra originally agree to a five-year term, but after only three years Boris wants to quit or Alexandra runs out of money, they can decide together to terminate the agency.

- *Agency at will.* If they make no agreement in advance about the term of the agreement, either principal or agent can terminate at any time.

- *Wrongful termination.* An agency relationship is a personal relationship. Hiring an agent is not like buying a book. You might not care which copy of the book you buy, but you do care which agent you hire. If an agency relationship is not working out, the courts will not force the agent and principal to stay together. **Either party always has the *power* to walk out. They may not, however, have the *right*.** If one party's departure from the agency relationship violates the agreement and causes harm to the other party, the wrongful party must pay damages. He will nonetheless be permitted to leave. If Boris has agreed to work for Alexandra for five years but he wants to leave after three, he can leave, provided he pays Alexandra the cost of hiring and training a replacement.

PRINCIPAL OR AGENT CAN NO LONGER PERFORM REQUIRED DUTIES

If the principal or the agent is unable to perform the duties required under the agency agreement, the agreement terminates.

- **If either the agent or the principal fails to obtain (or keep) a license necessary to perform duties under the agency agreement, the agreement ends.** Caleb hires Allegra to represent him in a lawsuit. If she is disbarred, their agency agreement terminates because the agent is no longer licensed to practice law.

- **The bankruptcy of the agent or the principal terminates an agency relationship only if it affects their ability to perform.** Bankruptcy rarely interferes with an agent's responsibilities. After all, there is generally no reason why an agent cannot continue to act for the principal whether the agent is rich or poor. If Lewis, the real estate agent, becomes bankrupt, he can continue to represent Ida or anyone else who wants to sell a house. The bankruptcy of a principal is different, however, because after filing for bankruptcy, the principal loses control of his assets. Therefore, the bankruptcy of a principal is more likely to terminate an agency relationship.

- **An agency relationship terminates upon the death or incapacity of either the principal or the agent.** Agency is a personal relationship, and when the principal dies, the agent cannot act on behalf of a nonexistent person. Of course, a nonexistent person cannot act either, so the relationship also terminates when the agent dies. Incapacity has the same legal effect, because either the principal or the agent is, at least temporarily, unable to act.

- **If the agent violates her duty of loyalty, the agency agreement automatically terminates.** Agents are appointed to represent the principal's interest; if they fail to do so, there is no point to the relationship. Sam is negotiating a military procurement contract on behalf of his employer, Missiles R Us, Inc. In the midst of these negotiations, he becomes very friendly with Louisa, the government negotiator. One night over drinks, he tells Louisa what Missiles' real costs are on the project and the lowest bid it could possibly make. By passing on this confidential information, Sam has violated his duty of loyalty, and his agency relationship terminates.

CHANGE IN CIRCUMSTANCES

After the agency agreement is negotiated, circumstances may change. If these changes are significant enough to undermine the purpose of the agreement, then the relationship ends automatically. Andrew hires Melissa to sell his country farm for $100,000. Shortly thereafter, the largest oil reserve in North America is discovered nearby. The farm is now worth 10 times Andrew's asking price. Melissa's authority terminates automatically. Other changes in circumstance that affect an agency agreement are:

- *Loss or Destruction of Subject Matter.* Andrew hired Damian to sell his Palm Beach condominium, but before Damian could even measure the living room, Andrew's creditors attached the condo. Damian is no longer authorized to sell the real estate because Andrew has "lost" the subject matter of his agency agreement with Damian.

- *Change of Law.* If the agent's responsibilities become illegal, the agency agreement terminates. Oscar has hired Marta to ship him succulent avocados from California's Imperial Valley. Before she sends the shipment, Mediterranean fruit flies are discovered, and all fruits and vegetables in California are quarantined. The agency agreement terminates because it is now illegal to ship the California avocados.

EFFECT OF TERMINATION

Once an agency relationship ends, the agent no longer has the authority to act for the principal. If she continues to act, she is liable to the principal for any damages he incurs as a result. The Mediterranean fruit fly quarantine ended Marta's agency. If she sends Oscar the avocados anyway and he is fined for possession of a fruit fly, Marta must pay the fine.

The agent loses her authority to act, but some of the duties of both the principal and agent continue even after the relationship ends:

- *Principal's duty to indemnify agent.* Oscar must reimburse Marta for expenses she incurred before the agency ended. If Marta accumulated mileage on her car during her search for the perfect avocado, Oscar must pay her for gasoline and depreciation.

- *Confidential information.* Remember the "He's So Fine" case earlier in the chapter. George Harrison's agent used confidential information to negotiate, on his own behalf, the purchase of the "He's So Fine" copyright. An agent is not entitled to use confidential information, even after the agency relationship terminates.

Chapter Conclusion

Agency law affects us all, because each of us has been and will continue to be both an agent and a principal many times in our lives.

Chapter Review

1. In an agency relationship, a principal and an agent mutually consent that the agent will act on behalf of the principal and be subject to the principal's control, thereby creating a fiduciary relationship.

2. An agent owes these duties to the principal: duty of loyalty, duty to obey instructions, duty of care, and duty to provide information.

3. The principal has three potential remedies when the agent breaches her duty: recovery of damages the breach has caused, recovery of any profits earned by the agent from the breach, and rescission of any transaction with the agent.

4. The principal has two duties to the agent: to reimburse legitimate expenses, and to cooperate with the agent.

5. Both the agent and the principal have the power to terminate an agency relationship, but they may not have the right. If the termination violates the agency agreement and causes harm to the other party, the wrongful party must pay damages.

6. An agency relationship automatically terminates if the principal or agent can no longer perform the required duties or if a change in circumstances renders the agency relationship pointless.

PRACTICE TEST

Matching Questions

Match the following terms with their definitions:

___ **A.** Term agreement.

___ **B.** A duty of a principal.

___ **C.** Agency at will.

___ **D.** A duty of an agent.

___ **E.** A duty to cooperate.

1. Two parties make no agreement in advance about the duration of their agreement.

2. The agent must have the opportunity to work.

3. When two parties agree in advance on the duration of their agreement.

4. Duty to cooperate.

5. Duty of loyalty.

True/False Questions

Circle true or false:

1. T   F   For an agency agreement to be valid, the agent must receive payment.

2. T   F   The trustee of a trust must act for the benefit of the beneficiaries, but the beneficiaries have no right to control the trustee. Therefore, the trustee is not an agent.

3. T   F   An agent may receive profits from an agency relationship even if the principal does not know, as long as the principal is not harmed.

4. T   F   An agent may never act for two principals whose interests conflict.

5. T   F   An agent has a duty to provide the principal with all information in her possession that she has reason to believe the principal wants to know, even if he does not specifically ask for it.

Multiple-Choice Questions

6. CPA QUESTION: A principal and agent relationship requires a:
   (a) Written agreement.
   (b) Power of attorney.
   (c) Meeting of the minds and consent to act.
   (d) Specified consideration.

7. Dorris works in Morris's pet shop. She would *not* be liable for the following activity:
   (a) When a salesperson offers to sell the shop a rare parrot, Dorris buys it for her own account instead.
   (b) Dorris got drunk and did obscene parrot imitations in the window of the pet shop.
   (c) Morris has been trying to acquire a broad-headed snake for years, but they are an endangered species and therefore cannot be sold. Dorris hates snakes so she refuses to buy a broad-headed when it is offered for sale to the shop.
   (d) Dorris tells Morris that there are only 10 gerbils in the shop when really there are 20.
   (e) The rhesus monkey needed to take his medication every morning. Dorris forgot one day and the monkey died.

8. In the *Abkco* case, which of the following activities could Klein have done without incurring liability to George Harrison?
   (a) He could have shared the confidential information only with his wife.
   (b) He could have used any general business experience he gained while George Harrison's agent.
   (c) He could have waited until after his agency agreement expired to use the confidential information he learned.
   (d) He could have revealed the confidential information only to people with whom he had *not* negotiated on behalf of Harrison.
   (e) He could have informed Harrison that he was going to use the confidential information.

9. Which of the following duties does an agent *not* owe to her principal?
   (a) Duty of loyalty.
   (b) Duty to obey instructions.
   (c) Duty to reimburse.
   (d) Duty of care.
   (e) Duty to provide information.

10. Bess works in Emil's gun shop. Which of the following occurrences would *not* terminate the agency relationship between them?
    (a) Emil loses his license to sell firearms.
    (b) Bess dies.
    (c) Emil dies.
    (d) Bess becomes bankrupt.
    (e) Emil is declared mentally incompetent by a court.

Short-Answer Questions

11. The German-American Vocational League was formed in New York during World War II to serve as a propaganda agency for the German Reich. Under U.S. law all foreign agents were required to register. Neither the Vocational League nor its officers registered. When they were charged with violating U.S. law, they

argued that they were not agents of the German government because they had no formal agency agreement. Their one written agreement with the German Reich said nothing about being a propaganda agency. Is a formal contract necessary to establish an agency relationship?

12. ETHICS: Radio TV Reports (RTV) was in the business of recording, transcribing, and monitoring radio and video programming for its clients. The Department of Defense (DOD) in Washington, D.C. was one of RTV's major clients. Paul Ingersoll worked for RTV until August 31. In July the DOD solicited bids for a new contract for the following year. During this same month, Ingersoll formed his own media monitoring business, Transmedia. RTV and Transmedia were the only two bidders on the DOD contract, which was awarded to Transmedia. Did Ingersoll violate his fiduciary duty to RTV? Aside from his legal obligations, did Ingersoll behave ethically? How does his behavior look in the light of day? Was it right?

13. David and Fiona Rookard purchased tickets for a trip through Mexico from Mexicoach in San Diego. The company told them that the trip would be safe. It did not tell them, however, that their tickets had disclaimers written in Spanish warning that, under Mexican law, a bus company is not liable for any harm that befalls its passengers. The Rookards did not read Spanish. They were injured in a bus accident caused by gross negligence on the part of the driver. Did Mexicoach violate its duty to the Rookards?

14. Penny Wilson went to Arlington Chrysler-Plymouth-Dodge to buy an automobile. Penny told Arlington that, as a minor, she could not buy the car unless she obtained credit life insurance that would pay the balance of any loan owing if her mother died. She also disclosed that her mother had cancer. Arlington was an agent for Western Pioneer Life Insurance Co.

Western Pioneer reported that a credit insurance policy would be invalid if Mrs. Wilson died within six months. In fact, the policy was invalid if Mrs. Wilson died of cancer within one year. Seven months later, Mrs. Wilson died, and Western Pioneer refused to pay. Penny Wilson sued Western Pioneer and Arlington. The trial court found Western Pioneer liable, but not Arlington. Was Western Pioneer liable for Arlington's legal expenses?

15. This is a tale of marital woe. At the urging of her husband, Phyllis Thropp placed $40,000 in a brokerage account with her husband's friend Richard Gregory, a broker at Bache Halsey. Mrs. Thropp opened the account in her name alone and did not authorize Gregory to discuss the account with Mr. Thropp, nor did she authorize Mr. Thropp to act for her. Undeterred by this technicality, Mr. Thropp forged his wife's name to a power of attorney that authorized him to make decisions for her. He gave this document to Gregory. In the course of the next year, Mr. Thropp ordered Gregory to sell his wife's securities and issue checks to her. After forging her name to the checks, he cashed them and used the money to pay his gambling debts. Gregory did not process the power of attorney form according to standard Bache procedures. When the Thropps saw Gregory socially, Mrs. Thropp frequently asked him how her account was doing. Gregory somehow neglected to mention that it was not doing very well at all. He never told her about the numerous sales. Can this marriage be saved? No, the Thropps were divorced. Did Richard Gregory violate his fiduciary duty to Mrs. Thropp?

16. ROLE REVERSAL: Write a multiple-choice question that focuses on an employee's obligation to her company once she has decided to quit her job and join a competitor (but before she actually leaves).

Internet Research Problem

The Code of Ethics for the National Association of Realtors is at **http://www.realtor.org/mempolweb.nsf/pages/code**. Do these rules require realtors to treat clients better—or worse—than agency law demands? In what ways?

You can find further practice problems in the Online Quiz at **http://beatty.westbuslaw.com** or in the Study Guide that accompanies this text.

Agency: The Outside Relationship

Some people simply do not know their own best interest. Sarah's boss was like that. Jamie was a nice guy, but his business would have been more successful if he had listened to Sarah once in a while. His company supplied product demonstrators to grocery stores. He hired and trained the people who stand in the aisles offering samples of salsa-flavored taco chips or marshmallow chip cookies.

A manager from the Lone Star grocery store chain called to offer a contract for the Fort Worth area. It was a tempting offer, but Jamie told Sarah to refuse. At the price the chain was proposing, Jamie would barely be able to pay his workers the minimum wage. He doubted that he could find qualified staff at that price. Sarah disagreed. She believed you could always find good workers if you looked hard enough. Besides, Lone Star had thousands of stores nationwide, and this was a great opportunity to get a foot inside its very large door.

Against orders, but thinking only about what was best for Jamie, Sarah called back to accept the offer. She knew that he would be terribly grateful—someday. Unfortunately, on the day when Jamie did find out, he was furious. He was even angrier when he called his lawyer to rescind the contract and found out that he was legally committed to the deal Sarah had made. He then ordered Sarah to take personal responsibility for the contract and make sure there were no problems.

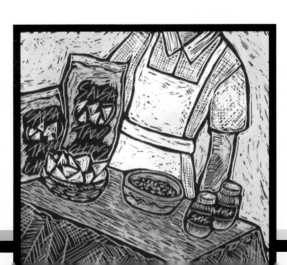

Sarah trained new workers and sent them off to demonstrate flavored popcorn. Eager to make a good impression, Hugo rushed to cook his first batch of popcorn, but forgot to read the instructions carefully. Instead of adding 1/3 cup of peppermint popcorn, he put in 3 cups. Attracted by the wonderful smell, Tori stood by Hugo's stand, waiting for the popcorn to finish. With a flourish, Hugo raised the lid of the pan, and the popcorn exploded in Tori's face, causing severe burns. ◾

It is virtually impossible to run a modern business without agents. However, having agents increases the risk of legal liability. A principal may be liable in contract for agreements that the agent signs and also liable in tort for any harm the agent causes. Indeed, once a principal hires an agent, he may be liable to third parties for her acts, even if she disobeys instructions. Although Jamie specifically told Sarah not to accept the Lone Star contract, Jamie is bound by the contract because Sarah appeared to act with authority. Jamie is also liable in tort to Tori, because his sub-agent (an agent hired by his agent) caused harm. This risk of liability means that it is important to understand agency law.

Principal's Liability for Contracts

Many agents are hired for the primary purpose of entering into contracts on behalf of their principals. Most of the time, the principal is delighted to be bound by these contracts. But even if the principal is unhappy, the principal generally cannot rescind contracts entered into by the agent. After all, if someone is going to be penalized, it should be the principal who hired the troublesome agent, not the innocent third party.

The principal is bound by the acts of an agent if (1) the agent had *authority*; or (2) the principal, for reasons of fairness, is *estopped* from denying that the agent had authority; or (3) the principal *ratifies* the acts of the agent. To say that the principal is "bound by the acts" of the agent means that the principal is as liable as if he had performed the acts himself.

AUTHORITY

A principal is bound by the acts of an agent if the agent has authority. There are three types of authority: express, implied, and apparent.

Express Authority

The principal grants express authority by words or conduct that reasonably cause the agent to believe the principal desires her to act. Craig calls his stockbroker, Alice, and asks her to buy 100 shares of Banshee Corp. for his account. She has *express authority* to carry out this transaction.

Implied Authority

Authority to conduct a transaction includes authority to do acts that are reasonably necessary to accomplish it. David has recently inherited a house from his grandmother. He hires Nell to auction off the house and its contents. She hires an auctioneer, advertises the event, rents a tent, and generally does everything necessary to conduct a successful auction. After withholding her expenses, she sends the tidy balance to David. Totally outraged, he calls her on the phone, "How dare you hire an auctioneer and rent a tent? I never gave you permission! I absolutely *refuse* to pay these expenses!"

David is wrong. A principal almost never gives an agent absolutely complete instructions. Unless some authority was implied, David would have had to say, "Open the car door, get in, put the key in the ignition, drive to the store, buy stickers, mark an auction number on each sticker . . ." and so forth. To solve this problem, the law assumes that the agent has authority to do anything that is reasonably necessary to accomplish her task.

Apparent Authority

A principal can be liable for the acts of an agent who is not, in fact, acting with authority if the principal's conduct causes a third party reasonably to believe that the agent is authorized. In the case of express and implied authority, the principal has authorized the agent to act. Apparent authority is different: The principal has *not* authorized the agent, but has done something to make an innocent third party *believe* the agent is authorized. As a result, the principal is every bit as liable to the third party as if the agent did have authority.

For example, Zbigniew Lambo and Scott Kennedy were brokers at Paulson Investment Co., a stock brokerage firm in Oregon. The two men violated securities laws by selling unregistered stock, which ultimately proved to be worthless. Kennedy and Lambo were liable, but they were unable to repay the money. Either Paulson or its customers would end up bearing the loss. What is the fair result?

Although the two brokers did not have *actual* or *implied* authority to sell the stock (Paulson had not authorized them to break the law), the company was nonetheless liable on the grounds that the brokers had *apparent* authority. Paulson had sent letters to its customers notifying them when it hired Kennedy. The two brokers made sales presentations at Paulson's offices. The company had never told customers that the two men were not authorized to sell this worthless stock.[1] Thus the agents *appeared* to have authority, even though they did not. Of course, Paulson had the right to recover from Kennedy and Lambo if it could ever compel them to pay.

Remember that the issue in apparent authority is always what the *principal* has done to make the *third party* believe that the agent has authority. Suppose that Kennedy and Lambo never worked for Paulson but, on their own, printed up Paulson stationery. The company would not be liable for the stock the two men sold, because it had never done or said anything that would reasonably make a third party believe that the men were its agents.

ESTOPPEL

No one may claim that a person was *not* his agent, if he knew that others thought the person *was* acting on his behalf, and he failed to correct their belief. He is *estopped* from denying an agency relationship. Paul Murphy approached the

---

[1] *Badger v. Paulson Investment Co.*, 311 Ore. 14, 803 P.2d 1178, 1991 Ore. LEXIS 7 (S. Ct. OR 1991).

Sperry Rand Corp. with a promising idea for marketing Remington shavers. He had a report from a dermatologist, Dr. William Hill, Jr., indicating that Remington shavers were superior. Sperry Rand publicized this report in full-page advertisements in newspapers and magazines. There was only one problem—Hill had not written the report and had not agreed to allow his name to be used in the ad campaign. Murphy was not, in fact, Hill's agent.

The court, however, found Sperry Rand *not* liable to Hill on a theory of estoppel. Hill discovered the ad campaign in March but did not complain to Sperry Rand until November. By the simple act of making a prompt phone call, the doctor could have prevented most of the harm the advertisements caused him.[2]

RATIFICATION

If a person accepts the benefit of an unauthorized transaction or fails to repudiate it, then he is bound by the act as if he had originally authorized it. He has *ratified* the act. Many of the cases in agency law involve instances in which one person acts without authority for another. To avoid liability, the alleged principal shows that he had not authorized the task at issue. But sometimes, after the fact, the principal decides that he approves of what the agent has done even though it was not authorized at the time. The law would be perverse if it did not permit the principal, under those circumstances, to agree to the deal the agent has made. The law is not perverse, but it is careful. Even if an agent acts without authority, the principal can decide later to be bound by her actions as long as these requirements are met:

- The "agent" indicates to the third party that she is acting for a principal.

- The "principal" knows all the material facts of the transaction.

- The "principal" accepts the benefit of the whole transaction, not just part.

- The third party does not withdraw from the contract before ratification.

A night clerk at the St. Regis Hotel in Detroit, Michigan was brutally murdered in the course of a robbery. *The Detroit News* reported that the St. Regis management had offered a $1,000 reward for any information leading to the arrest and conviction of the killer. Two days after the article appeared, Robert Jackson turned in the man who was subsequently convicted of the crime. But then it was Jackson's turn to be robbed—the hotel refused to pay the reward on the grounds that the manager who had made the offer had no authority. Jackson still had one weapon left: He convinced the court that the hotel had ratified the offer. One of the hotel's owners admitted he read *The Detroit News*, so he must have been aware of the offer. By failing to revoke the offer publicly, he had ratified it and the hotel was liable.[3]

SUBAGENTS

Many of the examples in this chapter involve a single agent acting for a principal. Real life is often more complex. Daniel, the owner of a restaurant, hires Michaela

---

[2] *Sperry Rand Corp. v. Hill,* 356 F.2d 181, 1966 U.S. App. LEXIS 7491 (1st Cir. 1966).

[3] *Jackson v. Goodman,* 69 Mich. App. 225, 244 N.W.2d 423, 1976 Mich. App. LEXIS 741 (Mich. Ct. App. 1976).

to manage it. She in turn hires chefs, waiters, and dishwashers. Daniel has never even met the restaurant help, yet they are also his agents, albeit a special category called **subagent.** Michaela is called an **intermediary agent**—someone who hires subagents for the principal.

When an agent is authorized to hire a subagent, the principal is as liable for the acts of the subagent as he is for the acts of a regular agent. Michaela hires Lydia to serve as produce buyer. When Lydia buys food for the restaurant, Daniel must pay the bill.

Agent's Liability for Contracts

The agent's liability on a contract depends upon how much the third party knows about the principal. Disclosure is the agent's best protection against liability.

FULLY DISCLOSED PRINCIPAL

An agent is not liable for any contracts she makes on behalf of a *fully* disclosed principal. A principal is fully disclosed if the third party knows of his *existence* and his *identity.* Augusta acts as agent for Parker when he buys Tracey's prize-winning show horse. Augusta and Tracey both grew up in posh Grosse Pointe, Michigan, where they attended the same elite schools. Tracey does not know Parker, but she figures any friend of Augusta's must be OK. She figures wrong—Parker is a charming deadbeat. He injures Tracey's horse, fails to pay the full contract price, and promptly disappears from the face of the earth. Tracey angrily demands that Augusta make good on Parker's debt. Unfortunately for Tracey, Parker was a fully disclosed principal—Tracey knew of his *existence* and his *identity.* Augusta is not liable because Tracey could have (should have) investigated him. Tracey's only recourse is against the principal, Parker (wherever he may be).

To avoid liability when signing a contract on behalf of a principal, an agent must clearly state that she is an agent and must also identify the principal. Augusta should sign a contract on behalf of her principal, Parker, as follows: "Augusta, as agent for Parker" or "Parker, by Augusta, Agent." ▪

PARTIALLY DISCLOSED PRINCIPAL

In the case of a *partially* disclosed principal, the third party can recover from either the agent or the principal. A principal is partially disclosed if the third party knew of his *existence* but not his *identity.* Suppose that, when approaching Tracey about the horse, Augusta simply says, "I have a friend who is interested in buying your champion." Parker is a partially disclosed principal because Tracey knows only that he exists, not who he is. She is not able to investigate him. Tracey relies solely on what she is able to learn from the agent, Augusta. Both Augusta and Parker are liable to Tracey. (They are jointly and severally liable, which means that Tracey can recover from either or both of them. She cannot, however, recover more than the total that she is owed: If her damages are $100,000, she can recover that amount from either Augusta or Parker, or partial amounts from both, but in no event more than $100,000.)

UNDISCLOSED PRINCIPAL

In the case of an *undisclosed* principal, the third party can recover from either the agent or the principal. A principal is undisclosed if the third party did not know of his existence. Suppose that Augusta simply asks to buy the horse herself, without mentioning that she is purchasing it for Parker. In this case Parker is an undisclosed principal, because Tracey does not know that Augusta is acting for someone else. Both Parker and Augusta are jointly and severally liable. As Exhibit 29.1 illustrates, the principal is always liable, but the agent is only liable when the principal's identity is a mystery.

In some ways the concept of an undisclosed principal violates principles of contract law. If Tracey does not even know that Parker exists, how can they have an agreement or a meeting of the minds? Is such an arrangement fair to Tracey? No matter, a contract with an undisclosed principal is binding. The following incident illustrates why.

William Zeckendorf was a man with a plan. For years he had been eyeing a six-block tract of land along New York's East River. It was a wasteland of slums and slaughterhouses, but he could see its potential. Finally, in 1946 he got the phone call he had been waiting for. The owners were willing to sell—but at $17 a square foot, when surrounding land cost less than $5. To make his investment worthwhile, he needed to buy the neighboring property—once the slaughterhouses were gone, this other land would be much more valuable. But Zeckendorf was well known as a wealthy real estate developer. If he personally tried to negotiate the purchase of the surrounding land, word would soon get out and prices would skyrocket. So he hired agents to purchase the land for him, and he took off to South America for a month. When he returned, his agents had completed 75 different purchases, and he owned 18 acres of land.

Shortly afterwards, the United Nations began seeking a site for its headquarters. President Truman favored Boston, Philadelphia, or a location in the Midwest. The UN committee suggested Greenwich or Stamford, Connecticut. But John

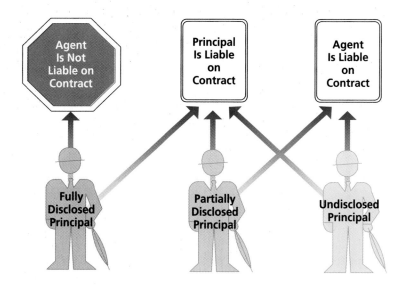

Exhibit 29.1

D. Rockefeller settled the question once and for all. He purchased Zeckendorf's land for $8.5 million and donated it to the UN (netting Zeckendorf a profit of $2 million). Without the cooperation of agency law, the UN headquarters would not be in New York today.

ETHICS | Did Zeckendorf behave ethically in purchasing this land secretly? What guidance would the Chapter 2 ethics checklist provide? Was this purchase legal? How would it look in the light of day? Has the process been fair?

UNAUTHORIZED AGENT

Thus far, we have been discussing an agent's liability to a third party for a transaction that was authorized by the principal. Sometimes, however, agents act without the authority of a principal. **If the agent has no authority (express, implied, or apparent), the principal is not liable to the third party, and the agent is.** Suppose that Augusta agrees to sell Peter's horse to Terrence. Unfortunately, Peter has never met Augusta and has certainly not authorized this transaction. Augusta is hoping that she can persuade him to sell, but Peter refuses. Augusta, but not Peter, is liable to Terrence for breach of contract.

Principal's Liability for Torts

A master is liable for physical harm caused by the negligent conduct of servants within the scope of employment. This principle of liability is called *respondeat superior,* which is a Latin phrase that means, "let the master answer." Under the theory of *respondeat superior,* the master (i.e., the principal) is liable for the servant's (i.e. the agent's) misbehavior, whether or not the principal was at fault. Indeed, the principal is liable even if he forbade or tried to prevent the agent from misbehaving. Because the principal controls the agent, he should be able to *prevent* misbehavior. If he cannot prevent it, at least he can *insure* against the risks. Furthermore, the principal may have deeper pockets than the agent or the injured third party and thus be better able to *afford* the cost of the agent's misbehavior.

To apply the principle of *respondeat superior,* it is important to understand each of the following terms: master and servant, scope of employment, negligent and intentional torts, and physical harm.

MASTER AND SERVANT

There are two kinds of agents: (1) *servants* and (2) *independent contractors.* A principal *may be* liable for the torts of a servant but generally is *not* liable for the torts of an independent contractor.

Servant or Independent Contractor?

The more control the principal has over an agent, the more likely that the agent will be considered a servant. Therefore, when determining if agents are servants or independent contractors, courts consider whether:

- The principal controls details of the work.

- The principal supplies the tools and place of work.

- The agents work full time for the principal.

- The agents are paid by time, not by the job.

- The work is part of the regular business of the principal.

- The principal and agents believe they have an employer-employee relationship.

- The principal is in business.

The Internal Revenue Service provides a thorough discussion of this issue at **http://www.irs.gov/pub/irs-pdf/p15a.pdf**.

Do not be misled by the term *servant*. A servant does not mean Jeeves, the butler, or Maisie, the maid. In fact, if Mrs. Dillworth hires Jeeves and Maisie for the evening from a catering firm, they are *not* her servants, they are independent contractors. On the other hand, the president of General Motors is a servant of that corporation.

Negligent Hiring

As a general rule, principals are not liable for the physical torts of an independent contractor. There is, however, one exception to this rule: **The principal is liable for the physical torts of an independent contractor *only if* the principal has been negligent in hiring or supervising her.** Was the supermarket at fault in the following case?

CASE SUMMARY

DURAN v. FURR'S SUPERMARKETS, INC.

921 S.W.2d 778, 1996 Tex. App. LEXIS 1345
Court of Appeals of Texas, 1996

FACTS: Steve Romero was an off-duty police officer working as a security guard for Furr's Supermarkets. He approached a car parked in the supermarket's fire lane and began yelling at a passenger to move it. The passenger, Graciela Duran, asked Romero for his name. He opened the car door and tried to pull her out, all the while threatening to arrest her. Duran ultimately required surgery to repair the injury that Romero caused to her arm. Duran filed suit against Furr's, but the trial court granted Furr's motion for summary judgment. Duran appealed.

ISSUE: Did the trial court properly grant Furr's motion for summary judgment? Is Duran entitled to a trial?

DECISION: Because issues of fact are still outstanding, the trial court's grant of summary judgment was improper. Duran is entitled to a trial.

REASONING: Furr's is liable only if it was negligent in hiring or retaining a servant whom it knew or should have known was incompetent, thereby creating an unreasonable risk of harm to others. Before hiring Romero, Furr's did not interview him, require him to complete a job application, or investigate his background as a police officer. If it had made reasonable inquiry, it would have discovered that a complaint had been filed against him for using vulgar and abusive language while on duty.

Duran argues that, if Furr's had discovered the complaint, it would have known that Romero had a tendency toward aggressive behavior. Furr's claims, however, that it could not have reasonably foreseen that Romero's verbal aggression would lead to physical assault. The case must return for trial to resolve this issue. ◢

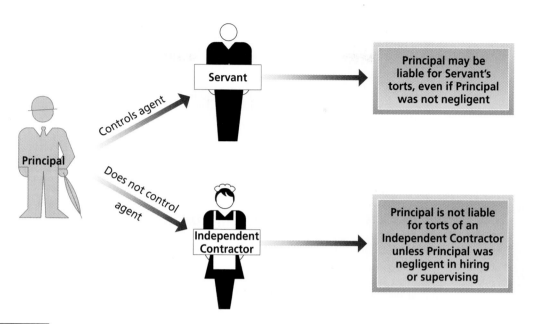

Exhibit 29.2

Exhibit 29.2 illustrates the difference in liability between a servant and an independent contractor.

SCOPE OF EMPLOYMENT

Principals are only liable for torts that a servant commits within the *scope of employment*. If an employee leaves a pool of water on the floor of a store and a customer slips and falls, the employer is liable. But if the same employee leaves water on his own kitchen floor and a friend falls, the employer is not liable because the employee is not acting within the scope of employment. A servant is acting within the scope of employment if the act:

- Is one that servants are generally responsible for.

- Takes place during hours that the servant is generally employed.

- Is part of the principal's business.

- Is similar to the one the principal authorized.

- Is one for which the principal supplied the tools; and

- Is not seriously criminal.

Scope of employment cases raise two major issues: authorization and abandonment.

Authorization

An act is within the scope of employment, even if expressly forbidden, if it is of the same general nature as that authorized. Although Jane has often told Hank not to speed when driving the delivery van, he ignores her instructions and plows into Bernadette. Hank was authorized to drive the van, but not to speed. However, his speeding was of the same general nature as the authorized act, so Jane is liable to Bernadette.

In the following case, an employee engaged in unauthorized behavior while on company business. Did his actions fall within the scope of his employment? You be the judge.

YOU BE THE JUDGE

CONNER v. MAGIC CITY TRUCKING SERVICE, INC.

592 So. 2d 1048, 1992 Ala. LEXIS 26
Supreme Court of Alabama, 1992

FACTS: Sarah Conner worked for A-Pac, which had hired Magic City to supply dirt for a roadway. Conner was responsible for punching holes in a ticket to tally the amount of dirt each Magic City truck brought in. When a driver was ready to dump the dirt from the truck, Conner would often release the truck's latch as a courtesy to the driver, who would otherwise have to climb out of the truck to release it.

Magic City employee David King drove up wearing a Halloween mask. Conner ignored the mask but punched King's load ticket. King later returned to Conner's post with a second load of dirt, this time without the mask. Conner punched his ticket, and King told her to release the latch on his truck quickly or else he would "put [his] friend" on her. Conner attempted to release the latch but could not budge it. Conner told King, who had a tool for forcing the release of the latch, to release it himself. King again threatened to "put [his] friend" on her if Conner did not quickly release the latch. King began chasing Conner with a very large snake. King's Magic City supervisor laughed as Conner ran from King. Eventually, King gave up the chase and threw the snake at Conner. She collapsed with severe medical problems.

YOU BE THE JUDGE: Under *respondeat superior*, is Magic City liable for the actions of its employee, King? Was King acting within the scope of his employment?

ARGUMENT FOR CONNER: An employee is acting within the scope of his employment if the conduct is of the same general nature as that authorized. Conner only met King because he was working for Magic City. He was angry at her because she did not release the latch on his truck. Their interaction was incidental to his job.

Respondeat superior is based on the concept of control. The principal is able to control the agent to prevent him from misbehaving. While David King was tormenting Sarah Conner, King's supervisor stood and laughed. He did not even tell King to stop. In all fairness, Magic City should bear liability for the harm caused by its employee.

ARGUMENT FOR MAGIC CITY: When King brought in the Halloween mask and snake, he was not acting in furtherance of his employer's business. Snakes have nothing to do with King's job, and his actions were not within the scope of his employment.

Conner blames Magic City because King's supervisor stood by and laughed. Consciously or not, people often react to bizarre antics with laughter even when they disapprove of the behavior. Magic City is sorry King behaved so badly. But the company did not authorize his actions and should not be liable for them.

Abandonment

The master is liable for the actions of the servant that occur while the servant is at work, but not for actions that occur after the servant has abandoned the master's business. The difficulty in interpreting this rule lies in determining when the employee has abandoned the master's business. The employer is liable if the employee is simply on a *detour* from company business, but the employer is not liable if the employee is off on a *frolic of his own.* Suppose that Hank, the delivery van driver, speeds during his afternoon commute home. While commuting, he is not within the scope of his employment, so his master, Jane, is not liable. On the other hand, if Hank stops at the Burger King drive-in window en route to making a delivery, Jane is liable when he crashes into Anna on the way out of the parking lot, because this time he is simply making a detour.

NEGLIGENT AND INTENTIONAL TORTS

The master is liable if the servant commits a negligent tort that causes physical harm to a person or property. When Hank crashes into Anna, he is committing a negligent tort, and Jane is liable if all the other requirements for *respondeat superior* are met.

A master is not liable for the *intentional* torts of the servant *unless* the servant was motivated, at least in part, by a desire to serve the master, or the conduct was reasonably foreseeable. Courts are generous in their definition of behavior that is intended to serve the master. In one case, a police trainee shot a fellow officer while practicing his quick draw technique. In another, a drunken sailor knocked a shipmate out of bed with the admonition, "Get up, you big son of a bitch, and turn to," after which the two men fought. The courts ruled that both the police trainee and the sailor were motivated by a desire to serve their master and, therefore, the master was liable for their intentional torts.[4]

PHYSICAL HARM

In the case of *physical* torts, a master is liable for the negligent conduct of a servant that occurs within the scope of employment. The rule for *nonphysical* torts (i.e., torts that harm only reputation, feelings, or wallet) is different. **Nonphysical torts are treated more like a contract claim, and the principal is liable only if the servant acted with actual, implied, or apparent authority.** For example, the Small Business Administration (SBA) granted Midwest Knitting Mills, Inc. more than $2 million in loans, but the SBA employee in charge of the case never told Midwest. (He was allegedly a drug addict.) The company sued the SBA for the negligence of its employee. Although the conduct had occurred within the scope of employment, it was a nonphysical tort. Since the employee had not acted with actual, implied, or apparent authority, the SBA was not liable.[5]

---

[4] *Nelson v. American-West African Line, Inc.,* 86 F.2d 730, 1936 U.S. App. LEXIS 3841 (2d Cir. 1936), and *Thompson v. United States,* 504 F. Supp. 1087, 1980 U.S. Dist. LEXIS 15834 (D.S.D. 1980).

[5] *Midwest Knitting Mills, Inc. v. United States,* 741 F. Supp. 1345, 1990 U.S. Dist. LEXIS 8663 (E.D. Wis. 1990).

Agent's Liability for Torts

The focus of this chapter has been on the principal's liability for the agent's torts. But it is important to remember that **agents are always liable for their own torts.** Agents who commit torts are personally responsible, whether or not their principal is also liable.

This rule makes obvious sense. If the agent were not liable, he would have little incentive to be careful. Imagine Hank driving his delivery van for Jane. If he were not personally liable for his own torts, he might think, "If I drive fast enough, I can make it through that light even though it just turned red. And if I don't, what the heck, it'll be Jane's problem, not mine." Agents, as a rule, may have fewer assets than their principal, but it is important that their personal assets be at risk in the event of their negligent behavior.

If the agent and principal are both liable, which does the injured third party sue? The principal and the agent are jointly and severally liable, which means, as we have seen, that the injured third party can sue either one or both, as she chooses. If she recovers from the principal, he can sue the agent.

Chapter Conclusion

Most people will, at some point in their lives, serve as a principal and as an agent. This is particularly true for those in business—few businesses operate without agents. Though essential, the agent-principal relationship is nonetheless a potential landmine of liability. By understanding agency law, principals and agents can both avoid liability.

Chapter Review

1. A principal is bound by the contracts of the agent if the agent has express, implied, or apparent authority.

2. The principal grants express authority by words or conduct that reasonably cause the agent to believe the principal desires her to act on the principal's account.

3. Authority to conduct a transaction includes authority to do acts that are reasonably necessary to accomplish it.

4. Apparent authority means that a principal is liable for the acts of an agent who is not, in fact, acting with authority if the principal's conduct causes a third party reasonably to believe that the agent is authorized.

5. The principal, but not the agent, is liable for any contract the agent makes on behalf of a fully disclosed principal. In the case of a partially disclosed or undis-

closed principal, both the agent and the principal are liable on the contract.

6. Under *respondeat superior,* a master is liable when a servant acting within the scope of employment commits a negligent tort that causes physical harm to a person or property. Under some limited circumstances, a master is also liable for a servant's intentional torts.

7. The principal is only liable for the physical torts of an independent contractor if the principal has been negligent in hiring or supervising him.

8. A principal is liable for nonphysical torts only if the servant acts with actual, implied, or apparent authority.

9. Agents are always liable for their own torts.

PRACTICE TEST

Matching Questions

Match the following terms with their definitions:

___ **A.** Apparent authority.

___ **B.** Fully disclosed principal.

___ **C.** Implied authority.

___ **D.** Partially disclosed principal.

___ **E.** Express authority.

1. The principal indicates that he desires the agent to act on his behalf.

2. Behavior by a principal convinces a third party that the agent is authorized, even though she is not.

3. The third party knows of the existence of, but not the identity of, the principal.

4. The third party knows of the existence and identity of the principal.

5. An agent has authority to do acts that are necessary to accomplish an assignment.

True/False Questions

Circle true or false:

1. T F An intermediary agent is someone who hires a subagent.

2. T F A principal is generally not liable for the acts of a subagent.

3. T F A principal is always liable on a contract, whether he is fully disclosed, partially disclosed or undisclosed.

4. T F When a contract goes wrong, a third party can always recover damages from the agent, whether the principal is fully disclosed, partially disclosed or undisclosed.

5. T F If an agent has no authority, then she is not liable to the third party.

Multiple-Choice Questions

6. CPA QUESTION: A principal will not be liable to a third party for a tort committed by an agent:

(a) Unless the principal instructed the agent to commit the tort.

(b) Unless the tort was committed within the scope of the agency relationship.

(c) If the agency agreement limits the principal's liability for the agent's tort.

(d) If the tort is also regarded as a criminal act.

7. CPA QUESTION: Cox engaged Datz as her agent. It was mutually agreed that Datz would not disclose that he was acting as Cox's agent. Instead he was to deal with prospective customers as if he were a principal acting on his own behalf. This he did and made several contracts for Cox. Assuming Cox, Datz, or the customer seeks to avoid liability on one of the contracts involved, which of the following statements is correct?

(a) Cox must ratify the Datz contracts in order to be held liable.

(b) Datz has no liability once he discloses that Cox was the real principal.

(c) The third party can avoid liability because he believed he was dealing with Datz as a principal.

(d) The third party may choose to hold either Datz or Cox liable.

8. In which of the following circumstances is the principal not necessarily bound by the acts of the agent?

(a) The agent has authority.

(b) The principal is undisclosed.

(c) The principal ratifies the acts of the agent.

(d) The agent is an independent contractor.

(e) The principal is partially disclosed.

9. Someone painting the outside of a building you own crashed through a window, injuring a visiting executive. Which of the following questions would your lawyer *not* need to ask to determine if the painter was your servant?

   (a) Did the painter work full-time for you?

   (b) Had you checked the painter's references?

   (c) Was the painter paid by the hour or the job?

   (d) Were you in the painting business?

   (e) Did the painter consider herself your employee?

10. Which of the following activities committed by an agent is *not* likely to create liability for the principal?

   (a) A car accident while driving to work.

   (b) Accidentally spilling a glass of water in the company cafeteria, causing another employee to fall.

   (c) Beating up a visitor because he was rude to the company receptionist.

   (d) A truck accident while driving drunk in the middle of the workday.

   (e) Accidentally catching the building on fire while taking a smoking break.

Short-Answer Questions

11. This article appeared in *The New York Times:*

    > A week after criminal charges were announced in the death of tennis star Vitas Gerulaitis, his mother filed suit yesterday against eight defendants, including the owner of the Long Island estate where Mr. Gerulaitis died of carbon monoxide poisoning last fall. Prosecutors have charged that a new swimming pool heater, installed at a cost of $8,000, was improperly vented and sent deadly fumes into a pool house where Mr. Gerulaitis was taking a nap. The lawsuit accuses the companies that manufactured, installed and maintained the pool heater, and the mechanic who installed it, with negligence and reckless disregard for human life. It makes similar charges against the owners of the oceanfront estate, Beatrice Raynes and her son Martin, a real-estate executive.[6]

    Why would the owners of the estate be liable?

12. ETHICS: Dr. James Leonard wrote Dr. Edward Jacobson offering him the position of Chief of Audiology at Jefferson Medical College in Philadelphia. In the letter, Leonard stated that this appointment would have to be approved by the promotion and appointment committee. Jacobson believed that the appointment committee acted only as a "rubber stamp" affirming whatever recommendation Leonard made. Jacobson accepted Leonard's offer and proceeded to sell his house and quit his job in Colorado. You can guess what happened next. Two weeks later, Leonard sent Jacobson another letter, rescinding his offer because of opposition from the appointment committee. On what grounds could Jacobson bring a lawsuit? Would he prevail? Regardless of the medical school's legal obligation, does the appointment committee have an ethical obligation to Dr. Jacobson? Would any of the questions on the ethics checklist in Chapter 2 make the committee members think twice about what they have done?

13. A. B. Rains worked as a broker for the Joseph Denunzio Fruit Co. Raymond Crane offered to sell Rains nine carloads of emperor grapes. Rains accepted the offer on behalf of Denunzio. Later, Rains and Denunzio discovered that Crane was an agent for John Kazanjian. Who is liable on this contract?

14. Roy Watson bought vacuum cleaners from T & F Distributing Co. and then resold them door-to-door. He was an independent contractor. Before hiring Watson, the president of T & F checked with two of his former employers but could not remember if he called Watson's two references. Watson had an extensive criminal record, primarily under the alias Leroy Turner, but he was listed in FBI records under both Leroy Turner and Roy Watson. T & F granted Watson sales territory that included Neptune City, New Jersey. This city required that all "peddlers" such as Watson be licensed. Applicants for this license were routinely fingerprinted. T & F never insisted that Watson apply for such a license. Watson attacked Miriam Bennett after selling a vacuum cleaner to her at her home in Neptune City. Is T & F liable to Bennett?

---

[6] Vivian S. Toy, "Gerulaitis's Mother Files Suit in Son's Carbon Monoxide Death," *The New York Times*, June 1, 1995, p. B5.

15. Sara Kearns went to an auction at Christie's to bid on a tapestry for her employer, Nardin Fine Arts Gallery. The good news is that she purchased a Dufy tapestry for $77,000. The bad news is that it was not the one her employer had told her to buy. In the excitement of the auction, she forgot her instructions. Nardin refused to pay, and Christie's filed suit. Is Nardin liable for the unauthorized act of its agent?

16. Jack and Rita Powers purchased 312 head of cattle at an auction conducted by Coffeyville Livestock Sales Co. They did not know who owned the cattle they bought. The Powers, in turn, sold 159 of this lot to Leonard Hoefling. He sued the Powers, alleging the cattle were diseased and dying in large numbers, and recovered $38,360. Are the Powers entitled to reimbursement from Coffeyville?

17. ROLE REVERSAL: Write a multiple choice question that deals with the liability of principals for the acts of their servants.

Internet Research Problem

Acting as an undisclosed principal, William Zeckendorf employed agents to purchase the land in New York on which the United Nations headquarters was ultimately built. Can you find any other examples on the Internet of business dealings in which agents made purchases for an undisclosed principal? Were these business arrangements ethical? What risks did the agents face?

You can find further practice problems in the Online Quiz at **http://beatty.westbuslaw.com** or in the Study Guide that accompanies this text.

Employment Law

"On the killing beds you were apt to be covered with blood, and it would freeze solid; if you leaned against a pillar, you would freeze to that, and if you put your hand upon the blade of your knife, you would run a chance of leaving your skin on it. The men would tie up their feet in newspapers and old sacks, and these would be soaked in blood and frozen, and then soaked again, and so on, until by nighttime a man would be walking on great lumps the size of the feet of an elephant. Now and then, when the bosses were not looking, you would see them plunging their feet and ankles into the steaming hot carcass of the steer . . . The cruelest thing of all was that nearly all of them—all of those who used knives—were unable to wear gloves, and their arms would be white with frost and their hands would grow numb, and then of course there would be accidents."[1]

---

[1] From Upton Sinclair, *The Jungle* (New York: Bantam Books, 1981), p. 80, a 1906 novel about the meat-packing industry.

Introduction

For most of history, the concept of career planning was unknown. By and large, people were born into their jobs. Whatever their parents had been—landowner, soldier, farmer, servant, merchant, or beggar—they became, too. Few people expected that their lives would be better than their parents'. The primary English law of employment reflected this simpler time. Unless the employee had a contract that said otherwise, he was hired for a year at a time. This rule was designed to prevent injustice in a farming society. If an employee worked through harvest time, the landowner could not fire him in the winter. Likewise, a worker could not stay the winter and then leave for greener pastures in the spring.

In the 18th and 19th centuries, the Industrial Revolution profoundly altered the employment relationship. Many workers left the farms and villages for large factories in the city. Bosses no longer knew their workers personally, so they felt little responsibility toward them. Since employees could quit their factory jobs whenever they wanted, it was thought to be only fair for employers to have the same freedom to fire a worker. Unless workers had an explicit employment contract, they were employees at will. **An *employee at will* could be fired for a good reason, a bad reason, or no reason at all.**

However evenhanded this common-law rule of employment may have sounded in theory, in practice it could lead to harsh results. The lives of factory workers were grim.[2] It was not as if they could simply pack up and leave; conditions were no better elsewhere. Courts and legislatures began to recognize that individual workers were generally unable to negotiate fair contracts with powerful employers. Since the beginning of the 20th century, employment law has changed dramatically. Now, the employment relationship is more strictly regulated by statutes and by the common law. **No longer can a boss discharge an employee for any reason whatsoever.**

Note that many of the statutes discussed in this chapter were passed by Congress and therefore apply nationally. The common law, however, comes from state courts and only applies locally. We will look at a sampling of cases that illustrates national trends, even though the law may not be the same in every state.

This chapter covers three topics in employment law: (1) employment security; (2) safety and privacy in the workplace; and (3) financial protection. Another important topic, employment discrimination, is covered in Chapter 31.

Employment Security

NATIONAL LABOR RELATIONS ACT

Without unions to represent employee interests, employers could simply fire any troublemaking workers who complained about conditions in factories or mines. By joining together, workers could bargain with their employers on more equal terms. Naturally, the owners fought against the unions, firing organizers and even hiring goons to beat them up. Distressed by anti-union violence, Congress passed

---

[2] For examples of some truly grim modern jobs, work your way over to **http://www.worstjob.com**.

the National Labor Relations Act in 1935. Known as the NLRA or the Wagner Act, this statute:

- Prohibits employers from penalizing workers who engage in union activity (for example, joining or forming a union); and

- Requires employers to "bargain in good faith" with unions.

FAMILY AND MEDICAL LEAVE ACT

When Randy Seale's wife went into premature labor with triplets, he stayed home from his job as a truck driver with Associated Milk Producers, Inc. However, the milk of human kindness did not flow in this company's veins: It promptly fired the expectant father. Since Seale was an employee at will, the company's action would have been perfectly legal without the Family and Medical Leave Act (FMLA).

The FMLA guarantees both men and women up to 12 weeks of unpaid leave each year for childbirth, adoption, or medical emergencies for themselves or a family member. An employee who takes a leave must be allowed to return to the same or an equivalent job with the same pay and benefits. The FMLA applies only to companies with at least 50 workers and to employees who have been with the company full time for at least a year—this is about 60% of all employees. The milk company ultimately agreed to pay Seale $10,000 for its violation of the FMLA. The Labor Department answers questions about this statute at **http://www.dol.gov/dol/esa/fmla.htm**.

WRONGFUL DISCHARGE

Olga Monge was a schoolteacher in her native Costa Rica. After moving to New Hampshire, she attended college in the evenings to earn a U.S. teaching degree. At night, she worked at the Beebe Rubber Co. During the day, she cared for her husband and three children. When she applied for a better job at her plant, the foreman offered to promote her if she would be "nice" and go out on a date with him. When she refused, he assigned her to a lower-wage job, took away her overtime, made her clean the washrooms, and ridiculed her. Finally, she collapsed at work and he fired her.

At that time an employee at will could be fired for any reason. But the New Hampshire Supreme Court decided to change the rule. It held that Monge's firing was a **wrongful discharge. Under the principle of** *wrongful discharge,* **an employer cannot fire a worker for a bad reason.** There are three categories of wrongful discharge claims: public policy, contract law, and tort law.

Public Policy

The *Monge* case is an example of the public policy rule. **This rule prohibits an employer from firing a worker for a reason that violates basic social rights, duties, or responsibilities.** The courts have primarily applied the public policy rule to protect an employee who has refused to violate the law or has insisted upon exercising a legal right or performing a legal duty.

Refusing to Violate the Law. Larry Downs went to Duke Hospital for surgery on his cleft palate. When he came out of the operating room, the doctor instructed a nurse, Marie Sides, to give Downs enough anesthetic to immobilize him. Sides refused because she thought the anesthetic was wrong for this patient. The doctor angrily administered the anesthetic himself. Shortly thereafter, Downs stopped breathing. Before the doctors could resuscitate him, he suffered permanent brain damage. When Downs's family sued the hospital, Sides was called to testify. A number of Duke doctors told her that she would be "in trouble" if she testified. She did testify and, after three months of harassment, was fired. When she sued Duke University, the court held that the university could not fire an employee for telling the truth in court.

As a general rule, employees may not be discharged for refusing to break the law. For example, courts have protected employees who refused to participate in an illegal price-fixing scheme, fake pollution control records required by state law, pollute waters in violation of federal law, or assist a supervisor in stealing from customers.

ETHICS   Does an employer *ever* have the right to require workers to participate in an illegal scheme? Suppose that state pollution control regulations would force a company out of business. When the life of the company is at stake, does the boss have a right to expect a worker to cooperate by fudging records? What guidance does the Chapter 2 Ethics Checklist offer? Is this behavior legal? How would it look in the light of day? ◼

Exercising a Legal Right.   Dorothy Frampton injured her arm while working at the Central Indiana Gas Co. Her employer (and its insurance company) paid her medical expenses and her salary during the four months she was out of work. When she discovered that she also qualified for benefits under the state's workers' compensation plan, she filed a claim and received payment. One month later, the company fired her. When she sued, the court held the company liable on the theory that if employers can penalize employees for filing workmen's compensation claims, then employees will not file and the whole purpose of the statute will be undermined. **As a general rule, an employer may not fire a worker for exercising a legal right.**

Performing a Legal Duty.   **Courts have consistently held that an employee may not be fired for serving on a jury.** Jury duty is an important civic obligation that employers are not permitted to undermine.

In the following case, an employee was fired for performing a good deed that was *not* legally required. Is that permitted?

CASE SUMMARY

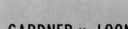

GARDNER v. LOOMIS ARMORED, INC.

913 P.2d 377, 1996 Wash. LEXIS 109 (1996)
Supreme Court of Washington

FACTS: Kevin Gardner had just parked his armored truck in front of a bank in Spokane, Washington, when he saw a man with a knife chase the manager out of the bank. While running past the truck, the manager looked directly at Gardner and yelled,

"Help me, help me." Gardner got out of his truck and locked its door. By then, the suspect had grabbed another woman, put his knife to her throat, and dragged her into the bank. Gardner followed them in, tackled the suspect, and disarmed him. The rescued woman hailed Gardner as a hero, but his employer fired him for violating a company rule that prohibited drivers from leaving their armored trucks unattended.

ISSUE: Does the public policy doctrine protect an employee who performs a good deed that is not legally required?

DECISION: The company did not have the right to fire Gardner.

REASONING: The court held for Gardner on the grounds that, although he had no legal duty to assist in such a situation, society values and encourages people to help out when a life is in danger. ◢

Whistleblowing. FMC Corp. sold 9,000 Bradley Fighting Vehicles to the U.S. Army for as much as $1.5 million each. But it was not clear the Bradley worked. Designed to carry soldiers around battlefields in Eastern Europe, its ability to "swim" across rivers and lakes was an important part of its job description. But Henry Boisvert, a testing supervisor for FMC, charged that the Bradley swam like a rock. He had one driven into a test pond and watched it quickly fill with water. FMC welders who worked on Bradleys claimed they were not given enough time to do their work properly and so would simply fill gaps with putty. FMC fired Boisvert when he refused to sign a false report. The jury sided with him.[3]

No one likes to be accused of wrongdoing even if (or, perhaps, especially if) the accusations are true. **This is exactly what whistleblowers do: They are employees who disclose illegal behavior on the part of their employer.** Not surprisingly, many companies, when faced with such an accusation by an employee, prefer to shoot the messenger.

Whistleblowers are protected in the following situations:

- *The False Claims Act.* Henry Boisvert refused to sign his name to a report he thought was inaccurate. As a result, he earned the right to sign a check from FMC for about $20 million. Boisvert recovered under the federal False Claims Act, a statute that permits anyone to bring suit against someone who defrauds the government. The Act also prohibits employers from firing workers who file suit under the statute. A successful whistleblower receives between 15% and 30% of any damages awarded to the government.

- *Employees of Public Companies.* The Sarbanes-Oxley Act of 2002 protects employees of public companies who provide evidence of fraud to investigators. A successful plaintiff must be rehired and given back pay.

- *Common Law.* Most state courts do not permit employers to fire workers who report illegal activity. For example, a Connecticut court held a company liable when it fired a quality control director who reported to his boss that some products had failed quality tests.

Thinking about blowing a whistle? The Web site **http://www.whistleblower.org** offers advice.

Contract Law

Traditionally, many employers (and employees) thought that only a formal, signed document qualified as an employment contract. Increasingly, however, courts

---

[3] Lee Gomes, "A Whistle-Blower Finds Jackpot at the End of His Quest," *The Wall Street Journal*, April 27, 1998, p. B1.

have been willing to enforce an employer's more casual promises, whether written or oral. Sometimes courts have also been willing to *imply* contract terms even when there is no *express* agreement.

Truth in Hiring. When the Tanana Valley Medical–Surgical Group, Inc. hired James Eales as a physician's assistant, it promised him that as long as he did his job, he could stay there until retirement age. Six years later the company fired him without cause. The Alaska Supreme Court held **oral promises made during the hiring process are enforceable.**

Employee Handbooks. The employee handbook at Blue Cross & Blue Shield stated that employees could be fired only for just cause and then only after warnings, notice, a hearing, and other procedures. Charles Toussaint was fired without warning five years after he joined the company. The court held that **an employee handbook creates a contract.**

Employers are now taking steps to protect themselves from liability for implied contracts. Some employers require new hires to sign a document admitting that (1) they are employees at will; (2) they can be terminated at any time for any reason; and (3) no one at the company has made any oral representations concerning the terms of employment. ◾

Tort Law

Workers have successfully sued their employers under the following tort theories.

Defamation. After Dean Witter fired John R. Glennon, Jr. as branch manager of the Nashville office it filed a notice with the National Association of Securities Dealers saying that Glennon had violated the law. This statement was untrue, and Witter had to pay $1.5 million in damages for defamation. **Employers may be liable for defamation when they give false and unfavorable references about a former employee.**

More than half of the states, however, recognize a *qualified privilege* for employers who give references about former employees. A **qualified privilege** means that employers are liable only for false statements that they know to be false or that are primarily motivated by ill will. After Becky Chambers left her job at American Trans Air, Inc., she discovered that her former boss was telling anyone who called for a reference that Chambers "does not work good with other people," is a "troublemaker," and "would not be a good person to rehire." However, Chambers was unable to prove that her boss had been primarily motivated by ill will. Neither Trans Air nor the boss was held liable for these statements because they were protected by the qualified privilege.

Even if the employer wins, a trial is expensive and takes a lot of time. Therefore, many companies tell their managers that, when asked for a reference, they should only reveal the person's salary and dates of employment and not offer an opinion on job performance.

Employers are afraid of liability if they give a negative reference, but are they liable if they tell less than the whole truth? **Generally, courts have held that employers do not have a legal obligation to disclose information about former employees.** For example, while Jeffrey St. Clair worked at the St. Joseph Nursing Home, he was disciplined 24 times for actions ranging from extreme violence to drug and alcohol use. When he applied for a job with Maintenance Management Corp. (MMC), St. Joseph refused to give any information other than St. Clair's dates of employment. After he savagely murdered a security guard at his new job, the guard's family sued, but the court dismissed the case.

In some recent cases, however, courts have held that, when a former worker is potentially dangerous, employers do have an obligation to disclose this information. For example, officials from two junior high schools gave Robert Gadams glowing letters of recommendation without mentioning that he had been fired for inappropriate sexual conduct with students. While an assistant principal at a new school, he molested a 13-year-old. Her parents sued the former employers. The court held that the writer of a letter of recommendation has "a duty not to misrepresent the facts in describing the qualifications and character of a former employee, if making these misrepresentations would present a substantial, foreseeable risk of physical injury to the third persons." As a result of cases such as this, it makes sense to disclose past violent behavior.

To assist employers who are asked for references, Lehigh economist Robert Thornton has written "The Lexicon of Intentional Ambiguous Recommendations" (LIAR). For a candidate with interpersonal problems, he suggests saying, "I am pleased to say that this person is a former colleague of mine." For the lazy worker, "In my opinion, you will be very fortunate to get this person to work for you." For the criminal, he suggests, "He's a man of many convictions" and "I'm sorry we let her get away." For the untrustworthy candidate, "Her true ability is deceiving."[4]

ETHICS

All joking aside, what if someone calls you to check references on a former employee who had a drinking problem? The job is driving a van for junior high school sports teams. What is the manager's ethical obligation in this situation? Many managers say that, in the case of a serious problem such as alcoholism, sexual harassment, or drug use, they will find a way to communicate that an employee is unsuitable. What if the ex-employee says she is reformed? Aren't people entitled to a second chance? Is it right to risk a defamation suit against your company to protect others from harm? What solutions does the Ethics Checklist in Chapter 2 suggest? Would it be just to reveal private information about a former employee? Is the process fair if you provide information that the job applicant has no opportunity to rebut because it is kept secret?

Intentional Infliction of Emotional Distress. **Employers who permit cruel treatment of their workers face liability under the tort of intentional infliction of emotional distress.** For example, the employer was held liable in the following cases:

- When a 57-year-old social work manager at Yale–New Haven Hospital was fired, she was forced to place her personal belongings in a plastic bag and was escorted out the door by security guards in full view of gaping coworkers. A supervisor told her that she would be arrested for trespassing if she returned. A jury awarded her $105,000.

- An employee swore at a coworker and threatened her with a knife because she rejected his sexual advances. Her superiors fired her for complaining about the incident.

---

[4] *The Wall Street Journal,* Mar. 22, 1994, p. 1.

SAFETY AND PRIVACY IN THE WORKPLACE

Workplace Safety

Congress passed the Occupational Safety and Health Act (OSHA) to ensure safe working conditions. Under OSHA:

- Employers are under a general obligation to keep their workplace free from hazards that could cause serious harm to employees.

- Employers must comply with specific health and safety standards. For example, health care personnel who work with blood are not permitted to eat or drink in areas where the blood is kept and must not put their mouths on any instruments used to store blood.

- Employers must keep records of all workplace injuries and accidents.

- The Occupational Safety and Health Administration (also known as OSHA) may inspect workplaces to ensure that they are safe. OSHA may assess fines for violations and order employers to correct unsafe conditions.

OSHA has done a lot to make the American workplace safer. In 1900, roughly 35,000 workers died and 350,000 were injured at work. One hundred years later, the workforce had grown five times larger but the number of annual deaths had fallen to 5,100.

EMPLOYEE PRIVACY

Upon opening the country's first moving assembly line in the early 1900s, Henry Ford issued a booklet, "Helpful Hints and Advice to Employees," that warned against drinking, gambling, borrowing money, taking in boarders, and practicing poor hygiene. Ford also created a department of 100 investigators for door-to-door checks on his employees' drinking habits, sexual practices, and housekeeping skills. It sounds pretty outrageous, but in modern times employees have been fired or disciplined for such extracurricular activities as playing dangerous sports, dating coworkers, or even having high cholesterol. What protection do workers have against intrusive employers?

Off-Duty Conduct

In an era of rapidly expanding health care costs, employers are concerned about the health of their workers. Some companies have banned off-duty smoking and have even fired employees who show traces of nicotine in their blood. In response, more than half the states have passed laws that protect the right of employees to smoke cigarettes while off duty. Some of these statutes permit any lawful activity when off duty, including drinking socially, having high cholesterol, being overweight, or engaging in dangerous hobbies—bungee jumping or rollerblading, for instance.

Alcohol and Drug Testing

Government employees can be tested for drug and alcohol use only if they show signs of use or if they are in a job where this type of abuse endangers the public. Most states permit private employers to administer alcohol and drug tests. According to one survey, more than 80% of large firms test employees for drugs.

Lie Detector Tests

Under the Employee Polygraph Protection Act of 1988, employers may not require, or even suggest, that an employee or job candidate submit to a lie detector test, except as part of an "ongoing investigation" into crimes that have occurred.

Electronic Monitoring of the Workplace

Technological advances in communications have raised a host of new privacy issues.

CYBERLAW

The Electronic Communications Privacy Act of 1986 (ECPA) permits employers to monitor workers' telephone calls and e-mail messages if (1) the employee consents; (2) the monitoring occurs in the ordinary course of business; or (3) in the case of e-mail, the employer provides the e-mail system. However, bosses may not disclose any private information revealed by the monitoring.

Although many workers feel that their e-mail should be private, employers argue that this monitoring improves employee productivity and protects the company from lawsuits. For example, a West Coast company fired a woman "because of a tough economy." When she sued, her attorneys demanded access to the company's e-mail system as part of the discovery process. They found a message from the woman's supervisor saying, "Get that bitch out of here as fast as you can. I don't care what it takes. Just do it." The supervisor had long since erased the message from his computer, but it had remained buried in the system. A few hours after the message was revealed in court, the company settled for $250,000. If the employee had known that his e-mail would be read by others, perhaps he would not have sent such an inflammatory statement.

Almost two thirds of companies also monitor employee use of the Internet. They are concerned not only about lawsuits but also that workers may be wasting time. During one month, employees at IBM, Apple Computer, and AT&T logged on to *Penthouse* magazine's Web site 12,823 times, using the equivalent of more than 347 workdays. Companies fear that even legal logging on to sexually explicit sites may give rise to sexual harassment claims. ◾

In the following case, two employees used company e-mail to trash-talk. Could they be fired for their indiscretion?

YOU BE THE JUDGE

MICHAEL A. SMYTH v. THE PILLSBURY CO.

914 F. Supp. 97, 1996 U.S. Dist. LEXIS 776
United States District Court for the Eastern District of Pennsylvania, 1996

FACTS: The Pillsbury Co. repeatedly assured its employees that all company e-mail was confidential. The company promised not to intercept e-mail or use it against employees. One evening at home, Michael Smyth and his supervisor engaged in a series of e-mail exchanges that threatened to "kill the backstabbing bastards" (that is, company sales managers) and referred to the planned holiday party as the "Jim Jones Koolaid affair." The company found out about these e-mails and fired both men. Smyth sued, alleging that the company had violated his right to privacy.

YOU BE THE JUDGE: Should employee e-mail be private if the company promises that it is?

ARGUMENT FOR SMYTH: Pillsbury violated Smyth's privacy rights because:

- It intruded into Smyth's life in a manner that any reasonable person would find offensive.

- Smyth had a reasonable expectation of privacy. The company had told him repeatedly that it would not read his e-mail.

ARGUMENT FOR PILLSBURY: The company had no choice but to fire him after he made death threats against other employees. What if the company had done nothing and he had carried out those threats? Furthermore, Smyth could not have a reasonable expectation of privacy with an e-mail system that the company established and maintained for the use of its employees. ▰

Financial Protection

Congress and the states have enacted laws that provide employees with a measure of financial security. All of the laws in this section were created by statute, not by the courts.

FAIR LABOR STANDARDS ACT

The Fair Labor Standards Act (FLSA) regulates wages and limits child labor. The wage provisions do not apply to managerial, administrative, or professional staff, which means that accounting, consulting, and law firms (among others) are free to require as many hours a week as their employees can humanly perform without having to pay overtime or the minimum wage.

The FLSA:

- Does not limit the number of hours a week that an employee can work but it does specify that **workers must be paid time and a half for any hours over 40 in one week.**

- **Prohibits "oppressive child labor,"** which means that children under 14 may work only in agriculture and entertainment. Fourteen- and 15-year-olds are permitted to work limited hours after school in nonhazardous jobs. Sixteen- and 17-year-olds may work unlimited hours in nonhazardous jobs.

- **Sets the federal minimum wage. It is currently $5.15 per hour,** although some states have established a higher minimum.

UPDATE Check the Department of Labor Web site **http://www.dol.gov** to see if Congress has raised the minimum wage. ▰

WORKERS' COMPENSATION

Workers' compensation statutes provide payment to employees for injuries incurred at work. In return, employees are not permitted to sue their employers for negligence. The amounts allowed (for medical expenses and lost wages) under workers' comp statutes are often less than a worker might recover in court, but the injured employee trades the certainty of some recovery for the higher risk of rolling the dice at trial.

SOCIAL SECURITY

The federal Social Security system began in 1935, during the depths of the Great Depression, to provide a basic safety net for the elderly, ill, and unemployed. **The Social Security system pays benefits to workers who are retired, disabled, or temporarily unemployed and to the spouses and children of disabled or deceased workers.** It also provides medical insurance to the retired and disabled. The Social Security program is financed through a tax on wages that is paid by employers, employees, and the self-employed.

Although the Social Security system has done much to reduce poverty among the elderly, many worry that it cannot survive in its current form. When workers pay taxes, the proceeds do not go into a savings account for their retirement, but instead are used to pay benefits to current retirees. In 1940, there were 40 workers for each retiree; currently, there are 3.3. By 2030, when the last Baby Boomers retire, there will be only two workers to support each retiree—a prohibitive burden. No wonder Baby Boomers are often cautioned not to count on Social Security when making their retirement plans.

The Federal Unemployment Tax Act (FUTA) is the part of the Social Security system that provides support to the unemployed. FUTA establishes some national standards, but states are free to set their own benefit levels and payment schedules. While receiving payments, a worker must make a good-faith effort to look for other employment. A worker who quits voluntarily or is fired for just cause is not entitled to benefits.

Chapter Conclusion

Although managers sometimes feel overwhelmed by the long list of laws that protect workers, the United States guarantees its workers fewer rights than virtually any other industrialized nation. For instance, Japan, Great Britain, France, Germany, and Canada all require employers to show just cause before terminating workers. Although American employers are no longer insulated from minimum standards of fairness, reasonable behavior, and compliance with important policies, they still have great freedom to manage their employees.

Chapter Review

1. Traditionally, an employee at will could be fired for a good reason, a bad reason, or no reason at all. This right is now modified by common law and by statute.

2. The National Labor Relations Act prohibits employers from penalizing workers for union activity.

3. The Family and Medical Leave Act guarantees workers

up to 12 weeks of unpaid leave each year for childbirth, adoption, or medical emergencies for themselves or a family member.

4. An employer who fires a worker for a bad reason is liable under a theory of wrongful discharge.

5. Generally, an employee may not be fired for refusing to break the law, exercising a legal right, or performing a legal duty.

6. Whistleblowers receive some protection under both federal and state laws.

7. Oral promises made during the hiring process may be enforceable. An employee handbook may create a contract.

8. Employers may be liable for defamation if they give false and unfavorable references.

9. The goal of the Occupational Safety and Health Act is to ensure safe conditions in the workplace.

10. The Electronic Communications Privacy Act of 1986 permits employers to monitor workers' telephone calls and e-mail messages if (1) the employee consents, (2) the monitoring occurs in the ordinary course of business, or (3) in the case of e-mail, the employer provides the e-mail system.

11. The Fair Labor Standards Act regulates minimum and overtime wages. It also limits child labor.

12. Workers' compensation statutes ensure that employees receive payment for injuries incurred at work.

13. The Social Security system pays benefits to workers who are retired, disabled, or temporarily unemployed and to the spouses and children of disabled or deceased workers.

PRACTICE TEST

Matching Questions

Match the following terms with their definitions:

___ **A.** Employee at will.

___ **B.** Public policy rule.

___ **C.** FLSA.

___ **D.** Wrongful discharge.

___ **E.** OSHA.

___ **F.** Whistleblower.

1. A federal statute that ensures safe working conditions.

2. When an employee is fired for a bad reason.

3. An employee who discloses illegal behavior on the part of his employer.

4. An employee without an explicit employment contract.

5. A federal statute that regulates wages and limits child labor.

6. An employer may not fire a worker for a reason that violates basic social rights, duties or responsibilities.

True/False Questions

Circle true or false:

1. T F An employee may be fired for a good reason, a bad reason, or no reason at all.

2. T F An employee may be fired if she disobeys a direct order from her boss not to join a labor union.

3. T F Promises made by the employer during the hiring process are not enforceable.

4. T F In some states, an employer is not liable for false statements they make about former employees unless they know these statements are false or are primarily motivated by ill will.

5. T F The federal government has the right to inspect workplaces to ensure that they are safe.

6. T F Any employer has the right to insist that employees submit to a lie detector test.

7. T F Federal law limits the number of hours an employee can work.

8. T F Children under 16 may not hold paid jobs.

9. T F Only workers, not their spouses or children, are entitled to benefits under the Social Security system.

Multiple-Choice Questions

10. Mike is an employee at will. "You're fired!," says Regina, his boss. "Why?" asks Mike. "Never mind why," Regina replies. "I can fire you for any reason at all. Scram!" Can Regina fire Mike for any reason at all?

    (a) Yes.

    (b) Regina must have a good reason to fire Mike if he has worked at the firm for more than one year.

    (c) Regina may fire Mike if he is out for more than three weeks while serving on a jury.

    (d) Regina may not fire Mike for logging onto pornographic Web sites at work.

    (e) Regina may not fire Mike for testifying in court that Regina was violating federal pollution laws.

11. Under the Family and Medical Leave Act:

    (a) Both men and women are entitled to leave from their jobs for childbirth, adoption, or medical emergencies.

    (b) An employee is entitled to 12 weeks of paid leave.

    (c) An employee is entitled to leave to care for any member of his household, including pets.

    (d) An employee who takes a leave is entitled to return to the exact job she left.

    (e) All employees in the country are covered.

12. Under the public policy doctrine:

    (a) An employee can be fired for any reason.

    (b) An employee can be fired for threatening a coworker.

    (c) An employee can be fired for filing a workers' compensation claim.

    (d) An employee can be fired for violating company policy even if he does so to save someone's life.

    (e) An employee can be fired for refusing to lie under oath on the witness stand.

13. A whistleblower

    (a) Is always protected by the law.

    (b) Is never protected by the law.

    (c) Is always protected when filing suit under the False Claims Act.

    (d) Is always protected if she is an employee of the federal government.

    (e) Is always protected if she works for a private company.

14. Jack was furious when Hermione left the company in the middle of a very busy sales period. He promised that he would get even with her. Another employer called to check Hermione's references. Which of the following statements should Jack make, if his goal is to limit his company's potential liability?

    (a) Hermione was generally a good worker, but she was often late arriving at the office. (This is true.)

    (b) Hermione tried to run over a coworker with her car. (This is true.)

    (c) Hermione wore inappropriate clothing. (This is not true.)

    (d) Hermione doesn't know her debits from her credits (This is not true.)

    (e) Hermione worked for this company for a year and a half. Her title was Chief Knowledge Officer. (This is true.)

15. CPA QUESTION: An unemployed CPA generally would receive unemployment compensation benefits if the CPA:

    (a) Was fired as a result of the employer's business reversals.

    (b) Refused to accept a job as an accountant while receiving extended benefits.

    (c) Was fired for embezzling from a client.

    (d) Left work voluntarily without good cause.

Short-Answer Questions

16. When Theodore Staats went to his company's "Council of Honor Convention," he was accompanied by a woman who was not his wife, although he told everyone she was. The company fired him. Has Staats's employer violated public policy?

17. ETHICS: When Walton Weiner interviewed for a job with McGraw-Hill, Inc., he was assured that the company would not terminate an employee without "just cause." McGraw-Hill's handbook said, "[The] company will resort to dismissal for just and sufficient cause only, and only after all practical steps toward rehabilitation or salvage of the employee have been taken and failed. However, if the welfare of the company indicates that dismissal is necessary, then that decision is arrived at and is carried out forthrightly." After eight years, Weiner was fired suddenly for "lack of application." Does Weiner have a valid claim against McGraw-Hill? Apart from the legal issue, did McGraw-Hill do the right thing? Was the process fair? Did the company's behavior violate important values?

18. Debra Agis worked in a Ground Round restaurant. The manager, Roger Dionne, informed the waitresses that "there was some stealing going on." Until he found out who was doing it, he intended to fire all the waitresses in alphabetical order, starting with the letter "A." Dionne then fired Agis. Does she have a valid claim against her employer?

19. Reginald Delaney managed a Taco Time restaurant in Portland, Oregon. Some of his customers told Mr. Ledbetter, the district manager, that they would not be eating there so often because there were too many black employees. Ledbetter told Delaney to fire Ms. White, who was black. Delaney did as he was told. Ledbetter's report on the incident said: "My notes show that Delaney told me that White asked him to sleep with her and that when he would not that she started causing dissension within the crew. She asked him to come over to her house and that he declined." Delaney refused to sign the report because it was untrue, so Ledbetter fired him. What claim might Delaney make against his former employer?

20. Nationwide Insurance Co. circulated a memorandum asking all employees to lobby in favor of a bill that had been introduced in the Pennsylvania House of Representatives. By limiting the damages that an injured motorist could recover from a person who caused an accident, this bill would have saved Nationwide significant money. Not only did John Novosel refuse to lobby, but he privately criticized the bill for harming consumers. Nationwide was definitely not on his side—it fired him. Novosel filed suit, alleging that his discharge had violated public policy by infringing his right to free speech. Did Nationwide violate public policy by firing Novosel?

21. ROLE REVERSAL: Prepare a short-answer question in which an employee alleges that his discharge violated public policy, but you think a court would not agree.

Internet Research Problem

Go to the Web site of a newspaper in your area or a national newspaper such as *The Wall Street Journal, USA Today,* or *The New York Times.* Find an article that deals with an employment law issue and write a short summary of the issue and the outcome.

Employment Discrimination

Imagine that you are on the hiring committee of a top San Francisco law firm. Sitting at your desk sorting through resumés, you come across one from a candidate who grew up on an isolated ranch in Arizona. Raised in a house without electricity or running water, he had worked alongside the ranch hands his entire childhood. At the age of 16, he had left home for Stanford University and from there he had gone on to Stanford law School, where he finished third in his class. "Hm," you think to yourself, "sounds like a real American success story. A great combination of hard work and intelligence." But without hesitation you toss the resumé into the wastebasket. No way you would consider hiring him.

This is a true story. Indeed, there was a candidate with these credentials who was unable to find a job in any San Francisco law firm. The only jobs on offer were as a secretary, because this candidate was a woman—Sandra Day O'Connor, who went on to become the first woman Supreme Court Justice and one of the most influential lawyers of her era. But when she graduated from law school, that is the way the world was. In the last four decades, Congress has enacted important legislation to prevent discrimination in the workplace. ▪▫

Equal Pay Act of 1963

Under the Equal Pay Act, an employee may not be paid at a lesser rate than employees of the opposite sex for equal work. "Equal work" means tasks that require equal skill, effort, and responsibility under similar working conditions. If the employee proves that she is not being paid equally, the employer will be found liable unless the pay difference is based on merit, productivity, seniority, or some factor other than sex. A "factor other than sex" includes prior wages, training, profitability, performance in an interview, and value to the company. For example, female agents sued Allstate Insurance Co. because its salary for new agents was based, in part, on prior salary. The women argued that this system was unfair because it perpetuated the historic wage differences between men and women. The court, however, held for Allstate.

To find out how much less women earn than men, in spite of the Equal Pay Act, click on **http://www.aflcio.org/issuespolitics/women/equalpay/calculate.cfm**. This site calculates how much the pay gap will cost a woman over her lifetime.

Title VII

Title VII of the Civil Rights Act of 1964 prohibits employers from discriminating on the basis of race, color, religion, sex, or national origin. (The text of Title VII is available at **http://www.eeoc.gov/abouteeo/overview_laws.html**.) Title VII prohibits (1) discrimination in the workplace; (2) sexual harassment; and (3) discrimination because of pregnancy. It also permits employers to develop affirmative action plans.

Discrimination under Title VII means firing, refusing to hire, failing to promote, or otherwise reducing a person's employment opportunities because of race, color, religion, sex, or national origin. This protection applies to every stage of the employment process from job ads to postemployment references and includes placement, wages, benefits, and working conditions.

PROOF OF DISCRIMINATION

Plaintiffs in Title VII cases can prove discrimination two different ways: disparate treatment and disparate impact.

Disparate Treatment

To prove a disparate treatment case, the plaintiff must show that she was *treated differently because of her sex, race, color, religion, or national origin.* The required steps in a disparate treatment case are:

Step 1. The plaintiff presents evidence that the defendant has discriminated against her because of a protected trait. This is called a *prima facie case.* The plaintiff is not required to prove discrimination; she need only create a *presumption* that discrimination occurred.

Suppose that Louisa applies for a job coaching a boys' high school ice hockey team. She was an All-American hockey star in college. Although Louisa is obviously qualified for the job, Harry, the school principal, rejects her and continues to interview other people. This is not proof of discrimination, because Harry may have a perfectly good, nondiscriminatory explanation. However, his behavior *could have been* motivated by discrimination.

Step 2. The defendant must present evidence that its decision was based on *legitimate, nondiscriminatory* reasons. Harry might say, for example, that he wanted someone with prior coaching experience. Although Louisa is clearly a great player, she has never coached before.

Step 3. To win, the plaintiff must now prove that the employer discriminated. She may do so by showing that the reasons offered were simply a *pretext*. Louisa might show that Harry had recently hired a male tennis coach who had no prior coaching experience. Or Harry's assistant might testify that Harry said, "No way I'm going to put a woman on the ice with those guys." If she can present evidence such as this, Louisa wins.

Disparate Impact

Disparate impact becomes an issue if the employer has a rule that, *on its face*, is not discriminatory, but *in practice* excludes too many people in a protected group. The steps in a disparate impact case are:

Step 1. The plaintiff must present a *prima facie* case. The plaintiff is not required to prove discrimination; he need only show a disparate impact—that the employment practice in question excludes a disproportionate number of people in a protected group (women and minorities, for instance).

Suppose that Harry will only hire teachers who are at least 5 feet 10 inches tall and weigh 170 pounds. He says he is afraid that students will literally push around anyone smaller. When Chou Ping, an Asian male, applies for a job, he cannot meet Harry's physical requirements. Chou Ping must show that Harry's rule, *in fact*, eliminates more women or minorities than white males. He might offer evidence that 50% of all white males can meet Harry's standard, but only 20% of white women and Asian males qualify.

Step 2. The defendant must offer some evidence that the employment practice was a *job-related business necessity*. Harry might produce evidence that teachers are regularly expected to wrestle students into their classroom seats. Further, he might cite studies showing his standards are essential for this task.

Step 3. To win, the plaintiff must now prove either that the employer's reason is a *pretext* or that other, *less discriminatory* rules would achieve the same results. Chou Ping might suggest that all teachers could take a self-defense course or engage in martial arts training.

Note that the mere existence of a disparate impact does not *necessarily* mean that an employment practice violates the law. When the Illinois Law Enforcement Officers Training Board created an exam to test aspiring police officers, a higher percentage of minority applicants than white candidates failed the test. Some of the unsuccessful aspirants filed suit, alleging that the exam was illegal because it had a disparate impact. In response, the board presented evidence that the exam had been very carefully prepared by a consulting company that specialized in creating such exams. The court held that the exam was legal because it was "demonstrably a reasonable measure of job performance."

RELIGION

Employers must make *reasonable accommodation* for a worker's religious beliefs unless the request would cause *undue hardship* for the business. Scott Hamby told his manager at Wal-Mart that he could never work on Sunday because that was his Sabbath. It also happened to be one of the store's busiest days. When the manager forced Hamby to quit, he sued on the grounds of religious discrimination. Lawsuits such as his are on the rise as more businesses remain open on Sundays. Wal-Mart denied wrongdoing but settled the case with a cash payment of undisclosed amount. It also established a company-wide training program on religious accommodation.

DEFENSES TO CHARGES OF DISCRIMINATION

Under Title VII, the defendant has three possible defenses.

Merit

A defendant is not liable if he shows that the person he favored was the most qualified. Test results, education, or productivity can all be used to demonstrate merit, provided they relate to the job in question. Harry can show that he hired Bruce instead of Louisa because Bruce has a master's degree in physical education and seven years of coaching experience. On the other hand, the fact that Bruce scored higher on the National Latin Exam in the eighth grade is not a good reason to hire him over Louisa for a coaching job.

ETHICS

It is easy to say that the most qualified person should be hired or promoted. But how do you measure merit? In Santa Clara, California, no woman had ever held the job of radio dispatcher. Although Diana Joyce scored two points lower than Paul Johnson on the dispatcher exam (his score was 75/100, hers was 73), the city hired her instead of him.[1] What *should* the city do in such a case? Is this two-point difference persuasive evidence that Johnson would be a better radio dispatcher than Joyce? Would the Ethics Checklist in Chapter 2 help in making such a decision?

Seniority

A legitimate seniority system is legal, even if it perpetuates past discrimination. Suppose that Harry has always chosen the most senior assistant coach to take over as head coach when a vacancy occurs. Since the majority of the senior assistant coaches are male, most of the head coaches are, too. Such a system does not violate Title VII.

Bona Fide Occupational Qualification

An employer is permitted to establish discriminatory job requirements if they are *essential* to the position in question. Such a requirement is called a **bona fide occupational qualification (BFOQ).** Catholic schools may, if they choose, refuse to hire non-Catholic teachers; mail order companies may refuse to hire men to model women's clothing. Generally, however, courts are not sympathetic to claims of BFOQ. They have, for example, almost always rejected BFOQ claims that are based

---

[1] This case ultimately reached the U.S. Supreme Court on the issue of whether a less qualified woman could be promoted over a more qualified man. The court ruled that she could.

on customer preference. Thus airlines could not refuse to hire male flight attendants even though travelers prefer female attendants. The major exception to this customer preference rule is sexual privacy: An employer may refuse to hire women to work in a men's bathroom and vice versa.

AFFIRMATIVE ACTION

Affirmative action is not required by Title VII, nor is it prohibited. Affirmative action programs have three different sources:

- *Litigation.* Courts have the power under Title VII to order affirmative action to remedy the effects of past discrimination.

- *Voluntary Action.* Employers can voluntarily introduce an affirmative action plan to remedy the effects of past practices or to achieve equitable representation of minorities and women.

- *Government Contracts.* In 1965, President Johnson signed Executive Order 11246, which prohibits discrimination by federal contractors. This order had a profound impact on the American workplace, because one third of all workers are employed by companies that do business with the federal government. If an employer found that women or minorities were underrepresented in its workplace, it was required to establish goals and timetables to correct the deficiency.

   In 1995, however, the Supreme Court ruled that these affirmative action programs are permissible only if (1) the government can show that the programs are needed to overcome specific past discrimination; (2) they have time limits; and (3) nondiscriminatory alternatives are not available.

SEXUAL HARASSMENT

When Professor Anita Hill accused Supreme Court nominee Clarence Thomas of sexually harassing her, people across the country were glued to their televisions, watching the Senate hearings on her charges. Thomas was ultimately confirmed to the Supreme Court, but "sexual harassment" became a household phrase. The number of cases—and the size of the damage awards—skyrocketed.

   Everyone has heard of sexual harassment, but few people know exactly what it is. Men fear that a casual comment or glance will be met with career-ruining charges; women claim that men "just don't get it." So what is sexual harassment, anyway? **Sexual harassment involves unwelcome sexual advances, requests for sexual favors, and other verbal or physical conduct of a sexual nature.** There are two major categories of sexual harassment:

- *Quid Pro Quo.* From a Latin phrase that means "this for that," *quid pro quo* harassment occurs if any aspect of a job is made contingent upon sexual activity. In other words, when a banker says to a secretary, "You can be promoted to teller if you sleep with me," that is *quid pro quo* sexual harassment.

- Hostile work environment. An employee has a valid claim of sexual harassment if sexual talk and innuendo are so pervasive that they interfere with her (or his) ability to work. Courts have found that offensive jokes, comments about clothes or body parts, and public displays of pornographic pictures create a hostile environment. In the following case, the company president repeatedly insulted and demeaned his female employees.

CASE SUMMARY

TERESA HARRIS v. FORKLIFT SYSTEMS, INC.

510 U.S. 17, 114 S. Ct. 367, 1993 U.S. LEXIS 7155
United States Supreme Court, 1993

FACTS: Teresa Harris was a manager at Forklift Systems; Charles Hardy was its president. Hardy frequently made inappropriate sexual comments to Harris and other women at the company. For example, he said to Harris, in the presence of others, "You're a woman, what do you know?" and "We need a man as the rental manager." He called her "a dumb ass woman" and suggested that the two of them "go to the Holiday Inn to negotiate her raise." He also asked Harris and other female employees to get coins from his front pants pocket. He insisted that Harris and other women pick up objects he had thrown on the ground. While Harris was arranging a deal with one of Forklift's customers he asked her, in front of other employees, "What did you do, promise the guy some sex Saturday night?"

Harris sued Forklift, claiming that Hardy had created an abusive work environment. The federal trial court ruled against Harris on the grounds that Hardy's comments might offend a reasonable woman, but they were not severe enough to have a serious impact on Harris's psychological well-being. The appeals court confirmed, and the Supreme Court agreed to hear the case.

ISSUE: To be a violation of Title VII, must sexual harassment seriously affect the employee's psychological well-being?

DECISION: A hostile or abusive environment violates Title VII, whether or not the plaintiff suffered psychological injury.

REASONING: Title VII is not limited to economic or tangible discrimination. A workplace loaded with intimidation, ridicule, and insult creates an abusive environment that violates Title VII.

Merely uttering a swear word or two is no violation, because a reasonable person would not find that hostile or abusive. But Title VII does come into play before the victim has a nervous breakdown. An abusive environment that does not seriously affect employees' psychological well-being may nonetheless detract from their job performance and keep them from advancing in their careers. If the environment would reasonably be perceived, and is perceived, as hostile or abusive, Title VII does not require it also to be psychologically injurious.[2]

Employees who commit sexual harassment are liable for their own wrongdoing. But is their company also liable? The Supreme Court has held that:

- If the victimized employee has suffered a "tangible employment action" such as firing, demotion, or reassignment, the company is liable to her for sexual harassment by a supervisor.

- Even if the victimized employee has *not* suffered a tangible employment action, the company is liable unless it can prove that (1) it used reasonable care to prevent and correct sexually harassing behavior; and (2) the employee unreasonably failed to take advantage of the company's complaint procedures.

 Corning Consumer Products Co. asks its employees to apply four tests in judging whether their behavior constitutes sexual harassment:

- Would you say or do this in front of your spouse or parents?

---

[2] The opinion in this case was written by Justice O'Connor.

- What about in front of a colleague of the opposite sex?
- Would you like your behavior reported in your local newspaper?
- Does it need to be said or done at all? ◾◾

PROCEDURES AND REMEDIES

Before a plaintiff in a Title VII case brings suit, she must first file a complaint with the federal Equal Employment Opportunity Commission (EEOC). The EEOC then has the right to sue on behalf of the plaintiff. This arrangement is favorable for the plaintiff because the government pays the legal bill. If the EEOC decides not to bring the case, or does not make a decision within six months, it issues a **right to sue letter,** and the plaintiff may proceed on her own in court. Many states also have their own version of the EEOC, but these state commissions are often understaffed.

Remedies available to the successful plaintiff include hiring, reinstatement, retroactive seniority, back pay, reasonable attorney's fees, and damages of up to $300,000. However, employers now often require new hires to agree in advance to arbitrate, not litigate, any future employment claims. Typically, employees receive worse results in the arbitrator's office than in the courtroom.

PREGNANCY

Under the Pregnancy Discrimination Act of 1978, **an employer may not fire or refuse to hire a woman because she is pregnant.** An employer must also treat pregnancy as any other temporary disability. If, for example, employees are allowed time off from work for other medical disabilities, women must also be allowed a maternity leave. The United States and Australia are the only industrialized nations that do not require employers to provide paid maternity leave.

Age Discrimination

The Age Discrimination in Employment Act (ADEA) of 1967 prohibits age discrimination against employees or job applicants who are at least 40 years old. An employer may not fire, refuse to hire, fail to promote, or otherwise reduce a person's employment opportunities because he is 40 or older. Employers may not require workers to retire at any age (with a few exceptions, such as police officers and top-level corporate executives).

The procedure for an age-bias claim is similar to that under Title VII—plaintiffs must first file a charge with the EEOC. If the EEOC does not take action, they can file suit themselves.

During tight economic times, companies often feel great pressure to lower costs. They are sometimes tempted to replace older, higher-paid workers with younger, less expensive employees. Courts traditionally held that replacing expensive, older workers with cheaper, younger ones was illegal discrimination under the ADEA. In some recent cases, however, courts have held that an employer is entitled to prefer *lower-paid* workers even if that preference results in the company also choosing *younger* workers. As the court put it in one case, "An action based on price differentials represents the very quintessence of a legitimate business decision."[3] The Supreme Court has suggested that the primary goal of the

---

[3] *Marks v. Loral Corp.,* 57 Cal. App. 4th 30, 1997 Cal. App. LEXIS 611 (Cal. Ct. App. 1997).

ADEA is to prevent employment decisions based on stereotypes about the productivity and competence of older workers.

ETHICS

A court summed up the age discrimination dilemma thus:

> We are not unmindful of the pain attendant with the loss of any job, particularly when the loss is sustained by an older worker for whom retraining may be more difficult. [W]e are [also] not unmindful that the image of some newly minted whippersnapper MBA who tries to increase corporate profits—and his or her own compensation—by across-the-board layoffs is not a pretty one. Even so, [Congress never] intended the age discrimination laws to inhibit the very process by which a free market economy—decision making on the basis of cost—is conducted and by which, ultimately, real jobs and wealth are created.

Apart from legal issues, does a "newly minted whippersnapper MBA" (or any other manager) have an ethical obligation to older employees for whom opportunities may be limited? What conclusions can you glean from the Ethics Checklist in Chapter 2? The Golden Rule suggests that you ask yourself how you would like to be treated when you are old. Would a layoff of older employees violate important values? ▪

Americans with Disabilities Act

Passed in 1990, the Americans with Disabilities Act (ADA) prohibits employers from discriminating on the basis of disability. (The text of the ADA is available at **http://www.eeoc.gov/types/ada.html**. The Justice Department's ADA home page is **http://www.usdoj.gov/crt/ada/adahom1.htm**.) As with Title VII, a plaintiff under the ADA must first file a charge with the EEOC. If the EEOC decides not to file suit, the individual may do so himself.

A disabled person is someone with a physical or mental impairment that substantially limits a major life activity. This definition includes people with mental illness, visual impairment, epilepsy, dyslexia, and AIDS, or who are *recovered* drug addicts and alcoholics. It does not cover people with sexual disorders, pyromania, exhibitionism, or compulsive gambling.

An employer may not refuse to hire or promote a disabled person as long as she can, with *reasonable accommodation*, perform the *essential functions* of the job. An accommodation is not reasonable if it would create *undue hardship* for the employer.

- *Reasonable accommodation:* This includes buying necessary equipment, providing readers or interpreters, or permitting employees to work a part-time schedule.

- *Undue hardship:* In determining what this term means, relative cost, not absolute cost, is the issue. Even an expensive accommodation—such as hiring a full-time reader—is not considered an undue hardship unless it imposes a significant burden on the overall finances of the company.

- *Essential functions:* In one case, a court held that a welder who could perform 88% of a job was doing the essential functions.

An employer may not ask about disabilities before making a job offer. The interviewer may ask only whether an applicant can perform the work. **Before making a job offer, an employer cannot require applicants to take a medical exam** unless the exam is (1) job-related; and (2) required of all applicants for similar jobs. However, drug testing is permitted. **After a job offer has been made, an employer may require a medical test, but it must be related to the essential functions of the job.** For example, an employer could not test the cholesterol of someone applying for an accounting job, because high cholesterol is no impediment to good accounting.

An employer may not discriminate against someone because of his relationship with a disabled person. For example, an employer cannot refuse to hire an applicant because he has a child with Down's syndrome or a spouse with AIDS.

Under EEOC rules, physical and mental disabilities are to be treated the same. The difficulty is that physical ailments such as diabetes and deafness may be easy to diagnose, but what does a supervisor do when an employee is chronically late, rude, or impulsive? Does this mean the worker is mentally disabled or just a lazy, irresponsible jerk? Among other accommodations, the EEOC rules indicated that employers should be willing to put up barriers to isolate people who have difficulty concentrating, provide detailed day-to-day feedback to those who need greater structure in performing their jobs, or allow workers on antidepressants to come to work later if they are groggy in the morning.

While lauding the ADA's objectives, many managers have been apprehensive about its impact on the workplace. Most acknowledge, however, that society is clearly better off if every member has the opportunity to work. And as advocates for the disabled point out, we are all, at best, only temporarily able-bodied. Even with the ADA, only 29% of the disabled population who are of working age are employed, while 79% of able-bodied persons have jobs.

When cases go to litigation, employers win more than 93% of the time. Workers are caught in something of a legal Catch-22: They must prove that they can perform the essential functions of the job, but they must also show that their disability limits a major life activity. In the following case, the Supreme Court takes a close look at the definition of "major life activity."

YOU BE THE JUDGE

TOYOTA v. WILLIAMS

534 U.S. 184, 122 S. Ct. 681, 2002 U.S. LEXIS 400
United States Supreme Court, 2002

FACTS: Ella Williams worked in a Toyota manufacturing plant in Georgetown, Kentucky. Her job required her to use pneumatic tools. When her arms and hands began to hurt, she went to see a doctor who diagnosed her with carpal tunnel syndrome. He advised her to avoid using pneumatic tools or lifting more than 20 pounds. Toyota transferred Williams to a position in Quality Control Inspection Operations (QCIO). Employees in this department typically performed four different jobs, but Williams was initially assigned only two tasks.

Toyota then changed its policy and required QCIO employees to rotate through all four jobs.

Williams began to perform the "shell body audit." After applying oil to the outside of cars, she visually inspected each car for flaws. To perform this task, she had to hold her hands and arms up around shoulder height for several hours at a time.

A short while after beginning this job, she began to experience pain in her neck and shoulders. She asked permission to perform only the two tasks that she could do without difficulty. Williams claimed that Toyota refused this request. Toyota said that Williams simply began missing work regularly. Ultimately, Williams's doctor told her she should not do work of any kind. Toyota fired her.

When Williams sued Toyota, alleging that the company had violated the Americans with Disabilities Act, the district court granted summary judgment to Toyota. The Court of Appeals for the Sixth Circuit reversed. The Supreme Court agreed to hear the case.

ISSUES: Was Williams disabled, within the terms of the Americans with Disabilities Act? Did Toyota violate the ADA?

ARGUMENT FOR WILLIAMS: Williams cannot perform a long list of manual activities. For example, she cannot sweep, dance, garden, or drive long distances. She sometimes needs help to get dressed and she cannot play with her children for extended periods. She is also unable to perform her job at Toyota.

With reasonable accommodation, Williams could perform the essential functions of her job—she could do two of the four tasks. All she wants is for Toyota to allow her to continue doing these jobs and not the ones that are crippling her. The ADA was passed for situations exactly like this—an employee who, with just a little assistance, could continue to work, to contribute to her employer, to her family, and to society. The accommodation she is requesting is ultimately reasonable and would certainly not impose an undue hardship on Toyota.

ARGUMENT FOR TOYOTA: When Congress enacted the ADA, it found that some 43,000,000 Americans have one or more physical or mental disabilities. If Congress intended everyone with a physical impairment that precluded the performance of some isolated, unimportant, or particularly difficult manual task to qualify as disabled, the number of disabled Americans would surely have been much higher.

The issue is not whether the employee can perform the tasks associated with a specific job, it is whether she can do activities that are central to most people's daily lives. Williams can brush her teeth, wash her face, bathe, fix breakfast, do laundry, and pick up around the house. Therefore, she is not disabled and not protected by the ADA. ▰

AT RISK

Every applicant feels slightly apprehensive before a job interview, but now the interviewer may be even more nervous—fearing that every question is a potential landmine of liability. Most interviewers (and students who have read this chapter) would know better than Delta Airlines interviewers, who allegedly asked applicants about their sexual preference, birth control methods, and abortion history. The following list provides guidelines for interviewers.

Don't Even Consider Asking	Go Ahead and Ask
Can you perform this function with or without reasonable accommodation?	Would you need reasonable accommodation in this job?
How many days were you sick last year?	How many days were you absent from work last year?
What medications are you currently taking?	Are you currently using drugs illegally?
Where were you born? Are you a United States citizen?	Are you authorized to work in the United States?
How old are you?	What work experience have you had?
How tall are you? How much do you weigh?	Could you carry a 100-pound weight, as required by this job?

(Continued)

Don't Even Consider Asking	Go Ahead and Ask
When did you graduate from college?	Where did you go to college?
How did you learn this language?	What languages do you speak and write fluently?
Have you ever been arrested?	Have you ever been convicted of a crime that would affect the performance of this job?
Do you plan to have children? How old are your children? What method of birth control do you use?	Can you work weekends? Travel extensively? Would you be willing to relocate?
What is your corrected vision?	Do you have 20/20 corrected vision?
Are you a man or a woman? Are you single or married? What does your spouse do? What will happen if your spouse is transferred? What clubs, societies, or lodges do you belong to?	Leave well enough alone!

The most common gaffe on the part of interviewers? Asking women about their child care arrangements. That question assumes the woman is responsible for child care. ▪

Chapter Conclusion

The statutes in this chapter have changed America—it is far different now than when Sandra Day O'Connor first looked for a job. People are more likely to be offered employment because of their efforts and talents rather than their age, appearance, faith, family background, or health.

Chapter Review

1. Under the Equal Pay Act, an employee may not be paid for equal work at a lesser rate than employees of the opposite sex.

2. Title VII of the Civil Rights Act of 1964 prohibits employers from discriminating on the basis of race, color, religion, sex, or national origin.

3. To prove a disparate treatment case under Title VII, the plaintiff must show that she was treated differently because of her sex, race, color, religion, or national origin.

4. To prove disparate impact under Title VII, the plaintiff must show that the employer has a rule that, on its face, is not discriminatory, but in practice excludes too many people in a protected group.

5. Employers must make reasonable accommodation for a worker's religious beliefs unless the request would cause undue hardship for the business.

6. A legitimate seniority system is legal, even if it perpetuates past discrimination.

7. Affirmative action is not required by Title VII, nor is it prohibited.

8. Sexual harassment involves unwelcome sexual advances, requests for sexual favors, and other verbal or physical conduct of a sexual nature.

9. Under the Pregnancy Discrimination Act of 1978, an employer may not fire or refuse to hire a woman because she is pregnant.

10. The Age Discrimination in Employment Act (ADEA) of 1967 prohibits age discrimination against employees or job applicants who are at least 40 years old.

11. Under the Americans with Disabilities Act an employer may not refuse to hire or promote a disabled person as long as she can, with reasonable accommodation, perform the essential functions of the job.

12. An accommodation is not reasonable if it would create undue hardship for the employer.

PRACTICE TEST

Matching Questions

Match the following terms with their definitions:

___ **A.** Equal Pay Act.

___ **B.** Right to sue letter.

___ **C.** ADEA.

___ **D.** Title VII.

___ **E.** ADA.

1. Statute that prohibits an employee from being paid at a lesser rate than employees of the opposite sex for equal work.

2. Statute that prohibits employers from discrimination on the basis of race, color, religion, sex, or national origin.

3. permission from the EEOC for a plaintiff to proceed with his case.

4. Statute that prohibits age discrimination.

5. Statute that prohibits discrimination against the disabled.

True/False Questions

Circle true or false:

1. T F In a disparate impact case, an employer may be liable for a rule that is not discriminatory on its face.

2. T F Title VII applies to all aspects of the employment relationship, including hiring, firing, and promotion.

3. T F If more whites than Native Americans pass an employment test, the test violates Title VII.

4. T F Employers that have contracts with the federal government are required to fill a quota of women and minority employees.

5. T F Employers do not have to accommodate an employee's religious beliefs if doing so would impose an undue hardship on the business.

Multiple-Choice Questions

6. Which of the following steps is *not* required in a disparate treatment case:

(a) The plaintiff must file with the EEOC.

(b) The plaintiff must submit to arbitration

(c) The plaintiff must present evidence of a *prima facie* case.

(d) The defendant must show that its action had a nondiscriminatory reason.

(e) The plaintiff must show that the defendant's excuse was a pretext.

7. An employer can legally require all employees to have a high school diploma if:

   (a) All of its competitors have such a requirement.

   (b) Most of the applicants in the area have a high school diploma.

   (c) Shareholders of the company are likely to pay a higher price for the company's stock if employees have at least a high school diploma.

   (d) The company intends to branch out into the high-tech field, in which case a high school diploma would be needed by its employees.

   (e) The nature of the job requires those skills.

8. Which of the following employers has violated VII?

   (a) Carlos promoted the most qualified employee.

   (b) Hans promoted five white males because they were the most senior.

   (c) Luke refused to hire a Buddhist to work on a Christian Science newspaper.

   (d) Max hired a male corporate lawyer because his clients had more confidence in male lawyers.

   (e) Dylan hired a man to work as an attendant in the men's locker room.

9. Which of the following activities would *not* be considered sexual harassment?

   (a) Shannon tells Connor she will promote him if he will sleep with her.

   (b) Kailen has a screen saver that shows various people having sex.

   (c) Paige says she wants "to negotiate Owen's raise at the Holiday Inn."

   (d) Nancy yells "crap" at the top of her lungs every time her rotisserie baseball team loses.

   (e) Quid pro quo.

10. Which of the following activities is *not* a violation of the law?

    (a) When Taggart comes to a job interview, he has a white cane. Ann asks him if he is blind.

    (b) Craig may refuse to hire Ben as a pilot because he wears contacts, although Ben has perfect vision with the contacts.

    (c) Concerned about his company's health insurance rates, Matt requires all job applicants to take a physical.

    (d) Concerned about his company's health insurance rates, Josh requires all new hires to take a physical so that he can encourage them to join some of the preventive treatment programs available at the company.

    (e) Jennifer may refuse to hire Alexis because she is a recovered alcoholic.

Short-Answer Questions

11. This article appeared in *The Wall Street Journal:*

    When Michelle Lawrence discovered she was pregnant, she avoided telling Ron Rogers, the owner of the Los Angeles public relations agency where she worked as manager of media relations. "I had heard he wasn't crazy about pregnant women," she says. Instead, she asked her immediate supervisor to pass along the news. Mr. Rogers didn't speak to her for a week. His first comment was, "Congratulations on your pregnancy. My sister vomited for months." A few weeks later, Ms. Lawrence was fired. Mr. Rogers told her the business was shifting away from her area of expertise.

    Does Lawrence have a valid claim against Rogers? Under what law?

12. ETHICS: John Mundorf hired three women to work for Gus Construction Co. as traffic controllers at road construction sites in Iowa. Male members of the construction crew incessantly referred to the women as "f—king flag girls." They repeatedly asked the women if they "wanted to f—k" or engage in oral sex. One crew member held a woman up to the cab window so other men could touch her. Another male employee exposed himself to the women. Male employees also urinated in a woman's water bottle and the gas tank of her car. Mundorf, the supervisor, was present during some of these incidents. He talked to crew members about their conduct, but the abuse continued until the women quit. What claim might the women make against their coworkers? Is Gus Construction Co. liable for the acts of its employees? What procedure must the women follow to pursue their

claim? Why do you think these men behaved this way? Why did they want to humiliate their coworkers? What should the supervisor have done when he observed these incidents? What would you have done if you were the supervisor? Or a fellow employee?

13. The Duke Power Co. refused to transfer any employees at its generating plant to better jobs unless they had a high school diploma or could pass an intelligence test. The company was willing to pay two thirds of the tuition for an employee's high school training. Neither a high school education nor the intelligence test was significantly related to successful job performance. Both requirements disqualified African Americans at a substantially higher rate than white applicants. Is the company in violation of Title VII?

14. The Lillie Rubin boutique in Phoenix would not permit Dick Kovacic to apply for a job as a salesperson. It only hired women to work in sales because fittings and alterations took place in the dressing room or immediately outside. The customers were buying expensive clothes and demanded a male-free dressing area. Has the Lillie Rubin store violated Title VII? What would its defense be?

15. When Thomas Lussier filled out a Postal Service employment application, he did not admit that he had twice pleaded guilty to charges of disorderly conduct. Lussier suffered from post-traumatic stress disorder (PTSD) acquired during military service in Vietnam. Because of this disorder, he sometimes had panic attacks that required him to leave meetings. He was also a recovered alcoholic and drug user. During his stint with the Postal Service, he had some personality conflicts with other employees. Once another employee hit him. He also had one episode of "erratic emotional behavior and verbal outburst." In the meantime, a postal employee in Ridgewood, New Jersey, killed four colleagues. The Postmaster General encouraged all supervisors to identify workers who had dangerous propensities. Lussier's boss discovered that he had lied on his employment application about the disorderly conduct charges and fired him. Is the Postal Service in violation of the law?

16. ROLE REVERSAL: Write a multiple choice question that highlights the differences between a disparate treatment and a disparate impact case.

Internet Research Problem

Go to **http://www.eeoc.gov/types/ada.html**. The EEOC offers advice on how to comply with some aspects of the Americans with Disabilities Act. Employers sometimes complain that the EEOC unfairly favors workers. What do you think of these EEOC guidelines? Are they fair and evenhanded? As an employee, would you like your company to follow these guidelines? If you were in a supervisory role, would your view of these guidelines be different?

Labor Law

A strike! For five weeks the union workers have been walking picket lines at JMJ, a manufacturer of small electrical engines. An entire town of 70,000 citizens, most of them blue-collar workers, is sharply divided, right down to the McNally kitchen table. Buddy, age 48, has worked on the assembly lines at JMJ for more than 25 years. Now he's sipping coffee in the house where he grew up. His sister Kristina, age 46, is a vice-president for personnel at JMJ. The two have always been close, but today, the conversation is halting.

"It's time to get back together, Buddy," Kristina murmurs. "The strike is hurting the whole company—and the town."

"Not the whole town, Kristina," he tries to quip lightly. "Your management pals still have fat incomes and nice houses."

"Oh yeah?" she attempts to joke, "you haven't seen our porch lately."

"Go talk to Tony Falcione," Buddy replies. "He can't pay his rent."

"Talk to the Ericksons," Kristina snaps back, "they don't even work for JMJ. Their sandwich shop is going under because none of you guys stop in for lunch. Come back to work."

"Not with that clause on the table."

That clause is management's proposal for the new union contract—one that Kristina helped draft. The company officers want the right to subcontract work, that is, to send it out for other companies to perform.

"Buddy, we need the flexibility. K-Ball is underselling us by 35%. If we can't compete, there won't be *any* jobs or *any* contract!"

"The way to save money is not by sending our jobs overseas, where a bunch of foreigners will work for 50 bucks a month."

"OK, fine. Tell me how we should save money."

"Kristina, I really do not know how you can sit at this table and say these things—in this household. You never would have got a fancy college degree if Dad hadn't made union wages."

"If we can't sell motors to Latin America, we're out of business. All we're asking is the right to subcontract some of the smallest components. Everything else gets built here."

"Next it'll be the wiring, then you'll assemble the whole thing over there—and that'll be it for me. You take that clause off the table, we'll be back in 15 minutes."

"Never."

Buddy stands up. They stare silently, sadly, at each other, and then Kristina says, in a barely audible voice, "I have to tell you this. My boss is starting to talk about hiring replacement workers." Buddy walks out. ▪

Unions Develop

During the 19th century, as industrialization spread across America, workers found employment conditions unbearable and wages inadequate. In factories, workers, often women and children, worked 60 to 70 hours per week and sometimes more, standing at assembly lines in suffocating, dimly lit factories, performing monotonous yet dangerous work with heavy machinery for pennies a day. Mines were different—they were worse.

Workers began to band together into unions, but courts and Congress were hostile. From the 1800s through the 1920s, judges routinely issued injunctions against strikes, ruling that unions were either criminal conspiracies or illegal monopolies. With the economic collapse of 1929, however, and the vast suffering of the Great Depression, public sympathy shifted to the workers.

In 1932 Congress passed the **Norris-LaGuardia Act,** which prohibited federal court injunctions in nonviolent labor disputes. Congress was declaring that workers should be permitted to organize unions and to use their collective power to achieve legitimate economic ends.

In 1935 Congress passed the Wagner Act, generally known as the **National Labor Relations Act (NLRA).** This is the most important of all labor laws. A fundamental aim of the NLRA is the establishment and maintenance of industrial peace, to preserve the flow of commerce. **Section 7 guarantees employees the right to organize and join unions, bargain collectively through representatives of their own choosing, and engage in other concerted activities.** Section 8 reinforces these rights by outlawing unfair labor practices.

Section 8(a) makes it an unfair labor practice (ULP) for an employer:

- To interfere with union organizing efforts.

- To dominate or interfere with any union.

- To discriminate against a union member; or

- To refuse to bargain collectively with a union.

The NLRA also established the **National Labor Relations Board (NLRB)** to administer and interpret the statute and to adjudicate labor cases. For example, when a union charges that an employer has committed an unfair labor practice—say, by refusing to bargain—the ULP charge goes first to the NLRB.

The Board, which sits in Washington, D.C., has five members, all appointed by the president. The NLRB makes final agency decisions about representation and ULP cases. But note that the Board has no power to *enforce* its orders. If it is evident that the losing party will not comply, the Board must petition a federal appeals court to enforce the order. Typically, the steps resulting in an appeal follow this pattern: The Board issues a decision, for example, finding that a company has unfairly refused to bargain with a union. The Board orders the company to bargain. The Board then appeals to the United States Court of Appeals to enforce its order, and the company cross-appeals, requesting the court not to enforce the Board's order. (The NLRB describes its mission and methods at **http://www.nlrb.gov/**.)

Throughout the 1930s and 1940s, unions grew in size and power, but employers complained of union abuse. In 1947 Congress responded with the Taft-Hartley Act, also known as the **Labor-Management Relations Act.** The statute amended Section 8 of the NLRA to outlaw certain unfair labor practices *by unions.*

Section 8(b) makes it an unfair labor practice for a union:

- To interfere with employees who are exercising their labor rights under Section 7.

- To encourage an employer to discriminate against a particular employee because of a union dispute.

- To refuse to bargain collectively; or

- To engage in an illegal strike or boycott, particularly secondary boycotts.

Finally, in the 1950s the public became aware that certain labor leaders were corrupt. Some officers stole money from large union treasuries, rigged union elections, and stifled opposition within the organization. In response, in 1959 Congress passed the Landrum-Griffin Act, generally called the Labor-Management Reporting and Disclosure Act (LMRDA). The LMRDA requires union leadership to make certain financial disclosures and guarantees free speech and fair elections within a union.

These landmark federal labor laws are outlined below:

Four Key Labor Statutes

Norris-LaGuardia Act (1932)	Prohibits federal court injunctions in peaceful strikes.
National Labor Relations Act (1935)	Guarantees workers' right to organize unions and bargain collectively. Prohibits an employer from interfering with union organizing or discriminating against union members. Requires an employer to bargain collectively.
Labor-Management Relations Act (1947)	Prohibits union abuses such as coercing employees to join. Outlaws secondary boycotts.
Labor-Management Reporting and Disclosure Act (1959)	Requires financial disclosures by union leadership. Guarantees union members free speech and fair elections.

LABOR UNIONS TODAY

In the 1950s about 25% of the workforce belonged to a union. Today, only about 13.5% of all workers are union members, yet labor law still affects many. About 16 million workers are union members. The largest unions are national in scope, with hundreds of affiliated locals throughout the country. A local is the regional union, which represents workers at a particular company. For example, over 2.2 million teachers belong to the National Education Association, with thousands of locals spread throughout the nation.

Unions are much more common in government offices than private companies. Full-time workers who are union members average earnings of $718 per week, compared to $575 for their nonunionized counterparts. Union membership is highest in the Northeastern, North Central, and Pacific states, and lowest in the South. Half of all union members live in just six states: California, New York, Illinois, Michigan, Ohio, and Pennsylvania. (For the most recent union statistics, work your way to the Bureau of Labor Statistics Web site, at **http://www.bls.gov/**.)

Organizing a Union

EXCLUSIVITY

Under Section 9 of the NLRA, a validly recognized union is the exclusive representative of the employees. This means that the union will represent all of the designated employees, regardless of whether a particular worker *wants* to be represented. The company may not bargain directly with any employee in the group, nor with any other organization representing the designated employees. A **collective bargaining unit** is the precisely defined group of employees who will be represented by a particular union.

It is the union's exclusive right to bargain for the unit that gives the organization its power. But some employees may be unhappy with the way a union exercises this power. In the following case, workers believed the union was failing to represent them on a vital issue. Should they be allowed to bargain on their own behalf? You be the judge.

YOU BE THE JUDGE

EMPORIUM CAPWELL CO. v. WESTERN ADDITIONAL COMMUNITY ORGANIZATION

420 U.S. 50, 95 S. Ct. 977, 1975 U.S. LEXIS 134
United States Supreme Court, 1975

FACTS: Emporium Capwell operated a department store in San Francisco. The Department Store Employees Union represented all stock workers. Several black union members complained to the union about racial discrimination in promotions, asserting that highly qualified black workers were routinely passed over in favor of less qualified whites. The union promised to pursue the issue with management, but the black employees were not satisfied with the union's effort. The unhappy workers demanded to speak with top management of the store and then, without the union's permission, picketed the store and handed out leaflets accusing the company of discrimination. Emporium Capwell fired the picketing employees. The resulting case went all the way to the Supreme Court.

In most labor cases, the union is on one side and management is on the other. In this case, the black employees were on one side, with the union on the other. The union argued that exclusivity prohibited any group of workers from demanding to meet separately with management. The black workers, on the other hand, argued that eliminating discrimination was more important than union exclusivity.

YOU BE THE JUDGE: Did the picketing employees violate the NLRA by demanding to bargain directly with management?

ARGUMENT FOR THE UNION: Your honors, exclusivity is the core of a union's strength. If management is free to talk with employees individually, the union has no leverage. An astute manager will quickly use worker conflicts as a tool to divide the union and destroy it. By cutting deals with favored employees, management could demonstrate to all workers that affiliation with the union is a losing tactic, and that the smart worker bargains for himself—and then does what management tells him to do.

Racial discrimination must be eradicated from the workplace. But the union must do it collectively. To allow this group of picketers to pursue a worthy goal with separate bargaining would be to destroy the union—and ensure that no valuable goals are obtained.

ARGUMENT FOR THE PICKETING WORKERS: Congress granted employees the right to organize for their mutual benefit, not to advance the cause of unions. When a union fails to support its members on a vital issue, employees must be free to fend for themselves. Race discrimination is not a simple bargaining issue like retirement benefits; it is a vital matter of human dignity.

We are not asking that union members be free to pursue every petty complaint directly with management. We merely ask that, when a union fails to protect its members concerning a profound issue such as this, the injured employees be allowed to speak for themselves. ▰

ORGANIZING

A union organizing effort generally involves the following pattern.

Campaign

Union organizers talk with employees—or attempt to talk—and interest them in forming a union. The organizers may be employees of the company, who simply chat with fellow workers about unsatisfactory conditions. Or a union may send nonemployees of the company to hand out union leaflets to workers as they arrive and depart from the factory.

Authorization Cards

Union organizers ask workers to sign authorization cards, which state that the particular worker requests the specified union to act as her sole bargaining representative.

Recognition

If a union obtains authorization cards from a sizable percentage of workers, it seeks recognition as the exclusive representative for the bargaining unit. The union may ask the employer to recognize it as the bargaining representative, but most of the time employers refuse to recognize the union voluntarily. The NLRA permits an employer to refuse recognition.

Petition

Assuming that the employer does not voluntarily recognize a union, the union generally petitions the NLRB for an election. It must submit to the NLRB authorization cards signed by at least 30% of the workers. If the NLRB determines that the union has identified an appropriate bargaining unit and has enough valid cards, it orders an election.

If more than 50% of the workers vote for the union, the NLRB designates that union as the exclusive representative of all members of the bargaining unit. The issues that most commonly arise during an organizing effort are: (1) What may a union do during its organizing campaign? (2) What may the employer do to defeat the campaign? (3) What is an appropriate bargaining unit?

WHAT WORKERS MAY DO

The NLRA guarantees employees the right to talk among themselves about forming a union, to hand out literature, and ultimately to join a union. Workers may urge other employees to sign authorization cards and may vigorously push their cause. When employees hand out leaflets, the employer generally may not limit the content. In one case a union distributed leaflets urging workers to vote against political candidates who opposed minimum wage laws. The employer objected to the union using company property to distribute the information, but the Supreme Court upheld the union's right. Even though the content of the writing was not directly related to the union, the connection was close enough that the NLRA protected the union's activity.

There are, of course, limits to what union organizers may do. The statute permits an employer to restrict organizing discussions if they interfere with discipline or production. A worker on a moving assembly line has no right to walk away from his task to talk with other employees about organizing a union.

WHAT EMPLOYERS MAY DO

An employer may prohibit employees from organizing if the efforts interfere with the company's work. In a retail store, for example, management may prohibit union discussions in the presence of customers, because the discussions could harm business.

May the employer speak out against a union organizing drive? Yes. **Management is entitled to communicate to the employees why it believes a union will be harmful to the company.** But the employer's efforts must be limited to explanation and advocacy. The employer may not use either threats or promises of benefits to defeat a union drive. The company is prohibited not only from threatening reprisals, such as firing a worker who favors the union, but also from offering benefits designed to defeat the union. A company that has vigorously rejected employee demands for higher wages may not suddenly grant a 10% pay increase in the midst of a union campaign.

It is an unfair labor practice for an employer to interfere with a union organizing effort. Normally, a union claiming such interference will file a ULP charge. If the Board upholds the union's claim, it will order the employer to stop its interference and permit a fair election.

APPROPRIATE BARGAINING UNIT

When a union petitions the NLRB for an election, the Board determines whether the proposed bargaining unit is appropriate. **The Board generally certifies a proposed bargaining unit if and only if the employees share a community of interest.** Employers frequently assert that the bargaining unit is inappropriate. If the Board agrees with the employer and rejects the proposed bargaining unit, it dismisses the union's request for an election.

Managerial employees must be excluded from the bargaining unit. An employee is managerial if she is so closely aligned with management that her membership in the bargaining unit would create a conflict of interest between her union membership and her actual work. For example, a factory worker who spends one third of his time performing assembly work but two thirds of his time supervising a dozen other workers could not fairly be part of the bargaining unit.

Once the Board has excluded managerial employees, it looks at various criteria to decide whether the remaining employees should logically be grouped in one bargaining unit, that is, whether they share a **community of interest.** The Board looks for rough similarity of training, skills, hours of work, and pay. The Board either certifies the bargaining unit or rejects the unit and dismisses the union's petition.

Collective Bargaining

The goal of bargaining is a contract, which is called a **collective bargaining agreement (CBA).** Problems arise as union and employer advocate their respective positions. Three of the most common conflicts are (1) whether an issue is a mandatory subject of bargaining; (2) whether the parties are bargaining in good faith; and (3) how to enforce the agreement. For a Web site devoted to articles and reports on collective bargaining, see **http://www.ilr.cornell.edu/depts/ICB/**.

SUBJECTS OF BARGAINING

The NLRA permits the parties to bargain almost any subject they wish, but *requires* them to bargain certain issues. **Mandatory subjects include wages, hours, and other terms and conditions of employment.** Either side may propose to bargain other subjects, but neither side may insist upon bargaining them.

Management and unions often disagree as to whether a particular topic is mandatory or not. Courts generally find these subjects to be mandatory: pay, benefits, order of layoffs and recalls, production quotas, work rules (such as safety practices), retirement benefits, and in-plant food service and prices (e.g., cafeteria food). Courts usually consider these subjects to be nonmandatory: product type and design, advertising, sales, financing, corporate organization, and location of plants.

Today, some of the angriest disputes between management and labor arise from a company's desire to subcontract work and/or to move plants to areas with cheaper costs. **Subcontracting** means that a manufacturer, rather than producing all parts of a product and then assembling them, contracts for other companies, frequently overseas, to make some of the parts. Is a business free to subcontract work? That depends on management's motive. A company that subcontracts in order to maintain its economic viability is probably not required to bargain first; however, **bargaining is mandatory if the subcontracting is designed to replace union workers with cheaper labor.**

Employer and Union Security

Both the employer and the union will seek clauses making their positions more secure. Management, above all, wants to be sure that there will be no strikes during the course of the agreement. For its part, the union tries to insure that its members cannot be turned away from work during the CBA's term, and that all newly hired workers will affiliate with the union. We look at several union security issues.

No Strike/No Lockout.   Most agreements include some form of no-strike clause, meaning that the union promises not to strike during the term of the contract. In turn, unions insist on a no-lockout clause, meaning that in the event of a labor dispute, management will not prevent union members from working. No-strike and no-lockout clauses are both legal.

Union Shop.   In a union shop, membership in the union becomes compulsory after the employee has been hired. Thus management retains an unfettered right to hire whom it pleases, but all new employees who fit into the bargaining unit must affiliate with the union. **A union shop is generally legal,** with two limitations. First, new members need not join the union for 30 days. Second, the new members, after joining the union, can only be required to pay initiation fees and union dues. If the new hire decides he does not want to participate in the union, the union may not compel him to do so.

DUTY TO BARGAIN

Both the union and the employer must bargain in good faith with an open mind. However, they are not obligated to reach an agreement. This means that the two sides must meet and make a reasonable effort to reach a contract. Suppose a union proposes a 15% pay increase, and management offers a 1% raise. Each side is required to attend bargaining sessions, listen to the other side's proposal, and consider its supporting argument. But neither side has to agree.

Sometimes an employer will attempt to make changes without bargaining the issues at all. However, **management may not unilaterally change wages, hours, or terms and conditions of employment without bargaining the issues to impasse.** "Bargaining to impasse" means that both parties must continue to meet and bargain in good faith until it is clear that they cannot reach an agreement. The goal in requiring collective bargaining is to bring the parties together, to reach an agreement that brings labor peace. In one case, the union won an election, but before bargaining could begin, management changed the schedule from five 8-hour days to four 10-hour days a week. The company also changed its layoff policy from one of strict seniority to one based on ability and began laying off employees based on alleged poor performance. The court held that each of these acts violated the company's duty to bargain. The employer ultimately might be allowed to make every one of these changes, but first it had to bargain the issues to impasse.

ENFORCEMENT

Virtually all collective bargaining agreements provide for their own enforcement, typically through **grievance-arbitration.** Suppose a company transfers an employee from the day shift to the night shift, and the worker believes the contract prohibits such a transfer for any employee with her seniority. The employee complains to the union, which files a **grievance,** that is, a formal complaint with the company, notifying management that the union claims a contract violation. Generally, the CBA establishes some kind of informal hearing, usually conducted by a member of management, at which the employee, represented by the union, may state her case.

After the manager's decision, if the employee is still dissatisfied, the union may file for **arbitration,** that is, a formal hearing before a neutral arbitrator. In the arbitration hearing, each side is represented by its lawyer. The arbitrator is required to decide the case based on the CBA. An arbitrator finds either for the employee, and orders the company to take certain corrective action, or for the employer, and dismisses the grievance.

In the vast majority of grievances, the arbitrator's decision is final. In a limited number of cases, a court may refuse to enforce an arbitrator's award that is contrary to public policy, but this exception is narrowly interpreted, as the following case illustrates.

CASE SUMMARY

UNITED PAPERWORKERS INTERNATIONAL UNION v. MISCO, INC.

484 U.S. 29, 108 S. Ct. 364, 1987 U.S. LEXIS 5028
United States Supreme Court, 1987

FACTS: Misco, Inc. (the Company), operated a paper plant in Louisiana. The Company had a collective bargaining agreement with the United Paperworkers (the Union), which permitted either side to file grievances and take them to final, binding arbitration. The CBA also permitted the Company to post work rules. Rule II.1 notified employees that they could be dismissed for bringing alcohol or drugs onto company premises or arriving for work under the influence of such substances.

Isiah Cooper, an employee covered by the CBA, operated a slitter-rewinder machine, which used sharp blades to cut rolling coils of paper. The machine was hazardous and had caused numerous injuries over the years. Cooper had twice been reprimanded for deficient performance. Two days after the second reprimand, police searched Cooper's house, pursuant to a search warrant, and discovered a large amount of marijuana. Later that day, police apprehended Cooper in the backseat of another worker's car, a white Cutlass, parked in the company lot. There was marijuana smoke in the air and a lighted marijuana cigarette in the ashtray in the front seat. Police arrested Cooper and then searched his car, where they found a plastic scales case and some marijuana.

When the Company learned of Cooper's presence in the white Cutlass, it discharged him for

having drugs on the premises. He filed a grievance. Eight months later, shortly before the arbitration hearing began, the Company learned that the police had found marijuana in Cooper's own car. The arbitrator found in Cooper's favor, stating that because he was in the backseat of the Cutlass and the marijuana was in the front, the Company had no evidence he had used or possessed an illegal substance on the premises. The arbitrator refused to consider the marijuana found in Cooper's own car because the Company had not known about it when it fired him.

The Company filed suit in United States District Court, which vacated the arbitrator's decision, holding that public policy prohibits the use of marijuana. The court of appeals affirmed the district court, and the union sought review by the Supreme Court.

ISSUE: Was the district court correct in overruling the arbitrator on public policy grounds?

DECISION: The arbitrator's decision stands. Reversed.

REASONING: Federal policy favors arbitration as the means to settle labor disputes. So a court plays a very limited role in reviewing an arbitrator's decision. Judges are not authorized to reconsider the merits of such a ruling.

These parties agreed on arbitration as their method of settling disputes. The collective bargaining agreement established procedures for employee hearings. One rule clearly left it to the arbitrator to decide what evidence to hear. This arbitrator determined that he should not consider information that the company itself had not known when it terminated Cooper, especially since the employee never received notice that this evidence might be allowed.

Even a possible violation of public policy (marijuana use) does not permit a court to do the arbitrator's work. The judgment of the court of appeals is reversed. ◢

Concerted Action

Concerted action refers to any tactics union members take in unison to gain some bargaining advantage. It is this power that gives a union strength. The NLRA guarantees the right of employees to engage in concerted action for mutual aid or protection. The most common forms of concerted action are strikes and picketing.

STRIKES

The NLRA guarantees employees the right to strike, but with some limitations. A union has a guaranteed right to call a strike if the parties are unable to reach a collective bargaining agreement. A union may call a strike to exert economic pressure on management, to protest an unfair labor practice, or to preserve work that the employer is considering sending elsewhere.

This right to strike can be waived. Management will generally insist that the CBA include a no-strike clause, which prohibits the union from striking while the CBA is in force. Other restrictions include a 60-day cooling-off period before many strikes, and in many states, a flat prohibition on strikes by public employees (police, teachers, and so forth). Violent strikes are always illegal.

ETHICS | Suppose state law prohibits teachers from striking, but the teachers' union is angry. Their contract expired a year ago, and the board of education has refused any pay raises. The teachers decide they will "work to rule," meaning they will teach classes, issues grades, and so forth . . . but will not write any college recommendations. What are the consequences? Is that just? What are the alternatives? ▪◾

REPLACEMENT WORKERS

When employees go on strike, management generally wants to replace them to keep the company operating. Are replacement workers legal? Yes. **Management has the right to hire replacement workers during a strike.** May the employer offer the replacement workers permanent jobs, or must the company give union members their jobs back when the strike is over? It depends on the type of strike.

After an *economic strike*, an employer may not discriminate against a striker, but the employer is not obligated to lay off a replacement worker to give a striker his job back. An economic strike is one intended to gain wages or benefits. When a union bargains for a pay raise but fails to get it and walks off the job, that is an economic strike. During such a strike, an employer may hire permanent replacement workers. When the strike is over, the company has no obligation to lay off the replacement workers to make room for the strikers. However, if the company does hire more workers, it may not discriminate against the strikers.

After a **ULP strike,** a union member is entitled to her job back, even if that means the employer must lay off a replacement worker. Suppose management refuses to bargain in good faith by claiming poverty without producing records to substantiate its claim. The union strikes. Management's refusal to bargain was an unfair labor practice, and the strike is a ULP strike. When it ends, the striking workers must get their jobs back.

PICKETING

Picketing the employer's workplace in support of a strike is generally lawful. Striking workers are permitted to establish picket lines at the employer's job site and to urge all others—employees, replacement workers, and customers—not to cross the line. But the picketers are not permitted to use physical force to prevent anyone from crossing the line.

LOCKOUTS

The workers have bargained with management for weeks, and discussions have turned belligerent. It is 6 a.m., the start of another day at the factory. But as 150 employees arrive for work, they are amazed to find the company's gate locked and armed guards standing on the other side. What is this? A lockout.

The power of a union comes ultimately from its potential to strike. But management, too, has weapons. In a lockout, management prohibits workers from entering the premises, denying the employees work and a chance to earn a paycheck.

A lockout is legal if the parties have reached a bargaining impasse. Management, bargaining a new CBA with a union, may wish to use a lockout to advance its position. It is allowed to do so provided the parties have reached an impasse. If there is no impasse, a lockout will probably be illegal. Most courts consider that a lockout before impasse indicates hostility to the union.

Regulating Union Affairs

Along with a union's exclusive bargaining power goes a duty of fairness to all of its members. The union's duty of fair representation was created by the NLRA and the Labor-Management Reporting and Disclosure Act. The **duty of fair representation** requires that a union represent all members fairly, impartially, and in good faith. A union is not entitled to favor some members over others. No union may discriminate against a member based on impermissible characteristics such as race or sex.

Unions must make reasonable decisions about whether to pursue an employee's grievance. A member may sue his union, claiming that the organization violated its duty of fair representation by deciding not to pursue a grievance on his behalf. But courts generally allow unions a wide range of latitude in deciding whether to pursue a grievance. A union's decision not to file a grievance is illegal only if it was arbitrary, discriminatory, or in bad faith.

Chapter Conclusion

Contemporary clashes between union and management are less likely to stem from sweltering temperatures in a mine than from a management decision to subcontract work, or from a teacher's refusal to write college recommendations. But although the flash points have changed, labor law is still dominated by issues of organizing, collective bargaining, and concerted action.

Chapter Review

1. Section 7 of the National Labor Relations Act (NLRA) guarantees employees the right to organize and join unions, bargain collectively, and engage in other concerted activities.

2. Section 8(a) of the NLRA makes it an unfair labor practice (ULP) for an employer to interfere with union organizing, discriminate against a union member, or refuse to bargain collectively.

3. Section 8(b) of the NLRA makes it a ULP for a union to interfere with employees who are exercising their rights under Section 7 or to engage in an illegal strike or boycott.

4. Section 9 of the NLRA makes a validly recognized union the exclusive representative of the employees.

5. During a union organizing campaign, an employer may vigorously present anti-union views to its employees, but it may not use threats or promises of benefits to defeat the union effort.

6. The National Labor Relations Board (NLRB) will certify a proposed bargaining unit only if the employees share a community of interest.

7. The employer and the union must bargain over wages, hours, and other terms and conditions of employment.

8. The union and the employer must bargain in good faith, but they are not obligated to reach an agreement.

9. The NLRA guarantees employees the right to strike, with some limitations.

10. During a strike, management may hire replacement workers.

11. Picketing the employer's workplace in support of a strike is generally lawful.

12. Lockouts are lawful if the parties have bargained to impasse.

13. The duty of fair representation requires that a union represent all members fairly, impartially, and in good faith.

PRACTICE TEST

Matching Questions

Match the following terms with their definitions:

___ **A.** ULP.

___ **B.** Exclusivity.

1. A specific group of employees that a union will represent.

2. The union's right to be the sole representative of workers.

___ **C.** Collective bargaining unit.

___ **D.** Union shop.

___ **E.** Concerted action.

3. Management interference with a union organizing effort.

4. Picketing and strikes.

5. Workers within specified categories are required to join the union.

True/False Questions

Circle true or false:

1. T   F   The union and management are both obligated to bargain until they reach a CBA or a court declares the bargaining futile.

2. T   F   Health benefits are a mandatory subject of bargaining.

3. T   F   During the last two decades, labor unions have grown by about 15% in the United States.

4. T   F   Workers are entitled to form a union whether management wants them to or not.

5. T   F   While organizing, workers may not discuss union issues on company property, but may do so off the premises.

Multiple-Choice Questions

6. During a union organizing drive, management urges workers not to join the union, and discusses a competing company which lost business after a union was formed. Management

(a) Committed a ULP by urging workers to reject the union, but did not do so by discussing a competing company.

(b) Committed a ULP by discussing a competing company, but did not do so by urging workers to reject the union.

(c) Committed a ULP both by urging workers to reject the union and by discussing a competitor.

(d) Committed no ULP.

(e) Has violated other sections of the NLRA.

7. Which of these does the NLRA *not* protect?

(a) Right to form a union.

(b) Right to picket.

(c) Right to strike.

(d) Right to block nonunion workers from company property.

(e) Right to bargain collectively.

8. The CBA at Grey Corp. has expired, as has the CBA at Blue Corp. At Grey, union and management have bargained a new CBA to impasse. Suddenly, Grey locks out all union workers. The next day, during a bargaining session at Blue, management announces that it will not discuss pay increases.

(a) Grey has committed a ULP but Blue has not.

(b) Blue has committed a ULP but Grey has not.

(c) Both Blue and Grey have committed ULPs.

(d) Neither company has committed a ULP.

(e) Grey and Blue have violated labor law, but not by committing ULPs.

9. About 30% of the union members at Blue Corp. believe their union is not representing them adequately. These workers have the right

(a) To leave the union.

(b) To bargain separately with management.

(c) To bargain separately with the union.

(d) To sue the union.

(e) To stop paying union dues.

10. When the union went on strike, the company replaced Ashley, a union member, with Ben, a nonunion member. The strike is now over, and a Federal court has ruled that this was a ULP strike. Does Ashley get her job back?

    (a) The company is obligated to hire Ashley, even if that requires laying off Ben.

    (b) The company is obligated to hire Ashley *unless* that would require laying off Ben.

    (c) The company is obligated to hire Ashley only if Ben voluntarily leaves.

    (d) The company's only obligation is to notify Ashley of future job availability.

    (e) The company has no obligation at all to Ashley.

Short-Answer Questions

11. Gibson Greetings, Inc., had a plant in Berea, Kentucky, where the workers belonged to the International Brotherhood of Firemen & Oilers. The old CBA expired, and the parties negotiated a new one, but were unable to reach an agreement on economic issues. The union struck. At the next bargaining session, the company claimed that the strike violated the old CBA, which had a no-strike clause and which stated that the terms of the old CBA would continue in force as long as the parties were bargaining a new CBA. The company refused to bargain until the union at least agreed that by bargaining, the company was not giving up its claim of an illegal strike. The two sides returned to bargaining, but meanwhile the company hired replacement workers. Eventually, the striking workers offered to return to work, but Gibson refused to rehire many of them. In court, the union claimed that the company had committed a ULP by (1) insisting the strike was illegal; and (2) refusing to bargain until the union acknowledged the company's position. Why is it very important to the union to establish the company's act as a ULP? Was it a ULP?

12. Plainville Ready Mix Concrete Co. was bargaining a CBA with the drivers' union. Negotiations went forward, on and off, over many months, with wages the major source of disagreement. Plainville made its final offer of $9.50 per hour, with step increases of $.25 per hour in a year and another $.25 per hour the following year. The plan also included certain incentive pay. The union refused to accept the offer, and the two sides reached an impasse. Plainville then announced it was implementing its plans. It established a wage rate of $9.50 per hour but eliminated the step increases and incentive pay. Was the company's implementation of the wage increase legal?

13. Fred Schipul taught English at the Thomaston (Connecticut) High School for 18 years. When the position of English Department chairperson became vacant, Schipul applied, but the Board of Education appointed a less senior teacher. Schipul filed a grievance, based on a CBA provision that required the Board to promote the most senior teacher where two or more applicants were equal in qualification. Before the arbitrator ruled on the grievance, the Board eliminated all department chairpersons. The arbitrator ruled in Schipul's favor. The Board then reinstated all department chairs—all but the English Department. Comment.

14. ETHICS: This chapter refers in several places to the contentious issue of subcontracting. Make an argument for management in favor of a company's ethical right to subcontract, and one for unions in opposition.

15. ROLE REVERSAL: Write an essay question involving a union organizing campaign and a management response that includes both permissible advocacy and illegal conduct.

Internet Research Problem

View **http://www.uniteunion.org/sweatshops/sweatshop.html**. What are sweatshops? Do they exist in the United States? Click on "College Students Against Sweatshops." Describe a current student campaign about this issue. Do you agree or disagree with what the students are doing? Why?

You can find further practice problems in the Online Quiz at **http://beatty.westbuslaw.com** or in the Study Guide that accompanies this text.

BUSINESS ORGANIZATIONS

UNIT 5

CHAPTER 33

Starting a Business

At long last, Rachel was in love. For years, she had yearned to start her own business, but the perfect concept always eluded her. Then, surfing the Net one day, she found the idea she had been searching for: movie theaters that show only classic films. Sure, you can rent the original *Star Wars* or *Gone with the Wind* anytime, but the little box at home cannot compete with a large screen and digital sound. At home, Atlanta simply does not burn as hot. According to the Internet, these theaters were already a rave success in Paris. Why not in Des Moines?

Rachel began looking for investors. Finally, at her 19th lunch meeting, she found Ross, who was as enthusiastic as she. Two days later, they signed a lease on a suitable property. Prospects for the business looked great. Then, while riding his bike on company business, Ross crashed into a pedestrian. Only when Rachel was served with a complaint did she learn that their business was a partnership, which meant that she and Ross were both personally liable for his accident.

In a panic, Rachel resumed surfing the Net, this time looking for legal information. She downloaded a sample corporate charter and formed a corporation, BigScreen, Inc. Now she and Ross enjoyed limited liability and could sell stock to outside investors. Their college

friend from Hong Kong, Bing, was the first to buy shares. But other prospective purchasers insisted that BigScreen be organized as an S corporation for tax reasons. Back to the Internet, where Rachel learned that nonresident aliens could not hold stock in S corporations. Bing's participation disqualified BigScreen.

By this time, Rachel was surfing in desperation. At last she found an answer: BigScreen could become a limited liability company. This form of business provided all the advantages of an S corp with none of the disadvantages. She and Ross immediately formed an LLC, transferred BigScreen's assets, and sighed in relief—until tax day. The Internal Revenue Service (IRS) considered their transfer of assets to be a sale. Suddenly, they faced a huge tax bill, with no way to pay it. Ross announced that he was quitting.

"You promised to stay five years." Rachel protested. "I trusted you!"

"Frankly, my dear, I don't give a damn," replied Ross, slamming the door as he left. ■

Many people dream of starting their own business. They look for exactly the right idea to power a company to success. Creativity is an important ingredient for any successful start-up. So are hard work and finely honed business skills. And so is the law. Legal issues can have as profound an impact on the success of a company as any business decision.

To begin, entrepreneurs must select a form of organization. The correct choice can reduce taxes, liability, and conflict while facilitating outside investment. At **http://www.onlinewbc.gov/docs/starting/test.html,** the U.S. Small Business Administration offers advice about starting a business and includes an entrepreneurial test to help you assess your potential as an entrepreneur.

Sole Proprietorships

A sole proprietorship is an unincorporated business owned by a single person. It is the most common form of business organization. Sole proprietorships are easy and inexpensive to create and operate. There is no need to hire a lawyer or register with the government. The company is not even required to file a separate tax return—all profits and losses are reported on the owner's personal return.

Sole proprietorships also have some serious disadvantages. For example, Linda runs ExSciTe (which stands for Excellence in Science Teaching), a company that helps teachers prepare hands-on science experiments in the classroom, using such basic items as vinegar, lemon juice, and red cabbage. As the owner of the business, Linda is responsible for all of the business's debts. If ExSciTe cannot pay its suppliers or if a student is injured by an exploding cabbage, Linda is personally liable. She may have to sell her house and car to pay the debt. Second, the owner of a sole proprietorship has limited options for financing her business. Debt is generally her only source of working capital because she has no stock or memberships to sell. If someone else brings in capital and helps with the management of the business, then it is a partnership, not a sole proprietorship. For this reason sole proprietorships work best for small businesses without large capital needs.

General Partnerships

Partnerships have two important advantages: They are *easy to form* and they do not pay *taxes*. Partnerships, however, also have some major disadvantages:

- *Liability.* Each partner is personally liable for the debts of the enterprise whether or not she caused them.

- *Funding.* Financing a partnership may be difficult because the firm cannot sell shares as a corporation does. The capital needs of the partnership must be met by contributions from partners or by borrowing.

- *Management.* Managing a partnership can also be difficult because, in the absence of an agreement to the contrary, all partners have an equal say in running the business.

- *Transferability.* A partner only has the right to transfer the *value* of her partnership interest, not the interest itself. Thus a mother who is a partner in a law firm can pass on to her son the value of her partnership interest, not the right to be a partner in the firm (or even the right to work there).

FORMATION

A partnership is an association of two or more co-owners who carry on a business for profit. Each co-owner is called a **general partner.** Like sole proprietorships, partnerships are easy to form. Although, practically speaking, a partnership *should* have a written agreement, the law generally does not require anything in the way of forms or filings or agreements.

TAXES

A partnership is not a taxable entity, which means it does not pay taxes itself. All income and losses are passed through to the partners and reported on their personal income tax returns. Corporations, by contrast, are taxable entities and pay income tax on their profits. Shareholders must then pay tax on dividends from the corporation. Thus a dollar is taxed only once before it ends up in a partner's bank account, but twice before it is deposited by a shareholder.

Exhibit 33.1 compares the single taxation of partnerships with the double taxation of corporations. Suppose, as shown in the exhibit, that a corporation and a partnership each receive $10,000 in additional income. The corporation pays tax at a top rate of 35%.[1] Thus the corporation pays $3,500 of the $10,000 in tax. The corporation pays out the remaining $6,500 as a dividend of $2,167 to each of its three shareholders. Then the shareholders are taxed at the special dividend rate of 15%, which means they each pay a tax of $325. They are each left with $1,842. Of the initial $10,000, almost 45% ($4,475) has gone to the IRS.

Compare the corporation to a partnership. The partnership itself pays no taxes, so it can pass on $3,333 to each of its partners. At a 35% individual rate, they will each pay an income tax of $1,167. As partners, they pocket $2,166, which is $324

---

[1] This is the federal tax rate; most states also levy a corporate tax.

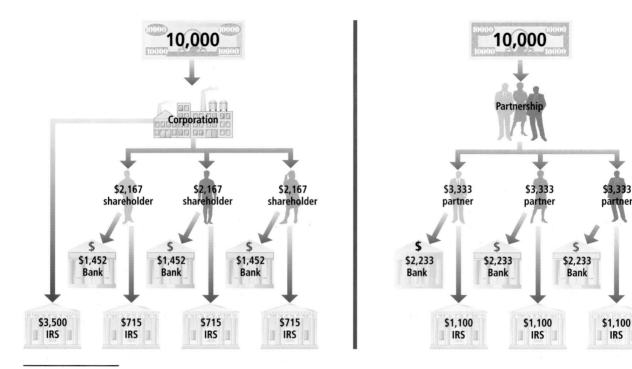

Exhibit 33.1

more than they could keep as shareholders. Of the partnership's initial $10,000, 35% ($3,501) has gone to the IRS—compared with the corporation's 45%.

LIABILITY

Every partner is an agent of the partnership. Thus the entire partnership is liable for the act of one partner in, say, signing a contract. **A partnership is also liable for any torts that a partner commits in the ordinary course of the partnership's business.** Thus, if one partner wields a careless calculator, the whole partnership is liable.

It gets worse. **If a partnership does not have enough assets to pay its debts, creditors may go after the personal property of individual partners, whether or not they were in any way responsible for the debt.** Because partners have **joint and several liability,** creditors can sue the partnership and the partners together or in separate lawsuits or in any combination. The partnership and the partners are all individually liable for the full amount of the debt, but, obviously, the creditor cannot keep collecting after he has already received the total amount owed. **Also note that, even if creditors have a judgment against an individual partner, they cannot go after that partner's assets until all the partnership's assets are exhausted.**

Letitia, one of the world's wealthiest people, enters into a partnership with penniless Harry to drill for oil on her estate. While driving on partnership business, Harry crashes into Gus, seriously injuring him. Gus can sue any combination of the partnership, Letitia, and Harry for the full amount, even though Letitia was 2,000 miles away on her Caribbean island when the accident occurred and she had many times cautioned Harry to drive carefully. Even if Gus obtains a judgment against Letitia, however, he cannot recover against her while the partnership still has assets. So, for all practical purposes, he must try to collect first against the partnership. If the partnership is bankrupt and he manages to collect the full amount from Letitia, he cannot then try to recover against Harry.

MANAGEMENT

The management of a partnership can be a significant challenge.

Management Rights

Unless the partnership agrees otherwise, partners share both profits and losses equally, and each partner has an equal right to manage the business. In a large partnership, with hundreds of partners, too many cooks can definitely spoil the firm's profitability. That is why large partnerships are almost always run by one or a few partners who are designated as **managing partners** or **members of the executive committee.**

Management Duties

Partners have a **fiduciary duty** to the partnership. This duty means that:

- *Partners are liable to the partnership for gross negligence or intentional misconduct.*

- *Partners cannot compete with the partnership.* Each partner must turn over to the partnership all earnings from any activity that is related to the partnership's business. Thus law firms would typically expect a partner to turn over any fees he earned as a director of a company, but he could keep royalties from his novel on scuba diving.

- *A partner may not take an opportunity away from the partnership unless the other partners consent.* If the partnership wants to buy a private plane and a partner hears of one for sale, she must give the partnership an opportunity to buy it before she purchases it herself.

- *If a partner engages in a conflict of interest, he must turn over to the partnership any profits he earned from that activity.* In the following case, one partner bought partnership property secretly. Is that a conflict of interest?

CASE SUMMARY

MARSH v. GENTRY

642 S.W.2d 574, 1982 Ky. LEXIS 315
Supreme Court of Kentucky, 1982

FACTS: Tom Gentry and John Marsh were partners in a business that bought and sold racehorses. The partnership paid $155,000 for Champagne Woman, who subsequently had a foal named Excitable Lady. The partners decided to sell Champagne Woman at the annual Keeneland auction, the world's premier Thoroughbred horse auction. On the day of the auction, Gentry decided to bid on the horse personally, without telling Marsh. Gentry bought Champagne Woman for $135,000. Later, he told Marsh that someone from California had approached him about buying Excitable Lady. Marsh agreed to the sale. Although he repeatedly asked Gentry the name of the purchaser, Gentry refused to tell him. Not until 11 months later, when Excitable Lady won a race at Churchill Downs, did Marsh learn that Gentry had been the purchaser. Marsh became the Excitable Man.

ISSUE: Did Gentry violate his fiduciary duty when he bought partnership property without telling his partner?

DECISION: Gentry violated his fiduciary duty to his partner.

REASONING: Kentucky partnership law required Gentry to make full disclosure to his partner before buying partnership property. Although Gentry did not know that he would be the winning bidder at auction, he had an obligation to tell Marsh that he intended to bid.

As for the private sale, although Marsh had agreed to the price, he still had a right to know that his partner was the offeror. He would certainly have looked more carefully at an offer from a partner than from an unknown third party. Indeed, Marsh said later that he would not have agreed to either sale if he had known Gentry was the purchaser.

Gentry claims that partners frequently place secret bids at auctions of partnership property. Whether or not this is true, such behavior violates the law and is unacceptable. Partners owe each other a high degree of good faith. ◢

TERMINATING A PARTNERSHIP

A partnership begins with an *association* of two or more people. Appropriately, the end of a partnership begins with a *dissociation*. **A dissociation occurs when a partner quits.**

Dissociation

A partner always has the *power* to leave a partnership but may not have the *right*. In other words, a partner can always dissociate, but she may have to pay damages for any harm that her departure causes.

A dissociation is a fork in the road: **The partnership can either buy out the departing partner(s) and continue in business or wind up the business and terminate the partnership.** Exhibit 33.2 illustrates the dissociation process. If the partnership chooses to terminate the business, it must follow three steps: dissolution, winding up, and termination.

Three Steps to Termination

Dissolution. The rules on dissolution depend, in part, on the type of partnership. If the partners have agreed in advance how long the partnership will last, it is a **term partnership.** At the end of the specified term, the partnership automatically ends. Otherwise, it is a **partnership at will**, which means that any of the partners can leave at any time, for any reason.

A partnership *automatically* dissolves:

- In a partnership at will, when a partner withdraws.

- In a term partnership when:

    (a) A partner is dissociated and half of the remaining partners vote to wind up the partnership business.

    (b) All the partners agree to dissolve.

    (c) The term expires or the partnership achieves its goal.

- In any partnership when:

    (a) An event occurs that the partners had agreed would cause dissolution.

    (b) The partnership business becomes illegal.

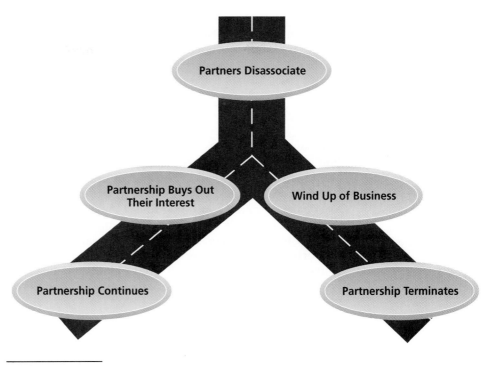

Exhibit 33.2

    (c) A court determines that the partnership is unlikely to succeed. If the partners simply cannot get along or they cannot make a profit, any partner has the right to ask a court to dissolve the partnership. For example, two men formed a partnership to buy *The San Juan Star*, Puerto Rico's English-language newspaper. They ended up in court, each bitterly accusing the other of having violated the partnership agreement. Their hostility was so great that the judge ultimately decided he could not tell who was at fault and, furthermore, the two men could never run a business together. The court ordered one partner to buy out the other. If the partners could not agree on a buyout, the judge was prepared to order a sale of the newspaper to outsiders.[2]

Winding Up.   During the winding up process, all debts of the partnership are paid, and the remaining proceeds are distributed to the partners.

Termination.   Termination happens automatically once the winding up is finished. The partnership is not required to do anything official; it can go out of the world even more quietly and simply than it came in.

Limited Liability Partnerships

A limited liability partnership (LLP) is a type of general partnership. There is a very important distinction, however, between these two forms of organization: **in an LLP, the partners are not liable for the debts of the partnership.** To form an

---

[2] *Nemazee Capital Corp. v. Angulo Capital Corp.,* 1996 U.S. Dist. LEXIS 10750 (S. Dist. NY, 1996).

LLP, the partners must file a statement of qualification with state officials. LLPs must also file annual reports. The other attributes of a partnership remain the same. Thus an LLP is not a taxable entity, and it has the right to choose its duration (that is, it can, but does not have to, survive the dissociation of a member).

Limited Partnerships

The owners of the Montreal Expos asked investment banker Jacques Menard to find a buyer for the baseball team. Instead, he found 11 other people to help him buy the team. They formed a limited partnership, and each purchaser invested between $1 million and $7 million. During their first year of ownership, the Expos lost nearly $5 million and their final 14 home games, finishing in the cellar of their division. Given this dismal showing, management had no choice but to fire the popular team manager. Then a concrete beam in the team's stadium collapsed.

Fortunately, the owners had formed a limited partnership. Limited partnerships and general partnerships have similar names but, like many siblings, they operate very differently. Here are the major differences between these two types of organizations.

Structure

General partnerships have only *general* partners. Limited partnerships have two types of partners—*limited* partners and *general* partners. A limited partnership must have at least one of each.

Liability

All the partners in a general partnership are *personally* liable for the debts of the partnership. **In a limited partnership, the general partners are personally liable but not the limited partners.** The limited partners are like corporate shareholders—they risk only their investment in the partnership (which is called their "capital contribution"). If the Expos lose money, creditors can go against the assets of the partnership and the personal property of the general partners, but the limited partners are safe.

Taxes

Limited partnerships, like general partnerships, are not taxable entities. Income is taxed only once before landing in a partner's pocket, and partners can deduct losses against their other income.

Formation

The general partners must file a certificate of limited partnership with their secretary of state. Although most limited partnerships do have a partnership agreement, it is not required. (A sample limited partnership agreement is available at **http://www.worldlawdirect.com/builddoc.php**.)

Management

General partners have the right to manage a limited partnership. Limited partners are essentially passive investors with few management rights beyond the right to be informed about the partnership business. Because limited partners are not allowed to manage, a limited partnership can handle a very large number of partners.

Transfer of Ownership

As is the case with a general partnership, limited partners always have the right to transfer the *value* of their partnership interest, but they can only sell or give away the interest itself if the partnership agreement permits. Thus, if Sadie is a limited partner in the Expos, but decides to invest in basketball instead, she does not have the automatic right to sell her limited partnership interest to Pedro. Although she could sell Pedro the right to receive profit distributions from the Expos, he would not *be* a limited partner, with the right to vote in meetings.

Duration

Unless the partnership agreement provides otherwise, limited partnerships enjoy perpetual existence—they continue even as partners come and go.

Corporations

Even as a child, Judy George dreamed of starting her own business. She realized her dream when she started Domain, an upscale, European-style chain of furniture stores.

George's lawyer suggested that she incorporate Domain. He explained that **a corporation offers the protection of *limited liability.*** If Domain flopped and could not pay its bills, George and her backers would lose their investment in the company, but not their other assets. He also explained that limited liability does not protect against *all* debts. Individuals are always responsible for their *own* acts. If a Domain employee was in an accident while driving a company van, Domain would be liable for any harm to the other driver, but its shareholders would not be personally liable. If George herself crashed the van, Domain would be liable, and *so would George.* If Domain did not pay the judgment, George would have to, from her personal assets if necessary. **A corporation protects managers and investors from personal liability for the debts of the corporation and the actions of others, but not against *personal* negligence (or other torts and crimes).**

Corporations have other advantages besides limited liability. They provide **flexibility** for enterprises small (with one owner) and large (with thousands of share-holders). For example, partnership interests are not transferable without the permission of the other partners, whereas corporate stock can be easily bought and sold. Further, when a sole proprietor dies, legally so does the business. But corporations have **perpetual existence:** They can continue without their founders.

The major disadvantage of a corporation is simply the expense and effort required to create and operate it. Because corporations are taxable entities, they must pay taxes and file returns. The cost of establishing a corporation may exceed $1,000 in legal and filing fees, not to mention the cost of the annual filings that states require. Corporations must also hold annual meetings for both shareholders and directors. Minutes of these meetings must be kept indefinitely in the company minute book.

Judy George knew that she needed at least $3 million to get Domain up and running. She could not borrow that much money, so she needed to sell stock. She

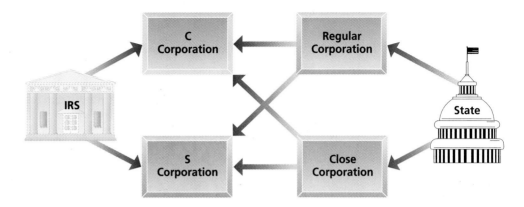

Exhibit 33.3
Both a regular and a close corporation can be either a C or an S corporation.

chose the corporate form of organization primarily because it would be the most convenient for raising funds.

Close Corporations

State laws regulate corporations, but federal statutes determine their tax status. Many states treat small corporations differently and even give them a different name: close corporations. The federal tax code also provides more favorable tax treatment to some small corporations and calls them S corporations. But the two sets of statutes are completely independent. Thus a close corporation or a regular (nonclose) corporation may or may not be an S corporation. Exhibit 33.3 illustrates the difference between state and IRS regulation of corporations.

Reynoldo, his son Juan, and Juan's girlfriend Marta have decided to open a restaurant featuring "cucina nueva"—modern, light Latin American food. Reynoldo will do the cooking in the back, while Juan and Marta run the front operation, everything from maître d' to accountant.

One of the first questions they face is: What form of organization? A sole proprietorship will not work, because there are three of them. They are concerned about the liability of a partnership. A corporation may be the best option, except it seems like an expensive bother. Who would be on their board of directors? Why do they even need a board? They have no plans to sell shares to the public. They want to act like a partnership, with all decisions made equally, but they need the legal protection of a corporation.

Their lawyer suggests that a close corporation might be the best choice. Although the provisions of close corporation statutes vary from state to state, they tend to have certain common themes:

- **Protection of Minority Shareholders.** Marta is concerned that Reynoldo and Juan may form an alliance and vote against her. Close corporations are permitted great leeway to prevent such problems. For example, *Abogado Verde, Inc.,* could require a unanimous vote of all shareholders to choose officers, set salaries, or pay dividends. It could grant each shareholder veto power over all important corporate decisions.

- **Transfer Restrictions.** What would happen if Reynoldo sold some of his shares to his other (irresponsible) children? Close corporation statutes often limit a shareholder's ability to sell shares without first offering them to the other owners. Similarly, if Reynoldo died, Juan and Marta would have the first option to buy his stock.

- **Flexibility.** Close corporations can typically operate without a board of directors, a formal set of bylaws, or annual shareholder meetings.

- **Dispute Resolution.** The three shareholders are allowed to agree in advance that any one of them can dissolve the corporation if some particular event occurs or, if they choose, for any reason at all. Marta could, for example, insist on the right to dissolve the corporation herself at any time, or if revenues for a month fall below a certain level. Even without such an agreement, a shareholder can ask a court to dissolve a close corporation if the other owners behave "oppressively" or "unfairly."

S Corporations

The majority of new businesses lose money in their early years. Only about half of all start-ups survive as long as eight years. Congress created S corporations (aka "S corps") to encourage entrepreneurship by offering tax breaks. **Shareholders of S corps have the best of all worlds: the limited liability of a corporation and the tax status of a partnership.** Like a partnership, an S corp is not a taxable entity—all of the company's profits and losses pass through to the shareholders, who pay tax at their individual rates. It avoids the double taxation of a regular corporation (called a "C corporation"). If, as is often the case, the start-up loses money, investors can deduct these losses against their other income.

A group of wealthy investors decided to start a magazine called *Living Alternatives*. The investors knew that magazines are risky and that most start-ups fail. But successful magazines are very profitable, and these investors believed in the magazine's mission—teaching consumers how to protect the environment. Unfortunately, the magazine failed after a year, but at least the investors could deduct these losses against their other (ample) income. Without this incentive, many of them would never have made the initial investment.

Eventually, however, most companies terminate their S election because of the limitations on this form of organization:

- There can be only one class of stock.

- There can be only 75 shareholders.

- Shareholders must be individuals, estates, charities, pension funds, or trusts, not partnerships or corporations.

- Shareholders must be citizens or residents of the United States, not nonresident aliens.

- All shareholders must agree that the company should be an S corporation.

Limited Liability Companies

You may be thinking that there are already as many different forms of organization as any entrepreneur could possibly need, but, as you have seen, none of them is perfect. In a continuing search for earthly perfection, states now permit limited liability companies (LLCs). **An LLC offers the limited liability of a corporation and the tax status of a partnership, without the limitations of an S corporation.**

An LLC is an extremely useful form of organization increasingly favored by entrepreneurs. However, state laws vary greatly. Thus, we can only discuss general trends in state laws. Before forming an LLC, you should carefully review the laws in your state.

Formation

To organize an LLC, you generally need two documents: a charter and an operating agreement. The charter contains basic information such as name and address. It must be filed with the secretary of state in your jurisdiction. An operating agreement sets out the rights and obligations of the owners, called members. Although some states do not require an operating agreement, lawyers recommend them as a way to avoid disputes. A sample is shown at **http://www.tannedfeet.com/simple_operating_Agreement_for_llc.doc.**

Limited Liability

As in a corporation, members are not personally liable for debts of the company. They risk only their investment. They are, however, personally liable for their own acts. The following case illustrates the scope of this protection.

CASE SUMMARY

ANTHONY v. BLUM

1999 Conn. Super. LEXIS 1037
Superior Court of Connecticut, 1999

FACTS: Leonard C. Blum, an attorney, was negligent in his representation of Louis Anthony, Sr. In settlement of Anthony's claim against him, Blum signed a promissory note for $10,400 on behalf of his law firm, Gladstone, Schwartz, Blum & Woods, LLC. When the law firm did not pay, Anthony filed suit against Blum. In his suit, Anthony alleged that Blum, as a member of the LLC, was personally liable for the promissory note.

ISSUE: Is a member personally liable for the debt of an LLC that was caused by his own negligence?

DECISION: Blum was not personally liable.

REASONING: Under the state statute, members of a limited liability company are not personally liable for any obligations of their LLC, whether arising in contract or tort, that are caused by other LLC members, agents, or employees. Members are personally liable only for their own negligent or wrongful acts.

Anthony argues Blum is personally liable because the promissory note was issued by the law firm to settle a claim based on Blum's negligence. Indeed, Blum might be liable if this case were for malpractice rather than breach of contract. But Anthony is seeking payment on a debt arising from a contract entered into by the LLC. Under the statute, Blum is not personally liable for such a claim. ◢

Tax Status

As in a partnership, income flows through the company to the individual members, avoiding the double taxation of a corporation.

Flexibility

Unlike S corporations, LLCs can have members that are corporations, partnerships, or nonresident aliens. LLCs can also have different classes of stock. Unlike corporations, LLCs are not required to hold annual meetings or maintain a minute book.

Transferability of Interests

In keeping with the flexible approach of LLCs, the members have a choice. If they want, the operating agreement can give them the right to transfer their interests freely to anyone. However, if the operating agreement is silent on this issue, then the members of the LLC must obtain the unanimous permission of the remaining members before transferring their ownership rights.

Duration

It used to be that LLCs automatically dissolved upon the withdrawal of a member (owing to, for example, death, resignation, or bankruptcy). The current trend in state laws, however, is to permit an LLC to continue in operation even after a member withdraws. Unless the operating agreement provides otherwise, the LLC must pay the departing member the value of her interest.

Going Public

Once an LLC goes public, it loses its favorable tax status and is taxed as a corporation, not a partnership. Thus, there is no real advantage to using the LLC form of organization for a publicly traded company. And there are some disadvantages: Unlike corporations, LLCs do not enjoy a well-established set of statutory and case law that is relatively consistent across the many states. For this reason, it may well turn out that most privately held companies begin as LLCs but change to corporations when they go public.

Changing Forms

Some companies that are now corporations might prefer to be LLCs. However, the IRS considers this change to be a sale of the corporate assets and levies a tax on the value of these assets. For this reason, few corporations have made the change. However, switching from a partnership to an LLC or from an LLC to a corporation is not considered a sale and does not have the same adverse tax impact.

Chapter Conclusion

Starting a business is immensely time-consuming. Eighteen-hour days are the norm. Not surprisingly, entrepreneurs are sometimes reluctant to spend their valuable time on legal issues that, after all, do not contribute directly to the bottom line. Wise entrepreneurs know, however, that careful attention to legal issues is an essential component of success. The form of organization affects everything from taxes to liability to management control. The idea for the business may come first, but legal considerations occupy a close second place.

Chapter Review

	Separate Taxable Entity	Personal Liability for Owners	Ease of Formation	Transferable Interests (Easily Bought and Sold)	Perpetual Existence	Other Features
Sole Proprietorship	No	Yes	Very easy	No, can only sell entire business	No	
General Partnership	No	Yes	Easy	No	Depends on the partnership agreement	
Limited Liability Partnership	No	No	Difficult	No	Depends on the partnership agreement	
Limited Partnership	No	Yes, for general partner No, for limited partners	Difficult	Yes, for limited partners, if partnership agreement permits	Yes	
Corporation	Yes	No	Difficult	Yes	Yes	
Close Corporation	Yes, for C corporation No, for S corporation	No	Difficult	Transfer restrictions	Yes	Protection of minority shareholders. No board of directors required.
S Corporation	No	No	Difficult	Transfer restrictions	Yes	Only 75 shareholders. Only one class of stock. Shareholders must be individuals, citizens or residents of the U.S. All shareholders must agree to S status.
Limited Liability Company	No	No	Difficult	Yes, if the operating agreement permits	Varies by state, but generally, yes	No limit on the number of shareholders, the number of classes of stock, or the type of shareholder.

PRACTICE TEST

Matching Questions

Match the following terms with their definitions:

___ **A.** S Corp

___ **B.** Dissociation

___ **C.** Close corp

___ **D.** Dissolution

___ **E.** Limited partnership

1. The first step in the process of terminating a partnership.

2. Created by federal law.

3. The general partner is liable.

4. Created by state law.

5. A partner leaves the partnership.

True/False Questions

Circle true or false:

1. T   F   Sole proprietorships must file a tax return.

2. T   F   Ownership in a partnership is not transferable.

3. T   F   Creditors of a partnership must first seek recovery from partnership assets before going after the personal assets of a partner.

4. T   F   In a limited partnership, neither the general partner nor the limited partners are personally liable for the debts of the partnership.

5. T   F   The laws regulating limited liability companies are generally consistent from state to state.

Multiple-Choice Questions

6. CPA QUESTION: Assuming all other requirements are met, a corporation may elect to be treated as an S corporation under the Internal Revenue Code if it has:

(a) Both common and preferred stockholders.

(b) A partnership as a stockholder.

(c) Seventy-five or fewer stockholders.

(d) The consent of a majority of the stockholders.

7. A partner's fiduciary duty does *not* include the following responsibilities:

(a) Partners are personally liable for negligent conduct.

(b) Partners must turn over to the partnership any earnings from an activity that is related to the partnership's business.

(c) If a partner is offered an opportunity that is related to the partnership business, he must first seek permission of the other partners before accepting it.

(d) A partner must turn over any profits from an activity that is a conflict of interest with the partnership.

(e) Partners are personally liable for intentional misconduct.

8. The following event does *not* automatically dissolve a term partnership:

(a) The partnership achieves its goals.

(b) A partnership is dissociated and all of the remaining partners vote to wind up the business.

(c) A court determines the partnership cannot be run at a profit.

(d) A partner withdraws.

(e) The partners agree to dissolve before the end of the term.

9. Joint and several liability means that:

   (a) A creditor of the partnership must sue all the partners together.

   (b) A creditor of the partnership must sue the partnership and all the partners together.

   (c) A creditor of the partnership can recover the full amount owed from the partnership or from any of the partners.

   (d) A creditor of the partnership can recover the full amount owed from the partnership or from each of the partners.

   (e) A creditor of the partnership must sue the partnership first, before suing the partners individually.

10. While working part-time at a Supercorp restaurant, Jenna spills a bucket of hot french fries on a customer. Who is liable to the customer?

   (a) Supercorp alone.

   (b) Jenna alone.

   (c) Both Jenna and Supercorp.

   (d) Jenna, Supercorp and the president of Supercorp.

   (e) Jenna, Supercorp and the shareholders of Supercorp.

Short-Answer Questions

11. Under Delaware law, a corporation cannot appear in court without a lawyer, but a partnership can. Fox Hollow Ventures, Ltd., was a limited liability company. One of its employees, who was not a lawyer, appeared in court to represent the company. Does an LLC more closely resemble a partnership, which may represent itself in court, or a corporation, which requires representation by a lawyer?

12. Alan Dershowitz, a law professor famous for his wealthy clients (O. J. Simpson, Claus von Bulow, Leona Helmsley), joined with other lawyers to open a kosher delicatessen, Maven's Court. Dershowitz met with greater success at the bar than in the kitchen—the deli failed after barely a year in business. One supplier sued for overdue bills. What form of organization would have been the best choice for Maven's Court?

13. Mrs. Meadows opened a biscuit shop called The Biscuit Bakery. The business was not incorporated. Whenever she ordered supplies, she was careful to sign the contract in the name of the business, not personally: The Biscuit Bakery by Daisy Meadows. Unfortunately, she had no money to pay her flour bill. When the vendor threatened to sue her, Mrs. Meadows told him that he could only sue the business, because all the contracts were in the business's name. Will Mrs. Meadows lose her dough?

14. The Logan Wright Foundation (LWF), an Oklahoma nonprofit corporation, was a partner in a partnership formed to operate two Sonic Drive-In restaurants. LWF argued that it was not responsible for Sonic's taxes because LWF was merely a limited partner, with limited liability to the partnership's creditors, including the IRS. The partnership had never filed a certificate of limited partnership with the secretary of state. Is it a valid limited partnership?

15. ROLE REVERSAL: Write a multiple-choice question that focuses on the difference between an LLC and an S corporation.

Internet Research Problem

Either go to **http://www.findlaw.com/casecode/#statelaw** or use Westlaw or LEXIS to find the statute on LLCs for your state. Fill out a sample certificate of organization for a business that you might like to start. Is an operating agreement required?

You can find further practice problems in the Online Quiz at **http://beatty.westbuslaw.com** or in the Study Guide that accompanies this text.

The Life and Death of a Corporation

Many people dream of starting their own business. For Judy George, the moment had come. She was ready to open Domain—a chain of upscale stores selling European-style furnishings and accessories. Her business plan was in place and her investors were ready; all she needed was to take care of legal matters. But she knew that legal issues were no small detail and that the choices she made would have a major impact on the success of her business.

In this chapter you will learn how to form a corporation and also how to avoid traps that await the unwary entrepreneur, before and after a business is formed. Finally, you will learn how to dissolve a corporation. ■

Before the Corporation Is Formed

To get Domain up and running, Judy George had more to do than seemed humanly possible. She had to find store locations, buy inventory, hire employees—it all seemed overwhelming. Her lawyer cautioned her not to do *too* much, *too* quickly. The corporation had not been formed, and she needed to be careful to avoid liability as a promoter.

The **promoter** is the person who creates the corporation. It is her idea; she raises the capital, hires the lawyers, calls the shots. Judy George was Domain's promoter.

Suppose that George finds the perfect location for Domain's flagship store before the corporation is legally formed. What would happen if she signs the lease? **A promoter is personally liable on any contract she signs before the corporation is formed.** After formation, the corporation can **adopt** the contract, in which case, both it and the promoter are liable. George could get off the hook personally only if the landlord agrees to a **novation,** that is, a new contract with the corporation alone.

Incorporation Process

The mechanics of incorporation are easy: Simply fill out the form and submit it online or mail it (with a check) to the secretary of state. Nonetheless, this document needs to be completed with some care. The corporate charter defines the corporation, including everything from the company's name to the number of shares it will issue. States use different terms to refer to a charter; some call it the "articles of incorporation," others use "articles of organization," and still others say "certificate" instead of "articles." All of these terms mean the same thing. Similarly, some states use the term "shareholders," and others use "stockholders"; they are both the same.

There is no federal corporation code, which means that a company can incorporate only under state, not federal, law. No matter where a company actually does business, it may incorporate in any state. This decision is important because the organization must live by the laws of whichever state it chooses for incorporation. To encourage similarity among state corporation statutes, the American Bar Association drafted the Model Business Corporation Act (the Model Act) as a guide. Many states do use the Model Act as a guide, although Delaware does not. Therefore, in this chapter we will give examples from both the Model Act and specific states, such as Delaware. Why Delaware? Despite its small size, it has a disproportionate influence on corporate law. More than 300,000 corporations are incorporated there, including 60% of Fortune 500 companies.

WHERE TO INCORPORATE?

A company is called a **domestic** corporation in the state where it incorporates and a **foreign** corporation everywhere else. Companies generally incorporate either in the state where they do most of their business or in Delaware. They typically must pay filing fees and franchise taxes in their state of incorporation as well as in any state in which they do business. To avoid this double set of fees, a business that will be operating primarily in one state would probably select that state for incorporation rather than Delaware. But if a company is going to do business in several states, it might consider choosing Delaware (or, perhaps, Ohio, Pennsylvania, Nevada, or one of the other states with sophisticated corporate laws). George incorporated Domain in Delaware because she planned to open stores in many states and also because outside investors felt more comfortable being incorporated in a state where they were familiar with the law. More information about Delaware law is available at **http://www.state.de.us/corp**. Or browse **http://www. findlaw.com/11stategov/indexcorp.html** for links to all state corporation Web sites.

Delaware offers corporations several advantages:

- *Laws that favor management.* For example, if the shareholders want to take a vote in writing instead of holding a meeting, many other states require the vote to be unanimous; Delaware requires only a majority to agree. The Delaware legislature also tries to keep up-to-date by changing its code to reflect new developments in corporate law.

- *An efficient court system.* Delaware has a special court (called "Chancery Court") that hears nothing but business cases and has judges who are experts in corporate law.

- *An established body of precedent.* Because so many businesses incorporate in the state, its courts hear a vast number of corporate cases, creating a large body of precedent. Thus lawyers feel they can more easily predict the outcome of a case in Delaware than in a state where few corporate disputes are tried each year.

THE CHARTER

Once a company has decided *where* to incorporate, the next step is to prepare and file the charter. The charter must always be filed with the secretary of state; some jurisdictions also require that it be filed in a county office. Sample articles of incorporation for Delaware are available at **http://www.state.de.us/corp**.

Name

The Model Act imposes two requirements in selecting a name. First, all corporations must use one of the following words in their name: "corporation," "incorporated," "company," or "limited." Delaware also accepts some additional terms, such as "association" or "institute." Second, under both the Model Act and Delaware law, a new corporate name must be different from that of any corporation, limited liability company, or limited partnership that already exists in that state. If your name is Freddy Dupont, you cannot name your corporation "Freddy Dupont, Inc.," because Delaware already has a company named E. I. Dupont de Nemours & Co. It does not matter that Freddy Dupont is your real name or that the existing company is a large chemical business while you want to open a video arcade. The names are too similar.

When Judy George started her company, she considered other names such as Intimacy and Sanctuary before settling on Ciao Italia, Inc. Afterwards, her advertising agency suggested a change to Domain. "It was probably the most emotional part of the process of putting this deal together," George explained. "When I heard 'Domain' I couldn't even talk. I couldn't work. All the heartfelt stuff about the concept just exploded. I just knew."

Address and Registered Agent

A company must have an official address in the state in which it is incorporated so that the secretary of state knows where to contact it and so that anyone who wants to sue the corporation can serve the complaint in-state. Since most companies incorporated in Delaware do not actually have an office there, they hire a registered agent to serve as their official presence in the state. Agents typically charge about $100 annually for this service.

Incorporator

The incorporator signs the charter and delivers it to the secretary of state for filing. Incorporators are not required to buy stock, nor do they necessarily have any future relationship with the company. Typically, the lawyer who forms the corporation serves as its incorporator. Domain's incorporator was William B. Simmons, Jr., the young lawyer who prepared the charter.

Purpose

The corporation is required to give its purpose for existence. Most companies use a very broad purpose clause such as Domain's:

> The nature of the business or purposes to be conducted or promoted is to engage in any lawful act or activity for which corporations may be organized under the General Corporation Law of Delaware.

Stock

The charter must provide three items of information about the company's stock.

Number of Shares. Before stock can be sold, it must first be authorized in the charter. The corporation can authorize as many shares as the incorporators choose, but usually the more shares, the higher the filing fee. If a company wants more shares after incorporation, it simply amends its charter and pays the additional fee. The Domain charter initially authorized 10,000 shares, but soon increased this number to over 10 million.

Stock that has been authorized but not yet sold is called **authorized and unissued.** Stock that has been sold is termed **authorized and issued** or **outstanding.** Stock that the company has sold but later bought back is **treasury stock.**

Par Value. The concept of par value was designed to protect investors. Originally, par value was supposed to be close to market price. A company could not issue stock at a price less than par, which meant that it could not sell to insiders at a sweetheart price well below market value. (Once the stock was *issued*, it could be *traded* at any price.) In modern times, par value does not relate to market value; it is usually some nominal figure such as 1¢ or $1 per share. Companies may even issue stock with no par value. Domain stock has a par value of 1¢ per share.

Classes and Series. Different shareholders often make different contributions to a company. Some may be involved in management, while others may simply contribute financially. Early investors may feel that they are entitled to more control than those who come along later (and who perhaps take less risk). Corporate

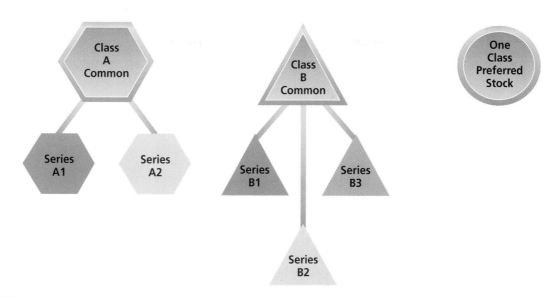

Exhibit 34.1

structure can be infinitely flexible in defining the rights of these various share-holders. Stock can be divided into categories called **classes,** and these classes can be further divided into subcategories called **series.** All stock in a series has the same rights, and all series in a class are fundamentally the same, except for minor distinctions. For example, in a class of preferred stock, all shareholders may be entitled to a dividend, but the amount of the dividend may vary by series. Different classes of stock, however, may have very different rights—a class of preferred stock is different from a class of common stock. Exhibit 34.1 illustrates the concept of class and series.

Defining the rights of a class or series of stock is like baking a cake—the stock can contain virtually any combination of the following ingredients (although the result may not be to everyone's taste):

- *Dividend rights.* The charter establishes whether the shareholder is entitled to dividends and, if so, in what amount.

- *Voting rights.* Shareholders are usually entitled to elect directors and vote on charter amendments, among other issues, but these rights can vary among different series and classes of stock. When Ford Motor Co. went public in 1956, it issued Class B common stock to members of the Ford family. This class of stock holds about 40% of the voting power and, thereby, effectively controls the company. Not surprisingly, the chairman of the company is often named "Ford."

- *Liquidation rights.* The charter specifies the order in which classes of stockholders will be paid upon dissolution of the company.

These are the ingredients for any class or series of stock. Some stock comes prepackaged like a cake mix. "Preferred" and "common" stock are two classic types. The Model Act does not use these terms, but many states still do.

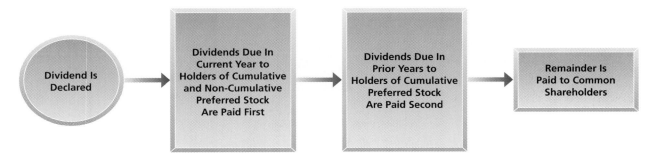

Exhibit 34.2

Owners of *preferred stock* have preference on dividends and also, typically, in liquidation. If a class of preferred stock is entitled to dividends, then it must receive its dividends before common stockholders are paid theirs. If holders of *cumulative* **preferred stock** miss their dividend one year, common shareholders cannot ever receive a dividend until the cumulative preferred shareholders have been paid, no matter how long that takes. Alternatively, holders of *non*-**cumulative preferred** stock lose an annual dividend for good if the company cannot afford it in the year it is due. When a company dissolves, preferred stockholders typically have the right to receive their share of corporate assets before common shareholders. Exhibit 34.2 illustrates the order of payment for dividends.

Common **stock is last in line for any corporate payouts, including dividends and liquidation payments.** If the company is liquidated, creditors of the company and preferred shareholders are paid before common shareholders.

The Domain charter demonstrates how flexible stock classes and series can be. The company began with common stock only. Then it added a class of cumulative preferred, which is divided into 11 series, one for each group of investors. Both classes have one vote for each share of stock, and the preferred shareholders may convert their stock into common shares, but the conversion rate is different for each series.

This ends our discussion of Domain. Like many businesses, the company has seen some lean times, but it has survived and flourished. There are now 30 Domain stores. For more information about the company, lounge over to **http://www.domain-home.com/**.

After Incorporation

DIRECTORS AND OFFICERS

Once the corporation is organized, the incorporators elect the first set of directors. Thereafter, shareholders elect directors. Under the Model Act, a corporation is required to have at least one director, unless (1) all the shareholders sign an agreement that eliminates the board; or (2) the corporation has 50 or fewer shareholders. To elect directors, the shareholders may hold a meeting, or, in the more typical case for a small company, they elect directors by written consent. A typical written consent looks like this:

Classic American Novels, Inc.
Written Consent

The undersigned shareholders of Classic American Novels, Inc., a corporation organized and existing under the General Corporation Law of the State of Wherever, hereby agree that the following action shall be taken with full force and effect as if voted at a validly called and held meeting of the shareholders of the corporation:

Agreed: That the following people are elected to serve as directors for one year, or until their successors have been duly elected and qualified:

Herman Melville

Louisa May Alcott

Mark Twain

Dated: _____ Signed: _____
Willa Cather

Dated: _____ Signed: _____
Nathaniel Hawthorne

Dated: _____ Signed: _____
Harriet Beecher Stowe

Once the incorporators or shareholders have chosen the directors, the directors must elect the officers of the corporation. They can use a consent form, if they wish. The Model Act is flexible. It simply requires a corporation to have whatever officers are described in the bylaws. The same person can hold more than one office.

The written consents and any records of actual meetings are kept in a **minute book,** which is the official record of the corporation. Entrepreneurs sometimes feel they are too busy to bother with all these details, but, if a corporation is ever sold, the lawyers for the buyers will insist on a well-organized and complete minute book. In one case, a company that was seeking a $100,000 bank loan could not find all of its minutes. Many of its early shareholders and directors were not available to re-authorize prior deeds. In the end, the company had to merge itself into a newly created corporation so it could start fresh with a new set of corporate records. The company spent $10,000 on this task, a large chunk out of the $100,000 loan.

BYLAWS

The bylaws list all the "housekeeping" details for the corporation. For example, bylaws set the date of the annual shareholders' meeting, define what a quorum is (i.e., what percentage of stock must be represented for a meeting to count), indicate how many directors there will be, give titles to officers, and establish the fiscal (i.e., tax) year of the corporation. A sample set of bylaws is available at **http://www.lectlaw.com/forms/f151.htm** and **http://www.tannedfeet.com/by-laws_ for_a_business_corporation.doc**. In the following case, the directors' ignorance of company bylaws led to disaster.

CASE SUMMARY

In Re BIGMAR

2002 Del. Ch. LEXIS 45
Court of Chancery, Delaware, 2002

FACTS: Bigmar was a Delaware corporation that manufactured and marketed pharmaceuticals in Europe. While trying to raise additional capital, the company's founder, John Tramontana, met Cynthia May. She lied to him about her education, wealth, and connections in the investment community. Unfortunately, he believed her. The upshot was that May became Bigmar's president and a director of the company. She soon took control of the company's financial records and refused to give Tramontana any information (always a bad sign).[1] When Bigmar ran out of money, Tramontana sent May an e-mail asking for her resignation. She did not respond. (Also a bad sign).

The company was in desperate financial shape, but Tramontana managed to find a bank willing to buy $1 million of Bigmar stock. He called a special meeting of the board of directors to approve the sale of shares and to fire May. The meeting was to take place by telephone. To establish a quorum necessary for the meeting to be valid, at least five of the nine directors had to take part. May and her three allies on the board refused to participate.

Tramontana testified that, at the appointed time, he met with two directors in his office. They used a speaker feature on a cell phone that Tramontana borrowed from Danilo Graticola to call two other directors, one of whom was in Heathrow Airport in London. The five directors unanimously resolved to issue the stock to the bank. The meeting then adjourned so that they could consult counsel. It was reconvened the next day, at which time they voted to fire May.

The following day, the bank transferred $1 million to Bigmar. Tramontana instructed the company's transfer agent to send stock certificates to the bank, but May contradicted his order. Tramontana and May went to court to determine if the director's meeting was valid.

ISSUE: Was the meeting of the Bigmar board of directors valid?

DECISION: The meeting of the board of directors was invalid.

REASONING: These two meetings evidently did take place; the issue is whether a quorum was present. Without a quorum, the meetings were invalid. Minutes of the meetings indicated that five directors were present. Four directors swore under oath that the minutes were accurate. Ordinarily that evidence would be sufficient, but this is not an ordinary case, for several reasons.

The minutes were prepared by a lawyer who was not present at the meetings but simply wrote down what Mr. Tramontana told him. No independent documentation or witnesses corroborated the directors' testimony. All notes taken at the meetings have been destroyed. Most of the relevant telephone records were not produced, and those that were contradict the directors' testimony. For example, the cell phone bills for the director who is supposed to have received a call in the London airport do not show any incoming calls to him at Heathrow Airport at 3 p.m., London time, which is when the meeting is said to have started. Moreover, Mr. Tramontana's telephone records show that he made an 11-minute telephone call to Mr. Graticola's cell phone number at 7:12 p.m.—a time that Mr. Tramontana claimed to have had Mr. Graticola's cell phone in his possession.

---

[1] She did, however, send him this e-mail: I wish for GOd's sake that you would GROW [UP] just a little . . . you've F the banking up here in Sweden so I can't get the money that I made [arrangements] for . . . damn idiot . . . take a shower and clean your ears out . . . you can't follow a straight line without having your ego and little hissy fits . . . Get off the play ground . . . before the big boys beat you up . . .

Although Mr. Tramontana had a speaker phone in his office, he claims that he conducted the board meeting on Mr. Graticola's borrowed cell phone. He explained that Mr. Graticola had described his new cell phone's technology in such glowing terms that he used the phone to ingratiate himself with Graticola. This story does have some plausibility, however slight, but it is difficult for the Court to accept that the same scenario occurred a second time, at the adjourned meeting. Accordingly, the Court finds that those directors' meetings were invalid.

Although the analysis could stop here, that would leave the Court (and perhaps a reader of this Opinion) with a sense of dissatisfaction, because Mr. Tramontana's testimony leaves unanswered questions. In purely human terms, the Court found this case most difficult and perplexing. Presumably, Mr. Tramontana tried to assemble all his colleagues for a telephonic meeting, but one director was unavailable because he was en route from London to Ireland. Without this director, there was no quorum. Mr. Tramontana believed that the problem could be solved by obtaining a written consent from each of the five directors. Unfortunately (and unbeknownst to Mr. Tramontana), Bigmar's bylaws provided that any action by written consent required a unanimous vote of the entire board. When Mr. Tramontana learned of this requirement, he decided to say that five directors had been present.

Mr. Tramontana and the other directors acted in the good-faith belief that unless the Bank received its shares, the Company would fall into the hands of Ms. May, who was incapable of saving it. They believed that at worst, they had failed to observe a highly technical legal requirement that was too insignificant to justify the ruination of the Company. ◢

ISSUING DEBT

Most start-up companies begin with some combination of equity and debt. Equity (i.e., stock) is described in the charter; debt is not. Authorizing debt is often one of the first steps a new company takes. There are several types of debt:

- **Bonds** are long-term debt secured by company assets. If the company is unable to pay the debt, creditors have a right to specific assets, such as accounts receivable or inventory.

- **Debentures** are long-term *unsecured* debt. If the company cannot meet its obligations, the debenture holders are paid after bondholders, but before stockholders.

- **Notes** are short-term debt, typically payable within five years. They may be either secured or unsecured.

Death of the Corporation

Sometimes, business ideas are not successful and the corporation fails. This death can be voluntary (the shareholders elect to terminate the corporation) or forced (by court order). Sometimes, a court takes a step that is much more damaging to shareholders than simply dissolving the corporation—it removes the shareholders' limited liability.

PIERCING THE CORPORATE VEIL

One of the major purposes of a corporation is to protect its owners—the shareholders—from personal liability for the debts of the organization. Sometimes, however, a court will **pierce the corporate veil;** that is, the court will hold shareholders personally liable for the debts of the corporation. Courts generally pierce a corporate veil in four circumstances:

- *Failure to observe formalities.* If an organization does not act like a corporation, it will not be treated like one. It must, for example, hold required shareholders' and directors' meetings (or sign consents), keep a minute book as a record of these meetings, and make all the required state filings. In addition, officers must be careful to sign all corporate documents with a corporate title, not as an individual. An officer should sign like this:

  Classic American Novels, Inc.

  By: *Stephen Crane*

  Stephen Crane, President

- *Commingling of assets.* Nothing makes a court more willing to pierce a corporate veil than evidence that shareholders have mixed their assets with those of the corporation. Sometimes, for example, shareholders may use corporate assets to pay their personal debts. If shareholders commingle assets, it is genuinely difficult for creditors to determine which assets belong to whom. This confusion is generally resolved in favor of the creditors—all assets are deemed to belong to the corporation.

- *Inadequate capitalization.* If the founders of a corporation do not raise enough capital (either through debt or equity) to give the business a fighting chance of paying its debts, courts may require shareholders to pay corporate obligations.

- *Fraud.* If fraud is committed in the name of a corporation, victims can make a claim against the personal assets of the shareholders who profited from the fraud.

Although it is difficult to feel sorry for shareholders who commit intentional wrongdoing such as fraud, some of these corporate sins involve carelessness more than anything else. What about the following case—was the wrongdoing careless or intentional?

CASE SUMMARY

RICE v. ORIENTAL FIREWORKS CO.

75 Or. App. 627, 707 P.2d 1250, 1985 Ore. App. LEXIS 3928
Oregon Court of Appeals, 1985

FACTS: Gregory Rice filed this claim against Oriental Fireworks and J. C. Chou for injuries Rice suffered while setting off fireworks he had bought from Oriental. The corporation had virtually no assets to pay a judgment. Although Rice had bought the fireworks from the corporation, he sought to pierce the corporate veil and obtain a judgment against Chou personally.

Chou and his wife owned all the stock of the six-year-old company. Chou was president, treasurer, and chairman of the board; his wife was vice-president. The Chous kept no records or minutes of any meetings of the shareholders or directors, except for a signed unanimous consent in lieu of the directors' first meeting. The corporation grossed from $230,000 to $400,000 annually, but its assets never exceeded $13,182. It had never obtained liability insurance, although, as Chou stated, accidents do occur, and lawsuits arise "as a general rule, right after July 4th." Chou also indicated that the lack of liability insurance motivated injured customers to bring actions against other defendants.

ISSUE: Can the plaintiff pierce the corporate veil and hold Chou personally liable?

DECISION: Chou is personally liable.

REASONING: A plaintiff has the right to pierce a corporate veil and hold shareholders liable if:

- The shareholder controlled the corporation.

- While in control, the shareholder acted improperly; and

- This improper conduct prevented the plaintiff from receiving adequate compensation from the corporation.

Under these three tests, Chou is personally liable because:

- He and his wife controlled all decisions made by officers, directors, and shareholders.

- Chou acted improperly by failing to observe corporate formalities and by inadequately capitalizing the business. A corporation is inadequately capitalized if its assets do not cover its reasonably foreseeable liabilities.

- Chou's failure to capitalize the corporation adequately or to purchase insurance prevented Rice from obtaining reasonable compensation. ◢

Termination

Terminating a corporation is a three-step process:

- *Vote.* The directors recommend to the shareholders that the corporation be dissolved, and a majority of the shareholders agree.

- *Filing.* The corporation files "Articles of Dissolution" with the secretary of state.

- *Winding up.* The officers of the corporation pay its debts and distribute the remaining property to shareholders. When the winding up is completed, the corporation ceases to exist.

The secretary of state may dissolve a corporation that violates state law by, for example, failing to pay the required annual fees. Indeed, many corporations, particularly small ones, do not bother with the formal dissolution process. They simply cease paying their required annual fees and let the secretary of state act.

A court may dissolve a corporation if it is insolvent or if its directors and shareholders cannot resolve conflict over how the corporation should be managed. The court will then appoint a receiver to oversee the winding up.

Chapter Conclusion

Most of the country's largest businesses, and many of its small ones, are corporations. Although corporations are an exceedingly useful form of organization, they are also exceedingly formal. State corporation codes contain precise rules that must be followed to the letter. To do otherwise is to court disaster.

Chapter Review

1. Promoters are personally liable for contracts they sign before the corporation is formed unless the corporation and the third party agree to a novation.

2. Companies generally incorporate in the state in which they will be doing business. However, if they intend to operate in several states, they may choose to incorporate in a jurisdiction known for its favorable corporate laws, such as Delaware or Nevada.

3. A corporate charter must generally include the company's name, address, registered agent, purpose, and a description of its stock.

4. A court may, under certain circumstances, pierce the corporate veil and hold shareholders personally liable for the debts of the corporation.

5. Termination of a corporation is a three-step process requiring a shareholder vote, the filing of "Articles of Dissolution," and the winding up of the enterprise's business.

PRACTICE TEST

Matching Questions

Match the following terms with their definitions:

___ **A.** Bond.

___ **B.** Note.

___ **C.** Debenture.

___ **D.** Incorporator.

___ **E.** Registered agent.

1. Short-term debt.

2. The company's representative in its state of incorporation.

3. Long-term secured debt.

4. The person who prepares and files the charter.

5. Long-term unsecured debt.

True/False Questions

Circle true or false:

1. T F A corporation can be formed in any state or under the federal corporate code.

2. T F Shareholders and stockholders are the same thing.

3. T F One of the reasons that corporations often incorporate in Delaware is that its laws are particularly fair to shareholders.

4. T F Most companies use a very broad purpose clause in their charter.

5. T F Stock cannot be traded at less than par value.

6. T F Preferred shareholders are entitled to receive dividends.

Multiple-Choice Questions

7. A promoter is liable for any contract he signs on behalf of a corporation before it is formed, unless:

(a) The corporation adopts the contract.

(b) The promoter notifies the other party that the corporation has not yet been formed.

(c) The promoter signs the contract on behalf of the corporation.

(d) The promoter forms the corporation within 72 hours of signing the contract.

(e) The other party agrees to a novation.

8. CPA QUESTION: A corporate stockholder is entitled to which of the following rights?

    (a) Elect officers.

    (b) Receive annual dividends.

    (c) Approve dissolution.

    (d) Prevent corporate borrowing.

9. CPA QUESTION: Generally, a corporation's articles of incorporation must include all of the following except the:

    (a) Name of the corporation's registered agent.

    (b) Name of each incorporator.

    (c) Number of authorized shares.

    (d) Quorum requirements.

10. Generally, a corporation's by-laws include all of the following except:

    (a) Par value of the stock.

    (b) The date of the shareholders meeting.

    (c) The number of directors.

    (d) The titles of officers.

    (e) The date of the fiscal year.

11. A corporation must have at least one of the following, except:

    (a) Promoter.

    (b) Incorporator.

    (c) Shareholder.

    (d) Director.

    (e) Officer.

Short-Answer Questions

12. Michael Ferns incorporated Erin Homes, Inc., to manufacture mobile homes. He issued himself a stock certificate for 100 shares for which he made no payment. He and his wife served as officers and directors of the organization, but, during the eight years of its existence, the corporation held only one meeting. Erin always had its own checking account, and all proceeds from the sales of mobile homes were deposited there. It filed federal income tax returns each year, using its own federal identification number. John and Thelma Laya paid $17,500 to purchase a mobile home from Erin, but the company never delivered it to them. The Layas sued Erin Homes and Michael Ferns, individually. Should the court "pierce the corporate veil" and hold Ferns personally liable?

13. Davis Ajouelo signed an employment contract with William Wilkerson. The contract stated: ". . . whatever company, partnership, or corporation that Wilkerson may form for the purpose of manufacturing shall succeed Wilkerson and exercise the rights and assume all of Wilkerson's obligations as fixed by this contract." Two months later, Wilkerson formed Auto-Soler Company. Ajouelo entered into a new contract with Auto-Soler providing that the company was liable for Wilkerson's obligations under the old contract. Neither Wilkerson nor the company ever paid Ajouelo the sums owed him under the contracts. Ajouelo sued Wilkerson personally. Does Wilkerson have any obligations to Ajouelo?

14. ETHICS: This case arises out of an unpaid hotel bill. An organization called the 21st Century Commission on African American Males made arrangements for a conference at the Omni Shoreham Hotel in Washington. J. D. Andrews signed the contract on behalf of the commission. Although the commission made some payments, $88,044.07 was still outstanding on the bill. The commission was not incorporated at the time of the conference, but it did subsequently incorporate. The Carnegie Corp., Xerox Corp., former Virginia Governor L. Douglas Wilder, and former United States Senator Terry Sanford were active participants in and organizers of the commission. Their employees served on a planning committee for the commission. This planning committee entered into the agreement with the Shoreham Hotel. Were Carnegie, Xerox, Wilder, and Sanford liable for the hotel bill as promoters of the commission? Whether or not the defendants were legally responsible for the debt, did they have an ethical obligation to pay? Did their wealth and fame lure the hotel into a contract with the commission? What would the Ethics Checklist in Chapter 2 suggest as a possible answer?

15. Angelica is planning to start a home security business in McGehee, Arkansas. She plans to start modestly but hopes to expand her business within 5 years to neighboring towns and, perhaps, within 10 years to neighboring states. Her inclination is to incorporate her business in Delaware. Is her inclination correct?

16. ROLE REVERSAL: Courts are willing to pierce the corporate veil if a company fails to comply with corporate technicalities. Write a short-answer question in which students are asked to identify several examples of such laxity.

Internet Research Problem

Think of an idea for a new company, and prepare a corporate charter for your business. You can find a sample Delaware charter at **http://www.state.de.us/corp**. For extra credit, find a sample charter for your own state.

You can find further practice problems in the Online Quiz at **http://beatty.westbuslaw.com** or in the Study Guide that accompanies this text.

CHAPTER 35

Corporate Management

Suppose that you are a shareholder of Wallace Computer Services, Inc. The company's stock is trading between $35 and $40 when, out of the blue, Moore Corp. offers to buy all the stock for $56 a share. A few days later, Moore raises its offer to $60. Wow! You quickly tender your stock to Moore and sit back to wait for the check, while visions of luxury dance in your head. You are in good company: The owners of nearly three quarters of Wallace stock also tender. But the check never comes because Wallace's board of directors turns down the offer. How is that?

The board says that the company is worth more. How much more? Well, a year after the board rejected Moore's $60 offer, Wallace stock was trading at $56. During the same period, the stock market had risen 20%. If you had sold your Wallace stock and invested the proceeds in the market, your $60 would now be worth $72. Wallace shareholders lost out on $74 million in that year alone. But the worst was not over. During the next few years, while the stock market continued to rise, Wallace stock hit a low of $15.44.[1]

---

[1] If you are interested in following the stock price of a particular company, click on **http://finance.yahoo.com/**. If you want to pretend to play the market for Hollywood movies, try **http://www.hsx.com**.

Before the Industrial Revolution in the 18th and 19th centuries, a business owner typically supplied both capital and management. However, the capital needs of the great manufacturing enterprises spawned by the Industrial Revolution were larger than any small group of individuals could supply. To find capital, firms sought outside investors, who often had neither the knowledge nor the desire to manage the enterprise. Investors without management skills complemented managers without capital. ("Manager" includes both directors and officers.)

Modern businesses still have the same vast need for capital and the same division between managers and investors. As businesses grow, shareholders are too numerous and too uninformed to manage the enterprises they own. Therefore, they elect directors to manage for them. The directors set policy and then appoint officers to implement corporate goals. The Model Business Corporation Act (the Model Act) describes the directors' role thus: "All corporate powers shall be exercised by or under the authority of, and the business and affairs of the corporation managed by or under the direction of, its board of directors . . ."

Directors have the authority to manage the corporate business, but they also have important responsibilities to shareholders and perhaps to other **stakeholders** who are affected by corporate decisions, such as employees, customers, creditors, suppliers, and neighbors. The interests of these various stakeholders often conflict. What are the rights—and responsibilities—of directors and officers to manage these conflicts?

Managers versus Shareholders: The Inherent Conflict

The following newspaper article illustrates the ongoing debate over corporate governance in America:

> The mood here in reaction to the sale of *The Los Angeles Times* to the Tribune Company may have been best summed up by Mark H. Willes, the company's chairman, when he left the board meeting that approved the transaction late Sunday evening. Mr. Willes burst into tears and wept openly, according to several people who saw him. The sale of the paper and its parent, the Times Mirror Company, would make Mr. Willes an immensely wealthy man. And it would earn tens of thousands of dollars, in some instances more, for each of the reporters, editors and many other employees of the Times Mirror Company who hold stock and stock options.
>
> But for many people in this city, both in *The Los Angeles Times* newsroom and outside, the deal felt humiliating, they said, as if something precious had been stolen away. "There is a feeling that yesterday, a part of this city's soul was *The Los Angeles Times*," said Geoffrey Cowan, dean of the Annenberg School of Communications at the University of Southern California. "I'm not sure how much that is true tomorrow." He added, "There is a loss of identity."
>
> Within the newsroom, many people expressed anger that the Chandler family, which has controlled the company for decades, had sold the company to an outsider, in spite of assurances in recent years that it never would. "The Chandler family long ago lost interest in running a newspaper and they're just interested in the profits," said Ken Reich, a columnist who has worked at *The Los Angeles Times* for 35 years.[2]

---

[2] James Sterngold, "In Los Angeles, Tears and a Feeling of Loss," *The New York Times,* Mar. 14, 2000, p. C16.

Managers serve at least three masters: themselves, shareholders, and other stakeholders. These masters have conflicting goals:

- **Managers** want, first, to keep their jobs and, second, to build an institution that will survive them. Mark Willes, chairman of *The Los Angeles Times,* wept when his company was sold, despite the immense wealth he received from the sale. To him, the job was what mattered.

- **Shareholders** want a high stock price, right now, not five years from now. As owners, the members of the Chandler family cared more about their own profits than they did about the newspaper and its important role in the life of the city.

- **Stakeholders,** those who work for the *LA Times,* read it, sell it ink, or own the food shop across the street from its plant, want the newspaper to stay in business. The speaker of the California State Assembly lamented the sale because the paper had been a booster for the whole city of Los Angeles. (Generally, managers are not included in the stakeholder category because their interests may be different from those of lower-level employees.)

Did the Chandler family have a legal or ethical obligation to consider the impact of this sale on the community and other stakeholders? Or should the stakeholders simply accept that shareholders—and their profits—come first? These are the difficult questions facing managers around the world. Only one thing is clear: Managers cannot please all the stakeholders all the time.

The basic rule is: **Managers have a fiduciary duty to act in the best interests of the corporation's shareholders.** Since shareholders are primarily concerned about their return on investment, managers must *maximize shareholder value,* which means providing shareholders with the highest possible financial return from dividends and stock price. However, reality is more complicated than this simple rule indicates. It is often difficult to determine which strategy will best maximize shareholder value. And what about stakeholders? A number of states have adopted statutes that permit directors to take into account the interests of stakeholders as well as stockholders. The Indiana Code, for example, permits directors to consider "both the short term and long term best interests of the corporation, taking into account, and weighing as the directors deem appropriate, the effects thereof on the corporation's shareholders and the other corporate constituent groups . . ."[3] The next section looks more closely at directors' responsibilities to their various constituencies.

The Business Judgment Rule

Officers and directors have a fiduciary duty to act in the best interests of their stockholders, but under the **business judgment rule,** the courts allow managers great leeway in carrying out this responsibility. The business judgment rule is a common-law concept that virtually every court in the country recognizes. In addition some states have enacted statutes that codify the business judgment rule.

---

[3] Indiana Code §23-1-35-1.

To be protected by the business judgment rule, managers must act in good faith:

Duty of Loyalty	1.	Without a conflict of interest.
Duty of Care	2.	With the care that an ordinarily prudent person would take in a similar situation; and
	3.	In a manner they reasonably believe to be in the best interests of the corporation.

The business judgment rule is two shields in one: It protects both the manager and her decision. If a manager has complied with the rule, a court will not hold her personally liable for any harm her decision has caused the company, nor will the court rescind her decision. If the manager violates the business judgment rule, then she has the burden of proving that her decision was fair to the shareholders. If it was not fair, she may be held personally liable, and the decision can be rescinded.

The business judgment rule accomplishes three goals:

- *It permits directors to do their job.* If directors were afraid they would be liable for every decision that led to a loss, they would never make a decision, or at least not a risky one.

- *It keeps judges out of corporate management.* Without the business judgment rule, judges would be tempted, if not required, to second-guess managers' decisions.

- *It encourages directors to serve.* No one in his right mind would serve as a director if he knew that every decision was open to attack in the courtroom.

Analysis of the business judgment rule is divided into two parts. The obligation of a manager to act without a conflict of interest is called the **duty of loyalty.** The requirements that a manager act with care and in the best interests of the corporation are referred to as the **duty of care.**

DUTY OF LOYALTY

The duty of loyalty prohibits managers from making a decision that benefits them at the expense of the corporation.

Self-Dealing

Self-dealing means that a manager makes a decision benefiting either himself or another company with which he has a relationship. While working at the Blue Moon restaurant, Zeke signs a contract on behalf of the restaurant to purchase bread from Rising Sun Bakery. Unbeknownst to anyone at Blue Moon, he is a part owner of Rising Sun. Zeke has engaged in self-dealing, which is a violation of the duty of loyalty.

Once a manager engages in self-dealing, the business judgment rule no longer applies. This does not mean the manager is automatically liable to the corporation or that his decision is automatically void. All it means is that the court will no longer *presume* that the transaction was acceptable. Instead, the court will scrutinize the deal more carefully. A self-dealing transaction is valid in any one of the following situations:

- **The transaction was entirely fair to the corporation.** In determining fairness, the courts will consider the impact of the transaction on the corporation and whether the price was reasonable.

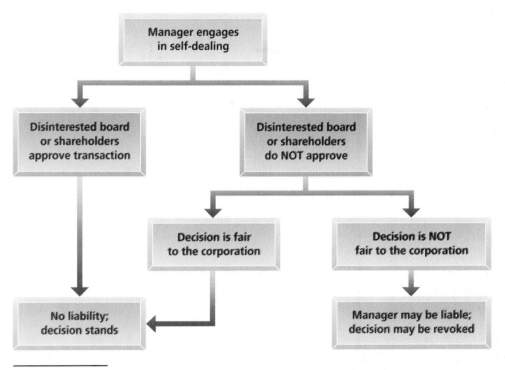

Exhibit 35.1

- **The disinterested members of the board of directors approve the transaction.** Disinterested directors are those who do not themselves benefit from the transaction.

- **The disinterested shareholders approve it.** The transaction is valid if the shareholders who do not benefit from it are willing to approve it.

Exhibit 35.1 illustrates the rules on self-dealing.

Corporate Opportunity

The self-dealing rules prevent managers from forcing their companies into unfair deals. The corporate opportunity doctrine is the reverse—it prohibits managers from excluding their company from favorable deals. **Managers are in violation of the corporate opportunity doctrine if they compete against the corporation without its consent.**

Charles Guth was president of Loft, Inc., which operated a chain of candy stores. These stores sold Coca-Cola. Guth purchased the Pepsi-Cola Co. personally, without offering the opportunity to Loft. The Delaware court found that Guth had violated the corporate opportunity doctrine and ordered him to transfer all his shares in Pepsi to Loft.[4] That was in 1939, and Pepsi-Cola was bankrupt; today, PepsiCo, Inc. is worth $88 billion.

---

[4] *Guth v. Loft*, 5 A.2d 503, 23 Del. Ch. 255, 1939 Del. LEXIS 13 (Del. 1939).

If a manager first offers an opportunity to disinterested directors or shareholders, and they turn it down, the manager then has the right to take advantage of the opportunity himself. (Remember that "disinterested directors or shareholders" are those who do not personally benefit from the transaction.) Sometimes, however, either through oversight or ignorance, managers do not seek permission in advance. To avoid violating the corporate opportunity doctrine, the manager must show after the fact that the company would not have been able to benefit from the opportunity. In the following case, a director took an opportunity without formally offering it to the company first. But all was not lost.

CASE SUMMARY

BROZ v. CELLULAR INFORMATION SYSTEMS, INC.

673 A.2d 148, 1996 Del. LEXIS 105
Supreme Court of Delaware, 1996

FACTS: Robert F. Broz was a director of Cellular Information Systems, Inc. (CIS), which had recently emerged from lengthy bankruptcy proceedings. Broz learned that a cellular telephone service license covering part of Michigan was for sale. The chief executive of CIS assured Broz that the company was not interested in the license. Broz then purchased the license himself. When new owners acquired CIS, they sued Broz on the grounds that he had violated the corporate opportunity doctrine. The Delaware trial court found in favor of the new owners of CIS and Broz appealed.

ISSUE: Did Broz violate the corporate opportunity doctrine?

DECISION: Reversed. Broz did not violate the corporate opportunity doctrine.

REASONING: When Broz purchased the Michigan license, CIS was in the process of selling off its cellular business. The company's business plan did not call for the acquisition of any new licenses. CIS's financial position was so precarious that it could not have afforded to buy the Michigan license anyway.

The trial court held that Broz should have formally submitted his purchase of the Michigan license to CIS's board of directors for approval. Indeed, the board's approval would have created a "safe harbor" and protected Broz from any claims that he had violated the corporate opportunity doctrine. But such approval is not required under Delaware law when the corporation lacks the interest or financial ability to undertake a transaction. ◢

DUTY OF CARE

In addition to the *duty of loyalty,* managers also owe a *duty of care.* **The duty of care requires officers and directors to act in the best interests of the corporation and to use the same care that an ordinarily prudent person would in the management of her own assets.**

Rational Business Purpose

Courts generally agree in principle that **directors and officers are liable for decisions that have no rational business purpose.** In practice, however, these same courts have been extremely supportive of managerial decisions, looking hard to find some justification. For decades, the Chicago Cubs baseball team refused to install lights in Wrigley Field. Cubs' fans could only take themselves out to the ballgame during the day. A shareholder sued on the grounds that the Cubs' revenues were peanuts and crackerjack compared with those generated by other teams that played at night. The Cubs defended their decision on the grounds that a large night crowd would cause the neighborhood to deteriorate, depressing the value of Wrigley Field (which the Cubs did not own). The court rooted for the home team and found that the Cubs' excuse was a "rational purpose" and a legitimate exercise of the business judgment rule.[5]

Legality

Courts are generally unsympathetic to managers who engage in illegal behavior, even if their goal is to help the company. For example, the managing director of an amusement park in New York State used corporate funds to purchase the silence of people who threatened to complain that the park was illegally operating on Sunday. The court ordered the director to repay the money he had spent on bribes, even though the company had earned large profits on Sundays.[6]

Informed Decision

Generally, courts will protect managers who make an *informed* decision, even if the decision ultimately harms the company. Making an informed decision means carefully investigating the facts. However, even if the decision is uninformed, the directors will not be held liable if the decision was entirely fair to the shareholders.

Exhibit 35.2 provides an overview of the duty of care.

Exhibit 35.2

[5] *Shlensky v. Wrigley*, 95 Ill. App. 2d 173, 237 N.E.2d 776, 1968 Ill. App. LEXIS 1107 (Ill. App. Ct. 1968).
[6] *Roth v. Robertson*, 64 Misc. 343, 118 N.Y.S. 351, 1909 N.Y. Misc. LEXIS 279 (N.Y. 1909).

In the following case, shareholders sued the board of directors for accepting a purchase price that they felt was too low. Did the directors violate their duty of care? You be the judge.

YOU BE THE JUDGE

SMITH v. VAN GORKOM

488 A.2d 858, 1985 Del. LEXIS 421
Supreme Court of Delaware, 1985

FACTS: Trans Union was a publicly traded company in the railcar leasing business. Jerome Van Gorkom, the company CEO, was nearing the mandatory retirement age of 65 and was concerned about maximizing the value of his 75,000 shares of Trans Union stock. In the preceding five years, Trans Union's stock had traded at a high of $39.50 and a low of $24.25 per share. The price was now about $37.

On September 13, Van Gorkom suggested to Jay Pritzker, a well-known corporate takeover specialist, that $55 per share would be a fair price for Trans Union. On Thursday, September 18, Pritzker offered to buy all of Trans Union's stock at this price. The offer expired three days later, on Sunday evening.

On Saturday, Van Gorkom met separately with senior managers and later with the board of directors. Salomon Brothers, the company's investment banker, was not invited to attend. At both meetings, Van Gorkom disclosed the offer and described its terms, but furnished no copies of the proposed agreement. The managers' reaction to the Pritzker proposal was completely negative—they feared losing their jobs, they did not like Pritzker, and they thought the price was too low.

The board was composed of five inside and five outside directors. Of the outside directors, four were corporate CEOs and one was the former Dean of the University of Chicago Business School. None was an investment banker or trained financial analyst. They had all recently reviewed the company's five-year forecast as well as a comprehensive 18-month study by a well-known consulting firm.

Van Gorkom explained that the company had the right to accept a higher offer, if one was made. Van Gorkom did not disclose to the board that he had first proposed the $55 price. The company's attorney advised the directors that they might be sued if they failed to accept the offer. The company's chief financial officer said that $55 was "in the range of a fair price," but "at the beginning of the range." The board approved the sale.

Van Gorkom executed the agreement at a formal social event that he hosted for the opening of the Chicago Lyric Opera. Neither he nor any other director read the agreement before signing it. The company hired Salomon Brothers to solicit other offers. No one else made a firm offer, perhaps because other bidders believed the company was already committed to Pritzker. On February 10, 69% of the stockholders of Trans Union voted in favor of the Pritzker proposal.

The plaintiff, Alden Smith, objected to the sale because he did not want to pay tax on the huge profits he realized.

YOU BE THE JUDGE: Did the directors of Trans Union violate their duty of care to the corporation by making an uninformed decision? Did the shareholders consent to the board's decision?

ARGUMENT FOR THE SHAREHOLDERS: The whole procedure for this sale was shockingly casual. Van Gorkom signed the final agreement at a social function. When the directors voted to sell the company, they had not (1) tried to negotiate a higher price with Pritzker; (2) read the agreement; (3) consulted their investment bankers; or (4) determined the intrinsic value of the company. The board did not know this important information and neither did the shareholders when they approved the sale. For that reason, the shareholder consent is invalid.

ARGUMENT FOR THE BOARD OF DIRECTORS:
Pritzker paid a fair price for the Trans Union stock. It represented a premium of (1) 62% over the average of the high and low price in the prior year; (2) 48% over the last closing price; and (3) 39% over the highest price at which the stock had *ever* traded. The plaintiffs suggest that the "intrinsic value" of the company was higher. Salomon would have earned millions of dollars if it had found a buyer willing to pay more than Pritzker, but it did not.

The five inside directors had collectively worked for the company for 116 years. The outside directors knew the company well, and they were experienced businesspeople. The board was forced to make a decision quickly because Pritzker's offer expired in three days. The Trans Union lawyer warned the directors that if they refused the offer, they would be sued.

Alden Smith's tax problems are not a legitimate reason to hold the board liable. The business judgment rule is meant to protect a board that makes a good-faith decision. This board did what it thought best for all of the company's shareholders, not for Alden Smith alone. /

Remember that managers are only liable if they make an uninformed decision and the transaction is unfair to the shareholders. If the appeals court in the Trans Union case determined that the directors had violated their duty of care, it would remand the case to the lower court to determine if $55 was a fair price.

Takeovers

The business judgment rule is an important guideline for officers and directors in the routine management of corporations. It also plays a crucial role in the regulation of hostile takeovers. In addition, both Congress and many state legislatures have passed statutes that define the roles of the various combatants in takeovers.

There are three ways to acquire control of a company:

- *Buy the company's assets.* Such a sale must be approved by both the shareholders and the board of directors of the acquired company.

- *Merge with the company.* In a merger, one company absorbs another. The acquired company ceases to exist. A merger must also be approved by the shareholders and the board of directors of the target company. If the current directors object, an acquiring company could buy enough stock to replace the board, but these battles are difficult and often end in defeat for the acquirer.

- *Buy stock from the shareholders.* This method is called a **tender offer** because the acquirer asks shareholders to "tender," or offer their stock for sale. Unlike the other methods of obtaining control, approval from the board of directors of the target company is not strictly necessary. As long as shareholders tender enough stock, the acquirer gains control. A tender offer is called a **hostile takeover** if the board of the target resists.

FEDERAL REGULATION OF TENDER OFFERS: THE WILLIAMS ACT

The Williams Act applies only if the target company's stock is publicly traded. **Under the Williams Act:**

- Any individual or group who together acquire more than 5% of a company's stock must file a public disclosure document (called a "Schedule 13D") with the Securities and Exchange Commission (SEC).

- On the day a tender offer begins, a bidder must file a disclosure statement with the SEC.

- A bidder must keep a tender offer open for at least 20 business days initially and for at least 10 business days after any substantial change in the terms of the offer.

- Any shareholder may withdraw acceptance of the tender offer at any time while the offer is still open.

- If the bidder raises the price offered, all selling shareholders must be paid the higher price, regardless of when they tendered; and

- If the stockholders tender more shares than the bidder wants to buy, the bidder must purchase shares pro rata (i.e., it must buy the same proportion from everyone, not first come, first served).

STATE REGULATION OF TAKEOVERS

Common Law of Takeovers

To fend off attack, potential targets often adopt defensive measures known as **antitakeover devices** or **shark repellents.** (Acquiring companies are sometimes called **sharks.**) **Shareholder rights plans** (aka **poison pills**) are among the most common antitakeover devices. A target company will, for example, amend its charter to provide that it can issue one share of preferred stock to each of its shareholders. If a shark purchases more than 20% of the target's stock and subsequently merges with the target, the preferred stock is convertible into 10 shares of the shark. This device makes a takeover much more expensive for the acquiring company.

Conventional wisdom views antitakeover devices as a mixed blessing—beneficial if used to ensure that shareholders receive the highest possible price for their stock in the event of a sale, but harmful to shareholders if used only to protect management from being fired. However, recent research indicates that the stock prices of companies with few shark repellents significantly outperform those of companies that provide more protection to their managers.[7]

When establishing takeover defenses, shareholder welfare must be the board's primary concern. The directors may institute shark repellents, but they must do so to ensure that bids are high, not to protect their own jobs.

In the chapter's opening vignette, Wallace Computer Services fought off a takeover attempt. Read on to find out how.

---

[7] P.A. Gompers, J. Ishii, A. Metrick, "Corporate Governance and Equity Prices," *Quarterly Journal of Economics,* 118(1), Feb. 2003.

CASE SUMMARY

MOORE CORP. LTD. v. WALLACE COMPUTER SERVICES, INC.

907 F. Supp. 1545, 1995 U.S. Dist. LEXIS 18882
United States District Court for the District of Delaware, 1995

FACTS: Under the terms of a poison pill adopted by Wallace Computer Services, Inc., each existing shareholder had the right to purchase Wallace stock at half price, in the event that 20% of Wallace's stock was acquired in a hostile takeover. Five years later, Moore Corp. offered to buy all Wallace's stock for $56 a share, which was 27% over the existing market price. However, the offer was contingent upon the Wallace board eliminating the poison pill.

Wallace consulted with Goldman, Sachs, its investment banker, which advised the company that the offer was inadequate, but did not indicate what the shares were really worth. Moore then raised its offer price to $60 per share, and again the bankers opined that the offer was inadequate. Both the board and Goldman believed that Wallace's recently adopted corporate strategy would lead to an increased stock price. Indeed, the company's recent financial results had been better than expected.

More than 73% of Wallace shareholders offered their shares to Moore. When Wallace refused to remove the poison pill, Moore filed suit.

ISSUE: Was the board's refusal to remove the poison pill a violation of the business judgment rule?

DECISION: No, the Wallace board did not violate the business judgment rule.

REASONING: In responding to a hostile tender offer, a board of directors must decide if the offer is in the best interests of the corporation and its shareholders. In making its decision, the Wallace board considered the company's strategy, its current and projected finances, and Goldman's opinion that the offer was too low. The board went through the same process again when Moore raised its offer.

A board of directors is not required to maximize shareholder value in the short term, even in the face of a takeover offer. The board believed that ultimately Wallace could achieve better returns for its shareholders than Moore and, indeed, the next set of quarterly results revealed that sales and profits had increased 32% over the prior year. The board feared that shareholders might be tempted to tender their shares because they did not know that Wallace's business strategy was beginning to pay off. Under these circumstances, the Wallace board had the right to keep the poison pill. ◢

UPDATE | As we saw at the beginning of the chapter, Wallace's favorable financial results turned out to be unsustainable. What has happened to the Wallace stock price in the last five years? How has it performed in comparison with the S&P 500? ◼

Neither the board of directors nor the court could see into the future. Did the court make the right decision with the information it had at the time? Does the business judgment rule adequately balance the rights of shareholders against those of company managers?

State Antitakeover Statutes

When fighting takeover battles, companies have also found support in state governments. Legislators may not care if a group of directors is thrown into the unemployment line, but they do fear the impact on the local economy if a major employer leaves. When the Belzberg family threatened a hostile takeover of auto parts manufacturer Arvin Industries, the second largest employer in Columbus, Indiana, the state legislature immediately passed a tough antitakeover bill that had been drafted by Arvin's own lawyers. Arvin and the Belzbergs quickly settled.

Most states have now passed laws to deter hostile takeovers. Among the common varieties:

- *Statutes that automatically impede hostile takeovers.* These statutes, for example, might ban hostile (but not friendly) mergers for five years after the acquirer buys 10% of a company.

- *Statutes that authorize companies to fight off hostile takeovers.* These statutes typically permit management, when responding to a hostile takeover, to consider the welfare of company stakeholders, such as the community, customers, suppliers, and employees. Some even go so far as to allow management to consider the regional or national economy.

Most of these statutes do not totally eliminate hostile takeovers. A determined, well-financed bidder can still be successful. But these state statutes do tip the playing field in favor of management. In the process they prevent some takeovers that shareholders might want, but they also insure that shareholders receive a high price in those takeovers that are successful.

ETHICS

Supporters of these state statutes argue that large, publicly traded corporations owe a duty to all of their constituencies. The loss of a large corporate presence can be immensely disruptive to a community. Perhaps a state should have the right to prevent economic upheaval within its borders.

Opponents contend that shareholders own the company, and their interests ought to be paramount. Antitakeover legislation entrenches management and prevents shareholders from obtaining the premium that accompanies a takeover. Opponents also argue that, if other stakeholders are so concerned with the well-being of the company, let them put their money where their mouths are and buy stock. And if current managers cannot offer shareholders as high a stock price as an outside raider, they ought to be replaced.

Delaware companies can choose not to accept the protection of the antitakeover statute. Is that the ethical choice for directors? What guidance does the Chapter 2 Ethics Checklist offer? Who are the stakeholders? What values are important to a company director? If a director owned stock in another company, how would she wish the directors of that company to respond to a takeover? ◼

Chapter Conclusion

Managers of corporations have a fiduciary duty to shareholders and are charged with running the organization for their benefit. The law, whether federal or state, common or statutory, grants managers great freedom in deciding how to promote the shareholders' interest. Particularly in the takeover arena, lawmakers have given managers considerable leeway in defending their organizations from outside attack.

Chapter Review

1. Officers and directors have a fiduciary duty to act in the best interests of the shareholders of the corporation.

2. The business judgment rule protects managers from liability for their decisions as long as the managers observe the duty of care and the duty of loyalty.

3. Under the duty of loyalty, managers may not take advantage of an opportunity that rightfully belongs to the corporation.

4. If managers enter into an agreement on behalf of their corporation that benefits them personally, then the business judgment rule does not apply. The managers may be liable unless the board of directors or the shareholders have first approved the transaction or it was fair to the corporation.

5. Under the duty of care, managers must make honest, informed decisions that have a rational business purpose.

6. The Williams Act regulates the activities of a bidder in a tender offer for stock in a publicly traded corporation.

7. When establishing takeover defenses, shareholder welfare must be the board's primary concern.

8. Most states have now passed laws to deter hostile takeovers.

PRACTICE TEST

Matching Questions

Match the following:

___ **A.** Stakeholders want

___ **B.** Shareholders want

___ **C.** Managers want

___ **D.** Duty of loyalty

___ **E.** Duty of care

1. To build an institution that will survive them.

2. Prohibits managers from making a decision that benefits them at the expense of the corporation.

3. To maximize the company's current stock price.

4. The company to stay in business.

5. Requires managers to act in the best interests of the corporation.

True/False Questions

Circle true or false:

1. T F Self-dealing means that a manager makes a decision benefiting another company with which she has a relationship.

2. T F In the *Broz* case, Broz was found not liable because he gained the approval of the president of the company.

3. T F A hostile takeover is a type of tender offer.

4. T F Takeovers are regulated solely under federal law.

5. T F Shareholders of Wallace Computer profited by the board's decision to reject the tender offer.

Multiple-Choice Questions

6. Under the duty of care, directors will be liable if they:

   (a) Make a decision that has a rational business purpose.

   (b) Use the same care as an ordinarily prudent person.

   (c) Make informed decisions.

   (d) Engage in illegal behavior that is profitable to the company.

   (e) Make an informed decision that ultimately harms the company.

7. A self-dealing transaction is invalid if:

   (a) It was fair to the corporation.

   (b) The disinterested shareholders approved it.

   (c) The price paid by the corporation was reasonable.

   (d) The disinterested members of the board of directors approved it.

   (e) A majority of the shareholders approved it.

8. Under the business judgment rule, managers must do all of the following, except one:

   (a) Act in good faith.

   (b) Act to maximize shareholder returns in the short and long run.

   (c) Act without a conflict of interest.

   (d) Act with the care of an ordinarily prudent person.

   (e) Act in the best interests of the corporation.

9. The business judgment rule does *not* achieve the following goal:

   (a) Insures the highest return to shareholders.

   (b) Protects directors from liability.

   (c) Permits directors to make the best decisions they can.

   (d) Keeps the courts from second-guessing managers' decisions.

   (e) Encourages directors to be willing to serve.

10. Under the Williams Act, the following statement is not true in regard to a publicly traded company:

    (a) Anyone who acquires more than 5% of the company's stock must file with the SEC.

    (b) Anyone who makes a tender offer must file with the SEC.

    (c) A bidder must keep a tender offer open for at least 20 calendar days.

    (d) The bidder must pay the same price to every purchaser.

    (e) A bidder must buy the same proportion of stock from everyone who tenders.

Short-Answer Questions

11. An appraiser valued a subsidiary of Signal Co. at between $230 million and $260 million. Six months later, Burmah Oil offered to buy the subsidiary at $480 million, giving Signal only three days to respond. The board of directors accepted the offer, without obtaining an updated evaluation of the subsidiary or determining if other companies would offer a higher price. Members of the board were sophisticated, with a great deal of experience in the oil industry. A Signal Co. shareholder sued to prevent the sale. Is the Signal board protected by the business judgment rule?

12. Asher Hyman and Stephen Stahl formed a corporation named "Ampersand" to produce plays. Both men were employed by the corporation. After producing one play, Stahl decided to write *Philly's Beat*, focusing on the history of rock and roll in Philadelphia. As the play went into production, the two men quarreled. Stahl resigned from Ampersand and formed another corporation to produce the play. Did the opportunity to produce *Philly's Beat* belong to Ampersand?

13. Klinicki and Lundgren started an air taxi service in Berlin, Germany, under the name Berlinair, Inc. Lundgren was approached by a group of travel agents who were interested in hiring an air charter business to take German tourists on vacation to warmer climes. Lundgren formed Air Berlin Charter Co. (ABC) and was its sole owner. On behalf of ABC, he entered into an air charter contract with the Berlin travel agents. Lundgren concealed his negotiations from Klinicki, even though he used Berlinair working time, staff, money, and facilities. Lundgren defended his behavior on the grounds that Berlinair could not afford to enter into a contract with the travel agents. Has Lundgren violated the corporate opportunity doctrine?

14. ETHICS: Ronald O. Perelman, chairman of the board and CEO of Pantry Pride, met with his counterpart at Revlon, Michel C. Bergerac, to discuss a friendly acquisition of Revlon by Pantry Pride. Revlon rebuffed Pantry Pride's overtures, perhaps in part because Bergerac did not like Perelman. The Revlon board of directors agreed to sell the company to Forstmann

Little & Co. at a price of $56 per share. Pantry Pride announced that it would engage in fractional bidding to top any Forstmann offer by a slightly higher one. To discourage Pantry Pride, the Revlon board granted Forstmann the right to purchase Revlon's Vision Care and National Health Laboratories divisions at a price some $100–$175 million below their value. Was the board within its rights in selling off these two divisions? Do the shareholders of Revlon have the right to prevent a sale of the company to Forstmann at a price lower than Pantry Pride offered? Is it ethical for a board to base a takeover decision on personal animosity? What are a board's ethical obligations to shareholders?

15. Vern Hayes owned 32% of Coast Oyster Co. and served as president and director. The company owned several large oyster beds, including two located in Washington State. Coast was struggling to pay its debts, so Hayes suggested that the company sell the Washington beds to Keypoint Co. After the sale, other officers at Coast discovered that Hayes owned 50% of Keypoint. They demanded that he give the Keypoint stock to Coast. Did Hayes violate his duty to Coast?

16. ROLE REVERSAL: Write a multiple choice question that deals with the duty of care under the business judgment rule.

Internet Research Problem

Using the Internet, find a newspaper article that discusses a failed takeover attempt. Track the stock price of the two companies involved in the dispute. Would the shareholders of the target company have been better or worse off if the company had been acquired?

You can find further practice problems in the Online Quiz at **http://beatty.westbuslaw.com** or in the Study Guide that accompanies this text.

Shareholders

In little more than a decade, Enron Corp. transformed itself from a modest pipeline company into a $65 billion global energy business. Enron's officers earned fabulous wealth and became major celebrities. But no sooner had the ink dried on articles lauding the Enron business model, when suddenly, shockingly, the company collapsed into bankruptcy court. What happened to Enron?

Enron had become, in essence, an energy trading enterprise that required a lot of cash. To obtain the cash, it created subsidiaries that held substantial sums in safe investments. Enron borrowed money that was secured by these subsidiaries, but—and here is the catch—excluded this debt from Enron's financial statements. In essence, the income from energy sales appeared as revenue for Enron, but the debt to support this income was off the books. None of these "special" arrangements was disclosed clearly to shareholders.

Moreover, compensation for top executives was tied directly to the company's stock price. So managers had a powerful incentive to raise the stock price in any way possible, legal or not. Stock manipulation and questionable accounting practices became standard operating procedure at Enron. The company would, for example, book as *current* revenues its (optimistic) assessment of what *future* revenues might be for new deals.

A few stock analysts began to ask tough questions. Ultimately, Enron restated its earnings by nearly $600 million. This restatement caused investors to lose confidence. Enron stock entered a death spiral into bankruptcy, destroying the net worth (and the dreams) of many employees and shareholders. It turned out, however, that not all employees suffered dramatic financial losses—the top executives had sold hundreds of millions of dollars in stock before the collapse, even as they were exhorting other employees and shareholders to continue buying.

Outrage and uproar ensued. Inquiring minds wanted to know: Why did the law fail to protect Enron shareholders? Why did the impressive board of directors miss—or ignore—obvious signs of trouble? At the same time, other prominent companies confessed to shady accounting practices: Xerox Corp., Merrill Lynch, Lucent, among others. The CEO of investment bank Goldman Sachs said, "I cannot think of a time when business over all has been held in less repute."

So what is the solution to this raft of corporate wrongdoing? Some commentators claim that there are simply a few bad apples in the executive orchard. More pessimistic commentators argue that wholesale changes are needed in the regulation of public companies. After reading this chapter, you decide. ◾

Introduction

Shareholders may technically own the companies in which they invest, but their power over these enterprises is very limited. As Chapter 35 revealed, *directors, not shareholders,* have the right to manage the corporate business. However, not all directors are created equal. Inside directors, who are also officers of the corporation, have typically controlled their company's board. Outside directors (als called independent directors) do not work for the company and have traditionally played a lesser role. They have been described scornfully as "ornaments on a corporate Christmas tree" or "parsley on the fish." Nominated by their friend, the chief executive (CEO), and elected by shareholders without question, these directors could collect handsome paychecks while simply rubber-stamping the CEO's decisions. Without a watchdog board, CEOs and other officers have great latitude in running their companies. As the Enron episode illustrates, they sometimes abuse this power. The results are predictable: Studies show that a weak board means higher pay for the boss and lower stock prices for the shareholders.

At one time, corporate stock was primarily owned by individuals, but now institutional investors—pension plans, mutual funds, insurance companies, banks, foundations, and university endowments—own more than 50% of all shares publicly traded in the United States. Institutional investors, with enormous sums to invest, have little choice but to buy the stock of large companies. If they are unhappy with management, it is difficult for them to do the "Wall Street walk"—that is, sell their shares—because a sale of their stock would depress the market price. And where would they invest the proceeds? Institutional investors cannot all profit simply by trading shares among themselves. For better or worse, the fate of fund managers hangs on the success of these large companies. So what can shareholders, large and small, do to protect their investments? This chapter discusses the ways in which existing laws do (and do not) safeguard their interests. At the end, we also discuss some of the many reform proposals that would provide greater protection to corporate owners.

ETHICS Enron was a "win at all cost" culture. Nothing, but nothing, was more important than keeping the stock price high. The company's focus was on short-term results, not long-term value. Its top executives worried about their income this year, not the impact on lower-level employees, shareholders, and society. Would the Ethics Checklist from Chapter 2 have been helpful to Enron executives? Should they have considered the consequences of their actions? What would happen to the economy if all executives behaved in a similar fashion? The New York Stock Exchange (NYSE) recently passed rules requiring each of its listed companies to publish a code of ethics. Would such a code have prevented abuses at Enron?

Rights of Shareholders

Shareholders have neither the *right* nor the *obligation* to manage the day-to-day business of the enterprise. If you own stock in Starbucks Corp., your share of stock plus $4.45 entitles you to a cup of mocha Valencia, the same as everyone else. By the same token, if the pipes freeze and the local Starbucks store floods, the manager has no right to call you, as a shareholder, to help clean up the mess. What rights do shareholders have?

RIGHT TO INFORMATION

Under the Model Business Corporation Act (Model Act), shareholders acting in good faith and with a proper purpose have the right to inspect and copy the corporation's minute book, accounting records, and shareholder lists. A **proper purpose** is one that aids the shareholder in managing and protecting her investment. If, for example, Celeste is convinced that the directors of Devil Desserts, Inc., are mismanaging the company, she might demand a list of other shareholders so that she can ask them to join her in a lawsuit. The company may not like this purpose, but it is proper and the company is required to give her the list. If, however, Celeste wants to use the shareholder list as a potential source for her new mail-order catalog featuring exercise equipment, the company could legitimately turn her down.

RIGHT TO VOTE

A corporation must have at least one class of stock with voting rights.

Proxies

Shareholders who do not wish to attend a shareholders' meeting may appoint someone else to vote for them. Confusingly, both this person and the document the shareholder signs to appoint the substitute voter are called a **proxy.** Under rules of the Securities Exchange Commission (SEC), companies are not *required* to solicit proxies. However, a meeting is invalid without a certain percentage of shareholders in attendance, either in person or by proxy. This attendance requirement is called a **quorum.** As a practical matter, if a public company with thousands of investors does not solicit proxies, it will not obtain a quorum. Therefore, virtually all public companies do solicit proxies. Along with the proxy, the company must also give shareholders a **proxy statement** and an **annual report.** The proxy statement provides information on everything from management compensation to a list of directors who miss too many meetings. The annual report contains detailed financial data.

CYBERLAW

Under SEC rules, companies can offer (but not require) electronic delivery of proxy statements and annual reports. Intel Corp. was one of the first companies to make its proxy statements and annual reports available on its Web site. See **http://www .intel.com/intel/finance/savethetrees.htm.** You can also read about Intel's policies on corporate governance at **http://www.intel.com/intel/finance/corp_gov.htm.** ∎

Typically, only the company itself solicits proxies for a shareholder meeting, but sometimes shareholders who disapprove of company policies try to convince other shareholders to appoint them as proxy instead of management. These dissident shareholders must also prepare a proxy statement that discloses, among other information, who they are, how they are financing their opposition, and how many other proxy contests they have participated in. If enough shareholders give their proxies to the dissidents, then the dissidents can elect themselves to the board of directors.

Shareholder Proposals

Some shareholders who oppose a company policy may not aspire to a board seat or perhaps cannot afford to send a proxy statement to other investors. Such shareholders may use an alternative method for communicating with fellow shareholders. **Under SEC rules, any shareholder who has continuously owned for one year at least 1% of the company or $2,000 of stock can require that one proposal be placed in the company's proxy statement to be voted on at the shareholder meeting.**

In practice, many of these resolutions have a political agenda: save the environment, withdraw from Myanmar, ban genetically modified ingredients. Others relate to corporate governance issues: reduce executive compensation and permit secret ballots. Each year, public companies vote on about 450 shareholder proposals. Prior to 1985, only two proposals had been approved—ever. Currently, about 10 to 20 receive a majority vote each year, a definite improvement (or deterioration, depending on your perspective). The Web sites at **http://www .socialfunds.com** and **http://www.irrc.org** provide information about recent shareholder proposals.

Despite the long history of shareholder proposals, an essential question remains unanswered: Are shareholder proposals binding on the company? The SEC recommends that proposals be couched in the form of a request or recommendation, because state laws sometimes prohibit binding resolutions. Although shareholders traditionally followed this advice, many activists have been angered by companies that refuse to implement proposals that receive a majority vote from shareholders. In response, an increasing number of shareholders have begun to propose binding resolutions. The Supreme Court of Oklahoma provided ammunition when it ruled that a shareholder vote on takeover defenses could be binding.[1]

Ironically, companies sometimes implement shareholder proposals that have not received support from a majority of the shareholders. Many companies are willing to negotiate, particularly with institutional investors, over issues of corporate governance. Nearly half of all shareholder proposals are now withdrawn before a vote because the company capitulates. For example, Colgate-Palmolive Co. agreed to a proposal by institutional investors to permit secret ballots at shareholder meetings.

Shareholder Meetings

A company must hold an **annual meeting** of shareholders, if for no other reason than to elect directors. Everyone who owns stock on the **record date** must be sent notice of a meeting.

CYBERLAW

Delaware law has entered cyberspace. It now permits companies to send official notices to their shareholders electronically and even allows shareholders to vote electronically both before and during a meeting. Shareholder meetings can be held in cyberspace as long as shareholders have a reasonable opportunity to participate in and vote at the meeting. But so far no company has held a meeting online, partly from fear of offending shareholders who suspect that they will not be able to confront corporate managers as effectively online as they can in person. ▪

Election and Removal of Directors

Shareholders have the right to elect directors and also to remove them from office. Under the Model Act, shareholders generally can remove directors at any time for any reason.

In theory, shareholders elect directors and directors then appoint officers. Typically, however, the real relationship between directors and shareholders in public companies is very different from this formula. Yes, shareholders elect the directors, but the shareholders almost always vote for nominees chosen by the board itself. And the board's nominating committee rarely chooses candidates that the CEO opposes. The officers are really choosing the directors, not the other way around.

In response to the recent spate of corporate scandals, involving Enron and others, Congress passed the Sarbanes-Oxley Act of 2002 (which applies to public companies). Under this statute:

- All members of the board's audit committee must be independent.

- A company's CEO and CFO must certify that the company's financial statements are accurate.

---

[1] International Bhd. of Teamsters Gen. Fund v. Fleming Cos., 1999 OK 3, 975 P.2d 907, 1999 Okla. LEXIS 3 (OK, 1999).

- If a company has to restate its earnings, its CEO and CFO must reimburse the company for any bonus or profits they have received from selling company stock within a year of the release of the flawed financials.

- A company cannot make personal loans to its directors or officers.

- Each company must develop a code of ethics for its senior financial officers.

- A Public Company Accounting Oversight Board was established to develop stricter accounting standards.

In addition, under New York Stock Exchange rules, only independent directors can serve on a listed company's audit, compensation, and nominating committees. Moreover, independent directors must comprise a majority of the total board. They also must meet regularly on their own without inside directors.

Compensation for Officers and Directors

To many investors, sky-high executive compensation has become the symbol of all that is wrong with corporate governance. Take the case of Golden Books Family Entertainment, Inc. For many children a Golden Book is their first book. *Pat the Bunny,* for example, contains few words but much interaction. "Readers" can pat the bunny, sniff the flowers, and play peekaboo with the blanket. After *Pat the Bunny,* many children graduate to other Golden Books such as *The Poky Little Puppy* and *Richard Scarry's Busy, Busy Town.*

Despite its portfolio of classics, Golden Books was having financial difficulties. The company hired Richard Snyder, an experienced publishing executive, to solve its distribution and sales problems. Such experience does not come cheap. At Golden Books he was the third-highest-paid executive in the publishing industry. But an executive does not live by pay alone. Snyder relocated the company to posh new quarters, hired a private chef, and used the corporate jet for vacations. He also hired other executives (including his wife) at salaries two to three times the industry average. In return, investors expected the stock price to zoom. They just did not expect it to zoom down. Not only did the stock price plummet 80%, but the company was put up for sale. In the midst of this turmoil, the board doubled Snyder's salary and paid him a $500,000 signing bonus for extending his contract two years. The stock promptly plummeted again. The company ended up filing for bankruptcy protection, not once, but twice, under Snyder's leadership. Ultimately, it was bought out and Snyder received close to $8 million in severance pay for a job well done. This sum was about 11% of the total purchase price for the company.

In 1980, CEOs earned on average 45 times more than an ordinary worker. By 1997, the ratio had risen to 305. In 2000, CEOs at large companies were earning 458 times as much as the typical employee, even though profits had only slightly increased since 1997.

If shareholders challenge executive compensation in court, an officer's salary is presumed to be reasonable unless she voted for it as a director of the company. Shareholders must prove that the board was grossly uninformed or that the amount was so high that it had no relation to the value of the services performed and was really a gift. As the following case illustrates, war has broken out even in the Magic Kingdom.

YOU BE THE JUDGE

BREHM v. EISNER

746 A.2d 244; 2000 Del. LEXIS 51
Supreme Court of Delaware, 2000

FACTS: Michael Ovitz was an important talent broker in Hollywood. He was also a long-time friend of Disney Chairman and CEO Michael Eisner. Although Ovitz lacked experience managing a diversified public company, Disney hired him to be its president. Eisner negotiated Ovitz's employment agreement on his own, and the board approved it.

After 14 months all parties agreed that the experiment had failed, so Ovitz left Disney—but not empty-handed. Under his contract he was entitled to $140 million in severance pay. When the board originally approved this agreement, it had known how the severance payment would be calculated, but it had not realized how high the total cost could be. Graef Crystal, the compensation expert who had advised the directors, later said that he wished he had done this calculation for them.

Shareholders of Disney sued to prevent payment or to obtain damages from the directors.

ISSUE: Did the Disney directors have the right to pay $140 million to an employee who had worked at the company unsuccessfully and for only 14 months?

ARGUMENT FOR THE SHAREHOLDERS: Both sides admit that Michael Ovitz was a failure at Disney. He was with the company only 14 months. Yet he was rewarded with a severance package of $140 million. This amount bore no relation to the value of the services he performed. Moreover, the directors were grossly uninformed—they were not even aware of the amount of his total compensation when they approved it.

ARGUMENT FOR DISNEY: A board is not *grossly* negligent simply because it does not know the exact *amount* of a severance payout as long as it is fully informed about the *manner* in which such a payout will be calculated. A board is not required to be informed of every fact, but rather it is required to be reasonably informed. The size and structure of executive compensation are inherently matters of judgment with which courts should not interfere, except in extreme cases of abuse.

Answer for Instructor's Manual, not the Text: The Supreme Court of Delaware dismissed most of the plaintiffs' claims, but it remanded the case to the trial court with instructions that the plaintiffs could conduct limited additional discovery to find support for one of their allegations. After this additional discovery was completed and the complaint repleaded, the trial court denied Disney's motion to dismiss the complaint and permitted the case to proceed to trial.

Directors not only set the salaries of company officers, they also determine their own compensation (unless the charter or bylaws provide otherwise). Directors of Fortune 200 companies are paid on average $137,000 annually, of which about $84,000 is in stock. Directors of small companies earn much less, but they are often granted substantial stock options, which could, in theory, increase dramatically in value. ▮

Fundamental Corporate Changes

A corporation must seek shareholder approval before undergoing any of the following fundamental changes: a merger, a sale of major assets, dissolution of the corporation, or an amendment to the charter or bylaws.

RIGHT TO DISSENT

If a corporation (that is not publicly traded) decides to undertake a fundamental change, the Model Act and many state laws require the company to buy back the stock of any shareholders who object. This process is referred to as **dissenters' rights,** and the company must pay "fair value" for the stock. Fundamental changes include a merger or a sale of most of the company's assets.

RIGHT TO PROTECTION FROM OTHER SHAREHOLDERS

Anyone who owns enough stock to control a corporation has a fiduciary duty to minority shareholders. (Minority shareholders are those with less than a controlling interest.) The courts have long recognized that minority shareholders are entitled to extra protection because it is easy (perhaps even natural) for controlling shareholders to take advantage of them. For example: A court refused to allow one brother, who was a majority shareholder of the family company, to force the other to sell his shares. According to the court, a minority shareholder can be ejected only for a reason that is fair or has a business purpose.[2]

In the following case, a controlling shareholder allowed his financial desperation to push him too far.

CASE SUMMARY

G & N AIRCRAFT, INC. v. BOEHM

743 N.E.2d 227, 2001 Ind. LEXIS 194
Supreme Court of Indiana, 2001

FACTS: G & N Aircraft, Inc., was in the business of repairing aircraft engines. Erich Boehm owned 34% of the stock, Paul Goldsmith 26%, and three other men owned 40%. G & N operated out of a hangar owned by Goldsmith and bought its parts from Edgecumbe, Inc., which was partly owned by Goldsmith.

Goldsmith also owned several other aviation companies, all of which were unprofitable. To help him out of what was becoming an increasingly unpleasant financial position, his tax adviser suggested that he purchase all the stock of G & N. The appraised value of the company was $961,000.

Although Boehm's stock in G & N was worth about $325,000, Goldsmith offered him only $200,000. Boehm refused to sell. To force him and the other shareholders out, Goldsmith threatened to increase the rent for G & N's hangar from $6,500 per month to $30,000. He also threatened to terminate Edgecumbe as G & N's parts supplier. The other G & N shareholders did sell their stock to Goldsmith.

At its next meeting, the G & N board decided, for the first time in many years, not to declare a dividend. Goldsmith again demanded that Boehm sell his stock in G & N, this time for $250,000. The letter threatened that the company would not pay dividends for at least three years.

Boehm filed suit, alleging that Goldsmith had breached his fiduciary duty. The trial court ordered G & N and Goldsmith to purchase Boehm's stock for $521,319. The court also awarded Boehm $175,000 in punitive damages. Goldsmith appealed.

ISSUE: Did Goldsmith violate his fiduciary duty to Boehm?

DECISION: Goldsmith violated his fiduciary duty and must pay the damages awarded by the trial court.

---

[2] *Lerner v. Lerner*, 306 Md. 771, 511 A.2d 501 (Md. App. 1986).

REASONING: As a controlling shareholder, Goldsmith owed Boehm a fiduciary duty. A fiduciary must deal fairly, honestly, and openly with his corporation and fellow stockholders. Goldsmith offered to purchase Boehm's shares of G & N for substantially less than the appraised value. In and of itself, this is not a breach of duty. There is no harm in making the offer. However, Goldsmith violated his duty when he tried to force Boehm to accept it.

As landlord, Goldsmith was free to charge whatever rent he wished. But as director and majority shareholder, he had an obligation to consider the welfare of the company. The eviction was a sham and Goldsmith knew it. Goldsmith also shut off dividends. He had the right to do this on behalf of the company for legitimate business reasons, but not for the purpose of forcing Boehm out.

Goldsmith must pay Boehm the fair market value of his shares plus punitive damages. ◢

Enforcing Shareholder Rights

Shareholders in serious conflict with management have three different mechanisms for enforcing their rights: a derivative lawsuit, a direct lawsuit, or a class action.

DERIVATIVE LAWSUITS

A derivative lawsuit is brought by *shareholders* **to remedy a wrong to the** *corporation.* **The suit is brought in the name of the corporation, and all proceeds of the litigation go to the corporation.** The shareholders of Disney were upset when the board of directors approved a $140 million severance package for Michael Ovitz. Technically, however, the directors had injured the *corporation*, not the *shareholders.* And who would authorize a suit by the corporation against the directors? The directors, of course. Because the directors are unlikely to file suit against themselves, shareholders are permitted to bring a *derivative* action, in the name of the corporation, against managers who have violated their duty to the corporation. All damages, however, go *to the corporation;* the individual shareholders benefit only to the extent that the settlement causes their stock to rise in value.

Litigation is tremendously expensive. How can shareholders afford to sue if they are not entitled to damages? A corporation that loses a derivative suit must pay the legal fees of the victorious shareholders. Most derivative lawsuits are brought by lawyers seeking to earn these fees. (Losing shareholders are generally not required to pay the corporation's legal fees.)

There is a complication, however: **Because a derivative lawsuit is brought in the name of the corporation, shareholders must** *make demand* **on the corporation, unless demand would** *clearly be futile.* That is, before filing a derivative suit, the shareholders must first ask the board to bring the suit itself. Understandably, boards almost always reject this request. Shareholders rarely have luck convincing a court that the board's rejection was a mistake. **Therefore, the shareholders' only real hope is to refuse to make demand on the grounds that such demand would clearly be futile, either because the directors had a conflict of interest or because the decision violated the business judgment rule.**

In the *Brehm* case, discussed earlier in this chapter, the Disney shareholders argued that demand would be futile, both because Michael Eisner controlled the board of directors and because the directors had violated the business judgment rule by making an uninformed decision. That case is still in the appeals process.

However, the court stated that, "[T]here is a very large—though not insurmountable—burden on stockholders who believe they should pursue the remedy of a derivative suit instead of selling their stock or seeking to reform or oust these directors from office."[3]

DIRECT LAWSUITS

Shareholders are permitted to sue the corporation directly only if their own rights have been harmed. If, for example, the corporation denies shareholders the right to inspect its books or to hold a shareholder meeting, they may sue in their own name and keep any damages awarded. The corporation is not required to pay the shareholders' legal fees; winning shareholders can use part of any damage award for this purpose.

CLASS ACTION LAWSUITS

If a group of shareholders all have the same claim, they can join together and file suit as a class action, rather than suing separately. By joining forces, they can share the expense and effort of litigation. It is also far more efficient for the judicial system for one court to try one case than for tens or hundreds of courts all over the country to try the same issue. For obvious reasons, companies tend to resist class actions. In such suits, management is assailed by many small shareholders who otherwise could not afford to (or would not bother to) sue individually.

Chapter Conclusion

At the beginning of this chapter, we asked the question: What happened to Enron (and Merrill Lynch and Xerox)? Commentators point to the following causes for trouble at Enron and other companies:

1. *A focus on stock prices.* Because corporate officers could earn vast wealth by exercising stock options, their incentive to raise stock prices was, for many, irresistible. They were willing to use complex (and even illegal) accounting methods. For instance, Yahoo! Inc. calculated its earnings one quarter by omitting depreciation, amortization, some payroll taxes, investment gains and losses, and acquisition-related and restructuring costs. In short, earnings were whatever Yahoo said they were.

2. *Ineffectual board of directors.* The Enron board was ignorant—either they did not know or they ignored many of the company's abuses. They also approved absurd compensation packages.

3. *Lax supervision by lawyers and accountants.* Financial reporting standards are not sufficiently rigorous, as the Yahoo example illustrates. Arthur Andersen, Enron's accounting firm, turned a blind eye to many dubious activities. Enron's lawyers did question a number of the company's activities but were not aggressive about reporting their concerns to the board.

---

[3] 2000 Del. LEXIS 51,67.

What can be done to improve corporate governance in America, to prevent other Enrons? Commentators have suggested:

1. Instead of stock options, base compensation on the company's growth in earnings compared with those of its competitors. Permit shareholders of all public companies to vote on stock option plans.

2. Hold boards of directors to higher standards:
   (a) Choose an independent director to serve as chairman of the board instead of the CEO.
   (b) Ask board members to evaluate each other on an annual basis.
   (c) Expect directors to own substantial stock in the company.
   (d) Ask the board to regularly evaluate and review the CEO.

ETHICS

In analyzing Enron and its aftermath, a *Wall Street Journal* article concluded: "[N]ot one of the instances of egregious abuse of shareholder interest could have occurred if the CEO had simply said, 'No!' It takes a person of character to know what lines you don't cross. That part of the equation of corporate management hasn't had the emphasis it should have had in the last decade or two."[4] Would you have the strength of character to resist the temptations faced by many CEOs?

Chapter Review

1. Shareholders have neither the right nor the obligation to manage the day-to-day business of the company.

2. Virtually all publicly held companies solicit proxies from their shareholders. A proxy authorizes someone else to vote in place of the shareholder.

3. Under certain circumstances public companies must include shareholder proposals in the proxy statement.

4. Shareholders have the right to:
   (a) Receive annual financial statements.
   (b) Inspect and copy the corporation's records (for a proper purpose).
   (c) Elect and remove directors; and
   (d) Approve fundamental corporate changes, such as a merger or a major sale of assets.

5. A shareholder of a privately held company who objects to a fundamental change in the corporation can insist that her shares be bought out at fair value. This protection is referred to as "dissenters' rights."

6. Controlling shareholders have a fiduciary duty to minority shareholders.

7. A derivative lawsuit is brought by shareholders to remedy a wrong to the corporation. The suit is brought in the name of the corporation, and all proceeds of the litigation go to the corporation.

8. If a group of shareholders all have the same claim against the corporation, they can join together and file a class action, rather than suing separately.

---

[4] David Wessel, "Why the Bad Guys of the Boardroom Emerged en Masse," *The Wall Street Journal*, June 20, 2002, p. A1.

PRACTICE TEST

Matching Questions

Match the following terms with their definitions:

___ **A.** Inside directors.

___ **B.** Proxy statement.

___ **C.** Derivative suit.

___ **D.** Independent directors.

___ **E.** Annual report.

___ **F.** Direct lawsuit.

1. Provides information to shareholders for the annual meeting.

2. Provides financial information to shareholders.

3. Officers of the corporation.

4. Do not work for the company.

5. Shareholders sue the corporation because their own rights have been harmed.

6. Shareholders bring a lawsuit in the name of their corporation.

True/False Questions

Circle true or false:

1. T   F   Shareholders have the right to manage the corporate business.

2. T   F   Under SEC rules, companies may not deliver proxy statements electronically to shareholders.

3. T   F   Shareholder proposals are generally binding on the company if approved by a majority of the shareholders.

4. T   F   Controlling shareholders have not special obligation to other shareholders.

5. T   F   Directors set the compensation for officers, while officers determine the compensation for directors.

Multiple-Choice Questions

6. Max is a shareholder of Helios, Inc. He is angry that the corporation has entered into a contract with a new supplier. Which of the following statements are true:

   I.   Max may file a direct lawsuit against Helios.

   II. Max may file a class action lawsuit against Helios on behalf of himself and other shareholders.

   III. Max may file a derivative lawsuit against Helios.

   (a) I, II and III.

   (b) Neither I, II nor III.

   (c) I and II.

   (d) II and III.

   (e) Only III.

7. Ella is not a shareholder of Dahlia Corp., but she is very unhappy with the company's environmental policies. Which of the following statements is true?

   (a) Ella has the right to place a proposal in the company proxy statement to be voted on at the next annual meeting.

   (b) Ella has the right to run for election to the board but must supply her own proxy statement.

   (c) Ella has the right to run for election to the board and must be included in the company's proxy statement.

   (d) Ella does not have the right to run for election unless nominated by the board.

   (e) Ella does not have the right to run for election unless she is a shareholder of the company.

8. Shareholders do not have the right to:

    (a) Inspect the books and records of the company.

    (b) Elect directors of the company.

    (c) Hire and fire officers.

    (d) Attend annual meetings.

    (e) Place a proposal in the company's proxy statement.

9. Which of the following is not a requirement of the Sarbanes-Oxley Act:

    (a) An independent director must serve as chairman of the board of directors.

    (b) All members of the board's audit committee must be independent.

    (c) A company cannot make loans to its directors or officers.

    (d) A company must develop a code of ethics for senior financial officers.

    (e) The CEO must certify the company's financial statements.

10. Which of the following statements are true?

    I. If a company is not publicly traded, it has an obligation to buy back the stock of any shareholder who objects to a fundamental change.

    II. Anyone who controls a corporation has a fiduciary responsibility to minority shareholders but minority shareholders have no responsibility to the majority.

    (a) Both I and II.

    (b) Neither I and II.

    (c) Just I.

    (d) Just II.

Short-Answer Questions

11. ETHICS: Edgar Bronfman, Jr., dropped out of high school to go to Hollywood and write songs and produce movies. Eventually, he left Hollywood to work in the family business—the Bronfmans owned 36% of Seagram Co., a liquor and beverage conglomerate. Promoted to president of the company at the age of 32, Bronfman seized a second chance to live his dream. Seagram received 70% of its earnings from its 24% ownership of DuPont Co. Bronfman sold this stock at less than market value to purchase (at an inflated price) 80% of MCA, a movie and music company that had been a financial disaster for its prior owners. Some observers thought Bronfman had gone Hollywood, others that he had gone crazy. After the deal was announced, the price of Seagram shares fell 18%. Was there anything Seagram shareholders could have done to prevent what to them was not a dream but a nightmare? Apart from legal issues, was Bronfman's decision ethical? What ethical obligations did he owe Seagram's shareholders?

12. Daniel Cowin was a minority shareholder of Bresler & Reiner, Inc., a public company that developed real estate in Washington, D.C. He alleged numerous instances of corporate mismanagement, fraud, self-dealing, and breach of fiduciary duty by the board of directors. He sought damages for the diminished value of his stock. Could Cowin bring this suit as a direct action, or must it be a derivative suit?

13. Two shareholders of Bruce Company, Harry and Yolan Gilbert, were fighting management for control of the company. They asked for permission to inspect Bruce's stockholder list so that they could either solicit support for their slate of directors at the upcoming stockholders' meeting, or attempt to buy additional stock from other stockholders, or both. Bruce's board refused to allow the Gilberts to see the shareholder list on the grounds that the Gilberts owned another corporation that competed with Bruce. Do the Gilberts have the right to see Bruce's shareholder list?

14. William H. Sullivan, Jr., purchased all the voting shares of the New England Patriots Football Club, Inc. (the Old Patriots). He organized a new corporation called the New Patriots Football Club, Inc. The boards of directors of the two companies agreed to merge. After the merger, the nonvoting stock in the Old Patriots was to be exchanged for cash. Do minority shareholders of the Old Patriots have the right to prevent the merger? If so, under what theory?

15. When Classic Corp. went public at $12 a share, its waterbed business was floating along nicely—the

company had annual sales of $23 million and turned a hefty profit. The company then sprang a leak and suffered through many years of losses. Isaac Fogel, who owned 64% of the stock, decided to take the company private again (by buying shareholders' stock) at a price of 20¢ a share. Classic hired two financial advisers who opined that the buyout price was fair. The board of directors voted in favor of the sale and then scheduled a special shareholder meeting to vote on the buyout. Do the minority shareholders have any rights?

16. ROLE REVERSAL: Write a short-answer question that focuses on whether a shareholder would be able to bring a derivative suit without first making demand.

Internet Research Problem

Starting at **http://www.corporateinformation.com**, find information on a company's shareholder proposals. (Type in a company name, then click on FreeEdgar Filings; choose View Filings and Proxy Statement.) What were these proposals about? What was the outcome of the shareholder vote? Can you find a proposal that shareholders supported?

You can find further practice problems in the Online Quiz at **http://beatty.westbuslaw.com** or in the Study Guide that accompanies this text.

Government Regulation: Securities and Antitrust

Sandy is a director of a public company. He tells his girlfriend, Carly, that the company is about to receive a buyout offer. Sandy does not buy any stock himself, but Carly does. When the offer is announced, the stock zooms up in price and Carly makes a handy profit.

Steve and Joe coach college wrestling teams that are in the same league. Both men are also about to hire an assistant coach. And they have very tight budgets. One day at a meet, Steve suggests to Joe that they agree to limit their new coach's salary to $32,000. That way neither of them will break their budget and they might even have more money to give in athletic scholarships. Joe thinks this is a great plan and agrees on the spot. ▪

Each of these people is about to find out, in a very unpleasant way, about government regulation. Sandy and Carly have violated securities laws on insider trading. Steve and Joe have engaged in price fixing that is illegal under antitrust laws. The moral of the story? It is important to be familiar with the most important government regulations. Ignorance can not only harm your business but also lead to fines and even imprisonment.

Securities Laws

There are two major securities laws: the Securities Act of 1933 (the 1933 Act) and the Securities Exchange Act of 1934 (1934 Act).

SECURITIES ACT OF 1933

The 1933 Act requires that, before offering or selling securities, the issuer must register the securities with the Securities and Exchange Commission (SEC), unless the securities qualify for an exemption. An **issuer** is the company that issues the stock. Registering securities with the SEC in a public offering is very time-consuming and expensive, but the 1933 Act permits some issuers to use simpler methods.

It is important to remember that **when an issuer registers securities, the SEC does not investigate the quality of the offering.** Permission from the SEC to sell securities does not mean that the company has a good product or will be successful. SEC approval simply means that, on the surface, the company has answered all relevant questions about itself and its major products. For example, the Green Bay Packers football team sold an offering of stock to finance stadium improvements. The prospectus admitted:

> IT IS VIRTUALLY IMPOSSIBLE that any investor will ever make a profit on the stock purchase. The company will pay no dividends, and the shares cannot be sold.

This does not sound like a stock you want in your retirement fund; on the other hand, the SEC will not prevent Green Bay from selling it, or you from buying it, as long as you understand what the risks are.

One last point: **The 1933 Act prohibits fraud in any securities transaction.** Anyone who issues fraudulent securities is in violation of the 1933 Act, whether or not the securities are registered. Both the SEC and any purchasers of the stock can sue the issuer.

CYBERLAW | Companies must deliver certain documents to investors and also file them with the SEC. Companies now make their required SEC filings electronically, using the EDGAR (Electronic Data Gathering, Analysis, and Retrieval) system. This information is available online (at **http://www.sec.gov**). ◼

Public Offerings

When a company wishes to raise significant amounts of capital from a large number of people, it is time for a public offering. A company's first public sale of securities is called an **initial public offering** or an **IPO.**

Registration Statement. To do a public offering, the company must file a registration statement with the SEC. The **registration statement** has two purposes: to notify the SEC that a sale of securities is pending and to disclose information to prospective purchasers. The registration statement must include detailed information about the issuer and its business, a description of the stock, the proposed use of the proceeds from the offering, and audited balance sheets and income statements. Preparing a registration statement is neither quick—it typically takes two to three months—nor inexpensive. A company can easily spend $1,000,000 on audits and other expenses.

Prospectus. Typically, buyers never see the registration statement; they are given the **prospectus** instead. (The prospectus is part of the registration statement that is sent to the SEC.) The prospectus includes all of the important disclosures about the company, while the registration statement includes additional information that is of interest to the SEC but not to the typical investor, such as the names and addresses of the lawyers for the issuer and underwriter. **All investors must receive a copy of the prospectus before purchasing the stock.**

Sales Effort. The SEC closely regulates an issuer's sales effort. In particular:

- The **quiet period** begins when a company hires an investment bank (called the "underwriter") to sell its stock and ends 25 days after the IPO. During this period, company officers must guard their words carefully to avoid any appearance of hyping the stock. For example, the SEC delayed an offering of stock by Webvan Group Inc. after its officers talked with reporters from *BusinessWeek* and *Forbes* magazines, giving out financial data on recent results that had not been included in the prospectus.

- The **waiting period** is the time after the registration statement has been filed but before the SEC has approved it. The underwriter may distribute the preliminary prospectus. It can also solicit offers, but cannot make sales.

- During the waiting period, the officers of the issuer go on a **road show**—the cross-country road trip to convince traders that their clients should buy this stock.

Going Effective. Once its review of the registration statement is complete, the SEC sends the issuer a **comment letter,** listing changes that must be made to the registration statement. An issuer almost always has to amend the registration statement at least once, and sometimes more than once. After the SEC has approved a final registration statement (which includes, of course, the final prospectus), the issuer then decides on a date to go effective, that is, to begin selling the stock.

Exemptions

Under the 1933 Act, an issuer is not required to register securities that are sold in a private offering, that is, an offering with only a few investors or a relatively small amount of money involved. Most small companies use private, not public, offerings to raise capital. The most common and important of these exemptions is **Regulation D** (often referred to as Reg D). For example, under Reg D, a company may sell up to $5 million of stock during each 12-month period, subject to the following restrictions:

- The company may not advertise the stock publicly.

- The issuer can sell to as many accredited investors as it wants, but is limited to only 35 unaccredited investors. **Accredited investors** are institutions (such as banks and insurance companies) or wealthy individuals (with a net worth of more than $1 million or an annual income of more than $200,000).

- The company need not provide information to accredited investors but must make some disclosure to unaccredited investors.

SECURITIES EXCHANGE ACT OF 1934

Most buyers do not purchase new securities from the issuer in an initial public offering. Rather they buy stock that is publicly traded in the open market. This stock is, in a sense, secondhand because others, perhaps many others, have already owned it. The purpose of the 1934 Act is to maintain the integrity of this secondary market.

The 1934 Act 13 requires public companies to file the following documents:

- **Annual reports** on Form 10-K, containing audited financial statements, a detailed analysis of the company's performance, and information about officers and directors.

- **Quarterly reports** on Form 10-Q, which are less detailed than 10-Ks and contain unaudited financials.

- **Form 8-K**s to report any significant developments, such as a change in control, the resignation of a director over a policy dispute, or a change in auditing firms.

A reporting company must send its annual report to shareholders. For particularly lively examples of this form of literature, check out the filings for Jack in the Box Inc. (**http://www.jackinthebox.com/investors/annualreport.php**).

INSIDER TRADING

Insider trading is immensely tempting. Anyone with reliable secret information can earn millions of dollars overnight. The downside? Insider trading is a crime punishable by fines and imprisonment. The guilty party may also be forced to turn over to the SEC three times the profit made. Ivan Boesky paid $100 million and spent two years in prison. Dennis Levine suffered an $11.6 million penalty and three years in prison.

Why is insider trading a crime? Who is harmed? Insider trading is illegal because:

- It offends our fundamental sense of fairness. No one wants to be in a poker game with marked cards.

- Investors will lose confidence in the market if they feel that insiders have an unfair advantage.

- Investment banks typically "make a market" in stocks, meaning that they hold extra shares so that orders can be filled smoothly. These marketmakers expect to earn a certain profit, but inside traders skim some of it off. So marketmakers simply raise the commission they charge. As a result, everyone who buys and sells stock pays a slightly higher price.

The rules on insider trading are as follows:

- *Stranger.* **Someone who trades on inside information is liable only if he has a fiduciary duty to the company whose stock he has traded.** Suppose that, while looking in a Dumpster, Harry finds correspondence indicating that MediSearch, Inc., will shortly announce a major breakthrough in the treatment of AIDS. Harry buys the stock, which promptly quadruples in value. Harry will be dining at the Ritz, not in the Dumpster nor in federal prison, because he has no fiduciary duty to MediSearch.

- *Fiduciaries.* Anyone who works for a company is a fiduciary. **A fiduciary may not trade stock of her company while in possession of important, secret information.** If the director of research for MediSearch learns of the promising new treatment for AIDS and buys stock in the company before the information is public, she is guilty of insider trading.

- *Tippers.* **Insiders who pass on important, secret information are liable, even if they do not trade themselves, as long as (1) they know the information is confidential; and (2) they expect some personal gain.** Personal gain is loosely defined. Essentially, any gift to a friend counts as personal gain. W. Paul Thayer was a corporate director, deputy secretary of defense, and former fighter pilot ace who gave stock tips to his girlfriend in lieu of paying her rent. That counted as personal gain and he spent a year and a half in prison.

- *Tippees.* **Those who receive tips—tippees—are liable for trading on inside information,** even if they do not have a fiduciary relationship to the company, as long as (1) they know the information is confidential; (2) they know it came from an insider who was violating his fiduciary duty; and (3) the insider expected some personal gain. Barry Switzer, then head football coach at the University of Oklahoma, went to a track meet to see his son compete. While sunbathing on the bleachers, he overheard someone talking about a company that was going to be acquired. Switzer bought the stock but was acquitted of insider trading charges, because the insider had not breached his fiduciary duty. He had not tipped anyone on purpose—he had simply been careless. Also, Switzer did not know that the insider was breaching a fiduciary duty, and the insider expected no personal gain.[1]

- *Misappropriation.* A person is liable if he trades in securities (1) for personal profit; (2) using confidential information; and (3) in breach of a fiduciary duty to the *source of the information.* This rule applies even if that source was not the company whose stock was traded. In the following case, the lawyer should have known better.

---

[1] *SEC v. Switzer,* 590 F. Supp. 756, 1984 U.S. Dist. LEXIS 15303 (W.D. Okla. 1984).

CASE SUMMARY

UNITED STATES v. O'HAGAN

521 U.S. 642, 117 S. Ct. 2199, 1997 U.S. LEXIS 4033
United States Supreme Court, 1997

FACTS: Grand Metropolitan PLC (Grand Met) hired the law firm of Dorsey & Whitney to represent it in a takeover of Pillsbury Co. James O'Hagan, a partner in Dorsey & Whitney, did not work for Grand Met, but he found out about the deal and purchased significant amounts of Pillsbury stock. After Grand Met publicly announced its takeover attempt, the price of Pillsbury stock rose dramatically. O'Hagan sold his stock at a profit of more than $4.3 million.

ISSUE: Did O'Hagan violate insider trading laws?

DECISION: O'Hagan was guilty of misappropriation, which is illegal under insider trading laws.

REASONING: Under the traditional law of insider trading, a corporate insider cannot use important,

secret information to trade in the securities of his corporation. The traditional theory applies not only to officers, directors, and other employees of a corporation, but also to attorneys, accountants, and others who *temporarily* become fiduciaries of a corporation.

The misappropriation theory applies to someone who is not a corporate insider, but nonetheless owes a fiduciary duty to the source of the information. Thus, in this case, O'Hagan did not work for Grand Met, the company whose stock he bought, but he did violate his fiduciary duty to his law firm. The theft of such information is the same thing as embezzlement. It makes no sense to find a lawyer like O'Hagan guilty if he works for a law firm representing the target of a tender offer, but not if he works for a law firm representing the bidder. ◢

AT RISK | If you learn confidential information about a company, what can you do? Of course, it is always safe not to trade. If you want to trade anyway, you should wait 24 to 48 hours after the information is disseminated through wire services or in the financial press. ◼

BLUE SKY LAWS

Currently, all states and the District of Columbia also regulate the sale of securities. These state statutes are called **blue sky laws** (because crooks were willing to sell naive investors a "piece of the great blue sky"). It can be an enormously complicated task for an issuer of securities to comply with federal securities laws and all the state laws as well.

Antitrust

Congress passed the Sherman Act in 1890 to prevent extreme concentrations of economic power. Because this statute was aimed at the Standard Oil Trust, which then controlled the oil industry throughout the country, it was termed **antitrust** legislation.

Violations of the antitrust laws are divided into two categories: *per se* and **rule of reason.** As the name implies, *per se* violations are automatic. Defendants charged with this type of violation cannot defend themselves by saying, "But the impact wasn't so bad" or "No one was hurt." The court will not listen to excuses, and violators may be sent to prison.

Rule of reason violations, on the other hand, are illegal only if they have an anticompetitive impact on the market. For example, mergers are illegal only if they harm competition in their industry. Those who commit rule of reason violations are not sent to prison.

Both the Justice Department and the Federal Trade Commission (FTC) have authority to enforce the antitrust laws. However, only the Justice Department can bring criminal proceedings; the FTC is limited to civil injunctions and other administrative remedies. In addition to the government, anyone injured by an antitrust violation has the right to sue for damages. The United States is unusual in this regard—in most other countries, only the government is able to sue antitrust violators. A successful plaintiff can recover treble (that is, triple) damages from the defendant.

THE SHERMAN ACT

Price-Fixing

Section 1 of the Sherman Act prohibits all agreements "in restraint of trade." The most common, and one of the most serious, violations of this provision involves price-fixing. **When competitors agree on the prices at which they will buy or sell products, their price-fixing is a *per se* violation of §1 of the Sherman Act.**

In an early case, the defendants argued that price-fixing was only wrong if the prices were unfair. The Supreme Court disagreed. In its view, prices should be set by markets, not by competitors—or judges. Moreover, "The reasonable price fixed today may through economic and business changes become the unreasonable price of tomorrow."[2]

For the better part of a century, price-fixing has been illegal, yet it never seems to go away. Here are some examples:

- *Dairy Industry.* Using a computer to analyze the bids that schools received on their milk contracts, the Florida Attorney General uncovered a pervasive price-fixing scheme. By some estimates, price-fixing raised milk prices in Florida by 14%. Forty-three companies were convicted or pleaded guilty; two dozen individuals went to prison. Companies paid fines in excess of $90 million.

- *College Athletics.* Colleges were concerned about the cost of their athletic programs. In particular, the cost of the coaching staffs seemed out of control. Some assistant coaches were being paid as much as $70,000 a year. In response, NCAA schools (that is, members of the National Collegiate Athletic Association) agreed to cap the salaries of assistant coaches at (a very stingy) $12,000. But a court blew the whistle, finding that the NCAA had engaged in illegal price-fixing. A jury awarded the coaches $66 million.

For information about new and interesting price-fixing cases, check out **http://www.antitrust.org**.

---

[2] *United States v. Trenton Potteries Co.*, 273 U.S. 392, 397, 1927 U.S. LEXIS 975 (1927).

ETHICS

The ethics discussion in Chapter 2 considered the possibility that illegal behavior could sometimes be ethical. Price-fixing is a per se violation of the law. Are there times when it might nonetheless be ethical? For example, every year the Council of Fashion Designers of America puts on a major fashion show under tents in New York's Bryant Park. This show offers an opportunity for up-and-coming designers to mix with more established names—and to attract media attention. The newcomers complained, however, that they could not compete with famous designers and attract vital media attention without hiring top models. But the price of these super-star models was too high: upwards of $10,000 for a three-hour show. Sympathetic to the newcomers' plight, the Council capped modeling fees at $750 an hour for super-models and $500 for rookies. Is this price-fixing illegal? Is it ethical to protect the inexperienced designers? From the Chapter 2 Ethics Checklist: What are the consequences of this alternative? Does the alternative violate important values? ◾

Monopolization

Under §2 of the Sherman Act, it is illegal to monopolize or attempt to monopolize a market. To monopolize means to acquire control over a market in the wrong way. *Having* a monopoly is legal unless it is *gained* or *maintained* by using wrongful tactics. To determine if a defendant has illegally monopolized, we must ask two questions:

- **Does the company control the market?** Without control, there is no monopoly.

- **How did the company acquire or maintain its control?** Monopolization is illegal only if gained or kept in the wrong way.

In the following case, the defendant had a large market share, but not control. The judge in the case sprinkled his opinion with movie titles. How many can you find?

CASE SUMMARY

UNITED STATES v. SYUFY ENTERPRISES

903 F.2d 659, 1990 U.S. App. LEXIS 7396
United States Court of Appeals for the Ninth Circuit, 1990

FACTS: Raymond Syufy entered the Las Vegas cinema market with a splash by opening a six-screen theater. His theaters are among the finest built and best run in the nation, making him something of a local hero. Syufy's entry into the Las Vegas market caused a stir, precipitating a titanic bidding war. Soon, theaters in Las Vegas were paying some of the highest license fees in the nation, while distributors sat back and watched the easy money roll in. After a hard-fought battle among several contenders, Syufy gained the upper hand. Three of his rivals saw their future as rocky and decided to sell out to Syufy, leaving a small exhibitor of mostly second-run films

as Syufy's only competitor in Las Vegas. The Justice Department brought this antitrust suit to force Syufy to sell off the theaters he had purchased from his former competitors.

ISSUE: Did Syufy have an illegal monopoly?

DECISION: No, Syufy had not violated antitrust laws.

REASONING: When Syufy purchased his theatres, he temporarily decreased the number of competitors in this market. But antitrust laws protect competition, not competitors. Unless there are significant barriers to entry, any attempt to raise prices will lure other competitors into the market.

After he purchased the theatres, Syufy had a 93% market share, but within three years this share had fallen to 75%. He clearly did not have the power to exclude competitors. Nor did Syufy have power over his suppliers. He was paying rental fees to Hollywood movie distributors far in excess of the national average. While a high market share does create an *inference* of monopoly power, this inference must be supported by evidence that a defendant can control prices or exclude competition. Syufy is not required to sell any theatres.

Even if a company does control a market, **monopolization is illegal only if "bad acts" are used to acquire or maintain it.** If the law prohibited the mere possession of a monopoly, it might discourage companies from producing excellent products or offering low prices. Anyone who can produce a better product cheaper is entitled to a monopoly. For an example of bad acts that would be illegal if used to acquire or maintain a monopoly, consider what British Airways (BA) did to Virgin Atlantic Airways:

- Approached Virgin's customers to persuade them to switch to BA flights.

- Obtained customers' files by tapping into Virgin's computer.

- Contacted customers and pretended to represent Virgin.

- Spread untrue, harmful rumors about Virgin's CEO.

Predatory Pricing

Predatory pricing occurs when a company lowers its prices below cost to drive competitors out of business. Once the predator has the market to itself, it raises prices to make up lost profits—and more besides.

Under §2 of the Sherman Act, it is illegal "to monopolize" and also to "attempt to monopolize." Typically, the goal of a predatory pricing scheme is either to win control of a market or to maintain it. A ban on these schemes prevents monopolization and attempts to monopolize. **To win a predatory pricing case, the plaintiff must prove three elements:**

- The defendant is selling its products *below cost*.

- The defendant *intends* that the plaintiff go out of business.

- If the plaintiff does go out of business, the defendant will be able to earn sufficient profits to *recover* its prior losses.

The classic example of predatory pricing is a large grocery store that comes into a small town offering exceptionally low prices that are subsidized by profits from its other branches. Once all the "Ma and Pa" corner groceries go out of business, MegaGrocery raises its prices to much higher levels.

Predatory pricing cases can be difficult to win. It is, for example, hard for Ma and Pa to prove that MegaGrocery intended for them to go out of business. It is also difficult for Ma and Pa to show that MegaGrocery will be able to make up all its lost profits once the corner grocery is out of the way. They need to prove, for example, that no other grocery chain will come to town. It is difficult to prove a negative proposition like that, especially in the grocery business where barriers to entry are low.

THE CLAYTON ACT

Mergers

The Clayton Act prohibits mergers that are anticompetitive. Companies with substantial assets must notify the Federal Trade Commission (FTC) before undertaking a merger.[3] This notification gives the government an opportunity to prevent a merger ahead of time, rather than trying to untangle one after the fact.

Tying Arrangements

A tying arrangement is an agreement to sell a product on the condition that the buyer also purchases a different (or tied) product. A tying arrangement is illegal under the Clayton Act if:

- Two products are clearly separate.

- The seller requires the buyer to purchase the two products together.

- The seller has significant power in the market for the tying product; and

- The seller is shutting out a significant part of the market for the tied product.

Six movie distributors refused to sell individual films to television stations. Instead, they insisted that a station buy an entire package of movies. To obtain classics such as *Treasure of the Sierra Madre* and *Casablanca* (the tying product), the station also had to purchase such forgettable films as *Gorilla Man* and *Tugboat Annie Sails Again* (the tied product).[4] This is an illegal tying arrangement if the answer to the following questions is "Yes."

- *Are the two products clearly separate?* A left and right shoe are not separate products, and a seller can legally require that they be purchased together. *Gorilla Man*, on the other hand, is a separate product from *Casablanca*.

- *Is the seller requiring the buyer to purchase the two products together?* Yes, that is the whole point of these "package deals."

- *Does the seller have significant power in the market for the tying product?* In this case, the tying products are the classic movies. Since they are copyrighted, no one else can show them without the distributor's permission. The six distributors controlled a great many classic movies. So, yes, they do have significant market power.

- *Is the seller shutting out a significant part of the market for the tied product?* In this case, the tied products are the undesirable films like *Tugboat Annie Sails Again*. Television stations forced to take the unwanted films did not buy "B" movies from other distributors. These other distributors were effectively foreclosed from a substantial part of the market.

---

[3] If, for example, the acquiring company is purchasing stock or assets of the acquired company that is worth more than $200 million in 2004 dollars.

[4] *United States v. Loew's Inc.*, 371 U.S. 38, 83 S. CT. 97, 1962 U.S. LEXIS 2332 (1962).

THE ROBINSON-PATMAN ACT

Under the Robinson-Patman Act (RPA), it is illegal to charge different prices to different purchasers if:

- The items are the same; and

- The price discrimination lessens competition.

However, it is legal to charge a lower price to a particular buyer if:

- The costs of serving this buyer are lower; or

- The seller is simply meeting competition.

Congress passed the RPA in 1936 to prevent large chains from driving small, local stores out of business. Owners of these "Ma and Pa" stores complained that the large chains could sell goods cheaper because suppliers charged them lower prices. As a result of the RPA, managers who would otherwise like to develop different pricing strategies for specific customers or regions may hesitate to do so for fear of violating this statute. In reality, however, they have little to fear.

Under the RPA, a plaintiff must prove both that price discrimination occurred and that it lessened competition. It is perfectly permissible, for example, for a supplier to sell at a different price to its Texas and California distributors, or to its health care and educational distributors, as long as the distributors are not in competition with each other.

The RPA also permits price variations that are based on differences in cost. Thus Amy's Kitchen would be perfectly within its legal rights to sell its frozen cheese enchiladas to Giant at a lower price than to Corner Grocery if Amy's costs are lower to do so. Giant often buys shipments the size of railroad containers that cost less to deliver than smaller boxes.

Chapter Conclusion

In this chapter, you have learned about some of the important government regulations that affect business. They can have a profound impact on your business and on your life.

Chapter Review

1. Before making a public offer or sale of securities, the issuer must register them with the SEC.

2. All investors must receive a copy of the prospectus before purchasing stock in a public offering.

3. The 1934 Act requires public companies to make regular filings with the SEC, including annual reports, quarterly reports and Form 8-Ks.

4. Insider trading is illegal.

5. State securities statutes are called blue sky laws.

6. When competitors agree on the prices at which they will buy or sell products, their price-fixing is a *per se* violation of §1 of the Sherman Act.

7. Under §2 of the Sherman Act, it is illegal to monopolize or attempt to monopolize a market.

8. Predatory pricing occurs when a company lowers its prices below cost to drive competitors out of business.

9. The Clayton Act prohibits mergers that are anticompetitive.

10. Certain tying arrangements are illegal under the Clayton Act.

11. Under the Robinson-Patman Act, it is illegal to charge different prices to different purchasers if the items are the same, and the price discrimination lessens competition.

PRACTICE TEST

Matching Questions

Match the following terms with their definitions:

___ **A.** Securities Act of 1933.

___ **B.** *Per se.*

___ **C.** Misappropriation.

___ **D.** Rule of reason.

___ **E.** Securities Exchange Act of 1934.

1. Only a violation if it has an anticompetitive impact.

2. Regulates companies once they have gone public.

3. Illegal insider trading.

4. Regulates the issuance of securities.

5. Automatic violation of the antitrust laws, punishable by imprisonment.

True/False Questions

Circle true or false:

1. T   F   Before permitting a company to issue new securities, the SEC investigates to ensure that the company has a promising future.

2. T   F   Small offerings of securities do not need to be registered with the SEC.

3. T   F   Price-fixing is legal as long as it does not have an anticompetitive impact.

4. T   F   Only the federal government regulates securities offerings; the states do not.

5. T   F   It is legal for a company to sell its product at a price below cost as long as it does not intend to drive competitors out of business.

Multiple-Choice Questions

6. An issuer is eligible for Regulation D, unless it:

   (a) Sells to a thousand accredited investors.

   (b) Sells to 27 unaccredited investors.

   (c) Fails to make disclosure to accredited investors.

   (d) Fails to make disclosure to unaccredited investors.

   (e) Fails to advertise the stock publicly.

7. Which of the following statements is *not* true about a public offering?

   (a) The issuer files a registration statement with the SEC.

   (b) The issuer files a prospectus with the SEC.

   (c) Company officers may not make public statements about the offering before the effective date.

   (d) After the effective date, company officers are free to make public statements about the offering.

   (e) Before the effective date, the issuer may solicit offers for the stock.

8. To have an illegal monopoly, a company must:

   I. Control the market.

   II. Maintain its control improperly.

   III. Have a market share greater than 50%.

   (a) I, II, and III.

   (b) I and II.

   (c) II and III.

   (d) I and III.

   (e) Neither I, II, nor III.

9. Lloyd sold car floor mats to Mercedes dealerships. Then Mercedes began to include floor mats as standard equipment. Mercedes has a 10% share of the luxury car market.

   (a) Mercedes has created an illegal tying arrangement because floor mats and cars are separate products.

   (b) Mercedes has not created an illegal tying arrangement because floor mats and cars are not separate products.

   (c) Mercedes has created an illegal tying arrangement because its market share is 10%.

   (d) Mercedes has not created an illegal tying arrangement because it is not tying the two products together.

   (e) Mercedes has created an illegal tying arrangement because it controls the market in floor mats.

10. Mike is director of sales for his company. Paige tells him that she can buy the same product cheaper elsewhere. He cuts the price for her, but not for his other customers. At the same time, he develops a crush on Lauren so offers to sell her the product at a lower price, too. Which statement is correct:

    (a) Mike can charge whatever price he wants to any customer.

    (b) Mike must charge all his customers the same price.

    (c) The price cut to Paige, but not Lauren is legal.

    (d) The price cut to Lauren, but not Paige is legal.

    (e) Mike is not required to charge all his customers the same price, but neither of these price cuts is legal.

Short-Answer Questions

11. ETHICS: Ira Waldbaum was president and controlling shareholder of Waldbaum, Inc., a large supermarket chain. After deciding to accept A & P's offer to purchase the chain, he told his sister, Shirley Witkin, about the offer so that she would be ready to sell her shares. He admonished her not to tell anyone, but she told her daughter, Susan Loeb, who passed the word (and the warning) on to her husband, Keith Loeb. The next day, Keith told his broker, Robert Chestman, about the impending sale and ordered some Waldbaum stock. Chestman purchased 11,000 shares of the stock for himself and his clients, at a price of roughly $25 per share. The A&P offer was for $50 per share. Did Chestman violate Rule 10b-5? Whether or not Chestman's trades were legal, did they harm anyone? How do they look in the light of day? Were Loeb's actions right? How might they have affected his wife (and other stakeholders)?

12. You're in line at the movie theater when you overhear a stranger say: "The FDA has just approved Hernstrom's new painkiller. When the announcement is made on Monday, Hernstrom stock will take off." What if you buy stock of the company before the announcement on Monday?

13. Fifty bakeries in New York agreed to raise the retail price of bread from 75¢ to 85¢. All the association's members printed the new price on their bread sleeves. Are the bakeries in violation of the antitrust laws?

14. BAR/BRI is a company that prepares law students for bar exams. With branches in 45 states, it has the largest share of the bar review market in the country. Barpassers is a much smaller company located only in Arizona and California. BAR/BRI distributed pamphlets on campuses falsely suggesting Barpassers was near bankruptcy. Enrollments in Barpassers' courses dropped, and the company was forced to postpone plans for expansion. Does Barpassers have an antitrust claim against BAR/BRI?

15. Reserve Supply Corp., a cooperative of 379 lumber dealers, charged that Owens-Corning Fiberglass Corp. violated the Robinson-Patman Act by selling at lower prices to Reserve's competitors. Owens-Corning had granted lower prices to a number of Reserve's

competitors to meet, but not beat, the prices of other insulation manufacturers. Is Owens-Corning in violation of the Robinson-Patman Act?

16. ROLE REVERSAL: Prepare a multiple-choice question that focuses on an issue involving insider trading.

Internet Research Problem

Choose a company, go to the EDGAR database at the SEC (**http://www.sec.gov**), and look at all filings this company has made during the last year. What filings has it made and why? Extra credit: search EDGAR for a prospectus for an initial public offering.

You can find further practice problems in the Online Quiz at **http://beatty.westbuslaw.com** or in the Study Guide that accompanies this text.

Accountants: Liability and Professional Responsibility

The accounting firm Arthur Andersen prided itself on its ethics. Old-timers would tell new recruits the legend of the firm's founder: how in 1914 the young Arthur Andersen had refused a client's request to certify a dubious earnings report. Although Andersen knew his firm would be fired, and he might not be able to meet payroll, he nonetheless stood on principle. He was vindicated a few months later when the client went bankrupt.

For its first 35 years, Andersen was primarily in the business of auditing public companies. Although its partners did not become rich, they made a good living. Then the firm entered the consulting business. Soon the consultants in the firm were generating much higher profits—and earning much higher salaries—than the auditors. Audits were fast becoming loss leaders to attract consulting business. Lower costs led to lower quality as Andersen (and other auditors) felt they could not afford to invest as many hours in their audits. And the audits were becoming less effective because partners were increasingly afraid to deliver bad news, for fear of losing both audit and consulting fees.

To save money, the firm began to force partners to retire at 56. This reduced the general level of experience and expertise. At the same time, accounting was becoming more complicated. Predictably, mistakes happened, lawsuits were filed, settlements were made.

Andersen's name was soiled by its role in a number of financial disasters such as Global Crossing and WorldCom. And then there was Enron. Andersen opened an office in Enron's headquarters staffed with more than 150 Andersen employees. When the federal government began investigating Enron's bankruptcy, panicked Andersen employees obstructed the government's investigation by shredding documents. And so, the firm that began as a model of ethics in the accounting profession collapsed in disgrace, the first major accounting firm ever to be convicted of a crime.[1] ◾

Introduction

To begin our study of the accounting industry, it is important to understand what accountants do. Many of the cases in this chapter involve audits that went awry, so we start there.

AUDITS

Accountants serve two masters—company management and the investing public. Management hires the accountants, but investors and creditors rely upon them to offer an independent evaluation of the financial statements that management issues.

When conducting an audit, accountants verify information provided by management. Since it is impossible to check each and every transaction, they verify a *sample* of various types of transactions. If these are accurate, they assume all are. To verify transactions, accountants use two mirror image processes—vouching and tracing.

In **vouching,** accountants choose a transaction listed in the company's books and check backwards to make sure that there are original data to support it. They might, for example, find in accounts payable a bill for the purchase of 1,000 reams of photocopy paper. They would check to ensure that all the paper had actually arrived and that the receiving department had properly signed and dated the invoice. The auditors would also check the original purchase order to ensure the acquisition was properly authorized in the first place.

In **tracing,** the accountant begins with an item of original data and traces it forward to insure that it has been properly recorded throughout the bookkeeping process. For example, the sales ledger might report that 1,000 copies of a software program were sold to a distributor. The accountant checks the information in the sales ledger against the original invoice to ensure that the date, price, quantity, and customer's name all match. The auditor then verifies each step along the paper trail until the software leaves the warehouse.

In performing their duties, accountants must follow two sets of rules: (1) generally accepted accounting principles (GAAP); and (2) generally accepted auditing standards (GAAS). **GAAP** are the rules for preparing financial statements, and **GAAS** are the rules for conducting audits. These two sets of standards include broadly phrased general principles as well as specific guidelines and

---

[1] Based in part on information in Ken Brown and Ianthe Jeanne Dugan, "Andersen's Fall from Grace Is a Tale of Greed and Miscues," *The Wall Street Journal,* June 7, 2002, p.1.

illustrations. The application and interpretation of these rules require acute professional skill.

OPINIONS

After an audit is complete, the accountant issues an opinion on the financial statements that indicates how accurately those statements reflect the company's true financial condition. The auditor has four choices:

- **Unqualified Opinion.** Also known as a **clean opinion,** this indicates that the company's financial statements fairly present its financial condition in accordance with GAAP. A less than clean opinion is a warning to potential investors and creditors that something may be wrong.

- **Qualified Opinion.** This opinion indicates that although the financial statements are generally accurate, there is nonetheless an outstanding, unresolved issue. For example, the company may face potential liability from environmental law violations, but the liability cannot yet be accurately estimated.

- **Adverse Opinion.** In the auditor's view, the company's financial statements do not accurately reflect its financial position. In other words, the company is lying about its finances.

- **Disclaimer of Opinion.** Although not as damning as an adverse opinion, a disclaimer is still not good news. It is issued when the auditor does not have enough information to form an opinion.

Liability to Clients

CONTRACT

A written contract between accountants and their clients is called an **engagement letter.** The contract has both express and implied terms. The accountant *expressly* promises to perform a particular project by a given date. The accountant also *implies* that she will work as carefully as an ordinarily prudent accountant would under the circumstances. If she fails to do either, she has breached her contract and may be liable for any damages that result.

NEGLIGENCE

An accountant is liable for negligence to a client who can prove both of the following elements:

- **The accountant breached his duty to his client by failing to exercise the degree of skill and competence that an ordinarily prudent accountant would under the circumstances.** For example, if the accountant fails to follow GAAP or GAAS, he has almost certainly breached his duty.

- **The accountant's violation of duty caused harm to the client.** For example, a new accountant failed to notify his client that the previous accountant had committed malpractice. But the new accountant was not liable because the former accountant could not have paid any damages. Thus the client had not suffered any harm from the new fellow's malpractice.[2]

FRAUD

An accountant is liable for fraud if (1) she makes a false statement of fact; (2) she either knows it is not true or recklessly disregards the truth; and (3) the client justifiably relies on the statement. William deliberately inflated numbers in the financials statements he prepared for Tess so that she would not discover that he had made some disastrous investments for her. Because of these errors, Tess did not realize her true financial position for some years. William committed fraud.

A fraud claim is an important weapon because it permits the client to ask for punitive damages. For example, an angry Billy Joel sued his business manager (and ex-wife's brother) for financial mismanagement. He claimed a mere $30 million on the negligence and breach of contract claims but asked for $60 million in punitive damages on a fraud claim.

BREACH OF TRUST

Accountants occupy a position of enormous trust because financial information is often sensitive and confidential. Clients may put as much trust in their accountant as they do in their lawyer, clergy, or psychiatrist. **Accountants have a legal obligation to (1) keep all client information confidential; and (2) use client information only for the benefit of the client.** What happens when an accounting firm discovers that one of its clients may injure other clients? In the following case, the firm made the wrong choice.

CASE SUMMARY

WAGENHEIM v. ALEXANDER GRANT & CO.

19 Ohio App. 3d 7, 482 N.E.2d 955, 1983 Ohio App. LEXIS 11194
Court of Appeals of Ohio, 1983

FACTS: Joel S. Wagenheim founded Consolidata Services, Inc. (CDS), to provide bookkeeping and payroll services to businesses. Each new payroll client was required to deposit money with CDS to insure that there would always be sufficient funds to cover the payroll checks. Upon termination of a contract, the deposit was to be returned within 30 days.

CDS hired Alexander Grant & Co. as its accounting firm. Many of the clients who used CDS's payroll services were also clients of Alexander Grant, and, in fact, many had chosen Alexander Grant upon the recommendation of CDS and vice versa. When accountants from Alexander Grant discovered that CDS was $150,000 short of cash in its payroll account, they insisted that CDS disclose its cash flow problems to its clients immediately before any further funds were received. Wagenheim asked for time to raise the missing money. If forced to notify clients, he wanted to do so himself. CDS had never failed to fulfill its payroll obligations or return its customers' deposits.

---

[2] *Hunter's Ambulance Service, Inc. v. Shernow*, 70 Conn. App. 96, 2002 Conn. App. LEXIS 290 (App. Ct., Conn. 2002).

The next day, without notifying Wagenheim, Alexander Grant began calling their mutual clients to advise them not to send additional payroll funds to CDS. Most of the clients canceled their contracts with CDS. Ten days later, CDS closed down operations. Wagenheim sued Alexander Grant for breach of trust. The jury returned an award of $1.32 million.

ISSUE: Did Alexander Grant breach its duty of trust to Wagenheim and CDS?

DECISION: Affirmed. Alexander Grant breached its duty.

REASONING: As a general rule, accountants cannot disclose information communicated by a client in confidence without the client's prior consent. This privilege is limited, however, because an accountant may reveal a client's confidential information during a court proceeding.

In this case, Alexander Grant violated its duty to Wagenheim and CDS.

Liability to Third Parties

No issue in the accounting field is more controversial than liability to third parties. Plaintiffs argue that auditors owe an important duty to a trusting public. The job of the auditor, they say, is to provide an independent, professional source of assurance that a company's audited financial statements are accurate. If the auditors do their job properly, they have nothing to fear. The accounting profession says in response, however, that if everyone who has ever been harmed even remotely by a faulty audit can recover damages, there will soon be no auditors left.

NEGLIGENCE

Accountants who fail to exercise due care are liable to (1) anyone they knew would rely on the information; and (2) anyone else in the same class. Suppose, for example, that Adrienne knows she is preparing financial statements for the BeachBall Corp. to use in obtaining a bank loan from the First National Bank of Tucson. If Adrienne is careless in preparing the statements and BeachBall bursts, she will be liable to First Bank. Suppose, however, that the company takes its financial statements to the Last National Bank of Tucson instead. She would also be liable, because the Last Bank is in the same class as the First Bank. Once Adrienne knows that a bank will rely on the statements she has prepared, the identity of the particular bank should not make any difference to her when doing her work.

Suppose, however, that BeachBall uses the financial statements to persuade a landlord to rent it a manufacturing facility. In this case, Adrienne would not be liable because the landlord is not in the same class as the First Bank, for whom Adrienne knew she was preparing the documents.

FRAUD

Courts consider fraud to be much worse than negligence because it is *intentional*. Therefore, the penalty is heavier. **An accountant who commits fraud is liable to any foreseeable user of the work product who justifiably relied on it.** For example, suppose that TechDisk manufactured disk drives. Customers were buying disk drives faster than the company could make them. Afraid that the stock price would plummet if investors found out about the shortage, company officers helped their sales numbers by shipping out bricks wrapped up to look like disk drives. Company accountants altered the financial statements to pretend that the bricks were indeed computer parts. These accountants would be liable to any fore-seeable users—including investors, creditors, and customers.

SECURITIES ACT OF 1933

The Securities Act of 1933 (1933 Act) requires a company to register securities before offering them for sale to the public. To do this, the company files a registration statement with the Securities and Exchange Commission (SEC). This registration statement must include audited financial statements. **Auditors are liable for any important misstatement or omission in the financial statements that they prepare for a registration statement.**

The plaintiff must prove only that (1) the registration statement contained an important misstatement or omission; and (2) she lost money. Ernst & Young served as the auditor for FP Investments, Inc., a company that sold tax shelter partnerships. These partnerships were formed to cultivate tropical plants in Hawaii. The prospectus for this investment neglected to mention that the partnerships did not have enough cash on hand to grow the plants. The investors lost their money. A jury ordered Ernst & Young to pay damages of $18.9 million.[3]

However, auditors can avoid liability by showing that they made a reasonable investigation of the financial statements. This investigation is called **due diligence.** Typically, auditors will not be liable if they can show that they complied with GAAP and GAAS.

In the following case, the registration statement revealed some, but not all, of an investment's risks. The fund declined in value—for a reason that *was* disclosed. Should the accountant be liable for the *undisclosed* risks?

YOU BE THE JUDGE

RODNEY v. KPMG PEAT MARWICK

143 F.3d 1140, 1998 U.S. App. LEXIS 9454
United States Court of Appeals for the Eighth Circuit, 1998

FACTS: The plaintiffs invested in the Piper Funds Institutional Government Income Portfolio (the Fund). The Fund invested heavily in a type of security, called a "derivative," that is very sensitive to changes in interest rates. If rates go up, the value of derivatives goes down, and vice versa. The Fund had disclosed this interesting fact in its registration statement. When the Federal Reserve Board tightened monetary policy, interest rates rose, and the price of Fund shares fell sharply. The investors filed suit against KPMG under the 1933 Act, alleging that its audit *should* have disclosed that:

- The Fund invested in a type of derivative that was not disclosed in the registration statement. This new type of investment was also sensitive to interest rate changes.

- The Fund's portfolio had a longer life expectancy than disclosed. For this type of investment, the longer the life expectancy, the higher the risk.

---

[3] *Hayes v. Haushalter,* 1994 U.S. App. LEXIS 23608 (9th Cir. 1994).

• The Fund's registration statement promised that it would not invest in illiquid securities (that is, securities that are not readily marketable). As much as 52% of the Fund's portfolio was illiquid.

YOU BE THE JUDGE: Was KPMG's failure to disclose this information an important omission? Should the accounting firm be liable to investors?

ARGUMENT FOR KPMG: After reading the registration statement, no reasonable person could fail to understand that the Fund intended to purchase highly risky investments. In particular, investors were on full notice that, if interest rates went up,

the value of their investment would go down. That is exactly what happened. The Fund's investments may not have complied exactly with the rules for registration statements, but the risk was the same.

ARGUMENT FOR THE INVESTORS: Plaintiffs need prove only that the registration statement contained an important misstatement and they lost money. The registration statement in this case was inaccurate. Although investors were warned about the danger of rising interest rates, they were not told about the other risks. Investors had the right to know not only that their purchase was risky, but how risky and why. ▮

SECURITIES EXCHANGE ACT OF 1934

Under the Securities Exchange Act of 1934 (1934 Act), public companies must file an annual report containing audited financial statements and quarterly reports with unaudited financials.

Fraud

In these filings under the 1934 Act, an auditor is liable for making (1) a misstatement or omission of an important fact; (2) knowingly or recklessly; (3) that the plaintiff relies on in purchasing or selling a security. Note that accountants are liable under this law only if they are *reckless*. For example, Price Waterhouse audited the financial statements of Altris Software. On the last day of the year, Altris recorded more than $500,000 as "start-up fees" from two of its customers. In the past, no start-up fee had exceeded $5,000. When Altris shareholders sued Price Waterhouse, the court agreed that the accountants had been *careless* and had not followed GAAP. But it held that the accountants had not been *reckless* and, therefore, were not liable. To show recklessness, the plaintiffs would have had to prove that "the accounting practices were so deficient that the audit amounted to no audit at all, or an egregious refusal to see the obvious, or to investigate the doubtful, or that the accounting judgments which were made were such that no reasonable accountant would have made the same decisions if confronted with the same facts."[4] Price Waterhouse's behavior had not been that bad.

Whistleblowing

Auditors who suspect that a client has committed an illegal act must notify the client's board of directors. If the board fails to take appropriate action, the auditors must issue an official report to the board. If the board receives such a report from its auditors, it must notify the SEC within one business day (and send a copy

---

[4] *DSAM Global Value Fund V. Altris Software, Inc.* 288 F.3d 385, 2002 U.S. App. LEXIS 7213.

of this notice to its accountant). If the auditors do not receive this copy, they must notify the SEC themselves.

Joint and Several Liability

Traditionally, liability under the 1934 Act was joint and several. When several different participants were potentially liable, a plaintiff could sue any one defendant or any group of defendants for the full amount of the damages. If a company committed fraud and then went bankrupt, its accounting firm might well be the only defendant with assets. Even if the accountants had caused only, say, 5% of the damages, they could be liable for the full amount.

Congress amended the 1934 Act to provide that accountants are liable *jointly and severally* only if they *knowingly* violate the law. Otherwise, the defendants are *proportionately* liable, meaning that they are liable only for the share of the damages that they themselves caused.

CRIMINAL LIABILITY

Some violations by accountants are criminal acts for which the punishment may be a fine and imprisonment:

- The Justice Department has the right to prosecute **willful violations** under either the 1933 Act or the 1934 Act.

- The Internal Revenue Code imposes various criminal penalties on accountants for **wrongdoing in the preparation of tax returns.**

- Many states prosecute violations of their securities laws.

Other Accountant-Client Issues

THE ACCOUNTANT-CLIENT RELATIONSHIP

An accountant who engages in unethical or improper professional conduct may be banned from practice before the SEC. Auditors who are banned or suspended cannot perform the audits that are required by the 1933 and 1934 Acts—quite a professional blow.

The SEC has long been concerned about the relationship between accountants and the companies they audit. Its rules require accountants to maintain independence from their clients. **An auditor or her family must not, for example, maintain a financial or business relationship with the client.**

Looking for Stock in All the Wrong Places

The SEC specifically prohibits accountants or their families from owning stock in a company that their firm audits. To take one woeful example, the SEC discovered that most of PricewaterhouseCoopers's partners were in violation of this rule, including half of the partners who were charged with enforcing it. Even worse, the firm had been caught violating the same rule only a few years before. The SEC notified 52 of the firm's clients that there were potential concerns about the integrity of their financial statements and even requested that some of the companies select a new auditor.

Consulting Services

Enron paid Arthur Andersen more for its consulting services than for its auditing efforts, which might have been one reason Andersen was reluctant to blow the whistle on Enron. For years, the SEC tried to restrict consulting by accounting firms, but the firms found powerful allies in Congress to protect them. In the aftermath of Enron's collapse, the Big Four accounting firms all reluctantly announced that they would henceforth refuse to sell consulting services to firms that they audited.

Stunned by a collapsing stock market and investor dismay, Congress then passed **the Sarbanes-Oxley Act, which prohibits accounting firms that audit public companies from providing consulting services on topics such as bookkeeping, financial information systems, human resources, and legal issues (unrelated to the audit).** This statute is not as tough as the one the accounting firms had already imposed on themselves. It is not clear at this writing which standard will prevail.

ETHICS | Your team arrives at a client's office to begin its audit. An eager young manager is introduced to you as your host for the week. After a warm welcome, he gives you an "audit planning memo," which lists meals at fancy restaurants, trips to NBA basketball games, and shopping. Should you accept this hospitality? Could it interfere with your ability to audit carefully? Could it create the appearance of a conflict of interest? From the Chapter 2 Ethics Checklist: How would these activities look in the light of day? Would they violate important values? ◾▪

ACCOUNTANT-CLIENT PRIVILEGE

Traditionally, an accountant-client privilege did not exist under federal law. Accountants were under no obligation to keep confidential any information they received from their clients. In one notorious case, the IRS suspected that the owner of a chain of pizza parlors was underreporting his income. The agency persuaded the owner's CPA, James Checksfield, to spy on him for eight years. (The IRS agreed to drop charges against Checksfield, who had not paid his own taxes for three years.) Thanks to the information that Checksfield passed to the IRS, his client was indicted on criminal charges of evading taxes by failing to report over $300,000 in income.

Congress passed the Internal Revenue Service Restructuring and Reform Act to reduce IRS abuse of taxpayers. This statute provides limited protection for tax advice that accountants give their clients. That is the good news. The bad news is the word "limited." **This new privilege applies only in civil cases involving the IRS or the U.S. government.** It does not apply to criminal cases, civil cases not involving the U.S. government, or cases with other federal agencies such as the SEC. Nor does it apply to advice about tax shelters. Thus, for example, this new accountant-client privilege would not have protected Checksfield's client because he was charged with a criminal offense.

Working Papers

When working for a client, accountants use the client's own documents and also prepare working papers of their own—notes, memoranda, research. In theory, each party owns whatever it has prepared itself. Thus accountants own the working papers they have created. In practice, however, the client controls even the accountant's working papers. **The accountant (1) cannot show the working papers to**

anyone without the client's permission (or a valid court order); and (2) must allow the client access to the working papers. Under the Sarbanes-Oxley Act, accountants for public companies must keep all audit work papers for at least seven years.

Professional Responsibility

The American Institute of Certified Public Accountants (AICPA) not only administers the CPA exam, it has also developed a long-standing Code of Professional Conduct (available at **http://www.aicpa.org**). This code affected more than just AICPA members because courts consistently held that all accountants, even those who are not members of AICPA, had to follow it. However, the Sarbanes-Oxley Act specifically gives a newly created Public Company Accounting Oversight Board authority to regulate ethical issues for public accounting firms. Therefore, the continued role of the AICPA in ethical issues is difficult to predict.

Chapter Conclusion

Accountants serve many masters and, therefore, face numerous potential conflicts. Clients, third parties, and the government all rely on their work. Privy to clients' most intimate financial secrets, accountants must decide which of these secrets to reveal and which to keep confidential. The wrong decision may destroy the client, impoverish its shareholders, and subject its auditors to substantial penalties.

Chapter Review

1. Accountants are liable to their clients for negligence if:
   - They breach their duty to their clients by failing to exercise the degree of skill and competence that an ordinarily prudent accountant would under the circumstances; and
   - The violation of this duty causes harm to the client.

2. Accountants are liable for fraud if:
   - They make a false statement of fact.
   - They know it is not true or recklessly disregard the truth; and
   - The client justifiably relies on the statement.

3. Accountants have a legal obligation to:
   - Keep all client information confidential; and
   - Use client information only for the benefit of the client.

4. Accountants who fail to exercise due care are liable to (1) any third party they knew would rely on the information; and (2) anyone else in the same class.

5. An accountant who commits fraud is liable to any foreseeable user of the work product who justifiably relies on it.

6. Auditors are liable for any important misstatement or omission in the financial statements that they provide the SEC with a registration statement.

7. Under the 1934 Act, an auditor is liable for making (1) any misstatement or omission of a material fact in financial statements; (2) knowingly or recklessly; (3) that the plaintiff relies on in purchasing or selling a security.

8. Auditors who suspect that a client has committed an illegal act must notify the client's board of directors.

9. Under the 1934 Act, accountants are liable jointly and severally only if they knowingly violate the law. Otherwise, they are proportionately liable.

10. The SEC prohibits auditors or their families from owning stock in companies that their firm audits.

11. The Sarbanes-Oxley Act prohibits accounting firms that audit public companies from providing consult- ing services on certain topics, such as bookkeeping, financial information systems, human resources, and legal issues (unrelated to the audit).

12. A limited accountant-client privilege exists under federal law.

PRACTICE TEST

Matching Questions

Match the following terms with their definitions:

___ **A.** GAAS.

___ **B.** Tracing.

___ **C.** Qualified opinion.

___ **D.** GAAP.

___ **E.** Vouching.

___ **F.** Unqualified opinion.

1. Rules for preparing financial statements.

2. Accountants check backwards to ensure there are data to support a transaction.

3. Clean opinion.

4. Rules for conducting audits.

5. Accountants check a transaction forward to ensure it has been properly recorded.

6. There is some uncertainty in the financial statements.

True/False Questions

Circle true or false:

1. T F Auditors are only liable under the 1933 Act if they intentionally misrepresent financial statements.

2. T F Auditors generally are not liable if they follow GAAP and GAAS.

3. T F Accountants are prohibited under federal law from disclosing a client's confidential information.

4. T F If auditors discover that company officers have committed an illegal act, they must immediately report this wrongdoing to the SEC.

5. T F Under federal law, accounting firms may not provide any consulting services to companies that they audit.

Multiple-Choice Questions

6. To be successful in a suit under the Securities Act of 1933, the plaintiff must prove

	Important Mistake In the Registration Statement	Plaintiff Lost Money
(a)	No	Yes
(b)	No	No
(c)	Yes	No
(d)	Yes	Yes

7. An accountant is liable to a client for conducting an audit negligently if the accountant:

   (a) Acted with intent.

   (b) Was a fiduciary of the client.

   (c) Failed to exercise due care.

   (d) Executed an engagement letter.

8. CPA QUESTION: A CPA's duty of due care to a client most likely will be breached when a CPA:

   (a) Gives a client an oral instead of a written report.

   (b) Gives a client incorrect advice based on an honest error judgment.

   (c) Fails to give tax advice that saves the client money.

   (d) Fails to follow generally accepted auditing standards.

9. To prove a case of fraud against an accountant, the following element is *not* required:

   (a) The client lost money.

   (b) The accountant made a false statement of fact.

   (c) The accountant relied on the false statement.

   (d) The accountant knew the statement was false.

   (e) The accountant was reckless.

10. Dusty is trying to buy an office building to house his growing consulting firm. When Luke, a landlord, asks to see a set of financials, Dusty asks his accountant Ellen to prepare a set for Luke. Dusty shows these financials to a number of landlords, including Carter. Dusty rents from Carter. Ellen has been careless and the financials are inaccurate. Dusty cannot pay his rent and Carter files suit against Ellen. Which of the following statements is true?

    (a) Carter will win because Ellen was careless.

    (b) Carter will win because Ellen knew that landlords would see the financials.

    (c) Carter will win because Ellen was careless and she knew that landlords would see the financials.

    (d) Carter will lose because Ellen did not know that he would see the financials.

    (e) Carter will lose because he had no contract with Ellen.

11. Ted prepared fraudulent financial statements for the Arbor Corp. Lacy read these statements before purchasing stock in the company. When Arbor goes bankrupt, Lacy sues Ted.

    (a) Lacy will win because it was foreseeable that she would rely on these statements.

    (b) Lacy will win because Ted was negligent.

    (c) Lacy will lose because she did not rely on these statements.

    (d) Lacy will lose because it was not foreseeable and she did not rely on these statements.

    (e) Lacy will lose because it is not foreseeable that she would rely on these statements.

Short-Answer Questions

12. Color-Dyne printed patterns on carpets. After reviewing the company's audited financial statements, the plaintiffs provided materials to Color-Dyne on credit. These financial statements showed that Color-Dyne owned $2 million in inventory. The audit failed to reveal, however, that various banks held secured interests in this inventory. The accountant did not know that the company intended to give the financial statements to plaintiffs or any other creditors. Color-Dyne went bankrupt. Is the accountant liable to plaintiffs?

13. James and Penelope Monroe purchased securities offered by Hughes Homes, Inc., a retailer of manufactured housing in Tacoma, Washington. During its audit, Deloitte & Touche found that Hughes Homes' internal controls had flaws. As a result, the accounting firm adjusted the scope of its audit to perform independent testing to verify the accuracy of the company's financial records. Satisfied that the internal controls were functional, Deloitte issued a clean opinion. After Hughes Homes went bankrupt, the Monroes sued Deloitte for violating the 1933 Act. They alleged that Deloitte's failure to disclose that it had found flaws in Hughes's internal control system was a material omission. GAAS did not require disclosure. Is Deloitte liable?

14. When Jeff Hall told one of the general partners of the Edge Energies limited partnerships that he did not wish to invest in these ventures, the general partner suggested he call Ronald W. Jackson, the partnerships' accountant. Jackson told Hall that Edge Energies partnerships were a "good deal," that they were "good

moneymakers," and "they were expecting something like a two-year payoff." In fact, Jackson knew that the operators were mismanaging these ventures, and that the partnerships were bad investments. Hall relied on Jackson's recommendation and invested in Edge Energies. He subsequently lost his entire investment. Is Jackson liable to Hall? Under what theory?

15. The British Broadcasting Corp. (BBC) broadcast a TV program alleging that Terry Venables, a former professional soccer coach, had fraudulently obtained a £1 million loan by misrepresenting the value of his company. Venables had been a sportscaster for the BBC but had switched to a competing network. The source of the BBC's story was "confidential working papers" from Venables's accountant. According to the accountant, the papers had been stolen. Who owns these working papers? Does the accountant have the right to disclose the content of working papers?

16. Medtrans, an ambulance company, was unable to pay its bills. In need of cash, it signed an engagement letter with Deloitte & Touche to perform an audit that could be used to attract investors. Unfortunately, the audit had the opposite effect. The unaudited statements showed earnings of $1.9 million, but the accountants calculated that the company had actually lost about $500,000. While in the process of negotiating adjustments to the financials, Deloitte resigned. Some time passed before Medtrans found another auditor, and, in that interim, a potential investor withdrew its $10 million offer. Is Deloitte liable for breach of contract?

17. ROLE REVERSAL: Prepare a multiple-choice question like those found on the CPA exam. The earlier question in the practice test provides an example.

Internet Research Problem

On the SEC Web site (**http://www.sec.gov**) find five examples of actions that the SEC has brought against accountants. (You might try typing the term "accounting violations" in the search box.) What does the SEC allege that the accountants have done? What provisions of the securities laws has the SEC accused them of violating?

You can find further practice problems in the Online Quiz at **http://beatty.westbuslaw.com** or in the Study Guide that accompanies this text.

PROPERTY AND CONSUMER LAW

UNIT 6

chapter 39

Consumer and Environmental Law

Three women signed up for a lesson at the Arthur Murray dance studio in Washington, D.C. Expecting a session of quiet fun, they instead found themselves in a nightmare of humiliation and coercion:

- "I tried to say no and get out of it and I got very, very upset because I got frightened at paying out all that money and having nothing to fall back on. I remember I started crying and couldn't stop crying. All I thought of was getting out of there. So finally after—I don't know how much time, Mr. Mara said, well, I could sign up for 250 hours, which was half the 500 Club, which would amount to $4,300. So I finally signed it. After that, I tried to raise the money from the bank and found I couldn't get a loan for that amount and I didn't have any savings and I had to get a bank loan to pay for it. That was when I went back and asked him to cancel that contract. But Mr. Mara said that he couldn't cancel it."

- "I did not join the carnival. I did not wish to join the carnival, and while it was only an additional $55, I had no desire to join. [My instructor] asked everyone in the room to sit down in a circle around me and he stood me up in that circle, in the middle of the circle, and said, 'Everybody, I want you to look at this woman here who is too cheap to join the carnival. I just want you to look at a woman like that. Isn't it awful?' "

Because of abuses such as these, the Federal Trade Commission (FTC) ordered the Arthur Murray dance studio to halt its high-pressure sales techniques, limit each contract to no more than $1,500 in dance lessons, and permit all contracts to be canceled within seven days.[1]

Introduction

Both consumer and environmental laws affect us in our daily lives—how accurate are the advertisements we see or the loan documents we sign, how clean the air we breathe or the water we drink. Also, both sets of laws have changed dramatically in the recent past as the attitudes of society have altered.

Years ago, consumers typically dealt with merchants they knew well. A dance instructor in a small town would not stay in business long if he tormented his elderly clients. As the population of the country grew and cities expanded, however, merchants became less and less subject to community pressure. The law has supplemented, if not replaced, these informal policing mechanisms. Both Congress and the states have passed statutes that protect consumers. But the legal system is generally too slow and expensive to handle small cases. The women who fell into the web of Arthur Murray had neither the wealth nor the energy to sue the studio themselves. To aid consumers such as these, Congress empowered federal agencies to enforce consumer laws. The Federal Trade Commission is the most important of these agencies.

Sales

Section 5 of the Federal Trade Commission Act (FTC Act) prohibits "unfair and deceptive acts or practices." You can report an unfair or deceptive practice to the FTC at its Web site (**http://www.ftc.gov**).

DECEPTIVE ACTS OR PRACTICES

Many deceptive acts or practices involve advertisements. **Under the FTC Act, an advertisement is deceptive if it contains an important misrepresentation or omission that is likely to mislead a reasonable consumer.** A company advertised that a pain-relief ointment called "Aspercreme" provided "the strong relief of aspirin right where you hurt." From this ad and the name of the product, do you assume that the ointment contains aspirin? Are you a reasonable consumer? Consumers surveyed in a shopping mall believed the product contained aspirin. In fact, it does not. The FTC required the company to disclose that there is no aspirin in Aspercreme.[2]

Was the company in the following case deceptive about its treatment for baldness?

---

[1] *In re Arthur Murray Studio of Washington, Inc.*, 78 F.T.C. 401, 1971 FTC LEXIS 75 (1971).
[2] *In re Thompson Medical Co.*, 104 F.T.C. 648, 1984 LEXIS 6 (1984).

CASE SUMMARY

FTC v. PANTRON I CORP.

33 F.3d 1088, 1994 U.S. App. LEXIS 22977
United States Court of Appeals for the Ninth Circuit, 1994

FACTS: Pantron I Corp. marketed the Helsinki Formula, a conditioner and shampoo costing $49.95 for a three-month supply. Pantron's advertisements (including late-night infomercials hosted by Robert Vaughn, star of the old TV show "The Man from U.N.C.L.E.") claimed scientific studies proved that the formula promoted growth of new hair on bald men.

At trial, three doctors testified that there was "no reason to believe" from current scientific data that the Helsinki Formula would cure or prevent baldness and that the studies on which Pantron relied did not meet generally accepted scientific standards. Users of the Helsinki Formula (or any other baldness cure) may indeed experience hair regrowth because of the so-called *placebo effect.* Frequently, products with no medicinal value work for psychological reasons. A patient who takes sugar pills believing they are pain relievers may feel better, although the pills themselves are worthless in treating pain. Hair growth products have a particularly strong placebo effect.

Pantron introduced evidence from 18 men who experienced hair regrowth or a reduction in hair loss after using the formula. It also introduced evidence of a "consumer satisfaction survey" that showed positive results in 70% of those who had used the product for six months or more. Over half of Pantron's orders came from repeat purchasers; it received very few written complaints; and fewer than 3% of its customers asked for their money back.

The trial court decided that Pantron could state, in its advertisements, that the Helsinki Formula was effective to some extent for some people in treating baldness. However, the ads must disclose that (1) the formula was more likely to stop hair loss than grow new hair; and (2) the claims were not supported by scientific studies that met U.S. standards.

ISSUE: Are the advertisements for the Helsinki Formula deceptive?

DECISION: Yes, these advertisements are deceptive.

REASONING: If a product's only benefit derives from the placebo effect, the product cannot be considered effective, even though some consumers experience positive results. Wesson Oil, promoted as a baldness cure, would probably produce results as good as the Helsinki Formula.

With the placebo effect, a product works because consumers believe that it works. The Helsinki Formula is effective because consumers believe the advertisements, even though the advertisements are, in fact, false. It would make no sense to permit false advertisements simply because consumers believe they are true. Otherwise, advertisers would have an incentive to create false, but credible, ads in the hope that consumers would believe them and therefore, that they would become true. Pantron's effectiveness claims are false.

UNFAIR PRACTICES

The FTC Act also prohibits unfair acts or practices. For example, a furnace repair company dismantled home furnaces for "inspection" and then refused to reassemble them until the consumers agreed to buy services or replacement parts.

BAIT AND SWITCH

FTC rules prohibit bait and switch advertisements: A merchant may not advertise a product and then try to get consumers to buy a different (more expensive) item. In addition, merchants must have enough stock on hand to meet reasonable demand for any advertised product.

Sears ran many advertisements like the following:

Portable Zig-Zag Sewing Machine

from SEARS

$58

Sews on buttons, sews buttonholes
Does zig-zag or straight stitching
monograms, appliqués, other fancy work
for household linens, gifts
Sews forward and reverse for her convenience

When eager customers went to buy this fabulous item, they were told that the machines were noisy, did not come with Sears's standard sewing machine guarantee, and could neither stitch in reverse nor do buttonholes. Also, the store was out of stock and would not be receiving any new machines for a long time.[3] Sears did not wish to sell the advertised merchandise; it wanted to switch consumers to another, higher-priced product. This practice violated FTC rules.

MAIL OR TELEPHONE ORDER MERCHANDISE

The FTC has established the following guidelines on mail or telephone order merchandise:

- Mail-order companies must ship an item within the time stated or, if no time is given, within 30 days after receipt of the order.

- If a company cannot ship the product when promised, it must send the customer a notice with the new shipping date and an opportunity to cancel. If the new shipping date is within 30 days of the original one, and the customer does not cancel, the order is still on.

- If the company cannot ship within 30 days of the original date, it must send the customer another notice. This time, however, the company must cancel the order unless the customer returns the notice, indicating that he still wants the item.

For example, Dell Computer Corp. advertised that its Dimension computer came with the "Dell Software Suite." In fact, the suite was not available for several

---

[3] *In re Sears, Roebuck and Co.*, 89 F.T.C. 229, 1977 FTC LEXIS 225 (1977).

months. Instead of the software, Dell sent customers a coupon for the suite "when available." Imagine having a coupon but no software. The FTC charged Dell with violations of the mail or telephone order rules.[4]

TELEMARKETING

The telephone rings: "Could I speak with Alexander Johannson? This is Denise from Master Chimney Sweeps." It is 7:30 p.m.; you have just straggled in from work and are looking forward to a peaceful dinner of takeout cuisine. You are known as Sandy, your last name is pronounced Yohannson, and you live in a modern apartment without a chimney. A telemarketer has struck again! What can you do to protect your peace and quiet?

The FTC has established a national do-not-call registry. You can register your telephone numbers with the FTC online at **http://www.donotcall.gov** or by telephone at (888)-382-1222. FTC rules also prohibit telemarketers from blocking their names and telephone numbers on Caller ID systems.

UNORDERED MERCHANDISE

Under §5 of the FTC Act, anyone who receives unordered merchandise in the mail can treat it as a gift. She can use it, throw it away, or do whatever else she wants with it.

There you are, watching an infomercial for Anushka products, guaranteed to fight that scourge of modern life—cellulite! Rushing to your phone, you place an order. The Anushka cosmetics arrive, but for some odd reason, the cellulite remains. A month later another bottle arrives, like magic, in the mail. The magic spell is broken, however, when you get your credit card bill and see that, without your authorization, the company has charged you for the new supply of Anushka. This company was in violation of FTC rules because it did not notify customers that they were free to treat the unauthorized products as a gift, to use or throw out as they wished.[5]

DOOR-TO-DOOR SALES

Consumers at home need special protection from salespeople. In a store, customers can simply walk out, but at home they may feel trapped. **Under the FTC door-to-door rules, a salesperson is required to notify the buyer that she has the right to cancel the transaction prior to midnight of the third business day thereafter.** This notice must be given both orally and in writing; the actual cancellation must be in writing. The seller must return the buyer's money within 10 days. For example, Tork & Associates violated FTC rules when it sold door-to-door magazine subscriptions. Customers were told that, to cancel, they had to submit a copy of the complete receipt, the canceled check, the salesperson's name, the magazine name, the date of the transaction, and the total cost. Salespeople never actually gave customers the complete receipt, so it was difficult for customers to comply with these requirements.

---

[4] *United States v. Dell Computer Corp.*, 1998 FTC LEXIS 30 (1998).
[5] *In the Matter of Synchronal Corp.*, 116 F.T.C. 1189, 1993 FTC LEXIS 280 (1993).

Consumer Credit

Most states limit the maximum interest rate a lender may charge. These laws are called **usury statutes.** The penalty for violating usury statutes varies among the states. Depending upon the jurisdiction, the borrower may be allowed to keep (1) the interest above the usury limit; (2) all of the interest; or (3) all of the loan and the interest.

TRUTH-IN-LENDING ACT

The federal Truth-in-Lending Act (TILA) does not regulate interest rates or the terms of a loan; these are set by state law. It simply requires lenders to disclose the terms of a loan in an understandable and complete manner.
   Under TILA:

- *The disclosure must be clear and in a sensible order.* A finance company violated TILA when it loaned money to Dorothy Allen. The company made all the required disclosures but scattered them throughout the loan document and intermixed them with confusing terms that were not required by TILA.[6] A TILA disclosure statement should not be a game of *Where's Waldo.*

- *The lender must disclose the finance charge.* The finance charge is the amount, in dollars, the consumer will pay in interest and fees over the life of the loan.

- *The creditor must disclose the annual percentage rate (APR).* This number is the actual rate of interest the consumer pays on an annual basis. Without this disclosure, it would be easy in a short-term loan to disguise a very high APR because the finance charge is low. Boris borrows $5 for lunch from his employer's credit union. Under the terms of the loan, he must repay $6 the following week. His finance charge is only $1, but his APR is astronomical—20% per week for a year.

FAIR CREDIT BILLING ACT

Is there anyone in America who has not sometime or other discovered an error in a credit card bill? Before Congress passed the Fair Credit Billing Act (FCBA), a dispute with a credit card company often deteriorated into an avalanche of threatening form letters that ignored any response from the hapless cardholder. **But under the FCBA:**

- If, within 60 days of receipt of a bill, a consumer writes to a credit card company to complain about the bill, the company must acknowledge receipt of the complaint within 30 days.

- Within two billing cycles (but no more than 90 days) the credit card company must investigate the complaint and respond.

- The credit card company cannot try to collect the disputed debt or close or suspend the account until it has responded to the consumer complaint.

- The credit card company cannot report to credit agencies that the consumer has an unpaid bill until 10 days after the response. If the consumer still disputes the charge, the credit card company may report the amount to a credit agency but must disclose that it is disputed.

---

[6] *Allen v. Beneficial Fin. Co. of Gary,* 531 F.2d 797, 1976 U.S. App. LEXIS 12935 (7th Cir. 1976).

At **http://www.ftc.gov/bcp/conline/pubs/credit/fcb.htm** the FTC provides a sample form letter to send to a credit card company if you want to dispute a bill.

In the following case, American Express made a big mistake picking on a law professor.

CASE SUMMARY

GRAY v. AMERICAN EXPRESS CO.

743 F.2d 10, 240 U.S. App. D.C. 10, 1984 U.S. App. LEXIS 19033
United States Court of Appeals for the District of Columbia Circuit, 1984

FACTS: In December, Oscar Gray used his American Express credit card to buy airline tickets costing $9,312. American Express agreed that Gray could pay for the tickets in 12 monthly installments. In January, Gray paid $3,500 and then in February an additional $1,156. In March, American Express billed Gray by mistake for the entire remaining balance, which he did not pay. In April, Gray and his wife went out for dinner to celebrate their wedding anniversary. When he tried to pay with his American Express card, the restaurant told him that the credit card company had not only refused to accept the charges for the meal, but had instructed the restaurant to confiscate and destroy the card. While still at the restaurant, Gray spoke to an American Express employee on the telephone who informed him, "Your account is canceled as of now."

Gray wrote to American Express, pointing out the error. For more than a year, the company failed to respond to Gray or to investigate his claim. It then turned the bill over to a collection agency. Gray sued American Express for violating the Fair Credit Billing Act. The trial court granted summary judgment to American Express and dismissed the complaint on the grounds that Gray had waived his rights under the act when he signed the application form.

ISSUE: Is American Express liable to Gray for violating the Fair Credit Billing Act?

DECISION: The district court's order of summary judgment and dismissal is vacated. American Express violated the Fair Credit Billing Act.

REASONING: When Gray applied for his American Express card the contract stated, "We can revoke your right to use [the card] at any time. We can do this without cause and without giving you notice." This contract directly conflicts with the FCBA, which provides that, while there is a dispute over the amount of a bill, the credit card company cannot close the account for failure to pay that bill. American Express argued that it had the right to cancel Gray's account for no reason or for a reason unrelated to the disputed amount. In short, American Express argued that Gray had waived the bulk of his rights under the Act.

The whole point of consumer protection legislation is to give consumers more bargaining power. To allow consumers to waive this protection by signing boilerplate language would undermine the purpose of the Act. A court ought not to attribute such nonsense to Congress. ◢

FAIR CREDIT REPORTING ACT

Most adults rely on credit—to acquire a house, credit cards, or overdraft privileges at the bank. A bad credit report makes life immensely more difficult. The goal of the Fair Credit Reporting Act (FCRA) is to ensure that consumer credit reports are accurate.

The FCRA regulates **consumer reporting agencies.** These are businesses that supply consumer reports to third parties such as credit card companies, banks, and employers. **Under the FCRA:**

- A consumer report can be used only for a legitimate business need. A nosy neighbor does not have the right to order a report.

- A consumer reporting agency cannot report information that is more than seven years old. (Except in the case of bankruptcies, the limit is 10 years.)

- An employer cannot request a consumer report on an employee without the employee's permission.

- Anyone who penalizes a consumer because of a credit report must reveal the name and address of the reporting agency that supplied the information.

- Upon request from a consumer, a reporting agency must disclose all information in his file.

- If a consumer tells an agency that some of the information in his file is incorrect, the agency must investigate. The consumer also has the right to give the agency a short report telling his side of the story.

A survey revealed that 70% of credit reports contain errors. Consumer advocates recommend that every year you check your credit reports from each of the three major reporting agencies: Equifax (**http://www.equifax.com**); Experian (**http://www.experian.com**); and TransUnion (**http://www.transunion.com**). A credit report generally costs $8, although, in some states, it is free. At **http://www.ftc.gov/bcp/conline/pubs/credit/crdtdis.htm**, the FTC offers advice on how to dispute credit report errors.

FAIR DEBT COLLECTION PRACTICES ACT

Debt collectors can be ruthless in tracking down their victims. Congress passed the Fair Debt Collection Practices Act (FDCPA) because it was concerned that abusive debt collection practices could contribute to the number of personal bankruptcies, to marital instability, to the loss of jobs, and to invasions of privacy. Debt collection practices can also disrupt Super Bowl Sunday. Debt collectors want to catch their prey off guard, and what better time than when the entire nation is at home, glued to the television? If the phone rings, sports fans assume it is a friend calling to gab about the game.

Is that legal? It depends. **Under the FDCPA, collectors may not:**

- Call or write a debtor who has notified the collector in writing that he wishes no further contact.

- Call or write a debtor who is represented by an attorney.

- Call a debtor before 8 a.m. or after 9 p.m.

- Threaten a debtor or use obscene or abusive language.

- Call or visit the debtor at work if the consumer's employer prohibits such contact.

- Threaten to arrest consumers who do not pay their debts.

- Make other false or deceptive threats, that is, threats that would be illegal if carried out or which the collector has no intention of doing—such as suing the debtor or seizing property.

- Contact acquaintances of the debtor for any reason other than to locate the debtor (and then only once); or

- Tell acquaintances that the consumer is in debt.

For example, after Sherri Gradisher bounced a check for $81.30 at Doug Born's Smokehouse, she received three notices on the letterhead of the local sheriff's department threatening to arrest her. It turns out that the notices were sent by a private company, not by the sheriff's department (although the sheriff's department had given its permission). These letters violated the FDCPA.[7]

AT RISK

If a debt collector calls you, what can you do? First of all, be sure to write down his name and the name of his agency. Tell the caller that you are recording the conversation and then do so. Send a letter to the agency, requesting that it not contact you. Report any violations to the FTC at **http://www.ftc.gov/bcp/conline/pubs/credit/fdc.htm**.

EQUAL CREDIT OPPORTUNITY ACT

The Equal Credit Opportunity Act (ECOA) prohibits any creditor from discriminating against a borrower because of race, color, religion, national origin, sex, marital status, age, or because the borrower is receiving welfare. A lender must respond to a credit application within 30 days. If a lender rejects an application, it must either tell the applicant why or notify him that he has the right to a written explanation of the reasons for the rejection.

For example, when an African-American couple applied for a mortgage, the lender repeatedly asked for information the couple had already supplied and also refused to believe their assurances that they planned to live in the house, which was 80 miles from their jobs. (Their son lived nearby.) The company turned down their mortgage, refusing to give either an oral or a written explanation. It was ordered to pay $35,000 for violating the ECOA.

CONSUMER LEASING ACT

If you, like many other consumers, lease a car rather than buy it, you are protected under the Consumer Leasing Act (CLA). The CLA does not apply to the rental of real property—that is, to house or apartment leases. **Before a lease is signed, a lessor must disclose the following in writing:**

- The number and amount of all required payments.

- The total amount the consumer will have paid by the end of the lease.

- Maintenance requirements and a description of the lessor's wear and use standards.

- The consumer's right to purchase the leased property and at what price.

- The consumer's right to terminate a lease early.

The government brochure "Keys to Vehicle Leasing" is available at **http://www.federalreserve.gov/pubs/leasing**. It lays out the lessor's rights and compares the advantages and disadvantages of leasing versus purchasing a car.

Magnuson-Moss Warranty Act

The Magnuson-Moss Warranty Act does not require manufacturers or sellers to provide a warranty on their products. **The Act does require any supplier that offers a written warranty on a consumer product that costs more than $15 to**

---

[7] *Gradisher V. Check Enforcement Unit, Inc.,* 2002 U.S. Dist. LEXIS 6003.

disclose the terms of the warranty in simple, understandable language before the sale. Required disclosure includes the following:

- The name and address of the person the consumer should contact to obtain warranty service.

- The parts that are covered and those that are not.

- What services the warrantor will provide, at whose expense, and for what period of time.

- A statement of what the consumer must do and what expenses he must pay.

Although suppliers are not required to offer a warranty, if they do offer one they must indicate whether it is *full* or *limited.* Under a **full warranty,** the warrantor must promise to fix a defective product for a reasonable time without charge; if, after a reasonable number of efforts to fix the defective product, it still does not work, the consumer must have the right to a refund or a replacement without charge; but the warrantor is not required to cover damage caused by the consumer's unreasonable use.

Consumer Product Safety

In 1969, the federal government estimated that consumer products caused 30,000 deaths, 110,000 disabling injuries, and 20 million trips to the doctor. Toys were among the worst offenders, injuring 700,000 children a year. Children were cut by Etch-a-Sketch glass panels, choked by Zulu gun darts, and burned by Little Lady toy ovens. Although injured consumers had the right to seek damages under tort law, the goal of the Consumer Product Safety Act (CPSA) was to prevent injuries in the first place. This act created the Consumer Product Safety Commission to evaluate consumer products and develop safety standards. The Commission can impose civil and criminal penalties on those who violate its standards. Individuals have the right to sue under the CPSA for damages, including attorney's fees, from anyone who knowingly violates a consumer product safety rule. You can find out about product recalls or file a report on an unsafe product at the Commission's Web site (**http://www.cpsc.gov**).

Environmental Law

Michelle has owned a building on Main Street for more than 20 years. At the beginning, one of the businesses in the building was a drycleaning shop. The operators of the shop disposed of the cleaning fluids legally. Recent testing of the groundwater in a nearby park revealed that it was contaminated by drycleaning chemicals from the shop in the building that Michelle owns. She is liable for the cost of cleaning up the chemicals, even though they were disposed of legally. The cost of the cleanup will far exceed the value of the building she owns.

This scenario is based on a true story. The environment is a complex issue. It is not enough simply to say, "We are against pollution." The question is: Who will pay? Who will pay for past damage inflicted before anyone understood the harm that pollutants cause?

AIR POLLUTION

The Clean Air Act of 1970 requires the Environmental Protection Agency (EPA) to establish national air quality standards. These standards must protect public health *without regard to cost*. To date, however, Denver is the only major city to meet Clean Air Act standards. About 62 million Americans breathe unhealthy air. To find out about the air quality in your community, feel your way over to **http://www.scorecard.org**.

In the following case, a power plant argued that the EPA had imposed a solution whose cost far outweighed its benefit. There is only one Grand Canyon. Should visibility there be preserved at any cost?

YOU BE THE JUDGE

CENTRAL ARIZONA WATER CONSERVATION DISTRICT v. EPA

990 F.2d 1531, 1993 U.S. App. LEXIS 5881
United States Court of Appeals for the Ninth Circuit, 1993

FACTS: The Navaho Generating Station (NGS) is a power plant 12 miles from the Grand Canyon. To protect the views of this national treasure, the EPA ordered NGS to reduce its sulfur dioxide emissions by 90%. To do so would cost NGS $430 million initially in capital expenditures and then $89.6 million annually. Average winter visibility in the Grand Canyon would be improved by at most 7%, but perhaps less. NGS sued to prevent implementation of the EPA's order. A court may nullify an EPA order if it determines that the agency action was arbitrary and capricious.

YOU BE THE JUDGE: Did the EPA act arbitrarily and capriciously in requiring NGS to spend half a billion dollars to improve winter visibility at the Grand Canyon by at most 7%?

ARGUMENT FOR NGS: This case is a perfect example of environmentalism run amok. Half a billion dollars for the chance of increasing winter visibility at the Grand Canyon by 7%? Winter visitors to the Grand Canyon would undoubtedly prefer that NGS provide them with a free lunch rather than a 7% improvement in visibility. The EPA order is simply a waste of money.

ARGUMENT FOR THE EPA: How can NGS, or anyone else, measure the benefit of protecting a national treasure like the Grand Canyon? Even people who never have and never will visit it during the winter sleep better at night knowing that the Canyon is protected. NGS has been causing harm to the Grand Canyon, and now it should remedy the damage.

WATER POLLUTION

The Clean Water Act (CWA) has two ambitious goals: (1) to make all navigable water suitable for swimming and fishing; and (2) to eliminate the discharge of pollutants into navigable water. Like the Clean Air Act, the CWA sets goals without regard to cost. **In support of its goals, the CWA prohibits anyone from discharging pollution into water without a permit from the EPA.** However, like the Clean Air Act, the CWA's goals have not been met.

SUPERFUND

Superfund's official name is the Comprehensive Environmental Response, Compensation, and Liability Act (CERCLA). Its goal is to clean up hazardous wastes that have been improperly dumped in the past.

The philosophy of Superfund is that "the polluter pays." **Therefore, anyone who has *ever* owned or operated a site on which hazardous wastes are found, or who has transported wastes to the site, or who has arranged for the disposal of wastes that were released at the site, is liable for (1) the cost of cleaning up the site; (2) any damage done to natural resources; and (3) any required health assessments.**

Since its creation in 1980, Superfund has been hugely controversial. Progress is slow because each cleanup typically costs more than $30 billion and has taken, on average, 11 years per site. There are 1,551 sites on the national priority list, of which 257 are completely cleaned up and 552 are almost completed. During the next decade, up to 500 sites could be added to the list, at an additional cost of $14 billion. Meanwhile, one in four Americans, including 10 million children below the age of 12, lives within four miles of a Superfund site. To find out about hazardous waste sites in your community, click on **http://www.epa.gov/oerrpage/superfund/sites**.

Chapter Conclusion

Virtually no one will go through life without reading an advertisement, ordering from a catalogue, borrowing money, or breathing air and drinking water. Consumer and environmental laws are important in our lives.

Chapter Review

1. The Federal Trade Commission (FTC) prohibits "unfair and deceptive acts or practices."

2. The FTC considers an advertisement to be deceptive if it contains an important misrepresentation or omission that is likely to mislead a reasonable consumer.

3. FTC rules prohibit bait and switch advertisements. A merchant may not advertise a product and then try to get consumers to buy a different (more expensive) item.

4. Under FTC rules on mail or telephone order merchandise, mail-order companies must ship an item within the time stated or, if no time is given, within 30 days after receipt of the order.

5. The FTC has established a national do-not-call registry.

6. Consumers may keep as a gift any unordered merchandise that they receive in the mail.

7. Under the FTC door-to-door rules, a salesperson is required to notify the buyer that she has the right to cancel the transaction prior to midnight of the third business day thereafter.

8. In all loans regulated by the Truth-in-Lending Act, the disclosure must be clear and in a sensible order. The lender must disclose the finance charge and the annual percentage rate.

9. Under the Fair Credit Billing Act, a credit card company must promptly investigate and respond to any consumer complaints about a credit card bill.

10. Under the Fair Credit Reporting Act:

    • A consumer report can be used only for a legitimate business need.

    • A consumer reporting agency cannot report out-of-date information.

    • An employer cannot request a consumer report on an employee without the employee's permission; and

    • Anyone who penalizes a consumer because of a credit report must reveal the name and address of the reporting agency that supplied the information.

11. Under the Fair Debt Collection Practices Act, a debt collector may not harass or abuse debtors.

12. The Equal Credit Opportunity Act prohibits any creditor from discriminating against a borrower on the basis of race, color, religion, national origin, sex, marital status, age, or because the borrower is receiving welfare.

13. The Magnuson-Moss Warranty Act requires any supplier that offers a written warranty on a consumer product costing more than $15 to disclose the terms of the warranty in simple and readily understandable language before the sale.

14. The Consumer Product Safety Commission evaluates consumer products and develops safety standards.

15. The Clean Air Act of 1970 requires the Environmental Protection Agency (EPA) to establish national air quality standards.

16. The Clean Water Act prohibits anyone from discharging pollution into water without a permit from the EPA.

17. The goal of Superfund is to clean up hazardous wastes that have been improperly dumped in the past.

PRACTICE TEST

Matching Questions

Match the following terms with their definitions:

___ **A.** FCBA.

___ **B.** FDCPA.

___ **C.** FCRA.

___ **D.** ECOA.

___ **E.** TILA.

1. Requires lenders to disclose the terms of a loan.

2. Regulates credit reports.

3. Regulates debt collectors.

4. Prohibits lenders from discriminating based on race, religion, and sex.

5. Regulates disputes between consumers and their credit card companies.

True/False Questions

Circle true or false:

1. T F If a store advertises a product, it must have enough stock on hand to fill every order.

2. T F The FTC has established a national do-not-call registry.

3. T F Under usury laws, lenders are limited in the amount of interest they can charge.

4. T F Under the Truth-in-Lending Act, it does not matter how the information is disclosed, as long as it is disclosed someplace on the first page of the loan document.

5. T F A consumer reporting agency has the right to keep information in its files secret.

6. T F In establishing national standards under the Clean Air Act, the EPA need not consider the cost of compliance.

7. T F The Clean Water Act requires anyone discharging pollution into water to obtain a permit from the EPA.

Multiple-Choice Questions

8. Which of the following statements is *not* true:

(a) Mail-order companies must ship a product within the time stated.

(b) If no time is stated, the mail-order company must ship within 30 days.

(c) If a company cannot ship a product when promised, the company must cancel the order unless the customer indicates he wants the item.

(d) If a company cannot ship the product within 30 days of the original shipping date, the company must cancel the order unless the customer indicates he still wants the item.

(e) Each time the shipping date changes, the company must notify the customer.

9. If you receive a product in the mail that you did not order:

(a) You must pay for it or return it.

(b) You must pay for it only if you use it.

(c) You must throw it away.

(d) It is a gift to you.

(e) You must pay for it but the company must reimburse you for postage.

10. Zach sells Cutco Knives door to door. Which of the following statements is *not* true?

(a) The buyer has three days to cancel the order.

(b) Zach must tell the buyer of her rights.

(c) Zach must give the buyer a written notice of her rights.

(d) The seller can cancel orally or in writing.

(e) If the seller cancels, Zach must return her money within 10 days.

11. Depending on state law, if a lender violates the usury laws, the borrower could possibly be allowed to keep:

I. The interest that exceeds the usury limit.

II. All the interest.

III. All of the loan and the interest.

(a) I, II, and III.

(b) Only I.

(c) Only II.

(d) Only III.

(e) Neither I, II, nor III.

12. Jodie is upset because her credit card bill shows a charge of $39 to a pornographic Web site that she never visited. Under the FCBA:

(a) She should call the credit card company to tell them that this charge is wrong.

(b) She should call her parents to let them handle the problem.

(c) The credit card company has 90 days to respond to a complaint by Jodie.

(d) The credit card company has the right to close out her account until the dispute is resolved.

(e) The credit card company must investigate a complaint and respond within 90 days.

13. Which of the following statements is true of Superfund?

I. Anyone who has ever owned a site is liable for clean-up costs.

II. Anyone who has ever transported waste to a site is liable for clean-up costs.

III. Anyone who has ever disposed of waste at a site is liable for clean-up costs.

(a) Neither I, II, nor III.

(b) I, II, and III.

(c) I and II.

(d) II and III.

(e) I and III.

Short-Answer Questions

14. Process cheese food slices must contain at least 51% natural cheese. Imitation cheese slices, by contrast, contain little or no natural cheese and consist primarily of water and vegetable oil. Kraft, Inc. makes Kraft Singles, which are individually wrapped process cheese food slices. When Kraft began losing market share to imitation slices that were advertised as both less expensive and equally nutritious as Singles, Kraft responded with a series of advertisements informing consumers that Kraft Singles cost more than imitation slices because they are made from five ounces of milk. Kraft does use five ounces of milk in making each Kraft Single, but 30% of the calcium contained in the milk is lost during processing. Imitation slices contain the same amount of calcium as Kraft Singles. Are the Kraft advertisements deceptive?

15. Josephine Rutyna was a 60-year-old widow who suffered from high blood pressure and epilepsy. A bill collector from Collections Accounts Terminal, Inc. called her and demanded that she pay $56 she owed to Cabrini Hospital Medical Group. She told him that Medicare was supposed to pay the bill. Shortly thereafter, Rutyna received a letter from Collections that stated:

> You have shown that you are unwilling to work out a friendly settlement with us to clear the above debt. Our field investigator has now been instructed to make an investigation in your neighborhood and to personally call on your employer. The immediate payment of the full amount, or a personal visit to this office, will spare you this embarrassment.

Has Collections violated the law?

16. Kathleen Carroll, a single woman, applied for an Exxon credit card. Exxon rejected her application without giving any specific reason and without providing the name of the credit bureau it had used. When Carroll asked for a reason for the rejection, she was told that the credit bureau did not have enough information about her to establish creditworthiness. In fact, Exxon had denied her credit application because she did not have a major credit card or a savings account, she had been employed for only one year, and she had no dependents. Did Exxon violate the law?

17.

> GET ENOUGH BROADLOOM TO CARPET ANY AREA OF YOUR HOME OR APARTMENT UP TO 150 SQUARE FEET CUT, MEASURED, AND READY FOR INSTALLATION FOR ONLY $77. GET 100% DUPONT CONTINUOUS FILAMENT NYLON PILE BROADLOOM.
> CALL COLLECT

When customers called the number provided, New Rapids Carpet Center, Inc. sent salespeople to visit them at home to sell them carpet that was not as advertised—it was not continuous filament nylon pile broadloom, and the price was not $77. Has New Rapids violated a consumer law?

18. ETHICS: After TNT Motor Express hired Joseph Bruce Drury as a truck driver, it ordered a background check from Robert Arden & Associates. TNT provided Drury's Social Security number and date of birth, but not his middle name. Arden discovered that a Joseph Thomas Drury, who coincidentally had the same birthdate as Joseph Bruce Drury, had served a prison sentence for drunk driving. Not knowing that it had the wrong Drury, Arden reported this information to TNT, which promptly fired Drury. When he asked why, the TNT executive merely stated, "We do not discuss these matters." Did TNT violate the law? Whether or not TNT was in violation, did its executives behave ethically? Who would have been harmed or helped if TNT managers had informed Drury of the Arden report?

19. In 1963, FMC Corp. purchased a manufacturing plant in Virginia from American Viscose Corp., the owner of the plant since 1937. During World War II, American Viscose had made rayon for Army airplanes and truck tires. In 1982, carbon disulfide, a chemical used to manufacture this rayon, was found in groundwater near the plant. American Viscose was out of business. Who is responsible for cleaning up the carbon disulfide? Under what statute?

20. ROLE REVERSAL: Prepare a short-answer question that focuses on deceptive advertisements. Include a sample ad in the question (either a real ad or one that you have made up).

Internet Research Problem

The Consumer Product Safety Commission (**http://www.cpsc.gov**) lists products that have been recalled and provides consumers with a telephone number for contacting the manufacturer. Choose a recalled product and telephone the manufacturer to find out how it is handling the problem. Also see if you can find the manufacturer's Web site to learn if it has disclosed the recall there. What do you think of the manner in which the manufacturer has handled the recall? Is the manufacturer providing adequate protection to consumers?

You can find further practice problems in the Online Quiz at **http://beatty.westbuslaw.com** or in the Study Guide that accompanies this text.

Cyberlaw

Jason always said that his computer was his best friend. He was online all the time, sending instant messages to his friends, listening to music, doing research for his courses, and, okay, maybe playing a few games now and again. Occasionally, the computer could be annoying. It would crash once in a while, trashing part of a paper he had forgotten to save. And there was the time that a copy of an e-mail he sent Lizzie complaining about Caroline somehow ended up in Caroline's mailbox. He was pretty irritated when the White Sox tickets he bought in an online auction turned out to be for a Little League team. And he was tired of all the spam advertising pornographic Web sites. But these things happen and, despite the petty annoyances, his computer was an important part of his life.

Then one day, Jason received a panicked instant message from a teammate on the college wrestling squad telling him to click on a certain Web site pronto to see someone they knew. Jason eagerly clicked on the Web site and discovered, to his total horror, that he was featured—in the nude. The Web site was selling videos showing him and other members of the wrestling team in the locker room in various states of undress. Other videos, from other locker and shower rooms, were for sale, too, showing football players and wrestlers from dozens of universities. No longer trusting technology, Jason pulled on his running shoes and dashed over to the office of his business law professor. ▪

More than two billion people use the Internet worldwide. While the Internet has opened up enormous opportunities in both our business and personal lives, it has also created the need for new laws, both to pave the way for these opportunities and to limit their dangers. This chapter deals with issues that are unique to the cyberworld, such as online privacy, hacking, and spam. If some of the words confuse you, the Web site at **http://www.matisse.net/files/glossary.html** provides a glossary of Internet terms.

Before beginning the chapter in earnest, let's return briefly to Jason, the wrestler. What recourse does Jason have for his Internet injuries? The nude video incident actually happened at Illinois State University and seven other colleges. Approximately 30 athletes filed suit against GTE and PSINet for selling the videos online. The outcome of that case is revealed later in this chapter. What about Jason's other computer injuries? Lizzie was not being a good friend, but it was perfectly legal for her to forward Jason's e-mail to Caroline. The seller of the White Sox tickets violated both federal and state fraud statutes. The federal Can-Spam Act prohibits spam—unsolicited commercial e-mail—but a lawsuit is a slow and awkward tool for killing such a flourishing weed. Thus far, the available legal tools have been relatively ineffectual (as you can tell from your e-mail inbox).

Privacy

Computerized communication can be wonderfully efficient but also alarmingly dangerous. Consumers enter the most personal data—credit card numbers, bank accounts, lists of friends, medical information, product preferences—on the Internet. Who will have access to this data? Who can see it, use it, sell it? Many people fear that the Internet is a very large window through which the government, employers, business, and criminals can find out more than they should about you and your money, habits, beliefs, and health. Even e-mail has its dangers: Who has not been embarrassed by an e-mail that ended up in the wrong mailbox?

Many commentators argue that, without significant changes in the law, our privacy will be obliterated. At the moment, however, privacy on the Internet is very much like the weather—everyone talks about it, but (so far) no one has done much about it. The three major sources of privacy concerns are Internet tracking, the hard drive, and e-mail.

INTERNET TRACKING

Of Cookies and Caches

If you order a book from Amazon.com, you may notice that the next time you log on, you will be greeted with the message, "Hello, [Your Name]. Explore today's featured recommendations." Click on the link and you may find that, because you bought a GMAT study guide the first time, Amazon will entice you with other guides for standardized tests. However did Amazon know? Many Web sites automatically place a cookie on the hard drive of your computer when you visit them. **A cookie is a small file that includes an identification number and may also include personal data such as your address, phone and credit card numbers, and searches you have made or advertisements you have clicked on.**

Cookies raise privacy issues. When you travel around the Internet, cookies create a file that could come back to haunt you. Although much of the information gathered is anonymous (that is, the consumer is identified only by a computer identification number), this anonymous information can be linked to **personally identifiable information (PII),** such as name and address. One company now markets a databank with the names of 150 million registered voters. Anyone can buy a list of voters that is sliced and diced however they want, say, Republicans between the ages of 45 and 60 with Hispanic surnames and incomes greater than $50,000. This company can also transmit specially tailored banner ads to voters surfing the Web.

If marketers can put together a databank of Hispanic Republican voters, they can also find out that you have visited a Web site for recovering alcoholics or unrecovered gamblers or Nazi sympathizers. Do you want information about every Web site you visit to be public?

Even without cookies, your computer creates a file about you. When you surf the Web, your computer stores a copy of the Web pages you visit in a cache file on your hard drive. Thus, anyone with access to your hard drive could get a good idea of your regular stopping places. Would you be concerned if your boss knew that you were visiting sites that specialized in job searches, cancer, or, for that matter, any non-job-related site?

The State of Privacy on the Internet

No matter what the dangers, many consumers reveal personal information about themselves over the Internet. The benefits of researching, shopping, and meeting others online are too tempting to resist. Who will protect consumers from themselves? At the moment, regulation of privacy over the Internet is incomplete and uncertain, a murky combination of self-regulation and government rules. (The Web site **http://www.consumerprivacyguide.org/topthings** offers advice on how to protect your privacy.)

SELF-REGULATION OF ONLINE PRIVACY

Voluntary Principles

The Network Advertising Initiative (NAI), an industry group, and the Federal Trade Commission (FTC) have agreed on the following NAI principles for Internet advertisers:

1. **Notice.** Before collecting personal information from consumers, a Web site must disclose its privacy policy in a "clear and conspicuous notice."

2. **Choice.** Consumers must be able to choose whether their data will be collected. Generally, consumers have the right to opt out; that is, a Web site can collect their data unless the consumer denies permission.

3. **Access.** A Web site must provide consumers reasonable access to their own data.

4. **Security.** Web sites that collect information should insure that nothing will be revealed without the consumer's permission.

5. **Sensitive Data.** Web sites must not use highly sensitive data (such as Social Security numbers, sexual behavior or preference, medical or financial information) to create profiles of individual consumers. (That is, they will not put together a list of gay men with AIDS who buy international index funds.)

6. **Enforcement.** An independent third party must monitor Web sites for compliance with these principles. Violators may be reported to the FTC. Consumers can register complaints at **http://www.truste.org/users/users_watchdog_intro.html**.

Although the NAI principles are an important first step, there is concern that they are insufficient because (1) 10% of Internet advertisers are not members of NAI; (2) Web sites that do not run advertisements are not covered by NAI rules; and (3) enforcement mechanisms are weak.

ETHICS

These NAI principles are simply guidelines, not laws. If you ran a Web site, what principles would you follow? What rules would be fair to you and Web users? From the Chapter 2 Ethics Checklist: What values are at stake? Which alternative is just?

Technology: P3P

Even as the NAI struggles to enforce its voluntary principles, new developments in technology may increase privacy protection online. The so-called Platform for Privacy Preferences (P3P), at least in theory, permits consumers to choose how much privacy they want. Each Web site answers a complex set of questions about its privacy policies. Then, each consumer indicates in her Web browser the level of privacy protection she desires. Her browser will not visit a Web site whose privacy policy does not meet the minimum standard she has set. For this system to work, Web sites must cooperate and consumers must take the time to configure their Web browsers. Microsoft has included P3P software in its Internet Explorer 6 so, for the first time, P3P will be tested in the real world. To learn more about P3P, sneak over to **http://www.w3.org/P3P**.

GOVERNMENT REGULATION OF ONLINE PRIVACY

Members of Congress have filed more than 300 bills to regulate online privacy. So intense, however, is the debate between industry and consumer advocates that no consensus—and little law—has emerged. There has, however, been some government regulation.

Children's Online Privacy Protection Act of 1998

The Children's Online Privacy Protection Act of 1998 (COPPA) prohibits Internet operators from collecting information from children under 13 without parental permission. It also requires sites to disclose how they will use any information they acquire. The standard for obtaining parental consent is on a sliding scale—a higher standard applies if the information will be disclosed publicly. If the Web site only intends to use information internally, it can obtain parental consent by e-mail. But if the personal data will be disclosed to third parties, parental consent must be obtained by regular mail, fax, e-mail with an official digital signature, a telephone call from the parent, or it must be accompanied by a credit card number.

Shortly after COPPA became law, the FTC brought an action against Young Investor (**http://www.younginvestor.com**). This site asked children about their weekly allowance, spending habits, work history, plans for college, and family finances. In addition, it asked for the child's name, address, age, and e-mail address. The site promised that all answers would be anonymous but, in fact, it could match names with surveys. In response to the FTC action, Young Investor agreed to post a privacy policy and obtain parental consent before collecting personal information from children.

Gramm-Leach-Bliley Privacy Act of 1999

The Gramm-Leach-Bliley Privacy Act of 1999 (GLB) requires banks and other financial institutions to tell a consumer if they plan to reveal any of her non-public information to third parties. A financial institution cannot disclose this private information if the consumer opts out (that is, denies permission). The Web site **http://www.privacyrights.org** offers advice on how to opt out.

State Regulation

A few states have passed their own online privacy statutes. Minnesota, for example, requires Internet service providers (ISPs) to obtain permission from consumers before disclosing PII.

YOUR HARD DRIVE AS WITNESS (AGAINST YOU)

Many people confide their deepest secrets to their computers. Would you want everything you have ever typed into your computer to be revealed publicly? Monica Lewinsky certainly did not. Investigators in the President Clinton impeachment case discovered damaging evidence on the hard drive of Lewinsky's computer—evidence she clearly thought was private, including copies of deleted e-mails and drafts of letters she had never sent. What protection do you have for information stored on your computer?

Criminal Law

The Fourth Amendment to the Constitution prohibits unreasonable searches and seizures by the government. In enforcing this provision of the Constitution, the courts ask: Did the person being searched have a legitimate expectation of privacy in the place searched or the item seized? If yes, then the government must obtain a warrant from a court before conducting the search.

The Fourth Amendment applies to computers. For example, an architecture professor at Oklahoma State University used his school computer to download more than 3,000 pornographic images of young boys. After viewing the images and printing some of them, he deleted the files. The university had the right, under its policies, to view any file stored on one of its computers or passing through its network. Tipped off by the professor's wife, police seized the computer and turned it over to a computer expert who retrieved the pornographic files that the professor had deleted. The court held that federal agents did not need a warrant to search the professor's computer because he had no expectation of privacy. He was sentenced to 51 months in prison.[1]

Civil Litigation

Increasingly, computers are fair game in civil litigation. Suppose that you sue your company for wrongful termination. The company counterclaims, alleging that you cheated on your expense account. During litigation, it might subpoena your computer to find support for its allegations.

E-MAIL

E-mails may feel ephemeral, but they can do lasting damage. They typically stay stored on your own computer and on your provider's system long after you have

---

[1] *United States of America v. Angevine*, 281 F.3d 1130, 2002 U.S. App. LEXIS 2746.

hit the delete button. For example, when the Justice Department sued Microsoft for antitrust violations, some of the most damaging evidence against the company was extracted from its own e-mail archives. E-mail that had long since been deleted rose from the dead to haunt the company. Even online chat rooms store all posted comments for years. The Electronic Communications Privacy Act of 1986 (ECPA) is a federal statute that regulates e-mail.

Electronic Communications Privacy Act of 1986

The ECPA prohibits unauthorized interception or disclosure of wire and electronic communications or unauthorized access to stored communications. The definition of electronic communication includes e-mail and transmissions from pagers and cellular phones. Violators are subject to both criminal and civil penalties. Under this statute:

1. **Any intended recipient of an e-mail has the right to disclose it.** Thus, if you complain to a friend about your boss, the friend may legally forward that e-mail to the boss or anyone else.

2. **An employer has the right to monitor workers' e-mail messages** if (1) the employee consents; (2) the monitoring occurs in the ordinary course of business; *or* (3) the employer provides the e-mail system.

3. **The government has the right to access e-mail messages if it first obtains a search warrant or court order.**

Common-Law Regulation of E-mail Privacy

Under the common law, intrusion into someone's private life is a tort if a reasonable person would find it offensive. Did Microsoft violate an employee's privacy? You be the judge.

YOU BE THE JUDGE

BILL McLAREN, JR. v. MICROSOFT CORPORATION

1999 Tex App. LEXIS 4103
Court of Appeals of Texas, 1999

FACTS: Microsoft suspended Bill McLaren from his job pending an investigation into allegations of sexual harassment and "inventory questions." In response, he sent a memorandum requesting that no one tamper with his Microsoft office workstation or his e-mail. Ignoring this request, Microsoft accessed e-mail files in the "personal folders" on McLaren's computer. These files were password-protected, but the company "decrypted" McLaren's personal password. The company then fired him.

McLaren filed suit against Microsoft for invasion of privacy. He alleged that he had a reasonable expectation of privacy in password-protected personal e-mail files.

YOU BE THE JUDGE: Would a reasonable person find this intrusion offensive? Does an employee have a reasonable expectation of privacy in his e-mail files?

ARGUMENT FOR McLAREN: When Microsoft developed a system that permitted employees to store e-mails in personal folders with password protection, the company was creating an expectation of privacy. The whole point of a password is to safeguard privacy. Microsoft lured McLaren into storing personal messages and then betrayed him by breaking into his folders.

ARGUMENT FOR MICROSOFT: These folders were part of an e-mail system owned and administered by Microsoft and made available to McLaren so that he could perform the functions of his job. These files were no more private than a locked file cabinet that Microsoft provided for his office. Moreover, these e-mail messages were transmitted over Microsoft's network and, thus, had already been accessible to third parties at some point. Therefore, any expectation of privacy on his part was unreasonable. ▮

Crime on the Internet

For the dishonest and unscrupulous, the Internet has also opened new frontiers in crime.

HACKING

Gaining unauthorized access to a computer system is called *hacking.* The goal of hackers is varied; some do it for little more than the thrill of the challenge. The objective for other hackers may be industrial espionage, extortion, or theft of credit card information. Whatever the motive, hacking is a major crime. American companies spend more than $6 billion annually on computer security systems.

Hacking is illegal under the federal Computer Fraud and Abuse Act of 1986 (CFAA). **The CFAA prohibits:**

- Theft of financial information.

- Theft of information from the U.S. government.

- Theft from a computer.

- Computer trespass.

- Computer fraud.

- Intentional, reckless, and negligent damage to a computer.

- Computer extortion.

Some states have also adopted statutes prohibiting computer crime. A list of these statutes is available at **http://www.cybercrimes.net/State/state_index.html**.

FRAUD

Fraud is the deception of another person for the purpose of obtaining money or property from him. Common scams include the sale of merchandise that is either defective or nonexistent; the so-called Nigerian letter scam;[2] billing for services that are touted as "free"; fraudulent stock offers; fake scholarship search services; business opportunity scams (for a small investment, you will get rich); and credit card scams (for a fee, you can get a credit card, even with a poor credit rating). Fraud can be prosecuted under state law or the Computer Fraud and Abuse Act. In addition, federal mail and wire fraud statutes prohibit the use of mail or wire communication in furtherance of a fraudulent scheme.

IDENTITY THEFT

Identity theft is one of the scariest crimes against property. Although it existed before computers, the Internet has made it much easier. Here is one person's story:

> I was working at Home Depot, where I'm a manager, when the Discover Card fraud unit called to find out why I'd requested an additional credit card. The Discover agent asked when I had moved to Norfolk, Va. My stomach turned inside out; I live on Long Island. I'd never even been to Virginia. The agent told me to notify the credit bureaus immediately.
>
> A woman at one bureau told me someone had applied for eight cards in my name within the last month. My heart raced as I called each company to confirm my worst fear—they were all carrying large balances in my name. Even though I was able to cancel each card, I was freaking out. Two weeks later, I received more credit reports. He had opened 21 accounts overall. After two computers were delivered to his Norfolk address, I called the Norfolk police. They refused to arrest him. My wife had to stop me from going to sit in front of his house myself. In less than a month, this guy spent more than $40,000.
>
> I finally contacted the FBI, which finally captured him. Turns out he conned 50 or 60 people out of more than $500,000. He plea-bargained and got six and a half years, but will probably get out earlier. This guy wrecked my credit history. What's worse is that he still knows my Social Security number. What would stop him from doing it again?[3]

The Identity Theft and Assumption Deterrence Act of 1998 prohibits the use of false identification to commit fraud or other crime and it also permits the victim to seek restitution in court.

What can you do to prevent the theft of your identity?

1. Check your credit reports at least once a year. (The addresses and Web sites for the three largest credit agencies are listed in Chapter 39 on consumer law.)

2. Subscribe to a credit monitoring service that will notify you each week if there are any major changes to your credit reports.

3. If you suspect that your identity has been stolen, contact the FTC at 877-IDTHEFT, 877-438-4338, or **http://www.consumer.gov/idtheft**. File a police report immediately and keep a copy to show creditors. Also, ask the three major credit agencies to place a security freeze on your credit reports. When a freeze is in place, thieves cannot obtain a credit card or loan in your name.

---

[2] Victims receive an e-mail from someone alleging to be a Nigerian government official who has stolen money from the government. He needs some place safe to park the money for a short time. The official promises that, if the victim will permit her account to be used for this purpose, she will be allowed to keep a percentage of the stolen money. Instead, of course, once the "official" has the victim's bank information, he cleans out the account. The highest average dollar losses are reported in this Internet scam—$5,575 per victim.

[3] Adam Ray, as told to Liz Welch, "Taken to the Bank," *The New York Times*, June 2, 2002, Sec. 6, p. 106.

Internet Service Providers and Web Hosts

Internet service providers (ISPs) are companies, such as America Online (AOL), that provide connection to the Internet. Web hosts post Web pages on the Internet.

SPAM

Spam is officially known as *unsolicited commercial e-mail (UCE)* or *unsolicited bulk e-mail (UBE)*. As much as 62% of all e-mail is spam. **The Controlling the Assault of Non-Solicited Pornography and Marketing Act (Can-Spam) prohibits spammers from using false or misleading return addresses and headers in their e-mail.** Also, spammers must provide a valid method for unsubscribing from their e-mail lists.

Although one can only applaud the effort, in truth, the Can-Spam Act has not noticeably decreased the amount of spam. Spammers operate in the netherworld of cyberspace where they are difficult to identify and locate. For the optimistic, **http://spamcop.net** offers a service where you can report spammers.

COMMUNICATIONS DECENCY ACT OF 1996

The Internet is an enormously powerful tool for disseminating information. But what if some of this information happens to be false or in violation of our privacy rights? Is an ISP liable for transmitting it to the world?

Under the Communications Decency Act of 1996 (CDA), an ISP or Web host is not liable for information that is provided by someone else. The following case (on which the chapter opener was based) illustrates how broadly this statute has been interpreted.

CASE SUMMARY

JOHN DOES v. FRANCO PRODUCTIONS

2000 U.S. Dist. LEXIS 8645
United States District Court for the Northern District of Illinois

FACTS: A group of college athletes was secretly videotaped in various states of undress by hidden cameras in restrooms, locker rooms, and showers. These videotapes were sold on Web sites hosted by GTE and PSINet. The Web sites also showed pictures taken from the videotapes. The athletes had not authorized the videotapes and only learned about their existence from a newspaper article. They brought suit against the producers and distributors of the videotapes, and against the Web hosts, GTE, and PSINet. The Court dismissed the plaintiffs' complaint against GTE and PSINet, finding that they were ISPs and therefore immune from suit under the CDA. The plaintiffs amended their complaint, alleging that GTE and PSINet were also liable in their capacity as Web site hosts. GTE and PSINet filed a motion to dismiss.

ISSUE: Are GTE and PSINet liable for the posting and sale of unauthorized videos? Should their motion to dismiss be granted?

DECISION: GTE and PSINet are not liable. The court granted the motion to dismiss.

REASONING: The CDA provides, "No provider or user of an interactive computer service shall be treated as the publisher or speaker of any information provided by another information content provider." Under this statute, ISPs are not liable for posting on the Internet information that a third party provides.

The plaintiffs claimed that GTE and PSINet were Web hosts, in addition to being ISPs, and that, as hosts, they were "information content providers" not protected by the CDA. According to the plaintiffs, the athletes were harmed twice—first, by the production of the videotapes and, second, by the posting of the advertisements and pictures on the Web. When GTE and PSINet posted the ads and images, they became content providers and, therefore, not protected by the statute.

This interpretation of the statute is wrong. Web hosting does not turn an ISP into a content provider.

Posting samples of the videotapes on the Web is not the same thing as making them. GTE and PSINet did not themselves sell the videotapes, they simply provided a mechanism through which others could sell them. By offering Web hosting services which enable someone to create a Web page, GTE and PSINet are not magically rendered the creators of those pages. Congress provided immunity even where the ISP has an active and aggressive role in posting content prepared by others. GTE's and PSINet's motions to dismiss are granted. ◢

ETHICS

1. An employee at AnswerThink Consulting group in Miami posted criticism of his boss on a Yahoo bulletin board. Without telling him, Yahoo revealed his identity to his employer and he was fired.

2. Four New Jersey boarding school students bought the drug DMX from eBay. After taking the drug, they began vomiting and became disoriented.

   Internet middlemen are not liable for what happens on their watch (i.e., on their Web site). Courts have generally taken the view that online providers are like the telephone company—simply transmitters of information. But do these companies have a moral obligation? Should eBay review listings before posting them to keep drugs and other illegal items at bay? Should Yahoo at least have notified the employee before revealing his identity? Should GTE and PSINet have asked questions about nude videos of college students? From the Chapter 2 Ethics Checklist: What important values are at stake? What answer would the Golden Rule suggest? ◼

Chapter Conclusion

The Internet has changed our lives in ways that were inconceivable a generation ago. Like a racer coming off a delayed start, the law is rushing to catch up. Not only will laws change, as legislators and courts learn from experience, but new laws will inevitably be needed.

Chapter Review

1. Currently, there is little regulation governing the collection or use of personal data on the Internet. Under principles established by the FTC and the Network Advertising Initiative, Web sites should provide notice, choice, access, security, and enforcement.

2. The Children's Online Privacy Protection Act of 1998 prohibits Internet operators from collecting information from children under 13 without parental permission. It also requires sites to disclose how they will use any information they acquire.

3. The Gramm-Leach-Bliley Privacy Act of 1999 requires banks and other financial institutions to tell a consumer if they plan to reveal any of her nonpublic information to third parties.

4. The Fourth Amendment to the Constitution prohibits unreasonable searches and seizures by government agents. This amendment applies to computers.

5. The Electronic Communications Privacy Act of 1986 prohibits unauthorized interception or disclosure of wire and electronic communications or unauthorized access to stored communications. Under this statute:

   - Any intended recipient of an e-mail has the right to disclose it.

   - An employer has the right to monitor workers' e-mail messages if (1) the employee consents; (2) the monitoring occurs in the ordinary course of business; or (3) the employer provides the e-mail system.

   - The government has the right to access e-mail messages if it first obtains a search warrant or court order.

6. Under the common law, intrusion into someone's private life is a tort if a reasonable person would find it offensive.

7. Hacking is illegal under the federal Computer Fraud and Abuse Act of 1986. The CFAA prohibits:

   - Theft of financial information.

   - Theft of information from the U.S. government.

   - Theft from a computer.

   - Computer trespass.

   - Computer fraud.

   - Intentional, reckless, and negligent damage to a computer.

   - Computer extortion.

8. Fraud is the deception of another person for the purpose of obtaining money or property from him.

9. The Identity Theft and Assumption Deterrence Act of 1998 prohibits the use of false identification to commit fraud or other crime.

10. The Controlling the Assault of Non-Solicited Pornography and Marketing Act prohibits spammers from using false or misleading return addresses and headers in their e-mail. Also, spammers must provide a valid method for unsubscribing from their e-mail lists.

11. Under the Communications Decency Act of 1996, ISPs and Web hosts are not liable for information that is provided by someone else.

PRACTICE TEST

Matching Questions

Match the following terms with their definitions:

___ **A.** ECPA

___ **B.** NAI principles

___ **C.** CFAA

___ **D.** COPPA

___ **E.** CDA

1. Regulates e-mail.

2. Regulates Internet service providers.

3. Regulates collection of information from children.

4. Regulate Internet advertising.

5. Regulates computer hacking.

True/False Questions

Circle true or false:

1. T   F   Under NAI principles, Internet advertisers may not collect sensitive personal data.

2. T   F   Under the Gramm-Leach-Bliley Act, a financial institution cannot disclose private information about consumers unless the consumers give permission.

3. T   F   The Fourth Amendment to the Constitution, which prohibits illegal searches and seizure, applies to computers.

4. T   F   Any intended recipient of an e-mail may forward it to whomever she wishes.

5. T   F   The police can read anyone's e-mail anytime as long as they have probable cause to believe that the e-mail will reveal evidence of a crime.

Multiple-Choice Questions

6. Rory is concerned that the employees in her division are wasting too much time on personal matters. She would like to monitor them. Which of the following activities is she *not* allowed to do?

    (a) Ask key employees to forward to her any e-mails they receive from their colleagues that contain jokes or other silly content.

    (b) Read all messages sent to employee pagers.

    (c) Read all employee e-mails sent through the office system.

    (d) Read employee's private e-mail accounts.

    (e) Read all e-mails sent in the ordinary course of business.

7. Three terrorists are plotting to blow up a high-rise office building, which could lead to thousands of deaths. The police capture their computers and read the files before obtaining a warrant. Which of the following searches would be illegal?

    I.   Marshall has written elaborate plans, which are stored on the hard drive of his laptop.

    II. Winston has violated school policies by downloading plans for bombs from the Internet through his school's network.

    III. Montgomery has made rental car reservations over the Internet in a cybercafé.

    (a) I, II, and III.

    (b) Neither I, II, nor III.

    (c) Just I.

    (d) Just II.

    (e) Just III.

8. The Computer Fraud and Abuse Act prohibits all of the following activities except:

    (a) Theft of financial information.

    (b) Illegal file sharing over the Internet.

    (c) Theft of information from the U.S. government.

    (d) Negligent damage to a computer.

    (e) Computer extortion.

9. Under the Can-Spam Act, it is legal to:

    (a) Send out advertisements for sexually explicit Web sites.

    (b) Send e-mails with false return addresses.

    (c) Send e-mails with fake headers

    (d) Refuse to unsubscribe recipients.

    (e) Send out e-mails with headers that, while technically accurate, are in fact misleading.

10. Your novel has just been published and is now for sale on Amazon.com. You access Amazon via AOL.com one day and are horrified to see that a reader (or alleged reader) has posted a bad review that is not only totally unfair but also totally inaccurate. (You did not plagiarize portions of the book!) Which of the following would be liable to you:

    I.   Amazon.com.

    II. AOL.com.

    III. The person who wrote the review.

    (a) I, II, and III.

    (b) Neither I, II, nor III.

    (c) I and III.

    (d) Just I.

    (e) Just III.

Short-Answer Questions

11. ETHICS: Matt Drudge published a report on his Web site (**http://www.drudgereport.com**) that White House aide Sidney Blumenthal "has a spousal abuse past that has been effectively covered up . . . There are court records of Blumenthal's violence against his wife." The Drudge Report is an electronic publication focusing on Hollywood and Washington gossip. AOL paid Drudge $3,000 a month to make the Drudge Report available to AOL subscribers. Drudge e-mailed his reports to AOL, which then posted them. Before posting, however, AOL had the right to edit content. Drudge ultimately retracted his allegations against Blumenthal, who sued AOL. He alleged that under the Communications Decency Act of 1996, AOL was a "content provider" because it paid Drudge and edited what he wrote. Do you agree? Putting liability aside, what moral obligation did AOL have to its members? To Blumenthal? Should AOL be liable for content it bought and provided to its members?

12. To demonstrate the inadequacies of existing computer security systems, Cornell student Robert Morris created a computer virus. His plan, however, went awry, as plans sometimes do. He thought his virus would be relatively harmless but it ran amok, crashing scores of computers at universities, military sites, and medical research sites. Under what statute might Morris be charged? Does it matter that he did not intend to cause damage?

13. Nancy Garrity and Joanne Clark worked for John Hancock Mutual Life Insurance Company. On their office computers they regularly received sexually explicit e-mails from friends and from Internet joke sites, which they then sent to coworkers. When a fellow employee complained, Hancock searched their e-mail folders and, finding inappropriate e-mails, fired the two women. The Hancock e-mail policy states: "Messages that are defamatory, abusive, obscene, profane, sexually oriented, threatening or racially offensive are prohibited. Company management reserves the right to access all e-mail files." The two employees filed suit against Hancock, alleging that the company had invaded their privacy. How would you rule as judge?

14. What can you do to protect your privacy online? Draw up a concrete list of steps that you might reasonably consider. Are there some actions that you would not be willing to take, either because they are not worth the effort or because they are too sneaky?

15. ROLE REVERSAL: Write a multiple-choice question that deals with an issue involving crime in cyberspace.

Internet Research Problems

1. The FTC offers advice to Web site operators about how to comply with the Children's Online Privacy Protection Act at **http://www.ftc.gov/bcp/conline/edcams/kidzprivacy/index.html**. Find two Web sites aimed at children. Do they comply?

2. The FTC provides an online brochure titled "Site Seeing on the Internet" (at **http://www.ftc.gov/bcp/conline/pubs/online/sitesee.htm**) that offers suggestions for safe travel on the Internet. Have you ever violated the FTC's advice on how to protect yourself in cyberspace?

You can find further practice problems in the Online Quiz at **http://beatty.westbuslaw.com** or in the Study Guide that accompanies this text.

Intellectual Property

It is hard to imagine that a Goliath like the $12 billion American music industry could see a 19-year-old college sophomore as a threat to its long-term financial health. But when Brian Matiash, a computer engineering major, boots up the computer in his dorm room at Syracuse University on a typical evening, several hundred e-mail messages will await him, each a request for digital copies of recorded music. He will fire up his computer, which is equipped with a hard drive that holds copies of literally hundreds of songs and a CD burner.

Mr. Matiash is part of a thriving underground network of digital music scavengers, mostly college students, who copy and trade music files globally over the Internet in violation of copyright laws. To the recording industry, Mr. Matiash's hobby is deeply disturbing. There are suddenly thousands of people around the globe creating vast electronic libraries of copy-protected music and posting it to the Internet in a format that allows for sound of near-CD quality. That means that potential consumers have a free alternative to buying music.

Mr. Matiash said, "I feel bad sometimes because I know I'm making a mess for the music companies. I know it's technically a crime."[1] ▪▪

---

[1] Jason Chervokas, "Internet CD Copying Tests Music Industry," *The New York Times, Apr. 6, 1998, p.D3.*

Introduction

For much of history, land was the most valuable form of property. It was the primary source of wealth and social status. Today, intellectual property is a major source of wealth. New ideas—for manufacturing processes, computer programs, medicines, books—bring both affluence and influence.

Although both can be valuable assets, land and intellectual property are fundamentally different. The value of land lies in the owner's right to exclude, to prevent others from entering it. Intellectual property, however, has little economic value unless others use it. This ability to share intellectual property is both good news and bad. On the one hand, the owner can produce and sell unlimited copies of, say, a software program, but, on the other hand, the owner has no easy way to determine if someone is using the program for free. The high cost of developing intellectual property, combined with the low cost of reproducing it, makes it particularly vulnerable to theft. As much as 35% of the software in use in America may be bootlegged (that is, copied and sold without permission).

Because intellectual property is nonexclusive, many people see no problem in using it for free. For example, students often argue that it is okay to copy CDs for their friends. How can copying a few CDs hurt a big recording studio? But if record companies earn lower royalties, they will produce fewer songs and music lovers everywhere will suffer. Some commentators suggest that the United States has been a technological leader partly because its laws have always provided strong protection for intellectual property. The Constitution provided for patent protection early in the country's history. In contrast, one of the oldest civilizations in the world, China, has been relatively slow in developing new technology. It did not institute a patent system until 1985.

Patents

A patent is a grant by the government that permits the inventor exclusive use of an invention for 20 years. During this period, no one may make, use, or sell the invention without permission. In return, the inventor publicly discloses information about the invention that anyone can use upon expiration of the patent.

A patent is not available solely for an idea, but only for its tangible application. Thus patents are available for:

Type of Invention	Example
Mechanical invention.	A hydraulic jack used to lift heavy aircraft.
Chemical invention.	The chemical 2-chloroethylphosphonic acid used as a plant growth regulator.
Process.	A method for applying a chemical to a plant—such as a process for applying a weed killer to rice.

Patents are not available for laws of nature, scientific principles, mathematical algorithms, or formulas such as $a^2 + b^2 = c^2$. In recent years, the status of computer software has been controversial: Is it an (unpatentable) mathematical formula or a (patentable) process or machine? The following case answers this question.

CASE SUMMARY

STATE STREET BANK & TRUST CO. v. SIGNATURE FINANCIAL GROUP, INC.

149 F.3d 1368, 1998 U.S. App. LEXIS 16869
United States Court of Appeals for the Federal Circuit, 1998

FACTS: Signature Financial Group, Inc., owns a patent on a computer software program that aids in the administration of mutual funds. The so-called Hub and Spoke System allows several mutual funds, or "Spokes," to pool their investment funds into a single portfolio, or "Hub." In this way, the funds can share administrative costs. Each Spoke sells shares to the public, and the cost of these shares depends upon the value of the assets pooled in the Hub. Therefore, each day within hours of the close of the stock market, each fund's administrator must know the value to the nearest penny of its pooled shares. The Signature software makes this calculation.

State Street Bank and Trust Co. negotiated with Signature for a license to use its software. When negotiations broke down, State Street brought suit alleging that the patent was invalid. The trial court granted State Street's motion for summary judgment.

ISSUE: Is data processing software patentable?

DECISION: Reversed and remanded. Yes, this software is patentable.

REASONING: Abstract ideas cannot be patented. Therefore, a mathematical algorithm is patentable only if it is applied in a useful way. The algorithm in this case does have a practical use—it calculates a final share price that is used both for record keeping and reporting purposes. This is a useful, concrete, and tangible result, even if it is expressed in numbers, such as price, profit, percentage, costs, or loss. ◢

CYBERLAW

The State Street case could have a profound impact on e-commerce as companies rush to patent techniques for doing business over the Internet. For example, Amazon.com received a patent for its One-Click method of instant ordering. The company then obtained an injunction to prevent barnesandnoble.com from using its Express Lane service that was similar to One-Click. The judge directed barnesandnoble.com to add an additional step to its ordering process.

Proponents of these e-commerce patents argue that they permit innovators on the Internet to protect their ideas. Otherwise, it is easy for copycats to open a rival Web site overnight. Critics counter that these patents could stifle e-commerce by limiting the use of new ideas. ◪

Requirements for a Patent

To obtain a patent, the inventor must show that her invention meets all of the following tests:

- **Novel.** An invention is not patentable if it (1) is known or has already been used in this country; or (2) has been described in a publication here or overseas. For example, an inventor discovered a new use for existing chemical compounds but was not permitted to patent it because the chemicals had already been described in prior publications, though the new use had not.[2]

---

[2] *In re Schoenwald,* 964 F.2d 1122, 1992 U.S. App. LEXIS 10181 (Fed. Cir. 1992).

- **Nonobvious.** An invention is not patentable if it is obvious to a person with ordinary skill in that particular area. An inventor was not allowed to patent a waterflush system designed to remove cow manure from the floor of a barn because it was obvious.[3]

- **Useful.** To be patented, an invention must be useful. It need not necessarily be commercially valuable, but it must have some current use. Being merely of scientific interest is not enough. Thus a company was denied a patent for a novel process for making steroids because they had no therapeutic value.[4]

A searchable database of all patents issued since 1976 is available at the Patent and Trademark Office's (PTO's) Web site: **http://www.uspto.gov/patft/index.html**. To find out just how creative inventors can be, check out the Wacky Patent of the Month at **http://www.colitz.com/site/wacky.htm**.

Provisional Patent Application

Investors who are unable to assess the market value of their ideas sometimes hesitate to file a patent application because the process is expensive and cumbersome. To solve this problem, the PTO now permits inventors to file a **provisional patent application (PPA).** The PPA is a simpler, shorter, cheaper application that gives inventors the opportunity to show their ideas to potential investors without incurring the full expense of a patent application. **PPA protection lasts only one year.** To maintain protection after that time, the inventor must file a regular patent application.

International Patent Treaties

Suppose you have a great idea that you want to protect around the world. It used to be that filing an application in other countries was a logistical nightmare because almost every country had its own unique filing procedures and standards. Several treaties now facilitate this process, although it is still not the one-stop (or one-click) effort that inventors desire. These treaties were drafted by the World Intellectual Property Organization (WIPO) of the United Nations and are available on its Web site at **http://www.wipo.org**.

The Paris Convention for the Protection of Industrial Property requires each member country to grant to citizens of other member countries the same rights under patent law as its own citizens enjoy. Thus, the patent office in each member country must accept and recognize all patent and trademark applications filed with it by anyone who lives in any member country. For example, the French patent office cannot refuse to accept an application from an American, as long as the American has complied with French law.

The Patent Law Treaty requires that countries use the same standards for the form and content of patent applications (whether submitted on paper or electronically). This treaty reduces the procedural conflicts over issues such as translations and fees. In short, it takes an important first step in standardizing the application process. Still to be worked out, however, is an international standard for the substance of patent laws. For instance, countries often have very different definitions of what constitutes "novelty" under patent law.

---

[3] *Sakraida v. Ag Pro, Inc.,* 425 U.S. 273, 96 S. Ct. 1532, 1976 U.S. LEXIS 146 (1976).
[4] *Brenner v. Manson,* 383 U.S. 519, 86 S. Ct. 1033, 1966 U.S. LEXIS 2907 (1966).

Copyrights

The holder of a copyright owns the *particular expression* of an idea, but not the underlying idea or method of operation. Abner Doubleday could copyright a book setting out his particular version of the rules of baseball, but he could not copyright the rules themselves nor could he require players to pay him a royalty.

Unlike patents, the ideas underlying copyrighted material need not be novel. Two movies that came out at the same time—*Armageddon* and *Deep Impact*—were both based on the idea of meteors destroying the earth. Neither violated the other's copyright because their expressions of the basic idea were different.

A copyright is valid until 70 years after the death of the work's last living author. In the case of works owned by a corporation—Mickey Mouse, for instance—the copyright lasts 95 years from publication or 120 years from creation. Once the copyright expires, anyone may use the material. Mark Twain died in 1910, so anyone may now publish *Tom Sawyer* without permission and without paying a copyright fee.

A work is automatically copyrighted once it is in tangible form. For example, once a songwriter puts notes on paper, the work is copyrighted without further ado. But if she whistles a happy tune without writing it down, the song is not copyrighted, and anyone else can use it without permission. Registration with the Copyright Office of the Library of Congress is necessary only if the holder wishes to bring suit to enforce the copyright. Although authors still routinely place the copyright symbol (©) on their works, such a precaution is not necessary in the United States. However, some lawyers still recommend using the copyright symbol because other countries recognize it. Also, the penalties for intentional copyright infringement are heavier than for unintentional violations, and the presence of a copyright notice is evidence that the infringer's actions were intentional.

INFRINGEMENT

Anyone who uses copyrighted material without permission is violating the Copyright Act. **To prove a violation, the plaintiff must present evidence that the work was original and that either:**

- The infringer actually copied the work; or

- The infringer had access to the original and the two works are substantially similar.

The story that opened this chapter illustrates how widespread copyright infringement has become.

FAIR USE

The purpose of copyright laws is to encourage creative work. A writer who can control, and profit from, artistic work will be inclined to produce more. If enforced oppressively, however, the copyright laws could stifle creativity by denying access to copyrighted work. **The doctrine of fair use permits limited use of copyrighted material without permission of the author for purposes such as criticism, news reporting, scholarship, or research.** Courts generally do not permit a use that will decrease revenues from the original work by, say, competing with it. A reviewer is permitted, for example, to quote from a book without the author's permission, but, as we see below, it is illegal to download entire versions of copyrighted songs without permission.

DIGITAL MUSIC AND MOVIES

As the chapter opener illustrates, much copyrighted music is now singing (for free) in cyberspace. Movie studios are facing the same issue with digitized movies on DVDs. A fierce war is currently raging in the entertainment world against online entrepreneurs (aka "pirates") who have figured out how to turn music and movies into downloadable files on the Internet.

Online Music

Napster was a truly brilliant—or diabolic—innovation, depending on your perspective. It was a so-called *peer-to-peer* file sharing system that connected individual computers so that anyone could copy any song from any linked computer. Napster also maintained a directory to facilitate finding the right files. If you hankered after your own copy of Cole Porter's *True Love,* you could download versions by 10 different artists in about 10 seconds. At its peak, Napster had 38 million users.

Napster did real damage to the recording industry. For the first time ever, CD sales declined nationally. One study found that the decline was particularly sharp in areas around college campuses. Perhaps even more insidious, Napster convinced a whole generation that music was, and should be, free. While an older sibling might in her teens and twenties have purchased a thousand CDs, her younger brother would buy none at all.

Eighteen music studios sued Napster for copyright violations.[5] In its defense, Napster claimed that it was protected under the fair use doctrine. The court disagreed, largely because Napster was competing with the music companies and reducing their revenues. According to the court, Napster was harming the music market in at least two ways: It reduced audio CD sales among college students and it raised barriers to entry for the music companies if they wanted to enter the online distribution business. The court entered an injunction against Napster, and the company ultimately filed for bankruptcy.

No sooner had the music companies killed Napster than, like the multiheaded hydra, other, tougher competitors appeared. Napster was particularly vulnerable to court action because it maintained its directory on a central server that could easily be shut down. Other companies, such as Gnutella and KaZaA, were more difficult to attack because they did not need a central directory. In theory, for a lawsuit to be effective the music companies would have to take action against each and every user. Traditionally, the music industry was reluctant to go after individual users (who might also be paying customers), but the Recording Industry Association of America has filed suit against the individuals with the largest offerings of songs on peer-to-peer services.

The Digital Millennium Copyright Act

Tom Tomorrow drew a cartoon that was syndicated to 100 newspapers, but, by the time the last papers received it, the cartoon had already gone zapping around

---

[5] *A&M Records v. Napster,* 239 F.3d 1004, 2001 U.S. App. LEXIS 5446, United States Court of Appeals (9th Cir. 2001).

cyberspace. Because his name had been deleted, some editors thought he had plagiarized it.

In response to incidents such as this, Congress passed the **Digital Millennium
Copyright Act (DMCA),** which provides that:

- **It is illegal to delete copyright information, such as the name of the author or
  the title of the article.** It is also illegal to distribute false copyright information.
  Thus, anyone who e-mailed Tom Tomorrow's cartoon without his name on it,
  or who claimed it was his own work, would be violating the law.

- **It is illegal to circumvent encryption or scrambling devices that protect copyrighted works.** For example, some software programs are designed so that
  they can only be copied once. Anyone who overrides this protective device to
  make another copy is violating the law.

- **It is illegal to distribute tools and technologies used to circumvent encryption devices.** If you help others to copy that software program, you have
  violated the statute.

INTERNATIONAL COPYRIGHT TREATIES

**The Berne Convention requires member countries to provide automatic copy-
right protection to any works created in another member country.** The protection
expires 50 years after the death of the author.

Trademarks

**A trademark is any combination of words and symbols that a business uses to
identify its products or services and distinguish them from others.** Trademarks
are important to both consumers and businesses. Consumers use trademarks
to distinguish between competing products. People who feel that Nike shoes
fit their feet best can rely on the Nike trademark to know they are buying the
shoe they want. A business with a high-quality product can use a trademark to
develop a loyal base of customers who are able to distinguish its product from
another.

OWNERSHIP AND REGISTRATION

Under common law, the first person to use a mark in trade owns it. Registration
under the federal Lanham Act is not necessary. However, registration has several
advantages:

- Even if a mark has been used in only one or two states, registration makes it
  valid nationally.

- Registration notifies the public that a mark is in use, because anyone who
  applies for registration first searches the Public Register to ensure that no one
  else has rights to the mark.

- The holder of a registered trademark generally has the right to use it as an
  Internet domain name.

Under the Lanham Act, the owner files an application with the PTO in Washington, D.C. The PTO will accept an application only if the owner has already used the mark attached to a product in interstate commerce or promises to use the mark within six months after the filing. In addition, the applicant must be the first to use the mark in interstate commerce. Initially, the trademark is valid for 10 years, but the owner can renew it for an unlimited number of 10-year terms as long as the mark is still in use. Trademark searches are free on the PTO's Web site: **http://www.uspto.gov/main/trademarks.htm**.

VALID TRADEMARKS

Words (Reebok); symbols (Microsoft's flying window logo); phrases ("Just do it"); shapes (a Coca-Cola bottle); sounds (NBC's three chimes); colors (pink for insulation); and even scents (plumeria blossoms on sewing thread) can be trademarked. To be valid, a trademark must be distinctive—that is, the mark must clearly distinguish one product from another.

The following categories are not distinctive and *cannot* be trademarked:

- **Similar to an existing mark.** To avoid confusion, the PTO will not grant a trademark that is similar to one already in existence on a similar product. Once the PTO had granted a trademark for "Pledge" furniture polish, it refused to trademark "Promise" for the same product.

- **Generic trademarks.** No one is permitted to trademark an item's ordinary name—"shoe" or "book," for example. Sometimes, however, a word begins as a trademark and later becomes a generic name. Zipper, escalator, aspirin, linoleum, thermos, yo-yo, band-aid, ping-pong, and nylon all started out as trademarks, but became generic. Once a name is generic, the owner loses the trademark because the name can no longer be used to distinguish one product from another—all products are called the same thing. That is why Xerox Corp. encourages people to say, "I'll photocopy this document," rather than "I'll xerox it."

- **Descriptive marks.** Words cannot be trademarked if they simply describe the product—such as "low-fat," "green," or "crunchy." Descriptive words can, however, be trademarked if they do not describe that particular product because they then become distinctive rather than descriptive. "Blue Diamond" is an acceptable trademark for nuts as long as the nuts are neither blue nor diamond shaped.

- **Names.** The PTO generally will not grant a trademark in a surname because other people are already using it and have the right to continue. No one could register "Jefferson" as a trademark.

- **Scandalous or immoral trademarks.** The PTO refused to register a mark that featured a nude man and woman embracing.[6]

DOMAIN NAMES

Internet addresses, known as domain names, can be immensely valuable. Suppose you want to buy a new pair of jeans. Without thinking twice, you type in

---

[6] *In re McGinley,* 660 F.2d 481, 211 U.S.P.Q. (BNA) 668, 1981 CCPA LEXIS 177 (C.C.P.A. 1981).

http://www.jcrew.com and there you are, ready to order. What if that address took you to a different site altogether, say, the personal site of one Jackie Crew? The store might lose out on a sale. Companies not only want to own their own domain name, they want to prevent complaint sites such as **http://www.untied.com** (about United Airlines) or **http://www.ihatestarbucks.com**. Generic domain names can be valuable, too. Shopping.com paid $750,000 to acquire its domain name from the previous (lucky) owner.

The Anticybersquatting Consumer Protection Act permits both trademark owners and famous people to sue anyone who registers their name as a domain name in "bad faith." The rightful owner of a trademark is entitled to damages of up to $100,000.

The good news about this statute is that it prevents Princeton Review from keeping the name kaplan.com, which the company acquired simply to inconvenience its archrival in the test preparation business. The bad news is that some businesses have used the law to threaten innocent holders of domain names. The maker of Pokey toys threatened a boy who had registered his nickname, Pokey, and Archie Comics went after a girl named Veronica. The Web site **http://www.chillingeffects.org** maintains a database of so-called "cease and desist" letters sent to holders of domain names.

INTERNATIONAL TRADEMARK TREATIES

Under the Madrid Agreement, any trademark registered with the international registry is valid in all signatory countries. The Trademark Law Treaty simplifies and harmonizes the process of applying for trademarks around the world.

Trade Secrets

Trade secrets—such as the formula for Coca-Cola—can be a company's most valuable asset. It has been estimated that the theft of trade secrets costs U.S. businesses $100 billion a year. Under the Uniform Trade Secrets Act (UTSA), **a trade secret is a formula, device, process, method, or compilation of information that, when used in business, gives the owner an advantage over competitors who do not know it.** In determining if information is a trade secret, courts consider:

- How difficult (and expensive) was the information to obtain? Was it readily available from other sources?

- Does the information create an important competitive advantage?

- Did the company make a reasonable effort to protect it?

Although a company can patent some types of trade secrets, it may be reluctant to do so because patent registration requires that the formula be disclosed publicly. In addition, patent protection expires after 20 years. Some types of trade secrets cannot be patented—customer lists, business plans, manufacturing processes, and marketing strategies.

The following case deals with a typical issue: Are customer lists trade secrets?

CASE SUMMARY

MORLIFE, INC. v. PERRY

56 Cal. App. 4th 1514, 1997 Cal. App. LEXIS 648
Court of Appeal of California, 1997

FACTS: Lloyd Perry was a sales representative for Morlife, Inc., which repaired roofs on commercial buildings. He signed an agreement not to disclose information about Morlife's customers if he ever left the company. When Perry resigned to start a competing business, he took with him the collection of business cards he had accumulated while at Morlife. These cards represented approximately 75% to 80% of the company's customers. Perry immediately began soliciting these clients, and 32 switched to him.

Morlife filed suit, claiming that Perry had violated the Uniform Trade Secrets Act. The court found for Morlife, awarded it $39,293.47 in damages, and ordered Perry not to use Morlife's trade secrets.

ISSUE: Did Perry violate the Uniform Trade Secrets Act?

DECISION: Affirmed. Perry did violate the Uniform Trade Secrets Act.

REASONING: The freedom to engage in the business or occupation of our choice is one of our most precious commercial rights. It is equally important, however, that the ingenuity and industry we invest in the success of that business or occupation be protected from misuse by others.

As a general principle, the more difficult information is to obtain, and the more time and resources an employer expends in gathering it, the more likely a court will find that such information is a trade secret. In this case, Morlife's president testified that it is difficult for the sales force to get past "gatekeepers" and contact the people who have authority to make a roofing decision. To develop its list, Morlife spent money on telemarketing, sales visits, mailings, advertisements, memberships in trade associations, referrals, and research. Only one in ten calls made by the telemarketing department actually results in a useful contact. For a Morlife sales representative to get in the door on an initial visit to a customer costs an estimated $238.

Morlife took reasonable steps to protect its customer information from disclosure. The data were stored on restricted computers. Perry signed an employment contract promising to keep customer information confidential. The Morlife employee handbook forbade employees, during or after their employment, to use or disclose confidential information, including lists of present and future customers. ◢

AT RISK

To be protected under the UTSA, the owner of a trade secret must make a reasonable effort to keep the information confidential. In formulating a policy on trade secrets, a company should:

- Identify specific information that is a trade secret.

- Set out the company's trade secret policy in writing (including what is secret) and require employees to sign this agreement.

- Allow access only to those employees who need the information to perform their jobs.

- Remind employees who leave the firm that they are still bound by the trade secret agreement. ▪

Chapter Conclusion

Intellectual property takes many different forms. It can be an Internet domain name, a software program, a cartoon character, a formula for motor oil, or a process for making anticancer drugs. Because of its great variety, intellectual property is difficult to protect. Yet, for many individuals and companies, intellectual property is the most valuable asset they will ever own. As its economic value increases, so does the need to understand the rules of intellectual property law.

Chapter Review

	Patent	Copyright	Trademark	Trade Secrets
Protects:	An invention that is the tangible application of an idea	The tangible expression of an idea, but not the idea itself.	Words and symbols that a business uses to identify its products or services.	Information that, when used in business, gives its own an advantage over competitors.
Requirements for protections:	Application approved by the PTO.	Automatic once it is in tangible form.	Must be used on the product in interstate commerce.	Must be kept confidential.
Duration:	20 years.	70 years after death of the author or, for a corporation, 95 years from publication.	10 years, but can be renewed an unlimited number of times.	As long as it is kept confidential.

PRACTICE TEST

Matching Questions

Match the following terms with their definitions:

___ **A.** Patent   **1.** Protects the particular expression of an idea.

___ **B.** Copyright   **2.** Words that a business uses to identify its products.

___ **C.** Trade secrets   **3.** Extends patent protection overseas.

___ **D.** Trademark   **4.** Grants the inventor exclusive use of an invention.

___ **E.** Paris Convention **5.** Compilation of information that would give its owner an advantage in business.

True/False Questions

Circle true or false:

1. T   F   Computer software is patentable.

2. T   F   A provisional patent lasts until the product is used in interstate commerce.

3. T   F   In the case of corporation, copyright protection lasts 120 years from the product's creation.

4. T   F   Under the fair use doctrine, you have the right to make a photocopy of this textbook for a classmate.

5. T   F   It is legal for you to download songs for free from the Internet only if the copyright holder gives permission.

Multiple-Choice Questions

6. To obtain a patent, an inventor must show that her invention meets all of the following tests, except:

   (a) It has not ever been used anyplace in the world.

   (b) It is a new idea.

   (c) It has never been described in a publication.

   (d) It is nonobvious.

   (e) It is useful.

7. After the death of Babe Ruth, one of the most famous baseball players of all time, his daughters registered the name, "Babe Ruth" as a trademark. Which of the following uses would be legal without the daughters' permission?

   I.   Publication of a baseball calendar with photos of Ruth.

   II. Sales of a "Babe Ruth" bat.

   III. Sales of Babe Ruth autographs.

   (a) Neither I, II, nor III.

   (b) Just I.

   (c) Just II.

   (d) Just III.

   (e) I and III.

8. To prove a violation of copyright law, the plaintiff does not need to prove that the infringer actually copied the work, but she does need to prove:

   I.   The item has a © symbol on it.

   II. The infringer had access to the original.

   III. The two works are similar.

   (a) I, II, and III.

   (b) II and III.

   (c) I and II.

   (d) I and III.

   (e) Neither I, II, nor III.

9. Eric is a clever fellow who knows all about computers. He:

   I.   Removed the author's name from an article he found on the Internet and sent it via e-mail to his lacrosse team, telling them he wrote it.

   II. Figured out how to unscramble his roommate's cable signal so they could watch cable on a second TV.

   III. Taught the rest of his lacrosse team how to unscramble cable signals.

   Which of these activities is legal under the Digital Millennium Copyright Act?

   (a) I, II, and III.

   (b) Neither I, II, nor III.

   (c) II and III.

   (d) Just III.

   (e) Just I.

10. Which of the following items *cannot* be trademarked?

   (a) Color.

   (b) Symbol.

   (c) Phrase.

   (d) Surname.

   (e) Shape.

Short-Answer Questions

11. Rebecca Reyher wrote (and copyrighted) a children's book entitled *My Mother Is the Most Beautiful Woman in the World*. The story was based on a Russian folktale told to her by her own mother. Years later, the children's TV show Sesame Street televised a skit entitled "The Most Beautiful Woman in the World." The Sesame Street version took place in a different locale and had fewer frills, but the sequence of events in both stories was identical. The author of the Sesame Street script denied he had ever seen Reyher's book but said his skit was based on a story told to his sister some 20 years before. Has Sesame Street infringed Reyher's copyright?

12. Roger Schlafly applied for a patent for two prime numbers. (A prime number cannot be evenly divided by any number other than itself and 1—3, 7, 11, and 13, for example.) Schlafly's numbers are a bit longer—one is 150 digits, the other is 300. His numbers, when used together, can help perform the type of mathematical operation necessary for exchanging coded messages by computer. Should the PTO issue this patent?

13. A man asked a question of the advice columnist at his local newspaper. His wife had thought of a clever name for an automobile. He wanted to know if there was any way they could own or register the name so that no one else could use it. If you were the columnist, how would you respond?

14. Frank B. McMahon wrote one of the first psychology textbooks to feature a light and easily readable style. He also included slang and examples that appealed to a youthful student market. Charles G. Morris wrote a psychology textbook that copied McMahon's style. Has Morris infringed McMahon's copyright?

15. ETHICS: After Edward Miller left his job as a salesperson at the New England Insurance Agency, Inc., he took some of his New England customers to his new employer. At New England, the customer lists had been kept in file cabinets. Although the company did not restrict access to these files, it said there was a "you do not peruse my files and I do not peruse yours" understanding. The lists were not marked "confidential" or "not to be disclosed." Did Miller steal New England's trade secrets? Whether or not he violated the law, was it ethical for him to use this information at his new job?

16. ROLE REVERSAL: Draft a multiple-choice question that focuses on an issue of copyright law.

Internet Research Problem

Think of a name for an interesting new product. Click on TESS (Trademark Electronic Search System) at **http://www. uspto.gov/main/trademarks.htm** to see if this name is available as a trademark. Also look at **http://www.verisign.com** to see if it is available as an Internet domain name.

You can find further practice problems in the Online Quiz at **http://beatty.westbuslaw.com** or in the Study Guide that accompanies this text.

Real Property

Some men have staked claims to land for its oil, others for its gold. But Paul Termarco and Gene Murdoch are staking their claim to an island using . . . hot dogs. Their quest to market frankfurters in the New Jersey wilderness has made their children blush with embarrassment, their wives shrug in bewilderment, and strangers burst into laughter. But for three years, the two friends from West Milford have sold chili dogs, cheese dogs, and the ever-traditional, hold-everything-but-the-mustard hot dogs from a tiny island in Greenwood Lake. Now it seems as though everyone knows about "Hot Dog Island."

"People love it," said Termarco. "They say, 'Thank you for being here.' I always say, 'No. Thank you.'" The personalized service and the inexpensive prices (hot dogs cost $1.75, chili dogs, cheese dogs, and sauerkraut $2) have cultivated a base of regulars. "I think it's great. It's better than going to a restaurant for two hours and spending a lot of money," said Joan Vaillant, who frequently jet-skis to the island for hot dogs slathered in mustard.

At two eighths of an acre, the island's pile of craggy rocks, scrubby bushes, and a few ash trees are difficult to spot. Termarco doesn't mind. "Not everyone can say they own an island," he boasted. Termarco and Murdoch decided to claim the slip of land after chatting with a local restaurateur a few years ago. Termarco had just finished suggesting that the man expand his lakeside business to the island when Murdoch kicked his friend under the table.

"We left thinking, 'We can do this ourselves,'" said Murdoch, who rushed to the township offices the following day to see who owned the island. Property records showed that the state owned the lake and lake floor, but nobody owned the island. An attorney told them about the law of adverse possession written in the 1820s. If Murdoch and Termarco could show that they used the island for five years, it would be theirs. As crazy as the scheme sounded, Murdoch figured it was worth trying.[1] ◾

Can two friends acquire an island simply by pretending they own it? Possibly. The law of adverse possession permits people to obtain title to land by using it if they meet certain criteria, which we examine later in the chapter. Real property law can provide surprises.

Nature of Real Property

We need to define a few terms. A **grantor** is an owner who conveys his property, or some interest in it, to someone else, called the **grantee**. If you sell your house to Veronica, you are the grantor and she is the grantee. Real property may be any of the following:

- **Land.** Land is the most common and important form of real property. In England, land was historically the greatest source of wealth, and so the law of real property has been of paramount importance for nearly 1,000 years.

- **Buildings.** Buildings are real property. Houses, office buildings, and factories all fall (or stand) in this category.

- **Subsurface Rights.** In most states, the owner of the land also owns anything under the surface, down to the center of the earth. The subsurface rights may be worth far more than the surface land, for example, if there is oil or gold underfoot. Although the landowner generally owns these rights, she may sell them, while retaining ownership of the surface land.

- **Air Rights.** The owner of land owns the airspace above the land. Suppose you own an urban parking lot. If the owner of an adjacent office building wishes to build a walkway across your property to join his building with a neighboring skyscraper, he needs your permission and will expect to pay handsomely for it.

- **Plant Life.** Plant life growing on land is real property, whether the plants are naturally occurring, such as trees, or cultivated crops. When a landowner sells his property, plant life is automatically included in the sale, unless the parties agree otherwise.

- **Fixtures.** Fixtures are goods that have become attached to real property. A house (which is real property) contains many fixtures. The furnace and heating ducts were goods when they were manufactured and when they were sold to the builder, because they were movable. But when the builder attached them to the house, the items became fixtures. By contrast, neither the refrigerator nor the grand piano is a fixture.

---

[1] Leslie Haggin, "Pair Stake Their Claim to Hot Dog Island," *Record* (Bergen, NJ), Sept. 5, 1994, p.A12. Excerpted with permission of the *Record*, Hackensack, NJ.

When an owner sells real property, the buyer normally takes the fixtures, unless the parties specify otherwise. Sometimes it is difficult to determine whether something is a fixture. The general rule is this: an object is a fixture if a reasonable person would consider the item to be a permanent part of the property. To decide the issue, courts look at:

Attachment. If an object is attached to property in such a way that removing it would damage the property, it is probably a fixture.

Adaptation. Something that is made or adapted especially for attachment to the particular property is probably a fixture, such as custom-made bookshelves fitted in a library.

Other manifestations of permanence. If the owner of the property clearly intends the item to remain permanently, it is probably a fixture. A homeowner who builds a large concrete platform in his backyard, then bolts a heavy metal shed to it, has created a fixture.

Estates in Real Property

Use and ownership of real estate can take many different legal forms. A person may own property outright, having the unrestricted use of the land and an unlimited right to sell it. However, someone may also own a lesser interest in real property. For example, you could inherit the use of a parcel of land during your lifetime, but have no power to leave the land to your heirs. The different rights that someone can hold in real property are known as **estates** or **interests.**

FREEHOLD ESTATES

The owner of a freehold estate has the present right to possess the property and to use it in any lawful way she wants. The three most important freehold estates are (1) fee simple absolute; (2) fee simple defeasible; and (3) life estate.

Fee Simple Absolute

A fee simple absolute provides the owner with the greatest possible control of the property. This is the most common form of land ownership. Suppose Cecily inherits a fee simple interest in a 30-acre vineyard. She may use the land for any purpose that the law allows. She may continue to raise grapes, or she may rip up the vines and build a bowling alley. Although zoning laws may regulate her use, nothing in Cecily's estate itself limits her use of the land. Cecily may pass on to her heirs her entire estate, that is, her full fee simple absolute.

Fee Simple Defeasible

Other estates contain more limited rights than the fee simple absolute. Wily establishes the Wily Church of Perfection. Upon his death, Wily leaves a 100-acre estate to the church for as long as it keeps the name "Wily Church of Perfection." Wily has included a significant limitation in the church's ownership. The church has a fee simple defeasible.

A fee simple defeasible may terminate upon the occurrence of some limiting event. If the congregation decides to rename itself the Happy Valley Church of Perfection, the church automatically loses its estate in the 100 acres. Ownership of the land then **reverts** to Wily's heirs, meaning title goes back to them. Because the heirs might someday inherit the land, they are said to have a future interest in the 100 acres. A landowner may create a fee simple defeasible to ensure that property is used in a particular way, or is not used in a specified manner (for example, as a casino). In the following case, a California city was surprised to learn that this ancient doctrine still has plenty of life.

CASE SUMMARY

WALTON v. CITY OF RED BLUFF

2 Cal. App. 4th 117, 3 Cal. Rptr. 2d 275, 1991 Cal. App. LEXIS 1474
California Court of Appeal, 1991

FACTS: In 1908 and 1916, Mrs. Elizabeth Kraft and her son, Edward Kraft, granted to the city of Red Bluff two adjoining properties, with buildings, for use as a public library. The grants from the Krafts required continuous use as a public library and stated that the property would return to the Kraft family if the city ever used it for other purposes.

In 1986, Red Bluff decided that the buildings were too small for its needs and moved all of the books to a new building nearby. The city used the Kraft property for other civic purposes such as town meetings, social gatherings, and school tutoring. Herbert Kraft Walton, a descendant and heir, filed suit seeking to have the property reconveyed to him. The trial court found for Red Bluff, and Walton appealed.

ISSUE: Did Red Bluff violate the terms of the grants, so the property must now revert to Walton?

DECISION: The property reverts to Walton. Reversed.

REASONING: The grant stated that if the property was used for anything but "library purposes" it would revert immediately to the Kraft family. The document defined "library purposes" broadly. However, once the books were removed, there was no evidence that Red Bluff conducted any of the described activities.

Red Bluff focused its argument on the "changed conditions" doctrine, which states that a power of termination expires when it becomes obsolete. For example, in one important case, a grant restricted property to residential use. Because the neighborhood had changed dramatically and was no longer residential, the court ruled that it would be unjust to enforce the reversionary clause.

Here, though, the change is simply that the city needs more space. Red Bluff does not claim that the present building cannot be used as a library, or that neighborhood changes have made such use impractical. There is nothing unfair about enforcing the restriction in this grant and Walton is entitled to the property. ◢

Life Estate

A life estate is exactly what you would think: **an estate for the life of some named person.** Aretha owns Respect Farm, and in her will she leaves it to Max, for his lifetime. Max is the **life tenant.** He is entitled to live on the property and work it as a normal farm during his lifetime, though he is obligated to maintain it properly. The moment Max dies, the farm reverts to Aretha or her heirs.

CONCURRENT ESTATES

When two or more people own real property at the same time, they have concurrent estates. In a **tenancy in common,** the owners have an equal interest in the entire property. Each co-tenant has the right to sell her interest to someone else, or to leave it to her heirs upon her death. A **joint tenancy** is similar, except that upon the death of one joint tenant (owner), his interest passes to the surviving joint tenants, not to his heirs.

To provide special rights for married couples, some states have created **tenancy by the entirety** and **community property.** These forms of ownership allow one spouse to protect some property from the other, and from the other's creditors.

Condominiums and cooperatives are most common in apartment buildings with multiple units, though they can be used in other settings, such as a cluster of houses on a single parcel of land. In a **condominium,** the owner of the apartment typically has a fee simple absolute in his particular unit. He is normally entitled to sell or lease the unit, must pay taxes on it, and may receive the normal tax deduction if he is carrying a mortgage. All unit owners belong to a condominium association, which manages the common areas. In a **cooperative,** the residents generally do not own their particular unit. Instead, they are shareholders in a corporation that owns the building and leases specified units to the shareholders.

Nonpossessory Interests

All of the estates and interests that we have examined thus far focused on one thing: possession of the land. Now we look at interests that *never* involve possession. These interests may be very valuable, even though the holder never lives on the land.

EASEMENTS

The Alabama Power Co. drove a flatbed truck over land owned by Thomas Burgess, damaging the property. The power company did this to reach its power lines and wooden transmission poles. Burgess had never given Alabama Power permission to enter his land, and he sued for the damage that the heavy trucks caused. He recovered—nothing. Alabama Power had an easement to use Burgess's land.

An easement gives one person the right to enter land belonging to another and make a limited use of it, without taking anything away. Burgess had bought his land from a man named Denton, who years earlier had sold an easement to Alabama Power. The easement gave the power company the right to construct several transmission poles on one section of Denton's land and to use reasonable means to reach the poles. Alabama Power owned that easement forever, and when Burgess bought the land, he took it subject to the easement. Alabama Power drove its trucks across a section of land where the power company had never gone before, and the easement did not explicitly give the company this right. But the court found that the company had no other way to reach its poles, and therefore the easement allowed this use. Burgess is stuck with his uninvited guest as long as he owns the land.

Property owners normally create easements in one of two ways. A **grant** occurs when a landowner expressly intends to convey an easement to someone else. This is how Alabama Power acquired its easement. A **reservation** occurs when an owner sells land but keeps some right to enter the property. A farmer might sell

40 acres to a developer but reserve an easement giving him the right to drive his equipment across a specified strip of the land.

Easements, whether created by grant or otherwise, come in all sizes. Is the easement in the following case too big?

YOU BE THE JUDGE

CARVIN v. ARKANSAS POWER AND LIGHT

14 F.3d 399, 1993 U.S. App. LEXIS 33986
United States Court of Appeals for the Eighth Circuit, 1993

FACTS: Between 1923 and 1947, Arkansas Power & Light (AP&L) constructed several dams on two Arkansas lakes, Hamilton and Catherine. The company then obtained "flood easements" on property adjoining the lakes. AP&L obtained some of the easements by grant and others by reservation, selling lakeside property and keeping the easement. These flood easements permitted AP&L to "clear of trees, brush and other obstructions and to submerge by water" certain acreage, which was described exactly. AP&L properly recorded the easements, and when the current landowners bought lakeside property, they were aware of the documents.

During one 12-hour period in May 1990, extraordinarily heavy rains fell in the Ouachita River Basin, including both lakes. In some areas, over 10 inches of rain fell, causing the water to reach the highest levels ever recorded. To avoid flooding Lake Hamilton, AP&L opened the gates of a dam called Carpenter. This caused Lake Catherine to flood, with water in some places rising 25 feet. This flood caused massive damage to the plaintiffs' houses, with water in some cases rising to the roof level.

Several dozen landowners sued, claiming that AP&L was negligent in opening one dam without simultaneously opening another and also in failing to warn homeowners of the intended action. The federal district court granted summary judgment for AP&L, based on the flood easements, and the landowners appealed.

YOU BE THE JUDGE: Did the easements relieve AP&L from liability for flooding?

ARGUMENT FOR THE LANDOWNERS: No sane homeowner would give a power company the right to do what this company has done. AP&L has destroyed land, demolished houses, and ruined lives. AP&L opened a dam knowing that this would flood the shores of Lake Catherine and inundate dozens of properties.

These flood easements were many years old, created long before many of the present owners bought their property. None of them ever dreamed something like this could happen. Even if the easements were once valid, they should not be enforced any longer.

Further, no easement authorizes negligence. At most the easements would permit some minimal flooding by a carefully controlled process, after adequate notice to everyone concerned. Here there was no notice, no care, no decency. AP&L should not be allowed to rely on ancient pieces of paper to wash away land and ruin lives.

ARGUMENT FOR AP&L: The flooding was caused by an act of God, not by anything AP&L did. The company opened the dam without notice because there was no time to give notice. AP&L had the duty to act quickly, to protect residents of a much wider area.

A flood easement exists for one reason: to allow a company, when necessary, to flood land. Although some of these owners did not grant the easements, their predecessors did. The value of the property would naturally decline somewhat with a flood easement attached, and as a result these owners paid less for their property. All of the owners made calculated decisions to accept the risk, and they must now live with their choices.

PROFIT

A profit gives one person the right to enter land belonging to another and take something away. You own 100 acres of vacation property, and suddenly a mining company informs you that the land contains valuable nickel deposits. You may choose to sell a profit to the mining company, allowing it to enter your land and take away the nickel. You receive cash up front, and the company earns money from the sale of the mineral.

LICENSE

A license gives the holder temporary permission to enter upon another's property. Unlike an easement or profit, a license is a temporary right. When you attend a basketball game by buying a ticket, the basketball club that sells you the ticket is the licensor and you are the licensee. You are entitled to enter the licensor's premises, namely the basketball arena, and to remain during the game, though the club can revoke the license if you behave unacceptably.

MORTGAGE

Generally, in order to buy a house, a prospective owner must borrow money. The bank or other lender will require security before it hands over its money, and the most common form of security for a real estate loan is a mortgage. **A mortgage is a security interest in real property.** The homeowner who borrows money is the **mortgagor,** because she is giving the mortgage to the lender. The lender, in turn, is the **mortgagee,** the party acquiring a security interest. The mortgagee in most cases obtains a lien on the house, meaning the right to foreclose on the property if the mortgagor fails to pay back the money borrowed.

Sale of Real Property

For most people, buying or selling a house is the biggest, most important financial transaction they will make. Here we consider several of the key issues that may arise. (For an instructive course on home buying, go to **http://mirage.towerauction.net** and find the link for homebuyer education.)

SELLER'S OBLIGATIONS CONCERNING THE PROPERTY

Historically, the common law recognized the rule of caveat emptor in the sale of real property—that is, let the buyer beware. If a buyer walked into his new living room and fell through the floor into a lake of toxic waste, it was his tough luck. But the common law changes, and today courts place an increasing burden of fairness on sellers. Two significant obligations are the implied warranty of habitability and the duty to disclose defects.

Implied Warranty of Habitability

Most states now impose an implied warranty of habitability on a builder who sells a new home. This means that, whether he wants to or not, the builder is guaranteeing that the new house contains **adequate materials** and **good workmanship.** The law implies this warranty because of the inherently unequal position of builder and buyer. Some defects might be obvious to a lay observer, such as a room with no roof or a front porch that sways whenever the neighbors sneeze. But only the builder will know if he made the frame with proper wood or if the heating system was second-rate. In most states the law implies this warranty to protect buyers of residential, but not commercial, property.

Duty to Disclose Defects

The seller of a home must disclose facts that a buyer does not know and cannot readily observe if they materially affect the property's value. Roy and Charlyne Terrell owned a house in the Florida Keys, where zoning codes required all living areas to be 15 feet above sea level. They knew that their house violated the code because a bedroom and bathroom were on the ground floor. They offered to sell the house to Robert Revitz, assuring him that the property complied with all codes and that flood insurance would cost about $350 per year. Revitz bought the house, moved in, and later learned that because of the code violations, flood insurance would be slightly more expensive—costing just over $36,000 per year. He sued and won. The court declared that the Terrells had a duty to disclose the code violations; it ordered a rescission of the contract, meaning that Revitz got his money back. The court mentioned that the duty to disclose was wide-ranging and included leaking roofs, insect infestation, cracks in walls and foundations, and any other problems that a buyer might be unable to discern.

SALES CONTRACT AND TITLE EXAMINATION

The statute of frauds requires that an agreement to sell real property must be in writing to be enforceable. A contract for the sale of a house is often several pages of dense legal reading, in which the lawyers for the buyer and seller attempt to allocate risks for every problem that might go wrong. Once the parties have agreed to the terms and signed a contract, the buyer's lawyer performs a **title examination,** that is, a search through the local land registry for all documents relating to the property. The purpose is to ensure that the seller actually has valid title to this land. Even if the seller owns the land, his title may be subject to other claims, such as an easement or a mortgage.

CLOSING AND DEEDS

While the buyer is checking the seller's title, she also probably needs to arrange financing, as described earlier in the section on mortgages. When the title work is complete and the buyer has arranged financing, the parties arrange a **closing,** a meeting at which the property is actually sold. The seller brings to the closing a **deed,** which is the document proving ownership of the land. The seller signs the deed over to the buyer in exchange for the purchase price. The buyer pays the price either with a certified check and/or by having her lender pay. If a lender pays part or all of the price, the buyer executes a mortgage to the lender as part of the closing.

RECORDING

Recording the deed means filing it with the official state registry. The registry clerk places a photocopy of the deed in the agency's bound volumes and indexes the deed by the name of the grantor and the grantee. Recording is a critical step in the sale of land, because it puts all the world on notice that the grantor has sold the land.

Adverse Possession

Recall Paul Termarco and Gene Murdoch, who opened this chapter by trying to sell us a hot dog from the middle of a New Jersey lake. The pair had their sights set on more than mustard and relish: They hoped that by using the island as if they owned it, they *would* own it. They were relying on the doctrine of adverse possession. **Adverse possession allows someone to take title to land if she demonstrates possession that is (1) exclusive; (2) notorious; (3) adverse to all others; and (4) continuous.**

ENTRY AND EXCLUSIVE POSSESSION

The user must take physical possession of the land and must be the only one to do so. If the owner is still occupying the land, or if other members of the public share its use, there can be no adverse possession.

OPEN AND NOTORIOUS POSSESSION

The user's presence must be visible and generally known in the area, so that the owner is on notice that his title is contested. This ensures that the owner can protect his property by ejecting the user. Someone making secret use of the land gives the owner no opportunity to do this, and hence acquires no rights in the land.

A CLAIM ADVERSE TO THE OWNER

The user must clearly assert that the land is his. He does not need to register a deed or take other legal steps, but he must act as though he is the sole owner. If the user occupies the land with the owner's permission, there is no adverse claim and the user acquires no rights in the property.

CONTINUOUS POSSESSION FOR THE STATUTORY PERIOD

State statutes on adverse possession prescribe a period of years for continuous use of the land. Originally, most states required about 20 years to gain adverse possession, but the trend has been to shorten this period. Many states now demand 10 years, but a few require only 5 years' use. The reason for shortening the period is to reward those who make use of land.

Regardless of the length required, the use must be continuous. In a residential area, the user would have to occupy the land year round for the prescribed period. In a wilderness area generally used only in the summer, a user could gain ownership by seasonal use.

How did Murdoch and Termarco fare? They certainly entered on the land and established themselves as the exclusive occupants. Their use has been open and notorious, allowing anyone who claimed ownership to take steps to eject them from the property. Their actions have been adverse to anyone else's claim. If the two hot dog entrepreneurs have grilled those dogs for the full statutory period, they should take title to the island.

In the following case, the couple claiming adverse possession have taken up residence in a ghost town.

CASE SUMMARY

RAY v. BEACON HUDSON MOUNTAIN CORP.

88 N.Y.2d 154, 666 N.E.2d 532, 1996 N.Y. LEXIS 676
Court of Appeals of New York, 1996

FACTS: In 1931, Rose Ray purchased a cottage in a mountaintop resort town in the Adirondacks, at the same time agreeing to rent the land on which the structure stood. The long-term lease required her to pay the real estate taxes and provided that when the tenancy ended, the landlord would buy back the cottage at fair market value. In 1960, the landlord terminated the lease of everyone in the town, so Ray and all other residents packed up and left. She died in 1962, without ever getting a penny for the cottage. The next year, Mt. Beacon Incline Lands, Inc., bought all rights to the abandoned 156-acre resort.

Robert and Margaret Ray, the son and daughter-in-law of Rose Ray, reentered the cottage and began to use it one month per year, every summer from 1963 to 1988. They paid taxes, insured the property, installed utilities, and posted "no trespassing" signs.

In 1978, Beacon Hudson bought the resort in a tax foreclosure sale. Finally, in 1988, the Rays filed suit, claiming title to the cottage by adverse possession. Beacon Hudson counterclaimed, seeking to eject the Rays. The trial court ruled for the couple. The appellate court reversed, stating that the Rays had been absent too frequently to achieve adverse possession. The Rays appealed to New York's highest court.

ISSUE: Did the Rays acquire title by adverse possession?

DECISION: The Rays acquired title by adverse possession. Reversed.

REASONING: To obtain property by adverse possession, the claiming party must prove continuous possession, among other elements. However, the actual occupancy need not be constant. The claimant must simply use the land as ordinary owners would.

Beacon Hudson argues that the Rays cannot demonstrate continuous possession because they only occupied the property one month per year. However, that argument fails to consider the Rays' other acts of control over the premises. The couple maintained and improved the cottage and installed utilities. They also repelled trespassers, posted the land, and padlocked the cottage. These acts demonstrated continuous control of the property.

The Rays' seasonal use of the cottage, along with the improvements described, put the owner on notice of the couple's hostile and exclusive claim of ownership, especially considering that all neighboring structures had collapsed due to vandalism and neglect. The Rays have obtained titled by adverse possession. ◢

Land Use Regulation

ZONING

Zoning statutes are state laws that permit local communities to regulate building and land use. The local communities, whether cities, towns, or counties, then pass zoning ordinances that control many aspects of land development. For example, a town's zoning ordinance may divide the community into an industrial zone where factories may be built, a commercial zone in which stores of a certain size are allowed, and several residential zones in which only houses may be constructed. Within the residential zones, there may be further divisions, for example, permitting two-family houses in certain areas and requiring larger lots in others.

ETHICS

Many people abhor "adult" businesses, such as strip clubs and pornography shops. Urban experts agree that a large number of these concerns in a neighborhood often causes crime to increase and property values to drop. Nonetheless, many people patronize such businesses, which can earn a good profit. Should a city have the right to restrict adult businesses? Some cities have passed zoning ordinances that prohibit adult businesses from all residential neighborhoods, from some commercial districts, or from being within 500 feet of schools, houses of worship, daycare centers, or other sex shops (to avoid clustering). Owners and patrons of these shops have protested, claiming the restrictions unfairly deny access to a form of entertainment that the public obviously desires. From the Chapter 2 Ethics Checklist: Who are the stakeholders? What are the consequences of these restrictions? Are there any superior alternatives?

EMINENT DOMAIN

Eminent domain is the power of the government to take private property for public use. A government may need land to construct a highway, an airport, a university, or public housing. All levels of government—federal, state, and local— have this power. But the Fifth Amendment to the United States Constitution states: ". . . nor shall private property be taken for public use, without just compensation." The Supreme Court has held that this clause, the Takings Clause, applies not only to the federal government but also to state and local governments. So, although all levels of government have the power to take property, they must pay the owner a fair price.

A "fair price" generally means the reasonable market value of the land. Generally, if the property owner refuses the government's offer, the government will file suit seeking **condemnation** of the land, that is, a court order specifying what compensation is just and awarding title to the government.

Chapter Conclusion

Real property law is ancient but forceful, as waterfront property owners discovered when a power company flooded their land and an old-fashioned easement deprived them of compensation. Had the owners truly understood nonpossessory interests when they bought their property, they would have realized the risk the investment represented. Similarly, a knowledge of the various freehold estates will enable a property owner to avoid the kind of error that cost the city of Red Bluff its library building. Although real property today is not the dominant source of wealth that it was in medieval England, it is still the greatest asset that most people will ever possess—and is worth understanding.

Chapter Review

1. Real property includes land, buildings, air and subsurface rights, plant life, and fixtures. A fixture is any good that has become attached to other real property.

2. A fee simple absolute provides the owner with the greatest possible control of the property, including the right to make any lawful use of it and to sell it.

3. A fee simple defeasible may terminate upon the occurrence of some limiting event.

4. A life estate permits the owner to possess the property during her life, but not to sell it or leave it to heirs.

5. When two or more people own real property at the same time, they have a concurrent estate.

6. An easement gives a person the right to enter land belonging to another and make a limited use of it, without taking anything away.

7. The implied warranty of habitability means that a builder selling a new home guarantees the adequacy of materials and workmanship.

8. The seller of a home must disclose facts that a buyer does not know and cannot readily observe, if they materially affect the property's value.

9. Adverse possession permits the user of land to gain title if he can prove entry and exclusive possession, open and notorious possession, a claim adverse to the owner, and continuous possession for the required statutory period.

10. Nuisance law, zoning ordinances, and eminent domain all permit a government to regulate property and in some cases to take it for public use.

PRACTICE TEST

Matching Questions

Match the following terms with their definitions:

___ **A.** Easement.

___ **B.** Fee simple defeasible.

___ **C.** Adverse possession.

___ **D.** Fixture.

___ **E.** License.

1. Temporary permission to enter upon another's property, for example, to attend a concert.

2. Gives one person the right to enter land belonging to another and make a limited use of it.

3. Goods that have become attached to real property.

4. A type of ownership that may terminate upon the occurrence of some limiting event.

5. A chance to own land without ever paying for it.

True/False Questions

Circle true or false:

1. T F The owner of a fee simple absolute could lose the property if she uses it in a prohibited manner.

2. T F If one joint tenant dies, his interest in the property passes to surviving joint tenants, not to his heirs.

3. T F If you sell the oil rights in your property while keeping the surface rights, the oil company has purchased a profit.

4. T F In the sale of a house, a seller may not make false statements about conditions, but is under no obligation to mention defective conditions unless the buyer asks about them.

5. T F The federal government has the power to take private property for public use, but local governments have no such power.

Multiple-Choice Questions

6. CPA QUESTION: On July 1, 1992, Quick, Onyx, and Nash were deeded a piece of land as tenants in common. The deed provided that Quick owned one half the property and Onyx and Nash owned one quarter each. If

Nash dies, the property will be owned as follows:

(a) Quick $\frac{1}{2}$, Onyx $\frac{1}{2}$.

(c) Quick $\frac{1}{3}$, Onyx $\frac{1}{3}$, Nash's heirs $\frac{1}{3}$.

(b) Quick $\frac{5}{8}$, Onyx $\frac{3}{8}$.

(d) Quick $\frac{1}{2}$, Onyx $\frac{1}{4}$, Nash's heirs $\frac{1}{4}$.

7. Marta places a large, prefabricated plastic greenhouse in her backyard, with the steel frame bolted into concrete that she poured specially for that purpose. She attaches gas heating ducts and builds a brick walkway around the greenhouse. Now the town wants to raise her real property taxes, claiming that her property has been improved. Marta argues that the greenhouse is not part of the real property. Is it?

(a) The greenhouse is not part of the real property because it was prefabricated.

(d) The greenhouse is a fixture and is part of the real property.

(b) The greenhouse is not part of the real property because it could be removed.

(e) The greenhouse is an easement, and is part of the real property.

(c) The greenhouse cannot be part of the real property if Marta owns a fee simple absolute.

8. A pro football team ejects five fans for rowdy behavior. The team is

(a) Revoking an easement.

(d) Revoking a license.

(b) Reserving an easement.

(e) Condemning certain use.

(c) Terminating a profit.

9. Takeoff Construction is struggling financially, and to save money, has "cut corners" in two construction projects: a three-story office building, and a large house. In both buildings, the company used cheap structural supports, pipes, and insulation, which it knows will not last long. Both properties sell, and neither buyer asks about those specific materials. Six months later, both buyers sue, based on Takeoff's shabby material and workmanship.

(a) The homeowner will win but the office buyer will lose.

(d) Both the homeowner and office buyer will lose.

(b) The office buyer will win but the homeowner will lose.

(e) In both cases, a jury will decide whether Takeoff "adequately responded to all questions the buyer posed."

(c) Both the homeowner and office buyer will win.

10. A common security interest in real property is

(a) A profit.

(d) A mortgage.

(b) A license.

(e) A warranty.

(c) An easement.

Short-Answer Questions

11. Paul and Shelly Higgins had two wood stoves in their home. Each rested on, but was not attached to, a built-in brick platform. The downstairs wood stove was connected to the chimney flue and was used as part of the main heating system for the house. The upstairs stove, in the master bedroom, was purely decorative. It had no stovepipe connecting it to the chimney. The Higginses sold their house to Jack Everitt, and neither party said anything about the two stoves. Is Everitt entitled to either stove? Both stoves?

12. In 1944, W. E. Collins conveyed land to the Church of God of Prophecy. The deed said: "This deed is made with the full understanding that should the property fail to be used for the Church of God, it is to be null and void and property to revert to W. E. Collins or heirs." In the late 1980s, the church wished to move to another property and sought a judicial ruling that it had the right to sell the land. The trial court ruled that the church owned a fee simple absolute and had the right to sell the property. Comment.

13. ETHICS: Mark Wasser negotiated to purchase a 67-year-old apartment building from Michael and Anna Sasoni. The Sasonis told Wasser that the building was "a very good building" and "an excellent deal." The contract stated that the Wassers took the building "as

is" and that there were no express or implied warranties or representations. After Wasser took over the building, he discovered that it needed major structural repairs. He sued the Sasonis, claiming that they had failed to disclose defects. Who wins? (Slow down before answering.) Ethically, who should win? Why?

14. In 1966, Arketex Ceramic Corp. sold land in rural Indiana to Malcolm Aukerman. The deed described the southern boundary as the section line between sections 11 and 14 of the land. Further south than this section line stood a dilapidated fence running east to west. Aukerman and Arketex both believed that this fence was the actual southern boundary of his new land, though in fact it lay on Arketex's property.

Aukerman installed a new electrified fence, cleared the land on "his" side of the new fence, and began to graze cattle there. In 1974, Harold Clark bought the land that bordered Aukerman's fence, assuming that the fence was the correct boundary. In 1989, Clark had his land surveyed and discovered that the true property line lay north of the electric fence. Aukerman filed suit, seeking a court order that he had acquired the disputed land by adverse possession. The statutory period in Indiana is 20 years. Who wins?

15. ROLE REVERSAL: Write a short-answer question focusing on one of these issues: a fixture, an easement, or adverse possession.

Internet Research Problem

A client interested in buying a condominium wants your advice on how that form of ownership differs from others, what problems might arise, and how he should protect himself. Read at least three articles on condominium disputes, and then write a short memo explaining advantages and disadvantages of condominium ownership.

You can find further practice problems in the Online Quiz at **http://beatty.westbuslaw.com** or in the Study Guide that accompanies this text.

Landlord-Tenant Law

On a January morning in Studio City, California, Alpha Donchin took her small Shih-Tzu for a walk. Suddenly, less than a block from her house, two large Rottweilers attacked Donchin and her pet. The heavy animals mauled the 14-pound Shih-Tzu, and when Donchin picked her dog up, the Rottweilers knocked her down, breaking her hip and causing other serious injuries.

Ubaldo Guerrero, who lived in a rented house nearby, owned the two Rottweilers, and Donchin sued him. But she also sued Guerrero's landlord, David Swift, who lived four blocks away from the rental property. Donchin claimed that the landlord was liable for her injuries, because he knew of the dogs' vicious nature and permitted them to escape from the property he rented to Guerrero. Should the landlord be liable for injuries caused by his tenant's dogs?

As is typical of many landlord-tenant issues, the law in this area is in flux. Under the common law, a landlord had no liability for injuries caused by animals belonging to a tenant, and many states adhere to that rule. But some states are expanding the landlord's liability for injuries caused on or near his property. The California court ruled that Donchin could maintain her suit against Swift. If Donchin could prove that Swift knew the dogs were dangerous and allowed them to escape through a defective fence, the landlord would be liable for her injuries. ◾

One reason for the erratic evolution of landlord-tenant law is that it is really a combination of three venerable areas of law: property, contract, and negligence. The confluence of these legal theories produces results that are unpredictable but interesting and important. (To survey a variety of articles and laws in this rapidly evolving area, visit **http://www.law.cornell.edu/topics/landlord_tenant.html**.) We begin our examination of landlord-tenant law with an analysis of the different types of tenancy.

Recall that a freehold estate is the right to possess real property and use it in any lawful manner. **When an owner of a freehold estate allows another person temporary, exclusive possession of the property, the parties have created a landlord-tenant relationship.** The freehold owner is the **landlord,** and the person allowed to possess the property is the **tenant.** The landlord has conveyed a **leasehold** interest to the tenant, meaning the right to temporary possession. Courts also use the word "tenancy" to describe the tenant's right to possession. A leasehold may be commercial or residential.

THREE LEGAL AREAS COMBINED

Property law influences landlord-tenant cases because the landlord is conveying rights in real property to the tenant. She is also keeping a **reversionary interest** in the property, meaning the right to possess the property when the lease ends. Contract law plays a role because the basic agreement between the landlord and tenant is a contract. **A lease is a contract that creates a landlord-tenant relationship.** And negligence law increasingly determines the liability of landlord and tenant when there is an injury to a person or property. Many states have combined these three legal issues into landlord-tenant statutes; you can see a typical statute by going to **http://www.law.cornell.edu/topics/landlord_tenant.html** and, under State Material, finding the link to the uniform residential landlord-tenant act.

LEASE

The statute of frauds generally requires that a lease be in writing. Some states will enforce an oral lease if it is for a short term, such as one year or less, but even when an oral lease is permitted, it is wiser for the parties to put their agreement in writing, because a written lease avoids many misunderstandings. At a minimum, a lease must state the names of the parties, the premises being leased, the duration of the agreement, and the rent. But a well-drafted lease generally includes many provisions, called covenants. A **covenant** is simply a promise by either the landlord or the tenant to do something or refrain from doing something. For example, most leases include a covenant concerning the tenant's payment of a security deposit and the landlord's return of the deposit, a covenant describing how the tenant may use the premises, and several covenants about who must maintain and repair the property, who is liable for damage, and so forth. The parties should also agree about how the lease may be terminated and whether the parties have the right to renew it.

Types of Tenancy

There are four types of tenancy: a tenancy for years, a periodic tenancy, a tenancy at will, and a tenancy at sufferance. The most important feature distinguishing one from the other is how each tenancy terminates. In some cases, a tenancy terminates automatically, while in others, one party must take certain steps to end the agreement.

TENANCY FOR YEARS

Any lease for a stated, fixed period is a tenancy for years. If a landlord rents a summer apartment for the months of June, July, and August of next year, that is a tenancy for years. A company that rents retail space in a mall beginning January 1, 2005, and ending December 31, 2008, also has a tenancy for years. A tenancy for years terminates automatically when the agreed period ends.

PERIODIC TENANCY

A periodic tenancy is created for a fixed period and then automatically continues for additional periods until either party notifies the other of termination. This is probably the most common variety of tenancy, and the parties may create one in either of two ways. Suppose a landlord agrees to rent you an apartment "from month to month, rent payable on the first." That is a periodic tenancy. The tenancy automatically renews itself every month, unless either party gives adequate notice to the other that she wishes to terminate. A periodic tenancy could also be for one-year periods—in which case it automatically renews for an additional year if neither party terminates—or for any other period.

TENANCY AT WILL

A tenancy at will has no fixed duration and may be terminated by either party at any time. Tenancies at will are unusual tenancies. Typically, the agreement is vague, with no specified rental period and with payment, perhaps, to be made in kind. The parties might agree, for example, that a tenant farmer could use a portion of his crop as rent. Since either party can end the agreement at any time, it provides no security for either landlord or tenant.

TENANCY AT SUFFERANCE

A tenancy at sufferance occurs when a tenant remains on the premises, against the wishes of the landlord, after the expiration of a true tenancy. Thus a tenancy at sufferance is not a true tenancy because the tenant is staying without the landlord's agreement. The landlord has the option of seeking to evict the tenant or of forcing the tenant to pay rent for a new rental period.

Landlord's Duties

DUTY TO DELIVER POSSESSION

The landlord's first important duty is to **deliver possession** of the premises at the beginning of the tenancy, that is, to make the rented space available to the tenant. In most cases, this presents no problems and the new tenant moves in. But what happens if the previous tenant has refused to leave when the new tenancy begins? In most states, the landlord is legally required to remove the previous tenant. In some states, it is up to the new tenant either to evict the existing occupant or begin charging him rent.

QUIET ENJOYMENT

All tenants are entitled to quiet enjoyment of the premises, meaning the right to use the property without the interference of the landlord. Most leases expressly state this covenant of quiet enjoyment. And if a lease includes no such covenant, the law implies the right of quiet enjoyment anyway, so all tenants are protected. If a landlord interferes with the tenant's quiet enjoyment, he has breached the lease, entitling the tenant to damages.

The most common interference with quiet enjoyment is an eviction, meaning some act that forces the tenant to abandon the premises. Of course, some evictions are legal, as when a tenant fails to pay the rent. But some evictions are illegal. There are two types of eviction: actual and constructive.

Actual Eviction

If a landlord prevents the tenant from possessing the premises, he has actually evicted her. Suppose a landlord decides that a group of students are "trouble-makers." Without going through lawful eviction procedures in court, the landlord simply waits until the students are out of the apartment and changes the locks. By denying the students access to the premises, the landlord has actually evicted them and has breached their right of quiet enjoyment.

Constructive Eviction

If a landlord substantially interferes with the tenant's use and enjoyment of the premises, he has constructively evicted her. Courts construe certain behavior as the equivalent of an eviction. In these cases, the landlord has not actually prevented the tenant from possessing the premises, but has instead interfered so greatly with her use and enjoyment that the law regards the landlord's actions as equivalent to an eviction. Suppose the heating system in an apartment house in Juneau, Alaska fails during January. The landlord, an avid sled-dog racer, tells the tenants he is too busy to fix the problem. If the tenants move out, the landlord has constructively evicted them and is liable for all expenses they suffer.

To claim a constructive eviction, the tenant must vacate the premises. The tenant must also prove that the interference was sufficiently serious and lasted long enough that she was forced to move out. A lack of hot water for two days is not fatal, but lack of any water for two weeks creates a constructive eviction.

DUTY TO MAINTAIN PREMISES

In most states, a landlord has a **duty to deliver the premises in a habitable condition** and a continuing duty to maintain the habitable condition. This duty overlaps with the quiet enjoyment obligation, but it is not identical. The tenant's right to quiet enjoyment focuses primarily on the tenant's ability to use the rented property. The landlord's duty to maintain the property focuses on whether the property meets a particular legal standard. The required standard may be stated in the lease, created by a state statute, or implied by law.

Lease

The lease itself generally obligates the landlord to maintain the exterior of any buildings and the common areas. If a lease does not do so, state law may imply the obligation.

Building Codes

Many state and local governments have passed building codes, which mandate minimum standards for commercial and/or residential property. The codes are likely to be stricter for residential property and may demand such things as minimum room size, sufficient hot water, secure locks, proper working kitchens and bathrooms, absence of insects and rodents, and other basics of decent housing. Generally, all rental property must comply with the building code, whether the lease mentions the code or not.

Implied Warranty of Habitability

Students Maria Ivanow, Thomas Tecza, and Kenneth Gearin rented a house from Les and Martha Vanlandingham. The monthly rent was $900. But the roommates failed to pay any rent for the final five months of the tenancy. After they moved out, the Vanlandinghams sued. How much did the landlords recover? Nothing. The landlords had breached the implied warranty of habitability.

The implied warranty of habitability requires that a landlord meet all standards set by the local building code, or that the premises be fit for human habitation. Most states, though not all, imply this warranty of habitability, meaning that the landlord must meet this standard whether the lease includes it or not.

The Vanlandinghams breached the implied warranty. The students had complained repeatedly about a variety of problems. The washer and dryer, which were included in the lease, frequently failed. A severe roof leak caused water damage in one of the bedrooms. Defective pipes flooded the bathroom. The refrigerator frequently malfunctioned, and the roommates repaired it several times. The basement often flooded, and when it was dry, rats and opossums lived in it. The heat sometimes failed.

In warranty of habitability cases, a court normally considers the severity of the problems and their duration. In the case of Maria Ivanow and friends, the court abated (reduced) the rent 50%. The students had already paid more than the abated rent to the landlord, so they owed nothing for the last five months.

Tenant Remedies for Defective Conditions

Different states allow various remedies for defective conditions. For tenant rights in your state, see **http://www.tenantsunion.org/tulist.html**, which provides links to tenant organizations throughout the nation. For a useful series of form letters concerning defective conditions, problems with neighbors, interference with quiet enjoyment, and other common tenant concerns, see **http://little.nhlink.net/nhlink/housing/cto/letters/letrs.htm.** Many states allow a tenant to withhold rent, representing the decreased value of the premises. In some states, if a tenant notifies the landlord of a serious defect and the landlord fails to remedy the problem, the tenant may deduct a reasonable amount of money from the rental payment and have the repair made himself. Also, a landlord who refuses to repair significant defects is breaching the lease and/or state law, and the tenant may simply sue for damages.

DUTY TO RETURN SECURITY DEPOSIT

Most landlords require tenants to pay a security deposit, in case the tenant damages the premises. In many states, a landlord must either return the security deposit soon after the tenant has moved out or notify the tenant of the damage and the cost of the repairs. A landlord who fails to do so may owe the tenant damages of two or even three times the deposit.

Your authors are always grateful when a litigant volunteers to illustrate half a dozen legal issues in one lawsuit. The landlord in the following case demonstrates problems of security deposit, quiet enjoyment, constructive eviction, and . . . well, see how many you can count.

CASE SUMMARY

HARRIS v. SOLEY

2000 Me. 150, 756 A.2d 499
Supreme Judicial Court of Maine, 2000

FACTS: Near Labor Day, Andrea Harris, Kimberly Nightingale, Karen Simard, and Michelle Dussault moved into a large apartment in the Old Port section of Portland, Maine. The apartment had been condemned by the city of Portland, but Joseph Soley, the landlord, assured the tenants that all problems would be repaired before they moved in. Not quite. When the women arrived, they found the condemnation notice still on the door, and the apartment an uninhabitable mess. Soley's agent told the tenants that if they cleaned the unit themselves, they would receive a $750 credit on their first month's rent of $1,000. So the four rented a steam cleaner, bought supplies, and cleaned the entire apartment. Unfortunately, their problems had only begun.

The tenants suffered a continuous problem with mice and cockroaches, along with a persistent odor of cat urine. They ultimately discovered a dead cat beneath the floorboards. During October, the apartment had no heat. One tenant slept with blankets over her head, to keep heat in and bugs out. In November, the women submitted a list of complaints to Soley, including a broken toilet, inoperable garbage disposal, and shattered skylight, as well as a leaking roof and cockroach infestation. Snow began to fall into the living room through the skylight.

Soley made no repairs and the women stopped paying the rent. He phoned them several times, aggressively demanding payments. The tenants found another place to live but before they had moved, Soley's agents broke into the apartment and took many of their belongings. The tenants located Soley at the restaurant he owned and asked for their possessions back, but he refused to return the belongings unless they paid him $3,000. He threatened

them by saying that he knew where their families lived.

The tenants sued, claiming breach of contract, conversion [wrongful taking of property], intentional infliction of emotional distress, wrongful eviction, and wrongful retention of a security deposit. Soley refused to respond to discovery requests, and eventually the trial court gave a default judgment for the plaintiffs. The judge instructed the jury that all allegations were deemed true, and their job was to award damages. The jury awarded damages for each of the claims, including $15,000 to each tenant for emotional distress and a total of *$1 million* in punitive damages. Soley appealed.

ISSUE: Are the tenants entitled to such large damages?

DECISION: The tenants are entitled to all damages. Affirmed.

REASONING: Soley argues that the identical awards to all four tenants indicates the verdict is a result of irrational thinking, passion, and prejudice. However, the jury could reasonably have found that the emotional distress suffered by each tenant deserved comparable compensation, even if the harm was not identical to each. Among the factual findings from the trial court was this statement:

The plaintiffs were shaken up, infuriated, violated, intimidated, and in fear for their physical safety. The conduct of [Soley] was so extreme and outrageous as to exceed all possible bounds of decency. Defendant acted intentionally, knowingly, willfully, wantonly, and with malice.

The jury was entirely justified in awarding substantial punitive damages. The tenants had to endure insect and rodent infestation, dead animals, and falling snow. Soley refused to repair conditions that made the apartment unfit for human habitation, violently removed the tenants' property, destroyed some of their belongings, and threatened the young women. His conduct was utterly intolerable and the verdict is reasonable. ◢

Tenant's Duties

DUTY TO PAY RENT

My landlord said he's gonna raise the rent. "Good," I said, "'cause I can't raise it."

—Slappy White, comedian (1921–1995)

Rent is the compensation the tenant pays the landlord for use of the premises, and paying the rent, despite Mr. White's wistful hope, is the tenant's foremost obligation. The lease normally specifies the amount of rent and when it must be paid. Typically, the landlord requires that rent be paid at the beginning of each rental period, whether that is monthly, annually, or otherwise.

If the tenant fails to pay rent on time, the landlord has several remedies. She is entitled to apply the security deposit to the unpaid rent. She may also sue the tenant for nonpayment of rent, demanding the unpaid sums, cost of collection, and interest. Finally, the landlord may evict a tenant who has failed to pay rent.

State statutes prescribe the steps a landlord must take to evict a tenant for nonpayment. Typically, the landlord must serve a termination notice on the tenant and wait for a court hearing. At the hearing, the landlord must prove that the tenant has failed to pay rent on time. If the tenant has no excuse for the nonpayment, the court grants an order evicting him. The order authorizes a sheriff to remove the tenant's goods and place them in storage, at the tenant's expense. However, if the tenant was withholding rent because of unlivable conditions, the court may refuse to evict.

Landlord's Duty to Mitigate

Pickwick & Perkins, Ltd., was a store in the Burlington Square Mall in Burlington, Vermont. Pickwick had a five-year lease, but abandoned the space almost two years early and ceased paying rent. The landlord waited eight months before renting the space to a new tenant and then sued, seeking the unpaid rent. Pickwick defended on the grounds that Burlington had failed to **mitigate damages,** that is, to keep its losses to a minimum by promptly seeking another tenant. The winner? Pickwick, the tenant. Today, most (but not all) courts rule that **when a tenant breaches the lease, the landlord must make a reasonable effort to mitigate damages.** Burlington failed to mitigate, so it also failed to recover its losses.

DUTY TO USE PREMISES PROPERLY

A lease normally lists what a tenant may do in the premises and prohibits other activities. For example, a residential lease allows the tenant to use the property for normal living purposes, but not for any retail, commercial, or industrial purpose. A tenant may never use the premises for an illegal activity, such as gambling or selling drugs, whether or not the lease mentions the issue. A tenant may not disturb other tenants, and a landlord has the right to evict anyone who unreasonably disturbs neighbors.

A tenant is liable to the landlord for any significant damage he causes to the property. The tenant is not liable for normal wear and tear. If, however, he knocks a hole in a wall or damages the plumbing, the landlord may collect the cost of repairs, either by using the security deposit or by suing if necessary.

Change in the Parties

Sometimes the parties to a lease change. This can happen when the landlord sells the property or when a tenant wants to turn the leased property over to another tenant.

SALE OF THE PROPERTY

Generally, the sale of leased property does not affect the lease but merely substitutes one landlord, the purchaser, for another, the seller. The lease remains valid, and the tenant enjoys all rights and obligations until the end of the term. The new landlord may not raise the rent during the period of the existing lease or make any other changes in the tenant's rights.

ASSIGNMENT AND SUBLEASE

A tenant who wishes to turn the property over to another tenant will attempt to assign the lease or to sublet it. In an **assignment,** the tenant transfers all of his legal interest to the other party. If a tenant validly assigns a lease, the new tenant obtains all rights and liabilities under the lease. The new tenant is permitted to use and enjoy the property and must pay the rent. **However, the original tenant remains liable to the landlord unless the landlord explicitly releases him, which the landlord is unlikely to do.** This means that if the new tenant fails to pay the rent on time, the landlord can sue *both* parties, old and new, seeking to evict both and to recover the unpaid rent from both.

A landlord generally insists on a covenant in the lease prohibiting the tenant from assigning without the landlord's written permission. Some states permit a landlord to deny permission for any reason at all, but a growing number of courts insist that a landlord act reasonably and grant permission to sublease unless he has a valid objection to the new tenant.

Injuries

TENANT'S LIABILITY

A tenant is generally liable for injuries occurring within the premises she is leasing, whether that is an apartment, a store, or otherwise. If a tenant permits grease to accumulate on a kitchen floor and a guest slips and falls, the tenant is liable. If a merchant negligently installs display shelving that tips onto a customer, the merchant pays for the harm. Generally, a tenant is not liable for injuries occurring in common areas over which she has no control, such as exterior walkways. If a tenant's dinner guest falls because the building's common stairway has loose steps, the landlord is probably liable.

LANDLORD'S LIABILITY

Historically, the common law held a landlord responsible only for injuries that occurred in the common areas, or due to the landlord's negligent maintenance of the property. Increasingly, though, the law holds landlords liable under the normal rules of negligence law. In many states, a landlord must use reasonable care to maintain safe premises and is liable for foreseeable harm. For example, most states now have building codes that require a landlord to maintain structural elements in safe condition. States further imply a warranty of habitability, which mandates reasonably safe living conditions.

As always, the common law advances in a disorderly fashion, and state courts disagree about what "reasonable care" requires. The following pair of cases illustrate the diversity of issues—and conflicting arguments—that a landlord must consider before renting units. You make the calls.

YOU BE THE JUDGE

McGUIRE v. K & G MANAGEMENT CO.

1998 Ohio App. LEXIS 4742
Ohio Court of Appeals, 1998

FACTS: The McGuire family rented a second-story apartment from K & G Management, which managed a residential complex on behalf of Avant Co. Robin McGuire notified K & G that a window screen in her son's bedroom was loose and had fallen out once. Neighbors had also complained about loose-fitting screens. Five days after Robin reported the loose screen, her son, 26-month-old Devin, was playing in his bedroom with his eight-year-old cousin. Somehow, Devin fell or leaned into the window screen, which gave way. Devin fell to the ground and was seriously hurt.

The McGuires filed suit against K & G and Avant, claiming negligence. In Ohio (and most states), a landlord has a statutory duty to "make all repairs and do whatever is reasonably necessary to put and keep the premises in a fit and habitable condition." The trial court granted summary judgment for both defendants, ruling that the defendants had no duty to install screens strong enough to restrain a child. The McGuires appealed.

YOU BE THE JUDGE: Are the McGuires entitled to a trial on their claim of negligence?

ARGUMENT FOR THE McGUIRES: Both defendants have a statutory duty to keep the apartment fit and habitable, and both failed to do that. The screen was loose and they knew it, but failed to fix it. The danger of a child falling was entirely foreseeable, and the defendants are responsible. No parent can watch a child 24 hours a day. Young children climb and play anywhere they can reach. A landlord who makes a profit renting apartments to families should use reasonable care to protect all family members, young and old.

ARGUMENT FOR K & G AND AVANT: A window screen is not a child restraint. A screen is designed to keep insects and birds out, not to hold children in. A normal window screen, no matter how tightly installed, would not restrain a child. If all landlords throughout the state are suddenly obligated to install childproof screens, let the legislature announce the new rule and provide time to comply. We do not think that the voters want to pay the additional rent required to cover such a huge expense.

YOU BE THE JUDGE

MATTHEWS v. AMBERWOOD ASSOCIATES LIMITED PARTNERSHIP, INC.

351 Md. 544, 719 A.2d 199, 1998 Md. LEXIS 807
Maryland Court of Appeals, 1998

FACTS: Shelly Morton leased an apartment owned by Amberwood and operated by Monocle Management. The lease permitted the landlord to evict any tenant who broke the "House Rules," one of which prohibited pets. Morton kept her boyfriend's pit bull, named Rampage, in her apartment. At times, she kept Rampage chained outside the apartment house. When Morton was near the dog, he was not violent, but when she was absent, Rampage would attempt to attack anyone who came near him. Numerous maintenance workers had been unable to perform service work because Rampage barked and lunged at them. The workers reported each of these incidents to Monocle.

Shanita Matthews and her 16-month-old son, Tevin, visited Morton and her child, something they had done many times. As the adults worked on a puzzle in the dining room, the children played in the living room. Morton briefly left the apartment, and suddenly Rampage attacked Tevin. The dog grabbed the boy by the neck and shook him. Matthews was unable to free her son. She yelled for help and called 911. Morton reentered the apartment, could not free the boy, grabbed a knife, and repeatedly stabbed the ani-

mal, which finally released Tevin. An ambulance arrived, but an hour after reaching the hospital, Tevin died from his injuries.

Matthews sued Amberwood and Monocle. The jury awarded her $5,018,750 for the wrongful death of her son. The defendants appealed.

YOU BE THE JUDGE: Does a landlord owe a duty to a social guest of a tenant for an attack within the tenant's apartment?

ARGUMENT FOR MATHEWS: The House Rules prohibited pets. Monocle knew that Morton was breaking the rule and keeping an especially dangerous animal. Monocle should have acted to protect the other residents and all guests to the complex. The companies' failure to enforce their own rules led directly to the death of a child.

ARGUMENT FOR THE DEFENDANTS: Neither the owner nor the management company has control over the apartment or what goes on inside it. The companies could not have foreseen this attack, nor could they have done anything to stop it. Matthews knew the dog's nature. She had no business leaving her son alone with such a vicious beast.

CRIME

Landlords may be liable in negligence to tenants or their guests for criminal attacks that occur on the premises. Courts have struggled with this issue and have reached opposing results in similar cases. The very prevalence of crime sharpens the debate. What must a landlord do to protect a tenant? Courts typically answer the question by looking at four factors.

- *Nature of the crime.* How did the crime occur? Could the landlord have prevented it?

- *Reasonable person standard.* What would a reasonable landlord have done to prevent this type of crime? What did the landlord actually do?

- *Foreseeability.* Was it reasonably foreseeable that such a crime might occur? Were there earlier incidents or warnings?

- *Prevalence of crime in the area.* If the general area, or the particular premises, has a high crime rate, courts are more likely to hold that the crime was foreseeable and the landlord responsible.

Chapter Conclusion

A century ago no plaintiff would even have argued that a landlord was responsible for bites inflicted by a tenant's dog or for children falling from windows. But living patterns alter, social mores reflect the change, and the law—in theory—responds to both. The current trend is clearly for expanded landlord liability, but how far that will continue is impossible to divine.

Chapter Review

1. When an owner of a freehold estate allows another person temporary, exclusive possession of the property, the parties have created a landlord-tenant relationship.

2. Any lease for a stated, fixed period is a tenancy for years. A periodic tenancy is created for a fixed period and then automatically continues for additional periods until either party notifies the other of termination. A tenancy at will has no fixed duration and may be terminated by either party at any time. A tenancy at sufferance occurs when a tenant remains, against the wishes of the landlord, after the expiration of a true tenancy.

3. All tenants are entitled to the quiet enjoyment of the premises, without the interference of the landlord.

4. A landlord may be liable for constructive eviction if he substantially interferes with the tenant's use and enjoyment of the premises.

5. The implied warranty of habitability requires that a landlord meet all standards set by the local building code and/or that the premises be fit for human habitation.

6. The tenant is obligated to pay the rent, and the landlord may evict for nonpayment. The modern trend is to require a landlord to mitigate damages caused by a tenant who abandons the premises before the lease expires.

7. A tenant is liable to the landlord for any significant damage he causes to the property.

8. A tenant typically may assign a lease or sublet the premises only with the landlord's permission, but the current trend is to prohibit a landlord from unreasonably withholding permission.

9. Many courts require a landlord to use reasonable care in maintaining the premises, and hold her liable for injuries that were foreseeable.

10. Landlords may be liable in negligence to tenants or their guests for criminal attacks on the premises. Courts determine liability by looking at factors such as the nature of the crime, what a reasonable landlord would have done to prevent it, and the foreseeability of the attack.

PRACTICE TEST

Matching Questions

Match the following terms with their definitions:

___ **A.** Warranty of habitability.

___ **B.** Tenancy at sufferance.

___ **C.** Periodic tenancy.

___ **D.** Constructive eviction.

___ **E.** Tenancy at will.

1. Landlord's substantial interference with a tenant's use and enjoyment of the premises.

2. A tenancy without fixed duration, which either party may terminate at any time.

3. Tenant remains on premises after expiration of true tenancy.

4. A tenancy that automatically renews unless one party terminates it.

5. Requires a landlord to meet state building code standards.

True/False Questions

Circle true or false:

1. T F A landlord must maintain an apartment in compliance with the state's building code, unless the lease specifically exempts that particular unit.

2. T F A landlord could be liable for a constructive eviction even if he never asked the tenant to leave.

3. T F A nonrenewable lease of a store, for six months, establishes a tenancy for years.

4. T F A landlord may charge a tenant for normal wear and tear on an apartment, but the charges must be reasonable.

5. T F A landlord is generally liable for personal injuries sustained within an apartment, but cannot be liable for criminal attacks that occur there.

Multiple-Choice Questions

6. CPA QUESTION: Which of the following forms of tenancy will be created if a tenant stays in possession of the leased premises without the landlord's consent, after the tenant's one-year written lease expires?

(a) Tenancy at will.

(b) Tenancy for years.

(c) Tenancy from period to period.

(d) Tenancy at sufferance.

7. CPA QUESTION: To be enforceable, a residential real estate lease must:

(a) Require the tenant to obtain liability insurance.

(b) Entitle the tenant to exclusive possession of the leased property.

(c) Specify a due date for rent.

(d) Be in writing.

8. CPA QUESTION: A tenant renting an apartment under a three-year written lease that does not contain any specific restrictions may be evicted for:

(a) Counterfeiting money in the apartment.

(b) Keeping a dog in the apartment.

(c) Failing to maintain a liability insurance policy on the apartment.

(d) Making structural repairs to the apartment.

9. In May, Sharon and Joanne, both sophomores, are looking for an apartment to share beginning in September. They find the perfect unit which Ralph, the landlord, is working on right then. The parties agree on a rent of $1,000 per month, for 12 months. "Come back in late August, when I'm finished working," says Ralph. "I'll have a lease ready, I'll take your deposit, and you can move right in." The young women return in August to discover that Ralph has rented the apartment for $1,500 to other students. When they sue Ralph, Sharon and Joanne will

(a) Win $12,000.

(b) Win $18,000.

(c) Win possession of the apartment.

(d) Win the difference between $12,000 and whatever they are forced to spend for a similar apartment.

(e) Lose.

10. Michael signs a lease for an apartment. The lease establishes a periodic tenancy for one year, starting September 1 and ending the following August 31. Rent is $800 per month. As August 31 approaches, Michael decides he would like to stay another year. He phones the landlord to tell him this, but the landlord is on holiday and Michael leaves a message. Michael sends in the September rent, but on September 15, the landlord tells him the rent is going up to $900 per month. He gives Michael the choice of paying the higher rent or leaving. Michael refuses to leave and continues to send checks for $800. The landlord sues. Landlord will

(a) Win possession of the apartment because the lease expired.

(b) Win possession of the apartment because Michael did not renew it in writing.

(c) Win possession of the apartment because he has the right to evict Michael at any time, for any reason.

(d) Win $1,200 (12 months times $100).

(e) Lose.

Short-Answer Questions

11. ETHICS: Lisa Preece rented an apartment from Turman Realty, paying a $300 security deposit. Georgia law states: "Any landlord who fails to return any part of a security deposit which is required to be returned to a tenant pursuant to this article shall be liable to the tenant in the amount of three times the sum improperly withheld plus reasonable attorney's fees." When Preece moved out, Turman did not return her security deposit, and she sued for triple damages plus attorney's fees, totaling $1,800. Turman offered evidence that its failure to return the deposit was inadvertent and that it had procedures reasonably designed to avoid such errors. Is Preece entitled to triple damages? Attorney's fees? What is the rationale behind a statute that requires triple damages? Is it ethical to force a landlord to pay $1,800 for a $300 debt?

12. Loren Andreo leased retail space in his shopping plaza to Tropical Isle Pet Shop for five years, at a monthly rent of $2,100. Tropical Isle vacated the premises 18 months early, turned in the key to Andreo, and acknowledged liability for the unpaid rent. Andreo placed a "for rent" sign in the store window and spoke to a commercial real estate broker about the space. But he did not enter into a formal listing agreement with the broker, or take any other steps to rent the space, for about nine months. With approximately nine months remaining on the unused part of Tropical's lease, Andreo hired a commercial broker to rent the space. He also sued Tropical for 18 months' rent. Comment.

13. Philip Schwachman owned a commercial building and leased space to Davis Radio Corp. for use as a retail store. In the same building, Schwachman leased other retail space to Pampered Pet, a dog grooming shop. Davis Radio complained repeatedly to Schwachman that foul odors from Pampered Pet entered its store and drove away customers and workers. Davis abandoned the premises, leaving many months' rent unpaid. Schwachman sued for unpaid rent and moved for summary judgment. What ruling would you make on the summary judgment motion?

14. Doris Rowley rented space from the city of Mobile, Alabama, to run the Back Porch Restaurant. Her lease prohibited assignment or subletting without the landlord's permission. Rowley's business became unprofitable, and she asked the city's real estate officer for permission to assign her lease. She told the officer that she had "someone who would accept if the lease was assigned." Rowley provided no other information about the assignee. The city refused permission. Rowley repeated her requests several times without success, and finally she sued. Rowley alleged that the city had unreasonably withheld permission to assign and had caused her serious financial losses as a result. Comment.

15. ROLE REVERSAL: Write a multiple-choice question concerning one of these issues: tenancy for years, security deposit, or sublease.

Internet Research Problem

Go to **http://www.tenantsunion.org/tulist.html,** and search for the law of your state concerning a landlord's obligation to provide a habitable apartment. Now assume that you are living in a rental unit with serious defects. Draft a letter to the landlord asking for prompt repairs. For sample letters, go to **http://little.nhlink.net/nhlink/housing/cto** and find the links to "Know Your Rental Rights" and "CTO Model Letters."

You can find further practice problems in the Online Quiz at **http://beatty.westbuslaw.com** or in the Study Guide that accompanies this text.

Personal Property
and Bailments

"My only child is a no-good thief," Riley murmurs sadly to his visitors. "He has always treated me contemptuously. Now he's been sentenced to five years for stealing from a children's charity. He is my only heir, but why should I leave him everything?" Riley continues talking to his three guests: a bishop, a rabbi, and Earnest, a Boy Scout leader. "I have $500,000 in stocks in my bank deposit box. Tomorrow morning I'm going to the bank and hand the shares to the Boy Scouts so that other kids won't turn out so bad." Everyone applauds. But the following morning, on his way to the bank, Riley is struck by an ambulance and killed. A dispute arises over the money. The three witnesses assure the court that Riley was on his way to give the money to the Boy Scouts. From prison, the ne'er-do-well son demands the money as Riley's sole heir. Who wins? This is a typical issue of personal property law. ▪▪

Personal property means all property other than real property. In Chapter 43 we saw that real property means land and things firmly attached to it, such as buildings, crops, and minerals. All other property is personal property—a bus, a toothbrush, a share of stock. In this chapter we look at several ways in which personal property can be acquired, including gifts and found property. In the section on gifts we learn that Riley's no-good son gets the money. Riley intended to give the stocks and bonds to the Boy Scouts the following day, but he never completed a valid gift because he failed to deliver the papers. Then we turn to disputes over found property. And finally we examine bailments, which occur when the owner of personal property permits another to possess it.

Gifts

A gift is a voluntary transfer of property from one person to another without any consideration. It is the lack of consideration that distinguishes a gift from a contract. Contracts usually consist of mutual promises to do something in the future. Each promise is consideration for the other one, and the mutual consideration makes each promise enforceable. But a gift is a one-way transaction, without consideration. The person who gives property away is the **donor** and the one who receives it is the **donee.**

   A gift involves three elements:

* The donor intends to transfer ownership of the property to the donee immediately.

* The donor delivers the property to the donee.

* The donee accepts the property.

INTENTION TO TRANSFER OWNERSHIP

The donor must intend to transfer ownership to the property right away, immediately giving up all control of the item. Notice that the donor's intention must be to give title to the donee. Merely proving that the owner handed you property does not guarantee that you have received a gift; if the owner only intended that you use the item, there is no gift and she can demand it back.

   The donor must also intend the property to transfer immediately. A promise to make a gift in the future is unenforceable. Promises about future behavior are governed by contract law, and a contract is unenforceable without consideration. That is why the Boy Scouts will never touch the promised stocks. If Riley had handed Earnest the shares as he spoke, the gift would have been complete. However, the promise to make a gift the next day is legally worthless. Nor does Earnest have an enforceable contract, since there was no consideration for Riley's promise.

   A *revocable gift* is a contradiction in terms, because it violates the rule just discussed. It is not a gift and the donee keeps nothing. Suppose Harold tells his daughter Faith, "The mule is yours from now on, but if you start acting stupid again, I'm taking her back." Harold has retained some control over the animal, which means he has not intended to transfer ownership. There is no gift, and Harold still owns the mule.

Delivery

Physical Delivery

The donor must deliver the property to the donee. Generally, this involves physical delivery. If Anna hands Eddie a Rembrandt drawing, saying, "I want you to have this forever," she has satisfied the delivery requirement.

Constructive Delivery

Physical delivery is the most common and the surest way to make a gift, but it is not always necessary. **A donor makes constructive delivery by transferring ownership without a physical delivery.** Most courts permit constructive delivery only when physical delivery is impossible or extremely inconvenient. Suppose Anna wants to give her niece Jen a blimp, which is parked in a hangar at the airport. The blimp will not fit through the doorway of Jen's dorm. Anna may simply deliver to Jen the certificate of title and the keys to the blimp.

Inter Vivos Gifts and Gifts *Causa Mortis*

A gift can be either *inter vivos* or *causa mortis*. An **inter vivos gift** means a gift made during life, that is, when the donor is not under any fear of impending death. The vast majority of gifts are *inter vivos*, involving a healthy donor and donee. Shirley, age 30 and in good health, gives her husband Terry an eraser for his birthday. This is an *inter vivos* gift, which is absolute. The gift becomes final upon delivery, and the donor may not revoke it. If Shirley and Terry have a fight the next day, Shirley has no power to erase her gift.

A **gift *causa mortis*** is one made in contemplation of approaching death. The gift is valid if the donor dies as expected, but is revoked if he recovers. Suppose Lance's doctors have told him he will probably die of a liver ailment within a month. Lance calls Jane to his bedside and hands her a fistful of emeralds, saying, "I'm dying; these are yours." Jane sheds a tear, then sprints to the bank. If Lance dies of the liver ailment within a few weeks, Jane gets to keep the emeralds. But note that this gift is revocable. Since a gift *causa mortis* is conditional (upon the donor's death), the donor has the right to revoke it at any time before he dies. If Lance telephones Jane the next day and says that he has changed his mind, he gets the jewels back. Further, if the donor recovers and does not die as expected, the gift is automatically revoked.

Acceptance

The donee must accept the gift. This rarely leads to disputes, but if a donee should refuse a gift and then change her mind, she is out of luck. Her repudiation of the donor's offer means there is no gift, and she has no rights in the property.

The following case offers a combination of love and anger, alcohol and diamonds—always a volatile mix.

YOU BE THE JUDGE

ALBINGER v. HARRIS

2002 Mont. 118, 2002 WL 1226858
Montana Supreme Court, 2002

FACTS: Michelle Harris and Michael Albinger lived together, on and off, for three years. Their roller-coaster relationship was marred by alcohol abuse and violence. When they announced their engagement, Albinger gave Harris a $29,000 diamond ring, but the couple broke off their wedding plans because of emotional and physical turmoil. Harris returned the ring. Later, they reconciled and resumed their marriage plans, and Albinger gave his fiancée the ring again. This cycle repeated several times over the three years. Each time they broke off their relationship, Harris returned the ring to Albinger, and each time they made up, he gave it back to her.

On one occasion Albinger held a knife over Harris as she lay in bed, threatening to chop off her finger if she didn't remove the ring. He beat her and forcibly removed the ring. Criminal charges were brought but then dropped when, inevitably, the couple reconciled. Another time, Albinger told her to "take the car, the horse, the dog, and the ring and get the hell out." Finally, mercifully, they ended their stormy affair, and Harris moved to Kentucky—keeping the ring.

Albinger sued for the value of the ring. The trial court found that the ring was a conditional gift, made in contemplation of marriage, and ordered Harris to pay its full value. She appealed. The Montana Supreme Court had to decide, in a case of first impression, whether an engagement ring was given in contemplation of marriage. (In Montana and in many states, neither party to a broken engagement may sue for breach of contract, because it is impossible to determine who is responsible for ending the relationship.)

YOU BE THE JUDGE: **Who owns the ring?**

ARGUMENT FOR HARRIS: The problem with calling the ring a "conditional gift" is that there is no such thing. The elements of a gift are intent, delivery, and acceptance, and Harris has proven all three. Once a gift has been accepted, the donor has no more rights in the property and may not demand its return. Hundreds of years of litigation have resulted in only one exception to this rule—a gift *causa mortis*—and despite some cynical claims to the contrary, marriage is not death. What is more, to create a special rule for engagement rings would be blatant gender bias, because the exception would only benefit men. This court should stick to settled law, and permit the recipient of a gift to keep it.

ARGUMENT FOR ALBINGER: The symbolism of an engagement ring is not exactly news. For decades, Americans have given rings—frequently diamond—in contemplation of marriage. All parties understand why the gift is made and what is expected if the engagement is called off: The ring must be returned. Albinger's intent, to focus on one element, was conditional—and Michelle Harris understood that. Each time the couple separated, she gave the ring back. She knew that she could wear this beautiful ring in anticipation of their marriage, but that custom and decency required its return if the wedding was off. We are not asking for new law, but for confirmation of what everyone has known for generations: There is no wedding ring when there is no wedding.

The following chart distinguishes between a contract and a gift.

A Contract and a Gift Distinguished

A Contract:

Lou: I will pay you $2,000 to paint the house, if you promise to finish by July 3.	Abby: I agree to paint the house by July 3, for $2,000.

Lou and Abby have a contract. Each promise is consideration in support of the other promise. Lou and Abby can each enforce the other's promise.

A Gift:

Lou hands Phil two opera tickets, while saying: I want you to have these two tickets to *Rigoletto*.	Phil: Hey, thanks.

This is a valid *inter vivos* gift. Lou intended to transfer ownership immediately and delivered the property to Phil, who now owns the tickets.

Neither Contract nor Gift:

Lou: You're a great guy. Next week, I'm going to give you two tickets to *Rigoletto*.	Jason: Hey, thanks.

There is no gift because Lou did not intend to transfer ownership immediately, and he did not deliver the tickets. There is no contract because Jason has given no consideration to support Lou's promise.

Found Property

As you stagger to your 8 a.m. class, there is a gleam of light, not in your mind (which is vacant), but right there on the sidewalk. A ring! You stop in at the local jewelry shop, where you learn this ruby marvel is worth just over $700,000. Is it yours to keep?

The primary goal of the common law has been to get found property back to its proper owner. The finder must make a good-faith effort to locate the owner. In some states, the finder is obligated to notify the police of what she has found and entrust the property to them until the owner can be located or a stated period has passed. A second policy has been to reward the finder if no owner can be located. But courts are loath to encourage trespassing, so finders who discover personal property on someone else's land generally cannot keep it. Those basic policies yield various outcomes, depending on the nature of the property. The common-law principles follow, although some states have modified them by statute.

- **Abandoned property** is something that the owner has knowingly discarded because she no longer wants it. A vase thrown into a garbage can is abandoned. Generally, the finder is permitted to keep abandoned property, provided he can prove that the owner intended to relinquish all rights.

- **Lost property** is something accidentally given up. A ring that falls off a finger into the street is lost property. Usually, the finder of lost property has rights superior to all the world except the true owner. If the true owner comes forward, he gets his property back; otherwise, the finder may keep it. However, if the finder has discovered the item on land belonging to another, the landowner is probably entitled to keep it.

- **Mislaid property** is something the owner has intentionally placed somewhere and then forgotten. A book deliberately placed on a bus seat by an owner who forgets to take it with her is mislaid property. Generally, the finder gets no rights in property that has simply been mislaid. If the true owner cannot be located, the mislaid item belongs to the owner of the premises where the item was found.

Bailment

A bailment is the rightful possession of goods by one who is not the owner. The one who delivers the goods is the bailor and the one in possession is the bailee. Bailments are common. Suppose you are going out of town for the weekend and loan your motorcycle to Stan. You are the bailor and your friend is the bailee. When you check your suitcase with the airline, you are again the bailor and the airline is the bailee. If you rent a car at your destination, you become the bailee while the rental agency is the bailor. In each case, someone other than the true owner has rightful, temporary possession of personal property.

The parties generally—but not always—create a bailment by agreement. In each of the examples, the parties agreed to the bailment. In two cases, the agreement included payment, which is common but not essential. When you buy your airline ticket, you pay for your ticket, and the price includes the airline's agreement, as bailee, to transport your suitcase. When you rent a car, you pay the bailor for the privilege of using it. By loaning your motorcycle, you engage in a bailment without either party paying compensation.

A bailment without any agreement is called a constructive, or involuntary, bailment. Suppose you find a wristwatch in your house that you know belongs to a friend. You are obligated to return the watch to the true owner, and until you do so, you are the bailee, liable for harm to the property. This is called a constructive bailment because, with no agreement between the parties, the law is construing a bailment.

CONTROL

To create a bailment, the bailee must assume physical control with intent to possess. A bailee may be liable for loss or damage to the property. But it is not fair to hold him liable unless he has taken physical control of the goods, intending to possess them.

Disputes about whether someone has taken control often arise in parking lot cases. When a car is damaged or stolen, the lot's owner may try to avoid liability by claiming it lacked control of the parked auto and therefore was not a bailee. If the lot is a "park and lock" facility, where the car's owner retains the key and the lot owner exercises no control at all, then there may be no bailment, and no liability for damage. (For a sample automobile bailment form, see **http://www .gate.net/~legalsvc/autobail.html.**)

Jack Sonneveldt was a guest at the O'Hare Marriott Hotel outside Chicago. Sonneveldt arrived at the hotel in a 40-foot customized coach. He attempted to park in the hotel's valet parking area, but employees asked him to leave the vehicle in the hotel's general parking lot across the street. During the night, the $265,000 coach was stolen. If the hotel was a bailee, it would be liable. Sonneveldt's insurance company, Michigan Mutual, sued the hotel—and lost. The court ruled:

> *The complaint indicates that the Sonneveldt driver drove the Prevost coach into the lot and parked the vehicle himself. Nowhere does it suggest that Marriott was left with a set of keys to the coach, or that the hotel otherwise accepted or obtained actual control over the vehicle. Without the keys, Marriott had neither partial nor complete control over the Prevost coach.*

By contrast, when a driver leaves her keys with a parking attendant, the lot clearly is exercising control of the auto, and the parties have created a bailment. The lot is probably liable for loss or damage. What about cases in the middle, where the driver keeps her keys but the lot owner exercises some other control? There is no uniform rule, but the trend is probably toward liability for the lot owner.

ETHICS | Many companies post their parking policies on the Internet, often including a disclaimer stating that use of their facility creates no bailment or liability. Find such a statement and analyze it. Why does the owner claim (or hope) that no bailment exists? If a parked car is damaged, will a court honor the disclaimer? Does the facility operator have any control of the cars as they enter, or while parked, or as they leave? Do you consider the facility's policy fair, or is it an unjust effort to escape responsibility? ▪

RIGHTS OF THE BAILEE

The bailee's primary right is possession of the property. **Anyone who interferes with the bailee's rightful possession is liable to her.** The bailee is typically, though not always, permitted to use the property. When a farmer loans his tractor to a neighbor, the bailee is entitled to use the machine for normal farm purposes. But some bailees have no authority to use the goods. If you store your furniture in a warehouse, the storage company is your bailee, but it has no right to curl up in your bed.

A bailee may or may not be entitled to compensation, depending on the parties' agreement. A warehouse will not store your furniture for free, but a friend might.

DUTIES OF THE BAILEE

The bailee is strictly liable to redeliver the goods on time to the bailor or to whomever the bailor designates. Strict liability means there are virtually no exceptions. Rudy stores his $6,000 drum set with Melissa's Warehouse while he is on vacation. Blake arrives at the warehouse and shows a forged letter, supposedly from Rudy, granting Blake permission to remove the drums. If Melissa permits Blake to take the drums, she will owe Rudy $6,000, even if the forgery was a high-quality job.

Due Care

The bailee is obligated to exercise due care. **The level of care required depends upon who receives the benefit of the bailment.** There are three possibilities:

- *Sole benefit of bailee.* If the bailment is for the sole benefit of the bailee, the bailee is required to use **extraordinary care** with the property. Generally, in these cases, the bailor loans something for free to the bailee. Since the bailee is paying nothing for the use of the goods, most courts consider her the only one to benefit from the bailment. If your neighbor loans you a power lawn mower, the bailment is probably for your sole benefit. You are liable if you are even slightly inattentive in handling the lawn mower and can expect to pay for virtually any harm done.

- *Mutual benefit.* When the bailment is for the mutual benefit of bailor and bailee, the bailee must use **ordinary care** with the property. Ordinary care is what a reasonably prudent person would use under the circumstances. When you rent a car, you benefit from the use of the car, and the agency profits from the fee you pay. When the airline hauls your suitcase to your destination, both parties benefit. Most bailments benefit both parties, and courts decide the majority of bailment disputes under this standard.

- *Sole benefit of bailor.* When the bailment benefits only the bailor, the bailee must use only **slight care.** This kind of bailment is called a gratuitous bailment, and the bailee is liable only for gross negligence. Sheila enters a greased-pig contest and asks you to hold her $140,000 diamond engagement ring while she competes. You put the ring in your pocket. Sheila wins the $20 first prize, but the ring has disappeared. This was a gratuitous bailment, and you are not liable to Sheila unless she can prove gross negligence on your part. If the ring dropped from your pocket or was stolen, you are not liable. If you used the ring to play catch with friends, you are liable.

Burden of Proof

In an ordinary negligence case, the plaintiff has the burden of proof to demonstrate that the defendant was negligent and caused the harm alleged. In bailment cases, the burden of proof is reversed. **Once the bailor has proven the existence of a bailment and loss or harm to the goods, a presumption of negligence arises,** and the burden shifts to the bailee to prove adequate care. This is a major change from ordinary negligence cases. Georgina rents Sam her sailboat for a month. At the end of the month, Sam announces that the boat is at the bottom of Lake Michigan. If Georgina sues Sam, she only needs to demonstrate that the parties had a bailment and that he failed to return the boat. The burden then shifts to Sam to prove that the boat was lost through no fault of his own. If he cannot meet that burden, Georgina recovers the full value of the boat.

In the following case, the court looks at the two principal issues we have examined: whether there was a bailment, and whether the bailee exercised adequate care.

CASE SUMMARY

GIN v. WACKENHUT CORP.

741 F. Supp. 1454, 1990 U.S. Dist. LEXIS 8718
United States District Court for the District of Hawaii, 1990

FACTS: Max Gin and Johnnie Fong had a partnership specializing in wholesale jewelry. Gin left a jewelry show in Miami and went to the airport, where he intended to catch a flight to another trade show. Gin checked his suitcases with a curbside skycap and proceeded to the departure gate. He held one carry-on bag, containing $140,000 in jewelry.

Wackenhut operated the security checkpoint at the entrance to the departure gate, with an x-ray machine for baggage and a magnetometer to detect metal. Gin waited at one side until the line of people waiting for the magnetometer had dwindled. He then placed his bag on the conveyor belt and stepped up to the magnetometer. Suddenly a woman wearing a heavy coat cut in front of Gin, passed through the magnetometer, and activated the alarm. The Wackenhut employee who operated the magnetometer motioned for Gin to wait, while the woman emptied her pockets onto a tray. She passed through the machine again and once more the alarm sounded. Only on the fourth attempt did she proceed through the magnetometer. Gin walked through the machine, went to pick up his jewelry bag, and found it gone.

Gin sued, alleging negligent bailment. Wackenhut defended, claiming that no bailment had arisen and that, even if it had, the company used adequate care.

ISSUES: Was there a bailment? If so, did Wackenhut use adequate care?

DECISION: There was a bailment and Wackenhut was negligent.

REASONING: Although Wackenhut's very brief possession makes this case unusual, the parties did create a bailment. From the moment Gin placed his bag on the x-ray conveyor belt, he surrendered control to the company. Wackenhut could stop the bag for prolonged inspection or order it opened for examination. Gin had no control over how long he was separated from his property. He could not retrieve the bag until permitted to do so by Wackenhut personnel. Because of the machine's configuration, Gin was unable to see his bag once he surrendered it.

A bailee who fails to return the goods is presumed negligent. To avoid liability, the bailee must demonstrate that he exercised adequate care. Wackenhut realized that passengers could not see their bags during inspection, and knew that two bags were lost per week due to theft or error. Yet the company took no steps to improve security, such as rearranging equipment so passengers could see their bags continuously, or simply posting a sign warning of potential theft.

Wackenhut was negligent and the plaintiffs are entitled to $140,000. ◢

RIGHTS AND DUTIES OF THE BAILOR

The bailor's rights and duties are the reverse of the bailee's. The bailor is entitled to the return of his property on the agreed-upon date. He is also entitled to receive the property in good condition and to recover damages for harm to the property if the bailee failed to use adequate care.

Liability for Defects

Depending upon the type of bailment, the bailor is potentially liable for known or even unknown defects in the property. **If the bailment is for the sole benefit of the bailee, the bailor must notify the bailee of any known defects.** Suppose Megan lends her stepladder to Dave. The top rung is loose and Megan knows it, but forgets to tell Dave. The top rung crumbles and Dave falls onto his girlfriend's iguana. Megan is liable to Dave and the girlfriend unless the defect in the ladder was obvious. Notice that Megan's liability is not only to the bailee, but also to any others injured by the defects. Megan would not be liable if she had notified Dave of the defective rung.

In a mutual-benefit bailment, the bailor is liable not only for known defects but also for unknown defects that the bailor could have discovered with reasonable diligence. Suppose RentaLot rents a power sander to Dan. RentaLot does not realize that the sander has faulty wiring, but a reasonable inspection would have revealed the problem. When Dan suffers a serious shock from the defect, RentaLot is liable to him, even though it was unaware of the problem.

COMMON CARRIERS AND CONTRACT CARRIERS

A carrier is a company that transports goods for others. It is a bailee of every shipment entrusted to it. There are two kinds of carriers: common carriers and contract carriers. The distinction is important because each type of company has a different level of liability.

A **common carrier** makes its services available on a regular basis to the general public. For example, a trucking company located in St. Louis that is willing to haul freight for anyone, to any destination in the country, is a common carrier. **Generally, a common carrier is strictly liable for harm to the bailor's goods.** A bailor needs only to establish that it delivered property to the carrier in good condition and that the cargo arrived damaged. The carrier is then liable unless it can show that it was not negligent *and* that the loss was caused by an act of God (such as a hurricane) or some other extraordinary event, such as war. These are hard defenses to prove, and in most cases a common carrier is liable for harm to the property.

A common carrier is, however, allowed to limit its liability by contract. For example, a common carrier might offer the bailor the choice of two shipping rates: a low rate, with a maximum liability, say, of $10,000, or a higher shipping rate, with full liability for any harm to the goods. In that case, if the bailor chooses the lower rate, the limitation on liability is enforceable. Even if the bailor proves a loss of $300,000, the carrier owes merely $10,000.

A **contract carrier** does not make its services available to the general public, but engages in continuing agreements with particular customers. Assume that Steel Curtain Shipping is a trucking company in Pittsburgh that hauls cargo to California for two or three steel producers and carries manufactured goods from California to Pennsylvania and New York for a few West Coast companies. Steel Curtain is a contract carrier. **A contract carrier does not incur strict liability.** The normal bailment rules apply, and a contract carrier can escape liability by demonstrating that it exercised due care of the property.

INNKEEPERS

Hotels, motels, and inns frequently act as bailees of their guests' property. Most states have special innkeeper statutes that regulate liability.

Hotel patrons often assume that anything they bring to a hotel is safe. But some state innkeeper statutes impose an absolute limit on a hotel's liability. Other statutes require guests to leave valuables in the inn's safe deposit box. And even that may not be enough to protect them fully. For example, a state statute might require the guest to register the nature and value of the goods with the hotel. If a guest fails to follow the statutory requirements, he receives no compensation for any losses suffered.

Chapter Conclusion

Personal property law plays an almost daily role in all of our lives. The manager of a parking lot, the finder of lost property, and the operator of an airport security system must all realize that they may incur substantial liability for personal property, whether they intend to accept that obligation or not. Understanding personal property law can be worth a lot of money—but never carry all of it with you.

Chapter Review

1. A gift is a voluntary transfer of property from one person to another without consideration. The elements of a gift are intention to transfer ownership immediately, delivery, and acceptance.

2. Found property:
   - The finder of property must attempt to locate the true owner, unless the property was abandoned. The following principles generally govern:
   - Abandoned property—the finder may keep it.
   - Lost property—the finder generally has rights superior to everyone but the true owner, except that if she found it on land belonging to another, the property owner generally is entitled to it.
   - Mislaid property—generally, the finder has no rights in the property.

3. A bailment is the rightful possession of goods by one who is not the owner. The one who delivers the goods is the bailor and the one in possession is the bailee. To create a bailment, the bailee must assume physical control with intent to possess.

4. The bailee is always entitled to possess the property, is frequently allowed to use it, and may be entitled to compensation.

5. The bailee is strictly liable to redeliver the goods to the bailor.

6. The bailee is obligated to exercise due care. The level of care required depends upon who receives the benefit of the bailment: If the bailee is the sole beneficiary, she must use extraordinary care; if the parties mutually benefit, the bailee must use ordinary care; and if the bailor is the sole beneficiary of the bailment, the bailee must use only slight care.

7. Once the bailor has proven the existence of a bailment and loss, a presumption of negligence arises, and the burden shifts to the bailee to prove adequate care.

8. The bailor must keep the property in suitable repair, free of any hidden defects. If the bailor is in the business of renting property, the bailment is probably subject to implied warranties.

9. Generally, a common carrier is strictly liable for harm to the bailor's goods. A contract carrier incurs only normal bailment liability.

10. The liability of an innkeeper is regulated by state statute. A guest intending to store valuables with an innkeeper must follow the statute to the letter.

PRACTICE TEST

Matching Questions

Match the following terms with their definitions:

___ **A.** Extraordinary care.

___ **B.** *Inter vivos* gift.

___ **C.** Ordinary care.

___ **D.** Gift *causa mortis*.

___ **E.** Slight care.

1. Cannot be revoked.

2. Required in a bailment for the sole benefit of the bailee.

3. Can be revoked.

4. Required in a bailment for the mutual benefit of bailor and bailee.

5. Required in a bailment for the sole benefit of the bailor.

True/False Questions

Circle true or false:

1. T F A gift is unenforceable unless both parties give consideration.

2. T F A gift *causa mortis* is automatically revoked if the donor dies shortly after making it.

3. T F A bailee always has the right to possess the property.

4. T F A finder of lost property generally may keep the property unless the true owner comes forward.

5. T F A common carrier is strictly liable for harm to the bailor's goods.

Multiple-Choice Questions

6. CPA QUESTION: Which of the following requirements must be met to create a bailment?

   I. Delivery of personal property to the intended bailee.

   II. Possession by the intended bailee.

   III. An absolute duty on the intended bailee to return or dispose of the property according to the bailor's directions.

   (a) I and II only.

   (b) I and III only.

   (c) II and III only.

   (d) I, II, and III.

7. Martin is a rich businessman in perfect health. Monday morning he tells his niece, Stephanie, "Tomorrow I'm going to give you my brand new Ferrari." Stephanie is ecstatic. That afternoon, Martin is killed in a car accident. Does Stephanie get the car?

   (a) Stephanie gets the car because this is a valid *inter vivos* gift.

   (b) Stephanie gets the car because this is a valid gift *causa mortis*.

   (c) Stephanie gets the car because there is no reason to dispute that Martin made the promise.

   (d) Stephanie gets the car unless Martin left a wife or children.

   (e) Stephanie does not get the car.

8. Margie has dinner at Bill's house. While helping with the dishes, she takes off her Rolex watch, and forgets to put it back on when she leaves for the night. Bill finds the watch in the morning and decides to keep it.

   (a) This is abandoned property and Bill is entitled to it.

   (b) This is lost property and Bill is entitled to it.

   (c) This is lost property and Margie is entitled to it.

   (d) This is mislaid property and Bill is entitled to it.

   (e) This is mislaid property and Margie is entitled to it.

9. Arriving at a restaurant, Max gives his car keys to the valet. When the valet returns the car three hours later, it has a large, new dent. The valet says he did not cause it. Max sues the valet service.

   (a) The burden is on the valet service to prove it did not cause the dent.

   (b) The burden is on Max to prove that the valet service caused the dent.

   (c) The valet service is strictly liable for harm to Max's car.

   (d) The valet service has no liability to Max, regardless of how the dent was caused.

   (e) The valet service is only liable for gross negligence.

10. Car Moves hauls autos anywhere in the country. Valerie hires Car Moves to take her Porsche from Chicago to Los Angeles. The Porsche arrives badly damaged, because the Car Moves truck was hit by a bus. The accident was caused by the bus driver's negligence. If Valerie sues Car Moves for the cost of repairs

    (a) Valerie will win.

    (b) Valerie will win only if she can prove Car Moves was partly negligent.

    (c) Valerie will win only if she can prove that Car Moves agreed to strict liability.

    (d) Valerie will lose because Car Moves did not cause the accident.

    (e) Valerie will lose because this was a bailment for mutual benefit.

Short-Answer Questions

11. While in her second year at the Juilliard School of Music in New York City, Ann Rylands had a chance to borrow for one month a rare Guadagnini violin, made in 1768. She returned the violin to the owner in Philadelphia, but telephoned her father to ask if he would buy it for her. He borrowed money from his pension fund and paid the owner. Ann traveled to Philadelphia to pick up the violin. She had exclusive possession of the violin for the next 20 years, using it in her professional career. Unfortunately, she became an alcoholic, and during one period when she was in a treatment center, she entrusted the violin to her mother for safekeeping. At about that time, her father died. When Ann was released from the center, she requested return of the violin, but her mother refused. Who owns the violin?

12. Ronald Armstead worked for First American Bank as a courier. His duties included making deliveries between the bank's branches in Washington, D.C. Armstead parked the bank's station wagon near the entrance of one branch in violation of a sign saying: "No Parking Rush Hour Zone." In the rear luggage section of the station wagon were four locked bank dispatch bags, containing checks and other valuable documents. Armstead had received tickets for illegal parking at this spot on five occasions. Shortly after Armstead entered the bank, a tow truck arrived and its operator prepared to tow the station wagon. Transportation Management, Inc., operated the towing service on behalf of the District of Columbia. Armstead ran out to the vehicle and told the tow truck operator that he was prepared to drive the vehicle away immediately. But the operator drove away with the station wagon in tow. One and one half hours later, a bank employee paid for the car's release, but one dispatch bag, containing documents

worth $107,000, was missing. First American sued Transportation Management and the District of Columbia. The defendants sought summary judgment, claiming they could not be liable. Were they correct?

13. The government accused Carlo Francia and another of stealing a purse belonging to Frances Bainlardi. A policeman saw Francia sorting through the contents of the purse, which included a photo identification of Bainlardi. Francia kept some items, such as cash, while discarding others. At trial, Francia claimed that he had thought the purse was lost or abandoned. Besides the fact that Francia's accomplice was holding burglary tools, what is the weakness in Francia's defense?

14. Eileen Murphy often cared for her elderly neighbor, Thomas Kenney. He paid her $25 per day for her help and once gave her a bank certificate of deposit worth $25,000. She spent the money. Murphy alleged that shortly before his death, Kenney gave her a large block of shares in three corporations. He called his broker, intending to instruct him to transfer the shares to Murphy's name, but the broker was ill and unavailable. So Kenney told Murphy to write her name on the shares and keep them, which she did. Two weeks later Kenney died. When Murphy presented the shares to Kenney's broker to transfer ownership to her, the broker refused because Kenney had never endorsed the shares as the law requires, that is, signed them over to Murphy. Was Murphy entitled to the $25,000? To the shares?

15. ROLE REVERSAL: Write a multiple-choice question focusing on one of these topics: a gift *causa mortis*, lost property, or a bailment.

Internet Research Problem

You own a helicopter worth $250,000. A business associate wishes to use it for one week to show prospective clients around various islands in the Caribbean. You are willing to let him use it, for a fee of $15,000. Draft a bailment agreement. Use the form supplied at **http://www.gate.net/~legalsvc/autobail.html** as a model.

You can find further practice problems in the Online Quiz at **http://beatty.westbuslaw.com** or in the Study Guide that accompanies this text.

Estate Planning

Pablo Picasso, the renowned artist, created hundreds of paintings and sculptures as well as thousands of drawings and sketches. His personal life was unconventional, featuring a series of wives, mistresses, and children, both legitimate and illegitimate. Despite this large group of feuding heirs, he died in France without a will.

After four years of litigation, the French court decided that his estate would be shared by his widow, Jacqueline (who later committed suicide); two grandchildren by his legitimate child, Paulo (who died of cirrhosis of the liver); and his three illegitimate children, Maya, Claude, and Paloma. By the time the decision was reached, legal fees had swallowed up all the cash in the estate, but there was still an enormous stock of artworks. His daughter Paloma recalls: "There was a day finally when we all met, everyone with their lawyers, their assistants, their au pairs, all the most prestigious lawyers in France, and we drew lots for all the different categories of art and my nephew, who was the youngest person present, pulled numbers out of a hat. There were a few tensions, like in every family."[1]

---

[1] Adapted from Barber, Lynn, "A Perfectly Packaged Picasso," *The Independent*, 12/9/90, p.8.

Introduction

There is one immutable law of the universe: "You can't take it with you." But you can control where your assets go after your death. Or you can decide not to bother with an estate plan and leave all in chaos behind you.

DEFINITIONS

Like many areas of the law, estate planning uses its own terminology:

Estate Planning. The process of giving away property after (or in anticipation of) death.

Estate. The legal entity that holds title to assets after the owner dies and before the property is distributed.

Decedent. The person who has died.

Testator or Testatrix. Someone who has signed a valid will. Testatrix is the female version (from the Latin).

Intestate. To die without a will.

Heir. Technically, the term "heir" refers to someone who inherits from a decedent who died intestate. **Devisee** means someone who inherits under a will. However, many courts use "heir" to refer to anyone who inherits property, and we follow that usage in this chapter.

Probate. The process of carrying out the terms of a will.

Executor or Executrix. A personal representative chosen by the decedent to carry out the terms of the will. An executrix is a female executor.

Administrator or Administratrix. A personal representative appointed by the probate court to oversee the probate process for someone who has died intestate. As you can guess, an administratrix is a female administrator.

Grantor or Settlor. Someone who creates a trust.

Donor. Someone who makes a gift or creates a trust.

PURPOSE

Estate planning has two primary goals: to ensure that property is distributed as the owner desires and to minimize estate taxes. Although tax issues are beyond the scope of this chapter, they are an important element of estate planning, often affecting not only how people transfer their property but, in some cases, to whom. For instance, wealthy people may give money to charity, at least in part, to minimize the taxes on the rest of their estate.

PROBATE LAW

The federal government and many states levy estate taxes, although the tax rate imposed by states is typically much lower. Only the states, and not the federal government, have probate codes to regulate the creation and implementation of wills and trusts. These codes vary from state to state. This chapter, therefore, speaks only of general trends among the states. Certainly, anyone who is preparing a will must consult the laws of the relevant state. To make probate law more consistent, the National Conference of Commissioners on Uniform State Laws issued a Uniform Probate Code (UPC). However, fewer than half of the states have adopted it.

Wills

A will is a legal document that disposes of the testator's property after death. It can be revoked or altered at any time until death. (To find out how much longer you will live, check out **http://moneycentral.msn.com/investor/calcs/n_expect/main.asp**.) Virtually every adult, even those with only modest assets, should have a will:

- To ensure that their assets (modest though they may be) are distributed in accordance with their wishes.

- To select a personal representative to oversee the estate. If the decedent does not name an executor in a will, the court will appoint an administrator. Generally, people prefer to have a friend, rather than a court, in charge of their property.

- To avoid unnecessary expenses. Those who die intestate often leave behind issues for lawyers to resolve. A properly drafted will can also reduce the estate tax bill.

- To provide guardians for minor children. If parents do not appoint a guardian before they die, a court will. Presumably, the parents are best able to make this choice.

Sample wills are available at **http://www.legalscribe.com/formslibrary.html**.

REQUIREMENTS FOR A VALID WILL

Generally speaking, a person may leave his assets to whomever he wants. However, the testatrix must be:

- Of **legal age** (which is 18).

- Of **sound mind.** That is, she must be able to understand what a will is, more or less what she owns, who her relatives are, and how she is disposing of her property.

- Acting without **undue influence.** Undue influence means that one person has enough power over another to force him to do something against his free will.

LEGAL TECHNICALITIES

A testator must comply with the legal requirements for executing a will: It must be in writing, and the testator must sign it or direct someone else to sign it for him, if he is too weak. Generally, two witnesses must also sign the will. No one named in a will should also serve as a witness because, in many states, a witness may not inherit under a will.

The following case illustrates the importance of legal technicalities in the execution of a will. The decedent clearly intended to leave her estate to her son, but because she failed to comply with the *exact* requirements of the statute, her will was undone.

CASE SUMMARY

SMITH v. WHARTON

349 Ark. 351, 2002 Ark. LEXIS 375
Supreme Court of Arkansas, 2002

FACTS: In 1980, Iola Wharton executed a will in which she left her property equally to her daughter Kathleen Smith and her son, Joseph Wharton. In 1997, she executed another will that left most of her property to Joseph. Iola had recently broken her arm, so the three witnesses traveled to her house to watch her execute this second will. When the will was being prepared in her attorney's office, one of the witnesses (who worked in the office) typed Iola's name on it and then brought the will to her house. Iola could not sign her name so she executed the will by making a mark on it. The three witnesses then signed the will and their signatures were notarized.

Arkansas law provides that:

(a) The execution of a will must be by the signature of the testator and of at least two witnesses.

(b) The testator shall declare to the attesting witnesses that the instrument is his will and either:

(1) Himself sign; or . . .

(3) Sign by mark, his name being written near it and witnessed by a person who writes his own name as witness to the signature; . . .

(5) In any of the above cases, the signature must be at the end of the instrument and the act must be done in the presence of two (2) or more attesting witnesses.

After Iola died, Kathleen challenged the 1997 will, alleging that Iola had not validly executed it. The trial court agreed and Joseph appealed.

ISSUE: Is Iola's second will invalid?

DECISION: Affirmed. The second will is invalid.

REASONING: To have a valid signature by mark, a witness must sign the testator's name to the document near the testator's mark. The witness must also sign his own name next to the testator's name. All of this must be done in the presence of two additional witnesses who then sign at the end of the instrument.

In this case, Iola's name had been typed in her lawyer's office earlier in the day, not in the presence of the two witnesses. Therefore, the second will was not executed in compliance with the statute. ◢

Holographic Will

Sometimes courts will accept a holographic will. **A holographic will is handwritten and signed by the testatrix, but not witnessed.** Suppose Rowena is on a plane that suffers engine trouble. For 15 minutes, the pilot struggles to control the plane. Despite his efforts, it crashes, killing everyone aboard. During those 15 minutes, Rowena writes on a Post-it note, "This is my last will and testament. I leave all my assets to the National Gallery of Art in Washington, D.C." She signs her name, but her fellow passengers are too frantic to witness it. This note is found in the wreckage of the plane. Her previous will, signed and witnessed in a lawyer's office, left everything to her friend, Ivan. If Rowena resides in one of the majority of states that accepts a holographic will, then Ivan is out of luck and the National Gallery will inherit all. One court has, indeed, accepted as a will a handwritten Post-it note that had not been witnessed.

Nuncupative Will

Some states will also accept a **nuncupative will.** This is the formal term for an oral will. For a nuncupative will to be valid, the testatrix must know she is dying, there must be three witnesses, and these witnesses must know that they are listening to her will. Suppose that Rowena survives the airplane crash for a few hours. Instead of writing a will on the plane, she whispers to a nurse in the hospital, "I'd like all my property to go to the Angell Memorial Cat Hospital." This oral will is valid if there are two other witnesses and Rowena also says, "I'm dying. Please witness my oral will."

SPOUSE'S SHARE

A spouse is entitled to a **forced share** of the decedent's estate. In community property states, a spouse can override the will and claim one half of all marital property acquired during the marriage, except property that the testator inherited or received as a gift.[2]

In most non-community property states, a spouse can override the will and claim some percentage (usually one third to one half) of the decedent's probate estate. Under the UPC, a surviving spouse is entitled to whichever is greater: $50,000, or a percentage of the decedent's assets. The percentage depends upon how long the couple was married. At 5 years, a spouse is entitled to 15%; at 10 years, 30%; and at 15 years, 50%. Suppose that, when Drew and Sandy marry, Drew has assets of $500,000 while Sandy has virtually nothing. If Drew dies anytime during the first five years of their marriage, Sandy is entitled to $50,000. At five years, the share automatically goes up to $75,000. After 15 years, it reaches the maximum of $250,000.

CHILDREN'S SHARE

Parents are not required to leave assets to their children. They may disinherit their children for any reason.[3] However, the law presumes that a **pretermitted child** (that is, a child left nothing in the parent's will) was omitted by accident, unless the parent clearly indicates in the will that he has omitted the child on purpose. To do so, he must either leave her some nominal amount, such as $1, or specifically write in the will that the omission was intentional: "I am making no bequest to my daughter because she has chosen a religion of which I disapprove."

If a pretermitted child is left out by accident, she is generally entitled to the same share she would have received if her parent had died intestate.

In drafting a will, lawyers almost always use the term **issue** instead of children. Issue means all descendants such as children, grandchildren, and so on. If the will leaves property to "my children" and one child dies before the testator, the child's children would not inherit their parent's share.

The will must also indicate whether issue are to inherit *per stirpes* or *per capita*. *Per stirpes* means that each *branch* of the family receives an equal share. Each child receives the same amount, and, if a child has already died, her heirs inherit her share. *Per capita* means that each *heir* receives the same amount. If the children have died, then each grandchild inherits the same amount.

Suppose that Gwendolyn has two children, Lance and Arthur. Lance has one child, Arthur has four. Both sons predecease their mother. If Gwendolyn's will

---

[2] Arizona, California, Idaho, Louisiana, Nevada, New Mexico, Texas, and Washington all have community property law; Wisconsin's system is a variation of the same principle.

[3] Except in Louisiana, whose laws are based on the French model.

says "per stirpes," Lance's child will inherit her father's entire share, which is half of Gwendolyn's estate. Arthur's four children will share their father's portion, so each will receive one eighth ($\frac{1}{4} \times \frac{1}{2}$). If Gwendolyn's will says, "per capita," each of her grandchildren will inherit one fifth of her estate. Although it might sound fairer to give all grandchildren the same inheritance, most people choose a *per stirpes* distribution, on the theory that they are treating their children equally. The following chart illustrates the difference between per stirpes and per capita.

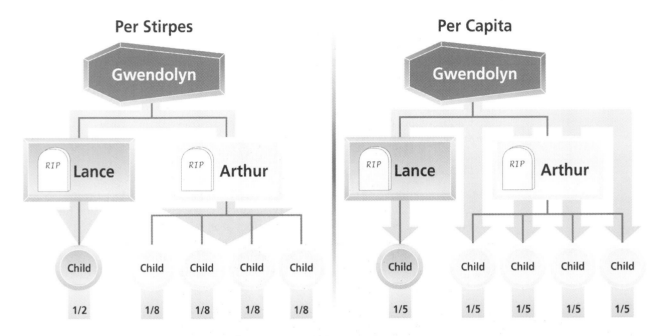

AMENDING A WILL

A testator can generally revoke or alter a will at any time prior to death. In most states, he can revoke a will by destroying it, putting an X through it, writing "revoked" (or some synonym) on it, or signing a new will. He can also execute an amendment—called a **codicil**—to change specific terms of the will, while keeping the rest of it intact. A codicil must meet all the requirements of a will, such as two witnesses. Suppose that Uncle Herman, who has a long and elaborate will, now wants his sterling silver Swiss Army knife to go to Cousin Larry rather than Niece Shannon. Instead of redoing his whole will, he can ask his lawyer to draw up a codicil changing only that one provision.

INTESTACY

When singer John Denver died unexpectedly in a plane accident, he had had several marriages, children, and platinum albums. His estate was worth $20 million. What he did not have was a will. He was in good company—almost three quarters of Americans die intestate, that is, without a will. In this event, the law steps in and determines how to distribute the decedent's property. Although, in theory, intestacy laws are supposed to be based on what most people would prefer, in practice, they are not. The vast majority of married people, for instance, leave all their assets to their surviving spouse. Most intestacy laws do not. In some states, if a married person dies intestate, some portion of her property (one half or two thirds) goes to her spouse, and the remainder to her issue (including grandchildren). Few people would actually want grandchildren to take a share of their estate in preference to their spouse.

POWER OF ATTORNEY

A **durable power of attorney** is a document that permits the **attorney-in-fact** to act for the principal. (An attorney-in-fact need not be a lawyer.) The power of attorney is effective until the principal dies or revokes it.

Lawyers generally recommend that their clients execute a durable power of attorney, particularly if they are elderly or in poor health. The power of attorney permits the client not only to choose the person who will act for him, but also to give advance instructions, such as "loan money to my son, Billy, if ever he needs it." If a client becomes incompetent and has no power of attorney, a court will appoint a guardian.

PROBATE

The testatrix cannot implement the terms of the will from beyond the grave, so she appoints an executor for this task. Typically, the executor is a family member, lawyer, or close friend. If the decedent does not select an executor, the probate court appoints an administrator to fulfill the same functions. Both the executor and the administrator are entitled to reasonable compensation—typically between 1% and 5% of the estate's value, although family members and friends often waive the fee.

ANATOMICAL GIFTS

Doctors have become increasingly successful at transplanting human organs. The demand for these organs—hearts, corneas, kidneys, pituitary glands, skin—is much greater than the supply. **The Uniform Anatomical Gift Act (UAGA) allows an individual to indicate her desire to be a donor either by putting a provision in her will or by signing an organ donation card in the presence of two witnesses.** A sample organ donation card is available at **http://www.delafe.com/ form/frmdonor.htm**. The UAGA also provides that, unless a decedent has affirmatively indicated her desire not to be a donor, family members have the right to make a gift of her organs after death.

LIVING WILLS

At the age of 25, Nancy Cruzan was in a devastating car accident. Deprived of oxygen for 14 minutes, a large part of her brain was destroyed. No one in her condition had ever recovered, but she could have continued to live for 25 years. In a rehabilitation hospital in Missouri, she lay in a fetal position, with her hands so twisted that her fingernails cut her wrists. She seemed to feel pain, and a nurse claimed that Cruzan cried once when read a Valentine's Day card. She seemed to sleep. When her eyes were open they gazed around the room randomly. Cruzan's parents believed that their daughter would rather be dead than live this way. They went to court to obtain permission to stop feeding her.

Yvette Williams was among a group that petitioned the Missouri courts to require that the feeding continue. Williams argued, "They said Nancy wouldn't want to live like this. Well, nobody would like to live like that. But everybody goes through hard times in their lives. I'm not happy all the time either. Nancy was a very healthy disabled person. She didn't even have bedsores. Like, what is a good quality of life?"[4]

Nancy Cruzan's tragedy led to a national debate over the right to die. **The Supreme Court ruled that family members can choose to discontinue treatment for an incompetent person if there is evidence the patient would have made that choice herself.**[5] After the Supreme Court decision, the probate court in Missouri heard new witnesses testify that Cruzan had said she would not want to live "like a vegetable." The lower court considered this clear and convincing evidence of Cruzan's wishes and granted the family permission to withhold feeding.

Spurred by the Cruzan case, many people executed so-called **living wills** or **advance directives.** Living wills permit adults to refuse extreme medical treatment that would prolong their lives, such as artificial feeding or cardiac resuscitation. In addition, a living will can be used to appoint a **health care proxy** to make decisions for a person who has become incompetent. A sample living will is available at **http://www.partnershipforcaring.org**. In addition, the Federal Patient Self-Determination Act requires hospitals to notify patients that they have the right to refuse lifesaving measures if they are near death.

Doctors are permitted to shorten a patient's life by withholding medical treatment. Can they go the next step and prescribe medication to end the life of a terminal patient who is suffering intolerably? In the following case, the court considered the legality of a statute in the state of Washington that makes **assisted suicide** a felony. Other states have similar statutes. Should a state have the right to punish someone for assisting the suicide of a terminally ill person? You be the judge.

YOU BE THE JUDGE

WASHINGTON v. GLUCKSBERG

521 U.S. 702, 117 S. Ct. 2258, 1997 U.S. LEXIS 4039
United States Supreme Court, 1997

FACTS: The state of Washington passed a statute making assisted suicide a felony punishable by up to five years in prison and a $10,000 fine. Plaintiffs argued that this statute was unconstitutional. The trial court found for the plaintiffs, but the court of appeals reversed. The Supreme Court agreed to hear the case.

YOU BE THE JUDGE: Does a state have the right to punish those who assist the terminally ill to commit suicide?

ARGUMENT FOR THE PLAINTIFFS: The Fourteenth Amendment of the United States Constitution declares that the state may not "deprive any person

---

[4] Pamela Warrick, "Protesters Plotted 'Rescue' – And Then It Was Too Late," *Los Angeles Times,* Jan. 10, 1991, p.E1.

[5] *Cruzan v. Director, Missouri Department of Health,* 497 U.S. 261, 110 S. Ct. 2841, 1990 U.S. LEXIS 3301 (1990).

of life, liberty, or property, without due process of law." The Supreme Court has, in the past, interpreted this provision to prevent the government from interfering in personal decisions relating to marriage, procreation, contraception, family relationships, child rearing, and education. For example, in *Roe v. Wade,* the Supreme Court held that a woman has the right to an abortion. If she has the right to terminate her pregnancy, surely she must have the right to terminate her own life. The choice to end one's life, to avoid unbearable pain, is among the most intimate and personal choices a person may make, a choice central to personal dignity and autonomy, central to the liberty protected by the Fourteenth Amendment.

In the *Cruzan* case, the Supreme Court suggested that an individual has the right to refuse lifesaving treatment. No constitutional distinction can be drawn between the withdrawal of medical treatment that results in death and the hastening of death by giving drugs. The plaintiffs in this case suffered horribly from incurable diseases. Would any of us want to be in their place? If we were, wouldn't we want the right to control when and how we die?

ARGUMENT FOR THE STATE OF WASHINGTON: There is an enormous difference between withholding aid and actively killing someone. This difference has long been recognized in tort law. You may not be liable for allowing someone to drown, but you will certainly be liable for pushing him into the pond.

The American Medical Association is concerned that physicians would be less diligent in fighting disease if killing patients were as acceptable an option as curing them.

Without an anti-suicide statute, the ill, the elderly, minorities, and the poor would all be pressured to consent to their own deaths. Pain is a significant factor in creating a desire for assisted suicide, and doctors are notoriously less aggressive in providing pain relief to the underprivileged.

For over 700 years, Anglo-American common law has punished those who help suicides. Most states that have considered this issue have decided that assisted suicide should be illegal. Given this history, it is difficult to argue that the Constitution somehow protects, as a fundamental liberty, the right to assisted suicide. ▮

Oregon is the only state that specifically allows doctors to prescribe a fatal dose of drugs to a dying patient. About 20 terminally ill Oregonians take advantage of this law each year.

Trusts

Trusts are an increasingly popular method for managing assets, both during life and after death. **A trust is an entity that separates legal and beneficial ownership.** It involves three people: the **grantor** (also called the **settlor** or **donor**), who creates and funds it; the **trustee,** who manages the assets; and the **beneficiary,** who receives the financial proceeds. A grantor can create a trust during her lifetime or after her death through her will.

ADVANTAGES AND DISADVANTAGES

Why do people use trusts? These are among the advantages:

- **Control.** The grantor can control her assets after her death. In the trust document, she can direct the trustees to follow a specific investment strategy, and she can determine how much income the beneficiaries receive. As an example, suppose the grantor has a husband and children. She wants to provide her husband with adequate income after her death, but she does not want him to spend so lavishly that nothing is left for the children. Nor does she want him to spend all her money on his second wife. The grantor could create a trust in her will that allows her husband to spend the income and, upon his death, gives the principal to their children.

- **Caring for children.** Minor children cannot legally manage property on their own, so parents or grandparents often establish trusts to take care of these assets until the children grow up.

- **Tax savings.** Although tax issues are beyond the scope of this chapter, it is worth noting that many married couples use a so-called **marital trust** to minimize their estate taxes.

- **Privacy.** A will is filed in probate court and becomes a matter of public record. Anyone can obtain a copy of it. Some companies are even in the business of providing copies to celebrity hounds. Jacqueline Kennedy Onassis's will is particularly popular. Trusts, however, are private documents and are not available to the public.

- **Probate.** A will must go through the often lengthy probate process, so the heirs may not receive assets for some time. Assets that are put into a trust *before the grantor dies* do not go through probate; the beneficiaries have immediate access to them.

The major *disadvantage* of a trust is expense. Although it is always possible for the grantor to establish a trust himself with the aid of software or form books, trusts are complex instruments with many potential pitfalls. Do-it-yourself trusts are a recipe for disaster. In addition to the legal fees required to establish a trust, the trustees may have to be paid. Professional trustees typically charge an annual fee of about 1.5% of the trust's assets. Family members usually do not expect payment.

TYPES OF TRUSTS

Depending upon the goal in establishing a trust, a grantor has several different choices.

Living Trust

Also known as an *inter vivos* trust, a living trust is established while the grantor is still alive. In the typical living trust, the grantor serves as trustee during his lifetime. He maintains total control over the assets and avoids a trustee's fee. If the grantor becomes disabled or dies, the successor trustee, who is named in the trust instrument, takes over automatically. All of the assets stay in the trust and avoid probate. Most living trusts are **revocable,** meaning that the grantor can undo the trust or change it at any time.

Testamentary Trust

A testamentary trust is created by a will. It goes into effect when the grantor dies. Naturally, it is **irrevocable** because the grantor is dead. The grantor's property must first go through probate, on its way to the trust.

Living trusts are particularly popular with older people because they want to ensure that their assets will be properly managed if they become disabled. Younger people typically opt for a testamentary trust because the probability they will become disabled anytime soon is remote. Also they want to avoid the effort of transferring their assets to the trust.

TRUST ADMINISTRATION

The primary obligation of trustees is to carry out the terms of the trust. They may exercise any powers expressly granted to them in the trust instrument and any implied powers reasonably necessary to implement the terms of the trust. In carrying out the terms of the trust, the trustees have a fiduciary duty to the beneficiary. This fiduciary duty includes:

- **A Duty of loyalty.** In managing the trust, the trustees must put the interests of the beneficiaries first. They must disclose any relevant information to the beneficiaries. They may not mix their own assets with those of the trust; do business with the trust (unless expressly permitted by the terms of the trust); or favor one beneficiary over another.

- **A Duty of care.** The trustee must act as a reasonable person would when managing the assets of another. The trustee must make careful investments, keep accurate records, and collect debts owed the trust.

A trustee is liable to the beneficiaries of the trust if she breaches her duty. W. Averell Harriman was a member of a wealthy New York family. When he died, he left half of his $65 million estate outright to his wife, Pamela Harriman, and half in trust for his two daughters from an earlier marriage (who were in their 70s). Pamela was a trustee and had the right to appoint the other trustees. She had been married twice before, to Winston Churchill's son and to Hollywood producer Leland Hayward. After Averell's death, she became ambassador to France, partly because of her generous contributions to the Democratic Party.

Under Pamela's care, the trust assets were invested in a series of risky real estate deals, including a seedy conference center in New Jersey that had once been a Playboy Club. The beneficiaries filed suit against her when they discovered that trust assets had declined in value from $30 million to $3 million. She and the children ultimately settled their litigation for an undisclosed sum, and then both sides filed suit against the two other trustees. This litigation also was settled.

TERMINATION

A trust ends upon the occurrence of any of these events:

- On the date indicated by the grantor.

- If the trust is revocable, when revoked by the grantor. Even if the trust is irrevocable, the grantor and all the beneficiaries can agree to revoke it.

- When the purpose of the trust has been fulfilled. If the grantor established the trust to pay college tuition for his grandchildren, the trust ends when the last grandchild graduates.

Chapter Conclusion

Attitudes toward inherited money vary greatly. Self-made Warren Buffet, whose holdings in Berkshire Hathaway Inc. are worth more than $12 billion, disapproves of inherited wealth. His children have occasionally borrowed money from him, but he insists that they sign formal loan documents and repay the loans. Other wealthy, and not so wealthy, people spend considerable time and effort minimizing their estate taxes and maximizing their children's inheritance. Neither view is right or wrong. People are perfectly entitled to dispose of their money as they see fit. The only wrong is in not deciding.

Chapter Review

1. A holographic will is handwritten by the testator but not witnessed.

2. A spouse is entitled to a certain share of the decedent's estate, but children have no automatic right to share in a parent's estate.

3. In a will, a *per stirpes* distribution means that each branch of the family receives an equal share. Per capita means that each heir receives the same amount.

4. A testator may generally revoke or alter a will at any time prior to death.

5. Almost three quarters of Americans die intestate—that is, without a will. In this event, the law determines how the decedent's property will be distributed.

6. A living will permits an adult to refuse medical treatment that would prolong life.

7. A trust is an entity that separates legal and beneficial ownership.

8. In carrying out the terms of a trust, the trustees have a fiduciary duty to the beneficiary.

PRACTICE TEST

Matching Questions

Match the following terms with their definitions:

___ **A.** Executor.

___ **B.** Intestate.

___ **C.** Testator.

___ **D.** Administrator.

___ **E.** Testatrix.

1. Woman who has signed a valid will.

2. Man who has signed a valid will.

3. Personal representative chosen by the decedent to carry out the terms of a will.

4. To die without a will.

5. Personal representative appointed by the probate court to oversee the probate process.

True/False Questions

Circle true or false:

1. T F Under the Uniform Probate Code, one spouse is not required to leave any money to the other spouse.

2. T F A holographic will need not be witnessed.

3. T F A nuncupative will need not be witnessed.

4. T F A principal may not revoke a durable power of attorney.

5. T F A grantor may not be the trustee of a trust.

Multiple-Choice Questions

6. CPA QUESTION: A decedent's will provided that the estate was to be divided among the decedent's issue, per capita and not per stirpes. If there are two surviving children and three grandchildren who are children of a pre-deceased child at the time the will is probated, how will the estate be divided?

   (a) $\frac{1}{2}$ to each surviving child.

   (b) $\frac{1}{3}$ to each surviving child and $\frac{1}{9}$ to each grandchild.

   (c) $\frac{1}{4}$ to each surviving child and $\frac{1}{6}$ to each grandchild.

   (d) $\frac{1}{5}$ to each surviving child and grandchild.

7. Hallie is telling her cousin Anne about the will she has just executed. "Because of my broken arm, I couldn't sign my name, so I just told Bertrand, the lawyer, to sign it for me. Bertrand also witnessed the will. Anne said, "You made a big mistake:

   I. You should have at least made some sort of mark on the paper yourself.

   II. The lawyer is not permitted to witness the will.

   III. You did not have enough witnesses."

   Which of Anne's statements is true:

   (a) I, II, and III.

   (b) Neither I, II, nor III.

   (c) Just I.

   (d) Just II.

   (e) Just III.

8. Owen does not want to leave any money to his son, Kevin. What must he do to achieve this goal?

   I. Nothing. If he dies without a will, Kevin will inherit nothing.

   II. Make a will that leaves nothing to Kevin.

   III. Leave Kevin $1 in his will.

   (a) I, II, or III.

   (b) II or III.

   (c) Just I.

   (d) Just II.

   (e) Just III.

9. Lauren is dying of cancer and suffering terribly. She has signed a living will directing her husband to make medical decisions for her. She is begging her husband and her doctors to kill her. Which of the following statements is true?

   I. If she goes into a coma, her husband has the right to direct her doctors to withhold treatment.

   II. Her doctor has the right to give her an overdose of pills that will kill her.

   III. Her husband has the right to give her an overdose of pills that will kill her.

   (a) I, II, and III.

   (b) Neither I, II, nor III.

   (c) Just I.

   (d) Just II.

   (e) Just III.

10. Blake tells his client that there are five good reasons to set up a trust. Which of the following is *not* a good reason?

    (a) To pay his grandchildren's college tuition if they go to the same college he attended.

    (b) To save money, since a trust is cheaper than a will.

    (c) To make sure the money is properly invested.

    (d) To avoid probate.

    (e) To safeguard his privacy.

Short-Answer Questions

11. When Frank Gilbert died, he left behind an eight-page typed will, prepared by an attorney, and handwritten notes dated two years later. The notes were found folded together in a sealed envelope. On the back of a business card, Frank had written: "Jim and Margaret I have appro $50,000.00 in Safe. See Buzz if anything happens [signed] Frank Gilbert." On the back of a pay stub, Frank had written: "Jim & Margaret $20,000.00 the Rest divided Equally the other Living Survivors Bro. & Sisters [signed] Frank Gilbert." He had written on the envelope: "I gave to Jim and Margaret this card which I Stated what to do." Jim was one of Frank's brothers; Margaret was Jim's wife. The typed will granted Jim a share of Frank's other assets besides the $50,000 in the safe. Jim's siblings argued that the handwritten notes were a new will that revoked the typed document and that, therefore, Jim and Margaret were entitled to $20,000 and nothing more. Jim argued that the handwritten notes were a codicil, giving him $20,000 in addition to his share under the will. Who is correct?

12. Kevin Fitzgerald represents the down-and-out Mission Hill and Roxbury Districts in the Massachusetts House of Representatives. A priest alerted him that Mary Guzelian, a street person who roamed his district, had trash bags in her ghetto apartment stuffed with cash, bonds, and bank books. Fitzgerald visited the apartment with his top aide, Patricia McDermott. Two weeks later, Guzelian signed a will, drafted by one of Fitzgerald's acquaintances, that left Guzelian's $400,000 estate to Fitzgerald and McDermott. Fitzgerald claimed not to know about the will until Guzelian's death four years later. Guzelian, 64, suffered from chronic paranoid schizophrenia and severe health problems. Would Guzelian's sister have a claim on Guzelian's estate?

13. Josh was a crotchety fellow, often at outs with his family. In his will, he left his son an autographed copy of his book, *A Guide to Federal Prisons*. He completely omitted his wife of 35 years and his daughter, instead leaving the rest of his substantial estate to the Society for the Assistance of Convicted Felons. Under the UPC, which member of his family fared best?

14. After nearly 40 years of marriage, Frank Honigman executed a new will that left his wife only the minimum required by law. The balance went to his brothers and sisters (the couple had no children). For some time before his death, Honigman had repeatedly told both friends and strangers, using obscene and abusive language, that his wife was unfaithful. Honigman was normal and rational in other respects but, by all evidence, his suspicions were untrue. They were based on such evidence as the fact that, when he left the house, his wife would ask him when he planned to return. Also, whenever the telephone rang, Mrs. Honigman answered it. For the last two years of his life he positively forbade her to answer the telephone. Is Mr. Honigman's will valid?

15. ROLE REVERSAL: Draft a multiple-choice question that compares *per stirpes* with *per capita*.

Internet Research Problem

Fill out your own organ donor card (available at **http://www.delafe.com/form/frmdonor.htm**) or advance directive (see **http://www.partnershipforcaring.org**).

Insurance

CHAPTER
46

In his job at the National Institutes of Health, Dr. James A. Magner analyzes the molecular structure of a hormone that stimulates the thyroid gland. One evening at home, he was trying to figure out the life insurance policy he purchased two years ago. Glancing at the rows of figures, Magner said, he could not understand precisely what the coverage was or what benefits the policy gave him, nor could he recall how much he was supposed to pay each year. "I try to be an intelligent consumer," he said. "It was inscrutable." Before deciding which coverage to buy, Magner said, he had asked a second agent for prices on an equivalent $100,000 policy. But when he got back a complicated set of numbers, he recalled, "I couldn't compare."

Like half the people who purchase life insurance in this country, Magner ended up buying a policy from someone he knew—in this case, his sister-in-law. He said he still does not know if he got the best buy. The physician is not alone. Even insurance company executives and other experts say there are so many variations in prices, benefits, and types of policies offered by life insurance companies that they cannot compare them accurately without a computer analysis.[1]

---

[1] Adapted from Kessler, Ronald, "Insurance: Costly Enigma," *The Washington Post*, 3/20/83, p.A1.

Introduction

No matter how careful our behavior, we are all subject to risk—from automobile accidents, injury, illness, fires, early death, and other catastrophes. No wonder that, from earliest times, people have sought insurance against these unpredictable and unpreventable dangers. Today, a typical family spends about 15% of its disposable income on insurance, more than on any other single category except food and housing.

It is important to begin by defining these key terms:

- **Person.** An individual, corporation, partnership, or any other legal entity.

- **Insurance.** A contract in which one person, in return for a fee, agrees to guarantee another against loss caused by a specific type of danger.

- **Insurer.** The person who issues the insurance policy and serves as guarantor.

- **Insured.** The person whose loss is the subject of the insurance policy.

- **Owner.** The person who enters into the insurance contract and pays the premiums.

- **Premium.** The consideration that the owner pays under the policy.

- **Beneficiary.** The person who receives the proceeds from the insurance policy.

The beneficiary, the insured, and the owner can be, but are not necessarily, the same person. If a homeowner buys fire insurance for her house, she is the insured, the owner, and the beneficiary because she bought the policy and receives the proceeds if her house burns down. If a mother buys a life insurance policy on her son that is payable to his children in the event of his death, then the mother is the owner, the son is the insured, and the grandchildren are the beneficiaries.

Before beginning a study of insurance law, it is important to understand the economics of the insurance industry. Suppose that you have recently purchased a $500,000 house. The probability your house will burn down in the next year is 1 in 1,000. That is a low risk, but the consequences would be devastating, especially since you could not afford to rebuild. Instead of bearing that risk yourself, you take out a fire insurance policy. You pay an insurance company $1,200 in return for a promise that, if your house burns down in the next 12 months, the company will pay you $500,000. The insurance company sells the same policy to 1,000 similar homeowners, expecting that on average one of these houses will burn down. If all 1,000 policyholders pay $1,200, the insurance company takes in $1.2 million each year, but expects to pay out only $500,000. It will put some money aside in case two houses burn down, or even worse, a major forest fire guts a whole tract of houses. It must also pay overhead expenses such as marketing and administration. And, of course, shareholders expect profits.

Insurance Contract

An insurance policy must meet all the common law requirements for a contract. There must be an offer, acceptance, and consideration. The owner must have legal capacity; that is, he must be an adult of sound mind. Fraud, duress, or undue influence invalidates a policy. In theory, insurance contracts need not be in writing because the statute of frauds does not apply to any contract that can be performed within one year and it is possible that the house may burn down or the car may crash within a year. Some states, however, specifically require insurance contracts to be in writing.

OFFER AND ACCEPTANCE

The purchaser of a policy makes an offer by delivering an application and a premium to the insurer. The insurance company then has the option of either accepting or rejecting the offer. **It can accept by oral notice, by written notice, or by delivery of the policy.** It also has a fourth option—a written binder. A **binder** is a short document acknowledging receipt of the application and premium. It indicates that a policy is *temporarily* in effect but does not constitute *final* acceptance. The insurer still has the right to reject the offer once it has examined the application carefully. Kyle buys a house on April 1 and wants insurance right away. The insurance company issues a binder to him the same day. If Kyle's house burns down on May 1, the insurer must pay, even though it has not yet issued the final policy. If, however, there is no fire, but on May 1 the company decides Kyle is a bad risk, it has the right to reject his application at that time because it has not yet issued the policy.

LIMITING CLAIMS BY THE INSURED

Insurance policies can sometimes look like a quick way to make easy money. More than one person suffering from overwhelming financial pressure has insured a building to the hilt and then burned it down for the insurance money. Unbelievably, more than one parent has killed a child to collect the proceeds of a life insurance policy. Therefore, the law has created a number of rules to protect insurance companies from fraud and bad faith on the part of insureds.

Insurable Interest

An insurance contract is not valid unless the owner has an *insurable interest* in the subject matter of the policy. To understand why an insurable interest is important, read this tragic story. Twenty-year-old Deana Wild was thrilled when James Coates proposed to her. To celebrate their engagement, they took a sightseeing trip along the California coast with Coates's mother, Virginia Rearden. They seemed to be just one big happy family. Only one problem: Wild slipped while walking along the edge of a cliff at Big Sur and fell to her death. That would have been the end of the story except that, the day before, Wild had taken out a $35,000 life insurance policy, naming Coates and Rearden as beneficiaries. When the insurance company investigated, it learned that Coates was married to someone else. Therefore, he could not be Wild's fiancé, and neither he nor Rearden had an insurable interest in Wild. It also turned out that Rearden had taken out the policy without Wild's knowledge. Rearden was convicted of first-degree murder and sentenced to life in prison without parole.

These are the rules on insurable interest:

- **Definition.** A person has an insurable interest if she would be harmed by the danger that she has insured against. If Jessica takes out a fire insurance policy on her own barn, she will presumably be reluctant to burn it down. However, if she buys a policy on Nathan's barn, she will not mind, she may even be delighted, when fire sweeps through the barn. It is a small step to saying that she might even burn the barn down herself.

- **Amount of loss.** The insurable interest can be no greater than the actual amount of loss suffered. If the barn is worth $50,000, but Jessica insures it (and pays premiums) for $100,000, she will recover only $50,000 when it burns down. Nor is she entitled to a refund of the excess premiums she has paid. The goal is to make sure that Jessica does not profit from the policy.

- **Life insurance.** A person always has an insurable interest in his own life and the life of his spouse or fiancée. Parents and minor children also have an insurable interest in each other.

- **Work relationships.** Business partners, employers, and employees have an insurable interest in each other if they would suffer some financial harm from the death of the insured. For example, a start-up company will often buy **key person life insurance** on its officers to compensate the company if an important person dies.

Misrepresentation

Insurers have the right to void a policy if, during the application process, the insured makes a material misstatement or conceals a material fact. The policy is voidable whether the misstatement was oral or in writing, intentional or unintentional. **Material** means that the misstatement or omission affected the insurer's willingness to issue the policy. In the following case, the applicant lied about his health. Were his misstatements material?

CASE SUMMARY

GOLDEN RULE INSURANCE CO. v. HOPKINS

788 F. Supp. 295, 1991 U.S. Dist. LEXIS 19970
United States District Court for the Southern District of Mississippi, 1991

FACTS: Brian Hopkins submitted an application to Golden Rule Insurance Co. for medical and life insurance. In filling out the application, he answered "no" to questions asking whether he had had any of the following conditions: heart murmur, growths, skin disorders, immune deficiencies, sexually transmitted diseases, or any disorders of the glands. In response to questions about past surgery, Hopkins reported that he had had tonsils and hemorrhoids removed.

A year later, Hopkins was hospitalized. While in the hospital, he was diagnosed with AIDS. In his discharge summary, Dr. William A. Causey stated that Hopkins had tested HIV positive three years before. (HIV is the virus that causes AIDS.) Shortly thereafter, Dr. Causey wrote to Golden Rule to say that he

was mistaken and that Hopkins was not HIV positive. During the trial, however, Dr. Causey admitted that he was reluctant to tell insurance companies information that would harm his patients. The following year, Hopkins died of AIDS. Golden Rule rescinded Hopkins's policies, contending that his application contained material misrepresentations.

ISSUES: Did Hopkins materially misrepresent his health when applying for insurance? Does Golden Rule have the right to rescind his insurance policies?

DECISION: Golden Rule had the right to rescind Hopkins's insurance policy because he made material misrepresentations in his application.

REASONING: An insurer has the right to rescind an insurance policy if the application contains a false statement that affects the insurer's risk. When Hopkins filled out the Golden Rule application, he was HIV positive and had a heart murmur as well as a history of skin disorders, swollen lymph glands, and rectal warts (which had been surgically removed). All of these conditions were material and would have affected Golden Rule's decision to issue the policy.

Golden Rule is entitled to rescind Hopkins's policy. The company is not obligated to pay any of his medical costs, but must refund the premiums it received from Hopkins. ◢

BAD FAITH BY THE INSURER

Insurance policies often contain a covenant of *good faith and fair dealing.* Even if the policy itself does not *explicitly* include such a provision, an increasing number of courts (but not all) *imply* this covenant. An insurance company can violate the covenant of good faith and fair dealing by (1) fraudulently inducing someone to buy a policy; (2) refusing to pay a valid claim; or (3) refusing to accept a reasonable settlement offer that has been made to an insured. When an insurance company violates the covenant of good faith and fair dealing, it becomes liable for both compensatory and punitive damages.

Fraud

In recent years, a number of insurance companies have paid substantial damages to settle fraud charges involving the sale of life insurance. For example, agents for Prudential Insurance Company of America tricked customers into trading in existing policies for new ones with higher coverage and bigger premiums. Sales agents promised the customers that their premiums would not increase, but that was not true. The higher premiums were disguised at the beginning because the company used cash reserves that had built up in the original policy to pay the premiums on the new policy. Eventually, however, all the cash in the old policy was used up and the customers began to receive bills for much higher premiums. In many cases, they could not afford to pay the premiums, so their policy lapsed. This meant that Prudential received premiums for years, but never had to pay benefits because the policies lapsed before anyone died.

In short, Prudential had trained its agents to commit fraud. Agents were also trained to target the elderly. The state of Florida found that Prudential had deliberately cheated its customers for more than 10 years. Prudential agreed to pay as much as $2 billion in refunds. In a similar case, State Farm Insurance agreed to pay its customers $200 million.

Refusing to Pay a Valid Claim

Perhaps because juries feel sympathy for those who must deal with an immovable bureaucracy, damage awards are often sizeable when an insurance company refuses to pay a legitimate claim. For example, a jury in Ohio entered a $13 million verdict against Buckeye Union Insurance Co. for its bad-faith refusal to pay a claim. An Ohio sheriff stopped the automobile of 19-year-old Eugene Leber. As the sheriff approached Leber's car, he slipped on ice and his gun discharged. By incredible bad luck, the bullet struck Leber, permanently paralyzing him from the rib cage down. The insurance company recognized that it was liable under the policy, but it nonetheless fought the case for *16 years.*

Consumers complain that insurance companies often "low-ball"—that is, they make an unreasonably low offer to settle a claim. Some insurance companies even set claims quotas that limit how much their adjusters can pay out each year, regardless of the merits of each individual claim. If juries continue to award multimillion-dollar verdicts, insurance companies may decide simply to pay the claims.

Refusing to Accept a Settlement Offer

An insurer also violates the covenant of good faith and fair dealing when it *wrongfully* refuses to settle a claim. Suppose that Dmitri has a $100,000 automobile insurance policy. After he injures Tanya in a car accident, she sues him for $5 million. As provided in the policy, Dmitri's insurance company defends him against Tanya's claim. She offers to settle for $100,000, but the insurance company refuses because it only has $100,000 at risk anyway. It may get lucky with the jury. Instead, a jury comes in with a $2 million verdict. The insurance company is only liable for $100,000, but Dmitri must pay $1.9 million. In the following case, the court found that an insurance company had acted in bad faith when it refused to accept a reasonable settlement offer.

CASE SUMMARY

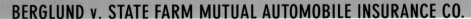

BERGLUND v. STATE FARM MUTUAL AUTOMOBILE INSURANCE CO.

121 F.3d 1225, 1997 U.S. App. LEXIS 22609
United States Court of Appeals for the Eighth Circuit, 1997

FACTS: At an intersection in rural Iowa, Thomas Berglund ran a stop sign and struck a van. Ronald Jalas and his wife were seriously injured, and their four-year-old daughter, Jazelle, was killed. Two of the Jalases' other children had previously died.

The Jalases sued the Berglunds, who had two insurance policies: a $500,000 automobile policy with State Farm and a $1 million excess liability insurance policy with Grinnell Mutual. The excess policy applied only after other insurance was exhausted. The Jalases offered to settle for $1.51 million. As required by the insurance contract, State Farm was defending the Berglunds. If State Farm had accepted this offer, the Berglunds would have had to contribute only $10,000. State Farm's claims committee officially valued the claim at $200,000. However, several committee members felt the claim was worth more, as did a consultant at corporate headquarters. This consultant recommended that the company offer the full $500,000. Instead, State Farm offered the Jalases $300,000, which they refused.

At trial, the jury awarded the Jalases $1,897,703.80. After the two insurance companies paid, the Berglunds owed about $400,000. The Berglunds brought this lawsuit, asserting that State Farm acted in bad faith. A jury awarded damages of $530,831.42, including punitive damages. State Farm appealed.

ISSUE: Did State Farm act in bad faith in its representation of the Berglunds?

DECISION: Yes, State Farm acted in bad faith.

REASONING: When an insurance company realizes that a verdict may exceed the policy's limits, it has an obligation to act in good faith on behalf of the insured. The company must negotiate a settlement as if policy limits did not exist. State Farm does not appear to have done so.

State Farm blames Grinnell Mutual for the large verdict. There was some evidence at trial that Grinnell would contribute no more than $300,000 towards settlement. Until State Farm offered the limit of its policy, however, there is no way to know what Grinnell would have done in response. Also, the Jalases' attorney testified that they might have been willing to accept a settlement offer of $800,000. About half the plaintiffs who initially demand over $1 million ultimately do settle for less. A jury could reasonably find that State Farm's failure to offer its policy limits caused the large judgment. ◢

Types of Insurance

Insurance is available for virtually any risk. Bruce Springsteen, Michael Jackson, Billy Joel, and the Rolling Stones have insured their voices. When Kerry Wallace shaved her head in the Star Trek films, she bought insurance in case her hair failed to grow back. Food critic Egon Ronay insured his taste buds. And an amateur dramatics group took out insurance to protect against the risk that a member of the audience might die laughing. Most people, however, get by with six different types of insurance: property, life, health, disability, liability, and automobile.

PROPERTY INSURANCE

Property insurance (also known as **casualty insurance**) covers physical damage to real estate, personal property (boats, furnishings), or inventory, from causes such as fire, smoke, lightning, wind, riot, vandalism, or theft.

LIFE INSURANCE

Life insurance is really death insurance—it provides for payments to a beneficiary upon the death of the insured. The purpose is to replace at least some of the insured's income so that her family will not be financially devastated. Sales of life insurance in the United States had been declining for years because Baby Boomers preferred to invest in the stock market to provide for their retirement rather than in life insurance. In the month after the terrorist attacks of September 11, 2001, sales of life insurance jumped by 9%.

Term Insurance

Term insurance is the simplest, cheapest life insurance option. It is purchased for a specific period, such as 1, 5, or 20 years. If the insured dies during the period of the policy, the insurance company pays the policy amount to the beneficiary. If the owner stops paying premiums, the policy terminates and the beneficiary receives nothing. As the probability of death rises with age, so do the premiums. A $200,000 policy on a 25-year-old nonsmoker costs about $180 annually; at age 60 the same policy costs $1,000. Term insurance is the best choice for a person who simply wants to protect his family by replacing his income if he dies young.

Whole Life Insurance

Whole life or **straight life** insurance is designed to cover the insured for his entire life. A portion of the premiums pays for insurance, and the remainder goes into savings. This savings portion is called the cash value of the policy. The company pays dividends on this cash value and typically, after some years, the dividends are large enough to cover the premium so that the owner does not have to pay any more. The cash value accrues without being taxed until the policy is cashed in. The owner can borrow against the cash value, in many cases at a below-market rate. In addition, if the owner cancels the policy, the insurance company will pay her the policy's cash value. When the owner purchases the policy, the company typically sets a premium that stays constant over the life of the policy. A 25-year-old nonsmoker pays annual premiums of roughly $2,000 per year on a $200,000 policy.

The advantage of a whole life policy is that it forces people to save. It also has some significant disadvantages:

- The investment returns from the savings portion of whole life insurance have traditionally been mediocre. Mutual funds may offer better investment opportunities.

- A significant portion of the premium for the first year goes to pay overhead and commissions. Agents have a great incentive to sell whole life policies, rather than term, because their commissions are much higher.

- Unless the customer holds a policy for about 20 years, it will typically generate little cash value. Half of all whole life policyholders drop their policies in the first seven or eight years. At that point, the policy has generated little more than commissions for the agent.

- Whole life insurance provides the same amount of insurance throughout the insured's life. In contrast, most people need more insurance when they have young children and less as they approach retirement age.

Universal Life

Universal life insurance is a flexible combination of whole life and term. The owner can adjust the premiums over the life of the policy and also adjust the allocation of the premiums between insurance and savings. The options are complex and often difficult for the customer to understand.

Annuities

As life expectancy has increased, people have begun to worry as much about supporting themselves in their old age as they do about dying young. Sales of life insurance have stagnated while the number of annuities sold each year is growing rapidly. **Annuities are the reverse of life insurance—they make payments *until* death whereas life insurance pays *after* death.** In the basic annuity contract, the owner makes a lump-sum payment to an insurance company in return for a fixed annual income for the rest of her life, no matter how long she lives. If she dies tomorrow, the insurance company makes a huge profit. If she lives to be 95, the company loses money. But whatever happens, she knows she will have an income until the day she dies.

In a **deferred annuity contract,** the owner makes a lump-sum payment but receives no income until some later date, say, in 10 or 20 years when he retires. From that date forward, he will receive payments for the rest of his life.

HEALTH INSURANCE

Traditional health insurance plans are **pay for service.** The insurer pays for virtually any treatment that any doctor orders. The good news under this system is that policyholders have the largest possible choice of doctor and treatment. The bad news is that doctors and patients have an incentive to overspend on health care because the insurance company picks up the tab. It has been estimated that as many as one third of the medical procedures performed in pay for service plans have little medical justification, which in the end is not good for the patient.

Instead of, or in addition to, pay for service plans, many insurers offer **managed care plans.** There are many variations on this theme, but they all work to limit treatment choices. In some plans, the patient has a primary care physician who must approve all visits to specialists. In **health maintenance organizations,** known as **HMOs,** the patient can be treated only by doctors in the organization, unless there is some extraordinary need for an outside specialist.

Neither type of plan is perfect. In pay for service plans, doctors have an incentive to overtreat. In managed care plans, they may have an incentive to undertreat. For example, a recent study revealed that managed care plans tend to treat mental illness primarily with drugs. A combination of drugs and therapy is more successful but also more expensive. Many managed care plans provide excellent care, but whatever their strengths and weaknesses, they seem destined to become the norm in American health care.

DISABILITY INSURANCE

Disability insurance replaces the insured's income if he becomes unable to work because of illness or injury. "Ah!" you think, "that will never happen to me." In fact, the average person is seven times more likely to be disabled for at least 90 days than she is to die before age 65. Half of all mortgage foreclosures are caused by an owner's disability. Everyone should have disability insurance to replace between 60% and 75% of their income. (There is no need for 100% replacement because expenses while unemployed are lower.) Many employers provide disability protection.

LIABILITY INSURANCE

Most insurance—property, life, health, disability—is designed to reimburse the insured (or her family) for any harm she suffers. Liability insurance is different. **Its purpose is to reimburse the insured for any liability she incurs by *(accidentally)* harming someone else.** (Note that this insurance does not cover any *intentional* torts the insured commits.) This type of insurance covers tort claims by:

- Those injured on property owned by the insured—the mail carrier who slips and falls on the front sidewalk or the child who drowns in the pool

- Those injured by the insured away from his home or business—the jogger crushed by an insured who loses control of his rollerblades; and

- Those whose property is damaged by the insured—the owner whose stone wall is pulverized by the insured's swerving car.

These are the types of claims covered in a *personal* liability policy. *Business* liability policies may also protect against other sorts of claims:

- Professional malpractice on the part of an accountant, architect, doctor, engineer, or lawyer.

- Product liability for any injuries caused by the company's products.

- Employment practices liability insurance to protect employers against claims of sexual harassment, discrimination, and wrongful termination. About 30% of American firms carry this type of insurance. Note that this insurance typically does not protect the person who actually commits the wrongdoing—the sexual harasser, for instance—but it does protect the innocent insureds, such as the company itself.

AUTOMOBILE INSURANCE

An automobile insurance policy is a combination of several different types of coverage that, depending on state law, are either mandatory or optional. These are the basic types of coverage:

- **Collision** covers the cost of repairing or replacing a car that is damaged in an accident.

- **Comprehensive** covers fire, theft, and vandalism—but not collision.

- **Liability** covers harm the owner causes to other people or their property—their body, car, or stone wall. Most states require drivers to carry liability insurance.

- **Uninsured motorist** covers the owner and anyone else in the car who is injured by an uninsured motorist.

Most Americans spend a considerable percentage of their disposable income on insurance. What can you do to reduce this expense?

- **Do not insure against every risk.** If you can afford the loss yourself, it is better not to purchase insurance. About half of every dollar that consumers spend on insurance is paid back in claims; the other half goes to the company's profits and overhead. For example, salespeople often try very hard to sell extended warranties on consumer electronic devices and appliances such as televisions and refrigerators. These warranties are simply insurance plans that require the store to fix the item if something goes wrong. Stores often make a larger profit from the warranty than from the product itself. If you self-insure, odds are you will come out ahead in the long run.

- **Do not buy "special occasion" insurance.** After a major plane crash, sales of flight accident insurance jump. If you need life insurance, you should have it, no matter how you die. Your family does not need more money because you die in a plane crash rather than a car accident. The same rule holds true for other special occasion policies such as cancer insurance. You need health insurance regardless of your illness. Indeed, to protect the elderly who buy most of these policies, some states have outlawed cancer insurance.

- **Select as high a deductible as you can afford.** The higher the deductible, the lower the premium. Over the lifetime of your house or car, you can save thousands of dollars by self-insuring the small losses and buying insurance to protect only against major catastrophes.

- **Shop for the best price.** The lowest-cost company may charge as little as two thirds as much as its highest-price competitor. The Internet offers a great opportunity to compare prices for different types of insurance. Try **http://www.quicken.com/insurance**, **http://www.insweb.com**, **http://quickquote.com**, or **http://www.insure.com**.

- **Shop for quality.** An insurance company can fail as easily as any other business. What a disaster to pay premiums, only to discover later that you are not in safe hands after all. ▪

Chapter Conclusion

Life is a risky business. Cars crash, people die, houses burn. So what can we do? Buy insurance, and get on with our lives, knowing that we have prepared as best we can.

Chapter Review

1. An insurance policy must meet all the common-law requirements for a contract—offer, acceptance, and consideration.

2. A person has an insurable interest if she would be harmed by the danger that she has insured against.

3. Insurers have the right to void a policy if the insured makes a material misstatement, or conceals a material fact.

4. Many courts have held that insurance policies contain a covenant of good faith and fair dealing and have found insurance companies liable for compensatory and punitive damages if they commit fraud, refuse to pay legitimate claims, or reject reasonable settlement offers.

5. Property insurance covers physical damage to real estate, personal property (boats, furnishings), or inventory from causes such as fire, smoke, lightning, wind, riot, vandalism, or theft.

6. Annuities are the reverse of life insurance policies; they make payments until death.

7. Health insurance is available in pay for service plans, managed care plans, or HMOs.

8. Disability insurance replaces the insured's income if he becomes unable to work because of illness or injury.

9. Liability insurance reimburses the insured for any liability she incurs by accidentally harming someone else.

PRACTICE TEST

Matching Questions

Match the following terms with their definitions:

___ **A.** Insured.

___ **B.** Insurer.

___ **C.** Owner.

___ **D.** Beneficiary.

___ **E.** Insurable interest.

1. The person who issues the insurance policy.

2. The person who receives the proceeds from insurance policy.

3. The person who takes out the policy would be harmed by the danger that she has insured against.

4. The person who enters into the policy and pays the premiums.

5. The person whose loss is the subject of an insurance policy.

True/False Questions

Circle true or false:

1. T   F   If the insured makes any false statement in the application process, the insurance policy is void.

2. T   F   Once an insurance company issues a binder, the policy is irrevocable.

3. T   F   Although whole life insurance is more expensive than term, it is the best choice because it forces the customer to save money.

4. T   F   You are more likely to die before 65 than to become disabled before 65.

5. T   F   An annuity is simply a type of life insurance.

Multiple-Choice Questions

1. Lucas has bought the following insurance this week:

   I. A life insurance policy on his brother.

   II. A life insurance policy on the partner in his accounting practice.

   III. A fire insurance policy on the fitness club he belongs to so that if it burns down, he will receive a large enough payment to enable him to join a different club.

   In which of these policies does he have an insurable interest?

   (a) I, II, and III.

   (b) Neither I, II, nor III.

   (c) I and II.

   (d) I and III.

   (e) II and III.

2. An insurance company does *not* violate its covenant of good faith and fair dealing if it:

   (a) Charges elderly customers higher premiums than it charges younger customers.

   (b) Tells potential customers that their premiums will decline when that is not true.

   (c) Tells potential customers that their returns on a whole life policy are certain to be higher than an equivalent amount invested in the stock market.

   (d) Refuses to pay a valid claim until after four years of litigation.

   (e) Refuses to accept a settlement offer on behalf of an insured that was reasonable, but not in the company's best interest.

3. If you are a smart consumer, you will:

   I. Insure against as many different kinds of risks as you can so that no matter what happens, you will be protected.

   II. Select as low a deductible as possible so that no matter what happens, you will not have to pay large sums out of pocket.

   III. Buy flight insurance when you take long airplane flights so that your family will be protected if your plane crashes.

   (a) I, II, and III.

   (b) Neither I, II, nor III.

   (c) I and II.

   (d) Just I.

   (e) Just II.

4. Hamish owned an office building with a fair market value of $250,000. He insured it for $300,000. When it burned down, he was entitled to:

   (a) Nothing.

   (b) $250,000 and a return of the excess premiums he paid on the $300,000 policy.

   (c) $250,000.

   (d) $300,000.

5. Troy is having a very bad week. On Monday, he found out that he had genital herpes. On Tuesday, he slept with a woman he met in a bar. On Friday, the woman called him to tell him that he had transmitted the herpes to her. On Saturday, his roommate forgot his key so climbed in the apartment window. Hearing the noise, Troy mistook his roommate for a burglar and shot him. Troy's liability insurance will:

   (a) Not cover his liability to the woman or his roommate because he caused both harms intentionally.

   (b) Will cover his liability to both the woman and his roommate because he did not cause either harm intentionally.

   (c) Not cover his liability to the woman because he caused that harm intentionally.

   (d) Not cover his liability to his roommate because he caused that harm intentionally.

   (e) Not cover his liability to the woman because his behavior was so careless as to be as bad as an intentional tort.

Short-Answer Questions

6. Linda Richmond and Eddie Durham had two children before they were divorced. Under the terms of their divorce decree, Durham obtained title to their house. When he died suddenly of a heart attack, the children inherited the house. Richmond moved into the house with the children and began paying the mortgage that was in Durham's name. She also took out fire insurance. Ten months later, fire totally destroyed the house. The insurance company refused to pay a benefit under the policy because Richmond did not have an insurable interest in the property. Do you agree?

7. Mark Zulcosky applied for life insurance with Farm Bureau Life Insurance Co. On the application he indicated that he had not received any traffic tickets in the preceding five years. In fact, he had received several such citations for driving while intoxicated. Two years later, Mark was shot to death. When Farm Bureau discovered the traffic tickets, it denied coverage to his beneficiary. Was Farm Bureau in the right?

8. Dannie Harvey sued her employer, O. R. Whitaker, for sexual harassment, discrimination, and defamation. Whitaker counterclaimed for libel and slander, requesting $1 million in punitive damages. Both Whitaker and Harvey were insured by Allstate, under identical homeowner's policies. This policy explicitly promised to defend Harvey against the exact claim Whitaker had made against her. Harvey's Allstate agent, however, told her that she was not covered. Because the agent kept all copies of Harvey's insurance policies in his office, she took him at his word. She had no choice but to defend against the claim on her own. Whitaker mounted an exceedingly hostile litigation attack, taking 80 depositions. After a year, Allstate agreed to defend Harvey. However, instead of hiring the lawyer who had been representing her, it chose another lawyer who had no expertise in this type of case and was a close friend of Whitaker's attorney. Harvey's new lawyer refused to meet her or to attend any depositions. Harvey and Whitaker finally settled. Whitaker had spent $1 million in legal fees, Harvey $169,000, and Allstate $2,513. Does Harvey have a claim against Allstate?

9. Clyde Anderson received a letter from his automobile insurance company notifying him that it would not renew his policy that was set to expire on February 28. Anderson did not obtain another policy, and, on March 1, at 2:30 a.m., he struck another vehicle, killing two men. Later that day, Anderson applied for insurance coverage. As part of this application, he indicated that he had not been involved in any accident in the last three years. The new policy was effective as of 12:01 a.m. on March 1. Will the estates of the two dead men be able to recover under this policy?

10. ETHICS: Donna and Carl Nichols each bought term life insurance from Prudential Insurance Company of America. These policies contained a rider providing that, if the insured became disabled, the premiums did not have to be paid and the policy would still stay in effect. This term is called a "waiver of premium." Carl became totally disabled and his premiums were waived. Some years later, two Prudential sales managers convinced the Nicholses to convert their term life insurance policies into whole life insurance policies. They promised that, once Carl made the conversion, he would only have to pay premiums on the new policy for a six-month waiting period. They even wrote "WP to be included in this policy" on the application form. "WP" stood for waiver of premium benefit. Only after the new policy was issued did the Nicholses learn that Prudential would not waive the premium. The Nicholses had exchanged a policy on which they owed nothing further for a policy on which they now had to pay premiums that they could not afford. Do the Nicholses have a claim against Prudential? Regardless of the legal outcome, did Prudential have an ethical obligation to the Nicholses?

11. ROLE REVERSAL: Write a short-answer question dealing with either misrepresentation on the part of an applicant for insurance or bad faith by an insurer.

Internet Research Problem

Go to **http://insurancefraud.org** and look up the latest insurance regulations and legislation in your state. What is the goal of these rules—to protect consumers or the insurance industry? While you are at this Web site, read about the Fraud Case of the Month.

The Constitution of the United States

Preamble   We the People of the United States, in Order to form a more perfect Union, establish Justice, insure domestic Tranquility, provide for the common defense, promote the general Welfare, and secure the Blessings of Liberty to ourselves and our Posterity, do ordain and establish this Constitution for the United States of America.

ARTICLE I

Section 1.

All legislative Powers herein granted shall be vested in a Congress of the United States, which shall consist of a Senate and House of Representatives.

Section 2.

The House of Representatives shall be composed of Members chosen every second Year by the People of the several States, and the Electors in each State shall have the Qualifications requisite for Electors of the most numerous Branch of the State Legislature.

No Person shall be a Representative who shall not have attained to the Age of twenty five Years, and been seven Years a Citizen of the United States, and who shall not, when elected, be an Inhabitant of that State in which he shall be chosen.

Representatives and direct Taxes shall be apportioned among the several States which may be included within this Union, according to their respective Numbers, which shall be determined by adding to the whole Number of free Persons, including those bound to Service for a Term of Years, and excluding Indians not taxed, three fifths of all other Persons. The actual Enumeration shall be made within three Years after the first Meeting of the Congress of the United States, and within every subsequent Term of ten Years, in such Manner as they shall by Law direct. The number of Representatives shall not exceed one for every thirty Thousand, but each State shall have at Least one Representative; and until such enumeration shall be made, the State of New Hampshire shall be entitled to chuse three, Massachusetts eight, Rhode Island and Providence Plantations one, Connecticut five, New-York six, New Jersey four, Pennsylvania eight, Delaware one, Maryland six, Virginia ten, North Carolina five, South Carolina five, and Georgia three.

When vacancies happen in the Representation from any State, the Executive Authority thereof shall issue Writs of Election to fill such vacancies.

The House of Representatives shall chuse their Speaker and other Officers; and shall have the sole Power of Impeachment.

Section 3.

The Senate of the United States shall be composed of two Senators from each State, chosen by the Legislature thereof, for six Years; and each Senator shall have one Vote.

Immediately after they shall be assembled in Consequence of the first Election, they shall be divided as equally as may be into three Classes. The Seats of the

Senators of the first Class shall be vacated at the Expiration of the second Year, of the second Class at the Expiration of the fourth Year, and of the third Class at the Expiration of the sixth Year, so that one third may be chosen every second Year; and if Vacancies happen by Resignation or otherwise, during the Recess of the Legislature of any State, the Executive thereof may make temporary Appointments until the next Meeting of the Legislature, which shall then fill such Vacancies.

No Person shall be a Senator who shall not have attained to the Age of thirty Years, and been nine Years a Citizen of the United States, and who shall not, when elected, be an Inhabitant of that State for which he shall be chosen.

The Vice President of the United States shall be President of the Senate, but shall have no Vote, unless they be equally divided.

The Senate shall chuse their other Officers, and also a President pro tempore, in the Absence of the Vice President, or when he shall exercise the Office of President of the United States.

The Senate shall have the sole power to try all Impeachments. When sitting for that Purpose, they shall be an Oath or Affirmation. When the President of the United States is tried, the Chief Justice shall preside: And no Person shall be convicted without the Concurrence of two thirds of the Members present.

Judgment in Cases of Impeachment shall not extend further than to removal from Office, and disqualification to hold and enjoy any Office of honor, Trust or Profit under the United States: but the Party convicted shall nevertheless be liable and subject to Indictment, Trial, Judgment and Punishment, according to Law.

Section 4.

The Times, Places and Manner of holding Elections for Senators and Representatives, shall be prescribed in each State by the Legislature thereof: but the Congress may at any time by Law make or alter such Regulations, except as to the Places of chusing Senators.

The Congress shall assemble at least once in every Year, and such Meeting shall be on the first Monday in December, unless they shall by Law appoint a different Day.

Section 5.

Each House shall be the Judge of the Elections, Returns and Qualifications of its own Members, and a Majority of each shall constitute a Quorum to do Business; but a smaller Number may adjourn from day to day, and may be authorized to compel the Attendance of absent Members, in such Manner, and under such Penalties as each House may provide.

Each House may determine the Rules of its Proceedings, punish its Members for disorderly Behaviour, and, with the Concurrence of two thirds, expel a Member.

Each House shall keep a Journal of its Proceedings, and from time to time publish the same, excepting such Parts as may in their Judgment require Secrecy; and the Yeas and Nays of the Members of either House on any question shall, at the Desire of one fifth of those Present, be entered on the Journal.

Neither House, during the Session of Congress, shall, without the Consent of the other, adjourn for more than three days, nor to any other Place than that in which the two Houses shall be sitting.

Section 6.

The Senators and Representatives shall receive a Compensation for their Services, to be ascertained by Law, and paid out of the Treasury of the United States. They shall in all Cases, except Treason, Felony and Breach of the Peace, be privileged from Arrest during their Attendance at the Session of their respective Houses, and in going to and returning from the same; and for any Speech or Debate in either House, they shall not be questioned in any other Place.

No Senator or Representative shall, during the Time for which he was elected, be appointed to any civil Office under the Authority of the United States, which shall have been created, or the Emoluments whereof shall have been encreased during such time; and no Person holding any Office under the United States, shall be a Member of either House during his Continuance in Office.

Section 7.

All Bills for raising Revenue shall originate in the House of Representatives; but the Senate may propose or concur with Amendments as on other Bills.

Every Bill which shall have passed the House of Representatives and the Senate, shall, before it become a Law, be presented to the President of the United States; If he approve he shall sign it, but if not he shall return it, with his Objections to that House in which it shall have originated, who shall enter the Objections at large on their Journal, and proceed to reconsider it. If after such Reconsideration two thirds of that House shall agree to pass the Bill, it shall be sent, together with the Objections, to the other House, by which it shall likewise be reconsidered, and if approved by two thirds of that House, it shall become a Law. But in all such Cases the Votes of both Houses shall be determined by Yeas and Nays, and the Names of the Persons voting for and against the Bill shall be entered on the Journal of each House respectively. If any Bill shall not be returned by the President within ten Days (Sundays excepted) after it shall have been presented to him, the Same shall be a Law, in like Manner as if he had signed it, unless the Congress by their Adjournment prevent its Return, in which Case it shall not be a Law.

Every Order, Resolution, or Vote to which the Concurrence of the Senate and House of Representatives may be necessary (except on a question of Adjournment) shall be presented to the President of the United States; and before the Same shall take Effect, shall be approved by him, or being disapproved by him, shall be repassed by two thirds of the Senate and House of Representatives, according to the Rules and Limitations prescribed in the Case of a Bill.

Section 8.

The Congress shall have Power to lay and collect Taxes, Duties, Imposts and Excises, to pay the Debts and provide for the common Defence and general Welfare of the United States; but all Duties, Imposts and Excises shall be uniform throughout the United States;

To borrow Money on the credit of the United States;

To regulate Commerce with foreign Nations, and among the several States, and with the Indian Tribes;

To establish an uniform Rule of Naturalization, and uniform Laws on the subject of Bankruptcies throughout the United States;

To coin Money, regulate the Value thereof, and of foreign Coin, and fix the Standard of Weights and Measures;

To provide for the Punishment of counterfeiting the Securities and current Coin of the United States;

To establish Post Offices and post Roads;

To promote the Progress of Science and useful Arts, by securing for limited Times to Authors and Inventors the exclusive Right to their respective Writings and Discoveries;

To constitute Tribunals inferior to the supreme Court;

To define and punish Piracies and Felonies committed on the high Seas, and Offenses against the Law of Nations;

To declare War, grant Letters of Marque and Reprisal, and make Rules concerning Captures on Land and Water;

To raise and support Armies, but no Appropriation of Money to that Use shall be for a longer Term than two Years;

To provide and maintain a Navy;

To make Rules for the Government and Regulation of the land and naval Forces;

To provide for calling forth the Militia to execute the Laws of the Union, suppress Insurrections and repel Invasions;

To provide for organizing, arming, and disciplining, the Militia, and for governing such Part of them as may be employed in the Service of the United States, reserving to the States respectively, the Appointment of the Officers, and the Authority of training the Militia according to the discipline described by Congress;

To exercise exclusive Legislation in all Cases whatsoever, over such District (not exceeding ten Miles square) as may, by Cession of particular States, and the Acceptance of Congress, become the Seat of the Government of the United States, and to exercise like Authority over all Places purchased by the Consent of the Legislature of the State in which the Same shall be, for the Erection of Forts, Magazines, Arsenals, dock-Yards, and other needful Buildings;—And

To make all Laws which shall be necessary and proper for carrying into Execution the foregoing Powers, and all other Powers vested by this Constitution in the Government of the United States, or in any Department or Officer thereof.

Section 9.

The Migration or Importation of such Persons as any of the States now existing shall think proper to admit, shall not be prohibited by the Congress prior to the Year one thousand eight hundred and eight, but a Tax or Duty may be imposed on such Importation, not exceeding ten dollars for each Person.

The Privilege of the Writ of Habeas Corpus shall not be suspended, unless when in Cases of Rebellion or Invasion the public Safety may require it.

No Bill of Attainder or ex post facto Law shall be passed.

No Capitation, or other direct, Tax shall be laid, unless in Proportion to the Census or Enumeration herein before directed to be taken.

No Tax or Duty shall be laid on Articles exported from any State.

No Preference shall be given by any Regulation of Commerce or Revenue to the Ports of one State over those of another; nor shall Vessels bound to, or from, one State, be obliged to enter, clear, or pay Duties in another.

No Money shall be drawn from the Treasury, but in Consequence of Appropriations made by Laws; and a regular Statement and Account of the Receipts and Expenditures of all public Money shall be published from time to time.

No Title of Nobility shall be granted by the United States: And no Person holding any Office of Profit or Trust under them, shall, without the Consent of the Congress, accept of any present, Emolument, Office, or Title, of any kind whatever, from any King, Prince, or foreign State.

Section 10.

No State shall enter into any Treaty, Alliance, or Confederation; grant Letters of Marque and Reprisal; coin Money; emit Bills of Credit; make any Thing but gold and silver Coin a Tender in Payment of Debts; pass any Bill of Attainder, ex post facto Law, or Law impairing the Obligation of Contracts, or grant any Title of Nobility.

No State shall, without the Consent of the Congress, lay any Imposts or Duties on Imports or Exports, except what may be absolutely necessary for executing its inspection Laws: and the net Produce of all Duties and Imposts, laid by any State on Imports or Exports, shall be for the Use of the Treasury of the United States; and all such Laws shall be subject to the Revision and Controul of the Congress.

No State shall, without the Consent of Congress, lay any Duty of Tonnage, keep Troops, or Ships of War in time of Peace, enter into any Agreement or Compact with another State, or with a foreign Power, or engage in War, unless actually invaded, or in such imminent Danger as will not admit of delay.

ARTICLE II

Section 1.

The executive Power shall be vested in a President of the United States of America. He shall hold his Office during the Term of four Years, and, together with the Vice President, chosen for the same Term, be elected, as follows:

Each State shall appoint, in such Manner as the Legislature thereof may direct, a Number of Electors, equal to the whole Number of Senators and Representatives to which the State may be entitled in the Congress: but no Senator or Representative, or Person holding an Office of Trust or Profit under the United States, shall be appointed an Elector.

The Electors shall meet in their respective States, and vote by Ballot for two Persons, of whom one at least shall not be an Inhabitant of the same State with themselves. And they shall make a list of all the Persons voted for, and of the Number of Votes for each; which List they shall sign and certify, and transmit sealed to the Seat of the Government of the United States, directed to the President of the Senate. The President of the Senate shall, in the presence of the Senate and House of Representatives, open all the Certificates, and the Votes shall be counted. The Person having the greatest Number of Votes shall be the President, if such Number be a Majority of the whole Number of Electors appointed; and if there be more than one who have such Majority, and have an equal Number of Votes, then the House of Representatives shall immediately chuse by Ballot one of them for President; and if no Person have a Majority, then from the five highest on the List the said House shall in like Manner chuse the President. But in chusing the President, the Votes shall be taken by States, the Representation from each State having one Vote; A quorum for this Purpose shall consist of a Member or Members from two thirds of the States, and a Majority of all the States shall be necessary to a Choice. In every Case, after the Choice of the President, the Person having the greatest Number of Votes of the Electors shall be the Vice President. But if there should remain two or more who have equal Votes, the Senate shall chuse from them by Ballot the Vice President.

The Congress may determine the Time of Chusing the Electors, and the Day on which they shall give their Votes; which Day shall be the same throughout the United States.

No Person except a natural born Citizen, or a Citizen of the United States, at the time of the Adoption of this Constitution, shall be eligible to the Office of President; neither shall any Person be eligible to that Office who shall not have attained to the Age of thirty five Years, and been fourteen Years a Resident within the United States.

In Case of the Removal of the President from Office, or of his Death, Resignation, or Inability to discharge the Powers and Duties of the said Office, the Same shall devolve on the Vice President, and the Congress may by Law provide for the Case of Removal, Death, Resignation or Inability, both of the President and Vice President, declaring what Officer shall then act as President, and such Officer shall act accordingly, until the Disability be removed, or a President shall be elected.

The President shall, at stated Times, receive for his Services, a Compensation, which shall neither be increased nor diminished during the Period for which he shall have been elected, and he shall not receive within that Period any other Emolument from the United States, or any of them.

Before he enter on the Execution of his Office, he shall take the following Oath or Affirmation:—"I do solemnly swear (or affirm) that I will faithfully execute the

Office of President of the United States, and will to the best of my Ability, preserve, protect and defend the Constitution of the United States."

Section 2.

The President shall be Commander in Chief of the Army and Navy of the United States, and of the Militia of the several States, when called into the actual Service of the United States; he may require the Opinion, in writing, of the principal Officer in each of the executive Departments, upon any Subject relating to the Duties of their respective Offices, and he shall have Power to grant Reprieves and Pardons for Offenses against the United States, except in Cases of Impeachment.

He shall have Power, by and with the Advice and Consent of the Senate, to make Treaties, providing two thirds of the Senators present concur; and he shall nominate, and by and with the Advice and Consent of the Senate, shall appoint Ambassadors, other public Ministers and Consuls, Judges of the supreme Court, and all other Officers of the United States, whose Appointments are not herein otherwise provided for, and which shall be established by Law: but the Congress may by Law vest the Appointment of such inferior Officers, as they think proper, in the President alone, in the Courts of Law, or in the Heads of Departments.

The President shall have Power to fill up all Vacancies that may happen during the Recess of the Senate, by granting Commissions which shall expire at the End of their next Session.

Section 3.

He shall from time to time give to the Congress Information of the State of the Union, and recommend to their Consideration such Measures as he shall judge necessary and expedient; he may, on extraordinary Occasions, convene both Houses, or either of them, and in Case of Disagreement between them, with Respect to the Time of Adjournment, he may adjourn them to such Time as he shall think proper, he shall receive Ambassadors and other public Ministers; he shall take Care that the Laws be faithfully executed, and shall Commission all the Offices of the United States.

Section 4.

The President, Vice President and all civil Officers of the United States, shall be removed from Office on Impeachment for, and Conviction of, Treason, Bribery, or other high Crimes and Misdemeanors.

ARTICLE III

Section 1.

The judicial Power of the United States, shall be vested in one supreme Court, and in such inferior Courts as the Congress may from time to time ordain and establish. The Judges, both of the supreme and inferior Courts, shall hold their Offices during good Behaviour, and shall, at Times, receive for their Services, a Compensation, which shall not be diminished during their Continuance in Office.

Section 2.

The judicial Power shall extend to all Cases, in Law and Equity, arising under this Constitution, the Laws of the United States, and Treaties made, or which shall be made, under their Authority;—to all Cases affecting Ambassadors, other public Ministers and Consuls;—to all Cases of admiralty and maritime Jurisdiction;—to Controversies to which the United States shall be a Party;—to controversies between two or more States;—between a State and Citizens of another State;—between Citizens of different States;—between Citizens of the same State claiming Lands under Grants of different States; and between a State, or the Citizens thereof, and foreign States, Citizens or Subjects.

In all Cases affecting Ambassadors, other public Ministers and Consuls, and those in which a State shall be Party, the supreme Court shall have original Jurisdiction. In all the other Cases before mentioned, the supreme Court shall have appellate Jurisdiction, both as to Law and Fact, with such Exceptions, and under such Regulations as the Congress shall make.

The Trial of all Crimes, except in Cases of Impeachment, shall be by Jury; and such Trial shall be held in the State where the said Crimes shall have been committed; but when not committed within any State, the Trial shall be at such Place or Places as the Congress may by Law have directed.

Section 3.

Treason against the United States, shall consist only in levying War against them, or in adhering to their Enemies, giving them Aid and Comfort. No Person shall be convicted of Treason unless on the Testimony of two Witnesses to the same overt Act, or on Confession in open Court.

The Congress shall have Power to declare the Punishment of Treason, but no Attainder of Treason shall work Corruption of Blood, or Forfeiture except during the Life of the Person attainted.

ARTICLE IV

Section 1.

Full Faith and Credit shall be given in each State to the public Acts, Records, and judicial Proceedings of every other State. And the Congress may by general Laws prescribe the Manner in which such Acts, Records and Proceedings shall be proved, and the Effect thereof.

Section 2.

The Citizens of each State shall be entitled to all Privileges and Immunities of Citizens in the several States.

A Person charged in any State with Treason, Felony, or other Crime, who shall flee from Justice, and be found in another State, shall on Demand of the executive Authority of the State from which he fled, be delivered up, to be removed to the State having Jurisdiction of the Crime.

No Person held to Service or Labour in one State, under the Laws thereof, escaping into another, shall, in Consequence of any Law or Regulation therein, be discharged from such Service or Labour, but shall be delivered up on Claim of the Party to whom such Service or Labour may be due.

Section 3.

New States may be admitted by the Congress into this Union; but no new State shall be formed or erected within the Jurisdiction of any other State; nor any State be formed by the Junction of two or more States, or Parts of States, without the Consent of the Legislatures of the States concerned as well as the Congress.

The Congress shall have Power to dispose of and make all needful Rules and Regulations respecting the Territory or other Property belonging to the United States; and nothing in this Constitution shall be so construed as to Prejudice any Claims of the United States, or of any particular State.

Section 4.

The United States shall guarantee to every State in this Union a Republican Form of Government, and shall protect each of them against Invasion; and on Application of the Legislature, or of the Executive (when the Legislature cannot be convened) against domestic Violence.

ARTICLE V

The Congress, whenever two thirds of both Houses shall deem it necessary, shall propose Amendments to this Constitution, or, on the Application of the Legislatures of two thirds of the several States, shall call a Convention for proposing Amendments, which, in either Case, shall be valid to all Intents and Purposes, as Part of this Constitution, when ratified by the Legislatures of three fourths of the several States, or by Conventions in three fourths thereof, as the one or the other Mode of Ratification may be proposed by the Congress; Provided that no Amendment which may be made prior to the Year One thousand eight hundred and eight shall in any Manner affect the first and fourth Clauses in the Ninth Section of the first Article; and that no State, without its Consent, shall be deprived of its equal Suffrage in the Senate.

ARTICLE VI

All Debts contracted and Engagements entered into, before the Adoption of this Constitution, shall be as valid against the United States under this Constitution, as under the Confederation.

This Constitution, and the Laws of the United States which shall be made in Pursuance thereof; and all Treaties made, or which shall be made, under the Authority of the United States, shall be the supreme Law of the Land; and the Judges in every State shall be bound thereby, any Thing in the Constitution or Laws of any State to the Contrary notwithstanding.

The Senators and Representatives before mentioned, and the Members of the several State Legislatures, and all executive and judicial Officers, both of the United States and of the Several States, shall be bound by Oath or Affirmation, to support this Constitution; but no religious Test shall ever be required as a Qualification to any Office or public Trust under the United States.

ARTICLE VII

The Ratification of the Conventions of nine States, shall be sufficient for the Establishment of this Constitution between the States so ratifying the Same.

Amendment I [1791].

Congress shall make no law respecting an establishment of religion, or prohibiting the free exercise thereof; or abridging the freedom of speech, or the press; or the right of the people peaceably to assemble, and to petition the Government for a redress of grievances.

Amendment II [1791].

A well regulated Militia, being necessary to the security for a free State, the right of the people to keep and bear Arms, shall not be infringed.

Amendment III [1791].

No Soldier shall, in time of peace be quartered in any house, without the consent of the Owner, nor in time of war, but in a manner to be prescribed by law.

Amendment IV [1791].

The right of the people to be secure in their persons, houses, papers, and effects, against unreasonable searches and seizures, shall not be violated, and no Warrants shall issue, but upon probable cause, supported by Oath or Affirmation, and particularly describing the place to be searched, and the persons or things to be seized.

Amendment V [1791].

No person shall be held to answer for a capital, or otherwise infamous crime, unless on a presentment or indictment of a Grand Jury, except in cases arising in the land or naval forces, or in the Militia, when in actual service in time of War or public danger; nor shall any person be subject for the same offense to be twice put in jeopardy of life or limb; nor shall be compelled in any criminal case to be a witness against himself, nor be deprived of life, liberty, or property, without due process of law; nor shall private property be taken for public use, without just compensation.

Amendment VI [1791].

In all criminal prosecutions, the accused shall enjoy the right to a speedy and public trial, by an impartial jury of the State and district wherein the crime shall have been committed, which district shall have been previously ascertained by law, and to be informed of the nature and cause of the accusation; to be confronted with the Witnesses against him; to have compulsory process for obtaining witnesses in his favor, and to have the Assistance of counsel for his defence.

Amendment VII [1791].

In suits at common law, where the value in controversy shall exceed twenty dollars, the right of trial by jury shall be preserved, and no fact tried by a jury, shall be otherwise re-examined in any Court of the United States, than according to the rules of the common law.

Amendment VIII [1791].

Excessive bail shall not be required, no excessive fines imposed, nor cruel and unusual punishments inflicted.

Amendment IX [1791].

The enumeration in the Constitution, of certain rights, shall not be construed to deny or disparage others retained by the people.

Amendment X [1791].

The powers not delegated to the United States by the Constitution, nor prohibited by it to the States, are reserved to the States respectively, or to the people.

Amendment XI [1798].

The judicial power of the United States shall not be construed to extend to any suit in law or equity, commenced or prosecuted against one of the United States by Citizens of another State, or by Citizens or Subjects of any Foreign State.

Amendment XII [1804].

The Electors shall meet in their respective states and vote by ballot for President and Vice-President, one of whom, at least, shall not be an inhabitant of the same state with themselves; they shall name in their ballots the person voted for as President, and in distinct ballots the person voted for as Vice-President, and they shall make distinct lists of all persons voted for as President, and of all persons voted for as Vice-President, and of the number of votes for each, which lists they shall sign and certify, and transmit sealed to the seat of the government of the United States, directed to the President of the Senate;—The President of the Senate shall, in the presence of the Senate and House of Representatives, open all the certificates and the votes shall then be counted;—The person having the greatest number of votes for President, shall be the President, if such number be a majority of the whole number of Electors appointed; and if no person have such majority, then from the persons having the highest numbers not exceeding three on the list of those voted for as President, the House of Representatives shall choose immediately, by ballot, the President. But in choosing the President, the votes shall be taken by states, the representation from each state having one vote; a quorum for this purpose shall consist of a member or members from two-thirds of the states, and a majority of all the states shall be necessary to a choice. And if the House of Representatives shall not choose a President whenever the right of choice shall devolve upon them, before the fourth day of March next following, then the Vice-President shall act as President, as in the case of the death or other constitutional disability of the President. The person having the greatest number of votes as Vice-President, shall be the Vice-President, if such number be a majority of the whole number of Electors appointed, and if no person have a majority, then from the two highest numbers on the list, the Senate shall choose the Vice-President; a quorum for the purpose shall consist of two-thirds of the whole number of Senators, and a majority of the whole number shall be necessary to a choice. But no person constitutionally ineligible to the office of President shall be eligible to that of the Vice-President of the United States.

Amendment XIII [1865].

Section 1. Neither slavery nor involuntary servitude, except as a punishment for crime whereof the party shall have been duly convicted, shall exist within the United States, or any place subject to their jurisdiction.

Section 2. Congress shall have power to enforce this article by appropriate legislation.

Amendment XIV [1868].

Section 1. All persons born or naturalized in the United States, and subject to the jurisdiction thereof, are citizens of the United States and of the State wherein they reside. No State shall make or enforce any law which shall abridge the privileges or immunities of citizens of the United States; nor shall any State deprive any person of life, liberty, or property, without due process of law; nor deny to any person within its jurisdiction the equal protection of the laws.

Section 2. Representatives shall be appointed among the several States according to their respective numbers, counting the whole number of persons in each State, excluding Indians not taxed. But when the right to vote at any election for the choice of electors for President and Vice President of the United States, Representatives in Congress, the Executive and Judicial officers of a State, or the members of the Legislature thereof, is denied to any of the male inhabitants of such State, being twenty-one years of age, and citizens of the United States, or in any way abridged, except for participation in rebellion, or other crime, the basis of representation therein shall be reduced in the proportion which the number of such male citizens shall bear the whole number of male citizens twenty-one years of age in such State.

Section 3. No person shall be a Senator or Representative in Congress, or elector of President and Vice President, or hold any office, civil or military, under the United States, or under any State, who, having previously taken an oath, as a member of Congress, or as an officer of the United States, or as a member of any State legislature, or as an executive or judicial officer of any State, to support the Constitution of the United States, shall have engaged in insurrection or rebellion against the same, or given aid or comfort to the enemies thereof. But Congress may by a vote of two-thirds of each House, remove such disability.

Section 4. The validity of the public debt of the United States, authorized by law, including debts incurred for payment of pensions and bounties for services in suppressing insurrection or rebellion, shall not be questioned. But neither the United States nor any State shall assume or pay any debt or obligation incurred in aid of insurrection of rebellion against the United States, or any claim for the loss or emancipation of any slave; but all such debts, obligations and claims shall be held illegal and void.

Section 5. The Congress shall have power to enforce, by appropriate legislation, the provisions of this article.

Amendment XV [1870].

Section 1. The right of citizens of the United States to vote shall not be denied or abridged by the United States or by any State on account of race, color, or previous condition of servitude.

Section 2. The Congress shall have power to enforce this article by appropriate legislation.

Amendment XVI [1913].

The Congress shall have power to lay and collect taxes on incomes, from whatever source derived, without apportionment among the several States, and without regard to any census or enumeration.

Amendment XVII [1913].

The Senate of the United States shall be composed of two Senators from each State, elected by the people thereof, for six years; and each Senator shall have one vote. The electors in each State shall have the qualifications requisite for electors of the most numerous branch of the State legislatures.

When vacancies happen in the representation of any State in the Senate, the executive authority of each State shall issue writs of election to fill such vacancies; *Provided,* That the legislature of any State may empower the executive thereof to make temporary appointments until the people fill the vacancies by election as the legislature may direct.

This amendment shall not be construed as to affect the election or term of any Senator chosen before it becomes valid as part of the Constitution.

Amendment XVIII [1919].

Section 1. After one year from the ratification of this article the manufacture, sale, or transportation of intoxicating liquors within, the importation thereof into, or the exportation thereof from the United States and all territory subject to the jurisdiction thereof for beverage purposes is hereby prohibited.

Section 2. The Congress and the several States shall have concurrent power to enforce this article by appropriate legislation.

Section 3. This article shall be inoperative unless it shall have been ratified as an amendment to the Constitution by the legislatures of the several States, as provided in the Constitution, within seven years from the date of the submission hereof to the States by the Congress.

Amendment XIX [1920].

The right of citizens of the United States to vote shall not be denied or abridged by the United States or by any State on account of sex.

Congress shall have power to enforce this article by appropriate legislation.

Amendment XX [1933].

Section 1. The terms of the President and Vice President shall end at noon on the 20th day of January, and the terms of Senators and Representatives at noon on the 3d day of January, of the years in which such terms would have ended if this article had not been ratified; and the terms of their successors shall then begin.

Section 2. The Congress shall assemble at least once in every year, and such meeting shall begin at noon on the 3d day of January, unless they shall by law appoint a different day.

Section 3. If, at the time fixed for the beginning of the term of the President, the President elect shall have died, the Vice President elect shall become President. If a President shall not have been chosen before the time fixed for the beginning of his term, or if the President elect shall have failed to qualify, then the Vice President elect shall act as President until a President shall have qualified; and the Congress may by law provide for the case wherein neither a President elect nor a Vice President elect shall have qualified, declaring who shall then act as President, or the manner in which one who is to act shall be selected, and such person shall act accordingly until a President or Vice President shall have qualified.

Section 4. The Congress may by law provide for the case of the death of any of the persons from whom the House of Representatives may choose a President whenever the right of choice shall have devolved upon them, and for the case of the death of any of the persons from whom the Senate may choose a Vice President whenever the right of choice shall have devolved upon them.

Section 5. Sections 1 and 2 shall take effect on the 15th day of October following the ratification of this article.

Section 6. This article shall be inoperative unless it shall have been ratified as an amendment to the Constitution by the legislatures of three-fourths of the several States within seven years from the date of its submission.

Amendment XXI [1933].

Section 1. The eighteenth article of amendment to the Constitution of the United States is hereby repealed.

Section 2. The transportation or importation into any State, Territory, or possession of the United States for delivery or use therein of intoxicating liquors, in violation of the laws thereof, is hereby prohibited.

Section 3. This article shall be inoperative unless it shall have been ratified as an amendment to the Constitution by conventions in the several States, as provided in the Constitution, within seven years from the date of the submission hereof to the States by the Congress.

Amendment XXII [1951].

Section 1. No person shall be elected to the office of the President more than twice, and no person who has held the office of President, or acted as President, for more than two years of a term to which some other person was elected President shall be elected to the office of the President more than once. But this Article shall not apply to any person holding the office of President when this Article was proposed by the Congress, and shall not prevent any person who may be holding the office of President, or acting as President, during the term within which this Article becomes operative from holding the office of President, or acting as President during the remainder of such term.

Section 2. This article shall be inoperative unless it shall have been ratified as an amendment to the Constitution by the legislatures of three-fourths of the several States within seven years from the date of its submission to the States by the Congress.

Amendment XXIII [1961].

Section 1. The District constituting the seat of Government of the United States shall appoint in such manner as the Congress may direct:

A number of electors of President and Vice President equal to the whole number of Senators and Representatives in Congress to which the District would be entitled if it were a State, but in no event more than the least populous State; they shall be in addition to those appointed by the States, but they shall be considered, for the purposes of the election of President and Vice President, to be electors appointed by a State; and they shall meet in the District and perform such duties as provided by the twelfth article of amendment.

Section 2. The Congress shall have power to enforce this article by appropriate legislation.

Amendment XXIV [1964].

Section 1. The right of citizens of the United States to vote in any primary or other election for President or Vice President, for electors for President or Vice President, or for Senator or Representative in Congress, shall not be denied or abridged by the United States or any State by reason of failure to pay any poll tax or other tax.

Section 2. The Congress shall have power to enforce this article by appropriate legislation.

Amendment XXV [1967].

Section 1. In case of the removal of the President from office or of his death or resignation, the Vice President shall become President.

Section 2. Whenever there is a vacancy in the office of the Vice President, the President shall nominate a Vice President who shall take office upon confirmation by a majority vote of both Houses of Congress.

Section 3. Whenever the President transmits to the President pro tempore of the Senate and the Speaker of the House of Representatives his written declaration that he is unable to discharge the powers and duties of his office, and until he transmits to them a written declaration to the contrary, such powers and duties shall be discharged by the Vice President as Acting President.

Section 4. Whenever the Vice President and a majority of either the principal officers of the executive departments or of such other body as Congress may by law provide, transmit to the President pro tempore of the Senate and the Speaker of the House of Representatives their written declaration that the President is unable to discharge the powers and duties of his office, the Vice President shall immediately assume the powers and duties of the office as Acting President.

Thereafter, when the President transmits to the President pro tempore of the Senate and the Speaker of the House of Representatives his written declaration that no inability exists, he shall resume the powers and duties of his office unless the Vice President and a majority of either the principal officers of the executive department or of such other body as Congress may by law provide, transmit within four days to the President pro tempore of the Senate and the Speaker of the House of Representatives their written declaration that the President is unable to discharge the powers and duties of his office. Thereupon Congress shall decide the issue, assembling within forty-eight hours for that purpose if not in session. If the Congress, within twenty-one days after receipt of the latter written declaration, or, if Congress is not in session, within twenty-one days after Congress is required to assemble, determines by two-thirds vote of both Houses that the President is unable to discharge the powers and duties of his office, the Vice President shall continue to discharge the same as Acting President; otherwise, the President shall resume the powers and duties of his office.

Amendment XXVI [1971].

Section 1. The right of citizens of the United States, who are eighteen years of age or older, to vote shall not be denied or abridged by the United States or by any State on account of age.

Section 2. The Congress shall have power to enforce this article by appropriate legislation.

Amendment XXVII [1992].

No law, varying the compensation for the services of the Senators and Representatives, shall take effect, until an election of Representatives shall have intervened.

APPENDIX
B

Uniform Commercial Code

The Uniform Commercial Code can be found at
http://www.nccusl.org/Update/ or **http://www.law.cornell.edu/**

Glossary

A

Accepted check A check that the drawee bank has signed. This signature is a promise that the bank will pay the check out of its own funds. (Chapter 24)

Accession The use of labor and/or materials to add value to the personal property of another. (Chapter 44)

Accommodation party Someone who does not benefit from an instrument but agrees to guarantee its payment. (Chapter 24)

Accord and satisfaction An agreement to settle a debt for less than the sum claimed. (Chapter 11)

Accounts Any right to receive payment for goods sold or leased, other than rights covered by chattel paper or instruments. (Chapter 26)

Accredited investor Under the Securities Act of 1933, an accredited investor is an institution (such as a bank or insurance company) or any individual with a net worth of more than $1 million or an annual income of more than $200,000. (Chapter 37)

Acquit To find the defendant not guilty of the crime for which he was tried. (Chapter 7)

Act of State doctrine A rule requiring American courts to abstain from cases if a court order would interfere with the ability of the President or Congress to conduct foreign policy. (Chapter 8)

Actus reus The guilty act. The prosecution must show that a criminal defendant committed some proscribed act. In a murder prosecution, taking another person's life is the *actus reus.* (Chapter 7)

Adhesion contract A standard form contract prepared by one party and presented to the other on a "take it or leave it" basis. (Chapter 12)

Adjudicate To hold a formal hearing in a disputed matter and issue an official decision. (Chapter 4)

Administrative law Concerns all agencies, boards, commissions, and other entities created by a federal or state legislature and charged with investigating, regulating, and adjudicating a particular industry or issue. (Chapter 1)

Administrator A person appointed by the court to oversee the probate process for someone who has died intestate (that is, without a will). (Chapter 45)

Administratrix A female administrator. (Chapter 45)

Adverse possession A means of gaining ownership of land belonging to another by entering upon the property, openly and notoriously, and claiming exclusive use of it for a period of years. (Chapter 42)

Affidavit A written statement signed under oath. (Chapter 7)

Affirm A decision by an appellate court to uphold the judgment of a lower court. (Chapter 1)

Affirmative action A plan introduced in a workplace for the purpose of either remedying the effects of past discrimination or achieving equitable representation of minorities and women. (Chapter 30)

After-acquired property Items that a debtor obtains after making a security agreement with the secured party. (Chapter 26)

Agent A person who acts for a principal. (Chapter 7)

Alternative dispute resolution Any method of resolving a legal conflict other than litigation, such as: negotiation, arbitration, mediation, mini-trials, and summary jury trials. (Chapter 3)

Amendment Any addition to a legal document. The constitutional amendments, the first ten of which are known collectively as the Bill of Rights, secure numerous liberties and protections directly for the people. (Chapter 1)

Annual report Each year, public companies must send their shareholders an annual report that contains detailed financial data. (Chapter 36)

Answer The pleading, filed by the defendant in court and served on the plaintiff, which responds to each allegation in the plaintiff's complaint. (Chapter 3)

Apparent authority A situation in which conduct of a principal causes a third party to believe that the principal consents to have an act done on his behalf by a person purporting to act for him when, in fact, that person is not acting for the principal. (Chapter 29)

Appellant   The party who appeals a lower court decision to a higher court. (Chapter 3)

Appellate court   Any court in a state or federal system that reviews cases that have already been tried. (Chapter 3)

Appellee   The party opposing an appeal from a lower court to a higher court. (Chapter 3)

Arbitration   A form of alternative dispute resolution in which the parties hire a neutral third party to hear their respective arguments, receive evidence, and then make a binding decision. (Chapter 3)

Arson   Malicious use of fire or explosives to damage or destroy real estate or personal property. (Chapter 7)

Assault   An intentional act that causes the plaintiff to fear an imminent battery. (Chapter 5)

Assignee   The party who receives an assignment of contract rights from a party to the contract. (Chapter 15)

Assignment   The act by which a party transfers contract rights to a third person. (Chapter 15)

Assignor   The party who assigns contract rights to a third person. (Chapter 15)

Attachment   A court order seizing property of a party to a civil action, so that there will be sufficient assets available to pay the judgment. (Chapter 4)

Authorized and unissued stock   Stock that has been approved by the corporation's charter, but has not yet been sold. (Chapter 34)

Authorized and issued stock   Stock that has been approved by the corporation's charter and subsequently sold. (Chapter 34)

B

Bailee   A person who rightfully possesses goods belonging to another. (Chapter 12)

Bailment   Giving possession and control of personal property to another person. (Chapter 12)

Bailor   One who creates a bailment by delivering goods to another. (Chapter 12)

Battery   The intentional touching of another person in a way that is unwanted or offensive. (Chapter 5)

Bearer paper   An instrument payable "to bearer." Any holder in due course can demand payment. (Chapter 22)

Bilateral contract   A binding agreement in which each party has made a promise to the other. (Chapter 9)

Bill of lading   A receipt for goods, given by a carrier such as a ship, that minutely describes the merchandise being shipped. A **negotiable** bill of lading may be transferred to other parties, and entitles any holder to collect the goods. (Chapter 8)

Bill of Rights   The first ten amendments to the Constitution. (Chapter 4)

Bill   A proposed statute that has been submitted for consideration to Congress or a state legislature. (Chapter 4)

Blue sky laws   State securities laws. (Chapter 37)

Bona fide occupational qualification   A job requirement that would otherwise be discriminatory is permitted in situations in which it is *essential* to the position in question. (Chapter 30)

Bona fide purchaser   Someone who buys goods in good faith, for value, typically from a seller who has merely voidable title. (Chapter 19)

Bonds   Long-term debt secured by some of the issuing company's assets. (Chapter 34)

Brief   The written legal argument that an attorney files with an appeal court. (Chapter 3)

Bulk sale   A transfer of most or all of a merchant's assets. (Chapter 19)

Burden of proof   The allocation of which party must prove its case. In a civil case, the plaintiff has the burden of proof to persuade the factfinder of every element of her case. In a criminal case, the government has the burden of proof. (Chapter 3)

Business judgment rule   A common law rule that protects managers from liability if they are acting without a conflict of interest, and make informed decisions that have a rational business purpose. (Chapter 35)

Buyer in ordinary course of business   Someone who buys goods in good faith from a seller who routinely deals in such goods. (Chapter 26)

Bylaws   A document that specifies the organizational rules of a corporation or other organization, such as the date of the annual meeting and the required number of directors. (Chapter 34)

C

Capacity   The legal ability to enter into a contract. (Chapter 9)

Certificate of deposit   An instrument issued by a bank which promises to repay a deposit, with interest, on a specified date. (Chapter 22)

Certified check A check that the drawee bank has signed. This signature is a promise that the bank will pay the check out of its own funds. (Chapter 24)

Certiorari, writ of Formal notice from the United States Supreme Court that it will accept a case for review. (Chapter 3)

Challenge for cause An attorney's request, during *voir dire,* to excuse a prospective juror because of apparent bias. (Chapter 3)

Chancery, court of In medieval England, the court originally operated by the Chancellor. (Chapter 1)

Charging order A court order granting the creditor of a partner the right to receive that partner's share of partnership profits. (Chapter 33)

Chattel paper Any writing that indicates two things: (1) a debtor owes money and (2) a secured party has a security interest in specific goods. The most common chattel paper is a document indicating a consumer sale on credit. (Chapter 26)

Check An instrument in which the drawer orders the drawee bank to pay money to the payee. (Chapter 22)

Chicago School A theory of antitrust law first developed at the University of Chicago. Adherents to this theory believe that antitrust enforcement should focus on promoting efficiency and should not generally be concerned about the size or number of competitors in any market. (Chapter 37)

CISG See Convention on Contracts for the International Sale of Goods. (Chapter 10)

Civil law The large body of law concerning the rights and duties between parties. It is distinguished from criminal law, which concerns behavior outlawed by a government. (Chapter 1)

Class action A method of litigating a civil lawsuit in which one or more plaintiffs (or occasionally defendants) seek to represent an entire group of people with similar claims against a common opponent. (Chapter 3)

Classification The process by which the Customs Service decides what label to attach to imported merchandise, and therefore what level of tariff to impose. (Chapter 8)

Close corporation A corporation with a small number of shareholders. Its stock is not publicly traded. (Chapter 33)

Codicil An amendment to a will. (Chapter 45)

Collateral The property subject to a security interest. (Chapter 26)

Collateral promises A promise to pay the debt of another person, as a favor to the debtor. (Chapter 14)

Collective bargaining Contract negotiations between an employer and a union. (Chapter 32)

Collective bargaining unit The precisely defined group of employees who are represented by a particular union. (Chapter 32)

Comity A doctrine that requires a court to abstain from hearing a case out of respect for another court that also has jurisdiction. **International comity** demands that an American court refuse to hear a case in which a foreign court shares jurisdiction if there is a conflict between the laws and if it is more logical for the foreign court to take the case. (Chapter 8)

Commerce clause One of the powers granted by Article I, §8 of the Constitution, it gives Congress exclusive power to regulate international commerce and concurrent power with the states to regulate domestic commerce. (Chapter 4)

Commercial impracticability After the creation of a contract, an entirely unforeseen event occurs which makes enforcement of the contract extraordinarily unfair. (Chapter 16)

Commercial paper Instruments such as checks and promissory notes that contain a promise to pay money. Commercial paper includes both negotiable and non-negotiable instruments. (Chapter 22)

Commercial speech Communication, such as television advertisements, that has the dominant theme of proposing a commercial transaction. (Chapter 4)

Common carrier A transportation company that makes its services available on a regular basis to the general public. (Chapter 44)

Common law Judge-made law, that is, the body of all decisions made by appellate courts over the years. (Chapter 1)

Common stock Certificates that reflect ownership in a corporation. Owners of this equity security are last in line for corporate pay-outs such as dividends and liquidation proceeds. (Chapter 34)

Comparative negligence A rule of tort law that permits a plaintiff to recover even when the defendant can show that the plaintiff's own conduct contributed in some way to her harm. (Chapter 6)

Compensatory damages Those that flow directly from the contract. (Chapter 17)

Complaint A pleading, filed by the plaintiff, providing a short statement of the claim. (Chapter 3)

Concerted action Tactics, such as a strike, used by a union to gain a bargaining advantage. (Chapter 32)

Condition A condition is an event that must occur in order for a party to be obligated under a contract. (Chapter 16)

Condition precedent A condition that must occur before a particular contract duty arises. (Chapter 16)

Condition subsequent A condition that must occur after a particular contract duty arises, or the duty will be discharged. (Chapter 16)

Confiscation Expropriation without adequate compensation of property owned by foreigners. (Chapter 8)

Conforming goods Items that satisfy the contract terms. If a contract calls for blue sailboats, then green sailboats are non-conforming. (Chapter 21)

Consent order An agreement entered into by a wrongdoer and an administrative agency (such as the Securities and Exchange Commission or the Federal Trade Commission) in which the wrongdoer agrees not to violate the law in the future. (Chapter 39)

Consequential damages Those resulting from the unique circumstances of *this injured party*. (Chapter 17)

Consideration In contract law, something of legal value that has been bargained for and given in exchange by the parties. (Chapter 11)

Constitution The supreme law of a political entity. The United States Constitution is the highest law in the country. (Chapter 1)

Contract A legally enforceable promise or set of promises. (Chapter 9)

Contract carrier A transportation company that does not make its services available to the general public but engages in continuing agreements with particular customers. (Chapter 44)

Contributory negligence A rule of tort law that permits a negligent defendant to escape liability if she can demonstrate that the plaintiff's own conduct contributed in any way to the plaintiff's harm. (Chapter 6)

Control security Stock owned by any officer or director of the issuer, or by any shareholder who holds more than 10 percent of a class of stock of the issuer. (Chapter 37)

Convention on Contracts for the International Sale of Goods A United Nations sponsored agreement that creates a neutral body of law for sale of goods contracts between companies from different countries. (Chapter 10)

Conversion A tort committed by taking or using someone else's personal property without his permission. (Chapter 5)

Cookie A small computer file that identifies the user of a computer. Internet sites typically place cookies on a computer's hard drive to track visitors to their site. (Chapter 40)

Copyright Under federal law, the holder of a copyright owns a particular expression of an idea, but not the idea itself. This ownership right applies to creative activities such as literature, music, drama, and software. (Chapter 41)

Corporation by estoppel Even if a corporation has not actually been formed, courts will sometimes enforce contracts entered into in the belief that the corporation did indeed exist. (Chapter 34)

Counter-claim A claim made by the defendant against the plaintiff. (Chapter 3)

Cover The buyer's right to obtain substitute goods when a seller has breached a contract. (Chapter 3)

Creditor beneficiary When one party to a contract intends to benefit a third party to whom he owes a debt, that third party is referred to as a creditor beneficiary. (Chapter 15)

Criminal law Rules that permit a government to punish certain behavior by fine or imprisonment. (Chapter 1)

Cross-examination During a hearing, for a lawyer to question an opposing witness. (Chapter 3)

Cure The seller's right to respond to a buyer's rejection of non-conforming goods; the seller accomplishes this by delivering conforming goods before the contract deadline. (Chapter 21)

D

Damages (1) The harm that a plaintiff complains of at trial, such as an injury to her person, or money lost because of a contract breach. (2) Money awarded by a trial court for injury suffered. (Chapter 5)

De facto corporation Occurs when a promoter makes a good faith effort to incorporate (although fails to complete the process entirely) and uses the corporation to conduct business. The state can challenge the validity of the corporation, but a third party cannot. (Chapter 34)

De jure corporation The promoter of the corporation has substantially complied with the requirements for incorporation, but has made some minor error. No one has the right to challenge the validity of the corporation. (Chapter 34)

De novo The power of an appellate court or appellate agency to make a new decision in a matter under appeal, entirely ignoring the findings and conclusions of the lower court or agency official. (Chapter 4)

Debentures Long-term, unsecured debt, typically issued by a corporation. (Chapter 34)

Debtor A person who owes money or some other obligation to another party. (Chapter 26)

Decedent A person who has died. (Chapter 45)

Defamation The act of injuring someone's reputation by stating something false about her to a third person. *Libel* is defamation done either in writing or by broadcast. *Slander* is defamation done orally. (Chapter 5)

Default The failure to perform an obligation, such as the failure to pay money when due. (Chapter 26)

Default judgment Court order awarding one party everything it requested because the opposing party failed to respond in time. (Chapter 3)

Default rules Under the Uniform Partnership Act, these rules govern the relationship among the partners unless the partners explicitly make a different agreement. (Chapter 33)

Definiteness A doctrine holding that a contract will only be enforced if its terms are sufficiently precise that a court can determine what the parties meant. (Chapter 10)

Delegation The act by which a party to a contract transfers duties to a third person who is not a party to the contract. (Chapter 15)

Deponent The person being questioned in a deposition. (Chapter 3)

Deposition A form of discovery in which a party's attorney has the right to ask oral questions of the other party or of a witness. Answers are given under oath. (Chapter 3)

Derivative action A lawsuit brought by shareholders in the name of the corporation to enforce a right of the corporation. (Chapter 36)

Deterrence Using punishment, such as imprisonment, to discourage criminal behavior. (Chapter 7)

Devisee Someone who inherits under a will. (Chapter 45)

Direct examination During a hearing, for a lawyer to question his own witness. (Chapter 3)

Directed verdict The decision by a court to instruct a jury that it must find in favor of a particular party because, in the judge's opinion, no reasonable person could disagree on the outcome. (Chapter 3)

Disaffirmance The act of notifying the other party to a contract that the party giving the notice refuses to be bound by the agreement. (Chapter 13)

Discharge (1) A party to a contract has no more duties. (2) A party to an instrument is released from liability. (Chapter 16)

Disclaimer A statement that a particular warranty does not apply. (Chapter 20)

Discovery A stage in litigation, after all pleadings have been served, in which each party seeks as much relevant information as possible about the opposing party's case. (Chapter 3)

Dishonor An obligor refuses to pay an instrument that is due. (Chapter 24)

Dismiss To terminate a lawsuit, often on procedural grounds, without reaching the merits of the case. (Chapter 3)

Dissociation A dissociation occurs when a partner leaves a partnership. (Chapter 33)

Diversity jurisdiction One of the two main types of civil cases that a United States district court has the power to hear. It involves a lawsuit between citizens of different states, in which at least one party makes a claim for more than $75,000. (Chapter 3)

Domestic corporation A corporation is a domestic corporation in the state in which it was formed. (Chapter 34)

Donee A person who receives a gift. (Chapter 44)

Donee beneficiary When one party to a contract intends to make a gift to a third party, that third party is referred to as a donee beneficiary. (Chapter 15)

Donor A person who makes a gift to another. (Chapter 44)

Draft The drawer of this instrument orders someone else to pay money. Checks are the most common form of draft. The drawer of a check orders a bank to pay money. (Chapter 22)

Drawee The person who pays a draft. In the case of a check, the bank is the drawee. (Chapter 22)

Drawer The person who issues a draft. (Chapter 22)

Due Process Clause Part of the Fifth Amendment. *Procedural due process* ensures that before depriving anyone of liberty or property, the government must go through procedures which ensure that the deprivation is fair. *Substantive due process* holds that certain rights, such as privacy, are so fundamental that the government may not eliminate them. (Chapter 4)

Dumping Selling merchandise at one price in the domestic market and at a cheaper, unfair price in an international market. (Chapter 8)

Durable power of attorney An instrument that permits an attorney-in-fact to act for a principal. A durable power is effective until the principal revokes it or dies. It continues in effect even if the principal becomes incapacitated. (Chapter 45)

Duress (1) A criminal defense in which the defendant shows that she committed the wrongful act because a third person threatened her with imminent physical harm. (2) An improper threat made to force another party to enter into a contract. (Chapter 7)

Duty A tax imposed on imported items. (Chapter 8)

E

Easement The right to enter land belonging to another and make a limited use of it, without taking anything away. (Chapter 42)

Economic loss doctrine A common law rule holding that when an injury is purely economic, and arises from a contract made between two businesses, the injured party may only sue under the UCC. (Chapter 20)

Element A fact that a party to a lawsuit must prove in order to prevail. (Chapter 5)

Embezzlement Fraudulent conversion of property already in the defendant's possession. (Chapter 7)

Eminent domain The power of the government to take private property for public use. (Chapter 4)

Employee at will A worker whose job does not have a specified duration. (Chapter 30)

Enabling legislation A statute authorizing the creation of a new administrative agency and specifying its powers and duties. (Chapter 4)

Entrapment A criminal defense in which the defendant demonstrates that the government induced him to break the law. (Chapter 7)

Equal Protection Clause Part of the Fourteenth Amendment, it generally requires the government to treat equally situated people the same. (Chapter 4)

Equity The broad powers of a court to fashion a remedy where justice demands it and no common law remedy exists. An injunction is an example of an equitable remedy. (Chapter 1)

Error of law A mistake made by a trial judge that concerns a legal issue as opposed to a factual matter. Permitting too many leading questions is a legal error; choosing to believe one witness rather than another is a factual matter. (Chapter 3)

Estate The legal entity that holds title to assets after the owner dies and before the property is distributed. (Chapter 45)

Estoppel Out of fairness, a person is denied the right to assert a claim. (Chapter 29)

Evidence, rules of Law governing the proof offered during a trial or formal hearing. These rules limit the questions that may be asked of witnesses and the introduction of physical objects. (Chapter 3)

Exclusionary rule In a criminal trial, a ban on the use of evidence obtained in violation of the Constitution. (Chapter 7)

Exclusive dealing agreement A potential violation of §1 of the Sherman Act, in which a distributor or retailer agrees with a supplier not to carry the products of any other supplier. (Chapter 37)

Exculpatory clause A contract provision that attempts to release one party from liability in the event the other party is injured. (Chapter 12)

Executed contract A binding agreement in which all parties have fulfilled all obligations. (Chapter 9)

Executive agency An administrative agency within the executive branch of government. (Chapter 4)

Executive order An order by a president or governor, having the full force of law. (Chapter 1)

Executor A person chosen by the decedent to oversee the probate process. (Chapter 14)

Executory contract A binding agreement in which one or more of the parties has not fulfilled its obligations. (Chapter 9)

Executrix A female executor. (Chapter 45)

Exhaustion of remedies A principle of administrative law that no party may appeal an agency action to a court until she has utilized all available appeals within the agency itself. (Chapter 4)

Expectation interest A remedy in a contract case that puts the injured party in the position he would have been in had both sides fully performed. (Chapter 17)

Expert witness A witness in a court case who has special training or qualifications to discuss a specific issue, and who is generally permitted to state an opinion. (Chapter 3)

Export   To transport goods or services out of a country. (Chapter 8)

Express authority   Conduct of a principal that, reasonably interpreted, causes the agent to believe that the principal desires him to do a specific act. (Chapter 29)

Express contract   A binding agreement in which the parties explicitly state all important terms. (Chapter 9)

Express warranty   A guarantee, created by the words or actions of the seller, that goods will meet certain standards. (Chapter 20)

Expropriation   A government's seizure of property or companies owned by foreigners. (Chapter 8)

F

Factfinder   The one responsible, during a trial, for deciding what occurred, that is, who did what to whom, when, how, and why. It is either the jury or, in a jury-waived case, the judge. (Chapter 4)

Fair representation, duty of   The union's obligation to act on behalf of all members impartially and in good faith. (Chapter 32)

False imprisonment   The intentional restraint of another person without reasonable cause and without her consent. (Chapter 5)

Federal question jurisdiction   One of the two main types of civil cases that a United States district court has the power to hear. It involves a federal statute or a constitutional provision. (Chapter 3)

Federalism   A form of national government in which power is shared between one central authority and numerous local authorities. (Chapter 1)

Fee simple absolute   The greatest possible ownership right in real property, including the right to possess, use, and dispose of the property in any lawful manner. (Chapter 42)

Fee simple defeasible   Ownership interest in real property that may terminate upon the occurrence of some limiting event. (Chapter 42)

Felony   The most serious crimes, typically those for which the defendant could be imprisoned for more than a year. (Chapter 7)

Fiduciary duty   An obligation to behave in a trustworthy and confidential fashion toward the object of that duty. (Chapter 28)

Financing statement   A document that a secured party files to give the general public notice that the secured party has a secured interest in the collateral. (Chapter 26)

Firm offer   A contract offer that cannot be withdrawn during a stated period. (Chapter 10)

Fixtures   Goods that are attached to real estate. (Chapter 26)

Foreign corporation   A corporation formed in another state. (Chapter 34)

Foreign Sovereign Immunity Act   A federal statute that protects other nations from suit in courts of the United States, except under specified circumstances. (Chapter 8)

Formal rulemaking   The process whereby an administrative agency notifies the public of a proposed new rule and then permits a formal hearing, with opportunity for evidence and cross-examination, before promulgating the final rule. (Chapter 4)

Founding Fathers   The authors of the United States Constitution, who participated in the Constitutional Convention in Philadelphia in 1787. (Chapter 1)

Framers   *See* Founding Fathers. (Chapter 4)

Franchise   An arrangement in which the franchisee buys from a franchiser the right to establish a business using the franchiser's trade name and selling the franchiser's products. Typically the franchiser also trains the franchisee in the proper operation of the business. (Chapter 33)

Fraud   Deception of another person to obtain money or property from her. (Chapter 5)

Freedom of Information Act (FOIA)   A federal statute giving private citizens and corporations access to many of the documents possessed by an administrative agency. (Chapter 4)

Freehold estate   The present right to possess property and to use it in any lawful manner. (Chapter 42)

Frustration of purpose   After the creation of a contract, an entirely unforeseen event occurs that eliminates the value of the contract for one of the parties. (Chapter 16)

Fully disclosed principal   If the third party in an agency relationship knows the identity of the principal, that principal is fully disclosed. (Chapter 29)

Fundamental rights   In constitutional law, those rights that are so basic that any governmental interference with them is suspect and likely to be unconstitutional. (Chapter 4)

G

GAAP   Generally accepted accounting principles. Rules set by the Financial Accounting Standards Board to be used in preparing financial statements. (Chapter 38)

GAAS   Generally accepted auditing standards. Rules set by the American Institute of Certified Public Accountants (AICPA) to be used in conducting audits. (Chapter 38)

GATT   *See* General Agreement on Tariffs and Trade. (Chapter 8)

General Agreement on Tariffs and Trade (GATT)   A massive international treaty, negotiated in stages between the 1940s and 1994 and signed by over 130 nations. (Chapter 8)

General deterrence   *See* Deterrence. (Chapter 7)

General intangibles   Potential sources of income such as copyrights, patents, trademarks, goodwill and certain other rights to payment. (Chapter 26)

Gift   A voluntary transfer of property from one person to another without consideration. (Chapter 44)

Gift *causa mortis*   A gift made in contemplation of approaching death. (Chapter 44)

Goods   Anything movable, except for money, securities, and certain legal rights. (Chapter 26)

Grantee   The person who receives property, or some interest in it, from the owner. (Chapter 42)

Grantor   (1) An owner who conveys property, or some interest in it. (2) Someone who creates a trust. (Chapter 42)

Greenmail   If a company is threatened with a hostile takeover, its board of directors may offer to buy the stock of the attacker at an above-market price with the hope that the attacker will take her profits and leave the company alone. (Chapter 35)

H

Hacking   Gaining unauthorized access to a computer system. (Chapter 40)

Harmless error   A ruling made by a trial court which an appeals court determines was legally wrong but not fatal to the decision. (Chapter 3)

Heir   Someone who inherits from a decedent who died intestate (that is, without a will). (Chapter 45)

Holder in due course   Someone who has given value for an instrument, in good faith, without notice of outstanding claims or other defenses. (Chapter 22)

Holographic will   A handwritten will that has not been witnessed. (Chapter 45)

Horizontal agreement or merger   An agreement or merger between two potential competitors. (Chapter 37)

Hybrid rulemaking   A method of administrative agency procedure incorporating some elements of formal and some elements of informal rulemaking, typically involving a limited public hearing with restricted rights of testimony and cross-examination. (Chapter 4)

I

Identify   In sales law, to designate the specific goods that are the subject of a contract. (Chapter 21)

Illegal contract   An agreement that is void because it violates a statute or public policy. (Chapter 12)

Illusory promise   An apparent promise that is unenforceable because the promisor makes no firm commitment. (Chapter 11)

Implied authority   When a principal directs an agent to undertake a transaction, the agent has the right to do acts that are incidental to it, usually accompany it, or are reasonably necessary to accomplish it. (Chapter 29)

Implied contract   A binding agreement created not by explicit language but by the informal words and conduct of the parties. (Chapter 9)

Implied warranty   Guarantees created by the Uniform Commercial Code and imposed on the seller of goods. (Chapter 20)

Implied warranty of habitability   A landlord must meet all standards set by the local building code, or otherwise ensure that the premises are fit for human habitation. (Chapter 42)

Import   To transport goods or services into a country. (Chapter 8)

In camera   "In the judge's chambers," meaning that the judge does something out of view of the jury and the public. (Chapter 3)

Incidental damages   The relatively minor costs, such as storage and advertising, that the injured party suffered when responding to a contract breach. (Chapter 17)

Incorporator   The person who signs a corporate charter. (Chapter 34)

Indemnification   A promise to pay someone else's obligations. (Chapter 28)

Independent agency An administrative agency outside the executive branch of government, such as the Interstate Commerce Commission. (Chapter 4)

Independent contractor Someone who undertakes tasks for others and whose work is not closely controlled. (Chapter 29)

Indictment The government's formal charge that a defendant has committed a crime. (Chapter 7)

Indorser Anyone, other than the issuer or acceptor, who signs an instrument. (Chapter 24)

Infliction of emotional distress A tort. It can be the *intentional infliction of emotional distress,* meaning that the defendant behaved outrageously and deliberately caused the plaintiff severe psychological injury, or it can be the *negligent infliction of emotional distress,* meaning that the defendant's conduct violated the rules of negligence. (Chapter 5)

Informal rulemaking The process whereby an administrative agency notifies the public of a proposed new rule and permits comment but is then free to promulgate the final rule without a public hearing. (Chapter 4)

Initial public offering (IPO) A company's first public sale of securities. (Chapter 37)

Injunction A court order that a person either do or stop doing something. (Chapter 1)

Instructions or charge The explanation given by a judge to a jury, outlining the jury's task in deciding a lawsuit and the underlying rules of law the jury should use in reaching its decision. (Chapter 3)

Instruments Drafts, checks, certificates of deposit and notes. (Chapter 26)

Insurable interest A person has an insurable interest if she would be harmed by the danger that she has insured against. (Chapter 12)

Insured A person whose loss is the subject of an insurance policy. (Chapter 46)

Insurer The person who issues an insurance policy. (Chapter 46)

Integrated contract A writing that the parties intend as the complete and final expression of their agreement. (Chapter 14)

Intentional tort An act deliberately performed that violates a legally imposed duty and injures someone. (Chapter 5)

***Inter vivos* gift** A gift made "during life," that is, when the donor is not under any fear of impending death. (Chapter 44)

***Inter vivos* trust** A trust established while the grantor is still living. (Chapter 44)

Interest A legal right in something, such as ownership or a mortgage or a tenancy. (Chapter 46)

Interference with a contract *See* Tortious interference with a contract. (Chapter 5)

Interference with a prospective advantage See Tortious interference with a prospective advantage. (Chapter 5)

Internet An international computer network that connects smaller groups of linked computer networks. (Chapter 40)

Interpretive rules A formal statement by an administrative agency expressing its view of what existing statutes or regulations mean. (Chapter 4)

Interrogatory A form of discovery in which one party sends to an opposing party written questions that must be answered under oath. (Chapter 3)

Intestate Without a will. (Chapter 45)

Inventory Goods that the seller is holding for sale or lease in the ordinary course of its business. (Chapter 26)

Invitee Someone who has the right to be on property, such as a customer in a shop. (Chapter 6)

Issue All direct descendants such as children, grandchildren, and so on. (Chapter 1)

Issuer The maker of a promissory note or the drawer of a draft. (Chapter 22)

J

Joint and several liability All members of a group are liable. They can be sued as a group, or any one of them can be sued individually for the full amount owing. (Chapter 33)

Joint liability All members of a group are liable and must be sued together. (Chapter 33)

Joint venture A partnership for a limited purpose. (Chapter 33)

Judgment *non obstante verdicto* (n.o.v.) "Judgment notwithstanding the verdict." A trial judge overturns the verdict of the jury and enters a judgment in favor of the opposing party. (Chapter 3)

Judicial activism The willingness shown by certain courts (and not by others) to decide issues of public policy, such as constitutional questions (free speech, equal protection, etc.) and matters of contract fairness (promissory estoppel, unconscionability, etc.). (Chapter 4)

Judicial restraint A court's preference to abstain from adjudicating major social issues and to leave such matters to legislatures. (Chapter 4)

Judicial review The power of the judicial system to examine, interpret, and even nullify actions taken by another branch of government. (Chapter 4)

Jurisdiction The power of a court to hear a particular dispute, civil or criminal, and to make a binding decision. (Chapter 3)

Jurisprudence The study of the purposes and philosophies of the law, as opposed to particular provisions of the law. (Chapter 1)

Justification A criminal defense in which the defendant establishes that he broke the law to avoid a greater harm. (Chapter 7)

L

Larceny Taking personal property with the intention of preventing the owner from ever using it. (Chapter 7)

Law merchant The body of rules and customs developed by traders and businesspersons throughout Europe from roughly the fifteenth to the eighteenth century. (Chapter 18)

Lease A contract creating a landlord-tenant relationship. (Chapter 43)

Legal positivism The legal philosophy holding that law is what the sovereign says it is, regardless of its moral content. (Chapter 1)

Legal realism The legal philosophy holding that what really influences law is who makes and enforces it, not what is put in writing. (Chapter 1)

Legal remedy Generally, money damages. It is distinguished from equitable remedy, which includes injunctions and other non-monetary relief. (Chapter 17)

Legislative history Used by courts to interpret the meaning of a statute, this is the record of hearings, speeches, and explanations that accompanied a statute as it made its way from newly proposed bill to final law. (Chapter 4)

Legislative rules Regulations issued by an administrative agency. (Chapter 4)

Letter of credit A commercial device used to guarantee payment in international trade, usually between parties that have not previously worked together. (Chapter 8)

Libel *See* Defamation. (Chapter 5)

License To grant permission to another person (1) to make or sell something or (2) to enter on property. (Chapter 42)

Licensee A person who is on the property of another for her own purposes, but with the owner's permission. A social guest is a typical licensee. (Chapter 6)

Lien A security interest created by rule of law, often based on labor that the secured party has expended on the collateral. (Chapter 26)

Life estate An ownership interest in real property entitling the holder to use the property during his lifetime, but which terminates upon his death. (Chapter 42)

Limited liability company An organization that has the limited liability of a corporation but is not a taxable entity. (Chapter 33)

Limited liability limited partnership In a limited liability limited partnership, the general partner is not personally liable for the debts of the partnership. (Chapter 33)

Limited partnership A partnership with two types of partners: (1) limited partners who have no personal liability for the debts of the enterprise nor any right to manage the business, and (2) general partners who are responsible for management and personally liable for all debts. (Chapter 33)

Liquidated damages A contract clause specifying how much a party must pay upon breach. (Chapter 17)

Liquidated debt The amount of the indebtedness is not in dispute. (Chapter 11)

Litigation The process of resolving disputes through formal court proceedings. (Chapter 3)

Living trust A trust established while the grantor is alive. *See inter vivos* trust. (Chapter 45)

Living will An instrument that permits adults to refuse medical treatment. It can also appoint a health care proxy to make medical decisions for a person who has become incompetent. (Chapter 45)

Lockout A management tactic, designed to gain a bargaining advantage, in which the company refuses to allow union members to work (and hence deprives them of their pay). (Chapter 32)

M

Mailbox rule A contract doctrine holding that acceptance is effective upon dispatch, that is, when it is mailed or otherwise taken out of the control of the offeree. (Chapter 10)

Maker The issuer of a promissory note. (Chapter 22)

Material Important or significant. Information that would affect a person's decision if he knew it. (Chapter 13)

Mediation The process of using a neutral person to aid in the settlement of a legal dispute. A mediator's decision is non-binding. (Chapter 3)

Mens rea Guilty state of mind. (Chapter 7)

Merger An acquisition of one company by another. (Chapter 36)

Mini-trial A form of alternative dispute resolution in which the parties present short versions of their cases to a panel of three "judges." (Chapter 3)

Minor A person under the age of 18. (Chapter 13)

Minority shareholders Shareholders who do not own enough stock to control their corporation. (Chapter 36)

Minute book Records of shareholder meetings and directors' meetings are kept in the corporation's minute book. (Chapter 34)

Mirror image rule A contract doctrine that requires acceptance to be on exactly the same terms as the offer. (Chapter 10)

Misdemeanor A less serious crime, typically one for which the maximum penalty is incarceration for less than a year, often in a jail, as opposed to a prison. (Chapter 7)

Misrepresentation A factually incorrect statement made during contract negotiations. (Chapter 13)

Mitigation One party acts to minimize its losses when the other party breaches a contract. (Chapter 17)

Modify An appellate court order changing a lower court ruling. (Chapter 3)

Money laundering Taking the profits of criminal acts and either (1) using the money to promote more crime or (2) attempting to conceal the money's source. (Chapter 7)

Monopolization A company acquires or maintains a monopoly through the commission of unacceptably aggressive acts. A violation of §2 of the Sherman Act. (Chapter 37)

Mortgage A security interest in real property. (Chapter 42)

Mortgagee A creditor who obtains a security interest in real property, typically in exchange for money

given to the mortgagor to buy the property. (Chapter 42)

Mortgagor A debtor who gives a mortgage (security interest) in real property to a creditor, typically in exchange for money used to buy the property. (Chapter 42)

Motion A formal request that a court take some specified step during litigation. A motion to compel discovery is a request that a trial judge order the other party to respond to discovery. (Chapter 3)

Motion to suppress A request that the court exclude evidence because it was obtained in violation of the Constitution. (Chapter 7)

Multinational enterprise A corporation that is doing business in more than one country simultaneously. (Chapter 8)

N

NAFTA *See* North American Free Trade Agreement. (Chapter 8)

National Labor Relations Board (NLRB) The administrative agency charged with overseeing labor law. (Chapter 4)

Nationalization A government's seizure of property or companies. (Chapter 8)

Natural law The theory that an unjust law is no law at all, and that a rule is only legitimate if based on an immutable morality. (Chapter 1)

Negative or dormant aspect of the Commerce Clause The doctrine that prohibits a state from any action that interferes with or discriminates against interstate commerce. (Chapter 4)

Negligence per se Violation of a standard of care set by statute. Driving while intoxicated is illegal; thus, if a drunk driver injures a pedestrian, he has committed negligence per se. (Chapter 6)

Negotiable instrument A type of commercial paper that is freely transferable. (Chapter 22)

Negotiation The transfer of an instrument. To be negotiated, order paper must be indorsed and then delivered to the transferee. For bearer paper, no indorsement is required—it must simply be delivered to the transferee. (Chapter 22)

Nominal damages A token sum, such as one dollar, given to an injured plaintiff who cannot prove damages. (Chapter 17)

Noncompetition agreement A contract in which one party agrees not to compete with another in a stated type of business. (Chapter 9)

North American Free Trade Agreement A commercial association among Canada, the United States, and Mexico designed to eliminate almost all trade barriers. (Chapter 8)

Note An unconditional, written promise that the maker of the instrument will pay a specific amount of money on demand or at a definite time. When issued by a corporation, a note refers to short-term debt, typically payable within five years. (Chapter 22)

Novation If there is an existing contract between *A* and *B*, a novation occurs when *A* agrees to release *B* from all liability on the contract in return for *C*'s willingness to accept *B*'s liability. (Chapter 15)

Nuncupative will An oral will. (Chapter 45)

O

Obligee The party to a contract who is entitled to receive performance from the other party. (Chapter 15)

Obligor The party to a contract who is required to do something for the benefit of the other party. (Chapter 15)

Obscenity Constitutional law doctrine holding that some works will receive no First Amendment protection because a court determines they depict sexual matters in an offensive way. (Chapter 4)

Offer In contract law, an act or statement that proposes definite terms and permits the other party to create a contract by accepting those terms. (Chapter 10)

Offeree The party in contract negotiations who receives the first offer. (Chapter 10)

Offeror The party in contract negotiations who makes the first offer. (Chapter 10)

Order paper An instrument that includes the words "pay to the order of" or their equivalent. (Chapter 22)

Output contract An agreement that obligates the seller of goods to sell everything he produces during a stated period to a particular buyer. (Chapter 10)

Override The power of Congress or a state legislature to pass legislation despite a veto by a president or governor. A congressional override requires a two-thirds vote in each house. (Chapter 4)

P

Parol evidence Written or oral evidence, outside the language of a contract, offered by one party to clarify interpretation of the agreement. (Chapter 14)

Parol evidence rule In the case of an integrated contract, neither party may use evidence outside the writing to contradict, vary, or add to its terms. (Chapter 14)

Part performance An exception to the statute of frauds permitting a buyer of real estate to enforce an oral contract if she paid part of the price, entered the property, and made improvements, with the owner's knowledge. (Chapter 14)

Partially disclosed principal If the third party in an agency relationship knows that the agent is acting for a principal, but does not know the identity of the principal, that principal is partially disclosed. (Chapter 29)

Partnership An association of two or more persons to carry on as co-owners of a business for profit. (Chapter 33)

Partnership at will A partnership that has no fixed duration. A partner has the right to resign from the partnership at any time. (Chapter 33)

Partnership by estoppel If a person who is not a partner implies that he is a partner or does not object when other people imply it, he is liable as if he really were a partner. (Chapter 33)

Patent The right to the exclusive use of an invention for 20 years. (Chapter 41)

Payable on demand The holder of an instrument is entitled to be paid whenever she asks. (Chapter 22)

Payee Someone who is owed money under the terms of an instrument. (Chapter 22)

***Per se* violation of an antitrust law** An automatic breach. Courts will generally not consider mitigating factors. (Chapter 37)

Peremptory challenge During *voir dire,* a request by one attorney that a prospective juror be excused for an unstated reason. (Chapter 3)

Perfect tender rule A rule permitting the buyer to reject goods if they fail in any respect to conform to the contract. (Chapter 21)

Perfection A series of steps a secured party must take to protect its rights in collateral against people other than the debtor. (Chapter 26)

Personal property All property other than real property. (Chapter 44)

Plain meaning rule In statutory interpretation, the premise that words with an ordinary, everyday significance will be so interpreted, unless there is some apparent reason not to. (Chapter 4)

Pleadings The documents that begin a lawsuit: the complaint, the answer, the counter-claim and reply. (Chapter 3)

Positive aspect of the Commerce Clause The power granted to Congress to regulate commerce between the states. (Chapter 4)

Precedent An earlier case that decided the same legal issue as that presently in dispute, and which therefore will control the outcome of the current case. (Chapter 1)

Predatory pricing A violation of §2 of the Sherman Act in which a company lowers its prices below cost to drive competitors out of business. (Chapter 37)

Preemption The doctrine, based on the Supremacy Clause, by which any federal statute takes priority whenever (1) a state statute conflicts or (2) there is no conflict but Congress indicated an intention to control the issue involved. (Chapter 4)

Preferred stock Owners of preferred stock have a right to receive dividends and liquidation proceeds of the company before common shareholders. (Chapter 34)

Preponderance of the evidence The level of proof that a plaintiff must meet to prevail in a civil lawsuit. It means that the plaintiff must offer evidence that, in sum, is slightly more persuasive than the defendant's evidence. (Chapter 3)

Presentment A holder of an instrument makes a demand for payment. (Chapter 24)

Pretermitted child A child omitted from a parent's will. (Chapter 45)

Prima facie "At first sight." A fact or conclusion that is presumed to be true unless someone presents evidence to disprove it. (Chapter 30)

Principal In an agency relationship, the principal is the person for whom the agent is acting. (Chapter 28)

Privacy Act A federal statute prohibiting federal agencies from divulging to other agencies or organizations information about private citizens. (Chapter 4)

Privity The relationship that exists between two parties who make a contract, as opposed to a third party who, though affected by the contract, is not a party to it. (Chapter 20)

Probable cause In a search and seizure case, it means that the information available indicates that it is more likely than not that a search will uncover particular criminal evidence. (Chapter 7)

Probate The process of carrying out the terms of a will. (Chapter 45)

Procedural due process *See* Due Process Clause. (Chapter 4)

Procedural law The rules establishing how the legal system itself is to operate in a particular kind of case. (Chapter 1)

Proceeds Anything that a debtor obtains from the sale or disposition of collateral. Normally, proceeds refers to cash obtained from the sale of the secured property. (Chapter 26)

Production of documents and things A form of discovery in which one party demands that the other furnish original documents or physical things, relating to the suit, for inspection and copying. (Chapter 3)

Product liability The potential responsibility that a manufacturer or seller has for injuries caused by defective goods. (Chapter 20)

Professional corporation A form of organization that permits professionals (such as doctors, lawyers, and accountants) to incorporate. Shareholders are not personally liable for the torts of other shareholders, or for the contract debts of the organization. (Chapter 33)

Profit The right to enter land belonging to another and take something away, such as minerals or timber. (Chapter 42)

Promissory estoppel A doctrine in which a court may enforce a promise made by the defendant even when there is no contract, if the defendant knew that the plaintiff was likely to rely on the promise, the plaintiff did in fact rely, and enforcement of it is the only way to avoid injustice. (Chapter 9)

Promissory note The maker of the instrument promises to pay a specific amount of money. (Chapter 22)

Promoter The person who creates a corporation by raising capital and undertaking the legal steps necessary for formation. (Chapter 34)

Promulgate To issue a new rule. (Chapter 4)

Prosecution The government's attempt to convict a defendant of a crime by charging him, trying the case, and forcing him to defend himself. (Chapter 7)

Prospectus Under the Securities Act of 1933, an issuer must provide this document to anyone who purchases a security in a public transaction. The prospectus contains detailed information about the issuer and its business, a description of the stock, and audited financial statements. (Chapter 37)

Protective order A court order limiting one party's discovery. (Chapter 3)

Proxy (1) A person whom the shareholder designates to vote in his place. (2) The written form (typically a card) that the shareholder uses to appoint a designated voter. (Chapter 36)

Proxy statement When a public company seeks proxy votes from its shareholders, it must include a proxy statement. This statement contains information about the company, such as a detailed description of management compensation. (Chapter 36)

Publicly traded corporation A company that (1) has completed a public offering under the Securities Act of 1933, or (2) has securities traded on a national exchange, or (3) has 500 shareholders and $10 million in assets. (Chapter 35)

Punitive damages Money awarded at trial not to compensate the plaintiff for harm but to punish the defendant for conduct that the factfinder considers extreme and outrageous. (Chapter 5)

Purchase money security interest A security interest taken by the person who sells the collateral to the debtor, or by a person who advances money so that the debtor may buy the collateral. (Chapter 26)

Q

Quantum meruit "As much as she deserves." The damages awarded in a quasi-contract case. (Chapter 9)

Quasi-contract A legal fiction in which, to avoid injustice, the court awards damages as if a contract had existed, although one did not. (Chapter 9)

Quid pro quo A Latin phrase meaning "this for that." It refers to a form of sexual harassment in which some aspect of a job is made contingent upon sexual activity. (Chapter 30)

Quiet enjoyment A tenant's right to use property without the interference of the landlord. (Chapter 43)

Quorum The number of voters that must be present for a meeting to count. (Chapter 36)

R

Ratification When someone accepts the benefit of an unauthorized transaction or fails to repudiate it once he has learned of it, he is then bound by it. (Chapter 29)

Real property Land, together with certain things associated with it, such as buildings, subsurface rights, air rights, plant life and fixtures. (Chapter 42)

Reasonable doubt The level of proof that the government must meet to convict the defendant in a criminal case. The factfinder must be persuaded to a very high degree of certainty that the defendant did what the government alleges. (Chapter 3)

Reciprocal dealing agreement An agreement under which Company *A* will purchase from Company *B* only if Company *B* also buys from Company *A*. These agreements are rule of reason violations of the Sherman Act. (Chapter 37)

Record date To vote at a shareholders meeting, a shareholder must own stock on the record date. (Chapter 36)

Red herring A preliminary prospectus. (Chapter 37)

Reformation The process by which a court rewrites a contract to ensure its accuracy or viability. (Chapter 17)

Refusal to deal An agreement among competitors that they will not trade with a particular supplier or buyer. Such an agreement is a rule of reason violation of the Sherman Act. (Chapter 37)

Registration statement A document filed with the Securities and Exchange Commission under the Securities Act of 1933 by an issuer seeking to sell securities in a public transaction. (Chapter 37)

Reliance interest A remedy in a contract case that puts the injured party in the position he would have been in had the parties never entered into a contract. (Chapter 17)

Remand The power of an appellate court to return a case to a lower court for additional action. (Chapter 1)

Reply A pleading, filed by the plaintiff in response to a defendant's counter-claim. (Chapter 3)

Repossess A secured party takes collateral because the debtor has defaulted on payments. (Chapter 26)

Repudiation An indication made by one contracting party to the other that it will not perform. (Chapter 21)

Request for admission A form of discovery in which one party demands that the opposing party either admit or deny particular factual or legal allegations. (Chapter 3)

Requirements contract An agreement that obligates a buyer of specified goods to purchase all of the goods she needs during a stated period from a particular seller. (Chapter 10)

Res ipsa loquitur A doctrine of tort law holding that the facts may imply negligence when the defendant had exclusive control of the thing that caused the harm, the accident would not normally have occurred without negligence, and the plaintiff played no role in causing the injury. (Chapter 6)

Resale price maintenance A *per se* violation of the Sherman Act in which a manufacturer enters into an agreement with retailers about the prices they will charge. (Chapter 37)

Rescind To cancel a contract. (Chapter 11)

Respondeat superior A rule of agency law holding that a principal is liable when a servant acting within the scope of employment commits a tort that causes physical harm to a person or property. (Chapter 29)

Restitution Restoring an injured party to its original position. (Chapter 13)

Restitution interest A remedy in a contract case that returns to the injured party a benefit that he has conferred on the other party, which it would be unjust to leave with that person. (Chapter 17)

Restricted security Any stock purchased in a private offering (such as one under Regulation D). (Chapter 37)

Retribution Giving a criminal defendant the punishment he deserves. (Chapter 7)

Reverse The power of an appellate court to overrule a lower court and grant judgment for the party that had lost in the lower court. (Chapter 3)

Revocation The act of disavowing a contract offer, so that the offeree no longer has the power to accept. (Chapter 10)

Rule of reason violation An action that breaches the antitrust laws only if it has an anticompetitive impact. (Chapter 37)

Rulemaking The power of an administrative agency to issue regulations. (Chapter 4)

S

S corporation A corporation that is not a taxable entity. (Chapter 33)

Sale on approval A transfer in which a buyer takes goods intending to use them herself, but has the right to return the goods to the seller. (Chapter 19)

Sale or return A transfer in which the buyer takes the goods intending to resell them, but has the right to return the goods to the original owner. (Chapter 19)

Scienter In a case of securities fraud, the plaintiff must prove that the defendant acted willfully, knowingly, or recklessly. (Chapter 37)

Secondary boycott Picketing, directed by a union against a company, designed to force that company to stop doing business with the union's employer. (Chapter 32)

Security Any purchase in which the buyer invests money in a common enterprise and expects to earn a profit predominantly from the efforts of others. (Chapter 37)

Security agreement A contract in which the debtor gives a security interest to the secured party. (Chapter 26)

Security interest An interest in personal property or fixtures that secures the performance of some obligation. (Chapter 26)

Separation of powers The principle, established by the first three articles of the Constitution, that authority should be divided among the legislative, executive, and judicial branches. (Chapter 4)

Servant An agent whose work is closely controlled by the principal. (Chapter 29)

Service mark A type of trademark used to identify services, not products. (Chapter 41)

Settlor Someone who creates a trust. (Chapter 45)

Sexual harassment Unwanted sexual advances, comments or touching, sufficiently severe to violate Title VII of the 1964 Civil Rights Act. (Chapter 30)

Shilling A seller at auction either bids on his own goods or agrees to cross-bid with a group of other sellers. (Chapter 40)

Short-swing trading Under §16 of the Securities Exchange Act, insiders must turn over to the corporation any profits they make from the purchase and sale or sale and purchase of company securities in a six-month period. (Chapter 37)

Signatory A person, company, or nation that has signed a legal document, such as a contract, agreement, or treaty. (Chapter 8)

Single recovery principle A rule of tort litigation that requires a plaintiff to claim all damages, present and future, at the time of trial, not afterwards. (Chapter 5)

Slander *See* Defamation. (Chapter 5)

Sole proprietorship An unincorporated business owned by a single person. (Chapter 33)

Sovereign immunity The right of a national government to be free of lawsuits brought in foreign courts. (Chapter 8)

Spam Unsolicited commercial or bulk e-mail. ("To spam" is to send such e-mail.) (Chapter 40)

Specific deterrence *See* Deterrence. (Chapter 7)

Specific performance A contract remedy requiring the breaching party to perform the contract, by conveying land or some unique asset, rather than by paying money damages. (Chapter 17)

Stakeholders Anyone who is affected by the activities of a corporation, such as employees, customers, creditors, suppliers, shareholders, and neighbors. (Chapter 35)

Stale check A check presented more than six months after its due date. (Chapter 25)

Stare decisis "Let the decision stand." A basic principle of the common law, it means that precedent is usually binding. (Chapter 1)

Statute A law passed by a legislative body, such as Congress. (Chapter 1)

Statute of frauds This law provides that certain contracts are not enforceable unless in writing. (Chapter 14)

Statute of limitations A statute that determines the period within which a particular kind of lawsuit must be filed. (Chapter 16)

Statute of repose A law that places an absolute limit on when a lawsuit may be filed, regardless of when the defect was discovered. (Chapter 20)

Statutory interpretation A court's power to give meaning to new legislation by clarifying ambiguities, providing limits, and ultimately applying it to a specific fact pattern in litigation. (Chapter 4)

Strict liability A tort doctrine holding to a very high standard all those who engage in ultrahazardous activity (e.g., using explosives) or who manufacture certain products. (Chapter 6)

Strike The ultimate weapon of a labor union, it occurs when all or most employees of a particular plant or employer walk off the job and refuse to work. (Chapter 32)

Strike suit A lawsuit without merit that defendants sometimes settle simply to avoid the nuisance of litigation. (Chapter 36)

Subpoena An order to appear, issued by a court or government body. (Chapter 4)

Subpoena *duces tecum* An order to produce certain documents or things before a court or government body. (Chapter 4)

Substantial performance The promisor performs contract duties well enough to be entitled to his full contract price, minus the value of any defects. (Chapter 16)

Substantive due process *See* Due Process Clause. (Chapter 4)

Substantive law Rules that establish the rights of parties. For example, the prohibition against slander is substantive law, as opposed to procedural law. (Chapter 1)

Summary judgment The power of a trial court to terminate a lawsuit before a trial has begun, on the grounds that no essential facts are in dispute. (Chapter 3)

Summary jury trial A form of alternative dispute resolution in which a small panel of jurors hears shortened, summarized versions of the evidence. (Chapter 3)

Supermajority voting Typically, shareholders can approve charter amendments by a majority vote. However, sometimes corporations require more than a majority of shareholders (e.g., 80 percent) to approve certain charter amendments, such as a merger. These provisions are designed to discourage hostile takeovers. (Chapter 35)

Superseding cause An event that interrupts the chain of causation and relieves a defendant from liability based on her own act. (Chapter 6)

Supremacy Clause From Article VI of the Constitution, it declares that federal statutes and treaties take priority over any state law, if there is a conflict between the two or, even absent a conflict, if Congress manifests an intent to preempt the field. (Chapter 4)

T

Takings Clause Part of the Fifth Amendment, it ensures that when any governmental unit takes private property for public use, it must compensate the owner. (Chapter 4)

Tariff A duty imposed on imported goods by the government of the importing nation. (Chapter 8)

Tenancy by the entirety A form of joint ownership available only to married couples. If one member of the couple dies, the property goes automatically to the survivor. Creditors cannot attach the property, nor can one owner sell the property without the other's permission. (Chapter 42)

Tender To make conforming goods available to the buyer. (Chapter 21)

Tender offer A public offer to buy a block of stock directly from shareholders. (Chapter 35)

Term partnership When the partners agree in advance on the duration of a partnership. (Chapter 33)

Testamentary trust A trust created by the grantor's will. (Chapter 45)

Testator Someone who dies having executed a will. (Chapter 45)

Testatrix A female testator. (Chapter 45)

Third party beneficiary Someone who stands to benefit from a contract to which she is not a party. An *intended* beneficiary may enforce such a contract; an *incidental* beneficiary may not. (Chapter 15)

Three-Fifths Clause A clause in Article 1, section 2 of the United States Constitution, now void and regarded as racist, which required that for purposes of taxation and representation, a slave should be counted as three-fifths of a person. (Chapter 4)

Tort A civil wrong, committed in violation of a duty that the law imposes. (Chapter 5)

Tortious interference with a contract A tort in which the defendant deliberately impedes an existing contract between the plaintiff and another. (Chapter 5)

Tortious interference with a prospective advantage A tort in which the defendant deliberately obstructs a developing venture or advantage that the plaintiff has created. (Chapter 5)

Trade acceptance A draft drawn by a seller of goods on the buyer and payable to the seller or some third party. (Chapter 22)

Trade secret A formula, device, process, method, or compilation of information that, when used in business, gives the owner an advantage over competitors who do not know it. (Chapter 41)

Trademark Any combination of words and symbols that a business uses to identify its products or services and that federal law will protect. (Chapter 41)

Treasury stock Stock that has been bought back by its issuing corporation. (Chapter 34)

Trespass A tort committed by intentionally entering land that belongs to someone else, or remaining on the land after being asked to leave. (Chapter 5)

Trial court Any court in a state or federal system that holds formal hearings to determine the facts in a civil or criminal case. (Chapter 3)

Trust An entity that separates legal and beneficial ownership. (Chapter 45)

Tying arrangement A violation of the Sherman and Clayton Acts in which a seller requires that two distinct products be purchased together. The seller uses its significant power in the market for the tying product to shut out a substantial part of the market for the tied product. (Chapter 37)

U

Ultra vires An activity that is not permitted by a corporation's charter. (Chapter 34)

Ultrahazardous activity Conduct that is lawful yet unusual and much more likely to cause injury than normal commercial activity. (Chapter 6)

Unconscionable contract An agreement that a court refuses to enforce because it is fundamentally unfair as a result of unequal bargaining power by one party. (Chapter 12)

Undisclosed principal If a third party in an agency relationship does not know that the agent is acting for a principal, that principal is undisclosed. (Chapter 29)

Undue influence One party so dominates the thinking of another party to a contract that the dominant party cannot truly consent to the agreement. (Chapter 13)

Unfair labor practice An act, committed by either a union or an employer, that violates the National Labor Relations Act, such as failing to bargain in good faith. (Chapter 32)

Unilateral contract A binding agreement in which one party has made an offer that the other can accept only by action, not words. (Chapter 9)

Unliquidated debt A claimed debt that is disputed, either because the parties disagree over whether there is in fact a debt or because they disagree over the amount. (Chapter 11)

Usury Charging interest at a rate that exceeds legal limits. (Chapter 12)

V

Valuation A process by which the Customs Service determines the fair value of goods being imported, for purposes of imposing a duty. (Chapter 8)

Verdict The decision of the factfinder in a case. (Chapter 3)

Vertical agreement or merger An agreement or merger between two companies at different stages of the production process, such as when a company acquires one of its suppliers or distributors. (Chapter 37)

Veto The power of the president to reject legislation passed by Congress, terminating the bill unless Congress votes by a $\frac{2}{3}$ majority to override. (Chapter 4)

Void agreement   An agreement that neither party may legally enforce, usually because the purpose of the bargain was illegal or because one of the parties lacked capacity to make it. (Chapter 9)

Voidable contract   An agreement that, because of some defect, may be terminated by one party, such as a minor, but not by both parties. (Chapter 9)

Voir dire   The process of selecting a jury. Attorneys for the parties and the judge may inquire of prospective jurors whether they are biased or incapable of rendering a fair and impartial verdict. (Chapter 3)

W

Warranty   A guarantee that goods will meet certain standards. (Chapter 20)

Warranty of fitness for a particular purpose   An assurance under the Uniform Commercial Code that the goods are fit for the special purpose for which the buyer intends them and of which the seller is aware. (Chapter 20)

Warranty of merchantability   An assurance under the Uniform Commercial Code that the goods are fit for their ordinary purpose. (Chapter 20)

Whistleblower   Someone who discloses wrongful behavior. (Chapter 30)

Winding up   The process whereby the assets of a partnership are sold and the proceeds distributed. (Chapter 33)

World Wide Web   A decentralized collection of documents containing text, pictures and sound that is accessible from Internet sites. It is a sub-network of the Internet. (Chapter 40)

Writ   An order from a government compelling someone to do a particular thing. (Chapter 1)

Table of Cases

Index

S